Nicaea and its Legacy

Nicaea and its Legacy

An Approach to Fourth-Century Trinitarian Theology

LEWIS AYRES

OXFORD
UNIVERSITY PRESS

Great Clarendon Street, Oxford OX2 6DP
Oxford University Press is a department of the University of Oxford.
It furthers the University's objective of excellence in research, scholarship,
and education by publishing worldwide in
Oxford New York
Auckland Cape Town Dar es Salaam Hong Kong Karachi
Kuala Lumpur Madrid Melbourne Mexico City Nairobi
New Delhi Shanghai Taipei Toronto
With offices in
Argentina Austria Brazil Chile Czech Republic France Greece
Guatemala Hungary Italy Japan South Korea Poland Portugal
Singapore Switzerland Thailand Turkey Ukraine Vietnam

Oxford is a registered trade mark of Oxford University Press
in the UK and in certain other countries

Published in the United States
by Oxford University Press Inc., New York

© Lewis Ayres 2004

The moral rights of the author have been asserted

Database right Oxford University Press (maker)

Reprinted 2009

All rights reserved. No part of this publication may be reproduced,
stored in a retrieval system, or transmitted, in any form or by any means,
without the prior permission in writing of Oxford University Press,
or as expressly permitted by law, or under terms agreed with the appropriate
reprographics rights organization. Enquiries concerning reproduction
outside the scope of the above should be sent to the Rights Department,
Oxford University Press, at the address above

You must not circulate this book in any other binding or cover
And you must impose this same condition on any acquirer

ISBN 978-0-19-875505-0

Printed in the United Kingdom by
Lightning Source UK Ltd., Milton Keynes

For Medi

Preface and Acknowledgements

I did not know that I would produce this book when I did. I had intended to finish a book on Augustine's Trinitarian theology first and then to turn to this project. Eventually it became apparent that this book was nearer completion and would provide a context for the appearance of my more detailed treatment of Augustine. I would like to offer very special thanks to those who read drafts of various chapters and who have been willing to talk through my sometimes idiosyncratic ideas and prose at length. I think especially of Michel Barnes, Roberta Bondi, Catherine Chin, Brian Daley SJ, Stephen E. Fowl, Stanley Hauerwas (who suggested I should write the book), Brooks Holifield, Luke Johnson, Andrew Louth, Bruce Marshall, Daniel H. Williams, and Rowan Williams. Their advice, theological wisdom, and sometimes their sheer skill at punctuation has been invaluable. Without the excellent editorial help of Brooks and Roberta in the final months readers would have been subjected to considerably more text.

I owe much to many others who have offered their support and advice in many ways during the writing of the text. In particular my parents have always offered their unconditional support as I pursue what must at times seem an odd career choice. I would also like to mention Jonathan Beswick, Frank Black, Lenny Briscoe, J. Patout Burns, Robert Dodaro, Mark Eliott, Carol Harrison, Stanley Hauerwas, Stephen Hildebrand, Augustine Holmes, Gareth Jones, John Lee, Mary Mclintock-Fulkerson, Ian Markham, Robert Markus, Tom Martin, John Milbank, Rik van Nieuwenhove, Jeffrey Steenson, Vincent Twomey, and Robert Wilken. They are not all named here, but among those to whom I owe a debt are my former friends and colleagues at Trinity College Dublin and at the Pontifical College of Maynooth for providing an environment in which much of this text was thought through.

I am especially grateful to Michel Barnes for discussing all the topics covered in this book with me over the past few years and for reading the manuscript closely in earlier drafts. His knowledge has made this a far better book than it could otherwise have been and it should be read as a product of our ongoing conversation. Michel's understanding of the necessity of television, film, and Coca-Cola products to the good life has also shaped me in ways that must, somehow, have worked their way into my reading of the fourth century. Elizabeth Clark was exceedingly generous with her friendship, support, and advice during a year at Duke University—and since. From her scholarly and human qualities—and it is by no means certain that excelling in one area entails excelling in the other!—I and many other students of early Christianity have learnt much. I am also deeply grateful to Ian Markham (now Dean of Hartford Seminary) for providing me with an academic environment in Liverpool during 2000–1. He is a true friend.

I also want to acknowledge the gratitude I feel towards Dean Russell E. Richey and my colleagues—too many to name here—at the Candler School of Theology for welcoming me into their community and enabling the actual completion of the manuscript. The care and attention they have shown to me and to my family over the past three years has been a lesson in Christian virtue. Besides those named above I think especially of Stephen Gunter, Carl Holladay, Rod Hunter, Steve Kraftchick, Charlotte McDaniel, Philip Reynolds, Karen Schreib, and Brent Strawn. Roberta Bondi has been a wonderful colleague in Early Christian Studies over the past three years, not only in her discussion of my work and in her efforts to teach me Syriac but also in her appreciation for a good pair of socks. Two graduate classes also offered extremely helpful comment on some of the chapters and saved me from some particularly egregious assertions. Andy Gallwitz and Annie Bullock have been particularly and persistently helpful. A number of research assistants, Denise Kettering, Johnathan Lace, Leanne Montgomery, and most extensively Catherine A. Boothe did the hard work of compiling the bibliography and standardizing my notes. Sandra Tucker and the staff of Candler Support Services were invaluable towards the end. I would also like to thank my editors at Oxford, Hilary O'Shea and especially Lucy Qureshi: they have both been extremely patient and wise. Enid Barker and Heather Watson guided the manuscript through the editorial process with admirable skill and showed remarkable calm at my endless changes.

An earlier version of Chapter 13 was published in *Modern Theology*, 18 (2002), 445–74, while an earlier version of Chapter 14 appears in Robert Dodaro and George Lawless (eds.), *Augustine and his Critics* (London and New York: Routledge, 1999), 51–76. A draft of the narrative argument of Chapters 1–10 appears as chapter 38 of Frances Young, Lewis Ayres, and Andrew Louth (eds.), *The Cambridge History of Early Christian Literature* (Cambridge: Cambridge University Press, 2004), 414–63.

The book is dedicated to my wife Medi Ann Volpe. As friend, conversation partner, and mother of Anna and Thomas I can see her only as a gift of the divine providence sent to display to me the love, power, understanding, and sheer wonderful mystery of the Triune wisdom.

Atlanta
Easter 2004

Contents

Abbreviations	xv
Introduction	1

I. Towards a Controversy

1. Points of Departure	11
Introduction: Where to Begin?	11
I: From Arius to Nicaea	15
II: Origen	20
III: Theology and the Reading of Scripture	31
2. Theological Trajectories in the Early Fourth Century: I	41
The Generation of the Son: Two Trends	41
Alexander, Athanasius, and Friends: Theologians of the True Wisdom	43
The 'Eusebians': Theologians of the 'One Unbegotten'	52
3. Theological Trajectories in the Early Fourth Century: II	62
'Marcellan' Theology: Theologians of the Undivided Monad	62
Western Anti-Adoptionism: A Son Born Without Division	70
Incarnation and Soteriology at 300	76
Heresy and Orthodoxy in the Early Fourth Century	78
4. Confusion and Controversy: AD 325–340	85
The Nicene Creed as a Standard of Faith	85
The Course of the Council	88
Ousia and *Hypostasis* in the Creed of Nicaea	92
Was there a 'Nicene' Theology in 325?	98
AD 325–342: Towards the Creation of 'Arianism'	100
5. The Creation of 'Arianism': AD 340–350	105
The Creation of 'Arianism'	105
The *Orations Against the Arians*	110
The 'Dedication' Council of Antioch	117

The Council of Serdica: East vs. West?	122
Confusion and Rapprochement: AD 344–350	126

II. The Emergence of Pro-Nicene Theology

6. Shaping the Alternatives: AD 350–360 — 133

Constantius and the Rise of the Homoians	133
Athanasius and the Defence of *Homoousios*	140
Aetius and Eunomius	144
The Rise and Fall of the 'Homoiousians'	149
Cyril of Jerusalem	153
The Events of AD 359–360	157

7. The Beginnings of Rapprochement — 167

Introduction	167
Church and Emperor: AD 360–378	168
Athanasius and the Beginnings of Rapprochement	171
The Pro-Nicene Reaction in the West: AD 360–365	177
Hilary's Theology	179
Conclusion	186

8. Basil of Caesarea and the Development of Pro-Nicene Theology — 187

Basil's Early Theology: Problems with *homoousios*	188
Basil's Developing Theology: Ἐπίνοια and Ἰδιώματα	191
Οὐσία and ἰδιώματα in Basil's Theology	198
Novelty and Tradition in Basil's Trinitarian Theology	204
The Unity of God and the Human Person	207
Developments in Technical Terminology	209
On the Holy Spirit and Pro-Nicene Pneumatology	211
Tradition and Contemplation	218
Conclusion	221

9. The East from Valens to Theodosius — 222

Basil and his Contemporaries	222
Ephrem the Syrian	229
The Meaning of the Term 'Pro-Nicene'	236
The Accession of Theodosius	240

10. Victory and the Struggle for Definition — 244

Gregory Nazianzen	244
Imperial Definition	251
The Council of Constantinople	253

The West: AD 365–400	260
On Not Ending the Story	267

III. Understanding Pro-Nicene Theology

11. **On the Contours of Mystery** — 273
    - Culture, *Habitus*, and the Life of the Mind — 274
    - Strategy I: Speaking of Unity and Diversity in the Trinity — 278
    - Speaking of God — 288
    - God and the Unity of Mind — 289
    - Inseparable Operation and Appropriation — 296
    - Conclusion — 300

12. **'The First and Brightest Light'** — 302
    - Strategy II: Christology and Cosmology — 302
    - Purification in Christ's Body — 304
    - Existence in the Word — 312
    - Interlude I: 'Participation' in Pro-Nicene Theology — 321

13. **'Walk Towards Him Shining'** — 325
    - Strategy III: Anthropology, Epistemology, and the Reading of Scripture — 325
    - Dual-Focus Purification — 325
    - Rereading Scripture — 335
    - Conclusion — 341
    - Interlude II: Ascetic Portability — 342

14. ***On Not Three Gods*: Gregory of Nyssa's Trinitarian Theology** — 344
    - Introduction — 344
    - The Polemical Context of *Ad Ablabium* — 345
    - The Structure of the *Ad Ablabium* — 347
    - Argument A: Creation and the Indivisibility of Natures — 349
    - Argument B: Natures, Powers, Activities, and Knowledge — 351
    - Conclusion: The Essential Nyssa — 359

15. **The Grammar of Augustine's Trinitarian Theology** — 364
    - Introduction: The Modern Attack on Augustine — 364
    - The Early Augustine: Pro-Nicene or Platonist? — 366
    - The Mature Augustine: Pro-Nicene Simplicity — 372
    - Conclusion: Theology in the Word — 381

16. In Spite of Hegel, Fire, and Sword — 384
    I. Narration from Modernity — 384
    II. The Forms of Systematics — 392
    III. Locating the 'Revival' — 404
    IV. After the Passing: A Theology of Theology — 414
    V. On the Development of Doctrine — 425

Epilogue: On Teaching the Fourth Century — 430

Bibliography — 436
Index — 465

Abbreviations

ACW	Ancient Christian Writers
ANRW	*Aufstieg und Niedergang der römischen Welt*
BA	Bibliothèque Augustinienne
CAG	*Commentaria in Aristotelem Graeca*
CAH	*Cambridge Ancient History*
CCSG	Corpus Christianorum Series Graeca
CCSL	Corpus Christianorum Series Latina
CHHP	*Cambridge History of Hellenistic Philosophy*
CPG	Clavis Patrum Graecorum
CPL	Clavis Patrum Latinorum
CSCO	Corpus Scriptorum Ecclesiasticorum Orientalium
CSEL	Corpus Scriptorum Ecclesiasticorum Latinorum
EOIMA	*Ecclesiae Occidentalis Monumenta Iuris Antiquissima*
FoC	Fathers of the Church
GCS	Die griechischen christlichen Schriftsteller
JECS	*Journal of Early Christian Studies*
JThS	*Journal of Theological Studies*
LCC	Library of Christian Classics
PG	Patrologia, Series Graeca
PGL	*Patristic Greek Lexicon*
PL	Patrologia, Series Latina
RAC	*Reallexikon für Antike und Christentum*
SC	Sources Chrétiennes
SP	*Studia Patristica*
TLG	*Thesaurus Linguae Graecae*
TRE	*Theologische Realenzyklopädie*
TU	Texte und Untersuchungen
VigChr	*Vigiliae Christianae*
ZNTW	*Zeitschrift für die neutestamentliche Wissenschaft*

In many and various ways God spoke of old to our fathers by the prophets; but in these last days he has spoken to us by a Son, whom he appointed heir of all things, through whom also he created the world. He reflects the glory of God and bears the very stamp of his nature, upholding the universe by his word of power.

Hebrews 1: 1–3

For wisdom is more mobile than any motion; because of her pureness she pervades all things. For she is a breath of the power of God, and a pure emanation of the glory of the Almighty; therefore nothing defiled gains entrance into her. For she is a reflection of eternal light, a spotless mirror of the working of God, and an image of his goodness.

Wisdom 7: 24–6

Introduction

The fourth century of the Christian era witnessed a controversy that produced some of the basic principles of classical Trinitarian and Christological doctrine, the most important creed in the history of Christianity, and theological texts that have remained points of departure for Christian theology in every subsequent generation. This book explores that controversy and is aimed at a variety of readers.

To students of early Christianity and late antiquity, I offer a new narrative of the Trinitarian and Christological disputes that takes further the attempts of recent scholarship to move beyond ancient heresiological categories.[1] The aim and core of my argument is a paradigm that I offer for exploring the theologies that came to be counted as 'orthodox' at the end of the century. This paradigm attempts to move beyond simplistic east/west divisions and to respect the diversity of 'pro-Nicene' theologies better than available accounts. The paradigm also tries to show the interweaving of pro-Nicene Trinitarian theologies with discussions of cosmology, epistemology, anthropology and—importantly—with conceptions of how to read Scripture. For pro-Nicenes, theological accounts of Scripture—and of human speech about God—provided the contexts for accounts of the Trinity itself. Eventually I will suggest that pro-Nicene theology should be considered as a theological 'culture'.

My second intended audience is modern Christian theologians.[2] To these readers I suggest that recent Trinitarian theology has engaged the legacy of Nicaea at a fairly shallow level, frequently relying on assumptions about Nicene theology that are historically indefensible and overlooking the wider theological matrices within which particular theological terminologies were situated. Chapters

---

[1] The focus of the book is the Trinitarian and Christological disputes, which means that a number of other controversies between Christians during this century are not covered. For example, I do not discuss the Donatist, Melitian, or Origenist controversies. I also do not discuss in any detail controversies between Christians and non-Christians.

[2] Of course, here I speak mainly of theologians who consider detailed engagement with Nicaea to be a necessary part of good Trinitarian theology—a set that should include all Catholic and Orthodox theologians, and those of many other communions. I hope that my arguments will also be of interest to theologians not so bound, in particular by showing how the complex theologies of pro-Nicenes involve an attention to Scripture that should claim the attention of all who define their faith as 'scriptural'.

11–14 attempt to demonstrate the need for a more detailed account of 'Nicene' Trinitarian theology by theologians wishing to appropriate its dynamics. In the last chapter I argue that pro-Nicene theologies offer accounts of theological language, of the reading of Scripture, of analogical reasoning, and of the doctrine of God itself that challenge modern Trinitarian theologians to rethink some of their most cherished assumptions.

While a vast amount of scholarship over the past thirty years has offered revisionist accounts of themes and figures from the fourth century, few clear summary narratives built on this scholarship have appeared. Accordingly, Parts I and II of the book, Chapters 1–10, offer a narrative of Trinitarian and Christological thought between approximately AD 300 and 383. In part, my aim has been to construct a narrative that will be useful for readers without much familiarity with this field. In these chapters I have tried, where possible, to refer to existing English translations and to point to English-language scholarship that offers further useful discussion.

The fundamental problem in understanding the course of these controversies stems from the nature of our sources. Above and beyond the usual difficulties in constructing any narrative of intellectual argument and development, the documentary evidence from this period is, in many cases, fragmentary. For some important historical events (such as the Council of Constantinople itself) we lack any detailed primary account and the writings of some leading figures (such as Arius and Marcellus of Ancyra) survive only in fragments. Even surviving accounts that seem less fragmentary are deeply shaped by heresiological categories honed during the controversies—'Arian', 'semi-Arian', and 'neo-Arian' being good examples. Such heresiological labels enabled early theologians and ecclesiastical historians to portray theologians to whom they were opposed as distinct and coherent groups and they enabled writers to tar enemies with the name of a figure already in disrepute. Most famously some participants in the debate described loosely related but clearly distinct thinkers as Arians. In fact, it is virtually impossible to identify a school of thought dependent on Arius' specific theology, and certainly impossible to show that even a bare majority of Arians had any extensive knowledge of Arius' writing. Arius was part of a wider theological trajectory; many of his ideas were opposed by others in this trajectory: he neither originated the trajectory nor uniquely exemplified it. One further result of this polemical move was to hide the ways in which the theologies typified as Arian draw on a variety of theological trajectories and cannot be understood as springing from one source. The heresiological label thus covers up the complexity of theological development. Given the increasing clarity with which we can trace the history of these heresiological terms, recent writers on the fourth century have tried to narrate the period with greater sensitivity to the continuities and divisions that these labels seek to hide.

Throughout the book I will argue that we should avoid thinking of these controversies as focusing on the status of Christ as 'divine' or 'not divine'. They focus, first, on debates about the generation of the Word or Son from the Father. Second, the controversies involve debates about the 'grammar' of human speech about the divine. Before explaining these two points in a little more detail, I need to note that two common ways of presenting the controversies are simply misleading. One often finds accounts of fourth-century theology arguing that these disputes are not 'simply' Christological or 'simply' Trinitarian, but it would be far better simply to avoid the categories. The writers considered in these pages see questions about Christ's ability to reveal and act salvifically to be closely related to his status as the Word of God. Indeed, the questions are so interrelated because the controversies originally focused on the nature and consequences of the Word's generation.

For fourth-century theologians, understanding how one should read scriptural discussion of the Word of God or the Son of God was at the heart of understanding the Christian gospel itself. Only in the context of an account of the Word's relationship to God did these theologians articulate an account of redemption. Thus, behind the original controversy lie conflicting approaches to the Word's generation: to what extent can we think of it as the emergence of one distinct thing from another? How does one understand the distinction between God and Word, Father and Son: is this the distinction of two separate beings? Are the two distinct in a way parallel to the seemingly necessary hierarchy of source and product that we see in the creation? Or is this distinction analogous to that of a person who speaks his or her word (the word being here only a dependent and temporary product of the speaker)?

These questions about the generation of the Son or Word—and consequently about the ontological status of the generated Son—then have immediate repercussions for how one understands incarnation and redemption. Should we understand the Incarnate Christ's revelation of God by thinking of the Word as an intermediary being, able to communicate something of the divine character because of an inherent mutability that makes communication possible? Even if we reject the Word's mutability and insist on its inseparability from God, how far can the Word reveal the immutable source of all? In what ways can a Son generated as inferior to the Father act to effect closeness to the Father of all? Different accounts of the Son's generation (in modern terms a Trinitarian question) were taken to have implications for accounts of the incarnate Word (in modern terms questions of soteriology and Christology).

Such questions were central, in part, because fourth-century theologians read Scripture differently from modern theologians. On the one hand, fourth-century assumptions about the Old Testament as Scripture provided points of departure for reflection on the Word's generation that many modern theologians treat with suspicion. Thus fourth-century writers treated texts such as Proverbs 8: 22, Wisdom 7: 25–6 and 8: 1, Isaiah 53: 8, Exodus 33: 18–23, Malachi 3: 6, James 1: 17 as fundamental points of reference and departure for discussing the divine being. On the other hand, fourth-century theologians made assumptions about the analogical and imaginative resources provided by the language of Scripture that, to many modern readers, seem only to rip terms or verses out of context. To appreciate fourth-century theology and controversy we need to appreciate better how such reading attended to the imaginative resources of Scripture. Before we assess the value of this reading practice against the standards of modern exegetical techniques, we need to understand how early Christian exegetical practice functioned as a key cultural context for the fourth-century disputes.

A second approach that we need to reject treats the fourth-century debates as focusing on the question of whether to place the Son on either side of a clear God/creation boundary. The ease with which this distinction can be made by modern theological readers is itself an achievement of the fourth century. Many fourth-century theologians (including some who were in no way anti-Nicene) made distinctions between being 'God' and being 'true God' that belie any simple account of the controversy in these terms. One of the key factors that enabled the achievement of a clear distinction between God and creation (such that 'true God' is synonymous with God) was the increasing subtlety and clarity with which late fourth-century theologians shaped their basic rules or grammar for all language about the divine life and action. As part of this grammar pro-Nicene theologians articulate a clear principle that whatever is God is necessarily at one with the simplicity of divinity and admits of no degrees: at this point 'true God' is a phrase that cannot be taken to imply the existence of lesser Gods.

Seeing how fourth-century questions initially concern the Word's generation from the Father also helps us to consider whether and how we may speak of continuity in fourth-century accounts of God. I argue that one link between many participants supposedly on different sides was an insistence that one must speak of the Son's incomprehensible generation from the Father as a sharing of the

Father's very being. Expressions of this position were initially varied, seemingly contradictory, and often highly metaphorical. For some the position entailed recognizing the coeternity of the Son, for many it did not. Nevertheless, because of this continuity, and over the course of the controversies, an account that was both more precise and which could draw together many who had thought themselves opposed gradually emerged.

These narrative chapters are not intended to replace the standard large surveys by Richard Hanson and Manlio Simonetti. My intention is to offer a narrative framework for the controversies that in some measure advances on their texts, and which can form the basis for the consideration of pro-Nicene theology that occupies Parts II and III of my text. This means that a number of figures who most certainly deserve treatment have not been accorded individual treatment in the interests of space: I have in mind Marius Victorinus, Eusebius of Emesa, Epiphanius of Salamis, and Didymus the Blind. Some, however, who do not usually receive sufficient consideration in the story of the fourth century have been considered, Ephrem the Syrian being a good example. The English reader also lacks an extended introduction to Basil of Caesarea's Trinitarian thought, and I have accordingly devoted considerable space to him. It is also important to note that my intention has not been to offer complete portraits of the figures I discuss, but to trace the story of the fourth-century controversies. In some cases major texts by authors are not extensively considered where their influence is hard to trace. Thus the reader will look in vain for any extended treatment of Athanasius' *On the Incarnation*: but the same reader will also look in vain for any substantive evidence that this treatise had any effect on the later fourth-century readers I discuss.

The type of 'historical theology' represented by this book has been somewhat displaced by scholarly styles that frequently locate doctrinal development as an epiphenomenon of political, cultural, and social contexts. Indeed, it is important to recognize that placing doctrinal history against such background has been one of the central achievements of scholarship on early Christianity in the last few decades. Nevertheless, unless one has an entirely materialist understanding of intellectual development, this should not be taken to mean that the sort of theological history offered here is no longer of importance. The practitioner of this style has, however, to bear in mind that his or her account is always open to supplementation from other styles of investigation in the field. Questions of causation will remain particularly contentious, implying as they do not merely decisions about causal factors in any given case but wider debates about intellectual development as such. I have indicated places where the development of doctrine during the fourth century seems to have been driven by political events in the empire: further study (and more space) would enable the indication of more points at which political and economic contexts had important influence. The argument of this book is thus intended to be porous to other styles of study. This is perhaps particularly the case with reference to material that would relate the theological shifts of the fourth century to shifts in the intellectual life of the empire during the period. I have been able to undertake little of such study here: such investigation will have to await future opportunity.

Chapters 11–15 turn to the shared contours of pro-Nicene Trinitarianism. By 'pro-Nicene' I mean those theologies, appearing from the 360s to the 380s, consisting of a set of arguments about the nature of the Trinity and about the enterprise of Trinitarian theology, and forming the basis of Nicene Christian belief in the 380s. Intrinsic to these theologies were compatible (but not identical) accounts of how the Nicene creed should be understood. These accounts constituted a set of arguments *for* Nicaea—hence *pro*-Nicene.[3] All of these theologies build closely on and adapt themes found earlier in the century, but none is identical with any original 'Nicene' theology apparent in the 320s or 330s. Further, pro-Nicene theology was itself constituted by a collection of overlapping yet distinct theologies. Pro-Nicene theologies share assumptions and practices that provided the context for the terminologies so frequently treated as the single legacy of pro-Nicene theology. Throughout this part of the book I also argue that the East/West or Greek/Latin division which is often used as a primary dividing marker between varieties of fourth- and fifth-century Trinitarian theology is of far less significance than is usually thought. Chapters 14 and 15 look in detail at probably the two most contested and frequently discussed pro-Nicene theologians: Gregory of Nyssa and Augustine. I postpone these treatments until this point in the hope that the previous summary chapters allow for fresh narrations of these figures.

Chapter 16 is a theological conclusion in which I explore ways in which modern theological cultures have failed to engage pro-Nicene theology. Even modern theologies wishing to uphold a Nicene faith have frequently failed to sustain the theological practices that shaped and made possible that faith. At the very end of Chapter 16 I consider briefly the nature of doctrinal development. I do not offer here a model that allows one to assert a continuity discernible or verifiable

---

[3] I take up the question of terminology, with reference to scholarly debates about 'Nicene', 'neo-Nicene', and 'pro-Nicene' in Ch. 9.

Introduction 7

to any objective historical observer (as has been the function of many theories of doctrinal development in the past two centuries). Instead I set out some perspectives within which the narration of continuity is possible and necessary for Christian theologians—even though that continuity eludes our full comprehension—and in which the process of historical investigation is ongoing and continually demanded of theologians and historians of theology. In many ways the argument of my last chapter is not that modern Trinitarianism has engaged with pro-Nicene theology badly, but that it has barely engaged with it at all. As a result the legacy of Nicaea remains paradoxically the unnoticed ghost at the modern Trinitarian feast.

I
Towards a Controversy

I
Points of Departure

The whole power of the mysterious dogma is at once established by the one word *homoousios*, which was sovereignly proclaimed at the Council of 318 [*sic*], because this word stands for both a real unity and a real distinction. It is impossible to mention without reverent fear and holy trepidation that moment—infinitely significant and unique in its philosophical and dogmatic importance—when the thunder of *Homoousios* first roared over the city of Victory ... And the single word *homoousios* expressed not only a christological dogma but also a spiritual evaluation of the rational laws of thought. Here rationality was given a death blow.[1]

INTRODUCTION: WHERE TO BEGIN?

In his wonderful dramatic prose Pavel Florensky epitomizes a centuries-old account of the Council of Nicaea: in one decision and with one pronouncement the Church identified a term that secured its Trinitarian and Christological beliefs against heresy and established a foundation for subsequent Christian thought. The narrative offered in Chapters 1–10 demonstrates why such older accounts are deeply mistaken and suggests a more credible alternative.[2]

The four decades since 1960 have produced much revisionary scholarship on the Trinitarian and Christological disputes of the fourth century. It is now a commonplace that these disputes cannot simply be understood as the product of the Church's struggle

---

[1] Pavel Florensky, *The Pillar and Ground of the Truth: An Essay in Orthodox Theodicy in Twelve Letters*, tr. Boris Jakim (Princeton: Princeton University Press, 1997), 41. When he speaks of the 'Council of 318' Florensky is referring to the legendary number of those present, not the date.

[2] Three articles of recent years offer similar accounts of the century as a whole in the light of recent scholarship: André de Halleux, 'La Reception du Symbole Œcumenique, de Nicée à Chalcédoine', *Ephemerides Theologicae Lovanienses*, 61 (1985), 5–47 (repr. in *Patrologie et Œcuménisme. Recueil d'études*, Bibliotheca Ephemeridum Theologicarum Lovaniensum, XCIII (Leuven: Leuven University Press, 1990), 25–67); Michel René Barnes, 'The Fourth Century as Trinitarian Canon', in Lewis Ayres and Gareth Jones (eds.), *Christian Origins: Theology, Rhetoric and Community* (London and New York: Routledge, 1998), 47–67; Joseph T. Lienhard, 'The Arian Controversy: Some Categories Reconsidered', *Theological Studies*, 48 (1987), 415–36. The perspective of Barnes' is closest to my own.

against a heretic and his followers grounded in a clear Nicene doctrine established in the controversy's earliest stages.[3] Rather, this controversy is a complex affair in which tensions between pre-existing theological traditions intensified as a result of dispute over Arius, and over events following the Council of Nicaea. The conflict that resulted eventually led to the emergence of a series of what I will term pro-Nicene[4] theologies interpreting the Council of Nicaea in ways that provided a persuasive solution to the conflicts of the century.

Pro-Nicene theologies combined both doctrinal propositions and a complex of intellectual theological strategies. Together these doctrines and the strategies within which those doctrines were intended to be read constitute a theological culture. By attention to this theological culture, I suggest, we best understand the theological propositions typically identified as Nicene.[5] My treatment is intended to contribute to a developing scholarly discussion of what it means to speak of Nicene theology between 325 and 381. I say developing because while revisionary scholarship during the past forty years has addressed the complexity of the term Arian, discussion of the term Nicene has been much more restricted.[6] In describing this period Richard Hanson's *The Search for the Christian Doctrine of God* (1988) and Manlio Simonetti's *La Crisi Ariana nel IV secolo* (1975) remain essential points of reference—as I stated in the Introduction. Simonetti is, it should be noted, considerably more successful as a piece of narrative history. Anyone who attempts to narrate these controversies is also indebted to Hanns Christof Brennecke's *Studien zur Geschichte der Homöer* (1988) for the later phases of the controversy. Most recently, Richard Vaggione's *Eunomius of Cyzicus and the Nicene Revolution* treats the dispute as

---

[3] Rowan D. Williams, *Arius: Heresy and Tradition* (London: DLT, 1987), 1–25, offers one of the best recent discussions of the way scholarship on this controversy has developed. Ironically, Williams's excellent book still reflects something of an older concern in using Arius himself as the pivot for comments about the controversy as a whole. As we shall see, the direction of recent work has been to focus on Arius as a catalyst for a controversy within which his particular theology rapidly becomes marginal. Michael Slusser also offers a very useful summary of the history of 4th cent. historiography in his 'Traditional Views of Late Arianism', in Michel Barnes and Daniel H. Williams (eds.), *Arianism after Arius* (Edinburgh: T. & T. Clark, 1993), 3–30.

[4] The term 'pro-Nicene' is defined and discussed in Ch. 9.

[5] My use of 'culture' is discussed at the beginning of Ch. 11. The definition I give there may be helpful here: 'a system of learned patterns of behaviour (including thought, speech, and human action), ideas, and products that together shape conceptions of the order of existence and interactions with other cultures'.

[6] There has been some discussion, but its focus has largely been the relationship between the 'Nicene' theology of Athanasius and the later theologies of the Cappadocians. I criticize this approach in Ch. 9.

Points of Departure

a whole, but through a focus on the Heterousian theologians Aetius and Eunomius.[7]

Existing descriptions of this period tend to emphasize differences between theologians and theological parties, mainly for the sake of clarity. This historiographical tactic, however, all too easily blurs the differences between theologians who may also share much in common and hides themes that will eventually result in new alliances. Speaking of theological groups or parties is a descriptive move fraught with difficulty when we fail to recognize the particular patterns of mutual interconnection and cohesiveness pertaining among members of any such party. Hence, my account pays particular attention to the difficulties of identifying discrete parties and positions during the course of the controversy. I have refrained from trying to construct a new typology of parties and movements, focusing instead on the complex texture of the alliances that marked the period.

Many summary accounts present the Arian controversy as a dispute over whether or not Christ was divine, initially provoked by a priest called Arius whose teaching angered his bishop, Alexander of Alexandria. Eventually, this traditional account tells us, the controversy extended throughout the century—even after the decisive statements of the Council of Nicaea—because a conspiracy of Arians against the Nicene tradition represented particularly by Athanasius perpetuated Arius' views.[8] Even when the century is understood as one of evolution in doctrine, scholars continue to talk as if there were a clear continuity among non-Nicene theologians by deploying such labels as Arians, semi-Arians, and neo-Arians. Such presentations are misleading in two very important ways.

First, this controversy is mistakenly called Arian. No clear party sought to preserve Arius' theology. Many who are termed Arian justly protested their ignorance of his teaching or works: their theologies often have significantly different concerns and preoccupations. Even those who initially supported Arius in his struggle with Alexander, the bishop of Alexandria, may be misleadingly termed Arian, if what they recognized in the controversy over Arius was not an attack on their teacher or main inspiration, but an attack on one who expressed ideas to which they (perhaps only in part) subscribed.

---

[7] Manlio Simonetti, *La Crisi Ariana nel IV secolo*, Studia Ephemerides Augustinianum, 11 (Rome: Augustinianum, 1975); Hanns Christof Brennecke, *Studien zur Geschichte der Homöer: Der Osten bis zum Ende der homöischen Reichskirche* (Tübingen: J. C. B. Mohr, 1988); Richard P. Vaggione, *Eunomius of Cyzicus and the Nicene Revolution* (Oxford: Oxford University Press, 2000). Of older accounts, one of the very best available in English is Jean-Rémy Palanque et al., *The Church in the Christian Roman Empire*, tr. Ernest C. Messenger (London: Oates & Washbourne, 1949). The chapters on doctrinal history are by Gustave Bardy.

[8] The extent to which one can speak of an original 'Nicene theology' is discussed in Ch. 4.

Many of Arius' earliest supporters appear to have rallied to him because they, like him, opposed Alexander's theology: we have little information about their allegiance to the emphases of Arius' own theology. For these reasons some scholars now simply refrain from using the term Arian other than as an adjective to describe Arius' own theology and I shall follow that practice.[9] The relationships between those termed Arian must be demonstrated, not assumed.

Second, it is misleading to assume that these controversies were about 'the divinity of Christ' if that implies either a priori agreement about the meaning of ascribing divinity to the Son, or if it means that these controversies focused on this specific question. Suggestions that the issue was one of placing Christ (and eventually the Spirit) on either side of a well-established dividing line between created and uncreated are particularly unhelpful. At issue until the last decades of the controversy was the very flexibility with which the term 'God' could be deployed.[10] Many fourth-century theologians easily distinguished between 'God' and 'true God'. In discussions of the relations between the Son and the Father, or between creation and generation, arguments about the 'grammar' for talking about God were also under way.

The use of the term 'grammar' in theological and philosophical discussions has become both frequent and at times confusing: when I use the term, I mean a set of rules or principles intrinsic to theological discourse, whether or not they are formally articulated. If, for instance, a theologian argues that the Son is 'God' but not 'true God', that argument implies the possibility of degrees of deity and a rule that will allow a flexible application of 'God'. Similarly, questions about whether or not the Logos was 'breathed forth' for interaction with the creation or just breathed forth eternally also imply principles about whether the rules for speaking about God will allow some sort of semi-temporal change in God's being. If not, then the Logos must be breathed forth eternally or in a pre-temporal state. Embedded within exegetical and philosophical arguments were

---

[9] There are a few figures active in the latter stages of the controversy among those condemned with Arius in the controversy's earliest stages: Euzoius, Homoian bishop of Antioch in the 360s and 370s, is one of the most famous. However, there is little evidence that these figures presented themselves as his defenders or successors and there is little evidence that they follow the particular emphases of his thought. George, bishop of Laodicea and, for a while, a close associate of Basil of Ancyra (see Ch. 6), is an excellent example of an earlier supporter of Arius whose theology takes a very different turn.

[10] Marianne Meye Thompson, *The God of the Gospel of John* (Grand Rapids, Mich.: Eerdmans, 2001), ch. 1, offers a very helpful discussion of the flexibility of 'God' language in the Old and New Testaments. She is particularly helpful on noting the ways in which this term (in its various Greek and Hebrew forms) to some extent shifts its significance depending on context. Much of what she discusses there is directly relevant to the situation at the turn of the 4th cent.

different rules for speaking about divinity. In some cases, especially in the latter years of the fourth century, these issues of 'grammar' become explicit topics for some theologians. Indeed, part of the solution to the fourth-century controversies consists in an increased clarity about the grammar of divinity, in particular, an insistence that all speech about Father, Son, and Spirit is governed by the same assumptions about the divine. Once these principles have been articulated theologians used them as the basis for further arguments about the adequacy of particular ways of speaking about God. Thus, throughout the century, one can understand accounts of the Son's role and nature only against the background of the grammar of divinity that provides the context for those accounts.

Having considered how *not* to approach this story, we can now move to consider the origins of the dispute, exploring four possible points of departure:

1. I will consider what initially might seem the most obvious point of departure: events concerning Arius up to the Council of Nicaea in 325. To begin here, however, is to risk missing the context within which this dispute occurred and why it came to interest so many across the Roman world.

2. Next I turn to the theology and legacy of Origen. Since Epiphanius in the late fourth century, historians have pointed to Origen as the source of Arius' theology and hence of the controversy as a whole. While Origen cannot be treated thus, his legacy was important in the theological debates of the early fourth century.

3. Then I consider exegesis in the period between Origen and the late fourth century, seeking to highlight the extent to which particular understandings of theological practice ground and shape these disputes.

4. Finally, in Chapters 2 and 3 I use themes from the first three points of departure to lay out the fourth: the variety of theological trajectories existing in tension at the beginning of the fourth century. One of my goals in offering this fourth point of departure is to relativize the first: the controversy surrounding Arius was an epiphenomenon of widespread existing tensions and understanding those tensions is essential to understanding how the controversy developed in the decades that followed.

I: FROM ARIUS TO NICAEA

From the first point of departure these controversies began with a dispute between the priest Arius and his bishop Alexander in the city of Alexandria, probably in AD 318 (but maybe as late as

322).[11] Alexander taught that God was always Father and that the Son was always Son, thus implying the eternal generation of the Son; as the Father's Word and Wisdom the Son must always have been with the Father. At the same time, he taught that the Son is the exact image of the Father and thus able to reveal and represent him. Arius saw his bishop's theology as implying two ultimate principles in the universe, and he thought that Alexander compromised the biblical insistence on the Father's being alone God and alone immortal (1 Tim. 6: 16). For Arius, any talk about Father and Son as coeternal ignored the hierarchy involved in the very language of Father and Son. Arius saw the Son as a being distinct from and inferior to the Father, and he seems to have played down metaphorical language that suggested continuity of being or existence between Father and Son.[12] The Son imaged the Father, but only by being created as a derivative copy of some of the Father's attributes.

Complex social issues were also at stake. The episcopacy of Alexander occurred during a time when the Church in Alexandria was still moving *towards* acceptance of a 'monarchial' vision of episcopacy in which the bishop's authority over matters of faith and practice was unique and exceeded all other authorities in the diocese. During the second century and some of the third, it seems that the Alexandrian Church maintained a sense of the bishop as *primus inter pares* (first among equals), as the head of the presbyters rather than as the one absolute authority in the diocese. Through the second half of the third century and on into the fourth, the Alexandrian bishops gradually assumed a more powerful role, copying a conception of episcopacy seemingly evident in most other eastern cities. Nevertheless, even while Alexandria moved towards a monarchical model, it apparently maintained a tradition of independent priests whose relationship with the bishop was complex.

Struggle over the role of the bishop may have been behind an earlier dispute in Egypt, known as the 'Melitian schism'.[13] During the persecution of 303–13 Melitius, bishop of Lycopolis, seems to have aroused the anger of some imprisoned fellow bishops because he ordained priests and interfered in dioceses without consulting the official visitors (designated by bishops to act in their absence), most notably annoying Peter of Alexandria (who was probably in hiding).

---

[11] Socrates (*Hist. eccl.* 1. 5) and Sozomen (*Hist eccl.* 1. 15) both report the controversy as initially coming to a head in the context of discussion between Alexander and his assembled clergy about the relationship of Son and Father. Theodoret (*Hist. eccl.* 1. 1) presents the origins much more cursorily, presenting Arius as teaching something new and immediately being opposed by his bishop, Alexander, who held 'strongly to the doctrines of the Apostles'.

[12] The theologies of Alexander and Arius are discussed in more detail in Ch. 2.

[13] On the relations between these various disputes in Egypt see Rowan D. Williams, 'Arius and the Melitian Schism', *JThS* NS 37 (1986), 35–52.

At the end of the persecution Melitius seems to have taken offence at the leniency of Peter's regulations for readmittance to the Church (Peter himself was only out of prison a short time before being martyred) and within a few years Egypt had an alternative hierarchy of bishops. Although Peter's leniency was important here, it is clear that the bishop's authority was also at issue. It is not likely, as was once argued, that Arius himself had an association with Melitius, the disputes around Arius and Melitius were both interwoven with the rise in Alexandria of a monarchial vision of episcopacy over against the independence of individual teachers.[14] That Arius' disputes with his bishop began against the background of struggles over 'Melitians' seems only to have made Alexander more determined to assert control. At various times through the century Melitius' supporters and non-Nicene Christians appear to have made ad hoc alliances, but lack of evidence prevents us asserting doctrinal commonalities.

Alexander and the Alexandrian clergy condemned Arius after he refused to sign a confession of faith presented by Alexander.[15] Over the next few years Arius gained support from some bishops in Palestine, Syria, and North Africa, especially Eusebius of Caesarea in Palestine and Eusebius of Nicomedia, near Constantinople. Many of his supporters appear to have greatly valued the teaching of Lucian of Antioch, a priest and teacher in Antioch martyred in 312 and some were Lucian's students. Although these supporters may have been wary of some aspects of Arius' theology—especially his insistence on the unknowability of the Father—they joined in opposition to Alexander. For all of them Alexander's theology seemed to compromise the unity of God and the unique status of the Father. Two small councils, one in Bithynia, the other in Palestine, vindicated Arius, and Alexander may have refused a conciliatory approach from Arius as involving insufficient concession.[16] For some of this period Arius seems to have left (or been expelled from) Alexandria and travelled to seek support; eventually he returned and openly opposed Alexander.

In 324 the Emperor Constantine, who had that year defeated

[14] An excellent view of Athanasius' episcopate from this perspective is provided by David Brakke, *Athanasius and the Politics of Asceticism* (Oxford: Clarendon Press, 1995). One should, however, be careful to differentiate this complex background to the dispute from the anachronistic and nonsensical attempt to present Arius as the upholder of a 'democratic' Christianity.

[15] A helpful summary of the confusing events between 318 and 322 is provided by Richard P. C. Hanson, *The Search for the Christian Doctrine of God: The Arian Controversy 318–381 AD* (Edinburgh: T. & T. Clark, 1988), 134–5, largely reliant on the earlier work of Opitz. See also the slightly different reconstruction of events by Williams, *Arius*, 48–61. For our purposes detailed discussion of the differences between these two versions is not necessary. See also Simonetti, *La Crisi*, 25–41.

[16] The letter is to be found at Athanasius, *Synod*. 16. The question here turns on whether or not one reads this letter as conciliatory!

Licinius, formerly his co-ruler in the east, and assumed control of the whole empire, took an interest in the dispute.[17] Constantine wrote to Alexander and Arius telling them to stop quarrelling about what seemed to him to be such a small matter. Soon, however, Constantine began to see their dispute as more serious. It is highly likely that a small council took place in Alexandria, attended by Ossius the bishop of Cordoba in Spain who apparently acted in some sort of advisory capacity to Constantine, and perhaps also served as his representative in these events. Soon afterwards, Constantine decided that decisive action was necessary, possibly persuaded by Ossius.

A few months later, probably early in 325, a council took place in Antioch, possibly under the presidency of Ossius. We know about this meeting because of the survival of a letter in Syriac (translated from a Greek original) probably from Ossius, reporting the council's decisions.[18] The meeting produced a statement of belief asserting that the Son is generated from the Father himself in an ineffable manner and that the transcendence and ineffability of this generation forbid us from speaking of the Son as in any way like the creation. The text distinguishes the language of the Son's 'generation' from language used about the 'creation' of the cosmos. This council also temporarily excommunicated one of Arius' senior supporters, Eusebius of Caesarea. This excommunication was treated as temporary because the Antiochene council knew that a larger meeting would gather within months.

This larger council met from late May to July 325 at Nicaea in Asia Minor. Constantine himself summoned the bishops, demonstrating his determination to stop this divisive dispute getting worse.[19] Originally Constantine seems to have summoned the council to Ancyra (modern Ankara in Turkey), but he changed the venue, possibly to have the bishops meet closer to the imperial capital. At Ancyra he would have had the support of Marcellus, bishop of Ancyra, who was either already known to Constantine, or had at

[17] The nature of Constantine's role at Nicaea is discussed in Ch. 4.

[18] For the evidence see Hanson, *The Search*, 146–51; Alistair H. B. Logan, 'Marcellus of Ancyra and the Councils of 325: Antioch, Ancyra, and Nicaea', *JThS* NS 43 (1992), 428–46. The key sections of the text (translated from a reconstruction of the Greek original) are discussed in Ch. 2. Recently the nature of this meeting has been reconsidered and its very existence come under renewed attack in Holger Strutwolf, *Die Trinitätstheologie und Christologie des Euseb von Caesarea: Eine Dogmengeschichte Untersuchung seiner Platonismusrezeption und Wirkungsgeschichte* (Göttingen: Vandenhoeck & Ruprecht, 1999), 31–44. I remain unconvinced: it is unfortunate that Strutwolf does not consider Logan's articles on the subject.

[19] This is the conjecture of Henry Chadwick, 'Ossius of Cordova and the Council of Antioch', *JThS* NS 9 (1958), 292–304. Part of the circumstantial evidence for this interpretation is that Constantine seems to have attempted to exert some control over the Donatist split in the North African Church at its inception, without any success. Here he hoped to have more success.

Points of Departure

least now been indicated as a strong opponent of the views held by Arius.[20] Around 250–300 attended, drawn almost entirely from the eastern half of the empire: Ossius probably presided.[21] Although other business was also considered—especially the problem of settling on a universal method for deciding the date of Easter—the crisis in Alexandria seems to have taken centre stage.

The decision of the council against Arius found expression in a short statement of faith, the creed of Nicaea:

We believe in one God, Father Almighty Maker of all things, seen and unseen; and in one Lord Jesus Christ the Son of God, begotten as only begotten of the Father, that is of the being of the Father (ἐκ τῆς οὐσίας τοῦ πατρός), God of God, Light of Light, true God of true God, begotten not made, consubstantial (ὁμοούσιον) with the Father, through whom all things came into existence, both things in heaven and things on earth; who for us men and for our salvation came down and was incarnate and became man, suffered and rose again the third day, ascended into the heavens, and is coming to judge the living and the dead.

And in the Holy Spirit.

But those who say 'there was a time when he did not exist', and 'before being begotten he did not exist', and that he came into being from non-existence, or who allege that the Son of God is from another *hypostasis* or *ousia* (ἐξ ἑτέρας ὑποστάσεως ἢ οὐσίας), or is alterable or changeable, these the Catholic and Apostolic Church condemns.[22]

After the council Constantine exiled Arius along with two Libyan bishops who had strongly supported him. The Emperor also exiled Eusebius of Nicomedia: it appears that Eusebius signed up to Nicaea but had then received into communion some of Arius' Alexandrian supporters, an action that angered Constantine. Others of Arius' supporters—such as Eusebius of Caesarea—signed the creed and survived unscathed (Eusebius thus succeeded in getting his condemnation at the Council of Antioch reversed). Within two or three years, however, Arius and the others exiled by Constantine were recalled, it seems at the behest of the Emperor, and readmitted to communion by a small gathering of bishops.[23]

Those who assume that this narrative of Arius and his conflict with Alexander is the most important point of departure for the fourth-century controversies interpret the events after Nicaea by narrating the emergence of an Arian conspiracy to keep alive his

---

[20] See Logan, 'Marcellus of Ancyra and the Councils of 325'.

[21] For surviving lists of those present see the new edition of H. Gelzer *et al.* (eds.), *Patrum Nicaenorum Nomina* (Stuttgart and Leipzig: Teubner, 1995).

[22] This translation is Hanson's, at *The Search*, 163. His n. 42 on the same page gives references to surviving early texts of the creed.

[23] These are murky events that need not detain us here: for reconstructions see Hanson, *The Search*, 172–8; Williams, *Arius*, 67–81; Simonetti, *La Crisi*, 99 ff.

20   *I. Towards a Controversy*

theology, to oppose Athanasius, and to contend against Nicaea and its theology. In fact, little evidence for any Arian conspiracy can be found. In these confusing events around and after Nicaea, we see the need to consider not simply Arius and his fortunes but the wider context within which that particular controversy occurred. If we are to make useful judgements about Nicaea's creed and about how the Christian community viewed the conflict over Arius, we need to understand the theological options available in the 300–25 period. For example, the initial opponents of Arius present him as distorting the Church's traditional faith; Arius argues, however, that Alexander's theology changes and distorts the traditional catechetical teaching in Alexandria. We can only assess these claims by understanding the wider context within which those claims were made. Indeed, through exploring this context we will find pre-existing deep theological tensions at the beginning of the fourth century. Controversy over Arius was the spark that ignited a fire waiting to happen, and the origins of the dispute do not lie simply in the beliefs of one thinker, but in existing tensions that formed his background. I want to approach this discussion of origins slowly, first turning to two other possible points of departure. The first is the theology and legacy of Origen.

II: ORIGEN

The greater one's ability to place theologies within the traditions that nurtured them, the better one understands their dynamics.[24] The theology of Origen of Alexandria (*c.*185–*c.*251) lies beneath the surface of many early fourth-century theologies. Scholars have long recognized his significance: for some over the last century Arius' own theology is a direct result of Origen's 'subordinationism'.[25]

---

[24] Similarly, the more one narrates the history of theology as a diachronic illustration of unchangeable logics inherent in Christian thought (as sets of constant opposing possibilities), the more one adheres to the ahistorical practices of modern 'systematic' theology and to a historiography that evolved in symbiosis with it. I have attempted to give some positive suggestions as to what should count as historical engagement in theology (partially reliant on Jauss's reading of Gadamer) in my 'On The Practice and Teaching of Christian Doctrine', *Gregorianum*, 80/1 (1999), 33–94. See also Ch. 16.

[25] For this reason Basil Studer, *Trinity and Incarnation: The Faith of the Early Church* (Edinburgh: T. & T. Clark, 1993), 102–3, talks of the beginning of the 4th cent. as 'the Origenist controversy'. Simonetti, *La Crisi*, pursues the same argument. Studer talks of a twofold controversy between, on the one hand, Origenists themselves (Arius and Alexander) and, on the other hand, between these groups and those who stood outside the Origenist tradition, such as Marcellus of Ancyra. As long as one emphasizes the extent to which both 'Origenist' sides are only partially indebted to Origen and to an already transformed version of his theology this designation is helpful. I have avoided it because the phrase 'Origenist controversy' is already a well-established term for the debate over Origen's work at the end of the 4th cent. See Elizabeth A. Clark, *The Origenist Controversy: The Cultural Construction of an Early Christian Debate* (Princeton: Princeton University Press, 1992).

Such a view is implausible for three reasons. First, Origen exercised influence on *all* sides in Alexandria, and on many beyond Egypt and Palestine (the two areas where he wrote and taught).[26] Second, *no* theologian adopted Origen's system wholesale: his influence is always partial and usually hard to trace with precision.[27] Origen's legacy is complex because some aspects of his work—discussed below—were controversial within a few years of his death. As Rebecca Lyman writes, 'his Christian commitment was unquestionable, but his theological conclusions stimulated passionate apologetic or repudiation; he was too right to be wrong, or too attractively wrong to be ignored'.[28]

Third, Origen's account of the Son as in some ways subordinate to the Father is in part simply that of his contemporaries: the aspects that seem most his own push in different directions from those pursued by Arius. Indeed, it is important to note the problematic status of the very term subordinationism. Insofar as it is understood to indicate an intent to present the Son as being inferior to the Father it does not accurately describe the character of many pre-Nicene and early fourth-century theologies. Consider, for example, a third- or fourth-century theologian who spends considerable effort showing how the Son can be said to possess some of the Father's attributes or to image those attributes because of the manner in which the Son is uniquely generated. In such a case describing the theologian's intent as one of subordinationism directs our attention away from the concern to emphasize continuity of being between the two. Consequently I have tried to reserve the term in this book for theologians whose clear intent is to subordinate the Son to the Father in opposition to the gradual emergence of Nicene and pro-Nicene theologies.

Origen did not, however, simply offer to future generations new terminological choices and theological formulations: his work as exegete helped to shape the character of theology and exegesis in the fourth century. Origen commented on a huge amount of the biblical text and at every turn he was determined to display the capacity of the Scripture to illumine the story of creation and redemption, and

---

[26] In the West in the early 4th cent. his work seems to have exercised no discernible influence on the areas of theology with which we are concerned.

[27] Perhaps the strongest recent repudiation of attempts to see Origen's work as the direct background to controversy over Arius is Richard P. C. Hanson, 'The Influence of Origen on the Arian Controversy', in L. Lies (ed.), *Origeniana Quarta*, Innsbrucker theologische Studien, 19 (Innsbruck: Tyrolia, 1987), 410–23. As ever Hanson states his case a little too starkly: even here he ultimately notes the partial appearance of Origen's thought in a wide variety of contexts.

[28] J. Rebecca Lyman, *Christology and Cosmology: Models of Divine Activity in Origen, Eusebius, and Athanasius* (Oxford: Oxford University Press, 1993), 39.

the ways in which the text draws Christians into a process of purification and salvation. For Origen the text yields its message in degrees as purity of heart and attention to the Logos grows.[29] To serve these he developed several styles of intertextual practice, allowing texts throughout Scripture to illuminate each other and the whole. Many of these interpretative practices are used throughout the fourth century.[30]

Turning to his account of Father and Son, we need to explore how Origen emphasizes both the unique status of the Father and the ways in which the relationship of Father and Son is constitutive of the divine life.[31] Father and Son are distinct beings and yet Origen begins to think of the Son, the image who is 'in' the Father (John 14: 10), as constituted by a mirroring of the Father's existence and as intrinsic to the nature of God. In part he negotiates this paradox by means of his insistence that the Son is eternally generated from the Father. For Origen, he who is God's Wisdom and Power must have always been with the Father.[32] Introducing an argument that will be developed in the fourth century, Origen argues that Father and Son are 'correlative' terms. The name Father implies the existence of a child, and if God is truly called Father, the Son's generation must be eternal. The Son's existence thus seems to be essential to God's

---

[29] On Origen's exegetical practice and his legacy in this area see Karen J. Torjesen, *Hermeneutical Procedure and Theological Method in Origen's Exegesis* (Berlin: De Gruyter, 1986); Rowan D. Williams, 'Origen: Between Orthodoxy and Heresy', in W. A. Bienert and U. Kuhneweg (eds.), *Origeniana Septima: Origenes in den Auseinandersetzungen des 4. Jahrhunderts*, BETL CXXXVII (Leuven: Leuven University Press, 1999), 3–14; David Dawson, *Figural Reading, the Fashioning of Identity and the Suppression of Origen* (Berkeley: University of California Press, 2002); Bernhardt Neuschafer, *Origenes als Philologe*, 2 vols. (Basle: Friedrich Reinhardt, 1987).

[30] The first book of Origen's *Comm. John* is a paradigmatic text in this regard.

[31] For literature on Origen see Henri Crouzel, *Bibliographie critique d'Origène* (The Hague: Nijhoff, 1971 (with suppl. 1982)), and his annual reports on Origenist scholarship in the *Bulletin de littérature ecclésiastique*. For my account of Origen here I am greatly indebted to Rowan Williams, *Arius*, 131–48 and Michel René Barnes, *The Power of God: Δύναμις in Gregory of Nyssa's Trinitarian Theology* (Washington, DC: Catholic University America Press, 2000), 111–24. See also Alistair H. B. Logan, 'Origen and Alexandrian Wisdom Christology', in Richard P. C. Hanson and Henri Crouzel (eds.), *Origeniana Tertia* (Rome: Edizioni dell'Ateneo, 1985), 123–9. For English-language readers very good summary material is also provided in John Behr, *The Way to Nicaea*, The Formation of Christian Theology, 1 (Crestwood, NY: St Vladimir's Seminary Press, 2001), ch. 7; Lyman, *Christology and Cosmology*, ch. 2; Mark Edwards, *Origen Against Plato* (Burlington, Vt.: Ashgate, 2002).

[32] See Origen, *Princ.* 1. 2. 2: 'And can anyone who has learned to regard God with feelings of reverence suppose or believe that God the Father ever existed, even for a single moment, without begetting this wisdom? ... Let him who assigns a beginning to the Word of God or the wisdom of God beware lest he utters impiety against the unbegotten Father himself, in denying that he was always a Father ...'. On the use of the Father and Son's correlativity see Peter Widdicombe, *The Fatherhood of God from Origen to Athanasius* (Oxford: Clarendon Press, 1994), esp. chs. 3, 9, 10. One question that Widdicombe does not sufficiently address is the extent to which Father–Son correlativity is being discussed because of the Father–Son analogy itself, or because of the ontological principle it can be seen to deliver.

being what God from all eternity wills to be. Thus we see that while the Father is superior to the Son, Origen works to make the Son intrinsic to the being of God: subordinationism is an inappropriate word for describing this theological dynamic.

We better see the complexity of this dynamic by noting the importance of Wisdom terminology in Origen's theology.[33] On a number of occasions he deploys a Christological exegesis which links Wisd. 7: 25–6 to Heb. 1: 3 and Col. 1: 15. Origen uses the first text's description of Wisdom as 'a pure emanation of the glory of the Almighty' and as 'a reflection of eternal light' to interpret the image language of Colossians and the description in Hebrews of the Son as '[reflecting] the glory of God'. Just as the light of the divine glory is eternal so too must be the radiance that comes from that light.[34] The Son is the image and revealer of the Father as light from light, or brightness from the Sun.[35] By the standards of the late fourth century these statements, which have what Michel Barnes calls an 'X from X' form,[36] reinforce the idea that the Son shares the Father's existence or mode of existence. For example, 'light from light' is easily read as equivalent to 'true God from true God', as the creed of Constantinople puts it in 381. In the early third century it is not necessarily so. One might, for instance, read 'light from light' as a phrase describing the appearance of a secondary and temporally consequent light from an original source of light.

Origen himself did not deploy language in this second way without reserve: for him, for instance, the Son is not temporally after the Father. Nevertheless, Origen *does* consider the Son to be a distinct being dependent on the Father for his existence. In *On First*

---

[33] In making use of the book of Wisdom, Origen is also arguing for its canonical status. See Robert M. Grant, 'The Book of Wisdom at Alexandria: Reflections on the History of the Canon and Theology', *SP* 7 (1966), 462–72. It is ironic that a terminology that seemed later to provide such a useful metaphorical base for envisaging the Son as sharing the Father's being should come into play precisely to combat modalism.

[34] See Logan, 'Origen and Alexandrian Wisdom Christology'.

[35] Origen, *Princ.* 1. 2. 11: 'In the third place, wisdom is said to be the brightness of the eternal light. The force of this expression we have explained in a previous passage, where we introduced the illustration of the sun and the brightness of its rays ... God's wisdom is the brightness of that light, not only insofar as it is light, but insofar as it is everlasting light. His wisdom is therefore an everlasting brightness, enduring eternally'; *Princ.* 1. 2. 2: 'And in this subsistence of Wisdom there was implicit every capacity and form of the creation that was to be.'

[36] Barnes, *Power of God*, 119: 'All sides in the early stage of the Nicene controversy could (and did) comfortably describe the production of the second Person from the first as an *X from X* causal relationship. Expressions like light from light or wisdom from wisdom occur in virtually everyone's writings. Clearly, in themselves, they do not specify that the cause reproduces its own nature or identity in the product. The value of *X from X* expressions turned upon the understanding one had of the meaning(s) of the two X's: were the two X's used in exactly the same sense, or were they used as a kind of homonym? Was X said of the cause in the same way that X was said of the effect?'

Principles, in a passage again using the language of Wisdom 7. 25–6, Origen writes,

> wisdom is a breath of the 'power' of God. Now the power must mean that by which he is strong, that by which he both established and also preserves and controls all things visible and invisible . . . The breath, then, or if I may so call it, the strength of all this power, comes to have a subsistence of its own; and although it proceeds from the power itself as will proceeding from mind, yet nevertheless the will of God comes itself to be a power of God. There comes into existence, therefore, another power, subsisting in its own proper nature, a kind of breath, as the passage of Scripture calls it, of the first and unbegotten power of God, drawing from this source whatever existence it has; and there is not time when it did not exist.[37]

Here Origen uses Wisdom's language about the 'breath of the power of God' to characterize the Son as Wisdom of God. The Son is not the *one* power of God, but another distinct power dependent on God's power for its existence. The Son is dependent on the Father and has an existence not intrinsic to the Father's existence in the sense of directly sharing or participating in it.[38]

Indeed, Origen is constantly concerned to describe the relationship of Father and Son without falling into the (for him) material-sounding language of a shared essence or nature. A few texts have, to some scholars, indicated otherwise, but Origen directly denies that the Son can come from the Father's *ousia*, as this would imply a material conception of the divine generation.[39] One famous passage in which he seems to use the term *homoousios* ('sharing the same being') of the Father and Son may have been adulterated by later writers.[40] Origen seems, on the one hand, to have associated the term with the perceived materialism of some Gnostic writers and, on the other hand, to have understood it as indicating two things to be co-ordinate members of the same class. If, as seems possible, Origen saw this latter sense of the term as its basic sense, we can understand why he avoided it.[41] Thus, *ousia* language in most forms seemed to Origen unsuitable for application to the divine existence.

---

[37] *Princ.* 1. 2. 9.   [38] See Barnes, *Power of God*, 116 ff.

[39] See *Comm. John* 20. 157: 'Others, however, interpret the statement, "I proceeded from God," to mean, "I have been begotten by God." These must say consequently that the Son has been begotten of the Father's essence, as one might understand this also in the case of those who are pregnant, and that God is diminished and lacking, as it were, in the essence that he formerly had, when he has begotten the Son.' Here Origen's target is very clearly Gnostic theologies which seem to him unavoidably materialistic in their language. Cf. *Comm. John* 1. 24, 11. 23, 20. 18, *Orat.* 15. 1.

[40] For discussion of this text, a fragment of Origen's lost commentary on Hebrews, see Williams, *Arius*, 134–7.

[41] This is the suggestion of Williams, *Arius*, 134–5. The question of Origen's possible use of *homoousios* continues to be debated. For a recent positive assessment see Mark Edwards, 'Did Origen Apply the Word *Homoousios* to the Son?', *JThS* NS 49 (1998), 658–70. Edwards's

Origen's use of the term *hypostasis* opens a debate that continues throughout the fourth century: he used the term to indicate 'real existence'—as opposed to existence only in thought—but also as 'individual, circumscribed existence'. Origen used the term in the former sense a number of times: for instance, in his John commentary, he argues against those who distinguish Father and Son only in thought (*epinoia*), not in *hypostasis*.[42] In his *Contra Celsum* Origen also speaks of Father and Son as two 'things (πράγματα) in *hypostasis*, but one in like-mindedness, harmony, and identity of will'.[43] Here 'in *hypostasis*' seems to mean 'in actual existence'. Origen is searching for a way to argue that Father and Son and Spirit each have a distinct existence. He seeks a term that asserts the true existence of each: he has no interest in offering a dense account of what Father or Son 'is', an account of what qualities and abilities mark an individual divine being. Here πρᾶγμα fills that role—as it occasionally will throughout the fourth century. Elsewhere, at *Commentary on John* 2. 75, Origen writes that 'we are persuaded that there are three *hypostases*, the Father, the Son, and the Holy Spirit'.[44] Here *hypostasis* indicates 'individual circumscribed existence'.[45] This is the only time Origen speaks of 'three *hypostases*' directly, but his usage appears to begin a tradition of using the term in this sense that—after much argument and clarification—became a part of pro-Nicene orthodoxy.

Origen's intention here is not to describe the three *hypostases* as ontologically equal in all senses. He is primarily concerned to state that the three are equal in being distinct as individuals. The language of three *hypostases* evolves as part of a continuing attempt to describe the participation and hierarchy existing among the three that are most definitely three. The question that Origen's usage stimulates is: 'if the three are truly three in distinct existence, by what mode of participation or action are they together?' His answer is not clear: difficult and often incompatible fragments are scattered throughout his corpus. In a number of places Origen emphasizes the

---

argument is a persuasive one, but the question remains in doubt. It is, however, noteworthy that Edwards's argument is ultimately that the term may have been used hesitantly here to expand on an analogy, *not* in a technical sense.

[42] *Comm. John* 10. 37. 212.

[43] *C. Celsum* 1. 23. See the discussion of this text and parallels at Williams, *Arius*, 132.

[44] On the place of the Spirit see Origen, *Comm. John* 2. 75: 'We are, however, persuaded that there are three *hypostases*, the Father, the Son, and the Holy Spirit, and we believe that only the Father is unbegotten. We admit, as most pious and true, that the Holy Spirit is the most honoured of all things made through the Word, and that he is [first] in the rank of all things which have been made by the Father through Christ.'

[45] This is a usage of the term Origen may have taken over from Gnostics writers. See Alistair H. B. Logan, 'Origen and the Development of Trinitarian Theology', in L. Lies (ed.) *Origeniana Quarta*, Innsbrucker Theologische Studien, 19 (Innsbruck: Tyrolia 1987), 424–9.

transcendence of the Father over all things, including Son and Spirit.[46] He argues in his *Commentary on John* that the Father transcends the Son and Spirit *more* than they transcend the created world,[47] an observation probably linked with his insistence in *Contra Celsum* that the Father is 'beyond νοῦς (mind) and *ousia*'. His claim that the Father exceeds the Son may, in the light of this comment, be more concerned with demonstrating the nature of the Father than with arguing for the subordination of the Son. Although Origen elsewhere seems happy using the language of mind to talk of God, he seems to have followed currents in Platonic thought in wanting to place the source of all beyond the realm of thought and ideas.[48] He associates that realm with the Son who contains all the structure of creation within himself. As Rowan Williams argues, Origen finds himself here in something of a dilemma. His philosophical perspective enables an exegesis of scriptural texts that emphasizes the Father's transcendence, but his commitment to the text makes him insist on the Son's function as revealer of the Father.[49]

Rowan Williams also offers a discussion of Origen's understanding of the Son's knowledge of the Father that illustrates the same dilemma. On the one hand, Origen presents the Son as contemplating the Father uninterruptedly and unmediatedly; because of this contemplation the Son can function as agent of the Father in creation and redemption. The Son, as truth and wisdom, transmits to us the 'hidden things of the Father' and contains in himself eternally the intelligible form of all things. And yet, Origen seems also to regard the Father as containing in his own depth, in his true simplicity (which the Son does not share) a mode of contemplation (θεωρία) which is reflected by the Son but not simply shared. The Son, writes Williams, knows the Father 'as an infinite depth never fully to be sounded'.[50] The significance of Williams's argument lies in its highlighting of the tensions in Origen's presentation of the relationship between Father and Son. Origen's account of shared but graded divine existence offers an initially clear, but complex language to describe this relationship.

---

[46] In his later works Origen may have moved to modify this account, making Father and Son closer.

[47] *Comm. John* 13. 151–3: '(151) The Father exceeds the Saviour himself and the Holy Spirit as much (or even more) as the Saviour himself and the Holy Spirit exceed the rest . . . (153) For he is an image of the goodness and brightness, not of God, but of God's glory and of his eternal light, and he is a vapour, not of the Father, but of his power . . .'. Note once again the use of terminology from Wisd. 7. 25–6 in this text.

[48] See Williams, *Arius*, 139 ff., 199 ff.   [49] Williams, *Arius*, 140.

[50] Rowan D. Williams, 'The Son's Knowledge of the Father in Origen', in L. Lies (ed.), *Origeniana Quarta*, Innsbrucker theologische Studien, 19 (Innsbruck: Tyrolia, 1987), 146–53, here 150.

On a number of occasions Origen deploys the idea that the Son is generated 'as the will from the mind'.⁵¹ This language serves not only to present the generation as non-material, but also to emphasize the Son's generation as an intimate expression of the Father's existence. Origen's understanding that the Son has no origin (ἀρχή) except the Father, including no origin in time, also emphasizes that the Son's existence is constituted *by* his imaging God from eternity.⁵² The Son may not share the *ousia* of the Father, but the Son is constantly *in* the Father. Similarly, Origen's insistence on the relationship of Father and Son offers a new argument in Christian tradition, an argument that depicts this relationship as intrinsic to the life of God. The Son for Origen exists in a certain subordination to the Father, and yet Origen's theology raises questions about the extent to which the Father's generation of *this* Word, *this* Son, is a constitutive part of being God.

In Origen's insistence that the Son is a product of the Father's will, not his essence, we might seem to see the outline of a key anti-Nicene argument in the fourth century: if the Son is from the will then he is *not* from the Father's essence. Williams points out, however, that things may not be so simple for Origen. On the one hand, Origen hesitates, for reasons we discussed, to talk of the Son as coming from the Father's essence. On the other hand, his sense of the Father's eternal will gives to the results of that will a quasi-necessity, and the paradigmatic example of the Father's eternal will is the Son's eternal existence. For Origen, to say that the Son is from the Father's will is to *emphasize* the eternal status of the Son as expression of the Father.⁵³

Similarly Origen seems to have spoken of the Son as created, as a κτίσμα.⁵⁴ It is difficult to know how we should read this. Origen says that the first act of creation, the creation of the original rational beings before the world as we know it came into being, resulted from the immediate and unimpeded expression of God's will. This primary creation he may have termed a κτίσμα as opposed to the κόσμος of our world. The Logos is the 'beginning' of this original creation and the medium through which it came into being. Describing the Son as a κτίσμα is very different from describing the material world as created.

In *On First Principles* Origen distinguishes the three *hypostases* by

---

⁵¹ e.g. *Princ.* 1. 2. 6; 1. 2. 9.
⁵² *Comm. John* 1. 16. 102–4: '"In the beginning was the Word", because what is said to be in the Father is in the beginning ... Since the firstborn of all creation is the image of the invisible God, the Father is his beginning.'
⁵³ Williams, *Arius*, 140–1.
⁵⁴ *Princ.* 4. 4. 1; Williams, *Arius*, 140.

attributing to them specific roles or activities in the world.⁵⁵ The Spirit is found only in the saints, while the Son is 'in' all rational beings. From one perspective this text might seem to reinforce the hierarchical side of Origen. And yet, his statement reflects his insistence that the Son shares the Father's nature to the extent that we may speak of there being one will, and that in the activity of three hypostases there is one 'movement'. Once again, Origen's concern is to distinguish Father, Son, and Spirit while maintaining the idea that the latter two reveal and bring to completion the one divine will and action.

Origen's account is, then, complex. He speaks of the Son as inferior to the Father, and yet his explanation of this inferiority turns, at many points, into an account of the necessity of the Son within the divine life. In *On First Principles* Origen writes:

As regards the power of his works, then, the Son is in no way whatever separate or different from the Father, nor is his work anything other than the Father's work, but there is one and the same movement, so to speak, in all they do.⁵⁶

Origen is here alluding to John 5: 19, which he took to mean that the Son does the works that the Father does because he is an image whose birth is 'as an act of [the Father's will] proceeding from the mind'. Once again we see the degree of closeness within difference that Origen seeks in his descriptions: on the one hand, the Son's will is so like the Father's that they can be said to be one;⁵⁷ on the other, the Son is generated like the will from the mind. Elsewhere Origen describes the Son as the image of the Father because his will directly mirrors the Father's.⁵⁸ These arguments reappear in a modified form in the later fourth century, when the common works of Father and Son are taken to indicate a common nature. Origen does not quite say this; he comes close while remaining at a distance.

Origen was not the direct source of Arius, or even of Arius *and* his opponents. Origen's influence was piecemeal. This is so in part

---

⁵⁵ Origen, *Princ*. 1. 3. 5: 'he who is "born again through God" to salvation has need of both Father and Son and Holy Spirit and will not obtain salvation apart from the entire Trinity, and ... it is impossible to become partaker of the Father or the Son without the Holy Spirit ... The God and Father, who holds the universe together, is superior to every being that exists, for he imparts to each one from his own existence that which is each one; the Son, being less than the Father, is superior to rational creatures alone ... the Holy Spirit is still less, and dwells within the saints alone.'

⁵⁶ *Princ*. 1. 2. 12.

⁵⁷ Cf. *Comm. John* 13. 228: 'It is proper food for the Son of God when he becomes a doer of the Father's will, that is, when he wills in himself what was also the Father's will, so that the will of God is in the will of the Son, and the will of the Son has become indistinguishable from the will of the Father, and there are no longer two wills but one.'

⁵⁸ *Comm. John* 13. 231.

simply because he did not exist in a vacuum. When Origen is presented as 'the' theologian in the third-century east and as the quintessential 'Alexandrian' thinker it is easy to see his thought as the one point of reference for subsequent generations. Origen wrote within an existing tradition and so even those partial to his work came to it with ideas from other writers and did not necessarily adopt it wholesale. He also met with a widespread critique in the second half of the third century, which demands our attention if we are to see Origen's legacy as early fourth-century writers would have done.

Particularly important was the suspicion that Origen's theology implied the eternal existence of the creation. This is a charge raised by Methodius of Olympus, writing in the last years of the third century—and one of our few witnesses to the period. In a dialogue that survives only in extracted fragments (probably called *Xeno: On Created Things*) Methodius presented a discussion between two groups, one of whom represented an Origenist position. Under attack is Origen's attempt to say both that all the first created spiritual things exist eternally in the Logos and that God is the beginning or *arche* of all things.[59] Methodius' 'Origenists' do not display the complexities of Origen's texts, they are a vehicle to expose the implications of Origen's thought. Lloyd Patterson argues that Methodius' critique reveals a great sensitivity toward an implicit cosmological dualism found in many of the 'heresies' of his own time. Fear of dualism has led him to emphasize the distinction between the one uncreated (the Father) and the creation, in ways that make him suspicious of Origen's thought. It is unclear how Methodius views the Logos; he seems to speak of eternal generation, but, as Patterson argues, the same language may indicate a generation at some point before the creation.[60] Methodius' doctrine of the Logos emphasizes that there is only one uncreated. His main concern is cosmological, but his arguments raise questions about how one understands the relationship between Father and Logos and between Father and world once much of Origen's participatory talk has been abandoned.

Methodius and others also rejected Origen's understanding that Christ had a human soul preserved from the fall of all other souls.[61] For Origen, while other souls were embodied for God's redemptive purpose (and this world thus created), Christ's soul remained in the

---

[59] See Lloyd G. Patterson, *Methodius of Olympus: Divine Sovereignty, Human Freedom, and Life in Christ* (Washington, DC: Catholic University of America Press, 1997), chs. 4–6; idem, 'Methodius, Origen and the Arian Dispute', *Studia Patristica*, 17/2 (1982), 912–23; Williams, *Arius*, 167–71.
[60] Patterson, 'Methodius', 916–19; idem, *Methodius*, 214 ff.
[61] Patterson, *Methodius*, 170–86.

spiritual realm until the incarnation. To abandon Origen's account of the creation and fall of souls, was to depart from his view of the higher part of the soul, the νοῦς, as a pre-existent reality not determined solely by *this* historical existence.[62] To abandon this theme, in turn, meant that one faced a challenge in describing the union of the Logos with Christ. If one's νοῦς was not that which ensured participation in the spiritual realm and hence enabled the human Christ to be taken up by the Logos, then how did the Logos act in Christ? One solution was to make the Logos ontologically less and mutable such that it could act in the human person, now devoid of a νοῦς.

In all these cases, rejection of Origen's cosmology entailed consequences for the rest of his theology. In the absence of that cosmology, the tensions in his account of the relationship between Father, Son, and creation intensified. While the reaction against Origen in the later third century may have led some to emphasize the distinction between the Father and the Logos, we can see, as Rowan Williams has argued, a separate and increasingly strong emphasis in Alexandria on formulae that emphasize the closeness of Father and Son. One of these is the Origenist-sounding phrase 'always Father, always Son' that Arius attributed to Alexander.[63]

Origen's theology thus encountered criticism but influenced many across the theological spectrum. His theology shaped many of the theological trajectories found in the early fourth century. While Origen may, however, serve as a temporal point of departure for understanding fourth-century theology, the constant ground of all fourth-century theologies is a conception of the reading of Scripture and the practice of theology. Narrations of these disputes tend to assume that readers are familiar with the exegetical practice of fourth-century Christians and understand how it may be understood as the core of early Christian 'theology'. This seems to me a considerable mistake.

---

[62] Part of the complexity in interpreting Origen's account stems from the question of what follows from his insistence that souls are inseparable from bodies and that only God is incorporeal. It seems that, at least, the original creation of the souls involved the creation of souls with already a certain form of body. A number of scholars have recently pushed further in a revisionary account of Origen and argued that he does not actually exhibit a two-stage account of creation and of the fall of souls in the way that his later detractors (and many modern scholars claim). This case is pursued with particular vigour in Edwards, *Origen Against Plato*.

[63] Williams, *Arius*, 170; idem, 'The Logic of Arianism,' *JThS* NS 34 (1983), 56–81, here 57–66.

III: THEOLOGY AND THE READING OF SCRIPTURE

Recent scholarship has argued that characterizing the fourth century as the culmination of Christianity's 'Hellenization' is misleading.[64] This is especially so if Hellenization is understood as resulting in a philosophically articulated doctrinal system only distantly related to the words of Scripture. The revisionary scholarship to which this book is indebted has tried to demonstrate the ways in which exegetical concerns shaped the theologies with which we are concerned here. Many of those scholars, however, who have themselves contributed to these post-Harnackian perspectives continue to offer negative judgements about fourth-century exegesis. Richard Hanson contends, for instance, that 'the expounders of the text of the Bible [in the fourth century] are incompetent and ill-prepared to expound it'.[65]

These negative judgements have usually resulted from comparisons between early Christian and modern academic exegetical practice, comparisons that assume the former is a deficient form of the latter. An implied comparison between fourth-century exegesis and modern historical-critical modes is also frequently embedded in reference, for instance, to post-Reformation divisions between allegory and typology,[66] or to some ways of distinguishing Alexandrian from Antiochene exegesis (particularly those which assume that Antiochenes were more interested in the historical, that they were somehow more modern).[67] Progress in understanding early Christian

---

[64] Harnack's account of 'Hellenization' is considerably more complex than usually stated. Nevertheless, even his account (in which the universalizing spirit intrinsic to *Hellenized* Judaism moves towards self-realization in Christianity) remains unable to treat exegetical questions in the evolution of doctrine as fundamental. For a summary of Harnack's position see William V. Rowe, 'Adolf von Harnack and the Concept of Hellenization', in Wendy Hellman (ed.), *Hellenization Revisited* (Lanham, NY: University Press of America, 1994), 69–98.

[65] Hanson, *The Search*, 848. Similarly (p. 474), Hanson sees Hilary's treatment of Matthew as 'a dreary jungle of empty fantasy'.

[66] The modern division between 'allegory' and 'typology' arose in Reformation debates about medieval Catholic practice. While allegory was condemned as a foisting of meaning upon the text to bolster Catholic ecclesial practices or to illuminate spiritual life without reference to the life of Christ, typology was explained as a closely governed attempt to show how events and prophecies described in the Old Testament were fulfilled in the events of the life of Christ. This polemical practice has been continued by a number of writers through the 20th cent. For those wishing to argue against the usefulness of the distinction Henri de Lubac's *Histoire et Esprit: L'Intelligence de l'Ecriture d'après Origène* (Paris: Aubier, 1950), and his article ' "Typologie" et "allegorisme" ', *Recherches de science religieuse*, 34 (1947), 180–226, remain fundamental points of reference.

[67] For example, Robert Wilken cites Kendrick Grobel's statement that if Theodore of Mopsuestia had been followed historical exegesis 'might have emerged a thousand years earlier than it did'. Robert L. Wilken, 'In Defense of Allegory', *Modern Theology*, 14 (1988), 197–212, here 197. For a recent account of Alexandrian and Antiochene exegesis by which I have been influenced see John O'Keefe, 'A Letter that Killeth: Toward a Reassessment of Antiochene Exegesis', *JECS*, 8 (2000), 83–104.

exegesis and theology can be made only by struggling to describe that exegesis outside explicit or implicit comparison with modern academic practices. Luckily we do not have to begin from scratch. Paralleling the rejection of Harnackian narratives, has been a sophisticated reappraisal of Patristic exegesis.[68] Some of the themes of this reappraisal help us to see how early Christian exegetical practice shapes modes of theological rationality apparent in the period's controversies. I begin by offering a terminology for discussing early Christian exegesis from Origen to the fifth century.[69]

Patristic exegesis takes as its point of departure the 'plain' sense of the text of Scripture. I avoid the term literal sense because it is frequently associated in modern discussion with the sense intended by the human author of a text or the sense that a text had for its initial readers. The plain sense is 'the way the words run' for a community in the light of that community's techniques for following the argument of texts.[70] The plain sense is, then, the sense that a text had for a Christian of the period versed in ancient literary critical skills.[71] The plain sense is pluralistic in a number of ways. First, a number of fourth- and fifth-century authors assume that one might understand 'the way the words run' in different ways. Augustine, for example, argues that one can read Rev. 20: 4—which speaks of the Saints reigning with Christ for a thousand years—as a prophecy of a literal thousand-year period *or* as a description of the Church's symbolic thousand-year existence.[72] The reading one adopts depends largely on which figure of speech one takes to be present.

[68] The following literature presents the major themes in this reassessment: Elizabeth A. Clark, *Reading Renunciation: Asceticism and Scripture in Early Christianity* (Princeton: Princeton University Press, 1999), esp. ch. 4; Stephen E. Fowl, *Engaging Scripture* (Malden, Mass.: Blackwells, 1999); David Dawson, *Allegorical Readers and Cultural Revision in Ancient Alexandria* (Berkeley: University of California Press, 1992), esp. 1–17; idem, *Figural Reading*; Wilken, 'In Defense of Allegory'. One other sign of this interest is the ongoing translation of de Lubac's *Medieval Exegesis*.

[69] When, in what follows I speak of 'early Christian exegesis' I refer only to the period designated in this sentence. My categories may or may not be useful for other periods.

[70] Three essays illustrate this view of the plain sense: Brevard Childs, 'The *sensus literalis* of Scripture: An Ancient and Modern Problem', in H. Donner *et al.* (eds.), *Beiträge zur Alttestamentlichen Theologie, Festschrift für Walter Zimmerli zum 70* (Göttingen: Vandenhoeck & Ruprecht, 1977), 80–93; Kathryn Tanner, 'Theology and the Plain Sense', in Garret Green (ed.), *Scriptural Authority and Narrative Interpretation* (Philadelphia, 1987), 59–87. The phrase 'the way the words run' I copy from Eugene Rogers's essay 'How the Virtues of an Interpreter Presuppose and Perfect Hermeneutics: The Case of Thomas Aquinas', *Journal of Religion*, 76 (1996), 64–81, where he uses the phrase as a translation of Aquinas' *circumstantia litterae* at *De Potentia*, q. 4, a.1, c.

[71] This does not of course mean that a less well-educated reader will simply not be able to discern the plain sense. The situation is directly parallel to the relative abilities of formally and less formally educated English speakers reading a newspaper. Many skills formally taught are related to those reading strategies inherent in cultural practice more widely. Different dimensions of the plain sense will appear to readers with different degrees of education.

[72] Augustine, *Civ.* 20. 7.

Some writers explicitly state that God providentially ordered the words so that they could be taken in different ways. For virtually all the flexibility of the plain sense results from its speaking about realities that are beyond comprehension.

Of course, early Christian readers do frequently equate the author's presumed intention with a text's plain sense. This equation needs, however, to be qualified. On the one hand, it is qualified by the frequent claim that the ultimate author of a text is God. By the shaping of events or the inspiration of human authors God may intend the words of a text to carry a multiple plain sense. On the other hand, early Christian exegetes assume that the mind of the author is to be discerned by a focus on elucidating the text, not by reconstructing the world within which the author wrote and by assuming that such a world was marked by a symbolic universe and by social structures distinct from those of the reader. This elision or lack of recognition of distinctions between the imaginative universe of reader and writer or text[73] enables patterns in the text to serve as direct descriptors of the reader's world and community. The absence of modern historicist and social scientific concerns gives a different texture to interest in authorial intention. While many modern readers will, no doubt, see this difference as indicating a theoretical *naïveté*, one will better understand early Christian exegesis the more one reserves judgement and considers how this 'lack' resulted in particular styles of attention to the text.[74]

A second way in which the plain sense was pluralistic stems from assumptions that the scriptural text could have a variety of functions in the education of the Christian mind. Almost all early Christian authors assume that one may read the plain sense of many scriptural passages using different techniques and in different ways as a 'figural' resource for the Christian seeking to grow in understanding of the mystery of God's action and the process of purification in

---

[73] It is sometimes said that ancient exegetes do not have a modern historical sense. This statement is far too imprecise. These exegetes understood that they stood within a tradition of Christians stretching back to the Apostles, but they did not presuppose a gap between their own imaginative worlds and those of the earliest Christians.

[74] At times, for modern readers, it is the recognition of historical 'distance' that is taken to enable the interpretative 'gap' between text and reader that enables ongoing and vital interpretation and dispute about meaning. Such a person might ask, 'On what basis did ancient readers feel the "gap" that enables interpretative dispute?' The question is one that demands multiple answers. On the one hand, some points of departure may be indicated: the sense that a scriptural text is inherently mysterious and demands ongoing attention; the mere existence of interpretative dispute within one's tradition enables the possibility of continuing debate by offering new readings. On the other hand, ancient readers do recognize certain sorts of historical 'gap': for instance, a recognition that the text may contain references and terminology whose meaning may not now be clear. This historical sense may enable multiple interpretation even though the text is still read as speaking immediately to one's 'imaginative universe'.

Christ. When we seek to understand this variety of ways of reading the text, it is more helpful to speak of different reading practices than different levels of the text. The plain sense is not abandoned as the reader moves to different levels of the text; the plain sense contains different senses. The 'way the words run' still governs the shape of the sense discovered.[75]

Early Christian authors do sometimes use metaphors of ascent to describe the progress from one reading technique to another, and they speak of uncovering what remains hidden. They did not necessarily believe, however, in distinct levels of texts or that non-literal senses are to be discerned without reference to 'the way the words run'.[76] While they deploy these terminologies of uncovering and ascending, they also insist that progress is made by learning how to apply (when appropriate) different reading techniques to the plain sense. As we shall see, the words and flow of the plain sense still shape and police figural readings.

Having contended that early Christian exegesis focuses on the plain sense, I suggest we now divide early Christian exegetical/ hermeneutical strategies into two categories, the grammatical and the figural.[77] These categories are not mutually exclusive: grammatical techniques are also used within figural practices. Grammatical techniques are, however, the fundamental reading tools, essential for the good reading of Scripture.[78] They are particularly important when considering exegesis of Trinitarian and Christological texts, and they form the core of the exegesis that we will discuss throughout this book.

---

[75] Patricia Cox Miller, 'Origen and the Witch of Endor', in *The Poetry of Thought in Late Antiquity: Essays in Imagination and Religion* (Aldershot, Burlington, Vt.: Ashgate, 2001), offers a particularly interesting attempt to note the complexity of the relationships between the different 'senses'.

[76] Such an assumption is frequently cited as a reason for rejecting the readings of these other senses by modern scholars arguing that Christians should abandon early Christian exegetical techniques.

[77] These terms owe something to Frances Young's division between rhetorical and philosophical exegesis, modes dependent on noting their non-Christian origins. See her essay 'The Rhetorical Schools and their Influence on Patristic Exegesis', in Rowan D. Williams (ed.), *The Making of Orthodoxy: Essays in Honour of Henry Chadwick* (Cambridge: Cambridge University Press, 1989), 182–99. In this essay she argues that much of the 'Antiochene' critique of Origen is not a critique of his 'allegorical' method for neglecting the 'historical' dimension of the text, but a dispute between two different techniques for treating the 'literal' sense of a text. The term 'figural' is intended as a term that intentionally avoids the opposition between 'allegory' and 'typology'. Its usage in modern writing always invokes the figure of Erich Auerbach. Auerbach, as Andrew Louth reminds me, assumed that this practice was long dead. In Dawson's work the term is defined with explicit acknowledgement of the legacy and of the need to understand the term beyond his usage.

[78] For recent scholarship which takes this principle to be fundamental in understanding early Christian exegesis see Neuschafer, *Origenes* and Frances Young, *Biblical Exegesis and the Formation of Christian Culture* (Cambridge: Cambridge University Press, 1997).

Grammatical techniques have at their core skills learned at the hands of the γραμματικός (or *grammaticus*).[79] The γραμματικός was broadly responsible for the education of children in the teenage years, but ancient education was highly flexible: grammatical studies were, however, the foundation of any later studies.[80] They provided students not only with techniques and skills for reading, but also with a sense of the appropriate order to be followed in applying these techniques and of the ends of textual interpretation. A student was taught to begin with textual and manuscript criticism, especially important in an age when texts were hand copied. Then came practice in reading a text aloud. In an age without punctuation, this combination of literary critical and oral techniques enabled students to identify who was speaking at a given point, and how to attribute passages to the characters speaking in the text. This literary technique would have doctrinal significance, focusing the minds of Christian readers of Scripture on questions of who might be speaking in Christologically significant texts, the Word, the incarnate Word, or the human being assumed by the Word.[81]

Next, students learned to identify historical and literary references and to apply appropriate medical, scientific, or philosophical knowledge to understand the vocabulary or argument. Of course, many of the figures considered in this book received higher levels of technical education beyond what a γραμματικός would have taught. Others received advanced training in exegetical technique through apprenticeship to Christian teachers. This would have included advanced philosophical training, including skill in logic and dialectic but also additional areas of study such as medicine. While in some cases this material did teach new reading techniques (discussed

---

[79] On the teaching of the γραμματικός see for introduction the classic study of H. I. Marrou, *Education in Antiquity*, tr. George Lamb (Madison: University of Wisconsin Press, 1956), 160–85, 274–91. See also Martin Irvine, *The Making of Textual Culture: Grammatica and Literary Theory 350–1100* (Cambridge: Cambridge University Press, 1994). Fundamental for current study of grammarians and their role in late antique society is Robert A. Kaster, *Guardians of Language: The Grammarian and Society in Late Antiquity* (Berkeley: University of California Press, 1988). Kaster's chs. 4 and 5 give the two extremely useful accounts of individual grammarians at work with a text. For an introduction to Jewish exegesis in this period and beyond see David Weiss Halvini, *Plain and Applied Meaning in Rabbinic Exegesis* (New York: Oxford University Press, 1991).

[80] The flexibility of ancient educational practice is helpfully explored in Teresa Morgan, *Literate Education in the Hellenistic and Roman Worlds* (Cambridge: Cambridge University Press, 1998), esp. chs. 5 and 6. See also Robert A. Kaster, 'Notes on Primary and Secondary Schools in Late Antiquity', *Transactions of the American Philological Association*, 113 (1983), 323–46.

[81] For an example of how this technique influenced the development of Christological terminology see Hubertus R. Drobner, *Person-Exegese und Christologie bei Augustinus* (Leiden: Brill, 1986). A summary is provided in his 'Grammatical Exegesis and Christology in St. Augustine', *SP* 18 (1990), 49–63.

below under 'figural' techniques), it mainly provided resources for an interpreter to expand on techniques learnt under the γραμματικός.

Faced with difficult passages, students would also learn to identify rhetorical techniques used and the plot and direction of a text, its σκοπός or οἰκονομία.[82] When modern historical-critical scholars describe early Christian exegesis, they often identify an apparent lack of interest in interpreting terms within their immediate textual context. While this is by no means universally so, it is indeed true that Christian adaptation of ancient reading practices pushed Christians in certain directions. On the one hand, when Christians talk about the σκοπός of Scripture (or its synonyms) they usually refer to Scripture understood *as a unit*. Especially in the case of debate over fundamental doctrinal themes, they took the text of Scripture as a resource enabling a consistent, unitary vision of God and the order of creation. The function of Scripture for the Christian community pushes Christians to search for a canonical unity beyond that provided by any one discrete passage. On the other hand, perception of the unity of scriptural teaching—as a necessary result of Scripture's function in the economy of salvation—makes Christians attentive to the individual terms used in Scripture. The function of Scripture as Scripture pushes Christians toward particular applications and adaptations of grammatical practice.

The final stage of textual analysis as taught by the γραμματικός was judgement of a text, evaluating its moral content and drawing its lessons. This was both the capstone and the foundation of grammatical study. Greek and Roman children learned to treat this aspect of exegesis as its culmination *and*, from the very beginning of their education, to absorb moral maxims that they could find illustrated in classical texts. Understanding this moral aspect of education helps to clarify the ambiguous feelings of many intellectual Christians toward Roman education. Roman educators wanted students to learn the right lessons from the right texts. Education in reading technique, therefore, became a contested cultural area and Christians eventually if slowly sought to adapt these teaching techniques by focusing them on Scripture. This feature of Roman education also helps to explain why Christians so naturally read scriptural texts as shaping a form of life, and it reminds modern readers to be clear about the distinction between figural practices—especially allegory—and moral readings.

Some readers will be puzzled by my inattention so far to parallels between Christian and Jewish exegesis. Such parallels can be found,

---

[82] It is important to note that part of what a γραμματικός taught was how to recognize a textual element *as* 'difficult.' The γραμματικός taught students to notice obscure references or unusual grammatical forms as appropriate subjects for interpretation.

for the origins of Christian exegesis lie within Second Temple Judaism, but by the fourth century very few Christians had the detailed knowledge of Judaism that would enable Jewish practices to be a continuing source. In any case, Jewish education itself drew on Roman and Greek models, although it continued to be centred around the study of Jewish texts. Many early Christian exegetes, moreover, experienced higher levels of ancient education, especially in rhetoric: the techniques learnt here supplemented the basic grammatical education, and thus I include them under grammatical techniques.

Alongside grammatical techniques early Christians used figural reading practices. David Dawson has helped us see how Christian figural techniques describe relationships between one scriptural text (usually from the Old Testament) and an aspect of the incarnate Word's mission as described in the New Testament, using the former to inform a reading of the latter.[83] The phrase 'an aspect of the incarnate Word's mission' requires further discussion. For early Christian readers the progress of purification or sanctification that constitutes Christian life is intrinsically connected to the life, activity, and purpose of Christ, the incarnate Word. The mystery of the incarnation includes the mystery by which members of the Christian community are united to the person of Christ and purified toward the vision of God. Using a text from the Old Testament to illustrate the course and struggles of this mystery is of a piece with using Old Testament texts to illustrate Christ's actions and life. The figural reader seeks figures within the text both to understand the incarnate Word and to participate in the divine speech and action in creation.

For Dawson, these readings do not depend on a binary division between what texts literally say and what they non-literally mean. In other words, they do not assert that (say) a given Old Testament text is 'really about' some event or experience that can be clearly stated apart from that text without loss. The assumption that this is the formal structure of figural practices has often prompted their rejection by post-Reformation scholars. Dawson argues, however, that for figural readers the relationship between the particularities of one text and the event or text conjoined with it is *fundamental*. Only by taking the two poles together can one engage in good exegesis: attention to the letter of the text read figurally illumines the event or text being illustrated and explored.

Dawson does, however, distinguish figural from figurative

---

[83] David Dawson, 'Figural Reading and the Fashioning of Christian Identity in Boyarin, Auerbach and Frei', *Modern Theology*, 14 (1998), 181–96.

exegesis, preserving the latter term for an exegesis that begins with the plain text but loses the link with it. I prefer to speak more simply of figural and bad figural exegesis. The tendency for the figural to go bad is in some authors constant, but discerning how and where the shift has been made is complex. Several Christians after Origen saw his exegesis of Genesis as a key example of the figural going bad. Whether a given reading displays appropriate attention to the words of the text—and the way those words 'run'—cannot always be 'objectively' assessed. What counts as good figural exegesis is established within a tradition's development and internal argument.

This sketch of scriptural reading techniques helps us understand the nature of theological practice in the period. Early Christians did not distinguish 'exegesis' and 'theology' in the way that modern scholars tend to do. At the same time, no one term designated the practice of talking and writing about the divine and about things in relationship to the divine among Christians in this period, certainly none that can helpfully be translated by the modern English 'theology'. Christians used a variety of terms—such as φιλοσοφία, θεολογία, and θεωρία—all of which had long non-Christian histories. We can, however, make some progress in understanding how the reading of Scripture functioned for talking about God (and the world) by noting that the Christian adaptation of such words added distinct teleological and epistemological concerns to their sense. When Christian authors use terms such as θεολογία, they understand talk about God to be governed by a soteriological narrative. This narrative enables them to speak of the goal to which they are heading (or are drawn), and it positions all talk about God at a point within the narrative.

The narrative structure of faith shaped Christian discussions of human nature and transformation in teleological directions: discussions of human transformation came to be seen as appropriately focused on shaping progress toward the goals of life with God and the (increasingly eschatological) contemplation of the divine being. This view stands in some contrast to the ways in which ancient philosophical traditions sustained discussion about the ends of human nature and the possibility of attaining them. At the same time those narratives also position talk about God and the world by offering perspectives on human capacity and incapacity and the role of Scripture in aiding and shaping human reflection: Christian narratives thus also shape epistemological concerns. Despite their constant debate about human capacity, Christians insisted that the text of Scripture is, at this stage in the drama of redemption, the fundamental resource for knowledge of God and a resource that shapes how we engage existing human perceptions of the world and all it contains. As we shall see, this understanding of Scripture attains new sophistication during the fourth-century controversies as the extent to which the plain sense can be said to describe the divine being comes into question.

Thus, at this point in the divinely governed drama of redemption Christians explore and debate the transformation that constitutes Christian life by attention to the scriptural text. Christians summarized the narrative and σκοπός of the text in the 'rule of faith' or in the creeds that formed early Christian catechesis, and this received faith was the assumed context for one's reading of Scripture. Of course, these expressions of faith were frequently unclear on some central points of debate during the fourth century, and different local traditions favoured different expressions. Nevertheless, in all contexts the perceived traditional faith was the guide for interpretation. The terminology and phraseology of these statements of received faith were taken to reflect the content of Scripture and careful attention to 'the way the words run' was taken to be the fundamental point of reference in discussion.

Reading the scriptural text to discern the character of God and the structure of Christian existence involved early Christians in a constant discussion about which terminologies and philosophical resources are best suited to explicate the plain sense. Christian writers negotiated between the text and other resources that seemed attractive and persuasive. We might think of Scripture in the fourth century as the fundamental resource for the Christian imagination. The phrase recognizes the existence of a variety of *other* resources and the necessity of negotiating between competing attractions. To speak of the 'Christian imagination' is to indicate that Scripture provided a resource for thinking about the structure of the world and our perception and understanding of it. The better we understand the process of adapting (and transforming) technical terminologies and persuasive non-Christian ideas to read the resource of the plain sense, the better we understand early Christian 'theology'. The rest of this book provides a variety of extended examples of this process of adaptation and transformation. In general terms, and in an essay that takes Thomas Aquinas as its primary example, Bruce Marshall offers an outline applicable to fourth-century Christian practice:

To say the plain sense is primary in the order of justification is to say that one does not take Scripture to be false, although what we identify as its plain sense may at any given point be false . . . When the plain sense is thought of in this way, it is possible to retain the primacy of the plain sense in the order of justification, while still allowing that external arguments may lead to a change in the way the plain sense is construed. This is because, while it is always possible for external arguments to foster a reconsideration of the plain sense, no interpretation can count as an identification of the plain sense, no matter how well supported by external argument, which fails to agree with the way the words go ... Thus beliefs cannot be justified, as a criterion for the justification of other beliefs, which do not agree with the way the words go, that is, which cannot count as or cohere with the plain sense ... So, when confronted with evident conflict between ranges of internal and external beliefs both of which we would like to hold true, there are basically two courses of action consistent with the justificatory primacy of the plain sense—that is, with the requirement that beliefs held true be consistent with the way the words go: i) we can revise our identification of the plain sense in light of external beliefs; ii) we can revise our estimate of our external beliefs in light of the requirements of the plain sense.[84]

Thus, while it might seem that the mere prominence of scriptural material in texts would serve to indicate the biblical character of fourth-century theology, I suggest that understanding what it means for fourth-century theologies to be focused around the text of Scripture can best proceed by examining the range of functions of Scripture within fourth-century theological cultures. Only by such a wider investigation could we see the many ways in which philosophical traditions and terminologies were brought into an ongoing negotiation with—and about the sense of—the plain sense of Scripture. These negotiations were at the very heart of Christian intellectual cultures throughout the period covered in this book.[85] Chapters 11–15 offer an extended discussion of how pro-Nicenes viewed such negotiations at the end of the century; discussions of earlier theologians in previous chapters should offer some sense of the ways in which the origin and source of these controversies is in one sense an emerging Christian culture or cultures focused around engaging the plain sense of Scripture.

[84] Bruce D. Marshall, 'Absorbing the World: Christianity and the Universe of Truths', in Bruce Marshall (ed.), *Theology and Dialogue: Essays in Conversation with George Lindbeck* (Notre Dame, Ind.: Notre Dame University Press, 1990), 69–102, here 94–5.

[85] For the purposes of my argument the distinction between 'Alexandrian' and 'Antiochene' exegesis is irrelevant. Attempts to trace 'Arianism' to a source in proto-Antiochene exegesis (such as one finds in Newman) are unsustainable. In particular they assume that it is possible to identify an 'Antiochene' exegetical tradition as a virtually constant discrete tradition.

2
Theological Trajectories in the Early Fourth Century: I

THE GENERATION OF THE SON: TWO TRENDS

The first chapter discussed three different points of departure for the fourth-century controversies. In this chapter I turn to my fourth point of departure. To understand how the story of Arius and Alexander quickly spread beyond Alexandria we need to get some sense of the existing theological trajectories and tensions present in the early years of the fourth century. I have set out four distinct theological trajectories through this chapter and the next, but by way of introduction we can identify two distinct trends through these trajectories.[1] In talking about the status of the Son (the Spirit is, at least initially, much less a focus of attention), some prefer language that emphasizes the *sameness* of Father and Son, while others emphasize *diversity* between the two. Most theologians combine these tendencies, but almost all use one set as primary, as governing how the other should be understood.

Those who emphasize sameness frequently use language which predicates the same quality univocally of Father and Son—for example, Father is God, Son is God; Father is light, Son is light. These theologians also use terminologies that emphasize the Son derivatively sharing in almost all the Father's characteristics—for example, the Son is the Father's Wisdom, Power, or Word. The language of the Son's 'generation' here implies not just a 'mirroring'

---

[1] My account of these two tendencies is based on that of Barnes, 'Trinitarian Canon', 50. Both Barnes and I are also engaging with Joseph Lienhard, 'The Arian Controversy'. Lienhard offers the terms 'miahypostatic' and 'duohypostatic' as descriptive of the two most basic trends in early 4th-cent. theology. One problem with this terminology is its simplicity: the nature and degree of shared theology and personal connection between the various Eusebians, on the one hand, and between Alexander, Athanasius, and Marcellus, on the other hand, is unknown to us. Nor can we paint a picture of theology in the second half of the 3rd cent. in terms of these categories without a great deal of speculation. A second problem with this terminology lies in its supposition that *hypostasis* is the decisive factor in the controversies. While this term is certainly the focus of much debate and confusion—and here Lienhard's thesis is a very useful heuristic tool—the focus of the debate lies in competing accounts of the Son's generation and in different understandings of the way that inherited terminologies and metaphors maintained or did not seem to maintain the unity of God. Debate over whether God is one or more *hypostasis* is, in part, only one feature of and, in part, an epiphenomenon of this wider debate. Hence, while I have found Lienhard's account helpful, I have avoided his terminology.

of the Father by the Son—as the reflection of an object shares only the appearance of that object—but a real sharing of nature and qualities. These theologians also deploy analogical resources that liken the Son to one aspect or feature of the Father's existence; for example, the Son may be conceived as the Father's Wisdom and the argument made that the Son is eternal because a person can never be without their wisdom. Some of the analogies deployed here are also highly material; following Wisd. 7: 25–6, the Son is often likened to the rays of the sun or to a stream that flows from a spring.

Those who emphasize difference between Father and Son tend to make use of relational language, frequently of a hierarchical nature. Thus, for example, such theologians speak of the Son as image and the Father as the archetype, or of the Son as the first creature—or sometimes 'a creature unlike the other creatures'—and the Father as the creator. Father and Son language is, however, something of a special case. This language is sometimes used to indicate that there must be a relationship of clear hierarchy between the two, but because of its usage by Origen to indicate eternal correlativity such usage is less frequent than one might imagine.

Theologians who emphasize difference understand the Logos to be a subordinate and independent being. To theologians emphasizing sameness Logos implies something intrinsically connected to that of which it is Logos. This is especially so when Logos is understood to mean something like 'rational capacity'. In disputes with modalists and monarchians running back to the late second century the use of Logos was controversial because these groups seem to have taken the term to indicate something possessing a temporary status, as does a spoken word. In this context the use of the term as governing metaphor seemed to imply a temporary reality dependent on, if not merely part of, the One who speaks. Origen's argument that Logos must be understood in the context of other biblical titles for the second person represents a key anti-monarchian reading. Many other terms were equally multivalent: the context of their usage is all-important.

The difference between these tendencies can further be seen in the polemic strategies used by the two groups against each other. When those who emphasize difference between Father and Son attack those who emphasize sameness, they argue that the latter group speaks materially of God, implying a division of God's being in the Son's generation. They also criticize what seems to be an envisaging of two eternal principles. On the other hand, when those who emphasize sameness between Father and Son criticize those who emphasize diversity they tend to argue that the implications of some key scriptural terminologies are being ignored—

especially such terms as Word, Wisdom, and Power. They also see a fundamental impiety in speaking of the Son as in any way like one of the creatures. Charges of using inappropriate language are, thus, at the heart of the matter. In fact, *both* sides accuse each other of thinking materially about God. The clear difference and diversity spoken of by one camp seems to the other to be the result of thinking about God as two (or three) distinct beings, separated like material entities. Indeed, this concern to secure the language of diversity between Father and Son from being understood according to the grammar of materiality will eventually become a focus of pro-Nicene theology.

Modern Trinitarian theologians often speak as if there have always been two basic tendencies, one which emphasizes unity in God, one which emphasizes diversity. The division between sameness and diversity language may seem to be repeating that commonplace: this is not so. To speak about unity and diversity *in* God, one must already have agreed that Father and Son (let alone Spirit) are all 'part' of the one God. Theologians at the beginning of the fourth century are still grappling with the problem of whether Father and Son are both 'true God', with the question of whether it is possible to speak of degrees of divinity. The division I have tried to make here is between groups who favour different primary metaphors and analogies for speaking about the relationship between God and Word, Father and Son.

ALEXANDER, ATHANASIUS, AND FRIENDS: THEOLOGIANS OF THE TRUE WISDOM

The first trajectory is found in Alexander of Alexandria and in the early Athanasius. This trajectory emphasizes the *eternally* correlative status of Father and Son in ways close to Origen's understanding of eternal generation, but is also resistant to speaking of three *hypostases*. This tradition is not limited to Alexandria, we can identify a number of third-century predecessors and a few other early fourth-century representatives in Antioch, in Asia Minor, and in Thrace and northern Greece.

Alexander's theology is best preserved in a letter sent to Alexander of Byzantium refuting the errors of Arius. There is also an encyclical letter (known from its first two words as *Henos somatos*) sent to rally anti-Arian support, but possibly drafted by his then secretary Athanasius. A brief text by Alexander is also to be found quoted in a section of Athanasius' *First Letter to Virgins*.[2] As he describes his teaching in the letter to his namesake of Byzantium, Alexander insists that the relationship of Father and Son cannot be

---

[2] This text is translated in Brakke, *Athanasius and the Politics of Asceticism*, 286–8.

conceived: this mystery is known to the Father alone. There is no distance (διάστημα) between the two, and the Son is the brightness of the eternal light—Alexander using the language of Hebrews and seeming to allude to the language of Wisdom 7. Alexander deploys this language in an argument that the Father's perfection is *constituted by* the eternal begetting and presence of the Son: the Father is termed Father *because of* the Son's presence.³ To say that the Father's Power or Word began and does not eternally complement the Father denigrates the character of the Father. Similarly, if one denies the eternal presence of the brightness then the light itself cannot be eternal. In his encyclical letter *Henos somatos*, Alexander argues that as Word or Wisdom the Son must be eternal or the Father would, nonsensically, have been at one time bereft of both.⁴

In the letter to Alexander of Byzantium we also see some themes already shaped by debate with Arius. Alexander insists, for instance, on the immutability of the Logos against Arius' claim that the Logos was not by nature immune from error or sin. Alexander argues that Arius and his associates use scriptural texts that refer to the mutability of the *incarnate* Word to describe the eternal Word as such. Alexander distinguishes between texts which refer to the Incarnate Word alone and those that speak of the Word's eternal relationship to the Father.

Alexander also denies that one must either admit that the Son is created or that there are two unbegotten Gods. He argues for a 'great distance' between the unbegotten Father and the created order, and then describes the nature (φύσις) of the only-begotten Word as mediating between these two, 'holding the middle place' (μεσιτεύουσα).⁵ Alexander is here at the limit of what his language will allow. He is clear that in his status as 'exact and identical' image (ἀπηκριβωμένη καὶ ἀπαράλλακτος) the Son lacks 'only [the Father's] unbegotten character'.⁶ Yet, Alexander sees the Son's quality as begotten implying a mediating role, but he does not want this role to indicate a subordinate ontological status. He also understands the Son to have a distinct role in the creation. Nevertheless, Alexander

---

³ Alexander, *Ep. Alex.* 26: 'But he is Father of the always present Son, on account of whom he is called Father; and with the Son always present with him, the Father is always perfect, unfailing in goodness, who begot the only-begotten Son not temporally or in an interval or from nothing.'

⁴ Alexander, *Ep. om.* 3: 'Or how is He unlike to the substance of the Father, who is the perfect image and brightness of the father . . . And how, if the Son is the Word or Wisdom and Reason of God, was there a time when He was not? It is all one as if they said, that there was a time when God was without reason and wisdom.'

⁵ *Ep. Alex.* 45. This term carries the sense of something that occupies a mediating function. Some sense of its function will be gained from the entry in *PGL*.

⁶ *Ep. Alex.* 47.

understands the character of this action to result from the Word's position 'in the bosom of the Father'. The Word is not (as for the Eusebians) an intermediate being necessary because the Father cannot directly act on the creation. Alexander also insists (quoting Isa. 53: 8) that the Son's generation and nature are incomprehensible, and not to be understood materially. Interestingly his reason for asserting the Son's incomprehensibility is that the Son shares the Father's nature.[7] The Son as true image shares the qualities of the one he reflects: this argument we will see again in pro-Nicene theology.

Alexander clearly distinguishes Father and Son, but his terminology for doing so is not precise. At one point he speaks of Father and Son being two φύσεις. Alexander also speaks of two πράγματα or things—a usage which some have seen as owing to Origen's influence.[8] Alexander also uses the term *hypostasis*, but in the majority of his uses—even where he talks of the Son's *hypostasis*—the term seems to mean 'existence' or 'nature'. We never find him using *hypostasis* as a technical term for the individual existence of one of the divine persons, and he never speaks of there being two or three *hypostases*.

We do not know if this lack of use of *hypostasis* in Origen's technical sense represents ignorance of Origen's usage, active dislike, or simply continuing adherence to a tradition that never adopted Origen's suggestion. There are, however, some features of his thought that do indicate a debt to Origen. To his use of Hebrews and Wisdom terminology may be added his insistence on the Son's eternal generation. Alexander writes,

> Therefore the characteristic high status must be preserved for the unbegotten Father by saying that no one is the cause of his being. But the befitting honor must be assigned to the Son by ascribing to him generation without beginning from the Father.[9]

Alexander's theology found its most famous advocate in his successor Athanasius. Athanasius' thought and career is covered throughout the first eight chapters of this book; here I draw attention to some themes from his early writings. While it is possible that even the earliest of Athanasius' writings was already shaped by dispute with Arius, we see clear continuity with Alexander's theology as expressed in the *Letter to Alexander of Byzantium* and thus we

---

[7] Alexander, *Ep. Alex.* 47.
[8] Alexander, *Ep. Alex.* 37–8: '... "I and the Father are one." The Lord says this, not proclaiming himself the Father or explaining that the two φύσεις in the *hypostasis* are one, but saying that the Son of the Father is disposed by nature accurately to preserve the Father's likeness.' For the use of πράγματα see *Ep. Alex.* 15.
[9] Alexander, *Ep. Alex.* 52.

can use these texts as witnesses to this theological trajectory. In his *Against the Nations* (probably *c*.335–8) Athanasius follows Alexander in not linking the Word's appearance directly to the act of creation and in arguing that the Word is the one in whom all things exist *because of* his closeness to the Father:

being present with Him as his Wisdom and his Word, looking at the Father He fashioned the Universe, and organized it and gave it order . . .

Athanasius also follows Alexander in speaking of the Son as 'unchanging image' (εἰκὼν ἀπαράλλακτος):

He is the unchanging image of his own Father. For men, composed of parts and made out of nothing, have their discourse composite and divisible. But God possesses true existence and is not composite, wherefore his Word also has true existence and is not composite, but is the one and only begotten God, who proceeds in his goodness from the Father as from a good fountain . . .[10]

Athanasius played down Alexander's conception of the Word's mediating status, and avoided statements that implied an intermediate ontological status. Athanasius argues both that the Word has a derivative existence from the Father, and that the existence he is given comes from the Father's own being. Athanasius' account here is, however, still inchoate: in the *Against the Nations* Athanasius never directly speaks of God's *ousia*, making use of a variety of metaphors and biblical titles to emphasize the Son's closeness to the Father. Mostly importantly—and mostly clearly revealing of how undeveloped his account is as yet—he frequently speaks simply of 'the Word of the Father' (*Logos tou patros*).[11]

It should also be clear from the foregoing examples that Athanasius' most basic language and analogies for describing the relationship between Father and Son primarily present the two as intrinsic aspects of one reality or person. Nevertheless, Athanasius is not a modalist: he does not directly want to describe the Son as an aspect of the Father or as a name for one way in which the Father appears. In the first of his *Orations against the Arians* Athanasius will write, 'for the Father is ever Father and could never become Son, so the Son is ever Son and could never become Father'.[12] In these earlier texts, however, Athanasius does not make use of the correlativity of Father and Son. Only as he began to cast himself as the opponent of 'Arians' at the end of the 330s did he turn to this resource—recovering an argument deployed by his mentor Alexander. In *Against the Nations* and *On the Incarnation* Athanasius does speak of

---

[10] Athanasius, *C. Gen.* 41. 1. [11] *C. Gen.* 27, 40, 42, 44, 47. [12] *C. Ar.* 1. 22.

the 'Son of God' to indicate the Word's unique status, but he possesses no clear language for articulating the distinction as yet.[13]

At this early stage in his theology Athanasius emphasizes the closeness of Word to Father by repetition and by the accumulation of titles: most clearly in *Against the Nations* 46 he strings together intensifying adjectives to indicate that the Logos is the Father's own and is in himself the various attributes Scripture accords him:

> he is absolute wisdom, true word, and himself the Father's own power, absolute light, absolute truth, absolute justice, absolute virtue, and indeed, stamp, effulgence, and image. In short, he is the supremely perfect issue of the Father, and is also alone Son, the express image of the Father.

Athanasius here may be using material from Eusebius and Origen to emphasize the closeness of Son to Father,[14] but none of the terms expressing the Son's status as 'absolute X' ever achieves the status of a frequent and technical terminology for him: he gives the impression of using whatever is to hand to emphasize closeness of relationship but not yet of having a precise way of describing that relationship.

Athanasius also insists strongly and consistently on the distinction between the Creator and the creation.[15] The background to Alexander and Athanasius' usage may perhaps be the reaction against aspects of Origen's cosmology discussed in the last chapter. For these two theologians Origen's attempt to present the Son as intrinsic to the life of God has been taken up and followed through (without his worries about the use of *ousia* language in this context), but that aspect of his account which was taken to link the eternal generation of the Son and the eternal generation of the initial creation has been rejected. Generation and creation have become, for these theologians, entirely distinct activities.

One of the distinguishing features of this theological trajectory can be seen in Athanasius' use of the term *hypostasis*. At this stage in his writing Athanasius does not know or ignores the tradition stemming from Origen of using *hypostasis* to designate the individual reality of Father or Son. Up to the mid-340s Athanasius *never* uses *hypostasis* to indicate the individual existence of something and *never* uses the term in a technical sense to indicate the distinct persons. A key to his early usage is given in *Against the Nations* 6. Athanasius is here discussing the Manichaean teaching that there are two principles, one the source of Good and one the source of Evil. This doctrine proposes another *hypostasis* besides 'the Father of our

---

[13] e.g. Athanasius, *Incarn.* 19–20.   [14] Cf. Eusebius, *Prep.* 7. 10. 12; *Eccl. theol.* 1. 8.
[15] This theme is the subject of Khaled Anatolios, *Athanasius: The Coherence of his Thought* (London and New York: Routledge, 1998).

Lord Jesus Christ'. Athanasius does not, however, show any consistent usage of the term at this stage: elsewhere in the text *hypostasis* is used to describe the idea of actual existence, God brings things into *hypostasis* from nothing.[16] Nevertheless, this text does help us to see that Athanasius' gut reaction is that there can be only one eternal reality and source, and that proposing more than one *hypostasis* would imply a dualism. Interestingly, it is not quite accurate to say Athanasius insists there is only one *hypostasis* in God: while that is a clear inference from his usage he never actually uses the term to designate what is one in God. Indeed, even throughout the three *Orations against the Arians* Athanasius never uses the term other than in direct quotation of, or in allusion to, Heb. 1: 3.

Alexander and Athanasius are members of a trajectory that is also found beyond Alexandria and that had a long history. Later, during the 350s, Athanasius will point to the theology of Dionysius of Alexandria as a precedent for his own.[17] In a short work arguing against some 'Arians' who have taken Dionysius' talk of the Son being 'created' as a precedent, Athanasius argues that his use of 'created' must be understood as secondary to Dionysius' assertion of the Son's eternal relationship to the Father. He quotes Dionysius as saying

being the brightness of light eternal, certainly he is himself eternal, for as the light exists always, it is evident that the brightness must exist always as well.[18]

For Dionysius, the Son's existence is not connected exclusively with the creating and maintaining of the created order. Metaphors of light and water indicate closeness of relationship, the ability of the Son to reveal the Father, and the eternal correlation of the two.

Athanasius also claims Theognostus, who taught in Alexandria in the latter half of the third century, as a predecessor. He quotes the following:

The essence (οὐσία) of the Son is not derived from outside, nor was he produced out of nothing, but issued from the essence of the Father (ἐκ τῆς τοῦ πατρὸς οὐσίας) like radiance from light and like vapour from water; for

---

[16] *C. Gen.* 40–1.

[17] Hanson, *The Search*, 72, accepts the view that Dionysius was a possible forerunner of Arius because of his insistence that the Son was created; Williams, *Arius*, 149 ff., prefers to think of Dionysius as being not easily assimilable to one or other early 4th-cent. tradition but as also providing an indication that Athanasius' language was traditional in Alexandria and thus that Athanasius could plausibly claim Dionysius as his own. My own reading follows Williams rather than Hanson. Williams argues that κτίσμα (Dionysius' word) is significantly different from ποίημα in connotation and had a venerable history of being used to indicate the Son's generation without implying the same as *poiema*.

[18] Athanasius, *Sent.* 15. On this text see now Uta Heil, *Athanasius von Alexandria: de Sententia Dionysii*, PTS 52 (Berlin: De Gruyter, 1999).

neither the radiance, nor the vapour is the water itself or the sun itself, nor is the one alien to another, so too [the nature of the Son] is an outflowing (ἀπόρροια) of the Father's essence, without the Father's essence being divided. For as the sun remains the same, and is not impaired by the rays poured forth by it, so neither does the Father's essence suffer change, though it has the Son as an image of itself.[19]

It is a fascinating question whether Athanasius can fairly make a claim on Theognostus. Theognostus is criticized by other fourth-century writers (most notably Gregory of Nyssa) for teaching that the Son was created. We should, however, note that here we have another case of a writer whose language about the Son's production seemed dangerous to late fourth-century pro-Nicene ears, but may well have been less surprising in its immediate context. Both Dionysius of Alexandria and Theognostus use a terminology of 'creating' as one among a range of terms, and we simply cannot be certain how this was heard in third-century Alexandria. This problem aside, Theognostus insists clearly that the Son comes from the Father's being or essence. The metaphors on which Origen places so much weight are here understood to imply that the Son comes from what the Father truly is.

One figure who may stand as an independent witness to a post-Origenist tradition that strongly emphasized the closeness between Father and Son, is the late third-century writer Gregory Thaumaturgus. Gregory studied with Origen in Caesarea and later became bishop of Caesarea in Pontus.[20] Towards the end of the fourth century Gregory was treated as a significant forerunner by the Cappadocians. Among his surviving works is a short discussion of the unity of God and the distinctions between the persons.[21] For Gregory God is a simple and indivisible unity. The Word comes forth without division, like the production of a word in the

---

[19] Athanasius, *Decr.* 25. 2. The four fragments of Theognostus are collected and commented on by Adolf von Harnack, 'Die Hypotyposen des Theognost', *Texte und Untersuchungen*, 9 (1903), 73–92. On Theognostus see Leslie W. Barnard, 'The Antecedents of Arius', *Vigchr*, 24 (1970), 172–88, esp. 179–82; Aloys Grillmeier, *Christ in Christian Tradition*, 2nd ed. (London: Mowbrays, 1975), 159–62. With this text should be compared the fourth fragment, which demonstrates a strong theology of the Son as the image of the Father's *ousia*.

[20] There are a confusing number of Caesareas for the modern reader unfamiliar with ancient geography. Caesarea in Pontus is neither Eusebius' Caesarea in Palestine nor Basil's Caesarea in Cappadocia.

[21] Gregory Thaumaturgus, *To Philagrius* [*On Consubstantiality*] (c.240–60). Accepting that the 'On Consubstantiality' section of the title is almost certainly a later addition, there seem to be two reasons for accepting the authenticity of the text. First, there is no mention of any of the key disputed 4th-cent. terminology. Secondly, Gregory uses the metaphor of a spring and two rivers in a way that seems unimaginable by mid- or late 4th-cent. standards, especially in its en passant subordinationism. Other reasons for the authenticity of the text are reinforced by Michael Slusser in 'The "To Philagrius On Consubstantiality" of Gregory Thaumaturgus', *SP* 19 (1989), 230–5.

immaterial and indivisible soul. Gregory parallels this analogy with that of the sun and its rays, although he offers an idiosyncratic version that eventually turns to the analogy of the eye and the ray of light which supposedly comes from it in the process of vision. Gregory ends with the metaphor of two rivers flowing from a spring:

> But also just as from a certain spring of water which ungrudgingly wells forth water like nectar ... an abundant stream ... is carved into rivers which may be two as regards their stream, but have a single flow from the beginning ... even if each of the aforesaid rivers should seem to be defined for a long way, and to be very remote from the spring, at least it has its beginning united to its origin ... In very much the same way also, therefore, the God of all good things ... though he sent us as an intelligible grace a certain double flow of the Son and the Holy Spirit, did not himself suffer anything as if damaged in substance ....[22]

Gregory here deploys the traditional metaphor of a stream and a fountain to indicate that the Father gives from his inexhaustible existence in generating Son and Spirit. No technical language of shared existence or being is present, but the analogy itself points in a direction very different from that of Arius. Nevertheless, Gregory deploys this language while still speaking of the Son and Spirit as 'very remote from the Spring'. If this text is authentic then it indicates the presence of something like this trajectory in third-century Asia Minor. In discussing Marcellus' theology in the next chapter I will note possible links with 'Monarchian' and anti-Monarchian theologies in Asia Minor in the third century. Those links provide further context for a variety of theologies emphasizing the unity of Father and Son in this region.

There are other indications that this style of theology was to be found far beyond Alexandria. First, there is the synodical letter from the Council of Antioch early in 325. Alexander himself was not in attendance, and although his influence must have been of importance at the council, we can also fairly read the text as demonstrating a very similar theological tradition at work in Antioch. The text speaks of the only begotten Son as,

> begotten not from that which is not but from the Father, not as made but as properly an offspring, but begotten in an ineffable, indescribable manner, because only the Father who begot and the Son who was begotten know (for no one knows the Father but the Son, nor the Son but the Father), who exists everlastingly and did not at one time not exist. For we have learned from the Holy Scriptures that he alone is the sole image ... we confess him to have been begotten of the unbegotten Father, God the Word, true light, righteousness, Jesus Christ, Lord and Saviour of all. For he is the image,

---

[22] Gregory Thaumaturgus, *Phil.* 8.

not of the will or of anything else, but of his Father's very *qnômâ* (*hypostasis*).[23]

This text makes no use of the *ousia* language that we see in Nicaea's creed. Instead it relies on a very strong image theology. As 'sole image' of the Father the Son must be truly (and eternally) begotten from the Father. If we are right to read *hypostasis* in the text here it probably alludes to Heb. 1: 3 and indicates the Father's nature, as it does in Alexander. Against Arius the text also asserts very strongly that Father and Son know each other, even as far as both knowing the manner of the Son's generation, which is incomprehensible to all others.

The text also uses the terminology of the Son as 'true light'. We cannot identify with certainty the sources on which this text draws, we can see here reference to John 1: 9's reference to 'the true light that enlightens every man' and possibly allusion to the importance of Christ as 'true image'. It is not going too far, I think, to see behind this language a soteriological concern: the Son's status as revealer of the Father, as light of the world and as saviour is seen as resting on his being the true image eternally generated from the Father. Once again a strong assertion of the ability of the Son to image the Father to the world is seen as requiring a strong statement of the Son's origin from or 'in' the Father's being. If the Son is truly to reflect the Father then there is also a strong pull towards acknowledging the eternity of his existence.

Alexander's *Letter to Alexander of Byzantium* indicates (unless we attribute simple *naïveté* to the bishop of Alexandria) that he expected his theology to be recognized as orthodox by its intended audience. We may, thus, also be able to point to northern Greece and Thrace as an area that followed this theological trajectory. The bishops of Thessalonica in the early fourth century understood themselves to owe allegiance to the bishop of Rome and were strong supporters of Athanasius: Alexander wrote in defence of Athanasius when he was deposed and his successor Aetius was an important member of a council of 'western' bishops at Serdica in 343. Many of these 'westerners' were from Greece, Thrace, and the Balkans. That the Emperor Theodosius was himself baptized by Acholius, bishop of Thessalonica, and from there issued his famous edict defining Christian orthodoxy by reference to that taught in Rome and Alexandria is probably no accident.[24]

---

[23] The text is preserved only in Syriac. An English translation is to be found in J. Stevenson (ed.), *A New Eusebius: Documents Illustrating the History of the Church to AD 337*, rev. W. H. C. Frend (London: SPCK, 1987), 334–5.

[24] Were Alexander's letter to his namesake of Byzantium actually to Alexander of Thessalonica this would add greatly to these suppositions, but the case for that attribution is not

This is just one example of the diverse local theological traditions that existed, but it does enable us to point to an important conclusion. Some writers still persist in assuming that theologies in the early fourth century can be divided between east and west, the westerners resolutely 'beginning' from the unity of God, easterners somehow naturally prone to a more diverse account of Father, Son, and Spirit. This is obviously rendered highly problematic by the theology of Alexander and Athanasius, and nonsensical when we note the geographically widespread examples I have discussed here.[25]

THE 'EUSEBIANS': THEOLOGIANS OF THE 'ONE UNBEGOTTEN'

My second theological trajectory is the one in which we locate Arius himself. This loose alliance I will term 'Eusebian'. When I use this term I mean to designate any who would have found common ground with *either* of Arius' most prominent supporters, Eusebius of Nicomedia or Eusebius of Caesarea. Using the term in this way reflects but changes the early fourth-century phrase 'those around Eusebius'. This phrase is first used to describe those who supported Eusebius of Nicomedia in his theological and ecclesiastical policies by Alexander of Alexandria. Eusebius of Nicomedia was a supporter of Arius and a bishop influential with the Emperors Licinius, Constantine, and Constantius. However, I will use the term 'Eusebian' more broadly and with a primarily theological reference: the theological positions of Eusebius of Nicomedia and Eusebius of Caesarea are distinct and yet close enough for them to be allied in opposition to Alexander.[26] Many eastern bishops rallied around the Eusebii even while differing among themselves. Eventually these differences became more marked and those who sought to inherit guiding roles in this group found themselves on opposite sides of some key fences.

I begin here with three figures who share a common allegiance to the shadowy Lucian of Antioch, martyred around 312. The first of

---

convincing. For Alexander's support of Athanasius see Athanasius, *Apol. sec.* 16 and 66. At *Apol. sec.* 16 Athanasius does admit that his opponents expected Alexander to take their side. But, however we should take that hint, note that at *Apol. sec.* 66, Alexander is happy to accuse Athanasius' opponents of being 'Arians', which seems to indicate an early willingness to adopt Athanasius' heresiological terminology.

[25] One rarely finds in modern scholarship the older presentation of Alexandria as an 'outpost of western theology', and for good reason. Identifying 'western' as a type of theology and then typifying comparable eastern theologians as actually 'western' has a wonderful illogicality.

[26] My wide usage of 'Eusebians' mirrors that of Joseph T. Lienhard, *Contra Marcellum: Marcellus of Ancyra and Fourth Century Theology* (Washington, DC: Catholic University of America Press, 1999).

Theological Trajectories: I

these is Eusebius of Nicomedia. Little survives of Eusebius' writing—one complete letter and a few fragments. Writing to Paulinus the bishop of Tyre to encourage support for Arius, Eusebius writes:

> [There is] one, the unoriginated, and one produced by him truly and not from his substance, not participating at all in the unoriginated nature nor in his substance, but produced as altogether different in his nature and in his power, being in complete likeness of disposition and power to him who made him . . .
>
> There is, indeed, nothing of his *ousia*, yet everything that exists has been called into being by his will (βούλημα) . . .[27]

For Eusebius the status of the Word does not stem from sharing in the divine attributes as the only one generated from the divine being, but from a decision of the divine will. The theme of generation from the will we will meet many time again: for many it served both to secure the generation of the Word against materialist division of God, and to emphasize the unique character of the Father as true God. We do see some reference to the Son being like the Father, but unfortunately this letter does not provide us with any information about how Eusebius made use of this theme.

The second figure is Asterius, known as the 'sophist'. Asterius had sacrificed to the gods during the last great persecution and was thus ineligible for ordination. Nevertheless, Asterius was an important defender of Arius before Nicaea, and after Nicaea his theology became one of the main sparks for the continuing controversy as he attempted to defend Eusebius of Nicomedia against the attacks of Marcellus of Ancyra: unfortunately only fragments of his works survive. Asterius distinguishes between a number of distinct powers and wisdoms.[28] God's own power and wisdom is the source of Christ and of all things (it is God's own power and wisdom that Paul describes as being seen in the creation at Rom. 1: 20), but Christ himself is a recent power and wisdom, the first and 'only begotten' of the many powers created by the Father:

> The blessed Paul said not that he preached Christ the power of God or the wisdom of God, but, without the article, 'God's power and God's wisdom';

---

[27] Ed. Opitz, *Werke*, III/1, U.8.

[28] For brief introductions to Asterius' theology see Hanson, *The Search*, 32–8; Thomas A. Kopecek, *A History of Neo-Arianism*, 2 vols. (Philadelphia: Philadelphia Patristic Foundation, 1979), I. 28–34; Lienhard, *Contra Marcellum*, 89–98. Markus Vinzent, *Asterius von Kappadokien: Die Theologische Fragmente. Einleitung, Kritischer Text, Übersetzung und Kommentar* (Leiden: Brill, 1993), offers an excellent edition and discussion of what remains. There is also a set of homilies on the Psalms that have by some been attributed to Asterius. I am persuaded by the argument of Wolfram Kinzig, *In Search of Asterius: Studies on the Authorship of the Psalms* (Göttingen: Vandenhoeck & Ruprecht, 1990), at least that it is extremely doubtful that these homilies are by Asterius and thus I have not referred to them.

thus preaching that the proper power of God Himself, which is natural to him and coexistent with him unoriginatedly, is something besides.[29]

Asterius understands the terminology of power and wisdom in a manner directly opposed to that found in Alexander, and in Athanasius, where Christ is the one power and wisdom of the Father. Asterius argues that the Son was generated because the Father foresaw the inability of created nature to bear his direct touch.[30] Asterius insists also that Father, Son, and Spirit are three *hypostases* and he uses the logical formula that 'the Father is truly Father, the Son truly Son and the Spirit likewise' to emphasize that the distinctions between the three are implied by the names we accord them.

As Michel Barnes remarks, however, while we seem to see in Asterius a doctrine similar to Origen's insistence that the Son is one of the many powers, it is noteworthy that Asterius uses this doctrine not to support an account of the Son's separate existence from the Father, but to emphasize Christ's status as the first of many.[31] Indeed, Asterius does clearly emphasize the uniqueness of the Son's status as the first and as the one who can effect a transformation of all created things. The Son is 'Logos for the sake of rational things, and Wisdom for the sake of things endowed with wisdom. . . .'[32]

Eusebius of Caesarea quotes with approval a fragment from Asterius of particular importance: 'the only begotten Logos (John 1: 18) and first born of all creation, the alone [begetting] the alone, perfect the perfect, King the King, Lord the Lord, God [begetting] God, exact image of the being (οὐσίας . . . ἀπαράλλακτον εἰκόνα) and will and power and glory'.[33] Here Asterius shows himself happy to speak of the Logos as the image of the Father's *ousia*, presumably because for him the term image carries a clear sense of difference and subordination. This text reappears at an important council in 341, as we shall see in Chapter 5

The third figure is Arius himself. Again, little of his own writing survives.[34] Arius insists that the Father is alone God, simple and immutable. The Son is born from the Father before the creation and

---

[29] Quoted in Athanasius, *C. Ar.* 1. 32 (Vinzent fr. 64).

[30] Quoted in Athanasius, *C. Ar.* 2. 24 (Vinzent fr. 26): 'The God of all, wanting to create originate nature, when he saw that it could not endure the untempered hand of the Father, and to be created by him, makes and creates first and alone one only, and calls him Son and Word, that, through him as a medium, all things might thereupon be brought to be.'

[31] Barnes, *Power of God*, 126–7.   [32] Quoted at Athanasius, *C. Ar.* 2. 38.

[33] Eusebius, *C. Marcellus* 1. 4.

[34] Apart from some letters, we have only some fragments of Arius' own theology from his *Thalia*. While the placing of Arius as one among a number of Eusebian theologies may make the point obvious, it is worth noting directly that, unlike a number of accounts over the past 150 years, I have made no attempt to isolate one controlling theme or concept in his theology. The range of his concerns should emerge from seeing him against the background of his peers and immediate sources.

although we cannot describe the Son's birth in temporal categories, we should not say that the Son is coeternal. Such language circumvents the implications of the Son being *born* from the Father. In his *Thalia* ('the banquet', composed *c*.323) he writes,

> The one without beginning established the Son as the beginning of all creatures ... He [the Son] possesses nothing proper (ἴδιος) to God, in the real sense of propriety, for he is not equal to God, nor yet is he of the same substance (ὁμοούσιος) ... there exists a Trinity in unequal glories, for their subsistencies (*hypostases*) are not mixed with each other ... The Father is other than the Son in substance (κατ' οὐσίαν) because he is without beginning ... By God's will the Son is such as he is, by God's will he is as great as he is, from [the time] when, since the very moment when he took his subsistence from God; Mighty God as he is, he sings the praises of the Higher One with only partial adequacy. To put it briefly, God is inexpressible to the Son ... For it is impossible to search out the mysteries of the Father, who exists in himself ... What scheme of thought, then, could admit the idea that he who has his being from the Father (τὸν ἐκ πατρὸς ὄντα) should know by comprehension the one who gave him birth.[35]

For Arius, the three *hypostaseis* have different levels of glory befitting their different status. The Son does not know the Father and is unable fully to praise the Father. The Son exists because of the Father's will: and thus some of the central characteristics that govern all products of the Father must govern the Son. In his *Thalia* Arius may also have asserted that the Son is 'from the things that did not exist (ἐξ οὐκ ὄντων)'.[36] Although he later seems to have retracted such language, Arius seems to have continued to insist that the Logos is potentially changeable: only the Father is by nature immutable (1 Tim. 6: 16). Arius also talks of two wisdoms and powers, speaking of a *Logos* that was not distinct from the Father's *hypostasis*, after whom the Son is designated Word.

Arius still speaks of the Son as image, reflection (Heb. 1: 3), and light. Although the surviving fragments of Arius' work do not contain a direct parallel, Athanasius reports that he copied Asterius' account of the necessity of a mediator for the purpose of creation. In their 1981 book *Early Arianism: A View of Salvation* Robert Gregg and Denis Groh argued that Arius was motivated primarily by soteriological concerns. They argued that for Arius the mutable Son becomes incarnate, adopts a human life and thus provides a model for us of how to grow in moral excellence and holiness so that we too may be adopted as 'Sons' of God. Gregg and Groh argued

---

[35] The longest section of this work to survive is quoted by Athanasius at *Synod.* 15. The best translation (quoted here) and discussion is provided by Williams, *Arius*, 101 ff. (see also Hanson's translation at *The Search* 14 ff.).

[36] Athanasius, *C. Ar.* 1. 5.

that Arius' account of the relations between Father and Son should be read as part of a fully rounded conception of Christian existence. Nevertheless, in its details this thesis has met with only partial acceptance. Evidence is lacking for the adoptionist Christology they describe (Gregg and Groh rely over-heavily on the 'evidence' of Athanasius' description of Arius): there is also something very modern about explaining a cosmology as *really* about the practicalities of soteriology. For Arius and his followers preserving an appropriate account of the true God and of the Word may have been motivation enough.

Nevertheless, it does seem that Arius saw his opponents' account of the Word as distorting some central aspects of Christian life and practice. Rowan Williams has pointed to a possible Alexandrian liturgical context within which we might see Arius' views of the Son's status linked to concerns about prayer, worship, and the possibility of our interceding with the Father.[37] In Alexandria it seems likely that the words of the *sanctus* were understood as the prayers of the Son and the Spirit to the Father. The angels and the Christian community join in this act of praise because the Son and the Spirit act as mediators. Against this liturgical context Arius may have seen his picture of the Son as having important ramifications for how one understood the whole structure of Christian existence.

Williams also situates Arius' emphasis on the distinction between Father and Son within the context of late third-century developments in philosophical understandings of participation. Williams does not argue that Arius had a detailed knowledge of these categories, but some general awareness of the shifts that were occurring.[38] During the third century those whom modern scholars call 'neoplatonists' increasingly insisted on the transcendence of the One over all other things and developed accounts of participation in which lower realms of being can only paradoxically image features of higher realms: they represent the character of the *activity* of those higher realms but not their *essence*.

It is important to note that while much revisionary scholarship on the fourth century has focused on Arius himself, Arius' own theology is of little importance in understanding the major debates of the rest of the century. The *Thalia*, appears, for instance, to have circulated only in Alexandria; what is known of him elsewhere

---

[37] Rowan D. Williams, 'Angels Unawares: Heavenly Liturgy and Earthly Theology in Alexandria', *SP*, 30 (1997), 350–63.

[38] Particularly in the third part of his *Arius*. The necessity of the move has not gone unchallenged, especially by Christopher Stead in his 'Was Arius a Neoplatonist?', *SP*, 33 (1997), 39–52. Stead denies that some of the philosophical shifts Williams identifies actually occurred, and locates Arius firmly within 'middle Platonic' tradition.

seems to stem from Athanasius' quotations. We also even have only sporadic evidence of his texts being used by later 'Arians'.

I have linked together these three Eusebians because of their relationship to the theologian and martyr Lucian of Antioch.[39] The ancient sources seem to identify a particular group of Eusebian theologians as 'Lucianists'. Arius himself writes to Eusebius of Nicomedia using the epithet 'co-Lucianist'. The historian Sozomen reports that some of the key Eusebians after Nicaea sought to cultivate Lucian's memory by presenting the 341 second Antiochene creed as Lucian's.[40] The 'Heterousian'[41] historian Philostorgius, writing in the early fifth century, presents Lucian as one of the key sources for the non-Nicene tradition and is able to list his 'students' or followers among the supporters of Arius. In some cases there, 'students' probably lived in Antioch for a time and were actively taught by Lucian, but we should be wary of imagining anything like a formal programme of study. In other cases a 'student' of Lucian may have had only a small degree of actual contact with Lucian, but liked to acknowledge a relationship of dependence.

Unfortunately so little survives of Lucian that we cannot know what his students learnt from him.[42] We can fairly assume that he emphasized three distinct *hypostases* and taught a theology of the Son as revelatory but subordinate image. Much of Lucian's theology was probably available in other teachers as well and it seems best that we consider Lucian a prominent exponent of a theology that did not originate with him. Interestingly, although Arius was able to invoke a common bond with 'Lucianists', it also seems that he emphasized the transcendence of the Father in ways that distanced him from the others: Arius' teaching that the Son does not know the Father seems to have been at odds with the theologies of other 'Lucianists'—and with other Eusebians.

Moving on from these 'Lucianists' we come to the other Eusebius,

---

[39] The fundamental text for the study of Lucian remains Gustave Bardy, *Recherches sur Saint Lucien d'Antioche et son école* (Paris: Beauchesne, 1936); for the most recent summaries of Lucian see Williams, *Arius*, 162–7; Hanson, *The Search*, 79–84. Williams's account is the most careful, but Hanson is particularly clear on the basic problem here (79): 'the practice indulged in by many scholars of first explaining Lucian by Arius and, then, this accomplished, Arius by Lucian, may suffice to amuse the learned but is a most unsatisfactory mode of procedure which has resulted in a good deal of erudite but useless speculation'. See also Hanns Cristof Brennecke, 'Lukian von Antiochien in der Geschichte arianischen Streites', *Logos: Festschrift für Luise Abramowski* (Berlin: De Gruyter, 1993), 170–92. Brennecke adds strongly to the case that the particular emphases of Arius' theology were *not* shared by other 'Lucianists'.
[40] See below, Ch. 5 esp. p. 119. [41] A term defined in Ch. 6
[42] As Hanson points out, *The Search*, 83, the one teaching that we seem to be able clearly to identify with Lucian is the belief that the Word assumed a body without a soul.

Eusebius of Caesarea, the historian and theologian.[43] Eusebius knew Origen and drew on aspects of his thought. This Eusebius was not, however, a 'student' of Lucian. He insists on the closeness of Father and Son (like a light and its rays) and that the Son was created for the work of creation:

> He subsists, not like the rest of begotten things, nor does he have life as the things begotten through him do; but he alone was born of the Father himself and is life itself. It was fitting for the God above all, before everything that came to be and before all ages, to bring forth the unique Begotten like a foundation or an unbreakable fundament (ὥσπερ τινὰ κρηπῖδα καὶ θεμέλιον ἀρραγῆ) for the things that would come to be through him. So he begot the Son before all things that were going to be, like a ray of light and a source of life (ζωῆς πηγήν) and a treasury of goods, 'in which all the treasures of wisdom and knowledge are hidden'.[44]

At the same time Eusebius presents the Son as the product of the Father's will, and thus not coeternal or distinct in authority. The Son's existence as 'life itself' is a delegated participation that does not infringe the eternity and self-sufficiency of the Father:

> He is not unbegotten, but is offspring of an unbegotten Father. He is only-begotten, Logos, God from God, put forth from the being of the Father (ἐκ τῆς τοῦ πατρὸς οὐσίας προσεσλημένον), not by a partaking or a cutting or a division, but unspeakably and, for us, unexplainably. He is from time or rather before all time. He has his being from the inexpressible and incomprehensible will and power of the Father (ἐκ τῆς τοῦ πατρὸς ... βουλῆς τε καὶ δυνάμεως οὐσιούμενον διδάσκοντα).[45]

Eusebius' focus on the Father's will is subtly different from that of Arius: he describes the Son as 'life itself' and as the 'ray' of the Father's 'light', expressions that have no place in Arius' surviving texts. The notion of the Father's will in Eusebius shows both that the Son is not generated by a division of the Father's essence and how God gives himself in the creation of the world: at one point he remarks that the will of God is the original material (ὕλη) for all things.[46]

Eusebius clearly attributes to Father and Son different ontological status, envisaging the Son worshipping the Father. Like other Euseb-

---

[43] The usefulness and prominence of his *Ecclesiastical History* has led to his erroneously being considered a 'historian' rather than a 'theologian'. Very useful introductory descriptions of his theology with translated quotations are to be found in Colm Luibhéid, *Eusebius of Caesarea and the Arian Crisis* (Dublin: Irish Academic Press, 1981), ch. 2 and ch. 5, pp. 83–97; Lienhard, *Contra Marcellum*, ch. 5. For his theology see also Hanson, *The Search*, 46–59; Barnes, *Power of God*, 129 ff.; Lyman, *Christology and Cosmology*; Strutwolf, *Trinitätstheologie*.

[44] Eusebius, *Eccl. theol.* 1. 8. 2–4 (Lienhard, *Contra Marcellum*, 114–15).

[45] Eusebius, *Dem. evang.* 4. 3. 13 (Luibhéid, *Eusebius*, 36–7).

[46] Eusebius, *Dem. evang.* 4. 1. 6–7.

ians he speaks of two powers in God: the power of God unique to his nature and a second power, the Word, who is the first principle of creation.[47] Eusebius speaks of distinct *hypostases* but his use of this term is not consistent: he sometimes uses *hypostasis* in other senses and occasionally, early on, speaks also of two οὐσιαι. The Father is true God and the Son is appropriately called God: early in his career he is happy to speak of the Son as 'a second God' in a clearly subordinationist sense. Nevertheless, he insists strongly that the Son is the image of the Father's *ousia*[48] and frequently turn to the image of perfume or fragrance to describe the Son's relationship to the Father:

Perhaps one might say that the Son originated like a perfume and a ray of light from the Father's unoriginated nature and ineffable substance (τῆς τοῦ πατρὸς ἀγεννήτου φύσεως καὶ τῆς ἀνεκφράστου οὐσίας) infinite ages ago, or rather before all ages.

It is is noteworthy that this text occurs straight after Eusebius cites Isaiah 53: 8. Soon after this text Eusebius struggles to define the Son's status:

[the Son] is the image of God, in a way mysterious and incalculable to us, the living image of the living God and existing in its own right immaterially ... but not like an image in our experience, when the form is distinct from the image, but himself wholly the form, and assimilated in his own reality to the Father (ἀλλ' ὅλον αὐτὸ, εἶδος ὢν καὶ αδτοουσίᾳ τῷ πατρὶ ἀφομοιούμενος), and so he is the most lively perfume of the Father, once again in a way mysterious and incalculable to us.[49]

Eusebius insists on the revelatory ability of the Son and characterizes the Son as possessing many of the Father's qualities by the Father's gift. Particularly interesting is the clarity with which he thinks of the Son as mirroring the Father's unity: as image the Son must mirror the Father's incomposite unity.[50] In this doctrine he may well have differed significantly from Arius, in whom the Son seems to have been a composite being not sharing the Father's simplicity. And yet it is essential to Eusebius that the two are distinct and the status of the one unbegotten is preserved. Eusebius of Caesarea is thus subtly different in his theology from Arius and perhaps from the other 'Lucianists'. Eusebius can speak of the Son

---

[47] In Eusebius' theology the role of the Spirit is defined in this context as a lesser power under the authority of the Son, presiding over the other lesser powers. But note that even when Eusebius speaks of the Son as a second power, the 'X from X' language of power from power is understood as a real mode of participation, see Barnes, *Power of God*, 129 ff.
[48] Indeed, Hanson describes this theme as 'Eusebius' favourite doctrine', *The Search*, 52.
[49] Eusebius, *Dem. evang.* 5. 1. 18–21. For Eusebius' reference to the Logos as 'the second God' see *Prep.* 7. 12–13.
[50] Eusebius, *Dem. evang.* 4. 5.

being generated in language that relies on analogies of the Father's being and goodness overflowing into the Son, and he can use the images of perfume or of a ray of light to describe the Son. This is of course always combined with a consistent emphasis on not using imagery of God and of the Son's generation that implies any material division within God or any change like that found in material creatures.

Nevertheless, it is also easy to see how and why Eusebius would have made common cause with the 'Lucianists' against Alexander. The acts of the second council of Nicaea in 787 preserve a letter of Eusebius written to Alexander *c.*320 complaining about Alexander's treatment of Arius. Eusebius writes:

> your letter accuses them as though they were saying that the Son has come into being as one of the created things ... they do not say this, but clearly determine that he is 'not as one of the created things' ... You censure them for saying that 'he who is' has begotten 'he who is not'. I marvel that someone is able to say otherwise.[51]

Eusebius here takes as axiomatic that the Son's status is something which comes via the Father's gift and act, and that it is consequently obvious that he was in some sense 'created'. It has been argued that during the years of controversy around Nicaea Eusebius gradually modified his position, increasingly subordinating the Son to the Father, dropping the language of scent and perfume, and ever more clearly using the notion of the Son's incomprehensible generation (Isa. 53: 8) to point to the error in theologies such as those espoused by Alexander and Athanasius. The evidence is, however, unclear and fragmentary. All we can say with certainty is that when arguing against Alexander and that bishop's associates, Eusebius found it easy to be clear about the distinction between Father and Son.

I have pointed here to only some of the most famous Eusebians: it is important to realize that many other bishops in the east also took leading roles in the decades after Nicaea, bishops whose individual places within the broad Eusebian trajectory (and the extent of their detailed theological knowledge) it is hard to judge. Indeed, over the decades after Nicaea one of the most important shifts that occurs is within this broad 'Eusebian' trajectory. Some emphasize the subordinate nature of the Son with increasing clarity, others discover that struggling to preserve the traditional languages which still figure strongly in Eusebius of Caesarea's theology forces them along a different path and eventually leads them to make a significant contribution to the formation of pro-Nicene orthodoxy. In the 330s and 340s many followed the ecclesiastical political lead of the

[51] Opitz, *Werke*, III/i, U.7.

'Eusebians' not primarily from theological conviction, but because they wanted to take a stand against Athanasius' actions in his diocese and against western interference in their ecclesiastical business. In these decades it is also important to note that the forces that came together under 'Eusebian' guidance would have included many who were strongly united in their opposition to the theology of Marcellus of Ancyra, even while their theologies fully reflected the diversity of Eusebian opinion that we have seen among a few more well-known figures. But that story is one we shall tell in subsequent chapters.

3
Theological Trajectories in the Early Fourth Century: II

'MARCELLAN' THEOLOGY: THEOLOGIANS OF THE UNDIVIDED MONAD

My third theological trajectory is primarily associated with Marcellus of Ancyra. Indeed, while other figures can be linked with this trajectory, the fragments of Marcellus' corpus constitute the bulk of the material surviving from it: he is accordingly the focus of attention here.[1] Marcellus was bishop of Ancyra by 314, he played a major role at Nicaea, and was subsequently deposed, probably in 336. His theology was one of the central points of contention in the years following Nicaea, as we shall see. His earliest surviving writing consists of fragments of a work written against Asterius: the fragments survive because of Eusebius of Caesarea's extensive writing against this text. After the *Contra Asterium*, Marcellus seems to have modified some of the more idiosyncratic aspects of his teaching, and thus we probably see here his theology as it would have been before the post-Nicene disputes.

Marcellus was concerned above all to preserve the unity of God: to describe the relationship between Word and God he deploys the analogy of a human person and her reason in ways that may have made even Athanasius blanch. Just as a human person possesses a reasoning faculty that is intrinsic to her existence, so too does the Word eternally exist with God.[2] One of his most idiosyncratic pieces

---

[1] For Marcellus' surviving corpus see Markus Vinzent, *Markell von Ankyra: Die Fragmente und Der Brief an Julius von Rom* (Leiden: Brill, 1997). I have referred to the fragments by Vinzent's numbering (which follows that of Seibt), and then by Klosterman's numbering in parentheses. An English translation is provided in Maurice James Dowling, *Marcellus of Ancyra: Problems of Christology and the Doctrine of the Trinity*, diss. (Queen's University, Belfast, 1987), 286 ff. Here I have followed Dowling's translation except for minor changes. On Marcellus' theology see also Lienhard, *Contra Marcellum*, 49–68; Vinzent, *Markell von Ankyra*, xxvi–lxxvi; Klaus Seibt, *Die Theologie des Markell von Ankyra*, AKG 59 (Berlin: De Gruyter, 1994); idem, 'Ein argumentum ad Constantium in der Logos- und Gotteslehre Markells von Ankyra', SP 26 (1993), 415–20; Alistair H. B. Logan, 'Marcellus of Ancyra, Defender of the Faith against Heretics—and Pagans', SP 37 (2001), 550–64. See also the other articles by Logan in the bibliography.

[2] e.g. *Frag.* 87 (61): 'Just as everything that was made by the Father was made through the Word, so too the things that are spoken by the Father are proclaimed through the Word . . . I

of exegesis sees the 'let us make' of Gen. 1: 26 as describing the 'internal' conversation of God and his Word just as a person might converse with her own reason!³ This may seem to present a modalism in which there are no true distinctions in God. However, Marcellus should not be interpreted within the context of modern psychologies in which the distinct existence of reason occurs only by way of logical abstraction. In some ancient psychologies one could speak of distinct faculties within a whole. Thus, although we do not know which ancient psychology Marcellus preferred, we do know contexts in which his strong insistence that he is not a Sabellian made sense.⁴

Marcellus knows Origen, but draws little from him: indeed Marcellus asserts the primacy of the title 'Word' over other scriptural titles, perhaps directly refuting Origen's assertion in the first book of the commentary on John that one understands the Son by interpreting 'Word' alongside the other scriptural titles.⁵ Thus, Marcellus sees any language which separates God and Word as distinct beings either as illogical or as sacrilegious. He is particularly incensed at the use of *hypostasis* or *ousia* in the plural. Marcellus has no theology of eternal generation: the Word does not come to be distinct eternally but eternally is in the Father.

Marcellus' theology of creation and incarnation is difficult to decipher from the fragments. He speaks of the Word 'coming out' of God or 'going forth':

For before the world existed the Word was in the Father. When the Almighty God decided to make all things in heaven and on earth, the coming into being of the universe required an accomplishing activity (ἐνεργείας ... δραστικῆς). For this reason, since there was no one apart from God (for, as everyone agrees, all things were made by him), the Word came

believe this can be easily perceived by those who think logically ... It is not possible for a man's reason to be separated from him as a power or as a *hypostasis*. For reason is one with a man and identical with him, and not to be distinguished from him in any other way except than as the energy of action (τῇ τῆς πράξεως ἐνεργείᾳ).'

³ *Frag.* 98 (58).

⁴ *Frag.* 44 (69): 'For Sabellius, who had also slipped and fallen away from the right faith, understood correctly neither God nor his holy Word. For in that he did not know the Word he was ignorant of the Father also. It says, indeed, "No one knows the Father except the Son", that is, the Word. For the Word mediates knowledge of the Father through himself.'

⁵ *Frag.* 3 (43): 'thus, from every point of view, it is clear that for the eternal Word no other name is fitting than the one used by John, the most holy disciple and apostle of God, at the beginning of his gospel. For whenever, following the assumption of the flesh he is called Christ and Jesus, or life, way, day, resurrection, door, bread ... at the same time we should not forget his first name, which was Word .... If there is a new and more recent name, it arose from the new and recent dispensation of his flesh.' Cf. *Frag.* 7 (42): 'For the Word "was in the beginning," and was not anything else other than the Word ... If anyone professes to be able to show that before the new covenant the name of Christ or Jesus was applied to the Word on his own, he will find that this is said prophetically ...'.

forth (προελθών) and became the maker of the universe, he who first of all prepared it in thought in his own being . . .⁶

Marcellus seems to assume that the act of creation requires a certain activity—elsewhere he is happy to speak of a rest or silence (ἡσυχία) in God before this.⁷ In some sense the Word is this activity and may be said to 'come forth' in the act.

Some scholars have linked the language of 'act' to fragments where Marcellus talks of power (δύναμις) and energy (ἐνέργεια) in God:

By saying, 'in the beginning was the Word,' he shows that the Word was in the Father as a power . . . By saying, 'and the Word was with God,' he teaches that the Word was with God as an [or 'in'] energy . . . And by saying that the Word was God he teaches that one should not divide the Godhead, since the Word is in him and he is in the Word. For he says, 'The Father is in me and I am in the Father.'⁸

Noticing that Marcellus distinguishes δύναμις and ἐνέργεια and that he speaks of the Word coming forth from God as ἐνέργεια, Theodor Zahn in 1867 suggested this pair means potency and act in Aristotelian terms. This is unlikely: Marcellus clearly describes the Word's eternal existence in both terms. The Word does not *become* ἐνέργεια, this would indicate for Marcellus a change in the eternal state of God.

It is better to interpret these terms separately. Δύναμις is not particularly frequent in the fragments of Marcellus,⁹ and it seems likely that he uses the term because of its prominence in his Eusebian opponents. In order to show the illegitimacy of two-power theologies he argues that as power (of reason) the Word must be intrinsic to God's existence. Ἐνέργεια, on the other hand, is a fairly frequent term and seems to bear a lot of weight. Because the term stops us imagining being separate from the Father's existence, Marcellus finds the term acceptable for indicating *both* the Word's eternal existence in the Father and the character of the Word's action when it 'goes forth'. Nevertheless, we should be careful about assuming that Marcellus uses the term in a technical philosophical sense: his actual usage bears further discussion.

---

⁶ *Frag.* 110 (60).

⁷ *Frag.* 76 (103): 'For before the world was created at all there was a certain silence (ἡσυχία)—as one might expect, for the Word was in God. Now if Asterius has come to believe that God is the maker of all things, then obviously even he will acknowledge with us that God has always existed, that he never had a beginning to his being (τοῦ εἶναι ἀρχὴν), and that everything was brought into being out of nothing . . . Now if he accepts this he must also acknowledge with us that there was no other (ἕτερον) apart from God. Therefore, the Word possessed his appropriate glory, as one who was in the Father.'

⁸ *Frag.* 70 (52). ⁹ Leinhard, *Contra Marcellum*, 54–6.

In *Fragment* 70 (52) quoted above, Marcellus deploys the concept of energy to explain 'the Word was with God', a clause whose conjunction 'with' is used by many fourth-century theologians to indicate the Word's presence with the Father as a distinct being. Marcellus, however, deploys energy here to assert that the three clauses of John 1: 1 serve together to assert the absolute unity of God.[10] None of the fragments clearly reveals Marcellus using the term ἐνέργεια in light of a specific technical background: he uses the term because of a general sense of its rhetorical force. Thus we can note that Marcellus sometimes combines ἐνέργεια with adjectives indicating effective action to emphasize the way in which the Word is distinct from God in action. The phrases that Marcellus creates with ἐνέργεια do not seem to have theological precedent: they have the appearance not of technical terminology but of ad hoc attempts to shape an acceptable language for describing the Word.

Marcellus is clear that we cannot explain the mystery of the Word's 'coming forth' in action while God remains one. He criticizes Asterius for using the language of Father and Son to emphasize the subordination of the Son and the distinction of Father from Son. Marcellus wishes to apply this language solely to the relationship between God and the incarnate Word: to apply it to the eternal nature of God is a result of inappropriately applying the categories of human existence to God.[11] This insistence on the unique nature of the divine existence is mirrored in *Fragment* 48 (67) where Marcellus describes the 'coming forth' of the Son as a 'hidden mystery being unveiled' (κεκρυμμένον ἀνακαλύπτεσθαι τι μυστήριον). Marcellus does not seem to mean that the Son's 'coming forth' is now comprehensible, but that the *idea*—the mystery—of God's 'broadening' or 'dilation' while still remaining one is revealed. Marcellus does not use a consistent terminology for the Word's 'going forth'. At times he follows biblical terminology, at other times he uses verbs that appear to have no obvious technical context or scriptural reference. Marcellus seems to be seeking an analogical language for speaking about an act that remains incomprehensible

---

[10] Cf. *Frags.* 68 (51) and 6 (53) where Marcellus quotes the whole of John 1. 1 at once and describes the purpose of the verse as demonstrating 'the eternity of the Word'. In the latter fragment he writes, 'It is for this reason that he begins with the eternity of the Word, saying, "In the beginning was the Word, and the Word was with God, and the Word was God." He wishes to declare the eternity of the Word (τὴν ἀιδιότητα τοῦ λόγον) by means of three pieces of testimony one after the other.'

[11] e.g. *Frag.* 85 (63): ' "for there are two *hypostases*, the Father and the Son," [Asterius] says as he considers the human flesh which the Word of God assumed, and through which he thus manifested himself. Thus he separates the Son of God from the Father, just as the son of a man might be distinguished from his natural father.' Cf. *Frag.* 1 (65). One confusing aspect of Marcellus' theology is that he uses Father as a synonym for God while denying that Son is a title applicable before the Incarnation.

because it is always to be confessed within the context of the unity of God.

In two places Marcellus speaks of a 'monad' expanding into a 'triad':

> in this text [John 16: 13] we have a plain reference to the monad which expands to form a triad while in no way allowing itself to be divided ... unless the undivided monad (ἡ μονὰς ἀδιαίρετος) expands (πλατύνοιτο) to a triad how could [Christ] say at one point of the Spirit, 'He proceeds out of the Father'?[12]

> If our consideration were of the Spirit only, then the Word would rightly appear to be one and the same with [or 'in'] God; but if the addition of the flesh be considered, then it seems (δοκεῖ) that the Godhead expanded in energy alone, so that it is rightly [said to be] a monad which is indeed undivided (ἀδιαίρετος).[13]

Marcellus here does not speak of the one God *changing* to become a triad. In both texts he emphasizes that the 'undivided monad' remains such even as the going forth of the Son and the Spirit occurs 'in energy'. It is evident also in this text that Marcellus did have a theology of the Spirit. I have not here discussed Marcellus' hints about the role of the Spirit, for our purposes we need only to note that the same language of going forth in energy is used for the Spirit as was used in the case of the Son.[14]

Marcellus' eschatology became particularly notorious in the fourth century. He interprets 1 Cor. 15: 28 to indicate that at the end of the process of redemption Christ's kingdom comes to an end. The kingdom of Christ is a partial state, only a part of the true rule of God.[15] Once Christ's purpose has been accomplished at the judgement this partial rule will end and God will be 'all in all'. For Marcellus this must necessarily involve a return of the Word to its pre-'going forth' status. Marcellus does *not* mean that the Word's distinctive existence ends: the Word is eternally 'in' the Father. He is most concerned to uphold God's rule as complete and unmediated, and thus the kingdom of Christ must end. Scholars have rarely noted that Marcellus realizes his account begs many

---

[12] *Frag.* 48 (67).

[13] *Frag.* 73 (71). Translation of this fragment is difficult, and my version differs from that of Dowling considerably.

[14] In *Frag.* 47 (66) Marcellus also links Son and Spirit as being the only things characterized by a 'oneness' (ἕνωσις) with God.

[15] *Frag.* 107 (119): 'And if it is clear that he assumed [flesh] for our sake, and all things in our world by his planning and working will arrive at their end at the time of judgment, then there will no longer be any need for this partial kingdom.' That the Kingdom under discussion is that of the incarnate Word or the man assumed by the Word is apparent from 78 (105): 'The man (ἄνθρωπος) received authority not only over things on earth but also over those in heaven, as was fitting.'

questions: One of his clearest statements in this regard turns to 1 Cor. 13: 12:

> And if anyone should ask what happens to [Christ's] flesh which has become immortal in the Word, how should we answer him? ... For now [the Apostle] says we see through a mirror dimly, but then face to face. Now we know in part, then we shall know just as we are known. Do not ask me about things that I have not clearly learned from the sacred Scriptures. Rather, I believe the sacred Scriptures, that there is one God and that God's Word came forth from the Father so that 'through him all things' might be made. And after the time of judgment, the restoration of all things and the destruction of the opposing power, 'he will then be subject to the one who subjected all things to him', 'to God and the Father', so that the Word might be in God just as he was at first before the world existed. For there existed nothing at first save God alone; and as all things were to be brought into being through the Word, the Word went forth as an accomplishing energy, and this Word was the Father's.[16]

It is not clear here how Marcellus understands the created order after the judgement. He both envisages the incarnation as resulting in a transformation of Christ's human flesh into an immortal form, and sees the creation itself as having a τέλος finally accomplished at the judgement.[17] Marcellus seems to rely on appeal to mystery. Unfortunately, none of the surviving sources offers us a clear statement of how Marcellus would have narrated the whole of creation and salvation history. We should note, in conclusion, that after 336 Marcellus seems to have abandoned the more idiosyncratic aspects of his eschatology—though lack of evidence makes it impossible to describe his later views.

Although it is difficult to place Marcellus' theology in an immediate context, some suggestions can be made. His account of the ending of the Son's kingdom represents the most idiosyncratic aspect of his theology, but much of the rest finds extensive parallels in the second-century Apologists. This is especially so in the case of his understanding of the 'Word' being present somehow in the Father eternally but coming forth in connection with the creation. Indeed, this link is not seen only in Marcellus: taking examples from very different trajectories examined in these two chapters, both the early theology of Hilary of Poitiers and that of Eusebius of Caesarea seem to envisage a state in which the Logos is 'in' the Father 'before' being generated. Marcellus seems to have emphasized this theme considerably more strongly than they and to have spoken more openly about the quasi-temporal point at which the Son's

---

[16] *Frag.* 109 (121).   [17] For the latter idea see *Frag.* 107 (119).

going-forth occurred, but the basic position has a long history and many contemporary adherents in the early fourth century.

Scholarship has also consistently linked Marcellus with 'Monarchian' theologies. Monarchian theologians in the second and third centuries appear to have focused on the unity of God centred in the person of the Father. By their opponents they are accused of teaching that the Son and the Spirit do not have real independent existence and are in fact simply modes of the Father's being. Unfortunately none of the opponents of Monarchians offers extensive quotation of their texts and so we are at a loss to describe their doctrine in any detail. Some scholarship has seen this theological tendency as a strong and persistent theological voice, both in Rome and in Asia through the third century, with Marcellus as the last prominent Monarchian voice.[18] Marcellus cannot be equated with Monarchian theologies—*or at least with their opponents' description of them*—in one important respect. Marcellus considers the Word to be eternally with the Father, and uses this belief to differentiate himself from his account of Sabellius, who is taken not to believe in the Word of the Father. Perhaps then Marcellus represents a theological tradition that had long engaged in debate with 'Monarchians'—both rejecting some of their emphases and adopting others.[19]

We can identify others who had more in common with Marcellus in doctrine than they did with the tradition of Alexander and Athanasius and we can also identify a continuing body of supporters of Marcellus himself well into the 370s. Photinus of Sirmium we will discuss in later chapters, and we will also mention again a continuing body of Marcellans writing to Athanasius in the early 370s. Eustathius, bishop of Antioch,[20] was deposed from his see soon after Nicaea,

---

[18] Advocated most strongly in recent writing by Reinhard M. Hübner, *Der paradox Eine: Antignosticher Monarchianismus im zweiten Jahrhundert*, ed. Markus Vinzent (Leiden: Brill, 1999).

[19] For instance, one might read his insistence on the Son's return to the Father as an attempt to resist Monarchian charges that the theology of the Apologists involves a division in the being and unity of God that is unacceptable. In response Marcellus (or his predecessors) have developed an account of the Son's going forth designed to forestall such charges at a number of points, including by insisting that the Son ultimately returns to his primordial state of being 'in' the Father. This is, however, only conjecture.

[20] On Eustathius see Hanson, *The Search*, 208–17; R. V. Sellers, *Eustathius of Antioch* (Cambridge: Cambridge University Press, 1928); Michel Spanneut, *Recherches sur les écrits d'Eustathe d'Antioche* (Lille, 1948); idem, 'La Position théologique d'Eustathe d'Antioche'; *JThS* NS, 5 (1954); 220–4; Rudolf Lorenz, 'Die Eustathius von Antiochien zugeschriebene Schrift gegen Photin', *ZNTW* 71 (1980), 109–28. One should now also consult the excellent edition of Eustathius and extensive introduction by José Declerck in CCSG 51. Hanson, *The Search*, 213–14, translates *Frag.* 38 (107) as follows (and presuming *hypostasis* stands behind *qnôma*); 'in this [*hypostasis*] both [Father and Son] accomplish wonders. The divine books over and over again refer their majesty to One, so that they produce duality out of singularity or

probably in 327, having been bishop only since 325. Nevertheless, Eustathius left behind a community preserving his doctrine that persisted into the 370s: the long survival of this community most likely reveals that its theology was well established in Antioch before Eustathius short tenure of office. The fragments of Eustathius that survive present a doctrine that is close to Marcellus, and to Alexander and Athanasius. Eustathius insists there is only one *hypostasis*. He speaks of a dyad being produced out of singularity (or a monad) even while the singularity is declared in the dyad. In such expressions Eustathius appears similar to Marcellus in his hesitancy about deploying terms that might deny the constant unity of God. On the other hand, he seems to use the terms Father and Son in ways that Marcellus would not: 'Son' for Eustathius appears to have some sort of eternal reference. We also see him describing the Son as image of the Father's substance. Nevertheless, Eustathius did not follow the Alexandrian/Athanasian pattern of using genetic metaphors to express the generation of the Word or Son, but preferred to insist on the Word or Son's eternal presence in the Father.

Even though we can identify a wider context for Marcellan theology, it is not at all clear that those we can link with Marcellus shared the idiosyncracies of his early theology. Grasping the peculiarities of his theology is important for understanding why he became such an object of condemnation in the decades after Nicaea. At the same time, in his fundamental emphases he is the most prominent witness of a wider theological trajectory. The characteristic emphasis of this trajectory is the insistence that discussion of Word and Spirit must manifest the constancy and eternity of the divine unity. Terminologies which speak of generation and of subordinate degrees of existence of Word and Spirit are taken to be breaches of that unity. In this we see perhaps the strongest point of tension between Marcellan theology and that of Alexander and Athanasius, even while Marcellus, Eustathius and Alexander were able to make common cause against the Eusebians, and even while Athanasius and Marcellus could come together in Rome. The perception that these two trajectories held to very similar beliefs would help to shape widespread eastern antipathy to both in the years after Nicaea.

---

declare singularity from duality, because there is one *hypostasis* of the Godhead.' Commenting on Deut. 13: 1–3 in *De Engastrimytho* 24 (65), Eustathius also writes, 'Here [the text] presents the Dyad of the Father and the only-begotten Son; naming one of them as the Lord who proves, but the other as well as this one as the Lord and God who is loved, so that it teaches the one Godhead out of the Dyad and the true divine begetting.'

WESTERN ANTI-ADOPTIONISM: A SON BORN WITHOUT DIVISION

All three of the trajectories I have so far outlined are found primarily in the eastern half of the empire. It is often said that Latin-speaking theologians 'began' with the unity of God, insisting that there was only one *substantia* or substance in God. It was also once a common assertion that, because of this commitment to the unity of God, westerners were naturally sympathetic to Athanasius and Nicaea. Ossius of Cordoba has sometimes been credited with introducing *homoousios* as a term that reflected this traditional western emphasis.

In actual fact our knowledge of Latin Christology and Trinitarian theology between 250 and 360 is extremely limited and certainly not such that we can make any certain judgements about its overall character. It is noticeable that attempts to describe the character of western theology in the early decades of this crucial century have been few and far between during the recent decades of scholarly activity on the fourth century; the standard summary accounts frequently ignore the question. Thus, for example, Meslin's *Les Ariens d'Occident* offers no consideration of the period, and Hanson's *The Search for the Christian Doctrine of God* offers only a few sentences.[21] Nevertheless, I suggest we can sketch some common themes among western writers in the 250–350 period and so identify what may have been the concerns of many western bishops when they began to encounter the energizing conflict between eastern theological trajectories. In so doing, however, I am not characterizing *all* western theology: these themes evolved against *other* western trajectories, monarchian and then adoptionist, and eventually found themselves in competition with western non-Nicene theologies.

The main Latin theologians writing in the 250–350 period with whom we can usefully compare the Latin theology that survives from the late 350s are Novatian (fl. *c*.250) and Lactantius (*c*.250–*c*.325). To this list we can add a few fragments of early fourth-century writing and Hilary's own commentary on Matthew written probably *c*.350. I will first consider Novatian and Lactantius; second, their relationship to Tertullian; and, third, Hilary's own early work.[22] Looking at Novatian and Lactantius for evidence of Latin theology in this period does not seem promising. In mid-career Novatian left the mainstream Church and founded a rigorist group

---

[21] Hanson, *The Search*, 169 writes 'The western theological tradition which Ossius represented at the Council (if anyone did) was largely dependent upon Tertullian.' Some useful material is contained in the introduction to Evans, *Tertullian's Treatise Against Praxeas*.

[22] I have excluded Cyprian (*c*.200–58) from this discussion because the details of his Trinitarianism remain unclear. Some hints can be extracted from his surviving collection of scriptural *testimonia* against the Jews.

that continued for a number of centuries. Modern scholars have treated Lactantius' theology as idiosyncratic and Lactantius as ignorant of other Latin theology. Nevertheless, Novatian's work on the Trinity seems to have been of influence even among those who rejected his schism. At the same time, the standard scholarly account of Lactantius as primarily indebted to non-Christian philosophy has long needed reconsideration: he may also be read as an admittedly eccentric witness to the Latin theological traditions of his day.

For both of these writers the theology of Tertullian (fl. *c.*200) is a fundamental source, but their adaptation of his theology demonstrates the different polemical concerns of the mid-third to midfourth century. Chapter 31 of Novatian's *On the Trinity* (*c.*250) speaks of the Son or the Word being understood, '[but] not as a sound that strikes the air nor the tone of the voice forced from the lungs, but rather ... in the substance of a power proceeding from God (*sed in substantia prolatae a Deo virtutis agnoscitur*).'[23] The Father, who has no origin, necessarily precedes the Son, and the Son—who is also God—receives his being only from the Father who is the one God.[24] The Son receives his being in a manner which does not compromise the divine unity and which involves an eternal connection between Father and Son. Novatian does not possess a theology of eternal generation: the Word is eternally 'in' the Father and at some stage the Word comes forth from the Father.[25] Novatian is clear that,

whether he is the Word, whether he is Power, whether he is Wisdom, whether he is Light, whether he is the Son—whatever he is of these, he is not from any other source but from the Father ... Owing his origin to the Father, he could not cause any disunion in the Godhead by making two Gods.[26]

---

[23] Novatian, *Trin.* 31. 2.   [24] Novatian, *Trin.* 4. 6.
[25] Novatian, *Trin.* 31. 3–4: 'He then, since He was begotten of the Father, is always in the Father. And I thus say always, that I may show Him not to be unborn, but born. But He who is before all time must be said to have been always in the Father; for no time can be assigned to Him who is before all time. And He is always in the Father, unless the Father be not always Father, only that the Father also precedes Him, in a certain sense, since it is necessary—in some degree—that He should be before He is Father. Because it is essential that He who knows no beginning must go before Him who has a beginning; even as He is the less as knowing that He is in Him, having an origin because He is born, and of like nature with the Father in some measure by His nativity, although He has a beginning in that He is born, inasmuch as He is born of that Father who alone has no beginning. He, then, when the Father willed it, proceeded from the Father, and He who was in the Father came forth from the Father; and He who was in the Father because He was of the Father, was subsequently with the Father, because He came forth from the Father, that is to say, that divine substance whose name is the Word (*substantia ... divina, cuius nomen est verbum*), whereby all things were made, and without whom nothing was made.'
[26] Novatian, *Trin.* 31. 12–31.

I. Towards a Controversy

Novatian is sensitive to the possibility that this account of the Son might seem to indicate two eternal realities (thus indicating that Arius' charge against Alexander was not a new fear). Immediately before the passage quoted in the previous paragraph he writes:

> Assuredly God proceeding from God (*Deus utique procedens ex Deo*), causing a person second to the Father as being the Son, but not taking from the Father that characteristic that He is one God. For if He had not been born (*natus*) as unborn He would have been compared with Him who was unborn (*Innatus comparatus cum eo qui esset innatus*). Since an equality would have appeared in both, He would have constituted a second unborn, and thus two Gods.... Had He been formed without beginning as the Father, and He Himself the beginning of all things as is the Father, this would have made two beginnings, and consequently would have shown to us two Gods also ... Had He been invisible, as compared with the Invisible, and declared equal, He would have shown forth two Invisibles, and thus also He would have proved them to be two Gods. If incomprehensible, if also whatever other attributes belong to the Father, reasonably we say, He would have given rise to the allegation of two Gods, as these people feign.[27]

In this text we see something of Novatian's Christology. The Son, having come forth, is the visible God as opposed to the invisible Father. The origins, persistence, and eventual transformation of this theme need not concern us, but we must consider Novatian's insistence that the visible Son nevertheless receives his being from the Father and is rightly called God.

Novatian appears to have been particularly concerned about 'adoptionism'. 'Adoptionists' seem to have spoken of the Son as assumed for a salvific function by the divine power. By such means 'Adoptionists' protected the unity of God and avoided attributing the suffering of Christ to God. For Novatian such theologies misunderstand the Son, failing to distinguish between the different natures of Christ (although here Novatian struggles to find an adequate vocabulary). Thus, in *anti*-adoptionist contexts we see strong assertions that the Son receives his being from the Father but without the Godhead being divided. Thus the unity of God does indeed occupy much of Novatian's attention, but it partially does so in order to enable a careful *distinguishing* of Father from Son.

Sixty years later, the fourth book of Lactantius' *The Divine Institutes* (c.310) offers an extensive account of the Son's generation. At 4. 6–9 the manner of the Son's generation is unknown, as is his true name, but from the Scriptures we can speak of the Son as the Word of the Father (citing Pss. 32: 6 and 44: 2). Lactantius differentiates the Word from the angels by speaking of the angels as the

---

[27] Novatian, *Trin.* 31. 6–11.

'breathings' from the Father's nose, while the Son is the intelligible Word from the mouth of the Father, representing the mind of the Father.[28] The Word's role is closely linked with creation, and there is no understanding of eternal generation—although the speaking of the Word creates a Word that is then necessarily eternal.

Lactantius asks how it is that we speak of two—God the Father and God the Son—but do not speak of different Gods. He insists first on the correlativity of Father and Son as terms, and then on X from X language to show their inseparability:

> When we speak of God the Father and God the Son, we do not speak of different things and do not separate the two, as neither can the Father be separated from the Son nor the Son from the Father. Since, therefore, the Father makes the Son and the Son the Father, there is one mind in each (*una utrique mens*), one spirit, one substance (*una substantia*): but the one is as an overflowing fount (*exuberans fons*), the other as though a stream flowing (*defluens*) from that, the one a sun, the other a direct ray from the sun.[29]

A few sentences later we hear that 'whatever is in the Father flows (*transfluit*) to the Son, and whatever is in the Son descends from the Father'. Lactantius' account of the Son is strongly focused around the Son's revelatory and mediatorial role, and he insists on the closeness of the two to ensure that the Son truly reveals the Father. Lactantius differs from Novatian in treating the Son as incomprehensible like the Father, as invisible and as known only to the Father. However, they both emphasize the origin of the Son in the Father and the dependence of the Son's being on the Father's breath or overflowing. Both authors also take these to preserve the unity of God.

Novatian and Lactantius share a similar debt to Tertullian and yet also differ from him in similar ways. In his *Against Praxeas* (*c.*210) Tertullian presents the Son as a 'substantial' word because nothing insubstantial can come from the Father.[30] Although, for Tertullian,

---

[28] *Inst. div.* 4. 8: 'Rightly, therefore, he is called the speech and Word of God, since God comprehends the vocal spirit proceeding from his mouth which he had conceived, not in the womb, but in the mind by a certain unfathomable strength and power of his majesty into an image, which has life and power by its own proper knowledge (... *in effigiem, quae proprio sensu ex sapientia vigeat* ...).'

[29] *Inst. div.* 4. 29.

[30] On Tertullian's Trinitarian theology see Eric Osborn, *Tertullian, First Theologian of the West* (Cambridge: Cambridge University Press, 1997), ch. 6; Joseph Moingt, *Théologie Trinitaire de Tertullian*, 4 vols. (Paris: Aubier, 1966–9), esp. the discussion of *Adv. Prax.* at i. 225 ff.; Ernest Evans, *Tertullian's Treatise*, 38 ff. I have not offered an extensive discussion of Tertullian's Trinitarian terminology here. Tertullian did not, as is sometimes assumed, deliver to later Latin thought a fixed and specific Trinitarian terminology. On the one hand, there are later writers for whom his terminology was simply not that important (e.g. Hilary) and, on the other hand, his own terminology is fluid (e.g. he uses *substantia* to designate that which Father and Son share, that which distinguishes them, and to distinguish the two natures in Christ).

the Son is second in order and comes from the Father in connection with the Father's decision to create, he also insists that the Son was always in the Father: the same two-stage conception we find in our two later Latin writers.[31] Tertullian also describes the relationship between Father and Son as being like that between a tree and its root, a river and a fountain, or a ray and the sun. He also insists that because the Son gets everything that he has from the Father the unity of the Godhead is not destroyed.[32] Tertullian's targets here are Monarchian theologians for whom the Word does not exist as a distinct existing thing. Thus, ironically, an anti-monarchian, anti-'modalist' polemic fundamentally shapes these early Latin theologians, and that is taken so often to be determining the future course of a unitary western theology![33] We can note two important differences between Tertullian and Lactantius and Novatian. Neither Novatian nor Lactantius is a materialist in Tertullian's sense (thinking of God as an infinitely diffuse intelligent matter). Both Novatian and, I suggest, Lactantius are concerned to oppose adoptionism. Although Lactantius makes no overt reference to adoptionism, he condemns a heretical (*not* pagan) group who could not understand how God could be confined in a woman's womb or subject to contempt and crucifixion. Condemnation of this group seems also to be involved in Lactantius' Christological insistence that the Son undergoes a double birth: because the distinct Son is truly born as Word and in the flesh, we have real access to the Father.

As Ernest Evans remarks in his discussion of the ways in which Novatian adapts Tertullian's account of the Son,

what [Tertullian] uses to prove that the Son is a second divine Person beside the Father, Novatian (whose adversaries admit Christ's personal existence) finds equally apposite to prove his deity (which Tertullian's adversaries did not deny).[34]

---

[31] Tertullian, *Adv. Prax.* 5: '... even before the creation God was not alone, since He had within Himself both Reason, and, inherent in Reason, His Word, which he made second to himself by agitating it within Himself.'

[32] Tertullian, *Adv. Prax.* 8: '... the tree is not severed from the root, nor the river from the fountain, nor the ray from the sun; nor indeed is the Word separated from God. Following, therefore the form of these analogies, I confess that I call God and his Word—the Father and His Son—two. For the root and the tree are two things (*res*) but joined (*coniunctae*), the spring and the river are two *species* but joined ... Everything that proceeds from something (*omne quod prodit ex aliquo*) must of necessity be another beside that from which it proceeds, but it is not for that reason separated ... In this way the Trinity, proceeding by intermingled and connected degrees from the Father, in no respect challenges the monarchy, while it conserves the state of the economy.'

[33] It is also worth noting clearly that the idea of *persona* as a term in Latin theology leading always towards a certain modalism because of its root meaning of 'mask' is nonsense. In the Christian era the term did not carry this connotation. Prestige in 1936 could describe this reading as 'a legend', but for some reason the legend continues!

[34] Evans, *Tertullian's Treatise*, 27.

Tertullian argues for the true existence of the Son as a distinct reality, Novatian argues that in Christ a distinct divine reality truly became incarnate: the same texts serve both purposes. The adoptionism of the later third and early fourth centuries is in some ways related to the Monarchianism opposed by Tertullian. Both had great problems speaking of a distinct divine reality being present in the man Jesus. In the adaptation of anti-Monarchian polemic to anti-adoptionist purposes Novatian and Lactantius emphasize that the distinct Son is truly born from the Father and that this birth does not involve a destruction of the divine unity or monarchy. It is also only on the basis of the Son's being a substantive word to whom the Father has given divine being that Novatian can make sense of the Son's incarnate role. In these theologies the closeness of the Son to the Father is central to the process of salvation.

Daniel Williams, following the work of Jean Doignon, has recently argued that Hilary's early *Commentary on Matthew* (c.350) is strongly marked by anti-adoptionist, rather than anti-'Arian' concerns.[35] Hilary's theological position and polemical context in this work is very different from his later *On the Trinity*: Hilary here seems to hold a two-stage Logos theory, rather than a theory of eternal generation, and is most concerned to argue against those who see the infirmities of Christ's flesh preventing our according him the true powers of divinity. Hilary argues that this is seen as the blasphemy against the Spirit and endangers salvation itself. The language and concerns evident in Hilary's account are, Williams argues, paralleled in the acts of a small Gallic council of 345 or 346, when one Eufrata was condemned for a form of adoptionism and hence for blaspheming the Spirit.[36] There various anti-adoptionist theologies are not best described as interested in the unity of God more than in the distinctions between the persons. Such a view fails to see how far a polemical need to distinguish the persons clearly has shaped their adaptation of previous tradition. It is also important to note that these Latin theologians have as far to travel towards later pro-Nicene theology as the eastern trajectories examined in this and the previous chapter. Questions of eternal generation, questions about degrees of divine being, and about the very character of divine being are handled in a very different manner from the strategies we will find at the end of the fourth century. However, a key emphasis here is on a mode of generation that sees the Son's role as Saviour as dependent on the Son's existence stemming directly from the

---

[35] Daniel H. Williams, 'Defining Orthodoxy in Hilary Poitiers' Commentarium in Matthaeum', *JECS*, 9 (2001), 151–71; Jean Doignon, *Hilaire de Poitiers avant l'exil* (Paris: Études Augustiniennes, 1971).

[36] Willims, 'Defining Orthodoxy', 164–5.

Father. The use of the language of light and ray, spring and fountain alongside the language of the Son 'flowing' from the Father to describe this generation may help us to see why many western theologians had difficulty with many Eusebian emphases in the early fourth century.

INCARNATION AND SOTERIOLOGY AT 300

Third-century theological disputes concerning soteriology provided little clarity or resolution for fourth-century theologians. A brief discussion of this legacy will help to make clearer the complexity of early fourth-century theology and provide a foil for the soteriological discussions of Chapter 12. As we have seen, the structure and possible implications of Origen's theology provided one focus of debate in the east during the last decades of the third century: one other significant source of controversy in those years was the Christology of Paul of Samosata, deposed by a council in Antioch in 268/9.[37] Although it is no longer possible to speak with certainty about Paul's theology, it seems that his opponents were unhappy with his insistence that Christ possessed a human soul and body and that the union of natures in Christ was not comparable to the union of soul and body in a human being. To his opponents, insisting that Christ had a soul meant that the Logos never truly entered into the man. For his opponents this theology could only result from semi-modalism. Paul is understood to have seen the Logos as God's own inner Word and not as a distinct separate being: he could not subsequently envisage that the Logos really became one with a human person. There is also some evidence that he did not think of the Word as 'Son' until the incarnation, in ways that do interestingly prefigure Marcellus of Ancyra (although wider associations made between these two for heresiological purposes in the fourth century reveal very little about Paul himself).

When we turn to the beginning of the fourth century, we find that for Arius the Logos was able to act as mediator *because* it was in some sense visible and changeable. In this Arius seems to be part of a tradition present in Paul's third-century opponents and also visible in Eusebius of Caesarea. But, for this tradition, while the mutability of the Logos enabled union with a human being, any such union involved the Logos replacing the human soul. In Eustathius of Antioch we do in fact find one thinker who criticized the Eusebians

---

[37] On Paul see Hanson, *The Search*, 70–2, and the literature in his n. 50. A particularly useful account of Paul, especially as he is used as a heretical topos in later controversies, is to be found in Behr, *The Way to Nicaea*, ch. 8. See also Uwe Lang, 'The Christological Controversy at the Synod of Antioch in 268/9', *JThS* NS 51 (2000), 54–80.

for not allowing Christ a human soul.[38] We may also be able to attribute a belief in Christ's human soul to Marcellus of Ancyra.[39] Thus, strangely to modern ears, there were many at the beginning of the fourth century who thought that confessing Christ to have a soul indicated a semi-modalist theology. It is also possible that emphasis on Christ not possessing a human soul was a reaction against Origen's very strong emphasis on *eternal* souls as the mediating principles between the Logos and the material world.[40] As this theology became the subject of a sustained critique, the Logos itself was treated as the eternal mediating principle and hence understood to replace Christ's human soul.

Although it is difficult to argue that the human soul of Christ plays much role in Athanasius' thought, it is clear that the closeness of the Logos to the Father is emphasized as the basis for the structure of salvation. Athanasius emphasizes God's unmediated action in the material world, and sees the Arian/Eusebian emphasis on the intermediate nature of the Logos as serving to prevent this connection, however intimate the union between the Logos and the human body of Christ that they envision. In the last chapter I discussed Gregg and Groh's attempt in their *Early Arianism: A View of Salvation* to show that, against 'Arian' exemplarism, Athanasius offers a soteriology in which the Logos is active in the world transforming and redeeming without the need for any mediation.[41] Whether or not their account of 'Arianism' can be sustained, their picture of Athanasius has a high degree of cogency—and is based on a long tradition of scholarship. Thus, Athanasius' theology is not easily located; while one might have expected him to accord Christ a human soul, he may have followed an Alexandrian post-Origenist tradition of seeing the Logos itself as replacing the human soul.

The situation is, then, both complex and confusing. On the one hand, according Christ a human soul seemed to many at the beginning of our period highly problematic and incompatible with a real distinction between Father and Son. On the other hand, one of the

---

[38] Grillmeier, *Christ*, 1. 299, translates a section of frg. 19 (Declerk) Eustathius as follows: 'Why do they [Arians] think it so important to show that Christ took a body without a soul, fabricating such gross deceptions? So that if only they can induce some to believe this false theory, they may then attribute the changes due to the passions to the divine *pneuma* and thus easily persuade them that what is changeable could not have been begotten from the unchangeable nature.'

[39] This question is also in dispute. My statement here is based on his insistence that the incarnate Christ willed in ways that did not accord with the will of the Father (*Frag.* 75 (74) among others). The question remains highly complex.

[40] On this question see Rowan D. Williams, 'Origen on the Soul of Jesus', in Richard P. C. Hanson (ed.), *Origeniana Tertia* (Rome: Edizioni dell'Ateneo, 1985), 131–7.

[41] See, for example, Robert C. Gregg and Denis E. Groh, *Early Arianism: A View of Salvation* (Philadelphia: Fortress Press, 1981), esp. the discussions in ch. 4 and at 177–83.

themes of those who resisted Eusebian theologians in which the Son acted as mediator between God and the creation was that God's Word was truly God acting in the world. As true Word and exact image of the Father, the Word's redemptive action was that of the one God. However, developing this theology of redemption and transformation while according Christ a human soul took a number of decades. The understandings of salvation which flowed from the different accounts of the Son's generation espoused in this century were constantly in dispute, although only rarely the direct focus of attention until well into the 360s.

HERESY AND ORTHODOXY IN THE EARLY FOURTH CENTURY

Many readers will ask if we can identify in or between these four trajectories a Christian 'orthodoxy' against which we may judge the theologies competing in Alexandria and even the original decisions of Nicaea. Older narratives tended to assume that 'heresies' were novel creations divergent from a pre-existing orthodoxy. In such narratives what is later defined as orthodox comes to be projected back into earlier controversies to enable a clear narrative of an unchanging orthodoxy ever victorious against novel heresies. Thus, for example, we still sometimes find Athanasius presented both as the upholder of the Church's unchanging tradition and as (necessarily) the representative of late fourth-century 'Nicene' orthodoxy—itself taken to be simply a restatement of the 'Apostolic tradition'. The problems with reading early Christian thought from this perspective were identified with particular clarity in Walter Bauer's seminal text from 1934, *Orthodoxy and Heresy in Earliest Christianity*.[42] Bauer's book concerns the struggle over Gnosticism in the second century rather than the fourth-century controversies, and the specifics of his treatment have been much contested. Nevertheless, at least one general point from Bauer's book has now become a key principle of critical scholarship: what later counts as heretical at times preceded what came to be counted as orthodoxy, and was itself seen as orthodox at that earlier stage.

In recent scholarship this principle has been modified away from the idea that the development of orthodoxy *necessarily* involved a wholesale reversal. Recent scholarship has come to see late fourth-century orthodoxy, in particular, as emerging from tensions among existing Christian theologies. These tensions lead to conflicts from which emerge positions counted as orthodox and others typified as

---

[42] Bauer, *Orthodoxy and Heresy in Earliest Christianity*, tr. and ed. Robert A. Kraft *et al.* (Philadelphia: Fortress Press, 1971).

heretical. Thus, within the tensions of pre-existing Christian belief are found the precursors *both* of what will come to be counted heretical and what will come to be counted orthodox. In the course of these controversies what will count as orthodox emerges and defines the heretical in contradistinction to itself.[43] The complexity of this process makes the task of identifying continuities in belief and all questions about the orthodoxy of options that are later counted as heretical extremely complex.

Understanding the nature of orthodoxy and heresy during the fourth century is further complicated by the need to note not only shifts in the content of Christian belief concerning Trinitarian and Christological issues, but also considerable change in the structures and practices within which right belief is assessed. When theologians in the early fourth century debate questions of right belief they accuse their opponents of misreading the Scriptures, of failing to deploy appropriately scriptural texts taken to be hermeneutical keys, of belonging to an existing group or geneaology designated as heretical, and of going against the inherited rule of faith.[44] However, in the early stages of this controversy appeals to the rule of faith, to 'apostolic' or 'evangelical' faith—even when couched in terms of an appeal to baptismal creeds and the faith they symbolize—are frequently appeals to the *implications* of short summaries that by themselves say little of direct relevance. Appeal to this faith is, then, often an appeal to what may have been tacitly understood in a given community; sometimes it may be an appeal to the way that local traditions or famous teachers have explicated shorter summary statements; sometimes it may be a sophisticated attempt to convince one's home audience that a newly developed position should be read as reflecting tacit belief. Such appeals succeed or fail by their ability to invoke the 'fittingness' of a given position with an audience's sense of the overall structure of Christian faith and the text of Scripture. Even in the very rare cases where appeal could be made to earlier conciliar decisions or controversies (such as the Council of

---

[43] But note the extent to which 'heresy' may be defined in different ways as within or without the Christian fold, and via a range of different images. Here the recent work of Rebecca Lyman offers a useful point of departure. See esp. her 'A Topography of Heresy: Mapping the Rhetorical Creation of Arianism', in Michel Barnes and Daniel H. Williams (eds.), *Arianism after Arius* (Edinburgh: T. & T. Clark, 1993), 45–62; eadem, 'Ascetics and Bishops: Epiphanius on Orthodoxy', in Susanna Elm, Eric Rebillard, and Antonella Romano (eds.), *Orthodoxie, christianisme, histoire* (Rome: École Française de Rome, 2000), 149–61.

[44] On the heresiological strategies of the 2nd and 3rd cent. see A. Le Boulluec, *La Notion d'hérésie dans la littérature Grecque IIe–IIIe siècles*, 2 vols. (Paris: Études Augustiniennes, 1985). In this context one would need also to note recent debate about the 'rule of faith' in recent writing. See esp. Paul M. Blowers, 'The *regula fidei* and the Narrative Character of Early Christian Faith', *Pro Ecclesia*, 6 (1997), 199–228, and Young, *Biblical Exegesis*.

Antioch in 268 or the controversy between the two Dionysii), there was no clear structure for such appeals.

Nevertheless, this flexibility occurred within a deeply traditioned context. In the case of every theological trajectory discussed here particular terminologies or scriptural texts came, over time, to be particularly significant as hermeneutical keys. Indeed, Richard Vaggione has helpfully pointed out that throughout the fourth-century disputes theologians have a highly differentiated sense of theological terms, some being treated as flexible, others as fundamental in defining orthodox belief. Frequently conciliar credal terminology falls into the former context, while inherited terms and analogies, sometimes traced to venerated teachers (and always terms taken to be either scriptural or implications of Scripture), fulfil the latter role.[45] Those terminologies taken to be of particular significance did not have credal warrant (as such a concept did not yet exist) and vary from trajectory to trajectory. Appeal to such terminologies should always be heard as the invocation of a particular tradition as the most fitting expression of Christian faith.

Thus, the gradual diffusion and reception of principles established in earlier polemical contexts had gradually come to provide dense traditioned contexts with which the rule of faith and baptismal creeds were understood. In many cases the boundaries of right belief remained fluid; the status of the Son providing an excellent example. In such contexts the boundaries of right belief could only be established by polemical interchange and by the attempted performance of a theology's unity within the community of belief. Thus, what (to modern historicist eyes) may appear to be simply undifferentiated and unconvincing appeals to a unitary apostolic tradition, are also invocations of particular historical traditions taken to best represent that apostolic faith.

By the end of the fourth-century theologians had not abandoned these styles of defining right belief, but they had developed a further range of tools for such acts of definition. After 381 theologians are able not only to appeal to the terminology and logic of a creed, but also to sets of logical principles concerning unity and differentiation in the Trinity that had emerged as principles of agreement between different traditions over the 360–80 period. Such statements even appear as key principles of definition in imperial legislation.[46] Traditional terminologies and favoured scriptural images are now interpreted and understood by pro-Nicene theologians within these new sets of logical principles and credal formulae. Definitions of

[45] Richard P. C. Vaggione, 'Οὐχ ὡς ἓν τῶν γεννημάτων: Some Aspects of Dogmatic Formulae in the Arian Controversy', *SP* 17 (1982), 181–7.
[46] e.g. Theodosius, *C.Th.* 16. 1. 1–3.

orthodoxy now also occasionally involve direct appeal to a set of authoritative theologians.[47] Thus it is not that discussion of right belief has utterly changed during the fourth century and now may be said to revolve around precise credal statements: such a reading misses the complexity of the context within which creeds exist. Rather, these new strategies exist alongside and offer a dense context for continuing direct appeals to the 'Apostolic faith' and to the Scriptures.

The evolution of pro-Nicene theology also involved the evolution of new modes of 'performing' orthodoxy. In using the term 'performance', I have two senses in mind. First, the development of pro-Nicene orthodoxy involved the evolution of styles of or strategies for performance and narration of orthodoxy within different literary forms. One might point, for example, to particular strategies for combining statements of the divine incomprehensibility with discussion of the relations between Trinitarian persons. Note that my concern here is not so much with open and public 'performance' of one's subscription to the Nicene creed or its terminology but with the display in speech and writing of interconnected principles and combinations of ideas that enable hearers and readers to recognize an orthodox theology even when terminology differs.

Second, a number of recent writers have demonstrated that the evolution of theology in the fourth century is also tied to an evolution in the culture of the Church and its role within wider late antique culture. One aspect of this evolution is the development in patterns of social interaction taken to be appropriate for bishops; development in what it means to perform the role of a bishop in the changed situation of the imperially sanctioned Church. A number of aspects of such performance have been considered in recent scholarship, from shifts in how bishops function in relation to civil authorities to how the performance of orthodoxy is possibly tied to particular patterns of gender performance.[48] For my purposes the

---

[47] e.g. Theodosius, *C.Th.* 16. 1. 3. Note that the construction of such authoritative theologians is seen not in the evolution of a clear style of citing other authors, but initially in the elevation and 'canonization' of particular 4th-cent. figures in the ecclesiastical historians and in texts such as Nazianzen's oration on Athanasius. We should be wary of assuming that this process immediately resulted in the large-scale citation of previous authors as authoritative per se. See, with regard to Augustine's development in this regard, the helpful discussion of Eric Rebillard, 'A New Style of Argument in Christian Polemic: Augustine and the Use of Patristic Citations', *JECS* 8 (2000), 559–70.

[48] For examples of such scholarship see Peter Brown, *Power and Persuasion in Late Antiquity: Towards a Christian Empire* (Madison: University of Wisconsin Press, 1992); Susanna Elm, 'The Diagnostic Gaze: Gregory of Nzaianzus' Theory of Orthodox Priesthood in his Orations 6 *De pace* and 2 *Apologia de fuga sua*', in Elm *et al.* (eds.), *Orthodoxie, christianisme, historie*, 83–100; Richard Lim, *Public Disputation, Power and Social Order in Late Antiquity* (Berkeley: University of California Press, 1995); Virginia Burrus, '*Begotten, not*

aspect of this process that is most directly of interest are developments in how bishops understand their own performance of the Church's unity in local contexts and in the Church more widely. Rowan Williams has indicated the importance of epistolary contact between bishops in the pre-Nicene period. In the later fourth century we see similar structures of inter-diocesan relationship understood as an intrinsic part of the performance of orthodoxy among bishops:[49] the practical performance of the unity of the body of Christ. These practices of orthodox performance include epistolatory forms, forms of behaviour at regular conciliar meetings, and forms of communication and interaction with other bishops.

How then can we proceed when we ask if a given figure in the early fourth century is or is not 'orthodox'? Is the question even a useful one? When the question is posed with the assumption that there are dense standards of judgement—even such as are found in the 380s—against which we can understand the relative standing of the various theologies in competition, it is better not asked. There are, however, some more complex questions that may be helpfully asked. One might be, 'given the structure of appeals to right belief in the early fourth century, are there individuals or trends whose emergence or development has significantly hampered the possibility of their existing (even in tension) with the wider range of contemporary traditions throughout the broader Christian community?' Asking such a question serves a number of useful purposes. On the one hand, attempting to answer the question may reveal the development of tensions that stretch existing patterns of theological coexistence such that we can understand more clearly how a particular controversy becomes widespread. On the other hand, learning to ask such questions can help us attend better to the historical complexity of the development of orthodoxy. These questions do not rely on attempting to assess deviation from a previous orthodoxy, rather they attempt to highlight the possibility of considering the place of thinkers within a shifting community that is itself part of a dynamic tradition.

I want to draw together these remarks by discussing a recent argument offered by Rowan Williams in an essay on Origen's

---

made': Conceiving Manhood in Late Antiquity (Stanford, Calif.: Stanford University Press, 2002). In general Averil Cameron, *Christianity and the Rhetoric of Empire: The Development of Christian Discourse* (Berkeley: University of California Press, 1991) provides an excellent introduction to a series of fundamental questions about how the shape of Christian discourse changes during our period: some of these themes are of direct relevance to an examination of the multidimensional nature of the evolution and performance of pro-Nicene orthodoxy.

[49] And although in this paragraph for the sake of clarity I consider only bishops, similar questions occur when we consider the place of other members of the Christian community.

theological practice.⁵⁰ Williams suggests that if we are to understand what Origen might have meant by orthodoxy we need to see the centrality of Origen's concern to display the unity of the Scriptures—and hence of God's action—in his exegesis. For Origen, one of the most basic intellectual and spiritual problems facing the rational being is to perceive a rational and harmonious unity in the multiplicity that confronts us. For Christians this problem is immediately also one of theodicy: how can one see the unity of divine purpose and order in the disjunctions and seeming chaos of the temporal world?

Williams suggests that we view Origen's understanding of exegesis as in part a response to this perceived need: with divine assistance the exegete demonstrates the unity of scriptural teaching, and in so doing demonstrates the rational ordering and saving work of the Logos. Appropriate deployment of grammatical and figural techniques plays the score of Scripture into a harmonious unity. The exegete thus demonstrates the shape, bounds, and style of Christian speech through displaying how the text should be read. For Origen, though, this display is always an indication that each Christian may make the journey, not a statement that the revelation of truth has now been achieved for all. For Williams, Origen's deep concern for the demonstration of this unity also partly stems from his early experience of a time of crisis in Alexandria when a multiplicity of Christian and para-Christian groups in the city served to hide the vision of divine unity for which Origen strived.

Williams goes on to suggest that this perception of the exegete's task may also partially account for suspicion of Origen in the fourth century. Origen's account of the unity of orthodoxy resting in the possibility of a display of the unity of Scripture by the spiritually aware exegete had become unintelligible for two reasons. On the one hand, the fourth-century Church became increasingly reliant on short, synchronic, and institutionally enforced statements of orthodoxy. On the other hand, the changing social situation of the Church meant that bishops made increasingly concerted appeals to a non-elite audience in ways that made Origen's sense of a necessary intensive spiritual pedagogy for the comprehension of Christianity seem unworkable.⁵¹ At this point I suggest we should beware of following Williams's argument too easily.

I will argue in Chapters 11–13 that pro-Nicene theology is best understood as a theological culture. One of my reasons for taking

---

⁵⁰ Williams, 'Origen: Between Orthodoxy and Heresy'.
⁵¹ Williams also notes that many of Origen's accusers in this period also accuse him of excessive plurality in his theology and argue for greater unity—exactly mirroring Origen's own self-perception.

this approach is the evidence that pro-Nicene authors realized the difficulty of defining 'orthodoxy' by reference to individual terminologies and credal formulae. Instead they pointed to sets of terminologies embodying similar logics, and assumed that such terminologies were read in the context of a set of wider theological assumptions and practices. Thus any easy contrast between Origen's exegete performing the unity of Christian faith through the crafting of intertextual harmony and a later (frequently episcopal) authority simply reproducing the statements of credal definition is to be resisted. We should perhaps think, instead, of slow and subtle modifications to the structure of a particular cultural vision occurring throughout this period.

4
Confusion and Controversy: AD 325–340

THE NICENE CREED AS A STANDARD OF FAITH

In Chapter 1 I told the story of a conflict in Alexandria that came to involve many prominent bishops and theologians in the eastern half of the empire. This story reached its culmination at the Council of Nicaea in 325. I then argued that we needed to begin again and see this controversy as occurring within and *because of* tension between existing theological trajectories. It is now time to resume the narrative: as my point of departure I will return to the Council of Nicaea.

Many modern readers assume that the Nicene creed was intended at its promulgation to stand as a binding and universal formula of Christian faith with a carefully chosen terminology defining the fundamental Christian account of the relationship between Father and Son. The idea that the creed would serve as a universal and precise marker of Christian faith was unlikely to have occurred to anyone at Nicaea simply because the idea that *any* creed might so serve was as yet unheard of.[1] All the bishops at Nicaea would have understood their local 'baptismal' creed to be a sufficient definition of Christian belief and summary of the faith Scripture taught. Baptismal creeds were central both to the process of catechesis and to the rite of Christian initiation. In those areas for which we have evidence baptismal creeds formed the focus of the catechetical teaching given to candidates in the weeks or days before baptism. During the fourth century the baptismal rite itself developed and in an increasingly important and formal section of the ritual candidates would recite, in response to questions, the creed they had learnt.

Local baptismal creeds were handed down through a community's liturgical practice and sometimes associated with the name of a local saint or church founder. A variety of comparable creeds were in use, but the identity of the faith they instantiated was assumed where the communities who used them could remain in contact and mutual recognition. Communication between leaders of local Christian communities and gatherings of bishops was thus vital. In this fluid context precise credal formulae were not used for

---

[1] On creeds see J. N. D. Kelly, *Early Christian Creeds*, 3rd edn. (London: Longman, 1972). On the course of discussion at Nicaea see Hanson, *The Search*, 157–72; Williams, *Arius*, 67–71; Simonetti, *La Crisi*, 77–87; Strutwolf, *Trinitätstheologie*, 44–61.

defining the boundaries of acceptable belief. Bishops were not expected to sign a universal statement of faith and, prior to Nicaea, there are only two documented uses of credal-type documents being used as conciliar tools for defining right belief. Both of these occurred in Antioch: in 268 a credal definition seems to have played some role in the action taken against Paul of Samosata, and a few months before Nicaea, we have the Antiochene creed of 325. It is also important to note that even up until the beginning of the fifth century, when Nicaea's position became more clearly established in liturgical contexts, local creeds continued to be used in catechesis, simply interpreted and taught within the terms of a pro-Nicene theology.[2]

Throughout the first forty years of the controversy councils of bishops formulated a number of creeds in words different from those used at Nicaea. While some were constructed by those who opposed Nicaea, others were understood as compatible with it. That one might, on an ad hoc basis, produce a creed which put the same faith a little more clearly was a near-universal assumption. Indeed, as we shall see, the idea that Nicaea would serve as a universal standard of faith, and as one whose precise wording and terminology was itself definitive, evolved *through* the fourth century, and was still evolving at the century's end.

Even if the use of credal formulae in a conciliar context was new, the holding of councils was not. Hamilton Hess nicely summarizes the evidence for pre-Nicene councils in the second edition of his classic text on the Council of Serdica. Although we can trace different types of gatherings of Christian members and leaders from the New Testament period, it is only in the third century that we have clear evidence of fairly regular meetings of bishops to discuss doctrinal and administrative questions. It is, however, a mistake to think of these councils as consisting only of bishops: in many cases large numbers of lay people and other clergy we present and seem to have taken a full part. Many of these debates still seem to have seen themselves as discussions on the model of the philosophical schools rather than deliberative assemblies with legal powers. Only from around 250–70 do we hear of councils acting in a more clearly parliamentary manner, hearing evidence on a question, reaching decisions, and expecting those decisions to be executed in local churches. As councils became more formal bodies they seem to have adopted methods of self-governance modelled on procedures used

---

[2] See Daniel H. Williams, 'Constantine and the "Fall" of the Church', in Lewis Ayres and Gareth Jones (eds.), *Christian Origins: Theology, Rhetoric and Community* (London: Routledge, 1998), 117–36; Kelly, *Early Christian Creeds*, 254–62. See also Ch. 13.

at a number of levels of Roman government, from the Senate in Rome down to provincial assemblies.[3] Thus by the time Nicaea met Church leaders accepted the idea of a council as a deliberative forum, but they had no precedent for the idea of a council that would legislate for the Church as a whole. The procedures of a council modelled on methods of Roman governance would have been familiar to Constantine, and we can assume that he saw it as the natural means to achieve consensus within the Church. We should also note that even at Nicaea not all of those invited were bishops: it is as we go through the fourth century that we see the emergence of the solely episcopal gathering.

The council was widely known in the east in the decades that followed, at least initially because of its sheer size and because of Constantine's role in organizing the council and in enforcing its decrees. Both Constantine himself and Eusebius in his life of Constantine emphasize the importance of convening so many bishops in such a large meeting.[4] In the west detailed knowledge of Nicaea was far patchier. In all cases, however, we should not necessarily identify knowledge of the council with detailed knowledge of its creed.[5] In a context when councils were not expected to produce precise statements of belief, there is no reason to think that Nicaea would be remembered *for* its creed in the years which immediately followed. We might say that the judgements of Nicaea could be known, while the terms in which those judgements were expressed were of only secondary interest.[6] We should note also that Nicaea's canons concern many organizational issues far beyond the crisis over Arius.

Constantine himself had become sole emperor only in 324 (after having ruled the western half since 310–12), and he seems to have promoted Christianity as a unifying religion for the empire (although his personal beliefs will almost certainly remain unclear). Unity of Christians as a body was of as much concern to Constantine as any doctrinal issue involved: and it initially took the efforts of

---

[3] Hamilton Hess, *The Early Development of Canon Law and the Council of Serdica* (Oxford: Clarendon Press, 2002), chs. 1–3.

[4] Eusebius of Caesrea, *Vit. Const.* 3. 6; Constantine at Opitz, *Werke* III/2, U. 32.

[5] Hess, *Canon Law*, 124 ff. shows that in the west the canons of Serdica 343 were frequently treated as those of Nicaea. This nicely demonstrates the lack of detailed knowledge of the council in the west. In general on the reception of Nicaea's theological terminology in the west see Jörg Ulrich, *Die Anfänge der Abendländischen Rezeption des Nizänums* (Berlin: De Gruyter, 1994).

[6] There is still much to be learnt from H.-J. Sieben's *Die Konzilsidee der Alten Kirche* (Paderborn: Schöningh, 1979), ch. 1. His discussion of how, in Athanasius' writing, Nicaea goes through various stages on the road to its full status as 'ecumenical' council, from being a universal judgement against Arius towards a sufficient summation of the Church's faith, is an excellent point of departure for a wider consideration of the status of Nicaea in a range of writers through our period.

bishops like Ossius and Alexander of Alexandri to persuade him that anything significant was at issue in Alexandria. We should not simply put this down to theological ignorance. On the one hand, Constantine's attitude reflects deeply embedded Roman attitudes about the social function of religion which were at odds with the increasing importance Christians placed on orthodoxy of belief. On the other hand, as Robert Markus noted, Constantine's attitude itself may actually reflect an older Christian attitude to the virtue of unity under threat of persecution, the partisans at Nicaea reflecting the emergence of a more fractious attitude.[7] These ideas are intriguing, but will remain conjectural in the face of our lack of evidence. We do know that Constantine took a deep interest in the council, and issued a number of letters attempting to enforce its decisions. Despite this interest, as we shall see there is no indication that even Constantine saw the creed as anything other than a statement designed to solve the current rift in the Church.[8] In general then we have to say that the creed stood as a particular statement of faith designed for a particular purpose: any further status it might have would be a subject for argument in the following decades.

THE COURSE OF THE COUNCIL

In older narratives of the fourth century it was reasonably easy to understand why the Nicene creed was agreed with little dissent: only the few 'heretics' would refuse such a clear acknowledgement of the Church's constant faith. Without this older narrative, matters are more complex. Unfortunately, we have no surviving detailed acts of the proceedings at Nicaea. Indeed, it is unlikely that detailed minutes of the council were kept, as happened at later councils.[9] Hence we have to construct an account of the debate from some surviving scraps of evidence. We can certainly see that Eusebians of all types were under pressure and seem to have been on the defensive. It is at least possible that Eusebius of Nicomedia made an opening speech to the Emperor, but the direction of the council was very clearly in

---

[7] Robert Markus, 'The Problem of Self-Definition: From Sect to Church', in E. P. Sanders (ed.), *Jewish and Christian Self-Definition*, i: *The Shaping of Christianity in the Second and Third Centuries* (London: SCM, 1980), 1–15.

[8] We should avoid reading Constantius' attitude to credal formulae back into the intentions of his father Constantine without further evidence (see below, Ch. 6). It is true that the Council of Nicaea had also been called to settle on a universal date for the celebration of Easter, and in this regard Constantine clearly saw the council as having a universal function. But this does not necessarily mean that the creed of Nicaea was intended as a universal statement of faith. For Constantine's letter to Alexander and Arius (c.324) see Opitz, U.17.

[9] Hanson, *The Search*, 158 and *passim* 157–63, for accounts of the surviving evidence, and Simonetti, *La Crisi*, 77–95. On the arguments at the council Kelly, *Early Christian Creeds*, ch. 7 is also helpful.

the hands of others. Ossius of Cordoba probably chaired the meeting; Eustathius of Antioch, Marcellus of Ancyra, and Alexander must all have been key players in the discussions. Tension among Eusebian bishops was caused by knowledge that Constantine had taken Alexander's part and by events at the council of Antioch only a few months before.

However, despite the prominence of Ossius, Eustathius, Marcellus, and Alexander, Eusebius of Caesarea must still be counted as one of the most senior and influential bishops present. Eusebius reports that he read a creed and appended explanatory text to the assembly—which he quotes for us—and he tells us that this was accepted wholeheartedly.[10] The text Eusebius read is in fact extremely cautious and offers very little description of, or terminology for, the Son's generation other than to say that the Son was 'begotten from the Father before all ages'. A fragment from Eustathius of Antioch reports a 'Eusebius' reading a text which was then very badly received.[11] Unless we think that either Eustathius or Eusebius of Caesarea is simply lying, then it seems Eustathius must be referring to the other Eusebius, Eusebius of Nicomedia (a view reinforced by Ambrose of Milan writing in the 380s).[12] Thus, at some point it seems that Eusebius of Nicomedia failed to get approval for *his* theology. Once the creed itself was being drafted it also seems likely that an attempt was made to argue against the direction of events—and maybe the term *homoousios* was particularly criticized—but this too was rebuffed.[13]

Thus we see the Eusebians under pressure, some willing to compromise, others not. The role played by Constantine himself is uncertain. The Emperor certainly opened the meeting and attended at least some sessions. In his opening address he was clear that an agreement about the structure of Christian faith was his goal. This imperial pressure coupled with the role of his advisers in broadly supporting the agenda of Alexander must have been a powerful force. When, however, we ask if we can also imagine a majority of those present personally belonging to non-Eusebian trajectories the answer must be tentative. We simply do not know in individual cases whether subscription to Nicaea's creed reveals personal

---

[10] Eusebius of Caesarea, *Ep. Caes.* 4–6. Some have taken Eusebius to assert here that the creed of Nicaea was really the creed he presented with a few additions. This claim is not sustainable; see Kelly, *Early Christian Creeds*, 211–26. However, as Kelly points out, we do better to read Eusebius as saying that the *doctrine* represented by Nicaea is the same as that of Caesarea.

[11] Theodoret, *Eccl. hist.* 1. 7. 43–4.   [12] Ambrose, *De fide* 3. 15. 125.

[13] Theodoret, *Eccl. hist.* 1. 7. 33. I follow Williams, *Arius*, 67 in identifying this as a separate event from Eusebius of Nicomedia's attempt to get his orthodoxy confirmed. But the evidence here is uncertain.

commitment or willingness to follow the pressure of the Emperor's presence and the direction of the council's leaders. Many of those attending were probably unaware of the detailed issues involved in the controversy over Arius and willing to follow the lead of either local leaders or those whose theology seemed best to resonate with their own local theological traditions or favoured terminologies. Even among those who we might think of as more committed to Eusebian language there may have been many willing to agree that the sort of gloss put on the creed by Eusebius of Caesarea writing to his own diocese after the council would be the prudent course. In general, we do not possess the evidence to identify the allegiances of those present, nor can we suppose that the disposition of bishops at Nicaea reflected the disposition of theological trajectories more widely in the Christian world. Throughout the century large councils such as Nicaea were not constituted as a representative selection of bishops.

It does seem clear that those who carried weight were determined to have Arius' theology condemned.[14] Indeed, the choice of the term *homoousios* seems to have been motivated in large part because Arius was known to reject it. Athanasius, in later accounts of the council, tells us that those running the council originally proposed describing the Son as 'like' the Father or 'exactly like the Father in all things' and as being 'from God'.[15] But these terms would not serve because everyone could agree to them—Arius' supporters could find parallel statements in the Bible describing aspects of the creation and the phrase 'from God' could also be used of created things, and to mean 'from the will of God not his essence'. Hence, *homoousios* and 'from the essence of the Father' were chosen specifically to exclude Arius' supporters. Athanasius' reports offer a plausible account of a discussion attempting to produce a compromise formula that will exclude some positions and yet still achieve a majority. But if something like this did occur, everyone would have known what they excluded; nobody needs to have been able to define what they positively included.[16]

Eusebius, in his *Letter to his Diocese* written in 326, writes that Constantine himself spoke, endorsing the term *homoousios*, but insisting that it did not imply any material division in God. Eusebius also reports that he himself secured clarity that the phrase 'from the essence of the Father' did not mean 'is part of the Father's

---

[14] Arius himself may have been in attendance, but there is no evidence that he took any part in the proceedings, and it seems unlikely.

[15] Athanasius, *Decr.* 20; *Ad Afros* 5. It is only in the latter text that he mentions the phrase 'from God'.

[16] For futher discussion of Athanasius' argument see Ch. 6.

substance'. It is noticeable that in Eusebius' reading of the text it is still possible to read Nicaea as implying a certain subordinationism; the creed's technical terms are all interpreted to mean that the Son is like the Father, and is truly from the Father. Eusebius interprets Nicaea's anathema against those who say 'before he was begotten he was not' to mean that the Son existed potentially in the Father before his actual begetting by referring to Constantine's own opinions (although it seems likely that he does not mean opinions expressed at Nicaea).[17] By such means Eusebius avoids the notion of eternal generation so dear to some of his opponents.

Whether or not one believes Eusebius' account of Constantine's interventions, his text does give us a very plausible account of how someone within his theological trajectory could have interpreted Nicaea's terms. Emphasis on the incomprehensibility of the Son's generation was important to all the trajectories I have discussed and it is no surprise that we find it being emphasized to placate Eusebians. All trajectories could agree on this principle, even if they could not agree on the consequences of its incomprehensibility! Eusebius' discussion nicely demonstrates the extent to which the promulgation of *homoousios* involved a conscious *lack* of positive definition of the term.

Of course, those who were broadly in the same trajectory as Alexander would have easily been able to sign up to Nicaea's terms but would have read them in a very different manner, although not necessarily one dependent on a more careful definition of their sense. They desired to secure the condemnation of Arius and to that end saw as essential a clear statement that the Son was produced from the Father's essence. In this they succeeded, but at the cost of a creed that could still be acknowledged by some Eusebians and which is simply vague on some key points. It is noticeable, for example, that the Son is not described as *eternally* begotten, probably reflecting the impossibility of getting agreement on this still contested term. Thus it is not quite accurate to say that the creed reflects the beliefs of those who held the initiative at Nicaea. Rather, the creed shows the extent to which those who held the initiative could push their perspective while still achieving sufficient support for victory at the council. These bishops assumed that they had every right to

---

[17] Eusebius, *Ep. Caes.* 16: 'Already our Emperor, the most beloved of God, affirmed in a discourse that even according to his divine generation he was before all the ages, since even before he was begotten in actuality, he was in the Father ingenerately in potentiality . . .'. Eusebius may well be referring to the *Oratio ad Sanctos* (CPG 3497) attributed to Constantine, some indications of a parallel doctrine may be found there. There is now considerable scholarship on this text: for a discussion which offers some evidence compatible with my suggestion here see Mark Edwards, 'The Arian Heresy and the Oration to the Saints', *VigChr* 49 (1995), 379–87.

take the council's decisions as licensing their own theologies as expressions of orthodox faith. In the years which followed Nicaea these bishops were to find that this was a matter still very much open to dispute. Nicaea's terminology is thus a window onto the confusion and complexity of the early fourth-century theological debates, not a revelation that a definitive turning-point had been reached. My conclusions here are close to those of Richard Hanson when he writes,

> The evidence available does not admit of our forming ingenious, elaborate and highly nuanced theories about the council of Nicaea ... It is improbable that all of the people who had previously seen nothing offensive in the doctrine of Arius should have surrendered tamely to an openly Sabellian creed. It is improbable that the heirs of any side of Origen's thought should have abandoned a doctrine of three *hypostases*. As N. [*sic*] does not openly mention the eternal generation of the Son, so it does not openly declare that there is only one *hypostasis* in the Godhead. The *homoousion* was probably not a flag to be nailed to the masthead, a word around which self-conscious schools of theology could rally. But it was an atropopaic formula for resisting Arianism ... [18]

OUSIA AND *HYPOSTASIS* IN THE CREED OF NICAEA

One of the most striking aspects of Nicaea in comparison to surviving baptismal creeds from the period, and even in comparison to the creed which survives from the council of Antioch in early 325, is its use of the technical terminology of *ousia* and *hypostasis*.[19] There is, however, a huge difference between deploying terms that appear to fulfil a technical clarifying function, and understanding those terms clearly. There is in fact evidence that these terms had been the subject of debate and confusion since the mid-third century. Hence, it is important to attempt to understand what meaning was attributed to these terms at the time of Nicaea. By way of a general warning, it is important to note that any attempt to define fourth-century theological terminologies by reference solely to their philological origins or to a history of non-Christian philosophical development runs the constant danger of resulting in an artificial clarity that is not reflected in actual theological usage. Rather, we need to be attentive to the histories of theological use of these terms prior to Nicaea.

---

[18] Hanson, *The Search*, 172.
[19] For further introductory discussion of these key terms see Hanson, *The Search*, 181–207; G. Christopher Stead, *Philosophy in Christian Antiquity* (Cambridge: Cambridge University Press, 1994). Hanson's notes list the appropriate German and French literature to 1988. Of this see in particular H. Dörrie, '*Hypostasis*, Wort- und Bedeutungsgeschichte', *Nachr. Akad. Göttingen*, 3 (1955), 35–92; J. Hammerstaedt, 'Hypostasis', *RAC* 16 (1985), 986–1035.

I will begin with Nicaea's use of *ousia* language. The creed uses this terminology at three crucial points.[20] First, the description of the Son as 'only-begotten' is glossed with the immediately following phrase 'that is, of the *ousia* of the Father'. Second, Father and Son are subsequently described as *homoousios*. Third, those people are anathematized who understand the Son as being 'of another *hypostasis* or *ousia*'. Of the three uses of *ousia* language the term *homoousios* has generated the most discussion, in large part because of its later significance.[21] As will become clear through this and the next chapter, it is not at all clear that at Nicaea the term *homoousios* was understood to be the technical focus of the creed. The term was adopted in the second century by Gnostics, probably to indicate 'same ontological status' or 'of a similar kind'. In this context, however, the term was used alongside notions of emanation and derived being which described the ontological links between the highest deity, lower deities, and that within the human being which enabled union with those deities.[22] The term was also used to describe the products of acts of creation in which semi-divine beings are made out of pre-existing (semi-material) substances.[23] For Christian writers such notions seemed irredeemably materialist, and made it easy for them to suppose that the mere use of *homoousios* implies a certain materiality. By the fourth century—and with some basis in fact—Manichees were also taken to teach a cosmology in which creation of deities happens through a semi-materialist division of divine being. Although we do not know of Manichees actually using the term *homoousios*, Nicaea's supporters are accused of 'Manichaeism' even before the council met.[24]

Homoousios was also conditioned by its use in theological contexts. As we saw in Chapter 1, Origen may have rejected the term or possibly used it in a carefully analogical sense. Only a decade after his death, *homoousios* appears in two disputes. In a dispute between Dionysius, bishop of Rome, and Dionysius, bishop of Alexandria,

---

[20] It used to be assumed that Aristotle's account of two key senses of *ousia* was determinative for 4th-cent. Christians: while this would enable an easy description of usage, there is no evidence that this distinction was at all frequently employed. This point is now so well established in scholarship that I have not discussed it further. See Stead, *Divine Substance* (Oxford: Clarendon Press, 1977).

[21] Much relevant material is gathered at Hanson, *The Search*, 190–202 and his summary is helpful (n. 49 cites the other main literature). See Stead, *Divine Substance*, chs. 7–9; idem, ' "Eusebius" and the Council of Nicaea', *JThS* NS 24 (1973), esp. 88–92.

[22] Origen, *Comm. John* 13. 25. 148. it should, however, be noted that later Christian assumption that a doctrine of emanation implies inherent materialism is, in many cases, unwarranted. Doctrines of emanation—as the history of later Platonism demonstrates—may be highly complex and look remarkably like doctrines of an incomprehensible *creatio ex nihilo*.

[23] e.g. Irenaeus, *Adv. haer.* 1. 5. 1. Epiphanius, *Panarion* 33. 7. 8.

[24] e.g. in Arius' *Ep. Alex.*

c.260, the term appears to have been something that Dionysius of Alexandria had denied but was then persuaded by his namesake of Rome to accept.[25] We cannot give a clear account of this dispute: it seems at least likely that Dionysius of Alexandria, in a campaign against some local Sabellians had denied the term to emphasize the Son's secondary status. Dionysius of Rome criticized this position and claimed that Father and Son were *homoousios*.[26] From what we saw of third-century Latin theology in the last chapter, Dionysius of Rome probably sought to emphasize that the Son shared the divine existence, not that Father and Son were one thing. Dionysius of Alexandria seems to have responded and admitted that the term was acceptable, but only when it is understood as synonymous with the term ὁμογενής ('belonging to the same class') used of a Father and a Son, a plant and a root, or a river and a well. He also seems to have insisted that the term should not be understood to imply any materialist diminution in the Father when the Son is generated.

The council that deposed Paul of Samosata in 268 condemned the use of *homoousios*. The condemnation of *homoousios* by this well-known council caused embarrassment to a number of figures in the fourth century, but it is unlikely we shall ever know clearly what was at stake. Paul may have used the term when arguing that the Word was from God and distinct from the man Jesus, thus breaking any identification of Christ with the Word of God. For Paul the term may have indicated the closeness of God and Word: to his opponents his usage seemed materialistic.[27] In the years immediately before Nicaea Arius himself rejected the term, assuming that it implied a materialistic division in God and Eusebius of Nicomedia also condemned the term as implying two eternal co-ordinate realities.[28] In continuity with this earlier evidence the term is criticized later in the fourth century, both for implying that two things described as *homoousios* must be of the same ontological status, and for being inherently materialistic, implying that the co-ordinate terms came from an underlying material.

Summing up this evidence, we can suggest the following. A standard connotation of the term *homoousios* was membership in a class, a

---

[25] The best account of this dispute is Williams, *Arius*, 150–3.

[26] There is, however, no evidence that the term *homoousios* was a term highly valued in Latin theology through the 3rd and 4th cents. It does not appear, as was once argued, to have been a distinctively western term.

[27] We do not know if Paul used the term before this council or only in response to accusation against him. As John Behr points out, the council's condemnation of the term must have been highly qualified as the acts and decisions were sent on to Dionysius of Rome! See Behr, *Way to Nicaea*, 220.

[28] Arius, *Ep. Alex.* 3, 5; Eusebius of Nicomedia apud Ambrose, *De fide* 3. 15 (Opitz, *Urkunde*, 21).

generic similarity between things that were, in some sense, co-ordinate. The term was used loosely to point to markers of commonality and did not at all exclude relationships between realities that were hierarchically distinct in other ways. The use of the term in Gnostic and Christian contexts meant that it was inextricably linked with the question of the derivation of the Son from the Father. This derivative or genetic sense derived from a biological or material analogical base. Thus, for some theologians, the term emphasized that the Father's generation of the Son was more like the generation of a human son by a human father, than like the creation of all other things. For their opponents the very genetic and materialistic connotations that rendered the term useful indicated the term's problematic status. Such theologians could bring to bear in their polemic all of the term's materialistic connotations as well as its implication that the realities described as *homoousios* were co-ordinate realities.

Johannes Zachhuber, in discussing Athanasius' and Apollinaris' defence of *homoousios* in the 350s, notes a possible parallel in third-century Neoplatonic writers.[29] Plotinus and Porphyry both argue that *ousia* is not a genus in Aristotle's sense as things that share *ousia* are ontologically prior and posterior. *Ousia* can, they argue, only be a category in the specific sense that a family or a race of people derive from a common founder. Calling things related by descent *homoousios* might thus be taken to indicate that they are members of a class, but not simply in the sense of being co-ordinate realities.[30] It is, however, unlikely that this philosophical development had much impact on Christian thinkers before the later fourth century. Whether or not this philosophical debate influenced theologians at the time of Nicaea, discussion of the manner in which *homoousios* could be used to indicate derivative or genetic relationship was already embedded in theological tradition. Thus, a loose generic sense existed alongside a tradition of reflection on how it might serve when applied to the relationship of Father and Son.

This tradition of reflection probably helped to make the term acceptable to the architects of Nicaea. It is unlikely that Alexander or Ossius would have chosen the term intending a simple co-ordinate sense even removed of materialist connotations: this would have played into the hands of those arguing that Alexander taught two eternal principles. Marcellus and Eustathius also seem likely to have endorsed *homoousios* because of the notion of shared being that was an accepted part of its semantic range, but not because they

---

[29] This topic is discussed in more detail in Ch. 8.
[30] Johannes Zachhuber, *Human Nature in Gregory of Nyssa: Philosophical Background and Theological Significance* (Leiden: Brill, 2000), 37–8.

thought it implied two distinct eternally co-ordinate realities. In the context of Nicaea's creed all the theologians mentioned in this paragraph also probably saw *homoousios* as expanding on and secondary to the phrase 'from the *ousia* of the Father', the sense of the term thus being governed by the genetic relationship indicated there. This last point finds an interesting parallel in Eusebius' *Letter to his Diocese*. When Eusebius writes that he asked for clarification regarding *homousios* and 'from the *ousia* of the Father', the latter phrase is the focus of his account. Eusebius tells us that once he had been assured that this phrase served only to indicate that the Son was truly from the Father he could agree even to *homoousios*.[31] Although we have no extended explanation of *homoousios* from the early fourth century, we see the same position in Athanasius' defence of the term in the early 350s. Athanasius presents *homoousios* as a supplement to 'from the *ousia* of the Father', which in turn defends the traditional language of Word and Wisdom. Thus, the cumulative evidence seems to indicate that later focus on *homoousios* as a stand-alone term is a shift from its use at Nicaea: at the council it served to qualify 'from the *ousia* of the Father.'

Richard Vaggione has argued recently that Eusebius and Athanasius repeat both versions of an 'official' interpretation of Nicaea promoted by Constantine himself.[32] In actual fact Eusebius directly ascribes to Constantine *only* an emphasis on understanding *homoousios* without reference to material division or the sorts of change associated with corporeal existence. It seems, then, more likely that there was not an official interpretation of the creed's terms, but merely that Constantine interceded on behalf of those unhappy with *homoousios*, insisting on the importance of understanding the term without material connotation. The rest he left, and may have wished to leave, vaguely defined.[33] We should note also that after Nicaea *homoousios* is not mentioned again in truly contemporary sources for two decades. In part, our surprise at its absence reflects later insistence on its importance: it may not be discussed simply because it was not seen as that useful or important. This lack of usage also results from the association of Nicaea with the theology of Marcellus of Ancyra. As we shall see, the language

---

[31] Eusebius, *Ep. Caes.* 12–13.

[32] Vaggione, *Eunomius of Cyzicus*, 58: 'As explained by the emperor, that sense was that all thoughts of passion, division or separation were to be excluded and *homoousios* was to be used to express three things and three things only: that the Son is not similar to any created being; that he is similar to the Father in every particular; and that he derives his existence, not from any alien substance or essence, but from the Father alone.'

[33] Eusebius, *Ep. Caes.* 7. No further evidence is provided by Constantine, *Ep. Nic.* 1–2 (Opitz, U.27). On this question see Ch. 6 and my 'Athanasius' Initial Defence of the Term ὁμοούσιος: Re-reading the *De decretis*' *JECS*, 12 (2004), 337–59.

of that creed seemed to offer no prophylactic against Marcellan doctrine, and increasingly came to be seen as implying such doctrine.[34]

The phrase 'from the *ousia* of the Father' also had a complex history of use before Nicaea, much of which revolved around its seemingly materialistic or inappropriately genetic implications.[35] Origen treats this phrase as implying something like a human birth and thus a materialistic understanding of divine being.[36] Eusebius of Nicomedia criticizes the phrase both for implying a materialist view of the Son's generation and for implying that the Son shares the nature of the Father. To share this nature would mean that the Son was unbegotten as is the Father. Eusebius insists that nothing is 'of the Father's *ousia*': things that are begotten or created do not share the Father's mode of existence.[37] Eusebius of Caesarea, also writing before Nicaea, demonstrates similar worries that the phrase implies a materialistic diminution of the Father's being in the generation of the Son. He also offers an interpretation of the phrase he finds acceptable, but it is hedged by his typical insistence on the incomprehensibility of the generation and alongside the analogy of the fragrance and the ray of light.[38] It is, then, no surprise that talk of the Son coming from the Father's *ousia*, or from the Father himself was also unacceptable to Arius. The phrase seems to have been used at Nicaea both to characterize the Son's generation as being distinct from the process by which all other things came to be, and to invoke a sense—which the previous tradition had done little to clarify—that the Son or the Word shared some aspects of the Father's mode of existence. Invoking such an inchoate notion of the Son's participation in the divine existence was to cause much controversy in the decades which followed.

The creed condemns anyone who says that the Son is from (ἐκ)

---

[34] Alleging that there was suspicion of *homoousios* because of its association with Marcellus is not dependent on the assumption that the term by itself indicates identity of being, that Father and Son were 'one thing'. Even though it seems unlikely that anyone assumed this basic meaning for the term, when read against the background of Marcellus' strong support for Nicaea it may well have seemed that he was implying a (temporary) materialistic division of the divine being. Thus throughout the century we have to be careful to see where an accusation is aimed at the term itself or at someone's theology as a whole, in which the term itself plays a small role. This complexity often lies at the heart of why the term seems to be the subject of so many different accusations.

[35] On this phrase see the very helpful discussion of Stead, *Divine Substance*, 223–33.

[36] Origen, *Comm. John* 20. 157–8: 'These must consequently say that the Son has been begotten of the Father's essence, as one might understand this also in the case of those who are pregnant, and that God is diminished and lacking, as it were, in the essence that he formerly had, when he has begotten the Son. These people must also say, as a consequence, that the Father and the Son are corporeal, and that the Father has been divided.'

[37] Eusebius of Nicomedia, *Ep. Paul.* 3.

[38] Eusebius, *Dem. evang.* 4. 3. 13 (quoted in Ch. 2).

anything else than the *ousia* or *hypostasis* of the Father. Christopher Stead offers a convincing argument that the phrase was intended as a reinforcement of 'from the *ousia* of the Father' and *homoousios*.[39] For Stead, the phrase invokes a traditional (and muddled) set of oppositions between the Son being 'from God' or being from nothing or from some other divine source. Nicaea thus reinforces its earlier phraseology by further insisting that the Son is 'from God': the 'from' (ἐκ) here provides the key to understanding the anathema. Even if this provides a relatively convincing explanation of the anathema it is still obvious that continuing terminological confusion is reflected in the seeming equation of *ousia* and *hypostasis*. It is only much later in the century that the two are more clearly distinguished by some. We have already seen that, following Origen, some eastern theologians used *hypostasis*, both in a specific sense to designate a circumscribed individual reality and in a range of other senses. At the same time there are other theological trajectories for whom *hypostasis* did not function as a technical term. Those who formulated Nicaea's creed appear to demonstrate at least a lack of interest in the technical Origenist sense of *hypostasis* and possibly deep hostility to it.

Thus we can identify a broad range of possible meaning for each of Nicaea's three uses of a technical terminology, and in each case we can also demonstrate major issues that remain unresolved. This use of terminology demonstrates the (temporary) victory of one side in early fourth-century debate over *ousia* language, but it does not demonstrate any substantial advance towards a resolution of that debate.

WAS THERE A 'NICENE' THEOLOGY IN 325?

In what sense can one speak of an original 'Nicene' theology? It is worth observing that while modern scholars are often very sophisticated in their understanding of the difficulties involved in speaking of 'Arians' as a unified group, far fewer display the same sophistication when speaking of 'Nicenes'. Much of this book constitutes an exploration of the complexity of the label 'Nicene': in these paragraphs I concern myself only with the state of affairs in 325 and in the immediate aftermath of the council. I suggest that we can speak of an original 'Nicene' theology in the sense that we can point to some common themes apparent in texts from those most directly responsible for Nicaea's language. We can point to Alexander of Alexandria's letter's to Alexander of Byzantium, some fragments of

[39] Stead, *Divine Substance*, 233–42.

Marcellus of Ancyra, the creed of Antioch 325, some fragments of Eustathius of Antioch, and the few fragments giving Constantine's own opinions.[40] To these we might add the Athanasius of *Contra gentes* and *De incarnatione*. In these he writes before 'Arianism' seems to be of any significance to him, and in a large degree of continuity with Alexander's writing.

To some this list will seem strange precisely because of its diversity. However, by suggesting that these texts represent the theology of Nicaea 325 I do not mean that they embody a unitary and clearly defined theology. I have argued that Nicaea's creed was not designed to do much more than: (*a*) earn the approval (however grudging) of a majority present and (*b*) make it clear that certain perceived errors of Arius and his early supporters were unacceptable. If this is so then perhaps Nicaea's creed was both intended to reflect the views of the coalition who framed its distinctive terminology, and yet had to hide some of their idiosyncrasies in order to provide a common front and to achieve wider consensus at the council.

Note that I point to a set of texts rather than trying to isolate a theology supposedly embodied in the creed itself and acknowledged by the signatories of Nicaea. Such a tactic would have been problematic because there were clearly many signatories of Nicaea who did not hold to the theological positions of those who framed the creed, even if they were able to agree to it. Far too much traditional discussion about the disputes immediately after Nicaea takes at face value the fourth-century polemical accusation that a given opponent is distorting Nicaea or its intention. Such tactics hide the pluralistic nature of this original Nicene theology. Athanasius and Marcellus can and should both be counted as 'original Nicene', but there are considerable differences between their theologies. In the controversies which erupted over Eustathius of Antioch and Marcellus after Nicaea, both thought their theologies faithful to Nicaea—and they had good grounds for so assuming. Both were influential at the council, and Nicaea's lapidary formulations were never intended to rule out their theological idiosyncrasies. Thus, original Nicene theology was a fluid and diverse phenomenon, and one that kept evolving. We can perhaps view both the 'western' text from Serdica (discussed in Chapter 5) and Athanasius' early anti-'Arian' writings as attempts to enlarge on and offer a convincing version of that original Nicene theology. It was to be many years before those attempts evolved into what I shall term pro-Nicene theology, or even

---

[40] We might be able to add Ossius of Cordoba to the list had we sufficient surviving material. As it is we can only suppose.

before that theology even loosely centred around an explicit defence of Nicaea's own terms.

AD 325–342: TOWARDS THE CREATION OF 'ARIANISM'

During the years 325–42 neither Arius nor the particular technical terminology used at Nicaea were at the heart of theological controversy. Although the council was probably widely known, within a few years there is a near-fifteen-year absence before the creed is mentioned again.[41] The fact that those around whom debate was now to focus had been strong supporters of Nicaea gives us one obvious reason why Nicaea's creed seemed problematic if not useless to many. At the same time, we must bear in mind that, as yet, the idea of one precise credal formula functioning as a universal standard of faith was some way off.

The story of debate over Arius himself after Nicaea need not detain us long.[42] Arius and most of his supporters were, at Constantine's request, readmitted to communion within two or three years of the council. Arius submitted a bland confession of faith to Constantine and in return the Emperor appears to have instructed a council of bishops (probably of a Eusebian turn of mind) to readmit him.[43] The bishops exiled after Nicaea were allowed back to their sees and Eusebius of Nicomedia quickly rose again to a position of importance, baptizing Constantine on his death-bed in 337 and becoming bishop of Constantinople in 338 or 339. Arius himself did not fare so well. Unfortunately for him Alexander and his successor as bishop, Athanasius (who took office in 328 while still only in his early thirties), refused to readmit Arius to communion in Alexandria. Arius eventually seems to have felt somewhat abandoned by his erstwhile supporters and made the mistake of writing to the emperor asking for redress and emphasizing the strength of his following in Libya. In 333 Constantine wrote to Arius with the anger he seems to have reserved particularly for those who threatened unity. Constantine also sent an edict with the letter ordering Arius' works to be burnt. Very quickly Constantine seems to have

---

[41] After the debate in 326–7 mentioned by Sozomen and Eusebius' *Ep. Caes.* the first text that might contain a mention of the creed is Ossius' letter to Julius of 343 or 344 (mentioned again in Ch. 5). Even in this text Ossius is concerned to show that the 'western' text from Serdica does not attempt to overturn Nicaea in general; he demonstrates no interest in the particular words of the Nicene creed itself.

[42] The period 325–36 is most clearly described by Williams, *Arius*, 67–81. See also Hanson, *The Search*, 172–8. Hanson's account largely repeats that of Simonetti, *La Crisi*, 99–134.

[43] From Socrates, *Hist. eccl.* 1. 25, and Gelasius, *Hist. eccl.* 3. 15. 1, it seems that Arius was asked to agree to the Nicene creed and that he did so at this point. Unfortunately we know little about what exactly he would have been asked to agree to and in what format.

returned to his former conciliatory position, and in 335 encouraged Arius to present his case to a synod of bishops assembled to consecrate a new church in Jerusalem.[44] We shall return in a moment to the end of Arius' story, but it is important to notice first the appearance of a much wider conflict that forms the background to Arius' last appearance on the stage.

The fifth-century ecclesiastical historian Sozomen reports a dispute immediately after the council, focused not on Arius, but on the correct interpretation of Nicaea and on the possibility of reading the creed in a semi-modalist way:

> ... the bishops had another dispute among themselves, concerning the precise meaning of the term *homoousios*. Some thought this term could not be admitted without blasphemy; that it implied the non-existence of the Son of God; and that it involved the error of Montanus and Sabellius ... Eusebius [of Caesarea] and Eustathius, Bishop of Antioch, took the lead in this dispute. They both confessed the Son of God to exist hypostatically, and yet contended together as if they had misunderstood each other. Eustathius accused Eusebius of altering the doctrines ratified by the council of Nicaea, while the latter declared that he approved of all the Nicaean doctrines, and reproached Eustathius for cleaving to the heresy of Sabellius.[45]

In this incident (probably in 326 or 327) Eusebius of Caesarea and Eustathius of Antioch play out for us the tensions between their respective theologies. Arius is not being discussed here: Nicaea has been a catalyst for conflict between pre-existing theological trajectories. Eustathius lost this battle and was deposed, at some point between 326 and 331, in a council presided over by Eusebius. Eustathius had been bishop of Antioch only since 324, but his reputation and, one must presume, the existence of a tradition in Antioch that valued his theology, ensured that his followers in Antioch would preserve a 'Eustathian' community into the 370s. This event was only one part of the conflict that now began. Asterius, whom we met in Chapter 2, had written in defence of Eusebius of Nicomedia's *Letter to Paulinus*. This letter appears to have become widely known and may even have been the statement by Eusebius read—and rejected—at Nicaea. Marcellus of Ancyra then wrote against Asterius *c*.330. In the next few years Eusebius of Caesarea produced his *Against Marcellus* and then the *Ecclesiastical Theology*, not in

---

[44] For Constantine's letter of 333 see Opitz, U.34. The confession of faith from Arius and Euzois printed by Opitz as u.30 may have been presented to Constantine around this time, but is more likely to date from his rehabilitation in 327

[45] Sozomen, *Hist. eccl.* 2. 8. This text, if accurate in its description of the conflict, may be the one exception to my earlier comment about the absence of reference the term immediately after 325.

order to defend Eusebius of Nicomedia or Asterius, but to attack Marcellus' own doctrine.[46] The controversy over Arius had already revealed that many Eusebians were prepared to make common cause against a theologian of Alexander's stripe. In the years after Nicaea we see how the theology of Marcellus and Eustathius, which skirted Sabellian and Monarchian waters much more closely than Alexander's, was able to provoke a strong and sustained reaction from the Eusebians, and one that seems to have gained wide support throughout the east. In the narrative that follows it is important not to forget that for many eastern bishops the controversy over Marcellus is much more foundational than prior conflict over Arius.

At the same time as this new debate was raging around Marcellan theology, Athanasius was attempting to consolidate his position as bishop of Alexandria.[47] Athanasius' election as bishop is shrouded in rumour and the details need not concern us. Hanson nicely sums up the best we can say about it: 'Athanasius was indeed elected, but not by immediate and unanimous acclamation, and not without suspicion of sharp practice.'[48] After his election Athanasius pursued a campaign against the Melitians in Egypt with great force. At Nicaea Alexander had come to an agreement with the Melitians to reincorporate them into a unified Egyptian Church. Athanasius seems to have been unhappy with this arrangement—and it is not at all clear that the Melitians were happy to concede either. Athanasius seems to have encouraged his supporters to act violently towards Melitians, on occasion barring them from churches, having some arrested, and at least acquiescing in the beating of some. Although in one notable case a Melitian charge that Athanasius had endorsed murder was refuted (by production of the victim), it is noticeable that in the face of considerable evidence Athanasius earned the opprobrium of many eastern bishops and seems to have made little direct attempt to defend himself from the accusations. At some point in the early 330s the Melitians, as part of a campaign to elicit support against Athanasius, found an ally in some of the Eusebians and probably in Eusebius of Nicomedia himself.

After refusing to appear before a council in Caesarea, Athanasius was summoned with imperial support to Tyre in Palestine in 335. The council immediately focused on the charges of Athanasius' use of violence, even sending a commission to the Mareotis region of Egypt to investigate charges. It is noteworthy that this commission involved a number of figures clearly opposed to Athanasius on

[46] For analyses of these works see Lienhard, *Contra Marcellum*, chs. 3–5.
[47] On Athanasius' career to 340 see Hanson, *The Search*, 246–69; T. D. Barnes, *Athanasius and Constantius* (Cambridge, Mass.: Harvard University Press, 1993), 19–33.
[48] Hanson, *The Search*, 249.

theological grounds, whatever would be found in Egypt. When the commission returned and upheld some charges, Athanasius was deposed. Athanasius himself left Tyre under cover of darkness and fled to Constantinople to press his case directly before the Emperor. Initially, Athanasius seems to have had some success, but when his enemies also charged him with interrupting the grain supply from Egypt Constantine turned against him: Athanasius was exiled to Trier. While the commission sent from Tyre to Egypt was away on its mission, many of the same bishops had adjourned to Jerusalem for the dedication of the new Church of the Holy Sepulchre. While they were there a letter was received from Constantine asking that Arius, who had made a new profession of his faith, be readmitted to communion. It seems likely that this meeting did so. Soon after, late in 335 or early in 336, Arius died, apparently while trying to have this decision practically acknowledged in Constantinople.[49] The death of Arius marks, however, no significant turning point in the story of these years. By this time the focus was elsewhere. Marcellus was possibly one of the subjects discussed at Tyre in 335 but appears not to have been present. Similarly he was not at Jerusalem later that year—and unsurprisingly rejected its decisions. It was in this year that he presented his work against Asterius to Constantine (we cannot be sure of its true title) and met with no success. In 336, and possibly after failing to fulfil a promise to burn this book, Marcellus was condemned and deposed by a meeting of bishops in Constantinople. Unlike Athanasius, Marcellus was clearly deposed for theological reasons.

In May 337 Constantine died and many things changed. Constantine appears to have wanted both his own three sons and some descendants of his stepmother Theodora to share in the dynastic inheritance.[50] During the summer of 337, probably at the behest of Constantius, Constantine's middle son, Theodora's descendants were massacred—the future emperor Julian being one of the few to escape.[51] At the end of the summer Constantine's three sons agreed on the division of the empire. Constantius controlled the east as he had done over the past few years (but now with the addition of Thrace). The eldest son, Constantine II, continued in control of Gaul, Spain, and Britain. The youngest, Constans, who was only a

---

[49] The reconstruction here largely follows Barnes, *Athanasius and Constantius*, ch. 3. The reader unaware of the details of Arius' death, as narrated by Athanasius and copied by Epiphanius, should certainly seek them out: see Epiphanius, *Panarion* 68. 6. 9.

[50] For a brief account of this division see Averil Cameron and Peter Garnsey (eds.), *Cambridge Ancient History, xiii: The Late Empire AD 337–425* (Cambridge: Cambridge University Press, 1998), ch. 1.

[51] Constantius' career is considered in a little more detail at the beginning of Ch. 5. He is sometimes referred to as Constantius II, Constantius I being Constantine's father.

teenager, received Italy, Africa, and much of the Former Yugoslavia (Illyria and Moesia). As we shall see, the three sons did not pursue the same ecclesiastical policies and their personal rivalry soon came to influence the course of the emerging controversy. After Constantine's death, all exiled bishops were allowed to return to their sees, Constantine II writing personally to the Alexandrians about Athanasius during the summer of 337. Not for the first or the last time in the fourth century we see a fascinating dislocation between civil and ecclesiastical authority. The civil banishment of these bishops was revoked, but their ecclesiastical, conciliar depositions remained in force. Bishops who wished to ignore the latter frequently chose to take advantage of the former. Participants from all sides in the debate could and did complain to whichever authority best served their purposes. In 338 Athanasius held a council in Alexandria which circulated a dossier directed against his enemies but to no avail. In 339 imperial soldiers arrived to enforce Constantius' approval of the Eusebians' reiteration of Athanasius' deposition at a council in Antioch which had met during the winter of 338/9. Athanasius made his way to Rome, as did Marcellus, who had also been deposed again.

5
The Creation of 'Arianism': AD 340–350

THE CREATION OF 'ARIANISM'

Were the depositions of Eustathius, Athanasius, and Marcellus the result of a conspiracy by the Eusebians against the architects of Nicaea?[1] While Athanasius came to represent the events of 325–35 as such, we cannot take his account at face value. From 325 to 327 Eusebius of Nicomedia, supposedly one of the architects, was in exile and can hardly have masterminded a conspiracy. We have no evidence that the same Eusebius controlled events at Tyre 335, or the deposition of Marcellus. Assuming such a simple conspiracy also overlooks the central differences between the deposition of Marcellus and Eustathius, on the one hand, and Athanasius, on the other: Athanasius was not deposed for heresy. Nevertheless, theological conflicts must have been interwoven with all that happened, and we can fairly see Nicaea as focusing this conflict. Conflict between Eusebians and Marcellans in the wake of Nicaea could hardly be unexpected and is not simply an epiphenomenon of the previous conflict in Alexandria. That theologians in the tradition of Marcellus and Eustathius presented their theologies as the natural context for Nicaea's creed and judgements can only have made the Eusebians determined to demonstrate the unorthodoxy of Marcellus and Eustathius. When the occasion arose we have, however, no indication that Athanasius made any immediate protest against the deposition of Marcellus or Eustathius.

It seems, however, also inescapable that many Eusebians would have jumped at the chance to intrigue against Athanasius, a close confidant of Alexander who was present at Nicaea and later the focus of resistance to the readmittance of Arius. News of Athanasius' tactics against the Meletians can have been nothing other than music to the ears of the Eusebians. We know that a number of other bishops were deposed from their sees during the decade after Nicaea, but lack of evidence makes it almost impossible to say why in most cases.[2] In some events we can trace the hand of Eusebius of

---

[1] The evidence for a conspiracy is rejected by Hanson, *The Search*, 274–84; see also Williams, *Arius*, 75–81; Simonetti; *La Crisi*, 99 ff.

[2] Chief among these are Asclepas of Gaza and Paul of Constantinople. Hanson, *The Search*, 274 ff.

Nicomedia after he returned from exile, but it is important to realize that there is a great difference between an attempt to shape ecclesiastical affairs in the light of a theological trajectory and an attempt to do so as part of an overt conspiracy to perpetuate the theology of Arius. So, while the events of these years are not the result of one intentional 'conspiracy' by 'Arians', there very probably were particular theological conflicts behind many depositions, and theological motives added to the eagerness with which the Eusebians turned on Athanasius when occasion permitted.

Events in Rome during the 339–40 period are of importance for our story because it is here that the exiled Athanasius and Marcellus made common cause against their eastern opponents. They may already have met at the Council of Tyre in 335 which deposed Athanasius, but we have no evidence that they considered themselves allies until their meeting in Rome. Although Athanasius' theology was by no means identical with Marcellus', the overlaps were significant enough for them to be at one on some of the vital issues—especially their common insistence that the Son was intrinsic to the Father's external existence. Just as Marcellus, Eustathius, and Alexander had worked together at Nicaea, Athanasius and Marcellus now seem to have made common cause again those who insisted on distinct *hypostases* in God. Marcellus himself also seems to have modified his theology a little by this time, in particular abandoning his account of the end of Christ's kingdom. Once this happened differences might have appeared even less marked. It is, in fact, no longer clear that Athanasius ever directly repudiated Marcellus, and he certainly seems to have been sympathetic to Marcellus' followers until the 360s.[3]

We know little of the interaction between Athanasius and Marcellus in Rome: it seems that from Marcellus Athanasius learnt to argue that Prov. 8: 22 referred to the incarnate Word, not to the Word as such and he was to deploy this exegesis in his *Orations against the Arians*. Whatever Athanasius took from Marcellus was woven into an increasingly sophisticated account of his enemies as 'Arians' seeking to perpetuate a theology stemming from Arius. It is thus in these years that we see the full flowering of a polemical strategy that was to shape accounts of the fourth century for over 1,500 years.[4] Thus, Athanasius' engagement with Marcellus in Rome seems to have encouraged Athanasius towards the development of a richer and

---

[3] See Joseph T. Lienhard, 'Did Athanasius Reject Marcellus?', in Michel Barnes and Daniel H. Williams (eds.), *Arianism after Arius: Essays on the Development of the Fourth Century Trinitarian Conflicts* (Edinburgh: T. & T. Clark, 1993), 65–80.

[4] On Athanasius' use of 'Arian' against the background of other 4th-cent. heresiological techniques see Lyman, 'A Topography of Heresy'.

The Creation of 'Arianism' AD 340–350

richer account of his enemies' fundamentally theological motivations. The result is a masterpiece of the rhetorical art: Athanasius draws together a complex genealogy of the 'Arian' heresy stemming from Arius himself. With this strategy Athanasius redescribes the controversies we have seen developing since 325.

An early version of this emerging Athanasian genealogy is to be found in the first of his three *Orations Against the Arians*, written 339–40. Athanasius' account begins by presenting Arius as the originator of a new heresy and all later proponents of such a theology as appropriately designated 'Arians'. To this end Athanasius quotes extensively from Arius' *Thalia*. Athanasius parallels 'Arians' and Manichees as both named not for allegiance to Christ but from the founder of their particular heresy.[5] The choice of Manichaeism is not random: Manichaeism was the archetypal heresy for early fourth-century Christian polemicists and so Athanasius also likens supposed 'Arian' materialism to Manichaean materialism. Because, Athanasius argues, Alexander expelled Arius from the Church he and his followers are no longer Christians but Arians. If one remains in the Church one does not take the name of one's catechist or teacher, but that of Christ.[6] Athanasius presents himself as the preserver of the one theological tradition that is equivalent with scriptural orthodoxy.[7] Note that while Arius is the fount of all subsequent 'Arians', Athanasius uses the picture to attack contemporary opponents whose theologies were distinct from Arius'. Thus, he both names in passing Eusebius of Nicomedia as the partial author of 'Arianism' and spends most of his time refuting Asterius who is treated as the standard-bearer of 'Arianism'.

In shaping this account Athanasius draws on what seems to have been a reasonably well-established presentation of Eusebius of Nicomedia as the mastermind behind an ecclesiastical grouping: Alexander himself speaks collectively of 'those around Eusebius' in the years before Nicaea to indicate the party of those who follow Eusebius.[8] At the same time Athanasius' use of the language of 'Arian' and 'Arian madmen' or 'Ariomaniacs' (Ἀρειομανίται) seems to have its origin in Eustathian or Marcellan circles. In a surviving fragment from a homily on Prov. 8: 22 Eustathius identifies as 'Arian madmen' those who secretly supported Eusebius but were prepared to sign to Nicaea when they saw how Eusebius' statement of faith was received.[9] Unfortunately Eustathius' extensive writings against

---

[5] *C. Ar.* 1. 3.   [6] *C. Ar.* 1. 3.
[7] *C. Ar.* 1. 9–10 shows Athanasius presenting the controversy as between two theologies.
[8] Alexander, *Ep. om.* 11.
[9] Theodoret, *Eccl. hist.* 1. 7. The date of Eustathius' death is unknown, but it seems most plausible that he died before 337 (Declerk frg. 79). If he were to have lived through the 340s and 350s, as some have alleged, then this fragment is of much less interest here.

'Arians' survive only in fragments and so we cannot assess the extent to which he enlarged on the same terminology there.[10]

The development of Athanasius' own polemical strategy seems to have begun only after his return from his first short exile (November 335–mid-337). He refers once and for the first time to his opponents as 'Arian madmen' in his festal letter for 338. Then, in 339, the encyclical letter resulting from the council held in Alexandria speaks of a conspiracy by those who deposed Athanasius at Tyre dating back to Nicaea and perpetrated by a group of 'Ariomanitai' who take their name from Arius. Their conspiracy is motivated solely by theological concerns and by Athanasius' strong opposition to Arius (but, subtly, narration of this conspiracy theory is offered alongside a refutation of the *actual* charges against Athanasius). The constant thrust of this refutation is the narration of a conspiracy: 'the subject of the drama was a contest of Arians ... [in order that] the supporters of the Arians in the garb of judges might drive away the enemies of their impiety ...'.[11] It is also noticeable that Athanasius speaks of Eusebius and his supporters both as 'Arians' and as *supporting* the 'Arians': his terminology remains fluid. In the same text Nicaea itself is referred to as the 'ecumenical' council[12] in opposition to all subsequent councils, especially those at which Athanasius was condemned. The argument is a strange one: those councils were appropriately constituted, and, one might say, were so on the basis of Nicaea's own insistence that regular provincial meetings be held. Having seen the story of Nicaea itself it is difficult to typify Tyre as not truly a council because of imperial support and involvement! Athanasius' argument demonstrates the difficulties inherent in arguing for the superiority of any one council at this point in the fourth century. These various themes emerging in the late 330s find their full expression during and immediately after Athanasius' time in Rome—as we saw in the first of the *Orations Against the Arians*. It is then no accident that Athanasius' account of 'Arians' was of considerable importance in the west.[13] As we shall see with the 'Cappadocians',[14] there were some areas of the Mediterranean where this strategy is rarely found, and others deployed. In these areas Arius' own writings are rarely quoted and he is treated largely as one

---

[10] We are unsure if 'Arians' were mentioned in the original title of Eustathius' work. It may be that directly or via Marcellus Eustathius played an important role in the creation of 'Arianism'.

[11] Athanasius, *Apol. sec.* 17.

[12] See Henry Chadwick, 'The Origin of the Title Oecumenical Council', *JThS* 23 (1972), 132–5

[13] See Barnes, 'Trinitarian Canon', 56–8.

[14] My use here of the modern term 'Cappadocians' should not be taken to presuppose complete agreement among these three.

half of a formal pairing of extremes: 'orthodoxy' avoids both Arius and Sabellius.

Athanasius appealed to Julius of Rome in 339–40 by using his strategy of narrating a theological conspiracy of 'Arians'. His success had a profound impact on the next few years of the controversy. The encyclical letter from the Alexandrian council of 339 may already have been addressed to Julius in Rome. Julius appears to have sent envoys to Antioch to suggest a council in Rome to investigate the charges against Athanasius, a proposal that was rejected. The order of events here is not entirely clear, but following the arrival of Athanasius in Rome and the arrival of a delegation from his supposed replacement in Alexandria, Gregory, Julius decided to hold his council anyway. The council was a small affair, consisting of around fifty bishops, and it quickly vindicated Marcellus and Athanasius. Julius wrote to the east in 341 in a letter which shows the strong influence of the emerging Athanasian account of 'Arianism'.[15]

Julius addresses 'those around Eusebius', charging them with accepting 'Arians' into communion despite their condemnation at Nicaea. Julius has used Athanasius' account of a Eusebian conspiracy to draw together the cases of Athanasius and Marcellus. Much of the argument in the first half of this extremely long letter focuses on the perceived attempt of the Eusebians to ignore or even overturn the decisions and canons of Nicaea. The status of Nicaea remained, however, uncertain. It is clear both that there had been much argument about one council overturning the results of another, and that there existed little precedent on which to decide the issue. Julius also claims that it is customary for decisions about Alexandria to be referred to him: while this claim may reflect both a long-standing relationship between the two sees and the growing claim of the bishop of Rome, it is one that few would have accepted without question.

Relations between Rome and the Eusebians were shaped for many years by Athanasius' account of events. Once Julius had acted we begin to see divisions between the Church in the eastern and western halves of the empire emerging. We should, however, be cautious in our reading of these divisions. The divisions we initially observe are between one group of eastern bishops taking their lead from Eusebius of Nicomedia and Julius and his immediate associates. We

---

[15] See Athanasius, *Apol. sec.* 21–35. On the council see Hanson, *The Search*, 270 ff., Simonetti, *La Crisi*, 145 ff., Hans Christoph Brennecke, *Hilarius von Poitiers und die Bischofsopposition gegen Konstantius*, ii: *Untersuchungen zur dritten Phase des arianischen Streites (337–361)* (Berlin: de Gruyter, 1984), 7 ff.

110   I. *Towards a Controversy*

must be wary of reading this as reflecting a simple division between eastern and western theology. Even when just such a division appears to come clearly into the open at the Council of Serdica in 343, even there the participants cannot usefully be divided in purely geographic terms. The divisions that occur between Julius and 'those around Eusebius' also have an important extra-ecclesial political dimension. Early in 340 Constantine II invaded northern Italy, part of the territory governed by his youngest brother, Constans, according to the agreement of 337. Constantine himself was killed and Constans gained control of the western provinces as a whole. Tensions between Constans and Constantius soon began to affect the growing ecclesial conflict. Constans soon seems to have offered some support to the anti-Eusebian forces in Rome. We could read this support as simple theological commitment, but it seems far more likely also to reflect Constans' realization that this cause could play a role in thwarting his brother's ambitions. Before following the events of 341–3 further, however, I want to consider Athanasius' *Orations* in more detail.

THE *ORATIONS AGAINST THE ARIANS*

Athanasius' creation of a genealogical rhetoric of 'Arians' and their relationship to Arius should not lead us to overlook that side of the *Orations* that consists of an attack on the theology of Eusebians engaged in the post-325 (in many ways 'post-Arian') controversy.[16] In the *Orations* Athanasius both constructs a genealogy of 'Arianism' for ecclesio-political reasons and enters an existing theological debate with some force. The third *Oration* is later than the other two, although we cannot be certain by how much: here I assume it was written *c.* 345 and treat its theology with that of the other two.

Once the genealogy of 'Arianism' is established in the first sections of the *First Oration*, Athanasius offers a refutation of the basic

---

[16] On the *Orations* see Charles Kannengiesser, *Athanase d'Alexandrie évêque et écrivain: Une lecture des traités contre les Ariens*, Théologie historique, 70 (Paris: Beauchesne, 1983); E. P. Meijering, 'Athanasius on the Father as the Origin of the Son', *God, Being, History: Studies in Patristic Philosophy* (Amsterdam: North Holland, 1975), 89–102; Widdicombe, *Fatherhood*, chs. 8–11; Anatolios, *Athanasius*, chs. 3, 4, and 9; Martin Tetz, 'Markellianer und Athanasios von Alexandrien: Die markellianische Expositio fidei ad Athanasium des Diakons Eugenios von Ankyra', *ZNTW* 64 (1973), 75–121. Kannengiesser's discussion of the structure of the *Orations* is extremely useful. He argues, however, that the third is by Apollinaris (or his school), rather than by Athanasius. His arguments have not generally been accepted: I also am not convinced. His arguments seem only to demonstrate some stylistic differences between the third and the previous two. This may indicate a later date for the third, but my suggestion of a fairly short period of 339–45 for the set is based on Athanasius' consistent focus throughout on refuting Asterius. This tactic seems to have most force during Asterius' lifetime or shortly thereafter. The argument, of course, is extremely circumstantial.

The Creation of 'Arianism' AD 340–350

principles of 'Arian' theology and then refutes 'Arian' exegesis of some key texts. It is the last task which occupies half the first and all of the second and third *Orations*. But if we can say that the purpose of the first half of the first *Oration* is to establish a foundation for the category 'Arian', then the purpose of the rest of the series is to refute Asterius as the chief theologian of the 'Arians'. Asterius is described in the *Third Oration* as 'the retained pleader for the heresy' and as 'the advocate for the heresy'.[17] Asterius is first quoted at I. 32 and takes centre stage until the end of the *Third Oration*. In Chapter 2 I discussed some themes from the *First Oration* in the course of sketching the theological trajectory to which Athanasius belonged: here three more themes should be noted.

Imagining Father and Son

Athanasius shapes the second half of his initial refutation of 'Arian' theology in the first *Oration* around questions raised by 'Arians'.[18] Four questions are discussed: one concerns the Son's mutability, while three attempt to demonstrate the Father's priority over and before the Son's existence. Athanasius' tactic is to refuse the alternatives these 'Arian' questions offer and to accuse his opponents of only thinking the questions to have force because of assumptions about God that are overly reliant on human or created analogies. Thus, for example, Athanasius refutes the 'Arian' question, 'did God make him who was not from nothing or from something pre-existing?' by critiquing 'Arian' habits of thought. For Athanasius the question, to which Arians intend us to reply 'from nothing', relies on the assumption that God's 'making' must be subject to the same logic as our own. At the same time, 'Arians' do not consistently apply this direct analogical logic: they deny the 'obvious' consequences of Scripture's Father and Son language. Athanasius argues that we should, in fact, begin by reflection on God's Fatherhood (understood as unique and as the type of human fatherhood). God the Father is then presented as eternal and immutable, eternally with his Word and Wisdom, the radiance of the eternal divine sun. Thus, the argument fights on more than one front: Athanasius' suggestion that 'Arians' arbitrarily use analogies from the created order without attention to when those analogies actually help us speak of the divine existence is combined with a continual attempt to

---

[17] Athanasius, *C. Ar.* 3. 2, 60. There may be some truth in Athanasius' claim that Asterius was viewed as one of the chief theological minds by some major Eusebians, especially Eusebius of Nicomedia, and that he had travelled widely to promote Eusebian theology. See, Athanasius, *Synod.* 18, Eusebius of Caesarea, *Marcell.* 1. 4. 48, Socrates, *Hist. eccl.* 1. 36.

[18] *C. Ar.* 1. 22 ff. The first half of his initial refutation offers an account, against Arius' *Thalia*, of the Son's existence as proper to the Father.

persuade his readers that Athanasius' favourite analogies are more appropriate.[19]

In the very next section of the text Athanasius considers more directly how one should appropriately deploy analogical resources. Reflection on analogies that seem to suggest themselves on the basis of scriptural terminology or its implications must proceed from an appropriate sense of the divine nature. It is on the basis of this conception that inappropriate analogical connotations are avoided. Thus, in the case of analogy between the Father and the Son and human fathers and sons, Athanasius argues that the core of the language is to convey a genetic relationship in which the son is 'from' the father in a unique sense. In the case of God we understand the divine being to be simple, indivisible, eternal, perfect, and immutable. Therefore we can speak of the Father generating the Son without being worried about the notions of passion and division which might seem to be invoked by such language. We can further proceed to assume the eternal generation of the Son because of the nature of divine being. Alongside this use of Father and Son terminology Athanasius again deploys the analogy of a person and his 'word': here also we have generation without passion or division.[20]

We may take this further and say that throughout the *Orations* Athanasius constantly interrelates three arguments. The first offers an account of Father and Son language as the primary scriptural motif for articulating what it means when he speaks of the Word of God.[21] The second describes the uniqueness of the divine nature, while the third deploys the analogy of a person and their word or wisdom.[22] In a manner that demonstrates one of the fundamental continuities in his thought, Athanasius assumes that this analogy serves as the best illustration of the closeness indicated when Father and Son language is predicated of the eternally generative immutable divine existence, and that it should qualify texts that seem to indicate co-operation between Father and Son as distinct entities. When Athanasius comes directly to the 'Arian' question as to whether there is one unoriginate or two, we see these interrelated arguments at work. Athanasius first distinguishes different senses of 'unoriginate', treating the two Greek terms ἀγένητος and ἀγέννητος as synonyms. Then he identifies the sense in which both Father and Son are so: the Son is also unoriginate if one means by that 'what is

---

[19] *C. Ar.* 1. 24–5.   [20] *C. Ar.* 1. 26–9.
[21] The centrality of this language is clear from *C. Ar.* 2. 5; '... when persons ask whether the Lord is a creature or a work, it is proper to ask of them this first, whether he is Son and Word and Wisdom. For if this is shown, the surmise about work and creation falls to the ground at once and is ended.'
[22] This theme is the subject of extended discussion at *C. Ar.* 2. 36 ff.

not a work and always was'. If by the term one means 'existing but not generated of any nor having a father' then only the Father is ungenerated.[23] Athanasius makes this argument against the background of his insistence on the priority of Father and Son language understood as revealing an eternal generation. At the same time we hear that the unique nature of God involves God existing with his eternal power and wisdom: it is this triangulation of arguments that both forces us to ask how we understand confession of the uniqueness of the divine nature to govern our habits of speech and that attempts to persuade us that only Athanasius' answer is appropriate.

I draw attention to Athanasius' discussion of 'unoriginate' because of its increasing prominence in some 'non-Nicene' theology over the next thirty years. Thomas Kopecek has argued that Athanasius' focus on the term and his decision to argue that the Son too is unoriginate in one sense actually stimulated some of his opponents to develop the theme of God's unoriginate nature more strongly.[24] While we lack sufficient evidence to show that this is definitely the case, there may be some merit in Kopecek's argument. Athanasius' discussion does show him drawing attention to a key theme in much Eusebian theology, especially in the theology of the more subordinationist Lucianists. Indeed, consideration of the term 'unoriginate' in the *Orations* also reflects a tradition we can trace back to the dispute between Alexander and Arius.[25] Athanasius' increasing clarity in treating the Son as intrinsic to the Father's being begins to make the lines of theological division more stark.

The Son's divine activity

Through the *Orations* Athanasius also appeals to the unity of action between Father and Son and hence to the truly divine nature of the Son's redemptive and 'deifying' activity. We can see this theme appearing in Athanasius' arguments against 'Arian' exegesis through the first and second *Orations*. All the texts he discusses appear to indicate the Son being created or changing status at some discernible point, Prov. 8: 22 being the subject of particularly extended consideration. One of Athanasius' basic strategies is to distinguish between passages that speak of the Word and those that speak of the body assumed by the Word and of the Word's

---

[23] *C. Ar.* 1. 30 ff. See also *C. Ar.* 2. 37–8. Athanasius treats the two terms ἀγέννητος and ἀγένητος as synonyms, using the latter far more frequently and distinguishing a range of meanings for them. His most extensive use of ἀγέννητος is at 2. 37, but in 2. 38 he seems to treat ἀγένητος as synonymous. Soon the two terms become more clearly distinguished. At the end of the 4th cent. pro-Nicenes assume that distinction: the Father alone is ἀγέννητος (ungenerated) while all three divine persons are ἀγένητος (uncreated). For a later summary of the distinction see John Damascene, *Fid. orth.* 1. 8.

[24] Kopecek, *Neo-Arianism*, I. 88 ff.   [25] See Alexander, *Ep. Alex.* 4, 12.

'economy'.²⁶ In the course of building up to his reading of Prov. 8: 22, Athanasius insists that this verse cannot refer to the 'creation' of the Word as such because the Word is intrinsic to the Father's action. The Word is not a mediator because the world cannot bear God's touch: rather, the Father creates and makes immediately through his Word.²⁷ There is no difference in willing, no communication between the two before any action occurs, the Word *is* the Father's will, intrinsic to the divine mode of action.²⁸ Athanasius' argument speaks not of two realities engaged in a common activity, but develops his most basic sense that the Son is intrinsic to the Father's being.²⁹ It is also, for Athanasius, because the Word and Son is proper to the Father's essence that redemption is possible in Christ. At 2. 70 Athanasius argues, first, that only 'true God' could overcome the created devil, and, second, that only one who was 'natural and true' Word could draw us into the Father's presence. Salvation is a union effected between created human beings and God that must be accomplished by a 'mediator' who is proper to God's essence. In these texts we see Athanasius repeating themes found in his *On the Incarnation*, but we see him—stimulated by the anti-Asterian polemical context—drawing out with increased clarity the necessity of the Word being the direct hand of God, the immediate mediator.³⁰

This focus goes along with some new technical terminology used in the *Orations* to emphasize the closeness of Father and Son. In the latter half of the *On the Incarnation* Athanasius had made use of the term *idios* ('proper' or 'own') to describe various qualities and activities as 'proper' to human nature and hence as possessed by the Incarnate Word. In the *Orations* the term is frequently used to describe the Son as ἴδιος ('proper') to the Father, a usage rare before this point.³¹ At the same time Athanasius also seems to turn to *ousia* language, and, especially in the first two *Orations*, to the phrase ἐκ τῆς οὐσίας ('from the essence of'), used at Nicaea. In fact when Athanasius uses this phrase it is almost always associated with the term as ἴδιος.³² Thus while many scholars rightly note the one

---

²⁶ See J. Roldanus, *Le Christ et le homme dans la théologie d'Athanase d'Alexandrie* (Leiden: Brill, 1968).

²⁷ *C. Ar.* 2. 24 ff. Here Athanasius quotes Asterius, Vinzent fr. 26; see Ch. 2, p. 54.

²⁸ *C. Ar.* 2. 31.

²⁹ Cf. *C. Ar.* 3. 11: '... when the Son works, the Father is the worker, and the Son coming to the saints, the Father is he who comes in the Son'.

³⁰ Cf. *Incarn.* 20. *Incarn.* has not received much discussion in this book for the simple reason that it is extremely difficult to show that it was influential on the course of 4th-cent. theology outside Egypt.

³¹ Twice of this relationship at *C. Gen.* 2, 40 and twice more at *Incarn.* 3, 32.

³² e.g. *C. Ar.* 1. 15, 16, 36; 2. 2, 32, 41, 51, 57, 70. Some of these citations involve clear reference to the phrase even if it is not fully quoted. On the use of ἴδιος language see Andrew

appearance of *homoousios* in the *Orations* as evidence of Athanasius' lack of commitment to Nicaea's terminology at this stage of his career, we need also to note the character of his growing engagement with Nicaea's creed.[33] In the context of anti-Eusebian polemic and in the context of his construction of the 'Arian' genealogy Athanasius has seen the virtues of *ousia* language to emphasize the closeness of the Son to the Father, especially the phrase 'from the *ousia* of the Father'. It is noticeable, however, that Athanasius never bothers to claim this terminology as credal; such a style of reference did not yet exist. Nevertheless, we do see here an engagement with Nicaea, a realization that the language used there serves an ongoing purpose. It is also noticeable that his interest in *ousia* language occurs at the same time as his growing use of ἴδιος in the same contexts. Initially used to indicate that certain qualities and activities are intrinsic to being human, the use of the term to indicate that the Son is ἴδιος to the Father's *ousia* serves to reinforce his tendency to present the Father/Son relationship as most like that of a person and their faculties. Thus while this language is an important tool in Athanasius' armoury it probably served only to reinforce his opponents' sense that the use of *ousia* language could only serve to confuse the clear distinction between Father and Son, God and Word.

Unity and distinction in God

The third theme concerns Athanasius' refutation of charges that his theology implies either two unbegottens or only one reality. In the *Third Oration*, possibly written c.345, Athanasius turns to texts from the Gospels, notably John. One of the most important discussions concerns John 14: 10: 'I am in the Father and the Father is in me'. Athanasius argues that Asterius reads the text materially and so interprets it as meaning only that the Son follows the Father's desires and works in the Father's power. Developing themes from the *First Oration*, Athanasius argues that just as the Father is perfect, so too the Son is the 'fullness of the Godhead'. The Father is thus not 'in' the Son because of the Son's lack, not 'in' him in order to give life or sustain him in existence. Rather, he writes:

For the Son is in the Father, as it is allowed us to know, because the whole being of the Son is proper to the Father's essence, as radiance from light and stream from fountain; so that whoever sees the Son sees the Father, and knows that the Son's being, because from the Father is therefore in the Father.

Louth, 'The Use of the Term ἴδιος in Alexandrian Theology from Alexander to Cyril', *SP*, 19 (1987), 198–202.

[33] Already Athanasius' 339 Festal Letter speaks of the importance of Nicaea because of its size, but the creed is not yet mentioned.

Athanasius explains that there are two, but not in such a way as to compromise the divine unity:

> ... they are two, because the Father is Father and is not also Son, and the Son is not also Father; but the nature is one (for the offspring is not unlike ἀνόμοιος its parent for it is its image), and all that is the Father's is the Son's ... if the Son be other, as offspring, still he is the same as God; and he and the Father are one in propriety and peculiarity of nature, and in the identity of the one Godhead. For the radiance also is light, not second to the Son ... So also the Godhead of the Son is the Father's; whence also it is indivisible; and thus there is one God.[34]

Once again, Athanasius' position develops from his basic principle that the Son's existence is intrinsic to the Father's nature and flows from the Father's existence. But here Athanasius is able to demonstrate a little more clearly than before that Father and Son are clearly distinct. It is, however, characteristic of Athanasius that he does not make use of any technical terms for identifying Father and Son as two: *hypostasis*, πρόσωπον, and πρᾶγμα are absent. While these themes show the third *Oration* to be following a direction sketched in the first two, they also show that the third seems to have been written a little later, responding more carefully to some of the hardest hitting accusations about Athanasius theology.

Throughout all three *Orations* Athanasius condemns Asterius' theology as itself implying some of the very same problems that Asterius sees in Athanasius. For example, in the second *Oration* Athanasius argues that if Asterius sees his account of God and his own proper Word and Wisdom as implying two unbegottens, then the same must be true of Asterius' account of the true Wisdom of God which is distinct from the Wisdom found in the Word.[35] In many ways this argument misses its mark: Asterius would, I imagine, simply argue that in the case of God and God's intrinsic Wisdom we cannot imagine a distinction between two individuals. In texts such as this we see one of Athanasius' earlier efforts to distinguish Father and Son. Criticizing the idea that Christ is a derivative Wisdom and not God's own wisdom he writes:

> Moreover, what folly is there in that thought of theirs that the unoriginate wisdom coexisting with God is God himself, for what coexists does not coexist with itself, but with someone else (τὸ γὰρ συνυπάρχον οὐχ ἑαυτῳ, τινὶ δὲ συνυπάρχει).

---

[34] *C. Ar.* 3. 3–4. Cf. 3. 6: '... he [the Son] is in that One, and First and Only, as being of that One ... And he too is the First, as the fullness of the Godhead of the First and Only, being whole and full God. This then is not said on his account, but to deny that there is other such as the Father and his Word.'

[35] e.g. *C. Ar.* 2. 37–40. Note that here too Athanasius is concerned with the unity of operations between Father and Son.

Throughout the *Orations* Athanasius already prefigures key elements of later pro-Nicene theologies. He is increasingly clear that, beyond stating the logical distinction of Father from Son, charges of modalism and materialism are most appropriately resisted by focusing attention on the character of the divine existence as unique and beyond comprehension. As we have seen, Athanasius is particularly clear in the *Third Oration* that the Father and the Son are logically distinct and that his position is not Sabellian because of the unique nature of the divine existence in which we must confess the perfect Son of the perfect Father in a simple and indivisible existence.

In summary, then, I suggest three statements. First, the *Orations* represent the first full appearance of the fourth century's consummate act of heresiology: the wide-ranging controversy and tension between existing theological strategies is sold to his readers as a conspiracy by a group of 'Arians' seeking to perpetuate the novel theology of a condemned heretic. Second, the *Orations* constitute one of the key early anti-Eusebian theological manifestos. Third, we have as yet seen little about the extent to which this narrative or this theology was taken on board by other theologians. We can show that Athanasius' heresiological genealogy was taken up by Julius and by some others who followed his lead. Our knowledge of the impact of Athanasius' theology in these years is, however, unclear. As we shall see throughout the fourth century Athanasius' influence on events is something on which we should hesitate to pass too quick a judgement.

THE 'DEDICATION' COUNCIL OF ANTIOCH

I left the narrative of events with Julius' support for Athanasius and Marcellus. Julius' letter to 'those around Eusebius' met with an immediate response. In 341 a group of bishops present in Antioch ostensibly to dedicate a church built by the Emperor Constantius also considered Julius' decision to vindicate Athanasius and Marcellus. Around ninety bishops were present in Antioch, including Eusebius formerly of Nicomedia who had recently been translated to Constantinople and Acacius of Caesarea who had succeeded Eusebius after his death *c*.339–40. Asterius and the Emperor Constantius were also present. From this council in Antioch and its immediate aftermath four credal-type documents emerged. The first occurs in a letter which begins with a preamble making clear one point that had come to anger the Eusebians: 'we have not been followers of Arius—how could bishops, such as we, follow a presbyter—nor did we receive any other faith beside that which has been handed down . . .'.³⁶ The bishops also assert that they were within their rights to judge the faith of Arius and admit him to communion. This short text seems to have been issued as an immediate response to Julius. It has an urgency that reveals something of the propaganda campaign already under way.

The second text is of considerable importance in our story. This creed seems to have been composed as a formal extended statement of faith by the council, and is known as the 'Dedication' creed. Its significance demands that it be quoted in full:

Following the evangelical and apostolic tradition, we believe in one God Father Almighty, artificer and maker and designer of the universe:

And in one Lord Jesus Christ his only-begotten Son, God, through whom are all things, who was begotten from the Father before the ages, God from God, whole from whole, sole from sole, perfect from perfect, King from King, Lord from Lord, Living word, Living Wisdom, true Light, Way, Truth, Resurrection, Shepherd, Door, unchanging and unaltering, exact image (ἀπαράλλακτον εἰκόνα) of the Godhead and the *ousia* and will and power and glory of the Father, first-born of all creation, who was in the beginning with God, God the Word according to the text in the Gospel, 'and the Word was God', by whom all things were made, and in whom all things exist; who at the end of the days came down from above and was born of a virgin, according to the Scriptures, and became man, mediator between God and men, the apostle of our faith, author of life, as he says . . . (John 6: 38), who suffered for us and rose again the third day and ascended into heaven and is seated on the right hand of the father and is coming again with glory and power to judge the living and the dead:

And in the Holy Spirit, who is given to those who believe for comfort and sanctification and perfection, just as our Lord Jesus Christ commanded his disciples, saying . . . (Matt. 28: 19) obviously (in the name) of the Father who is truly Father, and the Son who is truly Son and the Holy Spirit who is truly Holy Spirit, because the names are not given lightly or idly, but signify exactly the particular *hypostasis* and order and glory of each of those who are named, so that they are three in *hypostasis* but one in agreement (συμφωνίᾳ).

Since we hold this belief, and have held it from the beginning to the end, before God and Christ we condemn every form of heretical unorthodoxy. And if anybody teaches contrary to the sound, right faith of the Scriptures, alleging that either time or occasion or age exists or did exist before the Son was begotten, let him be anathema. And if anyone alleges that the Son is a creature like one of the creatures or a product (γέννημα) like one of the products, or something made (ποίημα) like one of the things that are made, and not as the Holy Scriptures have handed down concerning the subjects which have been treated one after another, or if anyone teaches or preaches anything apart from what we have laid down, let him be anathema. For we

---

³⁶ Athanasius, *Synod.* 1. 22. All the relevant texts are to be found in subsequent sections of *Synod*. See also Hanson, *The Search*, 284–92.

believe and follow everything that has been delivered from the Holy Scriptures by the prophets and apostles truly and reverently.[37]

The creed is divided into two halves, the first invoking a number of traditional images, the second section attempting to offer a more technical gloss. We can identify sources for a number of phrases in both halves of the creed. The reference to three *hypostases* being one in συμφωνίᾳ seems to go back to Origen, *Contra Celsum* 8. 12. The insistence that the Father is 'truly Father' and the Son 'truly Son' directly mirrors Asterius' fragment 20 and the creed that Eusebius of Caesarea presented to Nicaea.[38] The phrase describing the Son as 'exact image of the Godhead and the *ousia* and will and power and glory of the Father' is remarkably close to a fragment of Asterius discussed in Chapter 2. Asterius has the titles in a slightly different order, but the conclusion seems unavoidable that Asterius had a significant role in framing the Dedication creed. For some ancient authorities this creed was originally produced by Lucian of Antioch—at least they knew that its authors claimed such a provenance. Unfortunately there is no evidence with which we might verify this claim, and it would anyway be unsurprising if its authors claimed their formulation embodied the 'faith' of Lucian as part of their own propaganda.[39]

The creed has a clear anti-Sabellian and anti-Marcellan thrust. It has been noted that the creed does not include a phrase insisting that the Son's kingdom 'has no end'. Such a phrase appears in the first creed discussed above, and becomes a standard anti-Marcellan assertion. It is indeed an odd omission, but little should be made of it. The creed clearly and strongly argues against Sabellian emphases and those emphases were associated with Marcellan theology. We see these emphases, for instance, in the insistence that there are three names which 'signify exactly the particular *hypostasis* and order and glory of each'.

It is not clear if this text directly aims at supplanting Nicaea. Given the lack of a formal credal tradition at this point we need to ask ourselves what we would mean by 'supplanting'. The Dedication creed almost certainly intended to offer a better and clearer affirmation of faith than Nicaea, and certainly represents the views

---

[37] This translation is that of Hanson, *The Search*, 286–7, with some modifications.
[38] See also Eusebius, *Marcell.* 1. 4.
[39] Thus I suggest we avoid the term 'Lucianic creed' to describe this text: such a name is the product of wishful thinking. For instance, Lienhard, *Contra Marcellum*, 96–7 presents the Asterius fragment as copying from the Lucianic creed and thus being forced, because of the creed's authority, to modify some of his most subordinationist emphases. There is no evidence—other than the claims of its own partisans reported at second hand—that the creed pre-dated 341.

of those unhappy with some of the key architects of Nicaea. But we cannot be certain that even its own architects thought of Nicaea as having a universal status that might make necessary any such 'supplanting'. Some similarities and differences between the two creeds are, however, clearly apparent. Missing entirely is Nicaea's insistence on the Son being from the Father's *ousia*: the already contested nature of this theology in 325 can only have been enhanced by controversy over Marcellus. The 341 creed does anathematize doctrines associated by Nicaea with Arius. Thus, the Son's generation is not to be considered as preceded temporally in any way and he is not to be considered a creature 'like one of the creatures'. This second point is of course open to wide interpretation and probably all of those associated with Arius himself would have been happy to agree. The use of συμφωνία to describe the unity of the persons will of course seem wholly inadequate by the standards of later orthodoxy, but here we should probably note its minimalism: it is a term open to wide interpretation.

Positively, the creed focuses on the Son's revealing of the Father in a manner that reflects the theological trajectory we saw in Eusebius of Caesarea. The creed uses X from X terminology to indicate the unique nature of the Son and his relationship to the Father—he is God from God, whole from whole, perfect from perfect. The status of the Son as revealer of the Father is particularly clear in the phrase 'exact image of the Godhead and the substance and will and power and glory of the Father'. 'Exact image' had a widespread usage beyond 'Eusebian' circles: Alexander and Athanasius both make use of it. The creed also deploys a variety of titles to emphasize Christ's revelatory function—such as 'Living Word, Living Wisdom, true Light, Way, Truth, Resurrection, Shepherd, Door'.

Thus, it is difficult to pin down the theological origins of the creed: we have seen that it owes debts to Asterius (and possibly to the mysterious Lucian), to Eusebius of Caesarea and to some aspects of Origen's legacy. But it does not push the theological emphases of Arius. Richard Hanson describes it thus: '[The creed] represents the nearest approach we can make to discovering the views of the ordinary educated Eastern bishop who was no admirer of the extreme views of Arius but who had been shocked and disturbed by the apparent Sabellianism of Nicaea ...'.[40] I disagree with some of Hanson's phrasing: 'Eastern' is too broad a category. I do, however, agree that the creed shows us that many in Asia Minor, Syria, and Palestine followed a broad 'Eusebian' line without necessarily

---

[40] Hanson, *The Search*, 290.

having any great time for the particulars of a theology like Arius'. In the decades that followed this creed was read in many different ways. Indeed, just because the text commanded wide support—perhaps wider support than Nicaea in the east—does not mean that it was clearer in expression. The reference to vague traditional expressions in the first half and the minimalist nature of the more technical last sections may actually have enabled its wide-ranging appeal.

For Athanasius, this creed is 'Arian'. Around 360, however, Hilary of Poitiers treats it as pro-Nicene, arguing that its primary intention is anti-modalist.[41] Hilary's account is somewhat anachronistic: the writers of the Dedication creed were not attempting to argue for Nicaea. However, Hilary's account is important. He offers a narration of credal history appropriated from one of the parties that made a major contribution to the final emergence of pro-Nicene theology. In this context Hilary saw continuity between his own theology in the early 360s and a tradition within which the Dedication creed was of great significance. The creed was thus able to represent a variety of eastern theologies that eventually followed separate paths. But this is to jump ahead of our narrative.

The third creed from this meeting need not concern us, it is simply a personal statement of faith made by a certain Theophronius whose faith had been called into question. The so-called 'fourth creed', however, needs attention. This document was composed after the council as a short summary to be sent west with messengers to the Emperor Constans.[42] It reads:

We believe in One God, the Father Almighty, Creator and Maker of all things; from whom all fatherhood in heaven and on earth is named. And in his only-begotten Son, our Lord Jesus Christ, who before all ages was begotten from the Father, God from God, Light from Light, by whom all things were made in the heavens and on the earth, visible and invisible, being Word, and Wisdom, and Power, and Life, and True Light; who in the last days was made man for us, and was born of the Holy Virgin; who was crucified, and dead, and buried, and rose again from the dead the third day, and was taken up into heaven, and sat down on the right hand of the Father; and is coming at the consummation of the age, to judge the quick and the dead, and to render to everyone according to his works; whose kingdom endures indissolubly into the infinite ages; for he shall be seated on the right hand of the Father, not only in this age but in that which is to

---

[41] Hilary, *Synod.* 32–3. See also Sozomen's puzzlement at the phrase 'exact image of the essence of the Father' at *Hist eccl.* 3. 5. For an 'anti-Arian' historian such as Sozomen it can only seem strange that such a phrase occurs.

[42] Athanasius (*Synod.* 25) suggested a separate meeting in Antioch composed the creed before sending it west. Socrates (*Hist. eccl.* 2. 17) and Sozomen (*Eccl. hist.* 3. 10) present the three ambassadors as making up the creed for their own purposes during the embassy rather than delivering the second creed. Athanasius' story has more of a plausible ring.

come. And in the Holy Ghost, that is the Paraclete; which, having promised to the apostles, He sent forth after his ascension into heaven, to teach them and to remind them of all things; through whom also shall be sanctified the souls of those who sincerely believe in him. But those who say that the Son was from non-existence, or from a different *hypostasis* and not from God, and, there was time when he was not, the Catholic Church regards as aliens.[43]

It is noticeable that this creed uses no *ousia* or image language. Further, it has added a direct anti-Marcellan reference: the Son's kingdom has no end. Whoever drew up this creed seems to have been caught between a desire to be conciliatory to the west and personal inclination to prefer a more subordinationist creed than the Dedication creed. Over the next twenty years many creeds emanating from the Eusebians and their successors were deeply indebted to its still ambiguous formulations.

The ambassadors from Antioch presented this fourth Antiochene creed to Constans, and both Socrates and Sozomen report that the ambassadors were vigorous in their attempts to demonstrate their orthodoxy. Unfortunately their mission was not purely a matter of seeking doctrinal agreement; they were also attempting to get Constans and key western bishops to see that Athanasius' and Julius' charges against them were false and that Athanasius had rightly been condemned for malpractice: these attempts came to naught. The deeply interwoven doctrinal and ecclesio-political questions at issue resisted any simple solution.

THE COUNCIL OF SERDICA: EAST VS. WEST?

During these years dispute between Constans and his brother Constantius plays an important role. In later years, after Constans was dead, Athanasius had to defend himself to Constantius against charges that he had, in 342–3, encouraged Constans to oppose his brother. In his *Apology to Constantius* Athanasius claims that he never met with Constans alone, but he does tell us that 'certain bishops' encouraged Constans to write to his brother suggesting a joint council to resolve the disputes that had arisen.[44] Constantius was at war with the Persians and in a mood to be conciliatory. Invitations were sent out (we do not know how widely) to a council that would meet in 343 at Serdica (modern Sophia), a city near the

---

[43] Athansius, *Synod.* 25. The fact that the penultimate anathema condemns only those who think of the Son as coming from a different *hypostasis*, and does not parallel *ousia* is probably not significant. It may even serve as backing for the idea that the two terms in Nicaea's anathema were understood as synonymous.

[44] Athanasius, *Apol.* 3–4.

border between Constans' half of the empire and Constantius'. Constans himself attended.

The council was a disaster: the two sides, one from the west and the other from the east, never met as one. Before seeing why, we must consider the nomenclature of 'western' and 'eastern' used to describe the two parties. We cannot identify with certainty those who constituted the approximately 95 bishops who are counted as 'western', but we can make some progress.[45] Of these 95 we can identify 33 as coming from modern-day Greece, around 10 from the modern Balkans south of the Danube (Moesia, Pannonia, Dacia), and 5 from further east and south (including Athanasius and Marcellus). Fifteen of the remaining half came from Italy, the majority from northern Italy: the Gallic and Germanic provinces seem to have delivered only 2 or 3 bishops. These figures must remain tentative: around 20 of the 95 probable attendees are not identifiable. Nevertheless, clear conclusions can be drawn: at least half of those attending the 'western' meeting were from areas to the east of northern Italy and the largest single block of attendees were the Greek and Balkan bishops. The 'western' council was as localized as most during this century. The demographics of the council demonstrate the errors of assuming that Greek-speaking areas of the east divided clearly in theology from the Latin-speaking west. Just as northern Italy and the area of the former Yugoslavia sustained a strong anti-Nicene presence through the second half of the century, the area of modern-day Greece sustained a strong tradition of support for anti-Eusebian theologies. 'East' vs. 'West' is far too clumsy a tool of analysis for almost anything in the fourth century.

While Constans promoted the interests of the anti-Eusebian bishops who had prompted him to the idea of a council (he perhaps hoped to influence ecclesiastical affairs across the empire), so too Constantius attempted to assert his authority, sending imperial officials with the bishops who headed unwillingly towards Serdica. These bishops made their way to Philippopolis, 100 miles south-east of Serdica, and at the furthest edge of the area under Constantius' control. En masse they travelled to Serdica, and were quartered in

---

[45] On the council see Hanson, *The Search*, 293 ff.; Simonetti, *La Crisi*, 161 ff.; Hess, *Canon Law*; Leslie W. Barnard, *The Council of Serdica, 343 AD* (Sofia: Synodal Publishing House, 1983). The list of attendees at the 'western' council remains uncertain: four lists survive: at Athanasius, *Apol. sec.* 48; Hilary, *C. ant. Par.* B. 2. 3–4; in a letter from the council to the church of the Mareotis and in a letter from Athanasius to the same church, see *EOMIA* 1/2. 658, 660. See also the discussion of J. Zeiller, *Les Origines Chrétiennes dans les provinces danubiennes de l'empire romain* (Paris: De Boccard, 1918), 233 ff. For the best reconstructed texts and discussion of the 'western' creed see Martin Tetz, 'Ante omnia de sancta fide et de integritate veritatis: Glaubensfragen auf der Synode von Serdica (342)', *ZNTW* 76 (1985), 243–69.

the imperial palace there. Two of their number changed sides, but the majority refused to meet with the 'westerners' who wished Athanasius and Marcellus to be allowed normal participation in the meeting. The 'easterners' had no intention of allowing the 'westerners' to revoke the decisions of their councils. After much manoeuvring the 'eastern' bishops wrote what amounts to an apology and a statement of faith, excommunicated all the 'western' leaders at Serdica, and retreated to Philippopolis, where these documents were formally promulgated. The statement issued by the 'easterners' consists of the fourth creed of Antioch with its anathemas and an extra clause aimed at a variety of positions, including 'those who say ... that Christ is not God'.[46] This addition is obviously enough aimed at 'western' fears that the 'easterners' were 'Arians', but its ambiguity also reminds us of the variety of ways in which the term 'God' could be deployed at this point. While this statement of faith is of interest, the letter by which it is prefaced reveals much about how the 'easterners' viewed events at Serdica. The letter begins by condemning Marcellus, accusing him of stating that Christ becomes image, bread, door, and life only with the incarnation (in such accusations we see how the mere list of titles in the Dedication creed could itself be understood as anti-Marcellan polemic). Marcellus has also been legitimately deposed by a council in Constantinople at which Constantine himself was present (no doubt there is here a not so subtle jab at claims about Nicaea's condemnation of Arius). Only then does the letter turn to Athanasius, focusing on his tyrannical behaviour and previous condemnation. Finally, the 'easterners' justify their excommunication of the chief 'westerners' and reject their council 'made up of this curdled blend of lost souls'.

The 'western' bishops issued a number of documents,[47] the most important for our purposes being a long profession of faith. It is not clear that this text was a formal statement promulgated by the whole meeting, it seems more likely that some of the council's leaders drew up the text in response to a statement which does not survive from Ursacius and Valens, two members of the eastern council. These two were from the Roman region of Illyria (very roughly covering the area of former Yugoslavia). They had been present at Tyre when Athanasius was condemned and quickly gained a reputation for promoting the 'Arian' cause. It is at least intriguing to note that Arius himself was exiled to their homeland. The Serdican statement that they were 'born from the Arian asp' may reflect knowledge of actual contact with Arius. We shall meet them again over the next

---

[46] For the 'eastern' text see Hilary, *C. ant. Par.* A. 4. 1.

[47] Hanson, *The Search*, 299 provides a list. The profession of faith produced by the western council is most easily found at Theodoret, *Eccl. hist* 2. 8. The Latin original does not survive.

twenty to thirty years in promoting theologies which seem to owe much to 'Eusebian' influence, although their pragmatism led them to seek agreement with Athanasius when circumstances demanded.[48]

The statement itself refutes three 'Arian' arguments supposedly put forward by Valens and Ursacius: Christ is not true God and has a beginning before time;[49] the Logos suffered and died; the *hypostases* of Father, Son, and Spirit are different. The statement tells us that Father, Son, and Spirit have only one *hypostasis* or *ousia*. The Son has no beginning or end in time and exists eternally, the Son is from the Father as the Father's 'true' Wisdom and Power and Word. The Logos is only-begotten '[because] he always was, and is in the Father'. The names Father and Son indicate their correlative inseparability and yet there is one Godhead in both. The text goes on to insist that the two are distinct because 'the Father is Father, and the Son is the Father's Son' and also that the Father is superior to the Son 'not because of difference, but because the very name itself of the Father is greater than that of the Son'. One of the oddities of this text is its seeming lack of any doctrine of the Spirit: although Father, Son, and Spirit are all named and said to share a *hypostasis*, elsewhere the statement speaks as if the Spirit were identical with the Logos and once describes the Son as 'Logos-Spirit' ($\Lambda\acute{o}\gamma os\ \pi\nu\epsilon\hat{v}\mu a$). The statement offers no technical terminology for identifying what Father and Son are as distinct. One of the only helpful technical distinctions it makes clear is to distinguish carefully 'begotten' ($\gamma\epsilon\nu\nu\eta\tau os$) and 'created' ($\gamma\epsilon\nu\eta\tau os$): those who interpret begotten by means of created are condemned. 'Arianism' is also defined in such broad terms that almost any theology which was willing to insist on there being more than one *hypostasis* was in error.[50]

The fact that the letter openly invokes the name of Arius to describe the eastern bishops is one indication that an Athanasian account of the conflict had been influential. The text then does not simply serve as a window onto western theology in the early 340s. It does, however, serve as a window onto the increasingly divergent concerns of the theological trajectories now in conflict. Concerns

---

[48] Michel Meslin, *Les Ariens d'Occident* (Paris: Éditions du Seuil, 1967) asserts that as a border region, Illyria was influenced by both sides. This is unsustainable: to the east and south it seems likely that Illyria was bordered by regions that strongly supported what Meslin would think of as 'western' theologies. On the place of Valens and Ursacius in anti-'Arian' polemic see Barnes, 'Canon', 58.

[49] This clause oddly attributes both beginning and end to Christ: my account follows Hall's gloss and explanation of what is meant, Stuart Hall, 'The Creed of Sardica', *SP* 19 (1989), 178–9.

[50] Here I adapt Kopecek, *Neo-Arianism*, I. 85: 'it issued an encyclical which defined Arianism so broadly that nearly every easterner who had ever heard of Origen was considered Arian'.

among Eusebians about the Father's transcendence pushed in very different directions from theologians whose main concern was to show a direct continuity of being between Father and Son. Confusion and misunderstanding in terminology was accompanied by deep disagreement over models of participation and generation: conflict had the effect of highlighting long-existing tensions.

This text also tells us a little more about perceptions of Nicaea among its own partisans. Bishops such as Ossius, Athanasius, and Marcellus were present at Serdica and yet willing to turn to an alternative statement of faith, just as many of their eastern counterparts had done at Antioch two years before. This reflects not an attempt to overturn the decisions of Nicaea, but a context in which conciliar formulations were not seen as fixed. After the council Ossius and Protegenes the bishop of Serdica wrote to Julius of Rome. The letter begins by saying that while circumstances demanded a supplementary statement they in no way intended to alter Nicaea's decrees (and here we perhaps find the first direct mention of Nicaea's creed since 326–7).[51] Nicaea's specific terminology was not treated as the obvious starting point for setting out the theology it was taken to indicate as orthodox.

CONFUSION AND RAPPROCHEMENT: AD 344–350

The remainder of the 340s requires much less discussion. Richard Hanson rightly characterizes this period as one in which the failure of Serdica eventually prompted attempts at rapprochement.[52] These years do demonstrate that few as yet shared Athanasius' rhetorical presentation of this controversy as revolving solely around two opposed theological options. While some saw a clash between different theological trajectories, many others also assumed that political motives were behind much of what had happened in the previous fifteen years, and that some middle ground could be found.

Once again Constans appears to have taken a lead in events. Philostorgius and Socrates even quote from what they allege are letters in which Constans threatens his brother with civil war if he will not permit Athanasius to return to Alexandria.[53] There is a good chance that these letters are forgeries, it being unlikely that

---

[51] See *EOMIA* I. 644, tr. Hall, 'Sardica', 174. The relevant section runs, 'We remember and hold and keep that statement which contains the Catholic Faith composed at Nicaea, and all the bishops present agreed. But since the disciples of Arius stirred up blasphemies ... we set out a fuller and longer ⟨faith⟩ agreeing with the first. ... They [the bishops at Serdica?] decided that the former should be firm and fixed, and that these are to be worded more fully with a sufficiency of truth ...'

[52] Hanson, *The Search*, 306–14.

[53] See Socrates *Hist. eccl.* 2. 22–3, Sozomen, *Hist. eccl.* 3. 20.

Constans would have threatened war over Athanasius but the general impression that Constans was keen to assert his own ecclesiastical policy seems to be borne out by events. In 344 a delegation of three bishops made their way to Antioch to seek agreement. This meeting came to naught, largely because of the machinations of Stephen, the bishop of Antioch. For his part in this affair—which reads like a plot from an afternoon soap opera—Stephen was deposed.[54] His successor Leontius encouraged attempts at rapprochement and, in the very next year, we find an embassy from Antioch heading west with another credal statement. This statement is considered below. In the summer of 345 Constantius permitted Athanasius back to Alexandria, probably in the knowledge that the Gregory who had replaced Athanasius in 339 was dying. Athanasius made his way back cautiously, visiting Constantius, and did not arrive until 346. Probably in 345 and 347 we even find the two bishops Ursacius and Valens willing to enter into communion with Athanasius (although we have no knowledge of what this, if anything, meant in practice).[55] Athanasius' arrival in Alexandria marked the beginning of the longest stretch of his episcopate spent in possession of his see: he remained until 356.

The formula of faith brought west in 345 now demands our attention. This document, known as the 'Macrostich' creed ('long-lined'), consists of a slightly changed version of the fourth Antiochene creed with a long explanation.[56] While the Macrostich ('long-lined') creed appears to have been composed by theologians unhappy with the *ousia* language deployed in the Dedication creed, it also goes to considerable lengths to demonstrate that there is some sort of continuity of being between Father and Son. This paradox is clearest in the middle of the text where we find a concerted attempt to steer between presenting Christ as 'God before ages' and what is described as Paul of Samosata's teaching that Christ became God: 'though he be subordinate to his Father and God, yet, being before ages begotten of God, he is God according to his perfect and true nature (θεὸν κατὰ φύσιν τέλειον εἶναι καὶ ἀληθῆ)'. The text argues against Marcellan doctrines which (echoing Origen's presentation of Monarchian doctrine in his *Commentary on John*) treat the Word as 'mere word of God and unexisting, having his being in another' (ἐν ἑτέρῳ τὸ εἶναι ἔχοντα). Not only Marcellus is named, but also his disciple Photinus. Photinus had recently become bishop of Sirmium

---

[54] Theodoret, *Eccl. hist.* 2. 7–8. Stephen attempted to hide a prostitute in the bishops' quarters hoping to discredit their embassy.
[55] See Athanasius, *Apol. sec.* 58, Hilary. *C. ant. Par.* B. 2. 6 and 8.
[56] Hanson, *The Search*, 309–12. The text may be found at Socrates, *Hist. eccl.* 2. 19 and Athanasius, *Synod.* 26.

(modern Mistrovica in Serbia). He is of importance here because his theology seemed to many Latin theologians to imply a form of adoptionism and thus helped to secure some measure of western suspicion of Marcellus.

Against this theology the Macrostich confesses the Son as 'living God and Word, existing in himself'. (καθ' ἑαυτὸν ἐπάρχοντα). The Son, in a phrase that will have a long history in the fourth century, is 'like in all things to the Father' (τῷ πατρὶ κατὰ πάντα ὅμοιον εἶναι). Twice here the Son is also presented as 'image' of God, but the language is not deployed as a central terminology (again in contrast to the Dedication creed). This position is followed by condemnation of those who treat Father, Son, and Spirit as three names of one reality (πρᾶγμα) or person (πρόσωπον). Interestingly, this doctrine is described as the teaching that 'Romans call Patripassianism': that the writers go out of their way to demonstrate that what they condemn is also condemned in Rome shows the apologetic aim of the text.

The early sections of the Macrostich insist that the Son is not co-ingenerate and the Father alone is unbegun and ingenerate. That the text places this assertion so near its beginning leads Kopecek to read the Macrostich as a direct response to Athanasius' discussion of ingeneracy in his *First Oration*.[57] While this may well be the case, we have no direct evidence. The text goes on to argue that there are three realities (πράγματα) or persons (πρόσωπα), but makes no mention of *hypostases*. This does not, we are told, mean three Gods because there is only one ingenerate, unbegun and because the Father 'who alone has existence from himself, and alone gives this abundantly to all others' (τὸν μόνον μὲν ἐξ ἑαυτοῦ τὸ εἶναι ἔχοντα, μόνον δὲ τοῖς ἄλλοις πᾶσιν ἀφθόνως τοῦτο χαριζόμενον). This phrasing is confusing: the text describes some sort of shared being stemming from the Father as the guarantor of unity, but as throughout this text, the verb is used substantively in place of the noun *ousia*. By such a tactic the creed's framers both avoid any connotations that a material division in God is intended or that there are two divine principles. At the same time the substantive use of the verb leaves much ambiguous, the existence bestowed can much more easily be understood as secondary and in some ways inferior. The text does, however, endeavour to show that the three are not separated in any simplistic sense. At the end of the text we find that Father and Son 'are united with each other without mediation (ἀμεσιτεύτως) or distance (ἀδιαστάτως)' and that they 'exist inseparably (ἀχωρίστους

---

[57] One might also note the text's citation of Prov. 8: 22 to indicate the Son's subordination. But this text has a long history of being used thus and cannot be seen as directly anti-Athanasian here without further evidence.

ὑπάρχειν ἑαυτῶν)', all the Father embosoming the Son, and all the Son hanging and adhering to the Father. Again they are not two Gods, because there is 'one dignity of Godhead, and one exact harmony of dominion' (ἓν ... τῆς θεότητος ἀξίωμα καὶ μίαν ἀκριβῆ τῆς βασιλείας τὴν συμφωνίαν).

The text clearly moves beyond the theology of some of the earlier 'Lucianists' in not insisting that only the Father is true God and that assertions of unity in God are about the Father's status alone. For this document the Son is generated in such a way that the unity of God somehow encompasses Father and Son as distinct beings. In traditional Eusebian fashion, we read that the Son is generated from the Father's will as the only alternative to being generated by necessity. While this insistence is clearly aimed at presentations of the Son as intrinsic to the Father's being, it is notable that the text does not use generation by will to emphasize that the Father's nature is not shared. Once again the conciliatory tone of this text is clear.

This text is still far from later pro-Nicene orthodoxy, but it is noticeable that the two points at which it demonstrates the most development within its own trajectory form two constant areas of discussion over the following decades. First, the Macrostich searches to find ways of defining the Father's generation of the Son as a sharing of the divine existence, but without compromising the unity of God and without materialist connotation. The result is not particularly successful and the hierarchical scheme within which this occurs remains unaltered. Second, the text focuses quite directly on the logic of asserting three distinct 'realities' while still finding a way to indicate their unity: distinction need not mean a differentiation parallel to that found in creation. *Hypostasis* language is avoided in the hope of convincing westerners that a plurality of divine beings is not intended, but the continued strong hierarchy and refusal of eternal generation were no doubt central reasons why its intended audience seems to have refused the olive branch that was being offered. The creed was presented at a council in Milan in 345, but the easterners were required to condemn Arius before their creed could be discussed. This insult had a predictable result and the embassy returned east.

At the end of the 340s we have, then, a confusing situation. Political tensions between Constans and Constantius have shaped a controversy between a key group of eastern bishops and their Roman, Balkan, and some other 'western' counterparts. That controversy is indeed partly theological, in that controversies between Marcellan and Eusebian theology, and then between Eusebian theology and the theology expressed in the 'western' letter from Serdica have brought into renewed conflict the tensions between the trajectories we saw in the early part of the century. At the same time the conflict of the 340s is also deeply political, both in ecclesial terms (what form of appeal is possible following conciliar condemnation? can eastern and western councils interfere in each other's business? can one appeal to Rome?) and in extra-ecclesial terms. In the last years of the 340s not all saw the controversy in the simple terms offered to us by the *Orations against the Arians*. Indeed, when circumstances permitted, Athanasius himself could come to terms with Constantius, the Eusebians could try to explain themselves to westerners and Constans, and Serdica could be to some extent overlooked. But this period of rapprochement resolved nothing: the tensions remained.

11
The Emergence of Pro-Nicene Theology

6
Shaping the Alternatives: AD 350–360

CONSTANTIUS AND THE RISE OF THE HOMOIANS

Over the period AD 351–3, and after a complex civil war, the eastern Emperor Constantius achieved complete control of the whole empire.[1] Constantius' brother Constantine II had been killed in 340 during an attempt to encroach on his brother Constans' agreed area of influence. In early 350 one of Constans' leading generals, Magnentius, was proclaimed Augustus. Constans was killed, but Constantius rejected Magnentius' attempts to come to terms politically. Two other figures with connections to the Constantinian dynsaty were soon after also declared emperor: one, Nepotianus, was defeated and killed by Magnentius; the second, Vetranio, was able to keep Magnentius out of the Balkans, eventually gave way to Constantius and retired. Magnentius himself was able to hold off Constantius' forces for some time. Constantius was fighting the Persians when news of the rebellion came to him and was unable to head west until the latter months of 350. Constantius, after some setbacks, eventually pushed Magnentius out of Italy in 352 and then, in 353, he defeated Magnentius in Gaul and the usurper committed suicide. At this point Constantius found himself sole ruler of the Roman world and with the ability to push for a unified religious policy throughout his domains in a way no emperor had been able to do since the death of his father in 337. These political events had a profound effect on the course of the ecclesiastical controversies we have been following. The policies Constantius now pursued in the west were, in part, responsible for the emergence of a clearer theological conflict and—by the end of the decade—for pulling together many of those who together shaped what would come to be recognized as 'Nicene' orthodoxy during the early 380s.

Constantius has frequently been seen as a ruthless and brutal ruler and was painted by later pro-Nicene writers as a persecuter of supporters of Nicaea. The true picture is more complex: within the fourth-century context Constantius was a fairly mild ruler.[2]

---

[1] The story is introduced in *CAH* xiii, ch. 1. See also Hanson, *The Search*, 315–25.
[2] See Richard Klein, *Constantius II und die christliche Kirche* (Darmstadt: Wissenschaftliche Buchgesellschaft, 1977). Klein's account is overly partial and should be supplemented with Barnes, *Athanasius and Constantius*.

However we present his character, Constantius was certainly deeply interested in the affairs of the Church. As his control over the empire grew Constantius pursued a policy of encouraging rapprochement between ecclesiastical groups, but within the framework of the Eusebian theology that was so influential in the east. Although Constantius worked for the acceptance of *some* very precise ecclesio-political decisions—especially, for much of his reign, the condemnation of Athanasius—his policies were in general pragmatic. He seems to have desired a basic formulation of the theological issues at stake that would (within some bounds) enable as many as possible to agree, and he was not beyond subterfuge and force to achieve public agreement between factions. In this initial section of the chapter I want to sketch the course of the 350s by focusing on two councils that met as Constantius' control over the west grew.

The first council met at Sirmium in 351 while Constantius was present in the city on his way west.[3] The focus of this council was the examination and condemnation of Photinus, bishop of Sirmium. As perhaps the most visible representative of a Marcellan theology in these years Photinus had already been condemned at a number of councils during the latter half of the 340s. He seems to have been popular in Sirmium and to have successfully resisted his deposition for some years. The purpose of this council on Photinus' own territory seems to have been to enforce the deposition that had not followed those previous condemnations. Photinus' main accuser at the 351 council was Basil of Ancyra. Basil had succeeded the deposed Marcellus in 336 and came to play a highly significant role during this decade (his own theology will be discussed shortly). The creed issued by this council is of importance for our narrative, and is largely a copy of the fourth Antiochene creed with a series of anathemas attached. Two of these strongly condemn some uses of *ousia* language. From these anathemas it seems that the signatories to the creed were particularly worried that linking the Son and Father with *ousia* language implies the Father's being is 'extended' ($\pi\lambda\alpha\tau\acute{u}\nu\epsilon\sigma\theta\alpha\iota$) in the generation of the Son. There are also a number of attacks on the idea that Father and Son are coeternal or two (equal) Gods. While the Son is 'before the ages' he is not unbeginning or without origin, and is subordinate to the Father.[4]

---

[3] Hanson, *The Search*, 325–9, Simonetti, *La Crisi*, 202–6.

[4] For the creed see Athanasius, *Synod*. 27, Socrates, *Hist. eccl.* 2. 30. The sixth and seventh anathemas read, '(6) Whosoever shall pretend that the essence of God is dilated or contracted, be he anathema. (7) Whosoever shall say that the essence of God being dilated made the Son, or shall name the dilation of His essence Son, be he anathema.' For the subordination of the Son, the eighteenth anathema says, '. . . For we do not place the Son in the Father's order, but as subordinate to the Father.'

Some scholars have seen in the anathemas a direct attack on the language of Nicaea itself. We cannot be certain that this is so, but the combined attack on uses of *ousia* language that have materialistic implications and on the conception of two coeternal 'Gods' begs a number of questions. While the former seems aimed at Photinus, the latter seems to be aimed at other theologies that seem to exhibit Marcellan tendencies. We may at least see this as an only partially cloaked attack on Athanasius and the theologies of other early partisans of Nicaea. Photinus' 'materialism' is seen to be part of a range of problems, problems that we see combined as early as the attacks on Alexander by Arius' supporters. Those attacks now seem to be more clearly focused around the *ousia* language used at Nicaea. That an attack on *ousia* language in general should follow from anti-Photinian and anti-Marcellan concerns nicely illustrates why there was such strong resistance to Nicaea even among those who eventually came to recognize that they were travelling roads parallel to that of Athanasius—such as Basil of Ancyra himself. The opinions opposed in the 351 anathemas are the same as some of those opposed in the Macrostich; but here there is no conciliatory olive branch and the opposition itself is more directly and clearly stated.

The council of Sirmium in 351 set the trend for a series of councils in which Constantius attempted to get the condemnation of Athanasius and probably some sort of theological statement accepted throughout the west.[5] Timothy Barnes argues that the decisions of Sirmium 351 formed the basis for the decisions Constantius wished westerners to agree to at these subsequent meetings.[6] The evidence for such a precise link is not conclusive, but as his control over the west grew Constantius increased his attempts to get bishops to agree to the key eastern decisions of the previous few years. Constantius may also have sent the decisions of councils in Arles (353) and Milan (355) to non-attending bishops, forcing them to sign on pain of exile.

In most older presentations, 'western' bishops were taken to be natural and stalwart defenders of Nicaea throughout the fourth century. The 350s show how Nicaea only slowly came to be of importance in the west. We do not know how well the Nicene creed was known in the west between 325 and 350. We do know that some western Church leaders revered Nicaea's 'judgements', if not the

---

[5] We cannot be certain that a doctrinal statement always accompanied Constantius' demands for the condemnation of Athanasius. Hanson, *The Search*, 329–31 makes a strong case, based on a variation of the arguments in Klaus Martin Girardet, 'Constance II, Athanase et l'édit d'Arles (353): A propos de la politique religieuse de l'empereur Constance II', in Charles Kannengiesser (ed.), *Politique et Théologie chez Athanase d'Alexandrie* (Paris: Beauchesne, 1974), 63–91. The evidence of Sulpicius Severus, *Chron.* 2. 39 is important.
[6] See Barnes, *Athanasius and Constantius*, 109 ff.

wording of the creed: as we saw in the case of Ossius and Protogenes. Through the 350s, however, we seem to see a growing opposition to Constantius' attempts to force western councils to agree to the decrees of Sirmium 351, and at the core of this opposition are figures later central in the formation of Latin pro-Nicene theology. It seems unlikely that previous adherence to Nicaea motivated their growing opposition: it is much more likely that events in the second half of the decade prompted a turn to Nicaea as a focus for their already strong opposition. This opposition was both theological and political, and remained both even as the theological alternative became clearer in the 350s and 360s.

Julius of Rome died in 352 and was succeeded as pope by Liberius (352–66). A letter from Liberius to Constantius, written after the council at Arles in 353, demonstrates that the new Pope soon attempted to resist Constantius' policies. Liberius explains that although the easterners have condemned Athanasius he knows of a larger council of eighty Egyptian bishops in Alexandria that has vindicated him. It thus seems inappropriate to follow only the smaller gathering. Moreover, he notes, some of those in charge of the current 'eastern' strategy have shown themselves worryingly unwilling to condemn Arius' views. Liberius then calls on the Emperor to summon a council as his father Constantine had done.[7]

Liberius was not alone in his resistance. He sent the letter to Constantius with Lucifer, bishop of Cagliari. At the same time he wrote to Eusebius, bishop of Vercelli, encouraging him to take a similar stand. Both of these bishops seem already to have been important voices in Italy, and established defenders of Athanasius. In his letters Liberius is disturbed that even bishops he knows well agreed to the condemnation of Athanasius at Arles and, by implication, have consorted with those of Arian tendencies. Western bishops had been both willing to sacrifice Athanasius when threatened and either did not yet see the easterners as Arian or were ignorant of the theological undercurrents at work. Liberius' request for a council was granted and Constantius summoned all western bishops to Milan for 355.

In the first session of this meeting Eusebius of Vercelli attempted to divert the council from condemning Athanasius, Marcellus, and Photinus by demanding that all agree on the Nicene creed before other business.[8] The leaders of the 'easterners', including Valens and Ursacius, prevented this happening and either persuaded the council to issue or with a group of others issued decrees in the name of the council condemning Athanasius and the others. Eusebius and

---

[7] Liberius' letter is in Hilary, *C. ant. Par.* A. 7. 6

[8] Daniel H. Williams, *Ambrose of Milan and the End of the Arian–Nicene Conflicts* (Oxford: Clarendon Press, 1995), 52 ff.

Lucifer were exiled, along with Dionysius the bishop of Milan. Eusebius and Lucifer were sent east, where they were able to maintain some measure of correspondence with their allies and learn more about the theological situation outside Italy.

This last clause is of importance: as we shall see, both eventually returned to Italy having developed considerably. In this they were not alone. We have not so far mentioned Hilary, bishop of Poitiers, another victim of the new order in the west. Hilary was exiled to Phrygia in Asia Minor in 356 at a small council in Bitterae, which also met as part of this sequence of councils called to implement Constantius' policies. Although modern accounts have often presented Hilary as already an anti-'Arian' champion, there is no evidence for this. A compelling case has been made that Hilary fell foul of Saturninus, bishop of Arles, one of Constantius' main advisers in Gaul on largely political grounds.[9] Hilary demands mention here, however, because he is the most famous example of a bishop who returned from exile to play a significant role in the evolution of Latin pro-Nicene theology. Hilary was also present at Milan, and he claims that it was there he first heard the Nicene creed recited.[10] The statement need not mean he had not heard of the creed before that date, but that he had not heard the creed recited in a public context as an authoritative statement of faith.

We need now to move forward to another meeting of bishops at Sirmium in 357. Here we see a significant turning point, leading to deep shifts in allegiance and the emergence of new alliances and oppositions. This meeting was attended by only a few bishops,[11] and it is not clear whether we should think of it as a formal council or as a small gathering of like-minded bishops that offered a summary confession as a contribution to the ongoing theological struggle. The 'manifesto' was probably composed by Ursacius and Valens, possibly with Potamius, bishop of Lisbon. It is striking to note that Hilary presents Ossius of Cordoba as partly responsible.[12] Hilary's attribution seems to reflect anger at the aged Ossius (who may well have been approaching his hundredth year), rather than a likely supposition. Under considerable pressure Ossius signed, having resisted agreeing to the deposition of Athanasius for some years.

One of the notable things about the fourth Antiochene creed of 341, on which this document unsurprisingly draws, is the absence of

[9] See Daniel H. Williams, 'A Reassessment of the Early Career and Exile of Hilary of Poitiers', *Journal of Ecclesiastical History*, 42 (1991), 202–17.
[10] *Synod.* 91.
[11] Hanson, *The Search*, 343 ff. and Simonetti, *La Crisi*, 227 ff. indicate the confusion in the sources. On the role of Liberius and the theology of 357 see also Brennecke, *Hilarius*, 292–334.
[12] Hilary, *Synod.* 11; *C. Const.* 23.

II. The Emergence of Pro-Nicene Theology

ousia terminology (which some have read as a pointed absence). Sirmium 351 had not only omitted *ousia* language, but positively condemned some uses of that language. The confession of 357 even more strongly argues against *ousia* language, condemning use of it *tout court*:

> But as for the fact that some, or many, are concerned about substance (*substantia*) which is called *ousia* in Greek, that is, to speak more explicitly, *homoousion* or *homoiousion*, as it is called, there should be no mention of it whatever, nor should anyone preach it.[13]

Strong ambivalence to Nicaea, or a wish to ignore its terms, has turned to direct opposition. This text demonstrates growing clarity among some theologians that resulted in the emergence of 'Homoian' theology.[14] Ecclesiastical parties are complex and often fluid entities—and the Homoians were particularly so.[15]

Over the next two or three decades Homoian theologians come in different varieties, but are united in their strong resistance to any theologies that see commonality of essence between Father and Son. Homoians were willing to talk of Son being 'like' (ὅμοιος—*homoios*) the Father, or 'like according to the Scriptures', but all further technical terminology was avoided—although a clear subordination emphasis was understood to be implied by 'like'. The leadership of this alliance was always diverse. In the east Acacius of Caesarea (bishop from 340 to c.365), the successor of Eusebius of Caesarea, was a powerful figure, and a bishop who had significant influence with Constantius.[16] Eudoxius, bishop of Antioch from 357 and bishop of Constantinople 360–70, was also prominent.[17] It included bishops of different stripes united by the desire to find a solution to the ongoing controversy that would rule out any theologies seemingly tainted with Marcellan emphases. Homoians are found in east and west, but Greek- and Latin-speaking Homoians follow different

---

[13] Hilary, *Synod.* 11, this translation is that of Hanson, *The Search*, 344–5.

[14] Hanson, *The Search*, 557–97, offers an account of Homoian theology. Unfortunately Hanson does not differentiate eastern and western Homoianism. See also Roger Gryson, *Scolies Ariennes sur le Concile d'Aquilée*, SC 267 (Paris: Éditions du Cerf, 1980) 173–200; Brennecke, *Geschichte der Homöer*.

[15] For some scholars it is inappropriate to speak of Homoians until the Dated creed of 359 on the twin councils of that year. Such is the position of Daniel Williams in *Ambrose of Milan*. Such a strict dating may make us forget the slow emergence of this theological grouping during the 350s, let alone the presence of likeness language throughout the first half of the fourth century, and its presence in such credal documents as the Macrostich.

[16] For Acacius see Joseph T. Lienhard, 'Acacius of Caesarea: Contra Marcellum. Historical and Theological Considerations', *Cristianesimo nella Storia*, 10 (1989), 1–22; J. M. Leroux, 'Acace évêque de Césarée de Palestine (341–365)', *SP* 8 (1966), 82–5.

[17] Eudoxius initially supported the most radically subordinationist Homoians (see the discussion of Aetius and Eunomius later in the chapter), but broke with them and became a significant influence on the emperor Valens in the 360s.

lines of development. In particular, Latin Homoians managed to contain some of the distinctions that resulted in distinct groupings in the east.

Even as it formed, this group found itself fracturing with the emergence of those who push the subordinationist impulse of Homoian theology even further and increasingly interpret 'likeness' as indicating a fundamental distinction in essence (those whom we will term Heterousians). Once we have grasped the rifts between Sirmium 351 and Sirmium in 357 we can understand more clearly how theological opinion was now beginning to be more clearly divided and focused. Constantius' seeming support for this broad trajectory encouraged some of its partisans to push a subordinationist agenda with increasing clarity.[18] At the same time, as we shall see shortly, the same imperial support seems to have encouraged some opponents to turn to Nicaea as the only other possible standard of faith. Thus, with the emergence of Homoian theology the stage is set for the emergence of the groups who were to develop the solution to the controversies as a whole.

It is important to note the extent of western reactions to the Sirmium 357 manifesto. We have already seen the beginnings of attempts on the part of a few to turn to Nicaea as a standard against the direction of Constantius' policies. Events of 357 deeply shaped this movement. We have a number of surviving texts written in response: Phoebadius bishop of Agen in southern France wrote a short *Contra Arianos* in direct reaction and Hilary of Poitiers wrote his *De synodis* (discussed in the next chapter) partly in response.[19] The appearance of this literature seems to have further helped to raise consciousness in the west of the doctrinal issues that now seemed to be increasingly at stake.

From the discussion of Chapter 4 it will already be clear that the character of adherence to Nicaea changed significantly through the century: in the same way there is no single theology of opposition to Nicaea. Many of the theologies we have considered so far are non-Nicene more than anti-Nicene: only in the 350s do we begin to trace clearly the emergence of directly anti-Nicene accounts. It is because of this fluidity that I cannot follow Richard Vaggione in his excellent *Eunomius of Cyzicus and the Nicene Revolution* when he suggests

---

[18] One of the most striking examples from the late 350s concerns Eudoxius' arrival in Antioch in 357. He claimed authority for his presence from Constantius and proceeded to support Aetius. Such actions created the impression of a logical direction to the Homoian programme, but also reveals the fluidity of this alliance.

[19] It is sometimes alleged that the second book of Marius Victorinus' anti-Arian writings, the first *Letter to Candidus* was stimulated by the Sirmium manifesto. There is no evidence to support this claim. It seems more likely that the whole collection was composed after Basil of Ancyra's 358 council.

140   *II. The Emergence of Pro-Nicene Theology*

that we can conceive of the various theological strands of the fourth century as fitting into two 'interpretive frameworks', the Nicene and the non-Nicene.[20] While Vaggione handles the evidence with subtlety, allowing this architectonic assumption to stand gives a cast to the narrative that fights against attempts to explore the differences between different Nicenes and non-Nicenes. At the present moment in scholarship on the century it is far better to resist such general classifications.

ATHANASIUS AND THE DEFENCE OF *HOMOOUSIOS*

Constantius' religious policies, and the 357 Sirmium 'manifesto' also provide important background to developments in the thought of Athanasius. Athanasius' fortunes in the years between 335 and 361 frequently changed: he had first been in exile (mostly in what is now Trier in Germany) between 335 and the end of 337, and we saw him earlier during his second exile between 339 and 346.[21] Once Constantius was in sole charge of the empire, Athanasius' fortunes turned again, and he was probably deposed both at a small council in Antioch in 349 and at the 351 Sirmium council. However, it was not until 356 that Constantius sent troops to Alexandria to remove him. From the beginning of 356 to the end of 361 Athanasius could not openly occupy his see, and spent most of these years in hiding in Egypt.

During the 350s Athanasius honed his polemic, in particular developing a detailed defence of Nicaea's terminology. We see these developments first in Athanasius' letter *De decretis* (*On the Decrees of Nicaea*). The work is difficult to date, but was probably composed in either 353 or 355–6. It is addressed to an unknown correspondent (possibly Julius of Rome[22]) and attempts to refute questions raised by associates of Acacius of Caesarea about Nicaea's use of *homoousios* and 'of the *ousia* of the Father'. Athanasius begins by arguing that Acacius' predecessor Eusebius of Caesarea had himself interpreted Nicaea's language in a non-modalist, non-materialist sense.[23] As we shall see, this observation provides an important clue

---

[20] Vaggione, *Eunomius*, 49–50. Rowan Williams, in his review of Hanson, *The Search* (*Scottish Journal of Theology*, 45 (1992), 101–11), comments on Hanson's tendency to allow the story to be one of two opposing sides despite his attempt to show the diversity of the story. Hanson even goes so far as to provide a general account of the shape of 'Arian' dynamics that seem rarely to be borne out. Vaggione's account is far subtler, but in some ways similarly problematic.

[21] See Barnes, *Athanasius and Constantius*, 89–90.

[22] Such is the hypothesis of Barnes, *Athanasius and Constantius*, 110–11. The suggestion makes much sense, but it remains conjecture.

[23] *Decr.* 2–5.

Shaping the Alternatives AD 350–360

to the structure and sources of Athanasius' argument. At the same time Athanasius argues that Acacius' own theology is just another version of the theology of Asterius and Arius.[24] He then sets out an account of the Son's generation which emphasizes its immaterial character, and which tries to show that the Son is eternally with the Father and an eternal partner in the Father's action. Much here relies on the argument of the *Orations*. This discussion offers one of Athanasius' clearest statements that we must understand the generation of the Son within the context of the divine immateriality and simplicity.[25]

When Athanasius comes to defend the *ousia* language of Nicaea, his main strategy is to present it as necessary if the sense of scriptural titles for the Son such as Power, Wisdom, and Word is to be safeguarded. First Athanasius considers Nicaea's 'from the essence of the Father'. He begins by stating that the Word is the instrument of the Father's creative activity and the Lord of all creation, not part of it. The Son alone is 'from the Father'. Thus, Nicaea speaks of the Son as being 'of the essence of the Father, that we might believe the Word to be other than the nature of things originate, being alone truly from God'.[26] Then, in the second section of the argument Athanasius tell us that a number of phrases were suggested at Nicaea to describe the status of the one who was truly 'from God': 'true power', as 'exact image of the Father', as 'in [the Father] without division', and as 'existing everlastingly with the Father, as the radiance of light'. But, Athanasius claims, these phrases were intentionally misread by Eusebians, who argued that human beings are also the image of the Father or powers in some sense. Thus, in order to indicate the overall intention of these terms, and 'gathering up the sense of the Scriptures', *homoousios* was used, expanding on 'from the essence of the Father'. *Homoousios* safeguards the point that the Son's generation is unlike the generation of human beings and does not involve the creation of one thing that may be separated from its originator. *Homoousios* renders impossible descriptions of the Son as created and rules out such phrases as 'there was a time when he was not'.[27] Thus, throughout this

---

[24] *Decr.* 6 ff.
[25] See esp. Athanasius, *Decr.* 10 ff.: 'Is then the Son's generation one of human affection? ... in no wise; for God is not as men, nor men as God ... And if so be the same terms are used of God and man in divine Scripture, yet the clear-sighted, as Paul enjoins, will study it, and thereby discriminate, and dispose of what is written according to the nature of each subject ...'.
[26] *Decr.* 19.
[27] *Decr.* 19–23: '(19) For neither are other things as the Son, nor is the Word one among others, for he is Lord and Framer of all; and on this account did the Holy Council declare expressly that he was of the essence of the Father, that we might believe the Word to be other

discussion the core of Nicaea's terminology is the phrase 'from the *ousia* of the Father'—*homoousios* is only comprehensible as a necessary supplement.

Athanasius next adds a key argument. God is simple (ἁπλοῦς), uncompound, and terms such as 'God' and 'Father' must therefore denote the essence of God. There are, for Athanasius, no qualities (συμβέβηκοι) in God and thus God's name and essence are not distinct. But, when we speak of God's essence we do no more than say that God is, we do not know what God is:

> For though to understand what the essence of God is be impossible, yet if we only understand that God is, and if Scripture indicates Him by means of these titles, we, with the intention of indicating Him and none else, call Him God and Father and Lord. When then He says, 'I am that I am', and 'I am the Lord God', or when Scripture says, 'God', we understand nothing else by it but the intimation of His incomprehensible essence Itself, and that He Is, who is spoken of.[28]

Athanasius here describes with increasing clarity how speaking of God's 'essence' may have an important 'logical' or 'grammatical' function, helping to make clear the logic of the relationships implicit in looser language. Thus, Athanasius goes on to argue again that describing the Word as 'of the essence of God' is the same as saying that the Word is 'of God'. If the Son is truly a Son of the Father and not just the same as any other created thing then he should be spoken of as truly generated 'from God'. Similarly, the metaphor of light and its radiance indicates a closeness of relationship in generation that is best grasped by speaking about the Son being 'from the essence of the Father' and as '*homoousios* with the Father'. Essence language serves to rule out what Athanasius sees as intentional 'Arian' misreading of this scriptural language, but it does not inappropriately detract from the equally vital scriptural insistence that God's nature is unknown to us. *Homoousios* is thus defended not by reference to a detailed understanding of what the term implies in

---

than the nature of things originate, being alone truly from God ... (20) For bodies which are like each other may be separated and become at distances from each other, as are human sons relatively to their parents ... but since the generation of the Son from the Father is not according to the nature of men, and not only like, but also inseparable from the essence of the Father, and He and the Father are one, as He has said Himself, and the Word is ever in the Father and the Father in the Word, as the radiance stands towards the light (for this the phrase itself indicates), therefore the council, as understanding this, suitably wrote "one is essence" ... (23) For the saints have not said that the Word was related to God as fire kindled from the heat of the sun, which is commonly put out again, for this is an external work and a creature of its author, but they all preach of Him as radiance, thereby to signify His being from the essence, proper and indivisible, and his oneness with the Father.'

[28] *Decr.* 22.

itself, but by arguing that it is an important cipher for other terms and phrases.

Athanasius' arguments here rest on some unexpressed assumptions. Most importantly, his assumption of a complete break between the created and the uncreated undergirds his reading of what is implied when Eusebius and others speak of Christ as ontologically inferior to the Father. This assumption comes greatly into play in the last sections of the *De decretis* when Athanasius considers the use of 'unoriginate' to distinguish Father and Son. There Athanasius reads 'Arian' intention in using this term as placing the Son on the created side of the boundary between created and uncreated.[29] Even though Athanasius does not spend much time openly defending this ontological distinction, his constant and subtle deployment of it may well have led some to see its virtues. Whether or not later writers learnt directly from Athanasius,[30] the deployment of such a clear distinction between Creator and creation and the placing of all talk about the Word on the uncreated 'side' of the boundary will become a central plank of pro-Nicene theologies in the 360s.

Athanasius seems not only to allude to, but also to build on, the argument of Eusebius of Caesarea in his *Letter to his Diocese* written in 326. While Athanasius clearly argues against Eusebius' support for 'Arians', it is noticeable that he never argues directly against the letter although he refers to it and appended the text to the *De decretis*. I suggest that Athanasius actually directly draws on the basic structure of Eusebius' account of how *homoousios* is only intended to emphasize that the Son is 'from God'. Of course, his adoption of Eusebius' argument is also a careful adaptation: he has a very different understanding of what 'from God' entails.[31] Lastly, we should note that the *De decretis* fails to offer any terminology for the distinctions between the persons, while Athanasius is clear en passant that the Word subsists and exists eternally, his account still fails to move in any way towards a clearer terminology.

There are a number of ways in which we can read the *De decretis* as responding to the events of the 350s. Athanasius was probably in

---

[29] *Decr.* 28–32.

[30] Tracing the actual influence of Athanasius on his contemporaries is difficult, and a scholarly task that would benefit from much new consideration. While he may have influenced Basil of Ancyra (see below), his influence on the Cappadocians is much more difficult to demonstrate (see Ch. 8).

[31] For a more extensive version of this argument see my 'Athanasius' Initial Defense of the Term ὁμοούσιος: Re-reading the *De decretis* Vaggione, *Eunomius*, 58, argues that Athanasius points to Eusebius' letter because it states an officially agreed interpretation of the term *homoousios* promoted by Constantine. Evidence for such an 'official' interpretation is weak, and if we can speak of one it seems to have concerned only the point that *homoousios* did not imply material division.

part responding to a council in Antioch in 349, which had again condemned him,[32] but the text also seems to respond to later events. If we date this text to 353, just after the Sirmium council of 351, then we might be able to say that Athanasius constructed the *De decretis* as a response. If we date the text later, around 355–6, then he can be taken to be using the *De decretis* to respond to the situation at the time of Sirmium 357. Thus, in either case, Athanasius' decision to make Nicaea and *homoousios* central to his theology has its origins in the shifting climate of the 350s and the structure of emerging Homoian theology. In the final sections of the *De decretis* Athanasius spends considerable time arguing against 'Arian' use of 'ingenerate'.[33] His account here largely copies, sometimes word for word, the discussion we saw in Athanasius' first *Oration*. His decision to draw attention again to this pair of terms (ἀγέννητος/ἀγένητος) reflects the continued presence of the term in Eusebian theology and polemic, and perhaps marks an increased significance 'ingenerate' had in the late 340s and early 350s. It is noticeable, for instance, that the Macrostich creed of 345 places considerable emphasis on the Father's status as sole ingenerate (and consistently using ἀγέννητος). We do not know if Athanasius is directly responding to this text (as Thomas Kopecek thought), but the arguments of the Macrostich combined with the final sections of the *De decretis* do indicate that the Father's status as 'ingenerate' was an increasingly prominent topic for debate. Kopecek also offers an extended argument that it was Athanasius' continued emphasis on this question that prompted some of the most starkly subordinationist Homoians to make this term even more central. The argument remains unproven, but it does seem clear that the debate over 'Ingenerate' we see in these years played a role in stimulating the theological clarity displayed in those thinkers to whom I must now turn.

AETIUS AND EUNOMIUS

One of the most significant signs of the tensions within the Homoian alliance is the emergence of 'Heterousian' theology. Heterousians emphasized the differences between the *ousia* of Father and Son and thus had a significantly different account of the ways in

---

[32] See Barnes, *Athanasius and Constantius*, 94–100.
[33] Athanasius, *Decr.* 28–32. Kopecek's analysis is at *Neo-Arianism*, i. 116–20. Kopecek sees Athanasius in the *Decr.* as directly responding to the Macrostich. I am unpersuaded by this argument; for example Athanasius' discussion of the 'likeness in all things' at *Decr.* 20 is likely to be aimed as much at the Dedication creed as at the Macrostich The evidence does not allow us Kopecek's precision.

which the Son was an image of and represented the Father. The two key Heterousian figures were Aetius and Eunomius—these two were prominent for Heterousians in a way that no individual figures were for Homoians.³⁴ During the late 350s the appearance of Aetius' theology within the Homoian alliance was a significant factor in prompting some to reject it. To some who had broadly supported the emerging Homoian position, Aetius came to seem its logical and unacceptable end.

As elsewhere in this century we face a terminological problem. The habit is still widespread of calling this movement 'neo-Arian'. There are, however, significant differences between Arius' theology and that of Aetius and Eunomius, and neither ever appears to have made any claim on Arius' legacy. Their most persistent and important opponents, the Cappadocians, do not engage in an 'Athanasian'-style attempt to cast Aetius and Eunomius as new Ariuses.³⁵ Another term frequently used for them is 'Anomoians'—those who teach the 'unlikeness' of Father and Son. This term was coined by their opponents and both were keen to defend themselves against it, insisting that their concern was to teach 'unlikeness *according to essence*': there were many other ways in which Father and Son *were* alike. I have thus opted to use the term 'Heterousian' because of its precision in indicating exactly where they saw the key difference between Father and Son.

Aetius' biography need not concern us: we need only to note that he was educated in theology by two or three figures who appear to have been among Arius' supporters in the 320s.³⁶ Even in these circles he seems to have gained a reputation for pushing a strong subordinationism. Aetius' theology is highly dense and makes use of

---

[34] On Aetius and Eunomius see Hanson, *The Search*, ch. 19. His biographical sketches are very helpful: his summary of Eunomius' theology is weak. Now fundamental to the study of these figures is Vaggione, *Eunomius*. On Eunomius' theology see especially Barnes, *Power of God*, ch. 5; Raoul Mortley, *From Word to Silence*, ii: *The Way of Negation, Christian and Greek* (Bonn: Hanstein, 1986), ch. 8; Vaggione, *Eunomius*, esp. ch. 5; Elena Cavalcanti, *Studi Eunomioni* (Rome: Pontificium Institutum Orientalium Studiorum, 1976).

[35] Using the term 'Arius' as a term of abuse—as they do—is very different from making a detailed attempt to relate one's opponent to Arius' own words. At this point an interesting question arises. The 'Cappadocians' do not focus at any length on representing Eunomius as Arius *redivivus* and Eunomius seems to make no claim on Arius. However, the early 5th-cent. Heterousian historian Philostorgius constructed a narrative in which Aetius and Eunomius are the true heroes, preserving the legacy of Lucian of Antioch and correcting the errors of others who almost saw the truth—Arius included. When we notice the importance that Philostorgius' account plays in the reconstruction of even such a detailed and scholarly account as Richard Vaggione's recent *Eunomius*, we need to return in some detail to scrutinizing Philostorgius himself: how much of the standard reading of non-Nicene history did he himself invent?

[36] The evidence for Aetius' early years is collected in Kopecek, *Neo-Arianism*, vol. i, ch. 2; Vaggione, *Eunomius*, 14–26.

certain types of syllogism and logical argument.³⁷ In his one surviving work, the *Syntagmation* ('little book'), he refers to those who countenance either *homoousios* or ὅμοιος κατ' οὐσίαν (a term we meet later in this chapter) as χρονίται, a term which Philip Amidon nicely translates as 'temporists', those who speak about God in temporal terms. For Aetius the essence of God lies in being ingenerate (for which Aetius and Eunomius both consistently use ἀγέννητος), which also involves not consisting in a compound essence. If God is truly 'not generated', he argues, then no logical sense can be given to an act of generation that results in one who is either *homoousios* or *homoiousios* with God. All that is generated *and* all that generates from its own substance must be compound. God, not being compound, cannot generate in this way, but only by God's will or authority.³⁸ The Son is thus the product of God's will. Aetius was also highly suspicious of using Father and Son language to show that the generation of the Word involves a generation from God's essence. 'Father' is used only towards the end of the *Syntagmation* and only to indicate the relationship of Son to God: the term 'Son' is used much more frequently of the one generated and is taken to indicate that he is essentially subordinate.

Eunomius was around 25 years younger than Aetius and functioned for some years as a secretary to him (from about 355). He was made bishop of Cyzicus in 360, probably through the influence of Eudoxius.³⁹ Eunomius then appears to have fallen out with Eudoxius, possibly over Eudxoius' failure to support Aetius, and abandoned his bishopric. At some stage during the next decade Aetius and Eunomius together began setting up an alternative episcopate in areas where they had supporters. This 'Eunomian' Church survived well into the next century. Eunomius' writing survives a little more extensively than Aetius', and of particular importance is his *Apology*, a text that may originally have been delivered as a speech in his defence. In many sections of the *Apology* Eunomius uses arguments that are characteristically Homoian, and arguments we have seen in Aetius.

For example, at *Apology* 10–12 Eunomius argues that Father and Son must be distinct because the mere fact of the Son being 'begotten' signifies that his essence cannot share the Father's simplicity. Eunomius also appeals to Christ's own confession of the Father's superiority at John 14: 28. These arguments seem to have been taken

---

[37] Aetius' *Syntagmation* is preserved at Epiphanius, *Panarion* 76. 11. 1 ff. On Aetius see Lionel Wickham, 'The Syntagmation of Aetius the Anomean', *JThS* NS 19 (1968), 532–69; Kopecek, *Neo-Arianism*, vol. i, ch. 4.

[38] Aetius, *Synt.* 5–7.

[39] Eunomius died at Dakora near Cappadocian Caesarea in 394 or 395.

up with enthusiasm by many Homoians. In the same passage Eunomius also gives great weight to ingenerate as a term summing up the character of God's essence: Aetius' influence on this basically Homoian theology is clear. We could also note Eunomius' allusion to some key Homoian formulae: he describes the Son as 'like [the Father] according to the Scriptures', a phrasing embodied in the Homoian creed of 360 that we shall see towards the end of this chapter.[40]

Eunomius deploys the same argument as Aetius to explain why the Son cannot come from the Father's essence. He distinguishes between generation from essence and generation by will.[41] Anything generated from the essence shares the essence of that from which it is generated, and it is simply illogical to imagine that any generated thing shares God's ingenerate nature.[42] As generated by will the Son has a clearly subordinate status; Eunomius assumes that ingenerate defines God in a unique way: God's unity and simplicity imply that ingenerate is the only characteristic of God. At this point we see a distinction between Eunomius and the Homoians. Although they also would have spoken of the Father as the only ungenerate, the term had a philosophical significance and range of implication for Eunomius that were very much his and Aetius'.

It is sometimes argued that Heterousian use of 'ingenerate' was directly dependent on earlier 'Arian' use back to Arius' own in the *Thalia*. This argument has come under suspicion because Alexander of Alexandria never expresses disapproval of Arius' use of the term and he uses it himself to describe the Father. Rowan Williams even suggests that use of the term *begins* with Alexander.[43] Charges that Alexander teaches 'two unbegottens' appear a number of times in his opponents, and it may be that his seeming to imply that Father and Son both shared the title caused some Eusebians to focus on it. It needs, however, to be noted that in this early usage we do not see any of the developed reflection found in Aetius and Eunomius. Following from the discussions we have seen in Athanasius' *Orations*, the Macrostich creed, and Athanasius' *De decretis*, it seems best that we imagine a slow development in reflection on the term 'ingenerate', a development perhaps stimulated both by Eusebian recognition of its polemical utility and Alexander's own slightly confusing usage. The reflections of Athanasius and then the thought of Aetius and Eunomius reflect increasingly sophisticated usage (and, as we shall see, perhaps retrieval). The term is now deployed in denser theological and philosophical contexts.

[40] *Apol.* 22.   [41] *Apol.* 15.   [42] *Apol.* 9, 11.
[43] Williams, 'Logic of Arianism', 57. See also G. Christopher Stead, 'The Platonism of Arius', *JThS* NS 15 (1964), 17.

Eunomius does describe the Son as created, but he is concerned to show that the Son is distinct from the creation we inhabit: the Son is a product unlike other products and stands in the relationship of maker to all other things.[44] The Son holds a unique status because he is a uniquely direct product of the Father's will.[45] Again, Eunomius carefully distinguishes activity (ἐνεργεία) and will from essence. He makes use of a causal hierarchy to consider the relationships between the persons that we can schematize as essence–activity–product. In this sequence Eunomius is at pains to argue that activity is not coterminus with essence: an activity is distinct from an essence and is temporary. Only by understanding that God's activity is an effortless willing without any consequences for his existence can we appropriately preserve the unity and simplicity of God. The Son is thus a product of the Father's will and is the image of the Father's will: but he is the Father's power only in being an image of his power and activity.[46] The Spirit is understood on the same schema, not as an activity of God that is somehow also an essence, but as a product of the divine will created through the Son and inferior to the Son.[47]

This complex system has frequently been understood as philosophically motivated and alien to earlier Christian thought. It may be, however, that Eunomius not only provides new sophistication to the concept of ingeneracy in the fourth-century debates but that he does so partly via an act of retrieval. Michel Barnes points to a number of third-century parallels for Eunomius' usage. Although the particular position that ungeneracy defines God's essence is hard to find elsewhere in the fourth century—and it seems absent from earlier non-Nicenes—Dionysius of Alexandria seems to have held the doctrine.[48] The fragment of his work in which this doctrine is preserved occurs as part of Eusebius of Caesarea's arguments for *creatio ex nihilo* in his *Preparation for the Gospel*. These arguments draw on debates from the second half of the third century concerning

---

[44] *Apol.* 24, 15, 28.
[45] *Apol.* 15: '. . . on the basis of the will of the one who made him we establish a distinction between the Only-begotten and all other things, affording him the same pre-eminence which the maker must necessarily have of his own products.'
[46] *Apol.* 24: 'Accordingly, if this argument has demonstrated that God's will is an action, and that this action is not essence but that the Only-begotten exists by virtue of the will of the Father (ὑπέστη δὲ βουλήσει τοῦ πατρὸς ὁ μονογενής), then of necessity it is not with respect to the essence but with respect to the action (which is what the will is) that the Son preserves his similarity to the Father (οὐ πρὸς τὴν οὐσίαν, πρὸς δὲ τὴν ἐνέργειαν (ἥτις ἐστὶ καὶ βούλησις) ἀποσώζειν τὴν ὁμοιότητα τὸν υἱὸν ἀναγκαῖον).' On this hierarchy see Barnes, 'Eunomius of Cyzicus and Gregory of Nyssa: Two Traditions of Transcendental Causality', *VigChr* 52 (1998), 59–87.
[47] *Apol.* 25.
[48] See Barnes, *Power of God*, 181–9. The fragment of Dionysius is preserved at Eusebius, *Prep.* 7. 19. 3.

Origen's perceived belief in the eternity of the creation. Eusebius even quotes a passage from Methodius of Olympus that argues that actions or accidents come into being when an agent is present, but cease when the agent is absent. An activity is also described as a work of an essence. Thus it seems as if some of the distinction Eusebius uses in his attempt to distinguish God from all the 'products' may have a long history in theological contexts, although there is still much scholarly work to be done here.

One Eunomian theme that has gathered much attention is his insistence that names are related to things not by convention but by nature. Thus Eunomius is able to claim a strong degree of knowledge about God's essence through the name 'ingenerate'. Indeed, Socrates writes that for Eunomius God knows God's essence no better than we do. It is likely that this 'quotation' is put into Eunomius' mouth: his insistence that names are given by God most probably served the function of allowing him to critique those who emphasized the incomprehensibility of the divine nature.[49] At the same time Eunomius was able to identify 'ingenerate' (and other synonymous terms such as 'the one who is') as providing a dependable knowledge on which we can base our discussion of God.[50] In these developments we see Eunomius differing from Arius' insistence on the incomprehensibility of God while developing in a unique manner Eusebian and Homoian insistence that God is not in any way constituted by the generation of the Son. These complexities help to reveal ever more clearly how the distinct theology of Eunomius was for many seen as the natural term of Homoian theology.

THE RISE AND FALL OF THE 'HOMOIOUSIANS'

The emerging shape of Heterousian theology prompted a strong reaction from many who had broadly supported Constantius' policies. In the winter of 358, soon after the Sirmium 357 meeting, a

---

[49] The likelihood of this reading is increased when we see Epiphanius ascribing a very similar statement to Aetius at *Panarion* 76. 4. 2.

[50] Which thus indicates a soteriological concern in Eunomius' position. Something like this position is argued by Vaggione, *Eunomius*, and by Maurice Wiles 'Eunomius: Hair-Splitting Dialectitian or Defender of the Accessibility of Salvation?', in Rowan Williams (ed.), *The Making of Orthodoxy: Essays in Honour of Henry Chadwick* (Cambridge: Cambridge University Press, 1989), 157–72. On the question of the philosophical sources for Eunomius' account of language see Jean Daniélou, 'Eunome l'Arien et l'exégèse néo-platonicienne du Cratyle', *Revue des Études Grecques*, 49 (1956), 412–32. Daniélou is criticized by Mortley, *From Word to Silence*, ii. 146 ff. Kopecek, *Neo-Arianism*, ii. 331, suggests that we do not need to suppose a Neoplatonic context for this theory, seeing clear parallels in Albinus' middle Platonism. Much depends on how clearly we accept modern scholarly distinctions between 'Middle' and 'Neo' platonism.

II. The Emergence of Pro-Nicene Theology

small council met at Ancyra at the invitation of its bishop Basil. This meeting seems to have had both immediate and longer-term causes. Most immediately, the meeting was prompted by the teaching of Aetius in Antioch. Eudoxius became bishop of Antioch in 357 and Aetius followed him from Alexandria and began teaching there. Eudoxius had also convened a council that had endorsed the Sirmium 'manifesto' of 357.[51] The longer-term cause of this event seems to have been the realization that many of those shaping Constantius' policies during the 350s were pushing an agenda that was strongly and intentionally subordinationist. Basil and his supporters saw other themes running between the Dedication creed, the fourth Antiochene creed, and the credal activity of the early 350s that pointed towards their own theologies. The emergence of radical Homoians—who themselves saw the same credal activity as pointing in *their* direction—forced upon the 'Homoiousians' the need to identify their own position far more clearly.

From this gathering at least one extensive letter survives, written by Basil of Ancyra himself.[52] Although Basil made ad hoc alliances with theologians such as Acacius against Photinus and Marcellus, he was heir to a tradition in eastern theology that strongly emphasized the Son's nature as image and revealer of the Father. Basil himself emphasizes the ineffable depth of the Father's self-gift in generating the Son. Such a theology found more subordinationist Homoian theologies to be acceptable partners in anti-Marcellan contexts but theologically insufficient in themselves. Basil's theology is usually described as 'Homoiousian' (and I will continue to use this term), but the title is misleading if it leads us to understand Basil's theology as focused around defending a compromise term for the relationship between Father and Son. Homoiousian theology has also frequently been termed 'semi-Arian', again indicating that Basil should be read mainly as a compromise figure in the 350s rather than as a representative of a significant and persistent strand in earlier eastern theology. In fact, the term *homoiousios* plays no role in Basil's surviving texts, although condemnation of it in the 'manifesto' of

---

[51] Sozomen, *Hist. eccl.* 4. 13. Sozomen notes the presence of Acacius of Caesarea. This action can only have served to reinforce the sense that the emerging Homoian position led inexorably towards Aetius.

[52] The text is preserved in Epiphanius' *Panarion* 73. 2. 1 ff. Central to the study of Basil is now Jeffery N. Steenson, 'Basil of Ancyra and the Course of Nicene Orthodoxy', D.Phil. diss. (Oxford, 1983). Some of Steenson's approach can be seen in his 'Basil of Ancyra on the Meaning of *Homoousios*', in Robert C. Gregg (ed.), *Arianism: Historical and Theological Reassessments*, Patristic Monograph Series, 11 (Philadelphia: Philadelphia Patristic Foundation 1985), 267–7. There is also some useful historical material in Winrich Löhr, *Die Entstehung der homöischen und homöusianischen Kirchenparteien. Studien zur Synodalgeschichte des 4. Jahrhunderts* (Bonn: Wehle, 1986).

Sirmium 357 shows that some had begun to suggest it in the mid-350s, and it is present in some other Homoiousion texts.

In many ways Basil's contribution to these controversies (as we find it in the 358 letter[53]) is best approached via his epistemology. Basil frequently links the process of doctrinal formulation with the formation of appropriate 'concepts' (ἔννοιαι—*epinoiai*).[54] We develop appropriate ἔννοιαι when, on the one hand, we know which scriptural terms most closely deserve our attention and, on the other hand, when we know how to grasp those concepts apart from any materialistic or temporal connotations. Appropriate doctrinal conceptions should also follow Paul's avoidance of 'rationalizing' or 'wise' speech: Basil takes this to imply that doctrinal discussions of the Son's generation should offer no directly descriptive accounts of the mode of generation.

Against this background, Basil argues that the language of Father/Son indicates something distinct from the language of Creator and creature, but not something that we can directly grasp. Once we remove the corporeal connotations of the Father/Son relationship then we are left with 'only the generation of a living being like in essence'.[55] Thus we must confess Father and Son to be like according to essence (ὅμοιος κατ' οὐσίαν) if we are not to mistake the Father/Son relationship for a Creator/creature relationship.[56] When Basil demands that the language of essence is necessary if we are to form appropriate concepts of the relationship between Father and Son, he does not think that God's essence is comprehensible to us and that we are consequently able to judge this known essence to be shared. Rather, talk of likeness in essence is necessary to indicate the closeness that Father/Son language must indicate in a non-material context. 'Essence' language is thus the necessary way of symbolizing a relationship that remains unknown.

Basil makes interesting use of ἐνέργεια (energy) language here. On the one hand, he rejects the idea that the Son is an *energeia* by

---

[53] Basil's own background and possible other surviving writings deserve note. According to Jerome (*Vir. ill.* 89), Basil was originally a physician. There exists a *De virginitate* (PG 30. 669–809) that was attributed to Basil by F. Cavallera in 1905, but many have doubted its authenticity. The treatise is analysed in Susanna Elm, '*Virgins of God*': *The Making of Asceticism in Late Antiquity* (Oxford: Clarendon Press, 1994), 113 ff. Elm's argument, in this otherwise excellent book, is that there was a distinctively Homoiousian form of asceticism associated particularly with Eustathius of Sebaste. The argument is problematic because of the way Elm understands the Homoiousians to have constituted a firm and continuous 'party': what she does identify is an association between some of the main Homoiousians and some ascetic emphases. Whether these can be read as clearly opposed to a 'Nicene' asceticism seems unlikely.

[54] This concept and its origins are discussed much more fully in Ch. 8, pp. 191–4.
[55] Epiphanius, *Panarion* 73. 4. 2.
[56] The way in which Basil distinguishes Father/Son relationships from Creator/creature relationships is the core of Hanson's account of Basil at *The Search*, 352–3.

152   *II. The Emergence of Pro-Nicene Theology*

insisting that the Father is the Father of an *ousia* that exists according to the Father's ἐνέργεια.[57] This is an anti-Marcellan argument focusing on the substantive existence of the Son. On the other hand, Basil uses the term in a number of passages to argue that likeness in activities indicates likeness in essences. Offering an argument parallel to that offered by Athanasius in his *Orations*, Basil argues a number of times that the Son is like the Father in both activity and essence and that likeness in certain activities indicates likeness in essence.[58] Basil seems to argue, though he is by no means clear, that the Son demonstrates the sort of activities intrinsic to the divine nature that should draw us to recognize the Son's likeness to the Father. It is noticeable that in these uses of ἐνέργεια language Basil still wants to speak mainly of *essences* possessing activities that are alike: he does not yet speak of common activities revealing the *same* essence.

Basil also uses his account of God's incorporeality when he speaks of Christ as Word and Wisdom. The Father has wisdom in an incomposite way, and the Son is wisdom from the incomposite wisdom; we can do no other than speak of the two having a likeness in essence and wisdom even though the manner of this generation is unknown to us. Basil argues that if the Father gives the Son to have life in himself (John 5: 26), and if the Father's life is life itself without composition or generation, then the Son must have the same life and thus have 'everything according to essence and absolutely as does the Father'.[59] Basil's strong emphasis on Father and Son language can also be seen in his insistence that the New Testament (and especially Paul) supplements Old Testament discussion of the Creator in every case with language that indicates the closeness of Father and Son. In distinguishing himself from Heterousian theology, Basil argues for a sharing of the existence in the Son's relationship to the Father. He argues for a sharing of existence in the Father's generation of the Son, but insists that this sharing does not involve material division or any sort of change in God.

Basil's council sent a delegation to the Emperor Constantius, who was at Sirmium, and this embassy met with success.[60] The Emperor wrote to the Church of Antioch condemning Eudoxius for taking

---

[57] Epiphanius, *Panarion* 73. 4. 4, See Steenson, *Basil of Ancyra*, 174–5. While Kopecek, for one, has argued for direct influence of Athanasius on Basil, there is no clear proof, and while it is certainly possible it is just as likely that his theology is primarily a development of earlier Eusebian tradition.

[58] Epiphanius, *Panarion* 73. 8. 6, 9. 4, 11. 2.   [59] Epiphanius, *Panarion* 73. 6. 7.

[60] See Hanson, *The Search*, 357 ff. Barnes, *Athanasius and Constantius*, 232, attempts to deny the existence of this meeting altogether. His arguments are strong, but not conclusive. Simonetti, *La Crisi*, 234 ff., offers a useful account of these events, and assumes the existence of the 358 Sirmium 'council'.

the see under the pretext of Constantius' support and for promoting Aetius and his teaching. Eudoxius, Aetius, and Eunomius were all exiled and in the letter Constantius writes, 'when we first made a declaration of our belief . . . we confessed that our Saviour is the Son of God, and of like substance with the Father (κατ' οὐσίαν ὅμοιος τῳ πατρί)'.[61] This might seem a fascinating volte-face on the part of Constantius, but it seems very likely that Basil had been able to convince Constantius that his statement was the natural implication of the Dedication creed, which might be understood as the first declaration by Constantius. At the same time, he probably argued that creeds drawing on the fourth Antiochene creed were themselves summaries of the Dedication creed and that it was the radical Homoians or Heterousians that were abandoning Constantius' own established tradition. Basil may also have connected this 'extremism' with civil disorder, at least in the sense of noting that Eudoxius was illegitimately claiming imperial support.[62] This meeting with Constantius appears also to have drawn up a dossier of key texts dating from the Dedication creed to circulate among other bishops and Basil wrote a letter, which is not extant, on the difference between *homoousios* and *homoiousios*. This letter was circulated west, however, and was one way in which Homoiousian theology became more widely known. Basil's influence was at its height.

CYRIL OF JERUSALEM

Before moving on to the events of 359–60, it will be helpful to consider one figure who is difficult to place in the standard categories of the fourth century. The difficulty we have in placing Cyril, bishop of Jerusalem from 348 until his death in 386 or 387, should help us to recognize that many bishops would have found themselves without direct 'party' commitment and able to shift allegiance as long as they felt their favourite terminologies and principles were upheld. Cyril's theology also shows us something further of how many could find themselves against the Athanasian/Marcellan theologies in the 340s and 350s—and thus suspicious of Nicaea's terms—but would eventually shift allegiance with the emergence of a more clearly

---

[61] Sozomen, *Hist. eccl.* 4. 14.

[62] Although we can make some general suppositions about Constantius' theological preferences, we can only guess about his development during these years. Moreover, although we can see that Constantius seems to have favoured certain bishops as advisers during his reign (on the question of whether some bishops were permanently in attendance, whether there were so-called 'court bishops' see E. D. Hunt, 'Did Constantius II Have "Court Bishops"?', *SP* 21 (1989), 86–90), we know little about the details of who was and who was not in favour at court.

expressed Homoian position and particularly with the emergence of Heterousian theology.[63]

Cyril's episcopal career was turbulent. He was initially promoted by Acacius of Caesarea, although he seems previously to have had the support of the preceding bishop of Jerusalem, Maximus, who was a supporter of Athanasius. Jerome tells us that Maximus had consecrated one Heraclius on his death-bed. Cyril had been installed as bishop in a counter move by Acacius, on condition that he renounced his previous allegiance to Maximus and to *his* predecessor Macarius.[64] Following these events doubts about the legitimacy of Cyril's tenure of the see seem to have frequently surfaced. Cyril eventually lost Acacius' support and was deposed in 357 (on the charge of selling Church furniture for poor relief!). He was reinstated by the majority at the Council of Seleucia (who, as we shall see, opposed Acacius and the Homoian creed) but then exiled in 360 along with the many deposed at that stage. Socrates and Sozomen present Cyril as a Homoiousian at this stage, although this probably means little more than that he voted with the majority. He was back in Jerusalem from 361 to 365 or 366 and then sent into exile again by Valens. At some point he seems to have returned and was probably back in charge of his see in 378. He was on the pro-Nicene side at Constantinople and lived to 386 or 387. The complexity of his career has often made him seem a maverick figure, or a 'moderate'. However, I suggest that it is actually more accurate to read him as one of those who held strongly to the emphases we see in many Eusebians (although he was happy to speak of the Son's eternal generation, unlike either Eusebius of Caesarea or Eusebius of Nicomedia) and in the Dedication creed. At the same time, his theology also has some strong parallels to that of Alexander of Alexandria, although he never seems to have been a supporter of Athanasius. Cyril demonstrates the problematic status even of the flexible categories I have tried to outline.

From his small surviving corpus the text that best displays his Trinitarian theology is his series of *Catechetical Lectures* possibly delivered in Lent 348 or 350. Cyril's doctrine of God is best

---

[63] Scholarship on Cyril's Trinitarian theology has frequently focused around the attempt to place his theology in unhelpful categories. See Hanson, *The Search*, 398–413; A. A. Stephenson, 'St. Cyril of Jerusalem's Trinitarian Theology', *SP* 11 (1972), 234–41; J. Lebon, 'La Position de Saint Cyrille de Jerusalem dans les luttes provoquées par l'arianisme', *Revue d'Histoire Ecclésiastique*, 20 (1924), 181–210, 357–86; Robert C. Gregg, 'Cyril of Jerusalem and the Arians', in Gregg (ed.), *Arianism: Historical and Theological Reassessments*, 85–109. Alexis Doval, *Cyril of Jerusalem, Mystagogue* (Washington DC: Catholic University of America Press, 2001), provides a great deal of useful material in the course of considering the authorship of the mystagogical catecheses.

[64] See Jerome, *Chronicle*, sub. Ann. Constantius XII. Hanson, *The Search*, 398–400 sets out the problem well.

understood by beginning where he begins: with the unity and transcendence of the one God, the Father. Cyril is insistent that there is one God, 'alone, unbegotten, without beginning, immutable, unchangeable . . .'. This God 'is not circumscribed (περιγέγραπται) in any place . . . He is in all things and about all'.[65] These quotations are from the fourth of the lectures, where Cyril summarizes his theology around ten key points of doctrine; in Lecture 6, he discusses God's μοναρχία, and gives a longer, but similar account:

(7) . . . [God] is One, a God who is, who is eternal, who is ever the self-same . . . Who is honoured under many names, is all-powerful, and uniform in hypostasis (καὶ μονοειδῆ τὴν ὑπόστασιν) . . . (9) He is one, everywhere present, seeing all things, understanding all things, fashioning all things through Christ. He is a fountainhead of all good, immense and unfailing, a stream of blessings, light eternal shining unceasingly . . .[66]

Cyril is also clear that the one God, the divine *hypostasis*, is incomprehensible,[67] he is the 'unsearchable'.

When Cyril speaks of 'the one God' he is very clear that he is speaking of the Father.[68] Indeed, God is eternally Father and the name 'Father' refers to God's essence.[69] Thus, for Cyril, to speak of the one God is immediately to speak of Father and Son; 'Father' implies the eternal existence of the correlative 'Son'. Although the Father is the 'sole principle' for Cyril, he consistently speaks of the Son as sharing the 'dignity (ἀξίωμα) of Godhead' with the Father. To understand this paradox we need to grasp how Cyril deploys the principle that the incomprehensible generation of the Son occurs in the context of the Father's immateriality and immutability.

In the eleventh of his lectures Cyril writes '[think of "Son"] in a true sense, that is, a Son by nature . . . a Son begotten from all eternity by an inscrutable and incomprehensible generation'.[70] Immediately following this quotation Cyril argues that although the Son is 'first-born' we cannot interpret this on a parallel with human first-borns whose birth involves a change of status: 'He was not begotten to be other than He was before.' Once again Cyril argues

---

[65] *Cat. lect.* 4. 4–5.   [66] *Cat. lect.* 6. 7–9.   [67] *Cat. lect.* 6. 5.

[68] *Cat. lect.* 4. 4–5, 7. 1–2. He insists that the name 'Father' distingushes Christian from Jewish faith.

[69] *Cat. lect.*, 7. 1–5: '. . . let us now . . . take up the saving doctrines of the true faith, joining to the dignity of the Unity of God that of the Fatherhood, and believing in One God, Father . . . (2) Thus our thought will rise to a higher plane than that of the Jews who, while they teach that God is One . . . do not admit that He is also Father of our Lord Jesus Christ . . . (4) The very mention of the name of the Father suggests the thought of the Son, just as, in turn, the mention of Son implies the thought of the Father. (5) . . . He did not attain Fatherhood in the course of time, but He is eternally Father of the Only-begotten. Not that he was Sonless before and afterwards became a Father by a change of purpose, but before all substance and all intelligence, before times and all the ages, God has the prerogative of Father . . .'.

[70] *Cat. lect.* 11. 4.

that the generation of the Son occurs in the context of the Father's immutability and eternity. A few lines later he writes:

As the Son of David, He is subject to time, and He is palpable and his descent reckoned; but in His Godhead He is subject neither to time nor place nor genealogical reckoning. For 'Who shall declare his generation?' 'God is Spirit'; He who is spirit begot spiritually, being incorporeal, by an unsearchable and incomprehensible generation (ἀκατάληπτον γέννησιν). For the Son Himself says of the Father: 'The Lord said to me, "you are my Son; this day I have begotten you (Ps. 2: 7)".' Now 'this day' is not recent, but eternal; 'this day' is timeless, before all ages. 'From the womb before the daystar I have begotten you.'[71]

Cyril also repeatedly uses X from X language—drawn from the creed of Jerusalem—to explain what it is for the generation of a 'true' Son to occur from the unchangeable and eternal Father. At 11. 4, explaining what it means for the Son to be Son eternally Cyril has already written,

... He was begotten Son from the beginning, Son of the Father, like in all things to his Genitor, begotten Life of Life, Light of Light, Truth of Truth, Wisdom of Wisdom, King of King, God of God, Power of Power.

Then at the end of 11. 8 we read,

... He has the Son eternally, having begot Him not as men beget men, but as He Himself alone knows who begot Him before all ages, true God. (9) Since the Father is true God He begot the Son like to Himself, true God ...

It is noticeable, however, that Cyril attempts to gloss his usage of X from X terminology; a little later in the same lecture he insists that the result of this generation is that the 'characteristics (χαρακτῆρες) of the Godhead are in the Son without variation (ἀπαράλλακτοι)'.[72] Thus, for Cyril X from X phraseology points to a continuity of attributes between Father and Son, not simply a derivation of lesser from greater: indeed he seems to see this X from X quality as itself indicating that the generation must be incomprehensible (and hence that it cannot be understood on analogy with material generation). It is thus through deploying an account of the Son's incomprehensible generation and God's immutability that Cyril argues for the *closeness* of Father and Son.

In his interpretation of X from X language we also see how Cyril tries to prevent the Son from being considered as a second God. At 11. 17 Cyril writes 'Therefore the Son is true God, having the Father in Himself, not changed into the Father ...'. Following

---

[71] *Cat. lect.* 11. 5. [72] *Cat. lect.* 11. 18.

through his insistence that the Father remains the one principle (ἀρχή), Cyril here characterizes the Son as being God because of the Father's presence or self-gift. At 6. 1 Cyril also speaks of the Son's glory as 'flowing' from the Father's. Thus the character of the Son's dependence on the Father as typified by X from X language serves to preserve the Father's μοναρχία.

Cyril constantly returns to the incomprehensibility of the Son's generation. At 11. 11 he culminates his argument that the Son is 'true' Son and his generation unlike any seemingly analogous generation we can think of by insisting that no one can speak of the *hypostasis* of the Father, not even the angels (*hypostasis* here seems to be used with the sense of 'nature' or 'being').[73] Following Isaiah 53: 8, we can only say what it is not. Cyril seems to envision the catechist shaping patterns of thought and speech that will promote continual awareness of where and how we speak, following Scripture, of that which is beyond comprehension. Sabellian accounts that confuse the Father and Son (Cyril probably has Marcellus in mind) insufficiently respect the true Sonship, while accounts that distinguish the two by the application of inappropriate material or temporal language claim too much by ignoring the nature of the divine existence.

This account of Cyril's concern with right speech seems borne out when we notice that he makes little use of any technical terminology for distinguishing Father and Son, but focuses on repeating the logic of the relationship:[74]

> Of One Only Father there is One Only-begotten Son: neither two unbegotten, nor two only-begotten; but one Father, unbegotten; and One Son, eternally begotten of the Father . . . Neither thinking to honour the Son, let us call him the Father, nor from thinking to honour the Father, imagine the Son to be one of the creatures. But let One Son be worshipped through One Son, and let not their worship be separated.

THE EVENTS OF AD 359–360

In AD 359 Constantius decided to emulate his father's action in calling Nicaea and summon a general council.[75] We do not know whether the idea for the council itself was his: he seems to have been

---

[73] At *Cat. lect.* 7. 5 Cyril also insists that the Father is only truly Father of the Son, and the divine Fatherhood is spoken of elsewhere only by extension. Once again Cyril emphasizes that language which seems to provide an account of or an analogical basis for describing the Son's generation fails so to do.

[74] *Ousia* language is almost entirely absent. Cyril does use *hypostasis* to indicate 'truly existing as a distinct reality' (e.g. at *Cat lect.* 11. 10–11, see quotation above), but seems resistant to using it as a technical term for the persons because he does not think it is so used in Scripture (*Cat. lect.* 16. 24).

[75] Sozomen, *Hist. eccl.* 4. 16.

prompted at least in part by Valens and Ursacius. Eventually—in consultation with Basil—he decided to hold twin councils in east and west. A small group of bishops met at Sirmium to draw up a draft creed for discussion.[76] Those present included not only Basil, but also some who were far more suspicious of *ousia* language. The creed on which they finally agreed asserts, on the one hand, that the Son is 'like the Father in all respects, as the Holy Scriptures also declare and teach'. On the other hand, it asserts that all *ousia* language should be avoided, because it was inserted in the creed of Nicaea 'though not familiar to the masses', because it caused 'disturbance', and because it is unscriptural.

The creed caused Basil of Ancyra some difficulty and he only signed by adding, after his name, that this 'likeness' was also according to 'being' (τὸ εἶναι). Thus, although Basil of Ancyra was influential with the imperial authorities at one point during 358–9, it was not for long, and he never seems fully to have overcome longstanding Homoian influence at court.[77] Basil (and perhaps Constantius) may well have thought that a compromise could be reached between Basil's party and the more radical Homoians such as Acacius: in retrospect this creed seems to show how unlikely such a compromise already was. This creed is known as the 'Dated creed' because the prologue identifies the date of its promulgation and later pro-Nicene writers—taking every polemical opportunity afforded them—ridiculed the idea that a true creed had a date and was not simply true for all time!

Immediately following the letter from Basil of Ancyra that he preserves, Epiphanius also preserves a letter probably composed by George of Laodicea (or by George and Basil). The question of authorship may be an impossible one to settle with certainty, but the text was clearly written between the Dated creed and the opening of the Council of Seleucia in the autumn of 359.[78] In this letter, George primarily attacks the emerging Heterousians, but treats them as the logical term of the emerging Homoian theology. Towards the end of the text he sums up his opponents' teaching with the pithy 'like in

---

[76] The creed was originally published in Latin, but survives only in Greek at Athanasius, *Synod.* 8 and Socrates, *Hist. eccl.* 2. 37. See Hanson, *The Search*, 363–4.

[77] For an account of the influence Basil did have see Winrich Löhr, 'A Sense of Tradition: The Homoiousian Church Party', in Michel Barnes and Daniel H. Williams (eds.), *Arianism after Arius* (Edinburgh: T. & T. Clark, 1993), 81–100.

[78] The letter is preserved at Epiphanius, *Panarion* 73. 12. 1 ff. This precise dating appears probable on two pieces of internal evidence. First at 73. 14. 8 George speaks of 'those from the east who went up to Sirmium last year' refuting the Heterousians: this can only refer to the 358 meeting of Homoiousians with Constantius. Second, at 73. 22. 5 George refers clearly to the signatories of the 'Dated' creed, insisting that they signed up to 'like the Father in all things', whatever they actually professed. This charge would have little force once the creed of Niké/Constantinople was in effect at the end of 359 without this phrase.

will, unlike in essence' and argues that it is on the basis of this teaching that they seek to remove the word essence from discussion.[79] George then argues that this is illogical given that they have signed a creed that describes the Son as 'like the Father in all respects'.[80]

George also offers an extensive defence of essence language and an account of the Father/Son relationship that shows how close the Homoiousians had come to the language of pro-Nicene orthodoxy that we will examine in later chapters. While *ousia* is not used of God in Old or New Testaments, it is, he argues, implied throughout the Scriptures. The term has been drawn out explicitly because Paul of Samosata and the Sabellians denied the real existence of Father and Son. Thus George presents Heterousians as misunderstanding the prophylactic value of the term and sets the stage for showing how they too misunderstand the relationship of Father and Son.[81] Father is a name superior to that of 'ingenerate' because it signifies the power of God in generating a Son, not only that the Father has not been begotten. The Son was begotten 'perfect from perfect, before every concept and all processes of reasoning and times and ages'. In an attempt to defend the terminology of 'three *hypostases*' George argues that the easterners who use this terminology speak of God as 'one divinity and one kingship (βασιλεία) and one principle', but also 'recognize the persons (πρόσωπα) in the properties (ἰδιότητες) of the *hypostases*'. The one godhead 'encompasses' all things through the Son in the Spirit (ἐμπεριέχουσαν δι' υἱοῦ ἐν πνεύματι ἁγίῳ τὰ πάντα).[82] Much of this terminology we will meet again shortly in Basil of Caesarea: here we need to note here only that George struggles to offer a coherent account of the equality and differences between the persons.

In the following passage, which comes just a little later in the letter, one can almost sense the struggle for a clarity not yet achieved:

... inasmuch indeed as he is spirit from spirit, [he] is the same as the ⟨Father⟩ (just as inasmuch as he is flesh from Mary's flesh ⟨he is the same as human beings⟩), but inasmuch as he was begotten from the Father without effluence, passion and partition he is like the Father and is not himself ⟨the Father just as also⟩ the Son in the flesh is in the likeness of men and is not himself in every respect man.[83]

George goes on to say that as far as the 'concept' (ἔννοια—*ennoia*, a term we can take as virtually synonymous with ἐπίνοια) of spirit goes

---

[79] Epiphanius, *Panarion* 73. 22. 1–3.   [80] Epiphanius, *Panarion* 73. 22. 5 ff.
[81] Epiphanius, *Panarion* 73. 12. 1–6. Note also that at 73. 19. 3 George also insists on the correlativity of the terms Father and Son over against ingenerate and generate.
[82] Epiphanius, *Panarion* 73. 16. 3–4.   [83] Epiphanius, *Panarion* 73. 17. 5.

the Son is the same as the Father, just as according to the ἔννοια of flesh he is the same as us. In statements such as this George reveals himself to have something like a later two-natured Christology, but also that he has difficulty defining in what way the Father and Son are 'alike'.

Like Basil of Ancyra, George emphasizes the real sharing of existence in the generation of the Son but also the distinction between Father and Son. He does not seem to contemplate later insistence that at the level of personal properties the persons are distinct, while sharing in one essence. The Homoiousians could not yet see how the order and distinction of the persons could be maintained if they were the same in essence. They seem to have been worried that 'sameness' of essence implies a material notion of division and identity of substance.[84] It is noticeable that even while George deploys the language of three *hypostases* but one divinity he struggles to articulate an order among the persons that will ensure the Father's superiority to Son and Spirit. There seems for George to be a sense in which because the Son shares the Father's attributes derivatively the Father remains ontologically superior.

The two councils met in 359: the eastern council at Seleucia in Cilicia (near Antioch), the western at Ariminum in northern Italy (modern Rimini).[85] The western council met first, towards the end of May 359. Valens and Ursacius tried to get the council to adopt a creed virtually identical to the Dated creed without success: a majority of those present voted in favour of retaining the creed of Nicaea and not introducing any new creed. We should be careful of assuming that this preference reveals a detailed understanding of Nicaea: it probably reflects a growing suspicion that those who were pushing the Dated creed understood its somewhat vague terminology in subordinationist senses they found unacceptable. Nicaea was the obvious alternative, the most appropriate cipher for their own sensibilities. The council possibly also condemned the temporal

---

[84] See Steenson, 'Basil of Ancyra on the Meaning of *Homoousios*' for this problem. Part of the difficulty stems from the comment of Sozomen, *Hist. eccl.* 3. 18, that the Homoiousians thought that spiritual substances could only be ὅμοιος, not *homoousios*. Sozomen probably means that Homoiousians saw *homoousios* as a term which appropriately describes material beings of the same class and is thus inappropriate in non-material contexts. On this basis Steenson argues that 'identity' means sharing the same ontological status, not being the same 'thing'. As I have argued at a number of points in the book, while Steenson is certainly right in some circumstances, critique of *homoousios* was interwoven with critique of those of Nicaea's supporters (such as Marcellus) who seemed to give Nicaea's terms a modalist twist: this may have led to *homoousios* also being criticized as implying the identity of Father and Son.

[85] See Hanson, *The Search*, 371–86, Simonetti, *La Crisi*, 313–49. The best account of the Council of Ariminum is in Williams, *Ambrose of Milan*, 18 ff. See also Brennecke, *Geschichte*, 23 ff.

Shaping the Alternatives AD 350–360

generation of the Son and adoptionism.[86] Valens, Ursacius, and their associates were excommunicated and the council then sent a delegation to the Emperor in Adrianople. Those of the minority party sent their own delegation.

Constantius kept this delegation waiting for some weeks in midsummer and eventually had them moved to the town of Niké in Thrace, apparently because of its resemblance to 'Nicaea'. After much pressure the delegates of the majority at Ariminum accepted the Dated creed excepting only the phrase 'in all things' used to qualify the Son's likeness to the Father. The delegates returned west and much time was spent convincing the majority to change their minds. After a few weeks the opposition to this creed was very small. How did this reversal come about? Two factors help to explain what happened.

First, the lack of a clear sense that Nicaea was a unique cipher for orthodox theology meant that they were susceptible to the argument that the newly proposed creed might serve as a cipher for that very same theology. Second, deceit and imperial pressure combined to influence the bishops. We know that Constantius made it clear he was willing to exile those who resisted, and it seems also that the bishops were told that the eastern council had already agreed to this new creed.[87] At the same time, there seems to have been an important case of fraud perpetrated, in this case by Valens. During this second session of the council Valens publicly professed a series of anti-'Arian' anathemas, in particular insisting that he did not think the Son to be a creature. This profession helped to reassure some that the new creed was not intended as a cipher for such positions, but Valens is reported to have later insisted that he meant only that the Son was not a creature *like the other creatures*. This small incident seems to confirm the view common in the west very soon after the council that those who originally wanted to hold to Nicaea had been duped: the new creed could be interpreted as representing the concerns of these western bishops, but that was not the intention of its framers.

The eastern council met in September of 359 and was divided between those around Acacius and Eudoxius who were keen to promulgate a new creed as the universal faith of the empire, and a larger party (if the later historians are to be trusted) sympathetic to those

---

[86] See Y. M. Duval, 'Traduction latine inédite du symbole de Nicée et une condamnation d'Arius à Rimini: Nouveau fragment historique d'Hilaire ou pièces des actes du concile?', *Revue Bénédictine*, 82 (1972), 7–25; Williams, *Ambrose of Milan*, 24–5.

[87] On the question of fraud surrounding this second session of Ariminum see Williams, *Ambrose of Milan*, 26 ff.; Y. M. Duval, 'La "Manœuvre fraudulense" de Rimini à la recherche du Liber adversus Ursacium et Valentem,' in *Hilaire et son temps: Actes du colloque de Poitiers, 29 septembre – 3 octobre* (Paris, 1969), 51–103.

bishops who had recently stood with Basil of Ancyra.[88] Basil himself was not initially one of the leaders at the council: in circumstances that remain unclear Basil had been accused of a misdemeanour of some sort which prevented his participation in the initial discussion—or he failed to arrive at the first session to forestall such an accusation. Hilary of Poitiers was present and provides us with a few more details, insisting that there were also a number of Egyptian bishops present who favoured the *homoousios*, and that among the Homoians there were also some with Heterousian sympathies.[89]

In the initial discussion a majority affirmed the Dedication creed of 341. A couple of days later Basil joined the discussion against the protestations of Acacius' party. Acacius himself then presented a creed very much like the Dated creed. The text begins with an affirmation of the acceptability in principle of the Dedication creed, but goes on to state the importance now of moving beyond dispute over *ousia* terms—*homoousios*, *homoiousios*, and ἀνόμοιος (dissimilar) are all mentioned. Presumably the Dedication creed is seen as unsuitable because of its description of the Son as image of the *ousia* of the Father. The final sentence of the introduction holds up ὅμοιος as an alternative and quotes Col. 1: 15 in support.[90] The creed ends by stating its own compatibility with '[that] which was published recently at Sirmium'—that is, the Dated creed—but unlike that creed contains a list of titles: 'Word ... light, life, truth, wisdom power'. This list seems intentionally to echo the style of the Dedication creed. The complex moves and negotiations described here present a wonderful example of the attempts of these two evolving 'parties' to exert a claim over a common past.

We also see here the very fluidity of credal formulation in the early fourth century becoming an open point of appeal. Acacius claims that his opponents' appeal to the Dedication creed as a fixed point of reference makes little sense. Socrates reports Acacius as saying, 'since the Nicene creed has been altered not once only, but frequently, there is no hindrance to our publishing another at this time'.[91] Socrates then reports a telling comment by Eleusis of Cyzicus (a prominent Homoiousian bishop): 'the synod is at present convened not to learn what it had no previous knowledge of, nor to receive a creed which it had not assented to before, but to confirm

---

[88] Brennecke, *Geschichte*, 40 ff. is particularly helpful on Seleucia.
[89] Hilary, *C. Const.* 12.
[90] The linkage implied is, presumably, that ὅμοιος most accurately captures the import of εἰκών at Col. 1: 15.
[91] Socrates, *Hist. eccl.* 2. 40.

the faith of the fathers ...'.[92] The response is in part a lame one. Eleusis cannot offer a refutation of Acacius' basic point, he can only shift the ground of the argument, questioning whether or not Acacius' creed reflects 'the faith of the fathers', the ultimate point at issue.

Acacius' mention of Nicaea leads to the topic of how Nicaea itself was perceived at this council. The question is important because Socrates presents the initial discussion as a dispute over Nicaea: while Acacius opposed Nicaea, the other faction concurred 'in all the decisions of Nicaea, but criticized its adoption of *homoousion*'.[93] This is a difficult statement to interpret: it seems unlikely that the 'Homoiousians' introduced the Nicene creed for discussion. Socrates' also seems dependent on Athanasius' very similar description at *De synodis* 12. In that text, as we will see in the next chapter, Athanasius had already begun to cast Ariminium/Seleucia as an attempt to overturn Nicaea, and he had already begun to shape an account of the Homoiousians as willing to acknowledge Nicaea apart from a (misguided) reservation about *homoousios*.

Nevertheless, it seems clear from Acacius' words that the status of this meeting in distinction to that of Nicaea *was* in some way at issue. Given that these two councils were understood by Constantius and presumably by his ecclesiastical advisers as mirroring Nicaea, it is not unlikely that some of the Homoiousians did argue that the Dedication creed was not simply the best available summary of the faith but that it was itself just a restatement of Nicaea. Such an argument would have been only a short step from their previous attempts to present their own theology genealogically as preserving the legacy of Antioch 341. Thus, I suggest we hear in our sources echoes of a debate about the credal direction of the previous few decades and about the relationship of this process to Nicaea itself. That the question of Nicaea appeared at this point is not surprising given the events of the preceding decade: the emergence of a Homoian theology that rejected all *ousia* language; the increasingly sophisticated defence of Nicaea's terminology in Athanasius; the turn to Nicaea among some western theologians in the face of Constantius' policies.[94]

---

[92] Socrates, *Hist. eccl.* 2. 40. Socrates here is openly relying on the now lost collection of texts compiled by Sabinus of Heracleia, who had access to the *acta* of the council.

[93] Socrates, *Hist. eccl.* 2. 39.

[94] I further suggest (*a*) that Athanasius' presentation of the Homoiousians at the council as agreeing with Nicaea save the *homoousion may* actually reflect their own genealogical arguments in this context or in the months before: not in the sense that they wanted to introduce Nicaea's creed, but that they presented themselves as upholding the 'faith' represented, however insufficiently, by Nicaea; (*b*) that Hilary's description of the Homoiousians as being acceptable because of their insistence that the Son's generation 'from God' should be

II. The Emergence of Pro-Nicene Theology

Returning to the story of the council: Acacius' creed was ultimately rejected by the majority of those present. The next day one of the imperial officials overseeing the council attempted to dissolve it, to no avail. The majority met, ostensibly to adjudicate a dispute between Acacius and Cyril of Jerusalem, but Acacius and his supporters refused to attend. This meeting then deposed Acacius and a number of other bishops. Each group sent embassies to the Emperor in Constantinople. The Homoian delegation arrived first and agreed to a modified version of the Dated creed. After much pressure, in part involving assuring the bishops that the western council had unanimously agreed to this creed, the Homoiousian delegation finally agreed on the last night of 359.

Early in 360 a small council was held in Constantinople to ratify the decisions of Ariminum and Seleucia. This council was presided over by Acacius and seems to have been composed of mostly local bishops.[95] The main act of the meeting beyond ratifying the creed was to depose a series of figures, especially those associated with Basil and the Homoiousians. At this point Eudoxius became bishop of Constantinople after Macedonius was deposed and Eunomius was made bishop of Cyzicus. The Homoian creed of Niké/Constantinople ran as follows:

We believe in one God, Father Almighty, from whom are all things; And in the only-begotten Son of God, begotten from God before all ages and before every beginning, by whom all things were made, visible and invisible, and begotten as only-begotten, the only from the only Father, God from God, like to the Father who generated him, according to the Scriptures; whose origin no one knows, except the Father who generated him. As we know, this only-begotten Son of God came forth from the heavens, as it is written, for the undoing of sin and death, and was born from the Holy Spirit, and from Mary the virgin according to the flesh, as it is written, and taught the disciples and fulfilled the whole economy according to the Father's will, was crucified, died and was buried, and descended into the underworld, at whom Hades itself shuddered; who also rose from the dead on the third day and lived with the apostles, and when forty days were fulfilled was taken up into heaven and sits on the right hand of the Father to come in the last day of the resurrection in the Father's glory, to give to each according to their deeds.

And [we believe] in the Holy Spirit, whom the only-begotten Son of God, the Christ, the Lord and the God of us promised to send to the race of men as Paraclete, as it is written; 'the Spirit of truth' whom he sent to them when he ascended into the heavens.

understood as 'from the substance of God', may reflect another aspect of the discussion around Seleucia: the Homoiousians may well have presented this conception as the core insight, going back to Nicaea itself, that their theology preserved.

[95] See Sozomen, *Hist. eccl.* 4. 24–6; Socrates, *Hist. eccl.* 2. 42; Brennecke, *Geschichte*, 48 ff.

But the word *ousia*, which was simplistically put down by the Fathers, being unknown to the people, has become a scandal, because the Scriptures do not contain it, we have decided should be removed and that there should be absolutely no mention of it at all, since the Holy Scriptures never mention the *ousia* of the Father and the Son. For neither should *hypostasis* concerning the Father, the Son, and the Holy Spirit be used. But we say that the Son is like the Father as the Holy Scriptures say and teach. And all the heresies, those which have already been previously condemned, and any others which have recently begun, contrary to the creed set out here, let them be anathema.[96]

From this creed the phrase 'in all things' that appeared in the Dated creed has disappeared. All *ousia* language is strongly rejected. The creed also seems to move against the fourth Antiochene creed. The fourth Antiochene creed used traditional X from X language, especially 'God from God, light from light'. While this new creed uses 'God from God', the only other use of X from X language seems designed to indicate the difference between Father and Son. Thus 'the only from the only Father' uses as its common term μόνος (alone or only) to emphasize that the generation of the Son results in two distinct beings. In this context, other key terms such as 'only-begotten Son of God', function to distinguish the Son very clearly from the Father. It seems most likely that this is an anti-Homoiousian credal tactic. The Homoians appear to have recognized both the ambiguity in traditional X from X language and that the Homoiousians were making a claim on the past two decades of eastern credal tradition very different from their own. The creed of 360 is a deliberate attempt to render unorthodox any other way of construing that tradition than their own.

The events of 359–60 in part mark the victory of Homoian theology. Despite the turmoil of the next few years, this creed remained the imperially sanctioned statement of orthodoxy for almost two decades (especially clearly in the east). Nevertheless, this 'victory' was achieved in the face of widespread resistance. The attempts of eastern Homoians at Constantinople 360 to follow up their victory with depositions of those who seem to have represented the majority at Seleucia can only have served to reinforce the perception that whatever the supposed compromise qualities of this creed it was not so intended by its framers. The victory was thus a Pyrrhic one whose main effect may have been to promote increasingly clear thinking about the issues that divided the Homoians from a whole variety of different trajectories and thinkers: Athanasius; many western theologians; the Homoiousians. That this division had

---

[96] Athanasius, *Synod.* 30.

become increasingly clear was one thing: whether those groups would be able to find sufficient common ground and willingness to overcome the conflict of the previous decades and make common cause was as yet unclear.

7
The Beginnings of Rapprochement

INTRODUCTION

A year after the Homoian triumph of 360 much suddenly changed. Constantius died from a sudden illness as he moved west to suppress a rebellion by his cousin Julian. He was only 44. Just as Constantius' control over both east and west shaped the course of the controversies considerably during the 350s, so his death radically changed their course at the beginning of the new decade. But even without Constantius' death, the architects of Homoian theology do not seem to have had the widespread support that would have enabled them to gain wide-ranging acceptance of the 360 creed. Many were unconvinced by claims that this creed was a compromise enabling an end to the controversies of the previous decades. The course of the 350s seemed to demonstrate that the Homoian leaders intended to use the creed as a cipher for a highly subordinationist theology that excluded not only Athanasian theologies but also theologies of a broadly Homoiousian nature. Under the 'Homoiousian' banner we can, as I argued in the last chapter, place many of those who voted with them at Seleucia, agreeing with their view of tradition and valuing the same traditional phraseology, but not necessarily having anything invested in *homoiousios* as a credal term. Thus, just as we see a Homoian victory, we also begin to see an increasing number willing to adopt Nicaea as a standard during the early 360s. These years also see shifts in understandings of what it means to adopt a creed as a standard. Constantius' policies focused attention much more clearly on the precise wording of creeds and on their possible function as binding identifiers of orthodox belief. Although there was much development still to come, these years begin to see the emergence of a sense of credal function very different from anything imagined in 325.

In the period after 360, we also begin to see the emergence of what I have termed throughout the book so far 'pro-Nicene' theology: theologies which contain new arguments for or pro Nicaea. Towards the end of Chapter 9 I define the term more carefully: for the moment three points will suffice. First, I use the term primarily to describe the full flowering of this theology in the 380s. Second, I also use the term to refer to the precursors of that theology which emerged during the late 350s and 360s and developed during the 370s. Third, I take this theology to be in continuity with many previous emphases, but not to be simply the continuation of a one original Nicene theology surviving unchanged since 325. In some cases pro-Nicene theologies emerge from older Nicene theologies, in other cases these theologies emerge from traditions originally opposed to those older Nicene theologies.

Before we embark on the story of these developments, we need to note that the course of theological development during the period from 360–80 is frequently uncertain. Surviving records during this period are particularly unclear and difficult to synthesize. At least in part this is because the fifth-century ecclesiastical historians did not narrate the process by which their heroes (such bishops as Basil of Caesarea) developed their support for pro-Nicene theology. Rather, these later historians present such figures as always holding to their mature opinions, even when they leave us enough hints to know that this is not so.

Through this chapter and the next two, some sections characterize the period in fairly general terms, while others focus on significant events about which we are better informed and which can serve as windows onto the wider nature of the developments in this period. In this way I hope to make clear the complexity of the historiographical choices that must be made when one moves from narrating these particular episodes to offer general characterizations. My own account chooses in particular to emphasize the slow process of rapprochement between parties that seems to mark these two decades. In this chapter, after a general sketch of imperial politics during these years, I turn to Athanasius' work and activities after 359–60, events in the west, and to the work of Hilary of Poitiers.

CHURCH AND EMPEROR: AD 360–378

When Constantius died in 361 his immediate successor was his cousin Julian.[1] Julian had been appointed by Constantius to rule the western half of the empire at the end of 355 as Constantius' subordinate Caesar but had, in 360, proclaimed himself co-emperor (Augustus). In a move that prevented further war, Constantius bequeathed the empire to Julian on his death-bed. As Emperor, Julian soon became an active non-Christian, repudiating the Christianity that he had earlier professed. In his attempt to undermine the Church Julian tried to foment dissension between groups in the

---

[1] Julian's reign is described in *CAH*, xiii, ch. 2, pp. 44–77. See also G. Bowersock, *Julian the Apostate* (Cambridge, Mass.: Harvard University Press, 1978).

Church—initially by recalling all bishops who had been banished under Constantius.

After Julian's death in 363 (and the sudden death of his immediate successor Jovian, who briefly seemed to many to support the pro-Nicene cause), Constantius' most powerful successors emerged: in the east the Emperor Valens (364–78); in the west the Emperor Valentinian (364–75).[2] While Valens supported a broadly Homoian position, Valentinian had much greater sympathy for the Nicene position, but also took a light-handed approach, refusing to support strongly even the party he favoured. Although Valens, like Constantius, has gone down in history as an 'Arian' emperor he, again like Constantius, was a pragmatic ruler prepared to promote Homoians when possible, but not at any great cost to his civil administration.[3] Valens' pragmatism is evident in his eventual acceptance of Athanasius' position in Alexandria and in his ambiguous relationship with Basil of Caesarea, accepting Basil's significant role in the Church of Asia Minor while still offering support to the Homoian interests that worked against his growing influence. Valens was considerably more hostile towards Heterousian theology. At least in part this hostility must reflect the opinions of his theological advisers—bishops such as Eudoxius and Acacius. While we read the fourth century so easily in terms of a battle between Nicenes and their opponents, it is important to remember that differences between non-Nicenes were equally important.[4]

In 365–6 Valens faced a serious military revolt by one of Julian's generals, Procopius. During this rebellion Valens recalled bishops that had been exiled (including Athanasius) in the hopes of securing wider support. In such circumstances pragmatism overcame general support for the Homoians. Valens' pragmatism provides an important key for understanding theological developments in this period. Open and large-scale challenge to the Homoian creed would have been impossible in the east: the creed of 359–60 was maintained as a

---

[2] For an introduction to Valens and Valentinian see *CAH*, xiii. 80–101. On the relations between Valentinian and western bishops see Williams, *Ambrose of Milan*, ch. 3. The events surrounding the death of Valens in 378 are covered in Ch. 9.

[3] Central to interpreting Valens' religious policy is now Brennecke, *Geschichte*, 181–242. Brennecke strongly emphasizes the pragmatism of Valens in contrast to what he sees as the exclusivism of his successor Theodosius.

[4] It is, of course, extremely difficult to try and give any account of the relative strengths of the various parties and the regions in which they were strongest. In part this is simply because many bishops in smaller cities seem to have avoided too strong or open a commitment to changing parties and were able to negotiate a position that enabled them to withstand changes in ecclesiastical and imperial regimes. We can with some certainty identify the Heterousians as the smallest of the parties. Brennecke, *Geschichte*, 186–201 brings together much of the surviving evidence and sketches the disposition of forces. Brennecke's account is useful but still problematic precisely because of the paucity of evidence.

II. The Emergence of Pro-Nicene Theology

universal standard. However, underneath or alongside this public Homoian ascendancy theological discussion continued and the period saw a steadily strengthening group of those who recognized the creed of Nicaea as a superior standard to Constantius' creed. Local and provincial councils continued to be held, and we know that at some the Nicene creed was adopted as a standard of faith. Thus, in considering this period we should remember that the dislocations of Julian's reign meant that Valens' attempt to impose the Homoian creed after 363 was considerably more difficult than it might have been for Constantius had he lived. There had been no time for the Homoians to consolidate their power and Julian had afforded their opponents every opportunity to regroup and realign.

One key example of the shifts in allegiance and self-understanding that mark this period—and of the fluid nature of those shifts—is found in the fate of the Homoiousians after 360. Sozomen reports that after the death of Constantius some Homoiousians held a number of councils which affirmed the creeds of 341 and condemned Acacius and the 360 creed.[5] After the death of Julian a council of Homoiousians met at Lampsacus.[6] This council decided to send a deputation to Valentinian (who was technically the senior emperor) to seek the reversal of Constantinople 360. Although they were unable to meet with Valentinian, they travelled to Rome and made peace with Liberius. They did so by wording a confession of faith including the Nicene creed and its anathemas.[7] Liberius sent with them a letter that was read and accepted at a council held (probably) in 366 at Tyana in Cappadocia, which also endorsed Nicaea.[8] The leaders at Tyana then tried to convene a larger council in the east at Tarsus following this meeting but were prevented by Valens under the advice of Eudoxius.

These events demonstrate that many of the leading Homoiousians saw that the time was ripe for realignment and were prepared to go to some lengths to gain support against the Homoians. We should, however, be wary of assuming that the acceptance of Nicaea documented here represents a permanent or even a majority decision. Some Homoiousians were prepared to acknowledge Nicaea to gain friends against the Homoians, but that does not mean they yet saw Nicaea's terminology as preferable to that of the Dedication

---

[5] Sozomen, *Hist. eccl.* 5. 14.

[6] The dating of this council is difficult: see Hanson, *The Search*, 763 n. 128; Brennecke, *Geschichte*, 206 ff.

[7] The text carried west by this embassy and Liberius' reply are preserved at Socrates, *Hist. eccl.* 4. 12.

[8] See Socrates, *Hist. eccl.* 4. 12; Sozomen, *Hist. Eccl.* 6. 11. Only Sozomen refers to Tyana, listing those present (including Gregory Nazianzen the elder). See also Jospeh Hefele, *Histoire de Conciles*, i/2 (Paris: Letouzey et Ané, 1907), 973–9.

The Beginnings of Rapprochement

creed. Some would later repudiate Nicaea when opportunity arose in the mid-370s, others would gradually become defenders of Nicaea. The complex shifts in allegiance among the Homoiousians that we see in these events are both a general indication of the realignment under way and, in particular, the creation of a basis for new alliances to emerge.

ATHANASIUS AND THE BEGINNINGS OF RAPPROCHEMENT

Over the years 359–61 Athanasius wrote his *De synodis* (*On the Councils of Ariminum and Seleucia*). During these years, Athanasius was in hiding in Egypt but seems to have been able to communicate easily with his supporters. The first two-thirds of the *De synodis* describe events at the twin councils of Ariminum/Seleucia and locate those events as the culmination of a story that began with Arius. This section of the text may well have been written sometime in 359–60 and then revised later when the final section was added, perhaps in 361, after the final results of the councils and the anti-Homoiousian action of 360.

In the first section of the text, the majority of those present at Seleucia are represented as being opposed to Acacius, as willing to accept Nicaea except for doubts about *homoousios*, and Athanasius specifically mentions George of Laodicea.[9] At this point Athanasius is disparaging about their actions at Seleucia and their willingness to co-operate with the 'Arians' under Acacius. However, in the last section of the *De synodis* Athanasius takes a more eirenic line, and claims that he and they fundamentally teach the same doctrine.[10] In this section of the text Athanasius both argues against 'Arians' and reaches out to the Homoiousians by attempting to refute their objections to Nicaea's two uses of *ousia* language, 'of the Father's *ousia*' and *homoousios*. His argument follows the path laid out in the *De decretis*.[11] The phrase 'of the Father's *ousia*' is again the focus of discussion and Athanasius again argues that it protects the difference between the generation of the Son as it is described in Scripture and the creation of all else.[12] *Homoousios* is defended as a necessary consequence of the phrase 'of the Father's *ousia*'. Athanasius then seeks to expose as hypocrisy the charge that this

---

[9] Athanasius' pragmatism needs to be noted. Some theologians were unwilling to go this far. Marius Victorinus, for example, although possibly writing before Constantius' death, attacks Homoiousian theology mercilessly, e.g. *Adv. Ar.* IA, III, 1 ff.

[10] Athanasius, *Synod.* 12.

[11] See Ch. 6.

[12] e.g. Athanasius, *Synod.* 35: '. . . it is all one to say rightly "from God", and to say "from the essence". For all the creatures, though they be said to have come into being from God, yet are not from God as the Son is . . .'.

172   *II. The Emergence of Pro-Nicene Theology*

terminology is non-scriptural, because Acacius and Eusebius of Caeasarea were willing to sign up to 'exact image of the Father's *ousia*' in the Dedication creed of 341.

At *De synodis* 41, Athanasius argues that those 'who accept everything else that was defined at Nicaea, and doubt only about *homoousios*' are not to be condemned as 'Ariomaniacs'. He continues with this fascinating argument:

> For confessing that the Son is from the essence of the Father (ἐκ τῆς οὐσίας τοῦ πατρός), and not from another subsistence (*hypostasis*), and that he is not a creature (κτίσμα) nor work (ποίημα), but His genuine and natural offspring, and that He is eternally with the Father as being His Word and Wisdom, they are not far from accepting even the phrase *homoousios*. Now such is Basil, who wrote from Ancyra concerning the faith. For only to say 'like according to essence' (ὅμοιον κατ' οὐσίαν) is very far from signifying 'of the essence' ... But since they say that he is 'of the essence' and 'like in essence', what do they signify by these but *homoousios*?[13]

Athanasius also notes that this party insists terms used of God are not used with any material connotation.[14]

If Athanasius is speaking of Basil's 358 synodal letter (and although we see strong echoes of that letter, we cannot be certain), then we should note that the 358 letter *never* speaks of the Son being born 'of the Father's *ousia*'. Basil speaks of the Father being a Father 'of an essence like himself' (ὁμοίας ἑαυτῷ οὐσίας)[15] and seems consciously to avoid Nicaea's terminology (Epiphanius, in his commentary takes this phrase to be an intentional denial of *homoousios* although he too sees Homoiousian theology as almost pro-Nicene).[16] It is also noticeable that Athanasius studiously avoids commenting on the 358 letter's direct anathematization of *homoousios*.

However, in what is for him an extremely charitable reading, Athanasius has grasped a central dynamic of Basil's argument. We

---

[13] Athanasius, *Synod.* 41.

[14] For an example of this standard Athanasian argument here see esp. Athanansius, *Synod.* 41–2: 'For the Son is the Father's Word and Wisdom; whence we learn the impassibility and indivisibility of such a generation from the Father. For not even man's word is part of him, nor proceeds from him according to passion; much less God's Word; whom the Father has declared to be his own Son, lest, on the other hand, if we merely heard of "Word", we should suppose him, such as is the word of man, impersonal; but that hearing that He is Son, we may acknowledge Him to be living Word and substantive wisdom. (42) Accordingly, as in saying "offspring". We have no human thoughts, and, though we know God to be a Father, we entertain no material ideas concerning Him, but while we listen to these illustrations and terms, we think suitably of God, for He is not as man, so in like manner, when we hear "co-essential" we ought to transcend all sense, and, according to the Proverb, "understand by the understanding what is set before us" (Prov. 23: 1).'

[15] e.g. at Epiphanius, *Panarion* 73. 4. 4: '... "Father" does not mean the Father of an activity but of an essence (*ousia*) like himself, whose subsistence (*hypostasis*) corresponds with a particular activity (ἐνέργεια).'

[16] Epiphanius, *Panarion* 73. 36. 1.

can see that dynamic in one place where Basil does comes close to saying 'of the Father's *ousia*':

(7. 6) as Wisdom is Son of the Wise one, essence of essence (οὐσία οὐσίας), in this way the image of an essence is like it.[17]

Basil here argues that essence language is the most appropriate way to defend one of the very terms for the Son that Athanasius himself had long argued can only be protected by essence language. Basil and his supporters developed such arguments because the more radical Homoians seemed to be directly contradicting the long-standing insistence on the part of many eastern theologians that the Father's generation of the Son enabled a mirroring or even sharing in the Father's existence. Athanasius thus accurately reads Basil as following a theological path increasingly parallel to his own and is prepared to look beyond the large terminological difference between them. Athanasius' shift in the last third of the *De synodis* involves the rewriting of his own narrative of events since the 340s—although he never acknowledges that this is so even as he continues to narrate the history of the 'Arian' conspiracy: he now simply separates one group as only belonging to that tradition for political reasons. Narrative is, as ever, a subtle tool in Athanasius' hands.

After returning from exile in 361 (following Constantius' death), Athanasius called a council in Alexandria in 362.[18] Two documents survive from this council, showing us another stage in Athanasius' strategy of rapprochement. The first is the 'Catholic Epistle', only recently identified as a genuine document from the council. This text sets out some basic rules for re-establishing communion with bishops who had subscribed to the decisions of Ariminum and Seleucia. The council took the pragmatic decision to set fairly minimum conditions focused around subscription to Nicaea and an acknowledgement of the spirit's divinity.[19] This strategy follows the realization that many had subscribed to the Homoion creed without great conviction. This new policy recognizes both that Nicaea was the only obvious rallying point in opposition to the Homoion creed, but it also recognizes that Nicaea would have to draw together a number of different theologies as yet only heading towards convergence. The council designated bishops to carry its decisions to as many eastern and western bishops as possible, and that appears to

---

[17] Epiphanius, *Panarion* 73. 7. 6. Cf. 73. 8. 7.

[18] These events will probably remain confusing, see Hanson, *The Search*, 639 ff.; Barnes, *Athanasius and Constantius*, 155 ff.; Simonetti, *La Crisi*, 358 ff. Barnes offers the more nuanced account of the events (if not of the theology).

[19] For text and German translation see Martin Tetz, 'Ein enzyklisches Schreiben der Synode von Alexandrien (362)', *ZNTW* 79 (1988), 262–81. Athanasius' letter to Rufinianus describes the reasons for the council's pragmatism.

II. The Emergence of Pro-Nicene Theology

have been carried out with some success (events in the west are discussed later in this chapter).

Immediately after this council Athanasius and others wrote a letter to the Church in Antioch known as the 'Antiochene Tome'. In this text Athanasius makes a significant move beyond the *De synodis*. He accepts that not all those who teach three *hypostases* imply three hierarchically ranked beings, of which only one is true God. Thus, Athanasius admits that *hypostasis* might primarily indicate a logical distinction: indicating only that the persons are truly and eternally distinct, and doing so in the context of a belief that whatever is God is immaterial and simply God. The relevant section of text presents the Alexandrian council as questioning two groups from Antioch: first those who confess three *hypostases* are examined:

> For as to those whom some were blaming for speaking of three *hypostases*, on the ground that the phrase is unscriptural and therefore suspicious, we thought it right indeed to require nothing beyond the confession of Nicaea, but on account of the contention we made enquiry of them, whether they meant, like the Arian madmen, *hypostases* foreign and strange, and alien in essence from one another, and that each *hypostasis* was divided apart by itself, as is the case with other created things and with those who are begotten of men ... They assured us in reply that they neither meant this nor had ever held it ... [they said they used this expression] because they believed in a Holy Trinity, not a Trinity in name only, but existing and subsisting in truth (ἀληθῶς ὄντα καὶ ὑφεστῶτα), 'both a Father truly existing and subsisting, and a Son truly substantial and subsisting, and a Holy Spirit subsisting and really existing do we acknowledge', and that neither had they said there were three Gods or three beginnings (ἀρχάς) ... but one Godhead, and one beginning, and that the Son is *homoousios* with the Father, as the Fathers said; while the Holy Spirit is not a creature, nor external, but proper to (ἴδιον) and inseparable (ἀδιαίρετον) from the Father and the Son.[20]

Athanasius then parallels this admission with an insistence that those who confess only one *hypostasis* are doing so only to indicate that the divine is one reality distinct from the created order and not indicating a belief that Son and Spirit are not truly existent realities:

> ... we made inquiry of those blamed by [the party adhering to the terminology of three *hypostases*] for speaking of one *hypostasis*, whether they use the expression in the sense of Sabellius, to the negation of the Son and the Holy Spirit ... But they in their turn assured us that they neither meant this nor had ever held it, but 'we use the word *hypostasis* thinking it the same thing to say *hypostasis* or *ousia*'; 'but we hold that there is one because the Son is of the essence of the Father (ἐκ τῆς οὐσίας), and because of the identity of nature (τὴν ταυτότητα τῆς φύσεως). For we believe that there is

---

[20] Athanasius, *Tom.* 5.

one Godhead (θεότητα), and that it has one nature (φύσιν), and not that there is one nature of the Father, from which that of the Son and of the Holy Spirit are distinct.'[21]

Athanasius then exhorts the addressees of the letter to accept any who explain their theology in either of the ways described here. Once these minimum conditions have been met both parties should cease fighting over terminology and should also cease inquiring further about each other's opinions. Both sides should seek nothing beyond subscription to the Nicene creed for the sake of peace. The pragmatism of the text is here evident in its *failure* to produce a theological solution to these differences. Athanasius finds a way in which both sides can recognize each other, using Nicaea as a point of reference but without trying to seek unanimity.

Importantly, the text recognizes that theological terminology may indicate grammatical or logical principles: Athanasius recognizes that both sides here use different terminologies to protect common principles of unity and division. In order for Nicaea to become a standard point of reference for those opposed to the Homoian creed Athanasius has begun to consider a wider set of theological principles within which Nicaea can be understood as not Sabellian in intention. For the first time we have considered a text that offers the logic of unity at one 'level' and distinction at another as the context within which to understand the Son's generation. Of course, from this text we do not get any clear sense of the particular theology of divine unity behind the language, but a fundamental move appears to have been made. This text is not the first to make this distinction (other candidates are considered in Chapter 8) but it is one of the most important. The technique of subscription to Nicaea as a minimum condition for communion had a wide influence: and the decision to follow this course represents one of Athanasius' most important contributions to the course of these years.

We need now to consider the identity of the two groups discussed in this letter to Antioch. The Church in Antioch was frequently divided during the fourth century. The removal from office of Eustathius in the aftermath of Nicaea initiated a series of divisions in the Christian community there. In 361 Meletius, a bishop who had previously occupied sees in Armenia and Syria, was consecrated bishop of Antioch with the support of Eudoxius, now bishop of Constantinople.[22] Meletius delivered a sermon in front of the Emperor that seemed Homoiousian in tone (even though it makes no use of *ousia* language) and he was deposed by

---

[21] Athanasius, *Tom.* 6.   [22] On these events see Hanson, *The Search*, 382–4.

176   II. The Emergence of Pro-Nicene Theology

those who had supported him, possibly within a month of his consecration.[23]

Meletius' views seem to have soon shifted to a point where he was able to accept Nicaea as a standard of faith and he eventually received the support of many bishops throughout Asia Minor and Syria, most noticeably Basil of Caesarea. However, many of those in the Antiochene Church who had kept faith with the memory of Eustathius would not support Meletius, at least in part because of his initial Homoian support, and also because of his sympathy for the terminology of 'three *hypostases*'. The leader of the 'Eustathians' in Antioch during the 360s was one Paulinus who received the support of the bishop of Rome and a number of eastern bishops.[24] Thus, during the 360s and 370s there were two parties in Antioch, *both* of whom ostensibly were agreed to Nicaea. As well as these two parties in Antioch there was also a sizable Homoian community. Athanasius' letter to the Antiochenes was almost certainly designed to reconcile the party of Meletius and the party of 'Eustathians'.

The importance of Athanasius' attempts to reconcile these parties is clear when we realize Antioch was a cause of conflict for many throughout the empire. The Antiochene Tome did not resolve the situation, and different 'Nicene' sides attracted the support of different groups. Of especial importance was the long-standing refusal of westerners to accept the orthodoxy of Meletius despite—and perhaps because of—his strong support in the east. Similarly, Athanasius' antagonism towards Meletius—despite willingness to recognize his orthodoxy—made it difficult for Athanasius and Basil of Caesarea to achieve common purpose (I return to this topic in Ch. 9). Thus, while I have offered Athanasius' attempts at rapprochement as an excellent example of developments in the early 360s, it

---

[23] The sermon is preserved by Epiphanius within his refutation of Homoiousians at *Panarion* 73. 29. 1–33. 5; here 30. 4–7: '. . . we confess that the Son of God is God of God, One of One, only begotten of Ingenerate . . . the Word, Wisdom and Power of Him who transcends wisdom and power . . . He is the perfect and abiding offspring of Him who is perfect, and abides the same—not an overflow of the Father or a bit or piece of the Father, but come forth without passion and entire, from him who has lost none of what he had. And because the Son ⟨is⟩, and is called the Word, he is by no means to be conceived of as the Father's voice or verbal expression. For he subsists in himself and acts, and by him and in him are all things . . . an Offspring who is like the Father and bears the exact impress of the Father. For the Father, God, has sealed him; and he neither inheres in another nor subsists by himself, but ⟨is⟩ an Offspring at work, who has made this universe and preserves it.' For a useful discussion of the homily see Kelly McCarthy Spoerl, 'The Schism at Antioch since Cavallera', in Michel Barnes and Daniel H. Williams (eds.), *Arianism after Arius: Essays on the Development of the Fourth Century Trinitarian Conflicts* (Edinburgh: T. & T. Clark, 1993), 101–26.

[24] Paulinus was consecrated bishop by Lucifer of Caligari, the extreme western pro-Nicene in 361. Events here are confused. Even though he was not yet a bishop, Paulinus seems to have been officialy represented at the council of Alexandria, while Meletius' name is never mentioned. See Hanson, *The Search*, 642–4 for a helpful review of the problems.

The Beginnings of Rapprochement 177

also stands as the most important example of the difficulties in the path of such developments. Common cause against Homoians and Eunomians was not sufficient to overcome the fundamental distrust shaped by decades of controversy. Only over many years could these still developing theologies come to recognize each other's theologies fully.

THE PRO-NICENE REACTION IN THE WEST: AD 360–365

In the west we can trace a parallel realignment and turn to Nicaea, but one partly rendered easier by the lack of a Homoiousian party. Events following the councils of 359–60 are interwoven with the gradual rise to power of Julian. As Julian moved towards declaring himself emperor a political space was created in which open reaction against the Ariminum creed became possible. At the same time, these years also saw the return of a number of prominent exiles. At some point in 360, Hilary returned west. It does not seem that he did so with permission from Constantius: Daniel Williams suggests that he did so having lost hope that the Homoiousians might prevail with Constantius, and in the knowledge that Julian had now raised his standard in the west.[25] Hilary possibly passed through Rome to discuss with Liberius the Pope's own recent return from exile under very different circumstances, and began to act as a standard-bearer for the pro-Nicene cause.[26]

Hilary had already begun his *Against Valens and Ursacius* at some point before 359: before his death in 367 he added to that text further documentation of the pro-Nicene campaigns of the early 360s.[27] Although Hilary's movements during the 360–67 period are difficult to trace, we see from this collection of texts that he was an important influence at a council in Paris sometime in 360 or 361. This council issued a statement of faith in favour of Nicaea and the term *homoousios*. The statement is in language that closely reflects that used in the initial books of Hilary's *On the Trinity*, a text discussed in more detail later in this section. We also find a careful

---

[25] Williams, *Ambrose of Milan*, 41 ff. On these years, Williams' ch. 2 offers the most helpful current study.

[26] After his election in 352 Liberius had tried to steer a course between the parties, at first overturning his predecessor's support for Athanasius. He soon reversed his policy, resisted Constantius' policies, and was exiled to Thrace in 355. In 358 Liberius signed the 'Blasphemy of Sirmium', renounced Athanasius again, and was allowed to return to Rome. Once he had re-established himself there he seems to have returned quickly to his anti-Eusebian/Homoian position. His contemporaries were somewhat suspicious of these changes of mind, but Athanasius himself was surprisingly indulgent (*Apol. sec.* 89).

[27] The story of the compilation and modern editing of this text is highly complex. An excellent summary is to be found in the introduction to the translation by Lionel Wickham used here.

account of the Son's distinction from the Father—the Son's birth indicates both his unique status and his real existence—and a refutation of Marcellan doctrine. These emphases probably demonstrate some of the care Hilary has taken to adapt western theology to the concerns of eastern pro-Nicenes. The statement also presents 'the many who fell at Ariminum' (to use Eusebius of Vercelli's colourful phrase) as having done so through deceit and ignorance of the issues.

This council may have received official support from Julian's government: it is unlikely that it could have happened in Italy, where Constantius still held power. By the summer of 361 Julian had gained full control of Italy and the situation there also changed. Again it is difficult to offer a clear narrative, but Hilary provides us with some important documentation. The first is a letter from Liberius (who had now come to his pro-Nicene senses) to bishops in Italy (*c*.363), asking that those who wished to be accepted back should be asked nothing more than a commitment 'to the apostolic and catholic creed up to and including the meeting of the synod of Nicaea'.[28] This policy—for the laxity of which Liberius feels the need to offer some apology—was exactly that recommended by Athanasius and it had probably been conveyed to Liberius by Eusebius of Vercelli, who was commissioned by the Alexandria council to carry its decisions west. The second text is a letter from a council of Italian bishops to pro-Nicene bishops in Illyricum, probably from 363, claiming that 'the whole extent of Italy . . . has returned to the fathers' faith of old'. The 'Aetian' heresy is also condemned. The bishops call for subscription to Nicaea and a clear repudiation of Ariminum.

Although Hilary is the most well-known Latin pro-Nicene figure from these years, Eusebius of Vercelli was also of great importance. Towards the end of 362 he met with Hilary and the two travelled together in Gaul, Italy, and east as far as Sirmium promoting the pro-Nicene cause.[29] When Julian inherited the Empire as a whole his antagonism to the Church as a whole became much more apparent.

---

[28] Hilary, *C. ant. Par.*

[29] Eusebius is traditionally said to have died in 370, although it could have been any time in the late 360s. Assessing the importance of Eusebius in this story in part depends on whether or not we attribute to him the first seven books of the *De trinitate* edited by Bulhart in CCSL 9 (1957). Williams, *Ambrose of Milan*, 239–42, attempts to remove objections to his authorship of this document, while admitting that the case remains weak. If Eusebius is credited as the author then he stands as another key Latin pro-Nicene. A problem, however, not faced by Williams concerns the difficulty of demonstrating that this text had any influence on Latin pro-Nicene writing over the 360–80 period. We can trace the appearance of Hilary, Phoebadius, and Gregory of Elvira, but why not this text? This lack may by itself cast further doubt on the attribution to Eusebius.

On the one hand, Julian's lack of support for any one church grouping allowed resistance to the Homoian creed to continue to coalesce. On the other hand, pro-Nicenes could expect no government support for their programme. In Chapter 9 I return to the course of events in the west after Julian's death in 363.

HILARY'S THEOLOGY

As an example of the gradual development of Latin theology during these years, I want to consider Hilary's own development. Hilary's theology is deeply indebted to earlier Latin theology, placing great importance on understanding how the Son's birth from the Father guarantees a sharing of essence and yet real distinction (an anti-adoptionist tactic we saw in Chapter 3). At the same time Hilary demonstrates new concerns stemming from his growing knowledge of theological debates in the east. His Trinitarian theology is mainly contained in two texts, *On the Synods* and *On the Trinity*.[30] The *On the Synods* was begun in 358–9 (after Basil's synod in Ancyra, but before the council of Seleucia) and completed after his return from exile. It takes the form of an extended letter written to bishops in the west concerning developments in the east. Hilary is particularly concerned to argue for the orthodoxy of the Homoiousians.

Hilary's point of departure is the 'blasphemy of Sirmium', the 357 manifesto, and he seeks to convince his audience that most easterners have long condemned such doctrines. Hilary offers a genealogy of eastern credal history since the Dedication creed, emphasizing that anti-Sabellian concerns lie behind some of the texts that will seem most suspicious to his western brethren.[31] There are times at which his exposition seems a little strained, especially when he discusses the anathemas attached to the Sirmium 351 creed. Nevertheless, he provides further evidence that some easterners could read a straight line from 341 to 351 but see a clear break occurring after the 357 manifesto. Throughout the text Hilary speaks of Father and Son as possessing a likeness that means 'perfect equality'. By such means Hilary attempts to show that Father and Son are not one

---

[30] The original title of the book was almost certainly *De fide*, *De trinitate* being a later attribution. There is little useful to read on the theology of Hilary's *De trinitate* and *De synodis* in English: Hanson, *The Search*, 471 ff. is deeply unsatisfactory; but see Paul Burns, 'Hilary of Poitiers' Confrontation with Arianism', in Robert C. Gregg (ed.), *Arianism: Historical and Theological Reassessments*, Patristic Monograph Series, 11 (Philadelphia: Philadelphia Patristic Foundation, 1985), 287–302. The baseline for work on his theology remains the corpus of the late Jean Doignon: see also the extensive introduction to Figura and Doignon in SC 443 and the bibliography at 192 ff. (which references all of the important material by Doignon). There is also a useful summary at Simonetti, *La Crisi*, 298–312.
[31] *Synod.* 37, 51.

thing.³² Hilary also relies heavily on the notion of the Son's unique generation from the Father to point to a shared being even while there is distinction. Thus, at *On the Synods* 71, Hilary writes that,

> the one substance must be derived from the true character of the begotten nature (*ex naturae genitae proprietate*), not from any division, any confusion of persons, any sharing of an anterior substance.

We can best see how Hilary's thought marks a development in Latin pro-Nicene theology by turning to his *On the Trinity*, and by comparing his accounts of the Son's birth in book 2 and book 7. Books 1–3 (with the exception of some obviously later sections of the first book summarizing the whole twelve) were probably constructed first and have their own unity. Here we see Hilary learning from contemporary eastern concerns while still turning constantly to his own Latin traditions.³³ In both book 2 and 3 Hilary begins by trying to talk of the unity of Father, Son, and Spirit. The Father is the one from whom all things come, and is treated as the source of the Son and the Spirit, but at the same time Hilary clearly speaks of a perfection (*consummatio*) existing in Father, Son, and Spirit.³⁴ God is perfect in being a trinity of persons. The idea is one we encounter increasingly among pro-Nicenes and seems to be a development of analogies that see the Word and Spirit as necessary to the Father being the Father. It is a short leap from saying that the Word must be with the Father (for who can be without her Word?) to saying that Father and Word (and Spirit) express the perfection of God. There is also an order here based on powers and merits, but this seems intended to point to the significance of the Father as the one power from whom all things come rather than to identify the Son as a distinct lesser power. Son and Spirit are 'ranked' by their respective functions as image of the Father's power and as the gift of hope in the Father.

Hilary is concerned at the beginning of book 2 to resist both 'Sabellians' who do not treat the three names as indicating three realities, the three 'names of the nature' (*naturae nomina*), and some 'in this present age' who think that the Son was created from

---

³² *Synod.* 27. 68: *A vero si idcirco unius substantiae Pater et filius dicatur, ut hic subsistens, sub significatione licet duum nominum, unus ac solus sit: confessum nomine Filium conscientia non tenemus, si unam substantiam confitentes ipsum sibi unicum ac singularem et Patrem esse dicimus et Filium.* 27. 73: *Perfectae aequalitatis significantiam habet similitudo* . . .

³³ Dating here is complex: I assume that the three books were either drafted before exile and completed there or written early in his exile—thus being initially composed before the *De Synod*.

³⁴ *De trin.* 2. 1. Later, at 7. 22 Hilary writes 'the birth of God perfects God' (*nativitas Dei Deum perficit*). A few sentences later he adds 'The birth, therefore, maintains the nature from which it subsists' (*tenet itaque nativitas eam ex qua subsistit naturam*). Here the birth of the Son guarantees that the Son will maintain the same nature as the Father.

The Beginnings of Rapprochement

nothing and thus introduce a division of substances by using the differences in the names to divide the nature.[35] In using this tactic of presenting orthodoxy between the extremes of Sabellius and Arius—to which I shall return below—Hilary seems to be adopting an eastern polemical strategy emerging in just these years. When Hilary returns to the topic of the unity at the beginning of book 3 he begins with John 14: 11, 'I in the Father and the Father in me':[36]

... the eternity of God ... transcends places, times, appearances and whatever can be conceived by the human mind. He is outside of all things and within all things (*Ipse extra omnia et in omnibus*). He does not change either by increase or decrease, but is invisible, incomprehensible, complete, perfect and eternal ... (3) This unbegotten One, therefore, brought forth the Son from himself (*ex se Filium genuit*) before all time, not from any pre-existing matter, because all things are through the Son; nor from nothing, because the Son is from Him; nor as an ordinary birth, because there is nothing changeable or empty in God; nor as a part that is divided, cut off or extended ... But in an inconceivable and ineffable manner, before all time and ages ... (4) What is in the Father is in the Son also because the Son is from Him; the Son is in the Father because he is not a Son from anywhere else ... Thus they are mutually in each other (*in se invicem*), because as all things are perfect in the Father, so all things are perfect in the Son.[37]

The Son's generation is incomprehensible because it occurs within and from the incomprehensible being of God. In books 1–3 Hilary relies heavily on X from X arguments. At 2. 8, for example, description of the Son as 'the one from the one, the true from the true' and five more X from X phrases introduces an account of scriptural material describing the generation, summed up in the phrase 'He is the perfect one from the perfect one ...'. Because the Father gives the Son all that the Father is: sharing the incomprehensible divine life the Son is incomprehensibly close to the Father:

The nature of the Godhead (*natura divinitatis*) is not different in one and in the other, because both are one. The only-begotten God is from the one unbegotten God. There are not two gods, but one from one. There are not two unbegotten gods, because he is born from him who is unborn. The one is from the other and is not different in anything, because the life of the living one is in the living one.[38]

This account of the Son's generation develops a line of argument we earlier saw in the case of Tertullian and Novatian.[39]

When we turn to book 7 we see shifts that demonstrate Hilary's

---

[35] *De trin.* 2. 4.   [36] *De trin.* 3. 1.   [37] *De trin.* 3. 2–4.
[38] *De trin.* 2. 11.
[39] The use of the Son's birth in this way is also a feature of other contemporary Latin polemic probably uninfluenced by contemporary eastern thought. For example, Phoebadius, *C. Ar.* 9. 1 ff.

deeper engagement with eastern theological concerns. The form of his polemic now follows even more clearly a pattern of condemning both Sabellius and Arius, with Photinus named as the contemporary Sabellian representative. Interestingly, Hilary knows not only this polemical style, but also the 'Athanasian' tactic of quoting from and refuting Arius as an attack on all non-Nicenes.[40] The combination of the two tactics is rare. In book 7 Hilary has largely abandoned X from X arguments as a central point of reference, perhaps because of their ambiguity in contemporary eastern debates. Instead we see Hilary developing his account of the birth of the Son in the light of some emphases that seem to have an eastern provenance. Two can be noted.

First, we see increased attention to the metaphysical relationships between natures, powers, and operations. Hilary is not only critical of attempts to consider the Son as a property of the divine nature or as an operation—and hence not eternally a subsistent reality—he also offers a dense alternative account. Developing an argument begun in book 5, in book 7 Hilary argues that because the Son has the power to carry out the same acts as the Father he must have the same nature. Moreover, the Son works with the activity of the Father's power.[41] Both these phrases indicate Hilary's familiarity with a technical philosophical argument that a thing's 'power' is intrinsic to its nature and that observing an operation or activity which stems from a particular power enables us to identify the nature to which the power is intrinsic.[42] We will meet a very developed version of this argument in Chapter 12's consideration of Gregory of Nyssa: it is an argument that will have an extensive future in pro-Nicene theology.

Second, Hilary now offers a dense account of the ways in which the Son does the same work as the Father and must therefore be considered as equal in nature.[43] Much of his consideration of this theme comes from treatment of John 5: 19's statement that 'The Son can do nothing of himself, but only what he sees the Father doing.' Against a text that readily lent itself to non-Nicene usage, Hilary emphasizes other texts that indicate continuity of activity between Father and Son, such as John 5: 17's 'my Father works even

---

[40] *De trin.* 4. 12; 6. 5. He gives an extended version of the tactic of comparing Sabellius and Arius as the two extremes at 7. 6 ff.

[41] *De trin.* 7. 17–18.

[42] Cf. *De trin.* 9. 52. See Barnes, *Power of God*, 157–65. These arguments also dovetail well with Hilary's detailed account of the eternity of the Son's generation found in the later books, e.g. at 12. 26–8.

[43] Arguments based on the common operation of the persons are found in pro-Nicene writers who do not seem to demonstrate eastern influence, but not in the context of detailed exegesis of John 5: 19; e.g. Phoebadius, *C. Ar.* 5. 4.

until now, and I work'. At the same time he argues both that the Son's doing of the same things as the Father indicates unity of nature, and that not only do they do the same things, but 'the [Father] himself was working in whatever he did'.[44] Hilary also reads John 5: 21's insistence that the Son has the same power to give life to the dead as the Father as part of the way Scripture reveals to us the status of the Son. We are shown the Son's ability to perform common works so that we will recognize in faith the common nature.[45] Once again we meet in Hilary an argument that we will find important to a variety of Greek and Latin pro-Nicenes. John 5: 19 appears to have become an increasingly important battleground in the 360s probably both because of its utility to Homoians and because of increasingly clear pro-Nicene articulation of the common nature of the three.

At this most mature stage of his theology Hilary moves closer to a clear and consistent vocabulary for distinguishing persons and essence. At a number of points in the *De trinitate* Hilary pairs *natura* and *persona*, but only after book 3.[46] When he does pair *natura* and *persona* in the *De trinitate* it is noticeable that he does not speak of 'three persons' in the plural, but uses *persona* as a distinguishing category in the abstract.[47] As well as *natura* he also uses *substantia* to designate the unity of God. Unfortunately, he also uses *substantia* to designate the three persons at a number of points, especially in the *De synodis*, where his translations of *ousia* and *hypostasis* in eastern texts can be confusing. *Essentia* is not used in the *De trinitate*, but appears as a translation of *ousia* in the *De synodis*.[48] Two important points come out of these summary remarks. First, as I noted in Chapter 3, we must be cautious in our assumptions about Tertullian's influence on fourth-century Latin theology: his terminology of *natura* and *persona* was neither assumed as a given nor frequently used at this point. As we shall see, the terminology is a little more consistently used by Ambrose in the latter half of his *De fide* (c.380), but only *after* he appears to have made an active attempt to find Greek resources to use after the failure of the first two books. A lesser author such as Phoebadius managed to compose his *Contra Arianos* without using this pairing.[49] The rise to prominence of the

---

[44] *De trin.* 7. 19.   [45] *De trin.* 7. 19.   [46] e.g. *De trin.* 5. 10, 35.
[47] P. Smulders, *La Doctrine trinitaire de S. Hilaire de Poitiers* (Rome, 1944), 288 remarks that at *De trin.* 7. 39 Hilary actively repudiates the theatrical sense of persona as 'mask': this seems a little overstated, but Hilary does directly repudiate the monarchian (or adoptionist?) idea that the Father calls himself Son in Christ playing a 'theatrical role'.
[48] For these patterns of use see Hanson, *The Search*, 486–7, Smulders, *La Doctrine trinitaire*, 280–9.
[49] e.g. Ambrose, *De fide* 3. 15. The pairing occasionally occurs in the *De trinitate* attributed to Eusebius of Vercelli, but it is worth noting that on one or two occasions it appears to be a

formula has not been satisfactorily traced: it cannot be assumed simply as Tertullian's legacy. Second, as we shall see in a number of different circumstances, the logic of unity and distinction could be adopted before a consistent terminology for that distinction was used.

Alongside his new arguments, the Son's mysterious birth or generation is still presented as the great mystery of the faith and serves key functions in distinguishing Father and Son. At the beginning and end of book 7 Hilary speaks of 'the mystery of the true birth' as the core of Christian belief, and at 7. 31 he writes:

> The Son is in the Father and the Father in the Son, not by a mutual transfusion and flowing, but by the perfect birth of a living nature (*sed per viventis naturae perfectam nativitatem*) . . . There is not one person, therefore, in the confession of the one God, while the Son also completes the Father and the birth of the Son is from the Father. The nature, however, is not changed by the birth so that it would not be the same according to the likeness of the nature. It is the same in such a manner that by reason of the birth and generation we must confess the two as one and not as one thing (*Eadem autem ita est, ut per nativitatem et generationem uterque potius unum confitendus sit esse, non unus*).[50]

For Hilary, the more we understand the character of a perfect birth[51]—a birth within the context of the divine immateriality, infinity, and perfection—the more we understand the mysterious unity and distinction of the two. The centrality of this theme in Hilary not only shows the complex ways in which earlier traditions were adapted and transformed, but also one reason why common cause could emerge between Hilary and some of his eastern counterparts. In the theology of the Homoiousians we find a similar focus on the significance of the Son's generation from the perfect Father. We do not know if Hilary knew anything of Athanasius' theology, but it is interesting to note that just as Athanasius saw grounds for a rapprochement between himself and the Homoiousians, Hilary saw the same.

We must end this chapter by returning to Hilary's understanding of the Spirit. In the latter half of the *De trinitate* Hilary says

---

later redactor who has added the terminology, e.g. at 1. 37 (CCSL 60. 11). Others in the 370s seem to have accorded the terminology a central importance more quickly, e.g. the formal statement of Damasus, *Ep.* 2.

[50] *De trin.* 7. 31.

[51] Cf. *De trin.* 7. 27: 'He who says "I am and I change not", cannot be changed by parts, nor become different in nature. All these things, which have been pointed out above, are not found within him as portions, but are all one and perfect within him, for everything is the living God. Accordingly, there is the living God, and the eternal power of the living nature, and that which is born from him with the mystery of his own knowledge could not be born as anything else than from a living being.'

explicitly that the Spirit is neither generated nor created and that the Spirit exists with the Father.[52] In book 2 he similarly seems to treat the Spirit as part of the perfect 'whole' that is the Godhead. His account of the Spirit's role is, however, entirely economic. The Spirit is the gift that enables contemplation, understanding, and perseverance in faith. He makes the seemingly odd statement, '[F]or those who will adore God the Spirit in the Spirit, the one is to assist, the other to be worshipped, because a distinction is made in the manner that each one is worshipped.'[53] The statement probably refers to the just who adore the Father for eternity: for Hilary the worship the saints give to God the Spirit, to the Father, is enabled by the Spirit. There is a distinction in worship here not in the sense that Hilary is suggesting a clear subordinationism but that in the unity of the Godhead the Spirit enables the worship of the Father.

In book 8 Hilary pursues the same basic argument, the Spirit is that which enables us to live in Christ, the Spirit is the Spirit of Christ and the Spirit of God.[54] Hilary is concerned in both books 2 and 8 to show how the Spirit's individual subsistence is compatible with Scripture's insistence that God is Spirit. In both contexts he answers anyone who might raise such a question by using the ambiguity as an occasion to emphasize that the Spirit Christians receive from Christ is of the very nature of God. Hilary's reading is closely tied into his assertion of the inseparability of operation: because the Spirit is, as he says, a 'thing of the nature' (*res naturae*) we must understand Father and Son to be present in the Spirit's work. Hilary has, thus, a clear sense of the Spirit's work, and virtually nothing to say about the relationship of Spirit to Son and Father in the Godhead. Just about the only thing that Hilary can say is that the Spirit comes from the Father and through the Son. He does so on the basis, first, of John 16's statements and, second, on the assumption that the unity of nature means that whatever is the Son's is the Father's and vice versa.[55] In the next chapter I offer some general comments about pro-Nicene pneumatology: I can anticipate some of those general statements by noting that in the case of Hilary we find a pneumatology that is clear about the function of the Spirit, proceeds polemically by applying to the Spirit arguments developed in the case of the Son, and deeply austere about the place of the Spirit in the Trinity itself.

---

[52] Hilary, *De trin.* 8. 19; 12. 55.
[53] *De trin.* 2. 31: *Adoraturis autem in Spiritu Deum Spiritum, alter in officio, alter in honore est, quia discretum est in quo quisque sit adorandus.*
[54] *De trin.* 8. 19 ff.   [55] *De trin.* 8. 20.

CONCLUSION

The theological shifts that we have seen in this chapter and the last have set the scene for the full emergence of pro-Nicene theology. We have seen Athanasius, Basil of Ancyra, and Hilary all speak of the incomprehensible generation of the Son occurring within the bounds of the divine simplicity. In this context a theology of the incomprehensible generation serves both to demonstrate the closeness and distinction between Father and Son and to show that the generation can be understood as passionless and immaterial. The emergence of this combination of themes in different writers is a fundamental stage on the way to the development of fully pro-Nicene theologies. This set of themes leaves open a number of questions about how we envisage the order, hierarchy, and unity that pertains between Father and Son but it presses towards a further stage: the emergence of clear statements of unity of essence, power, and nature even while the persons are truly distinct. We have begun to see that further development here; in the next chapter we see it emerging with a new sophistication in Basil of Caesarea.

8
Basil of Caesarea and the Development of Pro-Nicene Theology

This chapter and the first section of the next focus on a figure who presents an excellent example of the complex process of theological development and intra-ecclesial accommodation that was central to the emergence of fully pro-Nicene theologies: Basil of Caesarea.[1] In some accounts Basil is the architect of the pro-Nicene triumph: he carries forward the Nicene torch long held by Athanasius, holds together different pro-Nicene factions, and develops an account of the distinctions between persons and essence of such power that the final victory of pro-Nicene theology under the Emperor Theodosius is inevitable. In other presentations the victory of pro-Nicene theology in the 380s is largely the result of secular political moves, the work of Basil being of little importance.[2] The truth lies somewhere in between: Basil's theological and ecclesio-political work was of importance, but he was one of many architects of pro-Nicene theology. At the same time the accession of Theodosius in 379 was nothing if not providential for pro-Nicenes. In this chapter I will discuss only Basil's theological development: at the beginning of the next I will take up his ecclesio-political role in the 370s.[3]

Basil was born around 330 into a family that was part of the emerging Christian aristocracy.[4] Basil was extremely well educated

---

[1] Since the 19th cent. scholars have spoken of 'the Cappadocians' as a unified group. It is, however, important to understand both development within 'Cappadocian' theology and differences among the Cappadocians. Hence I have consciously treated the three figures separately.

[2] A third approach is represented by John Henry Newman's *Arians of the Fourth Century*, 3rd edn. (London: Pickering, 1871), in which Basil's theology receives little substantive discussion because of the sheer difficulty of admitting substantive development in Nicene theology.

[3] The lack of any decent and extensive introductory treatment of Basil's theology in English also suggested him as an important candidate for this more extensive treatment.

[4] For Basil's biography see most recently Philip Rousseau, *Basil of Caesarea* (Berkeley: University of California Press, 1994) and the summary in Hanson, *The Search*, 679–86. While he has some useful observations on Basil's understanding of theological practice, Rousseau's treatment of the 4th-cent. Trinitarian controversies is dependent on earlier narratives. See also Raymond Van Dam, 'Emperor, Bishops, and Friends in Late Antique Cappadocia', *JThS* NS 37 (1986), 53–76. Hanson's discussion of Basil's theology, *The Search*, 687 ff., is weak (although the later separate discussion of pneumatology is more helpful). On Basil's theology see also the excellent survey by Bernard Sesboüé, *Saint Basile et La Trinité. Un acte théologique au IVe siècle* (Paris: Desclée, 1998). Volker Henning Drecoll, *Die Entwicklung der*

in rhetoric and philosophy in Caesarea, Constantinople, and then in Athens, where he stayed for nearly six years. In 355 he returned to Caesarea to teach rhetoric. In a manner that reveals much about emerging Christian ideals among the educated elite as well as some details of his biography, Basil tells us of a conversion experience that led to baptism and an extensive tour of ascetic communities in Egypt, Syria, and Palestine in 356–7.[5] He returned to Caesarea and became part of a small ascetic community at Annesi on his father's estates. This community included his mother, sister, and his friend Gregory, later bishop of Nazianzus.[6] Basil was gradually drawn into assuming a public role in the Church of Caesarea. He was ordained deacon in 360 and priest in 362 by Dianius, bishop of Caesarea.[7] Basil took an increasingly important role in the Church of Caesarea from 364 under Dianius' successor Eusebius. In 370, on Eusebius' death, Basil was elected bishop in a hard-fought contest (Gregory Nazianzen the elder appears to have played an instrumental role in the election). Until his early death in 379, Basil was one of the main pro-Nicene leaders in Asia Minor.

BASIL'S EARLY THEOLOGY: PROBLEMS WITH *HOMOOUSIOS*

It has been traditional to speak of Basil as initially a Homoiousian: this requires qualification. Basil does seem to have had some personal connection with Basil of Ancyra[8] and he was strongly opposed

---

Trinitätslehre des Basilius von Cäsarea: Sein Weg vom Homöusianer zum Neonizäner (Göttingen: Vandenhoeck & Ruprecht, 1996), must also be taken into account. My view of Drecoll is similar to that of Manlio Simonetti in his extensive review for *Zeitschrift für Antikes Christentum*, 2 (1998), 304–15. Drecoll's view of Basil's dependence on Athanasius is unconvincing and his insistence on the Basilian authorship of *Letter* 38 skews his account of Basil's Trinitarian theology. Lastly, see Simonetti, *La Crisi*, 401–34, 455–525: the latter chapter offers a very useful discussion of the theological contribution of Basil, while the first excellently (but perhaps over-optimistically) sketches Basil's ecclesio-political activities.

[5] Possibly in the company of Eustathius of Sebaste, who later became an enemy (see Ch. 9). See Jean Gribomont, 'Eustathe le philosophe et les voyages du jeune Basile de Césarée', *Revue d'histoire ecclésiastique*, 54 (1959), 115–24.

[6] Basil's ascetic writing is not examined here. For a brief introduction see Augustine Holmes, *A Life Pleasing to God: The Spirituality of the Rules of St. Basil* (London: DLT, 2000). See also Susanna Elm, '*Virgins of God*', 60–105.

[7] Dianius was present at the 'eastern' council of Serdica in 343, had signed the 360 creed, and yet was able to sustain a relationship with the young Basil. This provides us with yet another small window on the complexity of speaking about ecclesiastical 'parties' during the 4th cent.

[8] There are three main pieces of evidence for this linkage: first, the story preserved in Philostorgius (*Hist. eccl.* 4. 12) that Basil accompanied Basil of Ancyra to Constantinople in 360 and debated with Aetius; second, his friendship (later repudiated) with Eustathius of Sebaste (who, for instance, consulted with Basil before attending the council at Lampsacus in 364; see *Ep.* 223); third, Basil's exchange of letters with Apollinaris (*c.*360–1 if they are accepted as genuine) and his *Ep.* 9 to Maximus, in all of which he holds to a position only comprehensible from one originally operating in broadly Homoiousian circles.

to the 360 Homoian creed at the time of its promulgation. Nevertheless, we never encounter Basil as a partisan for a distinct Homoiousian party and his attitude to the phrase ὅμοιος κατ' οὐσίαν is already a complex one when we first hear his voice. Basil's early position is most comprehensible, first, against the background of the plurality of strands of opinion that broadly supported 'Homoiousian' theology in the late 350s and, second, against the background of the realignment of the early 360s.

If it is true that there were some among the 'Homoiousians' who saw themselves as upholding the basic sense of Nicaea itself despite worries about its terminology, then we can easily imagine Basil in this company. Through the 360s and especially in the 370s we see him gradually distancing himself from those who refused to travel his road towards pro-Nicene theology. Nevertheless, in the early and mid-360s we still find Basil discussing theological topics with those whom we can broadly term 'Homoiousian'. We may even think of Basil's major dogmatic work, the *Contra Eunomium*, as the logical conclusion of one strand of Homoiousian theology.

Basil's early theological corpus—from his early letters to his *Contra Eunomium*—reveals a thinker in constant development. I want to follow the course of this development by looking first to an early correspondence with Apollinaris of Laodicea, which is probably to be dated around 360–1.[9] Basil has written to Apollinaris asking how to interpret *homoousios*. In this letter Basil lets us know his preference for the phrase ὅμοιος κατ' οὐσίαν ἀκριβῶς ἀπαραλλάκτως ('invariably like according to essence') to describe the relationship of Father and Son. Basil has here added the traditional adverb ἀπαραλλάκτως to the standard Homoiousian phrase ὅμοιος κατ' οὐσίαν.

Basil also states to Apollinaris that those who oppose any *ousia* language are motivated by hatred of *homoousios*, a hatred he does not appear to feel.[10] Thus, Basil's preference for Homoiousian-sounding language does not occur because of deep antipathy to Nicaea. Rather, it seems to result from concern about the difficulty of understanding *homoousios* appropriately: a difficulty[11] explained in his first letter to Apollinaris:

---

[9] See G. L. Prestige, *St. Basil the Great and Apollinaris* (London: SPCK, 1956); Henri de Riedmatten, 'La Correspondance entre Basile de Césarée et Apollinaire de Laodicée', *JThS* NS 7 (1956), 199–210; 8 (1957), 53–70. In what follows I assume the authenticity of this correspondence: Prestige's arguments still seem to me conclusive. See also Drecoll, *Trinitätslehre*, 21–8. Translations of all letters are taken (with some minor changes) from the Loeb edition.

[10] Basil, *Ep.* 361: '... regarding *homoousios* itself (because of which I think they are getting up this affair, slandering *ousia* deeply, in order to leave no room for *homoousios*) ...'.

[11] For the distinction between Nicaea's 'judgements' and its phraseology see Ch. 4, p. 87.

[whatever] the substance of the Father is assumed to be, this must by all means be assumed as also that of the Son. So that if anyone should speak of the substance of the Father as intelligible light (φῶς νοητόν), eternal, unbegotten, he would also call the substance of the Only-begotten intelligible light, eternal, unbegotten. And in such a meaning the phrase 'like without a difference' seems to me to accord better than 'consubstantial'. For light which has no difference from light in the matter of greater and less cannot be the same—because each is in its own circumscription of existence (ἐν ἰδίᾳ περιγραφῇ τῆς οὐσίας)—but I think that 'like in substance without variation' could be said correctly.[12]

There are two ways of understanding the problem Basil describes here. On the one hand, Basil may be expressing an anti-Marcellan concern with *homoousios*. He might be arguing that when we speak of 'light from light' we must speak clearly of *two* realities, each 'light' being 'circumscribed' as an individual reality; *homoousios* may thus imply that Father and Son are the same one light.[13]

On the other hand, it has recently been suggested that there is another way of reading Basil's concern.[14] As we saw in Chapter 6, Basil of Ancyra in the Ancyran synodical letter of 358, was very possibly concerned that *homoousios* implies Father and Son are of identical ontological status. *Homoousios* is unacceptable because it implies the existence of two ultimate principles. This worry about the implications of *homoousios* has a long pedigree in the fourth century: we first encountered it with Arius' charge that Alexander's 'always Father, always Son' implies the existence of two principles. It may well be that Basil of Caesarea's concern in *Letter* 361 is of the same kind: when we speak of 'light from light', Basil thinks that each of the lights is the *ousia* or *hypostasis* it is by possession of a series of qualities and characteristics, by being 'circumscribed' in a particular way. Thus to speak of Father and Son as simply having the same *ousia* would be to ignore the differences that follow from the Son being the sort of *ousia* he is because of being generated from the Father and to present him as logically another God.

Whichever interpretation of Basil's problem with *homoousios* in Letter 361 we follow, he does not yet articulate his mature distinction between a unitary shared nature at one level, and the personal distinctions of Father, Son, and Spirit at another. Basil still seems to view the relationship between Father and Son in a fundamentally Homoiousian way: the Father generates the being of the Son in such

---

[12] Basil, *Ep.* 361.
[13] One might hope to solve this question by attention to Apollinaris' own understanding of Basil's problem. Unfortunately his response at the beginning of *Ep.* 362 can be interpreted reasonably easily to fit either description.
[14] See Johannes Zachhuber, *Human Nature*, 25–8.

a way that there is a mysterious unity between them, and yet the Son's existence as generated qualifies his existence as in some manner distinct from the Father's. It is only in the next few years that Basil will move towards the distinctions with which he is often identified.[15]

BASIL'S DEVELOPING THEOLOGY: Ἐπίνοια AND Ἰδιώματα

It is time now to turn to Basil's *Contra Eunomium*,[16] the three books of which were probably finished in 363 or 364.[17] In this section I will consider the first two books, emphasizing the interconnection of two themes: first, Basil's account of the nature of human speech about God; second, his account of the relationship between divine unity and the individualities of Father, Son, and Spirit.

The three books of the *Contra Eunomium* are arranged in a trinitarian structure.[18] The second and third books are respectively concerned with the generation of the Son and the status of the Spirit, while the first focuses on the nature of God, of human speech about God, and sketches much of what is to follow. The text is also a loose commentary on Eunomius' text. The first book begins by attacking the epistemological and methodological assumptions of Eunomius' position. Basil insists that God's *ousia* is unknown, citing Isaiah 53: 8 and Romans 11: 33: such knowledge exceeds the capacity of rational nature. Coming to a focal argument, Basil states that no one name can ever serve to identify God's existence. Rather, we know in theology by ἐπίνοια (*epinoia*), which for the moment we can gloss as 'the activity of reflecting on and identifying the distinct qualities or properties of something'. In focusing on this term Basil contradicts Eunomius' dismissal of the idea that we know God only in concepts

---

[15] One other text that may reveal something of Basil's theology in these early years is translated and helpfully discussed in N. A. Lipatov, 'The Statement of Faith Attributed to St Basil the Great', *SP* 37 (2001), 147–59.

[16] One text that might also have been considered here is Basil's *Ep.* 9. In this letter Basil appears to have moved much more clearly towards *homoousios* and accepts other formulations insofar as they accord with it. Although the letter is usually dated to 361 or 362, Steenson, *Basil of Ancyra*, 306 ff., makes out a good case for dating it in the mid-360s, in which case it will not help us narrate progress between *Ep.* 361 and *Eunom.* I have accordingly left it out of consideration here.

[17] The immediate context of *Eunom.* is unclear. It seems at least possible that the conversations in front of stenographers about 'the faith' before the synod of Lampsacus in 364 that Basil held with Eustathius of Sebaste (see *Ep.* 223) formed the initial stage in composition. The existence of these conversations at the least reveals that Basil was still part of a very fluid theological context. See Rousseau, *Basil*, 102.

[18] The text is not available in English. A French translation is available in SC 299 and 305. There is a useful English summary of Basil's argument in Milton V. Anastos, 'Basil's *Kata Eunomiou*, A Critical Analysis', in Paul J. Fedwick, *Basil of Caesarea: Christian, Humanist, Ascetic* (Toronto: Pontifical Institute of Medieval Studies, 1981), 67–136. There is also a good discussion of *Eunom.* in Kopecek, *Neo-Arianism*, ii. 361–92.

developed by the human mind.[19] In response Basil, at *Contra Eunomium* 1.6, offers a definition of the process of ἐπίνοια. Realities we initially perceive as simple and undifferentiated can, by a process of reflection and abstraction, be recognized as a conglomeration of attributes and qualities. In this process of ἐπίνοια we find ourselves in a somewhat paradoxical situation: we do not, strictly speaking, grasp the nature of something by ἐπίνοια, but ἐπίνοια, nevertheless, delivers an accurate and useful knowledge of something.

At 1.7 Basil gives a theological example. The divine speech (Scripture) accommodates itself to our capacities and reveals Christ's properties (ἰδιώματα) of being 'door, way, bread, light' (for example), but his simple essence (*ousia* or ὑποκείμενον) remains unknown. Each one of these titles enables us to conceptualize an aspect of Christ's work and grow in knowledge of him, even while we do not know his essence. In the same way Basil argues that we use 'unbegotten' of God by ἐπίνοια: we perceive that God's life must extend beyond all pasts we can imagine and thus that God precedes temporal generation even while we cannot say what God is. Thus, for Basil, ἐπίνοια, far from being an unreliable mode of knowing, is both a necessary feature of any advanced knowledge of things *and* a means of human knowledge directly addressed by the divine dispensation.

The term ἐπίνοια has a long history.[20] Possibly originating in a Stoic context, it had long been possible to speak of things existing: καθ' ὑπόστασιν, as a concrete reality, and κατ' ἐπίνοιαν, existing conceptually.[21] This was not necessarily a distinction between 'real' and 'unreal': the second sense could characterize properties that do not have independent concrete existence but which do reflect something true about an object—Richard Vaggione nicely points to a rock that

---

[19] Eunomius, *Apology* 8 (Vaggione, 41–3; tr. altered): 'when we say "unbegotten", then, we do not imagine that we ought to honour God only in name (ὀνόματι μόνον), in conformity with human invention (κατ' ἐπίνοιαν); rather, in conformity with truth (κατ' ἀλήθειαν), we ought to repay him the debt which above all others is most due to God: the acknowledgement that he is what he is. Expressions based on invention (κατ' ἐπίνοιαν) have their existence in name and utterance only . . .'.

[20] For brief accounts of ἐπίνοια see Vaggione, *Eunomius*, 241–6; Kopecek, *Neo-Arianism*, ii. 375–7 (though Vaggione is more trustworthy on the term's origins); Drecoll, *Trinitätslehre*, 75–8. For more extensive discussion one needs also to consult Antione Orbe, *La Epinoia: Algunos preliminaires históricos de la distinción kat' epinoian* (Rome, 1955) and I. Owen, '*Ἐπινοέω, ἐπίνοια* and Allied Words', *JThS* 35 (1934), 368–76.

[21] For two early uses see Posidonius, *Fr.* 16 ('for we said that substance differs from matter, being the same in reality, in thought only') and 92 (Edelstein/Kidd). See also Arius-Didymus, *Frg. Phys.* 20 (458. 8–11 Diels). Kopecek, *Neo-Arianism*, ii. 376, presents the theory as Epicurean in origin on the basis of Diogenes Laertius 10. 32 and 68. It is clear from the discussion of epistemology at 10. 33 ff. that despite Epicurus' use of the opposition it does not play a technical role in Epicurean language. 10. 68 offers no further evidence in favour of Kopecek's conjecture. It seems likely that by the time of Posidonius (c.135–51 BC), if not sometime before, the distinction had become a commonplace.

exists κατ' ὑπόστασιν and the triangular shape of the rock which exists κατ' ἐπίνοιαν.²² This distinction is found in a number of late antique philosophers and theologians.²³ When it appears in Christian tradition, the process of ἐπίνοια is understood as central to the process of an intellectual contemplation of the reality of things, a mode of knowledge that for Clement of Alexandria even characterizes divine knowing.²⁴ Origen uses the term of the many biblical terms for Christ that cannot be taken literally: titles such as 'door' and 'way' enable us to reflect on the different ἐπίνοιαι of Christ. For Origen, such a process of reflection is at the heart of the progress the theologian may make towards more spiritual knowledge of God.

As may already be clear, however, the distinction is very easily understood to imply a distinction between the real and the unreal. Indeed, the language of ἐπίνοια had also long been used to make these charges: in his commentary on John, Origen condemns those who think that the distinction between Father and Son exists only κατά τινας ἐπινοίας.²⁵ It is then no surprise that Athanasius condemns Arius for saying that terms such as Wisdom apply to the Son κατ' ἐπίνοιαν.²⁶ As we have seen, Eunomius himself has little time for ἐπίνοια as a mode of knowing God. Thus, against the background of this long history when Basil uses the term to characterize all human knowledge of God he begs a number of questions about the extent and reliability of our knowledge of God.

Within the long history of the term there are two immediate sources for Basil's account. Basil's discussion of Christ's titles in *Contra Eunomium* I echoes Origen's discussion in the first book of his commentary on John.²⁷ At the same time, Basil's use mirrors Basil of Ancyra's focus on the importance of the formation of concepts (ἔννοιαι) about the incomprehensible divine existence. Eunomius' own condemnation of ἐπίνοια as a mode of knowledge seems to

---

²² Vaggione, *Eunomius*, 241–2.

²³ The range of philosophical usage is nicely illustrated by Plotinus. At *Ennead* 2. 9. 1, 6. 2. 3, and 6. 6. 6 we see ἐπίνοια being used to describe aspects of the process of thinking. Ἐπίνοια necessarily involves differentiation and when we consider the three primary *hypostases*, it leads us to make basic mistakes about the unity of a reality we apprehend under different ἐπίνοιαι. At *Enn.* 5. 8. 7, the process of creation cannot have involved the sort of planning through ἐπίνοια involved in human planning because that involves thinking new ideas that previously did not exist. And thus, on occasion, Plotinus can simply contrast things that only exist in ἐπίνοια with those that exist in reality, e.g. *Enn.* 6. 6. 9.

²⁴ Clement, *Strom.* 6. 17. 156; 6. 11. 86.   ²⁵ Origen, *Comm. John* 10. 37. 246.

²⁶ Arius, *Thalia*, apud. Athanasius, *Synod.* 15, speaks of the Son being 'conceived in many ἐπίνοιαι'. Athanasius refers to the Arian use of ἐπίνοια dismissively at *Sent.* 23 and elsewhere (e.g. *Decr.* 16) he similarly condemns Arius and Asterius for seeing the Son's titles as 'merely names'.

²⁷ One should, however, note that there are no passages in the *Philocalia* compiled by Basil and Gregory Nazianzen that use the term, and Origen himself makes no use of the term in the *De Principiis*. It is in the *Contra Celsum* and his biblical commentaries that we find it used.

presuppose a pre-existing debate. Given that the *Apology* is aimed at Homoiousian trends as much as at (if not *more* than at) 'Nicene' theologies, it seems likely that Eunomius' target was the emphasis on ἔννοιαι in figures such as Basil of Ancyra. When we note that Basil of Caesarea treats ἔννοια as a synonym for ἐπίνοια, we can see more clearly that he builds on and adds new sophistication to a theme in his immediate predecessors.[28]

Returning to the early chapters of the *Contra Eunomium*, Basil uses his account of ἐπίνοια to insist that Eunomius' particular term 'ingenerate' is only a privative term, indicating God's lack of cause, and hence it is unsuitable as the primary name of God. Basil then argues that the choice of this term as primary can serve only to teach that Father and Son are unlike, ἀνόμοιος, which must thus be the intention of Eunomius, whatever he protests.[29] For Basil, arguing that Father and Son are 'unlike' flies in the face of biblical material such as Col. 1: 15, Heb. 1: 3, and Phil. 2: 6, all of which point to a community of essence (τὸ κοινὸν τῆς οὐσίας) between the generated and the one who has generated. Basil then explains that this community of essence is the core of his teaching and writes:

According to this, divinity (θεότης) is one. That is to say, it is according to the rationale (λόγος) of the substance (*ousia*) that the unity is thought, but, as in number (ἀριθμός), the difference of each rests in the particular properties and in the particular characteristics (ταῖς ἰδιότησι ταῖς χαρακτηριξούσαις).[30]

By ἐπίνοια we know that there is a unity of *ousia* between Father and Son, although what that essence is remains unknown. At the same time we know the ἰδιώματα or ἰδιότητες of Father and Son as distinct individuals. Basil thus moves beyond his earlier theology and speaks of unity of essence at one level and differentiation at another level. At one level, the persons are co-ordinate realities, with an identical ontological status. I return to this fundamental shift later in this chapter. Note here that my two themes—one concerning the logic of the Trinitarian persons and one concerning Basil's epistemology— are already inter-linked: the distinction between the divine essence and the personal particularities is directly paralleled with what is known and unknown of God.

A few sentences later, after explaining that God's image must

---

[28] Indeed, as his career progresses Basil seems to prefer ἔννοια to ἐπίνοια when describing this process.

[29] Basil's invocation of ἀνόμοιος here shows the polemical origins of this term as an accusation about the logical direction of Eunomius' thinking. For Eunomians there are a number of ways in which the Son is like the Father; 'unlike' is a term used infrequently and only with reference to the Son and the Father's essence.

[30] Basil, *Eunom.* 1. 19.

coexist (συνεῖναι) not only before time but before all the aeons, and commenting on Hebrews 1: 3, Basil writes,

And thus, because of this, 'radiance' is said, so that we know what is signified, and 'image of substance', so that *homoousios* is understood.[31]

This text is in some ways unrepresentative, as it is the only application of *homoousios* to the relationship of Father and Son in the *Contra Eunomium*. Nevertheless I think we can see how Basil's new distinctions have provided him with an understanding of *homoousios* that overcomes his earlier concerns. It is important to note that although Basil can now confess the *homoousios*, the term does not function as a point of departure for the argument.

These initial arguments are deeply shaped by Basil's polemical context. Eunomius' insistence that likeness according to essence is logically incoherent—and that, hence, there is only sameness or difference in essence[32]—has forced Basil to articulate a position clearer than that found in the key Homoiousian texts. Eunomius' insistence that if we know God only according to ἐπίνοια, then our knowledge is insignificant and our faith useless, has forced Basil to articulate more clearly the character of our knowledge of God. The genius of Basil's solution is to attack both problems simultaneously. Basil articulates a distinction between natures and individuated realities that enables him to assert that Father and Son are, indeed, the same in essence, but distinct at another level thus preserving a certain order among the persons.[33]

At the same time, Basil distinguishes the unknowability of the divine essence and the knowability of the particular characteristics, the ἰδιώματα, of Father and Son. This epistemological dynamic needs further consideration. I want to leap forward a decade to Basil's *Letter* 234, addressed in 376 to his friend Amphilochius of Iconium. Amphilochius has reported to Basil a line of probably Heterousian polemic arguing that if pro-Nicenes say the essence of God is unknown then they worship what they do not know. This attack is supplemented by the suggestion that if God is simple, then all divine attributes are necessarily names of God's substance. Basil uses two strategies in defence. First, he emphasizes the variety of ways in which we can be said to 'know' (τὸ εἰδέναι) God. Second, Basil argues that we gather together a 'sense' or 'concept' of God (ἔννοια) by attention to his activities (ἐνέργειαι) towards us.[34]

---

[31] Basil, *Eunom.* 1. 20.   [32] Eunomius, *Apol.* 10. 21–2.

[33] As will become clear below in discussion of Basil's account of the Father as source of the Trinity.

[34] Basil, *Ep.* 234: 'we know the greatness of God, and his power, and his wisdom ... not his very substance ... the concept of God (ἔννοια) is gathered by us from the many attributes

Similarly at *Contra Eunomium* 1. 8 Basil argues that the many names we use of God result from God's diverse activities (ἐνέργειαι) towards us.[35] Unlike the divine essence and power, the energies are diverse, possibly temporary[36] and provide the context within which ἐπίνοια can distinguish essence and particulars.[37]

By the 370s Basil had evolved a formula stating that the activities of God all come from the Father, are worked in the Son, and are completed in the Spirit. In this formula Basil seems not so much to outline a dense account of the divine co-operation and sharing, but to find a way to speak of the unity of divine action while still preserving the priority of the Father and the sense of the Spirit as the agent of salvation. In a way that foreshadows Gregory of Nyssa's more famous account of human knowledge as a striving towards a divine 'darkness', Basil presents God as acting without mediation and in a manner beyond our comprehension. The creation is not acted on heteronomously but willingly co-operates with the activity of its creator.[38] Human knowledge of God does thus not suffer from a constant and ruinous lack, but is actively shaped by God to draw a wounded humanity back towards its creator through a slow reshaping of human thought and imagination. In *Letters* 234 and 235 (also addressed to Amphilochius) Basil even blurs the distinction between knowledge and faith: knowledge that one who is just, loving, and almighty acts in the world as creator and redeemer is truly a form of knowledge, but, this 'knowledge' is also the faith (πίστις) that is an essential component of Christian life (alluding to Heb. 11: 6's insistence on the necessity of faith, and thence to Heb. 11's general opposition of faith to what is 'seen').[39]

Athanasian and Homoiousian accounts had already invoked the

---

which we have enumerated... we say that from his activities (ἐνέργειαι) we know our God, but his substance itself we do not profess to approach. For his activities descend to us, but his substance remains inaccessible... Knowledge of his divine substance is, then, knowledge of his incomprehensibility (ἀκατάληψις: "ungraspability").'

[35] e.g. *Eunom.* 1. 8.   [36] e.g. *Spir.* 7. 19.

[37] It is not clear that this distinction is the same as the distinction between essence and energies in later Orthodox theology. As we shall see below and in Ch. 14 Basil and his brother Gregory both rely on a *threefold* distinction between essence, power, and activity.

[38] *Spir.* 7. 19: 'divine energy surpasses everything in speed ... What passage of time is needed by Him who "upholds the universe by His word of power"? he does not work by bodily strength, nor does he need the use of hands in order to fashion things, but all created things follow Him, offering Him their willing cooperation.'

[39] *Ep.* 234: 'But I do know that he exists, but what his substance is I consider beyond understanding. How then am I saved? Through faith. And it is faith enough to know that God is, not what he is, and that he is a rewarder of those who seek him (Heb. 11: 6) ... and that is to be worshipped which is comprehended, not as to what its substance is, but as to that its substance exists.' Cf. The discussion in *Ep.* 235 of the way in which a certain knowledge of God from his activities in creation *precedes* faith. Basil seems both to want to show that pro-Nicene theology can be said to know what it worships, and to show that this 'knowing' is part of a continuum with faith, not in opposition to it.

Son's sharing of the Father's incomprehensibility against anti-Nicene theologies. As we saw in Chapter 6, Basil of Ancyra had already presented the Son as sharing the Father's incomprehensibility. In a way that almost directly mirrors Athanasius' use of a similar idea at *De decretis* 22, Basil seems to see this idea as not simply preserving the Son's generation from scrutiny but as also providing an index against which we can identify what may and may not appropriately be said of the Son. In the anti-Heterousian sermon by Meletius of Antioch also preserved by Epiphanius we find a clear insistence that we should realize that our own generation is incomprehensible, and in the light of this realization see the appropriateness of not claiming to understand the Son's incomprehensible generation.[40] In Basil of Caesarea's theology, this principle is given a new coherence because of his systematic principle that *no ousia* is known as such: we find here an even more thoroughgoing apophatic sense of theological method. This account of human knowledge of God raises important questions for any exploration of Basil's account of unity and diversity in the Trinity: how does this apophaticism qualify the analogies and terminologies Basil offers for the divine existence?

Before moving on let us note how Basil's position here represents a gradual shift in the use of ἐνέργεια language through the fourth century. Throughout the first sixty years of the fourth century we find a number of figures turning to the language of will or ἐνέργεια when they seek to explain the Son's generation without seeming to attribute passion and division to God. Thus, Eusebius of Caesarea speaks of the Son as generated by and expressing the will of the Father. Marcellus of Ancyra uses the language of ἐνέργεια to explain how it is that the Son can come forth and work without God being extended materially. The two authors share a concern to preserve the divine being from division or materiality despite their very distinct theologies. In an anti-Marcellan context Eusebians and Homoians argued that the Son had substantial existence and was not purely an ἐνέργεια. The Son imaged the Father's *ousia* and ἐνέργεια as a distinct subsistent: such a position seems to have been followed, for instance, by Acacius of Caesarea in his anti-Marcellan writing.[41] At the same time Homoians retained emphasis on the Son as generated by the

---

[40] Apud Epiphanius, *Panarion* 73. 32. 5. In its extended conception of a theological method focused around the learning of appropriate speech and appropriate silence about the mystery of God the sermon nicely prefigures a theme central to pro-Nicene theology and theological rhetoric. In this regard one can compare the similar emphases of Gregory Nazianzen's *Or.* 27 and 28, the first two *Theological Orations*.

[41] Epiphanius, *Panarion* 72. 9. 8. Here the Son is image both of the Father's will and his ἐνέργεια.

Father's will, a position now offered with clear subordinationist intent. Thus a standard Homoian question that we see posed to figures from Ambrose to Gregory of Nazianzen to Ephrem the Syrian is 'did the Father beget the Son willingly or unwillingly?'

These earlier anti-Marcellan and anti-Nicene arguments are both firmly continued in Eunomius and strengthened. Eunomius insists that the Son is the product of the Father's will and ἐνέργεια. The Father's ἐνέργεια or will is passionless and unique, and may be temporary: the Son is the product of this temporary activity. Once again deployment of will and activity language helps to preserve the Father from division or passion. Through the 340s and 350s we see a number of alternatives to this tradition of using ἐνέργεια and will language: Athanasius speaks of the unity of action revealing unity of nature, while Basil of Ancyra similarly uses energy language in connection with *ousia* language: the Son is similar in both to the Father as can be deduced from observing his activities.[42] Basil's argument here takes forward the anti-Marcellan principle that the Son images the Father in both *ousia* and ἐνέργεια, but in anti-Heterousian contexts now draws attention to the similarity that must follow rather than the distinction between Father and Son that follows for Acacius. After the early 360s pro-Nicenes use ἐνέργεια language only in a developed version of these two earlier arguments, insisting that there is one divine ἐνέργεια just as there is one nature. The development of arguments about the inseparable divine activity and about the relationship between the one divine nature, power, and activity has pushed the use of this language into new territory. It is important to note, however, that non-Nicenes continue to use the language of energy and will in very traditional ways.

Οὐσία AND ἰδιώματα IN BASIL'S THEOLOGY

What we have seen so far, in the first book of *Contra Eunomium*, is a distinction between *ousia* and ἰδιώματα or ἰδιότητες. We need to note what is not yet said. Basil has made no attempt to offer a generic terminology for divine 'persons' in the abstract. One of the most extensive accounts of the distinction between *ousia* and ἰδιότητες that Basil offers at this stage of his career is to be found at *Contra Eunomium* 2. 28:

Particularities (ἰδιότητες), being added onto the substance (*ousia*) like marks or forms, distinguish what is common by means of individual characteristics (τοῖς ἰδιάζουσι χαρακτῆρσι), but they do not cut [or break through] the

---

[42] For Athanasius see Chs. 6 and 7. For Basil see Epiphanius, *Panarion* 73. 4. 4; 11. It is also important to note Basil's engagement with John 5: 19 at 73: 8–9. 5.

identity in nature (ὁμοφυὲς) of the substance. For instance, deity (θεότης) is common, fatherhood and sonship are individualities (ἰδιώματα); from the intertwining of each, the common and particular, there comes to us a grasp (κατάληψις) of the truth, so that on the mention of the unbegotten light we understand the Father, and on that of begotten light we get the notion (ἔννοιαν) of the Son ... for this is the character of individualities, to reveal in the identity (ταυτότητι) of substance the otherness (ἑτερότητα).[43]

This passage shows clearly that one of Basil's main concerns is to demonstrate how this division helps us articulate what we come to know of God and speak appropriately of both identity and difference between Father and Son. The concern is as much epistemological as strictly ontological. We might even say that Basil's point implies a metaphysics (or at least an analogy with the metaphysics of creation), but the metaphysical distinction he makes is only vaguely defined in comparison with the precise epistemology which drives the clarity of the distinction.

Basil's account represents a complex engagement with and adaptation of a range of philosophical and theological sources. Basil's philosophical borrowings occur in the context of particular late antique transformations of ancient philosophy:[44] the mutual engagement between various ancient 'traditions' occurring in the previous three centuries; a revival in the study of Aristotle; the emergence of thinkers who built on both Stoic and Platonic tradition (such as Posidonius and Antiochus of Ascalon); the eventual emergence of that style of Platonism modern scholars call 'Neoplatonism'. Even if we are aware of this context Basil's borrowings are complex and he seems uninterested in terminological precision. These provisos apart, we can identify three basic influences on Basil's account.[45] The first is Stoic terminologies about the

---

[43] With this passage should be compared the other extensive account in *Ep.* 236 to Amphilochius. The accounts are broadly compatible, although the latter takes the distinction between *ousia* and *hypostasis* as a point of departure: this difference stems from developments to be considered later in the chapter.

[44] The developments in the Platonic tradition (and the extent to which those developments involved a particular mode of interaction between 'schools') are excellently narrated in John Dillon, *The Middle Platonists 80 BC to AD 220* (London: Duckworth, 1977). The appropriate chapters in A. H. Armstrong (ed.), *The Cambridge History of Later Greek and Early Medieval Philosophy* (Cambridge: Cambridge University Press, 1967) are also helpful, though where coverage is provided by Dillon he is to be preferred. For the character of the emergence of 'Neoplatonism' from earlier Platonic tradition see Maria Luisa Gatti, 'Plotnius: The Platonic Tradition and the Foundation of Neoplatonism', in Lloyd P. Gerson (ed.), *The Cambridge Companion to Plotinus* (Cambridge: Cambridge University Press, 1996), 10–37. G. R. Boys-Stones, *Post-Hellenistic Philosophy* (Oxford: Clarendon Press, 2002) discusses the character of philosophy in this period with particular reference to traditionalism as a persistent theme.

[45] It is important to note here that I do not consider the text printed as *Ep.* 38 to be by Basil. If it were taken to be by Basil then one would be able to read his theology as considerably more Aristotelian.

relationship between general and individuated existence.⁴⁶ Simplifying somewhat, in a materialistic context early Stoics posited a universal (frequently passive) and undifferentiated substrate (ὑποκείμενον or *ousia*) as the basis for individuated existence. At a conceptual level we can speak of this substrate differentiated by the addition of particular qualities (ἰδιότητες or ποιότητες). Finally, at the level of concrete existence individuals are also qualified by further qualities with the result that they exit in a particular manner depending on those qualifications (τὸ ἰδίως ποιόν).

This basic scheme seems to lie behind Basil's discussion of a ὑποκείμενον that is one between Father and Son and his insistence that the names of Father and Son do not reveal what God is, but only how he is (ὅπως ἐστίν), the ἰδιότητες.⁴⁷ It is at least likely that Basil would have encountered these themes in the Stoic logic handbooks that seem to have been widely used in the imperial period. It is important to note that Stoics saw the undifferentiated substrate as no more a purely logical reality than one's individuating qualities. Basil's insistence that human beings share in a common substrate as well as in individuating qualities may reflect something of this conception. If we are right in seeing a Stoic emphasis here then we must be very cautious about reading Basil's account of the Trinity as offering 'only' a generic unity between the persons.

Basil's account is not, however, solely Stoic: he also makes use of Aristotelian language, probably mediated through Neoplatonic writing. First, Basil speaks a number of times of the ὁ τοῦ εἶναι λόγος, the logos/rationale of being and of the rationale of Godhead (θεότης) and of *ousia*. Aristotle specifically speaks of a λόγος τῆς οὐσίας at the very beginning of his *Categories*.⁴⁸ Understanding exactly how Aristotle conceives of the phrase the 'formula of being' is difficult: for our purposes it is perhaps most helpful to ignore Aristotle's own possible intentions and move to his interpreters in the first few centuries AD. Johannes Zachhuber argues that for some later interpreters of Aristotle (including Porphyry in his *Isagoge*), there could only

---

⁴⁶ The clearest summary of the perspective I offer here is to be found in Sesboüé's introduction to his edition of *Eunom.* in SC 299, pp. 65–95. A fundamental point of reference for the debate on Basil's sources is Reinhard Hübner's, 'Gregor von Nyssa als Verfasser de Sog. Ep. 38 des Basilius', in Jacques Fontaine and Charles Kannengiesser (eds.), *Epektasis: Mélanges patristiques offerts au Cardinal Daniélou* (Paris: Beauchesne, 1972), 463–90. There is a very useful discussion of Hübner's argument in English in David G. Robertson, 'Stoic and Aristotelian Notions of Substance in Basil of Caesarea', *VigChr*, 52 (1998), 393–417. Some scholarship still rejects almost entirely any Stoic influence on Basil, preferring to locate him entirely within an Aristotelian tradition perhaps mediated by Porphyry, e.g. Drecoll, *Trinitätslehre*, 319–31.

⁴⁷ e.g. *Eunom.* 1. 15.

⁴⁸ Aristotle, *Categories* 1: 'Things are equivocally named when they have the name in common only, the formula of essence (λόγος τῆς οὐσίας) being different . . .'.

be a λόγος τῆς οὐσίας of the generic aspects of something, never of individuals per se.[49] Basil seems to presuppose this interpretation and is able to use an 'Aristotelian' logical concept alongside his basically Stoic division between general essence and individuating characteristics.

We also see an Aristotelian position mediated through Neoplatonic thought in Basil's definition of an individual as a bundle of properties.[50] At *Ennead* 6. 3 Plotinus uses an existing account of the sensible individual as a bundle of properties, but does not concern himself with non-perceptible qualities. His disciple Porphyry develops this concept, speaking of an individual man as being individuated by the unique possession of a conglomeration of properties not in themselves unique. Socrates is individuated by things as diverse as his colour, by his rationality, and by his relationship to his father.[51] We do not know if Basil knew Porphyry first hand, but at *Contra Eunomium* 2. 4 Paul is Paul by being a Jew from Tarsus, the student of Gamaliel, a Pharisee according to the law and the persecutor of the Church. These ἰδιώματα or ἰδιότητες do not reveal the nature of Paul qua human but they do characterize him as a particular individual.

This account of individuals enabled Basil to develop a sophisticated account of the ways in which names for the divine 'persons' indicate relationships. Basil is not the first, of course, to point to the mutual implications of the terms 'Father' or 'Son': But from the late 350s we find the same theme expressed in more technical Aristotelian language. In George of Laodicea, for instance, we find the specific statement that the names Father and Son denote a relationship to something (πρός τι σχέσις).[52] In Basil this theme has a new importance because of the clarity with which he has come to distinguish the

---

[49] Zachhuber, *Human Nature*, 71–4. For an introduction to Neoplatonic use of Aristotle's *Categories* see Stephen Strange, 'Plotinus, Porphyry, and the Neoplatonic Interpretation of the *Categories*', *ANRW* 2. 36. 2 (1987), 955–74.

[50] For a basic introduction to this concept see Lucian Turcescu, 'The Concept of Divine Persons in Gregory of Nyssa's *To his Brother Peter, On the Difference between Ousia and Hypostasis*', *Greek Orthodox Theological Review*, 42 (1997), 63–82; Zachhuber, *Human Nature*, 63 ff. offers a more extensive and complex account of the same text.

[51] Porphyry, *Isagoge* (*CAG* 4. 1. 2); '. . . each thing is composed of a collection of characteristics which can never be the same for another; for the characteristics of Socrates could not be the same for any other particular man'.

[52] Apud Epiphanius, *Panarion* 79. 19. 3. Although the use of this technical language appears with increasing frequency from this time, the same language is also used by Eusebius of Caesarea at *Eccl. theol.* 1. 10—on whom Homoiousian usage may be drawing. Once again, although the language is 'Aristotelian', there are a number of possible late antique and Neoplatonic sources that probably provided the context for its appearance in Christian literature. For example, we find the terminology in the Neoplatonic philosopher Iamblichus (c.250–c.325), in the rhetor, philosopher, and politician Themistius (c.318–85/7), and in the writings of the Emperor Julian (332–63).

II. The Emergence of Pro-Nicene Theology

unity of God at the level of *ousia* and plurality at the level of ἰδιότητες. The language of relationship (σχέσις) serves to emphasize that Father–Son terminology has important consequences for how we understand the nature of God even while telling us nothing about the *ousia* of God.[53] A particularly important text in this regard is *Contra Eunomium* 2. 9 where Basil distinguishes between absolute and relative names. The former designate an essence (such as 'man') while relative names (such as 'son' and 'the generated one') designate relationship, an aspect of something's ἰδιώματα. Thus Basil's account of the relationship between the divine essence and the individual 'persons' is eclectic. Neoplatonic-Aristotelian conceptions are used to interpret a basically Stoic scheme.[54]

We cannot, however, treat Basil's distinction against a purely philosophical background: his attempt at such a distinction is one among a number of similar distinctions found in roughly contemporary theological sources. We do not know who first articulates this distinction clearly; the question is difficult in part because a variety of examples survive that cannot be dated with certainty, and, in part because of the difficulty of understanding the nature of the shared being that is envisaged. It seems most likely that Basil's evolution of the distinction occurred within a context where some such distinction was already clearly in the air. Basil developed an existing discussion, adding clarity, detail, and a new acceptance that the three persons are co-ordinate realities. We have five possible candidates for the earliest version (the order of my list should not be taken as representing an order of likelihood):

1. Apollinaris of Laodicea may have made some of the key moves in his *Detailed Confession of Faith* (ἡ κατὰ μέρος πίστις), speaking of three πρόσωπα or *hypostases* and one divinity or θεότης.[55] We do not

---

[53] Although sometimes this concept is allied to originally Stoic discussions, most scholars agree that Basil's usage of the notion of relationship and his discussion of relative names seems closer to the extended discussion at Aristotle, *Categories* 7.

[54] One aspect of Neoplatonic thought that seems not to have had any noticeable affect on Basil's account at this stage is the discussion of the three *hypostases* of the One, νοῦς, and ψοχή. Only later in his career can we detect clear signs of engagement with this theme. In the 370s, in *Spir.*, we can at least detect reference to Plotinus' *Enneads* 5. 1 and 6. 9. The former is particularly interesting because of its extensive discussion of the relationship between the 'three primary hypostases'. My view of Basil's use of Plotinus is close to the conservative line of John Rist, 'Basil's "Neoplatonism": Its Background and Nature', in Paul J. Fedwick, *Basil of Caesarea. Christian, Humanist, Ascetic* (Toronto: Pontifical Institute of Medieval Studies, 1981), i. 137–220. I also doubt the Basilian authorship of the *De spiritu* (CPG 2838), which contains numerous Plotinian allusions, and thus ignore it here.

[55] See Kelly McCarthy Spoerl, *A Study of the* Kata Meros Pistis *by Apollonarius of Laodicea*, Ph.D. diss. (University of Toronto, 1991), appendix D. This dissertation also offers (pp. 378–97) the only translation of the text into English. Apollinaris writes (sects. 13–15), 'Certain men engage in a dangerous practice against the Holy Trinity, by denying that there are three πρόσωπα, thereby introducing, as it were, a πρόσωπον that is without a *hypostasis* . . . we believe

Basil of Caesarea 203

know if Basil read this text. Apollinaris, however, maintains that the shared divinity is that of the Father present in Son and Spirit: they are not co-ordinate realities. This text may also have originated as a confession presented to the Emperor Jovian in 364 and thus may not represent Apollinaris' earlier teaching.

2. George of Laodicea, as we saw in Chapter 7, argues in 359 that there are three *hypostases* and yet one divinity (θεότης) (because the Father truly originated the Son and the Spirit).[56] Once again, this position comes close to but is still distinct from Basil's own position in ways we have already explored.

3. The Antiochene Tome stemming from the Alexandrian council of 362 reports those who speak of three *hypostases* as also confessing that there is one Godhead (θεότης). The date is late, but the document seems to be presenting a fairly established teaching. If these people are followers of Meletius in Antioch, then it may be that some in Antioch were fundamental in evolving the distinction.

4. There is a short work entitled *Against Arius and Sabellius* which has survived among the works of Gregory of Nyssa but which is probably not by Gregory. This work speaks of the Father and Son as two in *hypostasis* but one in *ousia*, ἀξίωμα, γνώμη and φρόνησις.[57] Some of those scholars who doubt the attribution to Gregory and date the text before 360 have seen it as the earliest witness to a clear division between the two terms. Others date the text as late as the mid-370s. If the text is early then it may pre-date Basil's work: the

---

that three πρόσωπα, Father, Son and Holy Spirit, are shown to possess the divinity, which is one. For the divinity, attested as one by nature in Trinity, confirms the unity of the nature, precisely because this divinity is a characteristic of the Father ... On the one hand, the πρόσωπον manifests the being itself and the existence as a *hypostasis* of each, and on the other hand divinity is a characteristic of the Father, and whenever the divinity of the three is said to be one, Paul gives witness that the characteristic of the Father is present in the Son and the Spirit. So if the divinity will be said to be one in three πρόσωπα, the Trinity is confessed and the single entity is not severed and the natural unity of the Son and the Spirit with the Father is confessed.'

[56] George of Laodicea, apud Epiphanius, *Panarion* 73. 16. 1–4: 'And let not the word *hypostases* bother anyone. For the Orientals speak of *hypostases* for this reason: that they may point out the subsistent, existent properties (τάς ἰδιότητας τῶν προσώπων ὑφεστώσας καὶ ὑπαρχούσας ...) of the three persons ... although by no means do they speak of the three *hypostases* as three principles or three Gods. But neither do they call Father and Son two Gods. For they acknowledge that there is one divinity (θεότης) containing all things through the Son in the Holy Spirit.' George's theology is discussed in Ch. 7.

[57] The text is to be found at PG 45, 1281–1302 and GNO 3/1. 71–85. The only extensive discussion in English is in Lienhard, *Contra Marcellum*, 232–9. Johannes Quasten, *Patrology*, iii: *The Golden Age of Greek Patristic Literature* (Westminster, Md.; Christian Classics, 1992), 93 dates the work before 358 and hence sees this as the first text to speak of the supposedly key formula three *hypostases* and one *ousia*. As Lienhard points out, 'Ousia and Hypostasis: The Cappadocian Settlement and the Theology of "One Hypostasis" ', in Stephen T. Davis, David Kendall, and Gerald O'Collins (eds.), *The Trinity: An Interdisciplinary Symposium on the Doctrine of the Trinity* (Oxford and New York: Oxford University Press, 2000), 100, the text does not use the phrase in this form at all. The dating of the text is also extremely uncertain.

text appears to present Father and Son as in some sense co-ordinate realities.

5. Marius Victorinus, writing around 358, says that 'the Greeks' speak of three *hypostases* out of one *ousia* (ἐκ μιᾶς οὐσίας τρεῖς εἶναι τὰς ὑποστάσεις). However, it is not clear whether the reference is to Christian or non-Christian writers. Nevertheless, the text is witness *at least* to the wide variety of ways in which such a distinction was under discussion by Christian authors during these years.[58]

Thus we can see that during the 357–64 period similar distinctions had begun to appear across the eastern Mediterranean. Indeed, although Basil appears to have been the first to defend the distinction extensively and to describe the distinct persons as simply sharing an ontological status, within a decade parallels appear in a number of contexts where we do not seem to see influence from Basil. The relationship between these different accounts is taken up again in following chapters.

NOVELTY AND TRADITION IN BASIL'S TRINITARIAN THEOLOGY

I want now to consider some ways in which Basil's theology continues to maintain traditional dynamics even as it develops. Throughout *Contra Eunomium* 1–2 Basil continues to speak of essential 'likeness',[59] and does not yet treat the language of Nicaea as a fundamental point of departure for his theology. At 1. 23, for example, Basil takes up Eunomius' critique of the idea of a 'similarity' between the Father's essence and the Son's. The Father, as simple, must clearly be distinct from the one who has been 'generated'. Indeed, Eunomius continues, the language of similarity here can only imply total equality and who would claim that the Son is equal to the Father in the light of John 14: 28? Basil's reply makes no attempt to substitute the language of similarity: he argues that the Son, like the Father is simple and uncompound such that there is a ὅμοιος κατ' οὐσίαν. Almost immediately Basil presses his point by

---

[58] Victorinus, *Adv. Ar.* 3. 4. It is also noteworthy that although Victorinus gives his account of what the Greeks say in Greek, a *TLG* search shows up no uses of this phrase in any of its available texts and, moreover, it seems unlikely that any 4th-cent. Greek theologian would be happy to speak of the three coming 'out of' a prior *ousia*. However, from *Adv. Ar.* 3. 4–5 it seems that Victorinus was aware of contemporary Greek discussion: about how to relate these terms.

[59] Particularly helpful here is Steenson, *Basil of Ancyra*, ch. 3, 'Theological foundations of the thought of Basil of Caesarea'. After the first two books this language is absent. This may represent Basil's gradual abandonment of the terminology. As I noted earlier, however, Steenson has suggested dating *Ep.* 9, which continues to argue for the significance of ὅμοιος κατ' οὐσίαν alongside *homoousios*, to the later 360s. Were he to be right, we would have to date Basil's final shift away from such language a few years later.

using 1 Cor. 1: 24 to argue that there is also a ταυτότης τῆς δυνάμεως, an identity of power between the two. At 2. 22 Basil argues that in his rejection of the incomprehensible, ineffable, and necessarily passionless generation Eunomius has failed to grasp the κατ' οὐσίαν... ὁμοιότητα, the likeness of essence. Basil uses the phrase twice and states that the particular use of 'generation' is designed to protect this concept. In all these examples Basil treats as interchangeable terms we often assume to be incompatible. The fluidity of this usage is rendered possible because the 'likeness' of which he continues to speak is now governed by his distinction between *ousia* and ἰδιώματα.

Johannes Zachhuber's recent *Human Nature in Gregory of Nyssa*[60] offers a detailed account of Basil's acceptance of the three persons as co-ordinate realities, and sees it as a clear rejection of Apollinaris' suggestions to Basil in *Letter* 362. Apollinaris argues that *homoousios* most truly indicates the unity between the founder of a race and subsequent members—we are *homoousios* with Adam or David because of their role as the founder of our race, and the Son is *homoousios* with the Father because he is Son. While Zachhuber is right to identify a basic and important break between Basil and this 'genetic' interpretation of *homoousios*, in his *Letter* 52 (*c*.370) Basil writes:

Since, therefore, the Father is light without beginning, and the Son is begotten light, yet one is light and the other is light, they [the fathers of Nicaea] rightly declared them *homoousios* . . . For things which are brothers to one another cannot be *homoousios*, as some have supposed; on the contrary, when both the cause and that which has its existence from the cause are of the same existence, they are said to be *homoousios*.

---

[60] Beyond the discussion of this paragraph there are three main disagreements I have with his book. First, Zachhuber's account of Basil's possible dependence on a 'Eustathian' tradition with reference to Eustathius of Antioch (pp. 57 ff.) is highly implausible. The one fragment to which he points is deeply ambiguous: it is not at all clear that it is a verbatim quotation from Eustathius and it is not at all clear that even were it so the terminology concerning the persons is intended to convey the degree of discrete existence necessary for the parallel to work. Basil's consistent support for Meletius over Paulinus and his attitude to 'continuing Marcellans' also indicate the unlikeliness of this connection. Zachhuber, p. 59 n. 54 also appears to confuse Eustathius of Antioch with Eustathius of Sebaste: in *Letter* 263 Basil is accusing the latter not the former of tritheism. Second, Zachhuber treats Basil's position as if it were explicable as one instance of a common Cappadocian tradition in a way that blurs important differences. While he is carefully cautious to speak of the uncertain authorship of Basil's *Ep*. 38, he is happy to speak of it as representing a 'Cappadocian' position with little nuance. Third, his approach to the 'Cappadocian' use of analogies based on common humanity also surprisingly lacks nuance. Nowhere does he examine exactly what is at issue in the drawing of these analogies (see my own discussion in Ch. 10), nor does he attempt to argue for the significance of the analogy within 'Cappadocian' theology by showing its prominence over against other usage. Thus, the remarkable subtlety of Zachhuber's reading of the philosophical sources should not lead us to accept his conclusions *tout court*.

On the one hand, this account of *homoousios* relies on Basil's division between *ousia* and ἰδιώματα in that he is able to identify a common essence between the two. But, on the other hand, he argues—in a manner unique in his corpus—that *homoousios* is appropriately used in a 'genetic' sense. Thus, while he had made an important break from his predecessors, Basil tends to reinterpret earlier language rather than immediately reject it.

We see the same transformation of earlier tradition in the way Basil speaks of the Father. Basil consistently presents the Father as the source of the Trinitarian persons and of the essence that the three share. At *Contra Eunomium* 2. 25 Basil rejects Eunomius' charge that 'light from light' indicates the same distinction as ungenerated and generated. Basil states that the Son is 'the generated light, having received light from the ungenerated, and is life in himself and goodness in himself proceeding from the life-giving source (ἐκ τῆς ζωοποιοῦ πηγῆς) and the paternal goodness'. Earlier, at 1. 25, Basil interprets John 14: 28 ('the Father is greater than I') by first indicating the 'equality and identity' of power between Father and Son and then arguing that the distinction is one at the level of cause (αἰτία) and point of origin (ἀρχή). The Father is greater only by being the cause, not at the level of substance. This language is found throughout Basil's career.[61]

Throughout the fourth century the theme of the Father as the source of the Son's existence is used as a prophylactic against charges that pro-Nicenes teach a plurality of Gods or that the Godhead is divided. Nevertheless, in all the previous discussions of the term that emphasize the Son's sharing of the Father's attributes, a certain ontological subordination is at least implied.[62] One can even point to Athanasius' pointed lack of willingness to use *homoousios* of the Father's relationship to the Son and his consistent picture of the Son as proper to the Father, as the Father's own wisdom. Athanasius' theology demonstrates a highly conservative

---

[61] Note for example, *Ep.* 210. 4 (*c.*375): '. . . as to the saying, "I have come in the name of my Father", it is necessary to know this, that he speaks thus ascribing the Father as the cause and point of origin of himself'. Interestingly, although the Father's status as cause of all created things is happily asserted in *Spir.* (at e.g. 16. 38, a text discussed below) and it is clear that the Father is the source of Son and Spirit, the text seems to avoid explanations of the relative status of Son and Spirit through accounts of the Father's acting as the source of their being. This idea perhaps seemed unsuitable to Basil in that polemical context.

[62] This may be seen in the way that these documents press likeness language very strongly but still avoid certain forms of simple parallelism. For example, George of Laodicea (apud Epiphanius, *Panarion* 73. 14. 3) writes: 'The accurate knowledge of the persons consists of the following: The Father, who is everlastingly a Father, is incorporeal and immortal, while the Son, who is everlastingly a Son and never a Father, but is called everlasting because of his being's independence of time and incomprehensibility, has taken flesh by the will of the Father, and has undergone death for us.'

transformation of his predecessors' thought. In Basil, the Father's sharing of his being involves the generation of one identical in substance and power. The combination of distinguishing *ousia* and ἰδιώματα and yet maintaining the role of the Father as source heightens the paradox of the incomprehensible depth of the Father's self-giving, and emphasizes even more clearly that in the generation of the Son (and Spirit) God's perfection is eternally realized. At the same time, previous accounts of the Father's priority actually enabled Basil's transformation of that tradition. Apollinaris saw the 'genetic' sense of *homoousios* protecting the theologian from seeming to assert two or three equal principles in the universe, thus guarding against those who would see *homoousios* implying the very picture of co-ordinate realities Basil himself eventually adopted. Basil's skill was to see that one could in fact make use of an account of co-ordinate realities while a robust conception of the Father as source would protect against unacceptable consequences.

We can in fact raise some aspects of this discussion of Basil to the level of generalities about pro-Nicene theology. For all pro-Nicenes the Father is presented as first in an order in the Godhead, and as the source of Son and Spirit. It is not surprising that we find this commonality: pro-Nicene formulations of the coequal persons emerged from a context in which the generation of the Son from the Father as equal to the Father was the focus of argument. The development from this position, however, towards a fully pro-Nicene position, enabled pro-Nicenes also to incorporate earlier insistence on the necessity of the Son to the Father and assertions that the perfectness of the Father is found in the coequal existence of the Son and Word.

THE UNITY OF GOD AND THE HUMAN PERSON

It is important to note how easily the discussion has proceeded so far without any discussion of Basil's possible use of an analogy between the three divine 'persons' and three human persons. Through *Contra Eunomium* 1 and 2 Basil uses the distinction between individual characteristics and common essence but makes no attempt to describe the realities of which these characteristics are true. Even when Basil discusses the individuation of Peter and Paul as analogous to the individuation of Father and Son, he does not argue that we should understand the nature of an individual divine person by analogy with a human person. Basil's arguments would lose nothing if he had spoken of three cats or dogs (and note that in *Letter* 236 he uses the example of a 'living thing'). There are, however, clear reasons for Basil's assumption that human persons are particularly appropriate examples.⁶³

Human persons for Basil possess a peculiar dignity because in their rational minds they possess the image of God and are the most appropriate site for exploring the nature of God. At a number of points in the *Contra Eunomium* Basil treats the harmonious, passionless emergence of thought as an analogue for the emergence of Son from Father: the human *nous* stands as an ideal site for the exploration of the immediacy of relations between the immaterial divine 'persons'. In *Sermon* 343 Basil offers an extended discussion of the same theme, emphasizing here the presence of the full power of the mind in expressed speech.⁶⁴ At *On the Holy Spirit* 16. 40, the Spirit's closeness to Father and Son is dramatically likened to the closeness of a human person's spirit to the self:

> But the greatest proof that the Spirit is one with the Father and Son is that he is said to have the same relationship to God as the spirit within us has to us: 'for what person knows a man's thought except the spirit of the man which is in him? So also no one comprehends the thoughts of God except the Spirit of God' (1 Cor. 2: 11).

In these passages Basil relies on the analogies between God and one human person to make his points. And yet, to read this as evidence for a preference for thinking of God in terms of a 'psychological' rather than a 'social' analogy is to miss the point. Basil's concern is not with selecting any primary analogical base, but with articulating a process of thought, a way of exploring the usefulness of the mind as a site for reflection.

Thus, when it suits his purpose, Basil can make use of the dynamics of human experience to articulate the character of the Persons individuality. At *On the Holy Spirit* 16. 38 Basil wishes to emphasize the perfect quality of each divine person's activity and thus speaks of the Father *choosing* to work through the Son—not needing to. Similarly, the Son chooses to work through the Spirit, but does not need to. Throughout these examples human experience of self-determining activity functions not as a basis for presenting the divine persons as a Trinity by committee, but as an analogical site enabling Basil to emphasize the ultimately incomprehensible perfect quality of the divine existence which originates in the Father but which is freely given to the Son. It does not reflect the subtlety of his usage to say that the human mind is an analogy for the Trinity or for

---

⁶³ We should note that at the most basic level when he describes the individual as a bundle of properties, Basil adapts an argument in which Socrates is the traditional example: transposing apostles into the argument is a rhetorical flourish that should hardly surprise.

⁶⁴ *Serm.* 343. 3 (PG 31. 477–80). The sermon is quoted at Rousseau, *Basil*, 115–16.

an individual divine person in Basil: it seems better to speak of human individuality and creative, self-determining rationality as providing an analogical site that may be explored in multiple ways to think through a variety of aspects of divine existence and the distance between our existence and God's. This concept is taken up further in Chapter 10 where I turn directly to the question of whether Basil and other pro-Nicenes present the Trinity as sharing a generic or numerical unity.

DEVELOPMENTS IN TECHNICAL TERMINOLOGY

So far, although a number of forays have taken us beyond the early 360s, my discussion has focused on the first two books of Basil's *Contra Eunomium*. In this section of the chapter I explore two ways in which Basil seems to develop in his technical terminology, from the third book until his death in 379. I say 'seems' because from the 365–79 period the only extended treatise on Trinitarian theology we possess is the *On the Holy Spirit*. In this treatise Basil is strongly guarded about his vocabulary, and conclusions must be carefully drawn. From Basil's letters, however, some key developments can be traced.

I have not discussed the term *hypostasis* so far because it does not function as a technical term for the individual divine persons in the early books of the *Contra Eunomium*. *Hypostasis* is here synonymous with *ousia* and ὑποκείμενον in the interpretation of Heb. 1: 3.[65] Bernard Sesboüé argues that occasionally in book 2 Basil uses the term of the Son and the Spirit with the dynamic sense of 'existence resulting from an act of generation'.[66] Basil's avoidance of *hypostasis* for individual divine 'persons' in books 1–2 was probably motivated by polemical concerns: seeking to indicate the unity of *ousia*, it may have seemed to give too much to deploy the highly contested *hypostasis*. In *Contra Eunomium* 3, however, when the Seraphim at Isaiah 6: 3 cry 'Holy' three times we see that 'the holiness according to nature (φύσις) is contemplated in the three *hypostases*'.[67] This is the only time the phrase 'three *hypostases*' is used in the *Contra Eunomium*. After 364 Basil uses *hypostasis* more regularly to describe the individual persons (although he also continues to use the term in other senses).[68] In *Letters* 52, 125, and 236 (*c*.373–6), for example,

---

[65] Here I am following Sesboüé, *Saint Basile*, 130–7. But see also Lucian Turcescu, 'Prosōpon and Hypostasis in Basil of Caesarea's *Against Eunomius* and the Epistles', *VigChr* 51 (1997), 374–95.
[66] Sesboüé, *Saint Basile*, 135 (partly following Prestige), with reference to *Eunom*. 2. 13, 17, 19, 32.
[67] *Eunom*. 3. 3.   [68] e.g. *Spir*. 16. 38; 17. 41.

hypostasis seems to have become a standard and technical term. Letter 236 to Amphilochius is particularly important as there Basil offers his most extended definition of the distinction between nature and persons since that of *Contra Eunomium* 2. 28. Two things are particularly notable about this letter. First, in response to a question from Amphilochius concerning the distinction between *ousia* and *hypostasis*, Basil accepts the terms without question as if it were clear that *hypostasis* holds an accepted technical status. Secondly, Basil treats *hypostasis* and πρόσωπον (prosopon) as synonymous, but he also sees πρόσωπον as less appropriate, too close to Sabellianism.[69] *Hypostasis* indicates a reality of existence that he feels πρόσωπον may not.

Even though *hypostasis* has grown in importance, we should not assume this indicates Basil now has a dense understanding of divine person in the abstract. For example, much is often made of Basil's use of the phrase τρόπος ὑπάρξεως, ('mode of being') to explain *hypostasis*. Unfortunately Basil's actual usage will not bear the weight sometimes put upon it. Basil uses the phrase only three times clearly and in none of these does he offer an interpretative gloss or account of its meaning.[70] Brian Daley notes (in a manner parallel to the account of Sesboüé discussed above) that in Basil and Gregory of Nyssa *hypostasis* seems to be used not so much to identify a metaphysically dense notion of individuated being as to point to the fact that we know Son and Spirit only as the product of particular acts of generation and as acts of relationship to the Father: we know their *hypostasis* and their τρόπος ὑπάρξεως insofar as we know their mode of origination from the Father.[71] As in so many other aspects of Trinitarian theology, Basil's use of *hypostasis* and τρόπος ὑπάρξεως

---

[69] *Ep.* 236: '... both unity is preserved in the confession of the one Godhead, and that which is peculiar to the persons (τὸ τῶν προσώπων ἰδιάζον) is confessed in the distinction made in the characteristics attributed to each (ἐν τῷ ἀφορισμῷ τῶν περὶ ἕκαστον νοουμένων ἰδιωμάτων).'

[70] *Ep.* 235. 2; *Spir.* 18. 46; *C. Sab. et Ar. et An.* 34. It is important to note that in the case of the second two refs. the τρόπος ὑπάρξεως of a Trinitarian 'person' is mentioned as something we cannot know. Karl Holl, *Amphilochius von Ikonium in seinem Verhältnis zu den grossen Kappadoziern* (Tübingen: J. C. B. Mohr, 1904), 133 ff. saw Basil's explanations of the relationship between essence and persons as insufficient for describing the 'personal' realities of the Trinity. In one sense I can only agree—it is not Basil's intention to offer a description of what it is to be a divine person. In another sense Holl misses the point—the terminology is not intended to serve this function, Basil, I suggest, thinks it impossible to offer a dense ontological account of a divine person or their mode of communal and unitary coexistence.

[71] Brian E. Daley, 'Nature and the "Mode of Union": Late Patristic Models for the Personal Unity of Christ', in Stephen T. Davis, Daniel Kendall, and Gerald O'Collins (eds.), *The Incarnation: An Interdisciplinary Symposium on the Incarnation of the Son of God* (Oxford: Clarendon Press, 2001), 164–96. See also the excellent discussion of Polycarp Sherwood, *The Earlier Ambigua of Maximus the Confessor*, Studia Anselmiana, 36 (Rome: Pontificum Institutum S. Anselmi, 1955), 155–61. Sherwood notes, following Holl, that it is Amphilochius who first uses τρόπος ὑπάρξεως of all three persons. Using the phrase of the Father points only in a negative sense to the Father's status as unoriginate.

Basil of Caesarea

brings to prominence a terminology that only much later receives extensive definition.

Finally, it is during the mid-360s that Basil seems to have abandoned ὅμοιος language. Even by book 3 of the *Contra Eunomium*, Basil seems to have become wary of such language. In letters from the 370s Basil seems to make increasingly frequent use of *homoousios*. The *On the Holy Spirit* of 375 (discussed below) is notoriously reticent about using *homoousios* of the Spirit, but we have a number of letters in which Basil points to Nicaea, *homoousios*, and an extra confession of the Spirit's status as the standard for receiving people into communion. It seems that Basil here copies the practice Athanasius adopted at the Council of Alexandria in 362.[72]

ON THE HOLY SPIRIT AND PRO-NICENE PNEUMATOLOGY

This brings us directly to Basil's *On the Holy Spirit* of 375.[73] In general terms what we find in *On the Holy Spirit* is a more clearly and extensively articulated pneumatology whose basic lines are those of *Contra Eunomium* 3. In order to understand fully the context for Basil's *On the Holy Spirit*, we need to sketch something of the debate over the place of the Spirit that had taken shape since the late 350s. This section of the chapter will, thus, also provide the opportunity for some more general remarks about the evolving character of pro-Nicene pneumatology.

We must begin by turning to Egypt. Somewhere between 358 and 361 Athanasius addressed three letters to one of his Egyptian supporters, Serapion, bishop of Thumis in the Nile delta.[74] Serapion had reported a group who are 'orthodox' as far as the Son is concerned, but seem to regard the Spirit as a created and superior angel (quoting 1 Tim. 5: 21).[75] This group appears to be an isolated

---

[72] In *Ep.* 113 Basil suggests that, in the cause of ecclesiastical peace, the requirements for entering into communion with someone should be a confession of the Nicene creed and then a confession that the Spirit is not a creature (κτίσμα). The same basic procedure seems to be also hinted at in *Ep.* 114 and recommended to Eusebius of Samosata in *Ep.* 128. In *Ep.* 204 Basil attributes his policy of requiring the confession of Nicaea for communion and actively avoiding further detailed examination to a letter he received from Athanasius. The letter he has in mind may well be a copy of the encyclical following the Council of Alexandria in 362, or a letter advocating the policy adopted in 362.

[73] On Basil's pneumatology see Hanson, *The Search*, 772–80; Simonetti, *La Crisi*, 480–501; Drecoll, *Trinitätslehre*, chs. 4 and 5. These authors all provide extensive further bibliography.

[74] On what follows see now Michael A. G. Haykin, *The Spirit of God: The Exegesis of 1 and 2 Corinthians in the Pneumatomachian Controversy of the Fourth Century* (Leiden: Brill, 1994). W.-D. Hauschild, *Die Pneumatomachen: Eine Untersuchung zur Dogmengeschichte des vierten Jahrhunderts*, diss. (University of Hamburg, 1967), is still significant.

[75] For a brief summary of recent scholarship on these letters see Haykin, *Spirit of God*, 59–61.

phenomenon and trying to tease out the details of their thought need not concern us here. Athanasius' response attempts to defend the place of the Spirit in the Godhead using the resources developed during two decades of polemic over the Son. Athanasius pursues two strategies. On the one hand, he shows that the Spirit is closely linked to the Son, either present in the Son's activity or completing the Son's activity. Athanasius' account of the function of the Spirit depends upon articulating the Spirit's dependence on the Son:

> As then the Father is light and the Son is his radiance . . . we may see in the Son the Spirit also by whom we are enlightened. 'That he may give you', it says, 'the Spirit of wisdom and revelation in the knowledge of him, having the eyes of your heart enlightened'. But when we are enlightened by the Spirit it is Christ who enlightens us.[76]

The Spirit's dependence on Christ is the same as the Son's dependence on the Father; as the Father's own the Son has the Father present in him: just so the Spirit belongs to Christ and Christ is present in the Spirit's work. Once the Spirit has been implicated in the Son's work and been presented as completing that work, then all the arguments that have been used to link Father and Son can be used of the Spirit. Athanasius' concern here is a fundamentally soteriological one: just as he insists on God's immediate work in Christ, the Spirit too must be part of that immediate divine activity.[77] Athanasius' account is, however, highly traditional in its conception of the Spirit's work. Origen offers a picture in which the Spirit supplies the gifts of God to the saints, but he also argues that the Spirit's existence and virtue comes through participation in the Son and through the Son's constant ministry.[78] His reflection is a little more extended than his contemporaries and predecessors, but the basic account of the Spirit's function is the same. Irenaeus, for example, presents the Spirit as a gift from the Father, coming through the Son and acting to transform and sanctify the saints.[79] According the Spirit these functions eventually goes back to texts such as Gal. 4: 6, 1 Cor. 6: 11 and Rom. 5: 5.

In the first half of the fourth century we find the same basic sense of the Spirit's work, the same uncertainty about the Spirit's ontological status, but the beginnings of debate over the issue. Eusebius of Caesarea, for example, follows Origen's account closely in those few passages where he discusses the Spirit, but in his anti-Marcellan

---

[76] Athanasius, *Serap.* 1. 19.
[77] Athanasius, *Serap.* 1. 24: 'Further it is through the Spirit that we are all said to be partakers of God . . . If the Holy Spirit were a creature, we should have no participation in God in him.'
[78] Origen, *Comm. John* 2. 75–6. Cf. *Princ.* 1. 3. 4.   [79] Irenaeus, *Adv. haer.* 3. 17.

context he emphasizes more strongly than Origen the Spirit's status as only first among those things created by the Son.[80] Representatives of alternative traditions can also be found: for Cyril of Alexandria the Spirit is a 'power' and a 'sanctifying principle' who inspired the prophets and the apostles and illuminates the souls of the just. Cyril includes the Spirit in the Trinity, but does not tell us what this means. The Spirit has come from heaven, is honoured with Father and Son but is also 'made by God through the Son'—the phrasing is ambiguous: does he mean to place the Spirit on a different ontological plane?[81] We do not find here much more clarity than we find in Irenaeus or Origen, but we do find someone refusing Eusebius' active subordinationism. In the *Letters to Serapion* Athanasius is thus reworking these earlier traditions to emphasize that the sanctifying work of the Spirit must be directly the work of God.

Immediately after the passage quoted above Athanasius lists various texts which point to aspects of the Spirit's function. The purpose of his list is to show that the work of the Spirit is the same as that of the Son (e.g. comparing 1 Cor. 1: 13 and 1 Cor. 10: 4) and that just as the Son's presence is also the presence of the Father, so too the Spirit's presence is the presence of God (1 John 4: 12–13).[82] Just as the Son declares that his works are the Father's, so too Paul declares that the works of the Spirit are the works of Christ. The list serves to shape a vision of Father, Son, and Spirit working together in an ordered and harmonious manner:

> But if there is such co-ordination and unity within the holy Triad, who can separate either the Son from the Father or the Spirit from the Son or from the Father himself?[83]

It is only a small step from here to a clear statement of the doctrine of inseparable operation as part of his explanation of why the Spirit's sanctifying action reveals it to be God:

> The Son, like the Father, is creator; for he says 'What things I see the Father doing, these things I also do.' . . . But if the Son, being, like the Father, creator, is not a creature; and if, because all things were created through him, he does not belong to things created: then, clearly, neither is the Spirit a creature. For it is written, concerning him in Psalm 103: 'Thou shalt take away their spirit, and they shall die and return to their dust. Thou shalt put forth thy Spirit, and they shall be created, and thou shalt renew the face of the earth.' As it is thus written, it is clear that the Spirit is not a creature, but takes part in the action of creation. The Father creates

---

[80] Eusebius, *Eccl. theol.* 1. 6.   [81] Cyril, *Cat. lect.* 16. 3–4.
[82] Athanasius, *Serap.* 1. 20.
[83] Athanasius, *Serap.* 1. 20. 'Co-ordination' here is συστοιχία.

all things through the Word in the Spirit ... the Father himself, through the Word in the Spirit works and gives all things.[84]

We have so far encountered arguments about inseparable operation in Hilary, and arguments which almost state this principle in Basil of Ancyra. Athanasius' *Letters to Serapion* may well represent the earliest clear statement of the doctrine applied to all three persons.[85] The combination of a need to shape a polemic in favour of the Spirit as well as the clarity with which the unity of nature could be stated in anti-Heterousian contexts seems to have prompted clearer statement of the principle. We shall meet it extensively in Gregory of Nyssa and Augustine later in the book.

Just as his account of the Son can rely heavily on the picture of the Father as one person with his intrinsic word, so too he emphasizes the closeness of Spirit to Son by presenting the Spirit as the Son's 'energy':

> As the Son is an only-begotten offspring, so also the Spirit, being given and sent from the Son is himself one and not many, nor one from among many, but only Spirit. As the Son, the living Word, is one, so must the sanctifying and enlightening life-giving activity (ἐνέργεια), his gift, be one perfect and complete, which is said to proceed from the Father, because it is from the Word, who is confessed to be from the Father ...[86]

This picture has its virtues: Athanasius can clearly show that the Spirit's work is a continuation of the Son's just as the Son's work is that of the Father in him. Nevertheless the language also shows Athanasius trying out formulations that will soon be problematic. As we shall see, in Asia Minor 'the Cappadocians' will find the language of ἐνέργεια used of the Spirit (probably by Homoiousians) to be highly problematic, seeming to indicate a lack of real existence.

We can now move from Egypt to Asia Minor, and forward to the late 360s and early 370s. At this time and in this context we begin to hear of those who deny the divinity of the Spirit as a distinct group. It is unlikely that this group is a continuation in any direct sense of those whom Athanasius had encountered.[87] Many or most of these seem to have held positions on the Son that were close to pro-Nicene positions, but they seem to have been worried that the emerging pro-Nicene position was modalist. During the late 370s and 380s they are termed Macedonians (after Macedonius the bishop of Constantinople who was exiled in 360) or Pneumatomachoi ('Spirit fighters':

---

[84] e.g. Athanasius, *Serap.* 3. 4–5.

[85] The earliest is probably found in Marius Victorinus writing a year or two before this text. One should, however, also note the discussion of Origen, *Princ.* 1. 2. 12: the seeds of the doctrine had long been available. I am grateful to Michel Barnes for emphasizing the importance of the Origen text.

[86] Athanasius, *Serap.* 1. 20. [87] e.g. Hanson, *The Search*, 762.

a name first used by Athanasius of Serapion's opponents). During the 380–400 period this group appears to have separated into a distinct sect with a very limited alternative hierarchy. Some in this group were former Homoiousians: indeed the complexity of these years is illustrated by the fact that some Homoiousians who had accepted Nicaea continued to resist treating the Spirit as a sharer in the one divine power. Basil's early associate and ascetic mentor, Eustathius of Sebaste (who became a significant 'Macedonian' leader after 372), is an excellent example. Eustathius' ability to agree to Nicaea and yet maintain a subordinationist theology of the Spirit eventually led him into direct conflict with Basil, to whom such a position could only seem a disingenuous avoidance of Nicaea's 'obvious' implications. In the context of the early 360s it is not at all clear that this is so. A number of texts by Basil and the two Gregorys are directed at Pneumatomachians, most famously Basil's *On the Holy Spirit* and Nyssa's *On the Holy Trinity* and *To Ablabius*.[88] The main tactic of these texts is to apply to the Spirit arguments about the unity of activity and nature that had been developed in polemic over the Son's status.

Basil's own contribution in the *On the Holy Spirit* was dedicated to Amphilochius in 375. We do not know how wide a circulation this text was intended to have, but it seems to have quickly become well known. The first aspect of the text to which I wish to draw attention is Basil's use of ἐνέργεια or energy language.[89] This language is associated with discussion of the Spirit in both the *Contra Eunomium* and *On the Holy Spirit*. Two witnesses from the 360–80 period indicate that there were those who described the Spirit itself *as* an ἐνέργεια. In his *Apology* Eunomius himself ridicules those who call the Spirit an ἐνέργεια but who also place the Spirit in an order of essences.[90] It is possible that he is referring to some associated with Homoiousian strains of thought. Eunomius presents the Son and the Spirit as products of the ἐνέργεια of God's substance, ἐνέργεια here serving as an intermediary term taken to be synonymous with will and indicating the clear distinction between the products and the divine existence itself. He also presents the distinct ἐνέργειαι of the persons as evidence that they must be ontologically distinct beings. Two decades later Gregory Nazianzen speaks of a confusing range of opinions concerning the Spirit in Constantinople, including some who think of the Spirit as an ἐνέργεια.[91] Nazianzen here

---

[88] For which text see Ch. 14.
[89] On this language see particularly Barnes, *Power of God*, 297–305. Steenson, *Basil of Ancyra*, 166–95, offers an extensive discussion of ἐνέργεια and *ousia* terminology in Basil of Ancyra.
[90] Eunomius, *Apol.*, 26.   [91] Gregory of Nazianzen, *Or.* 31. 5.

may be referring to Heterousian arguments that as ἐνέργεια the Spirit is not a substantive reality. Nazianzen argues that Scripture clearly speaks of the Spirit as substantive agent.

Against these uses of ἐνέργεια language Basil deploys two tactics. The first is to argue that the Spirit participates in all the activities of Father and Son. This tactic may draw on the earlier Homoiousian argument that the likeness of Son to Father is seen in their both undertaking the same activities.[92] The second tactic is one we saw above: placing all discussion of ἐνέργεια language within the context of a causal sequence in which activity is caused by and reveals a power (δύναμις) which in turn is an inherent and constituting aspect of a substance. This sequence is discussed more fully in Chapter 13, here we need only to note how this sequence undergirds Basil's use of the first tactic. It is because of the presumption of this tactic that he can argue that common activity demonstrates a common essence. Basil's use of the theme of common activities in *On the Holy Spirit* is, however, subtly different from the same tactic as deployed in Gregory of Nyssa. In Nyssa, as we shall see, the three 'persons' are presented as all involved in each unitary action which 'flows' from Father, through Son, and is completed in the Spirit. In *On the Holy Spirit*, however, Basil presents the peculiar action of the Spirit, completing and sanctifying, as a constant part or aspect of God's activity. The actions of Father and Son in creating and saving intrinsically involve an action of perfecting and (where appropriate) sustaining in existence or perfection that is the work of the Spirit. This account follows lines laid out clearly in the third book of the *Contra Eunomium*.[93]

In *On the Holy Spirit* Basil continues to follow his insistence in *Contra Eunomium* 3 that while the Spirit is third in order and dignity (τῇ τάξει καὶ τῷ ἀξιώματι), the Spirit is not third in an order of essences.[94] Basil insists that the Spirit is to be accorded equal worship and honour with the Father and the Son, even if he is not willing to say directly that the Spirit is God in the same terms as Father and Son. In *On the Holy Spirit*, we find if anything a slightly greater reserve,[95] but a wide variety of expressions indicating the

---

[92] e.g. apud Epiphanius, *Panarion* 73. 7. 4, 9. 5, 11. 2. Note that in all these texts John 5. 19 is cited by the Homoiousian authors. It is puzzling that Basil does not pick up on this use of this text. But we should note that the text is also insignificant in Gregory of Nyssa. Basil may also be drawing on Athanasius' *Letters to Serapion*, but direct borrowing has not been proved.

[93] Esp. *Eunom.* 3. 4. Cf. *Spir.* 16. 37–40. At *Or.* 30. 11, Gregory of Nazianzen offers a parallel 'Basilian' reading of the son as completing the Father's work

[94] Basil, *Eunom.* 3. 1.

[95] For example, we find nothing parallel to the assertion of the Spirit as one of three equal *hypostases* at *Eunom.* 3. 4. See Anthony Meredith, 'The Pneumatology of the Cappadocian Fathers and the Creed of Constantinople', *Irish Theological Quarterly*, 48 (1981), 196–212.

Spirit's divine activity. The Spirit's function as the perfecter of divine action and the *telos* of all that is virtuous is used to shape an account of the Spirit incorporating traditional discussion of the Spirit as agent of sanctification, but placing that work within a pro-Nicene account of the loving God's immediate work in his creation.[96] The care with which Basil so clearly presents the Spirit as an intrinsic part of the divine activity, and yet avoids drawing the terminological conclusions that Gregory Nazianzen, for example, saw as 'obvious' is noteworthy. Basil's caution may have been motivated in large part by the circumstances of debate: he still seems to have been trying to entice his opponents into the pro-Nicene camp and is encouraging Amphilochius to do likewise.

While Basil and Athanasius have different pneumatologies they also exhibit common concerns. We might say that they and all pro-Nicenes face common pressures when they argue that the Spirit is a coequal member of the triune Godhead. The most important pressure is to find a place for the Spirit in the Trinity as distinct and not simply as another Son. The task is somewhat complicated by the lack of clear scriptural verbs enabling us to speak distinctly of the Spirit's origin—parallel to what 'generation' allows for the Son. Thus the Spirit's mode of procession remains even more mysterious than that of the Son: the distinction between generation and 'procession' used by some writers on the basis of John 15: 26 delivers a distinction but little more. For the most part the problem is negotiated by attention to the traditional functions of the Spirit in the economy of salvation and by working with the dependence of Spirit on Son articulated there. The culmination of this strategy is found in Basil and Gregory of Nyssa where the order of the Spirit is preserved insofar as the Spirit is third in the order of every divine action, completing and bringing to fruition what the Father accomplishes through the Son. Perhaps the major contribution of pro-Nicene pneumatology is the insistence that the work of the Spirit is inseparable from Father and Son: this profoundly affects how the work of sanctification is seen. Thus pro-Nicene pneumatology makes a vital contribution to the history of pneumatology in its clarity that the work of sanctification is the unmediated work of God: but on the subject of the Spirit's place in the Godhead as such little progress is made.

It is vitally important to note that the later question of the *filioque* is not an issue. The question of the respective roles of Father and Son is used as an occasion by virtually all pro-Nicenes to argue that

---

[96] I think especially of *Spir.* 9. 22–3. This famous passage is often treated also as evidence for Basil's mature engagement with Plotinus. On the problems with such a statement see Rist, 'Basil's "Neoplatonism" ', 199–202.

the unity of the Godhead means that we should not separate the Son's activity from the Father's. Progress will only be made with the study of fourth-century pneumatology when scholars stop summarizing the period by making the question of attitudes towards the *filioque* an important point of departure (as Hanson still does). Indeed, noting the prevalence with which this occurs should also make us note just how thin are our current narratives about the early development of pneumatology.

TRADITION AND CONTEMPLATION

I want now to return to Basil. At *On the Holy Spirit* 1. 3 he appeals to the Church's liturgical practice and to 'unwritten' tradition as a basis for his pneumatology, and towards the end of the same text Basil quotes from a variety of figures to support his insistence on using 'together with the Spirit' in the liturgy. Before citing these authorities Basil makes a distinction between teachings that fall into the category of κηρυγμάτα (publicly proclaimed) or δογμάτα (appropriate only for the baptized faithful): in both categories some things come from written sources, while some come from 'unwritten' tradition handed down in the Church.[97] In this latter category Basil includes physical practices such as making the sign of the cross and standing for prayer on Sunday, as well as the words in which candidates for baptism make their confessions of faith. Thus, Basil argues, candidates receive from tradition a phraseology that reinforces the use of his 'with the Spirit'. Basil also treats this 'unwritten' dogma as an outgrowth of a true understanding of the written Scripture and rehearses evidence from a variety of writers who speak of the Spirit in ways that support his case, the high point of the list being Gregory Thaumaturgus, a figure taken to be central in the history of the Cappadocian Church.[98]

We miss an important dimension of Basil's appeal to tradition unless we see how it is intertwined with his understanding of θεωρία ('contemplation'). At 21. 52 Basil terms the ability to read the Mosaic law's 'depth' beyond 'Jewish' meanings as θεωρία, but then parallels this case with that of one who is able to understand Scripture's account of the Spirit:

the veil on Moses' face is analogous to the obscurity of the instruction offered by the law, just as spiritual contemplation (τὴν πνευματικὴν θεωρίαν)

---

[97] *Spir.* 27. 66. On this topic see E. Amand de Mendieta, 'The Pair Κήρυγμα and Δόγμα in the Thought of Basil of Caesarea', *JThS* NS 16 (1965), 129–42; idem, *The 'Unwritten' and the 'Secret' Apostolic Traditions in the Theological Thought of Basil of Caesarea* (Edinburgh: Scottish Journal of Theology, 1965).

[98] *Spir.* 29.71 ff.

corresponds to Moses speaking to the Lord with face unveiled. He who throws away the letter and turns to the Lord when reading the Law (and now the Lord is called Spirit) becomes like Moses, whose face shone with the glory of God's manifestation ... he who fixes his gaze on the Spirit is transfigured to greater brightness, his heart illumined by the Spirit's truth.

Basil argues that the need for a special θεωρία to understand the Mosaic law is paralleled by the need for a special θεωρία to grasp the nature of the Spirit. Thus the contemplation of the Spirit necessary to understand the Spirit is itself at the core of Christian life, and through the work of the Spirit in the believer this contemplation is enabled. The one enabling the contemplation that is the goal of Christian life is the same as the one contemplated, both must be God.

This argument is seen again in the section that follows (22. 53). There Basil argues that the sort of contemplation necessary if we are to 'see' the Spirit is identical to that necessary if we are to 'see' the Father and Son. Just as Father and Son are incomprehensible to human conception, so too the 'Spirit of truth' cannot be seen by the 'world' (quoting John 14: 17). All three are 'seen' by Christians who have attained 'purity of heart'. And yet, this ability to 'see' the Trinity within is given by the Son's teaching and the Son's gift of the Spirit: it is the Spirit who completes the possibility of the pure in heart seeing God. Thus, in this passage not only does Basil argue that the Spirit is the subject of the same predicates as Father and Son, but that the Spirit is also the final agent of that contemplation in all cases. It seems probable that Basil pursues this argument because the text is addressed to Amphilochius, someone whom Basil perceived as sharing a common ascetic vision. The theme of the purity of heart that constitutes the true goal of asceticism is a fairly common one in late fourth-century ascetic literature, as is the assumption that it is God who grants the gift of this purity.[99]

This argument interweaves with Basil's discussions of unwritten tradition. Basil's admission that the full truth of the Spirit's divinity has gradually unfolded in the Church is closely allied to his assertion of the importance of correct contemplation. Just as understanding the 'depth' of the Mosaic law depends on understanding the essential dynamics of God's action in Christ, so too, grasping the shape and intention of the Church's teaching depends on grasping the inner dynamics of the contemplation of God that stands as the goal and ground of Christian life. We also see here that Basil's emphasis on understanding the ways in which Christian doctrines speak of God, involves constructing and arguing for a particular vision of the

---

[99] For examples see Evagrius, *De fide* (Basil, *Ep.* 8); Cassian, *Conf.* 1.

Christian life. Basil's asceticism at this point directly affects his account of theological practice.

In discussing the 'Cappadocians' much is often made of the distinction between θεολογία and οἰκονομία. Some caution is required here. Basil generally uses θεολογία of a mode of insight into the nature of God that comes as a result of an ability to see beyond material reality, or beyond the material-sounding phraseology of some scriptural passages.[100] Οἰκονομία is used to describe a wide range of acts of ordering of events and behaviour: in the case of divine ordering Basil can speak of an οἰκονομία in creation and an οἰκονομία in the work of redemption through the incarnation. In this latter case Basil speaks of God's οἰκονομία as the ordering of the incarnation so that it would appropriately accomplish its purpose. 'Appropriately' here means accomplishing its purpose in a way commensurate with God's original purposes in creation. God acts in Christ in a way that will attract, purify, and lead humanity towards a restored exercise of human freedom in Christ.

Basil rarely pairs these two terms: the only really clear example is at *Contra Eunomium* 2. 3 where Basil speaks of the apostle Peter at Acts 2: 36 ('God has created him Lord and Christ . . .') not teaching 'in the manner/style of *theologia*' (θεολογίας . . . τρόπον), but making clear the 'structures of the *oikonomia*' (τοὺς τῆς οἰκονομίας λόγους). On occasion elsewhere Basil also links οἰκονομία and θεωρία, speaking of the θεωρία necessary to grasp the sense of passages which speak of God's οἰκονομία.[101] Thus, while θεολογία and οἰκονομία are not a paired technical terminology in Basil,[102] his handling of these two terms further indicates the importance of epistemological and anthropological themes in his discussion. For Basil an account of the character of true Christian θεωρία provides both a context within which he can begin to articulate how one learns to speak appropriately of the divine being *and* a polemical tool for describing ways in which non-Nicene exegesis and theology fail. When we also note that Basil's mature appeal to unwritten tradition is part of his appeal to the centrality of true θεωρία, we see how the articulation of orthodoxy involved not only making a claim on the content of previous tradition. The articulation of orthodoxy also involved developing an account of the true theologian and arguing that behind any seeming

---

[100] e.g. *Eunom*. 2. 15, in discussion of John 1: 1 and of how one reads the accounts of Jesus' various 'origins'.

[101] e.g. *Eunom*. 1. 12.

[102] We should be particularly wary of treating them as synonymous with modern discussions of the 'immanent' and 'economic' Trinity. This latter, modern and post-Hegelian language is frequently used to contrast modes of divine existence in ways alien to Basil's thought. While θεολογία describes a mode of contemplation, οἰκονομία describes the ordering of God's action in the world.

diversity in pre-Nicene theology stood the figure of the true theologian embodying orthodoxy in his unexpressed θεωρία: through the handing down of true θεωρία, true doctrine is preserved even when the disputatious character of fallen minds leads to the need for more fulsome statements of the principles of Christian belief.

CONCLUSION

It has, perhaps, not gone unnoticed that I have been able to speak of the evolution in Basil's thought with little discussion of Basil's relationship to Athanasius. This is for the simple reason that while it seems probable, as I discussed earlier, that Basil took from Athanasius an understanding of how the Nicene creed might serve as a criterion for admission to communion, modern scholarship has failed to demonstrate with certainty any detailed engagement with Athanasius' theology on the part of Basil.[103] Much work here remains to be done, but even on the evidence we have seen so far, this lack of detailed interaction is one more piece of evidence that pro-Nicene theologies emerged in a variety of contexts and from a variety of traditions. One of the central problems of my treatment of Basil so far is the choice to focus initially on the development of Basil's theology. While I have tried to show that grasping a variety of polemical contexts is essential to understanding this theology, it is important also to place Basil's theological texts within the context of the political manoeuvring and alliance-building that formed a central part of Basil's life. It is to this task that I now turn.

[103] See most recently Marina Troiano (responding in large part to the arguments of Drecoll's *Trinitätslehre*), 'Il Contra Eunomium III di Basilio di Cesarea e le Epistolae ad Serapionem I–IV di Atanasio di Alexandria—nota comparativa', *Augustinianum*, 41 (2001), 59–91.

9
The East from Valens to Theodosius

BASIL AND HIS CONTEMPORARIES

The developments in Basil's theology discussed in the last chapter occurred within a complex social and political context, something of which was sketched in the first section of the last chapter. We might say that in his attempts at alliance-building Basil was creating an audience receptive to his theology, and in his theology Basil was shaping a vocabulary that would reflect his own evolving position while being persuasive to those he wished to bring into alliance. Once again, Basil is both important in his own right and serves as an example of the character of pro-Nicene activity during the two decades prior to 381, though in his caution and linguistic care Basil represents an ability at compromise that was rare. Thus, my intention here is not to attempt to tell the whole of the story of Basil's episcopate, but to highlight some of the key events, themes, and relationships that reveal to us the complex context for the intellectual developments explored in Chapter 8.

Two constant problems foiled Basil's attempts at alliance-building. The antipathy of Valens and the imperial government to pro-Nicenes made it difficult to act openly against Homoians, and the constant unpredictability of personal antipathies and personal ambitions made it difficult for Basil to achieve alliances even where doctrinal agreement seemed close. Philip Rousseau's recent biography of Basil very helpfully points to Basil's increasing realization that personal dispute among those whom he thought should be united in the pro-Nicene cause was as much a foil to his plans as the active opposition of non-Nicenes.[1] Basil's willingness to use friends and family as pawns in the service of the pro-Nicene cause sometimes provoked protest and could create tensions in previously close friendships.

Basil's interaction with the Emperor Valens provides an excellent point of departure for understanding this complexity. In 372 Valens travelled to Caesarea, was present for the feast of the Epiphany and met with Basil at some length. As early as Gregory Nazianzen's *Oration* 43 this encounter is presented as an archetypal encounter between heroic bishop and worldly authority. Basil faces down the

[1] Rousseau, *Basil*, ch. 7.

Emperor and gains his grudging respect. The episode may better be read as demonstrating Valens' pragmatism and as showing the complexity of 'party' allegiance in these years. It is noticeable that Basil gave Valens communion: he might well press strongly for pro-Nicene theology and episcopal appointments, but care had to be exercised with the imperial authorities. At the same time as we see Basil making overtures to Valens, we see Valens offering some support to Basil. Not only did Valens allow Basil to stay in possession of his see, Basil was even entrusted with the ecclesiastical reorganization of Armenia, which followed a pre-emptive Roman strike against Persian attempts to control this highly contested border region.[2] Valens seems to have accepted that Basil could prove useful in ensuring effective administration. There were times, then, when the dispute between theological parties in the Church could take second place to other concerns.

At around the same time, Valens divided the province of Cappadocia into two. Basil had previously been Metropolitan of the whole province: now the bishop of Tyana, the most important city in the new province, claimed control over the new province. Despite what Basil presents as the scheming of an Arian emperor, we do not know if this administrative move had anything to do with opposition to Basil. Raymond Van Dam points out that much of the region left to Basil consisted of imperial estates and we might perceive this as indicating the degree of trust Valens put in him.[3] Nevertheless, this division had the effect of weakening Basil's position. In order to try and increase his authority[4] Basil created new sees in both the old and new provinces and pushed forward his own friends and relatives. The most famous of his appointments were that of his brother Gregory to the town of Nyssa (newly raised to episcopal status) and his friend Gregory Nazianzen to the tiny and inhospitable see of Sasima (again a new epsicopal seat).[5] While the former stayed, the latter probably never entered the town as its bishop, a failure that led to a significant rift with Basil. One might read Basil's creation of new episcopal sees as resulting from a desire to maintain a pro-Nicene power base in the region. At the same time we might read these appointments as a far more personally focused attempt to

---

[2] On Roman interaction with Armenia see Rousseau, *Basil*, 278–83.

[3] Van Dam, 'Emperors, Bishops and Friends'. See also A. H. M. Jones, *The Cities of the Eastern Roman Empire* (Oxford: Clarendon Press, 1971), 184 ff.

[4] As Hanson, *The Search*, 682, remarks (no doubt bringing his own short experience as bishop to bear): 'It is as difficult to persuade a bishop to surrender part of his see to another as it is to persuade a dog to part with a bone.'

[5] John McGuckin, *Saint Gregory of Nazianzus: An Intellectual Biography* (Crestwood, NY: St Vladimir's Seminary Press, 2001), ch. 4, shows how Sasima was chosen by Basil because of its strategic position.

maintain power within the regional Church, which is how at least some in the new province read the course of events. When Basil's attempts were read in the latter manner then personal animosity could easily frustrate plans to build pro-Nicene alliances.

Basil's relationship with figures throughout his region shows the same mix of theological and personal complexity. As illustration we might compare his relations with Atarbius the bishop of Neocaesarea and Amphilochius of Iconium. The former city lay to the north of Basil's Caesarea, close to the Black Sea coast and very close to land owned by Basil's family—where he had earlier lived in ascetic retreat. Neocaesarea's bishop Musonius died in 371 and was replaced by Atarbius, a distant relative of Basil. We cannot trace any communication between them until 373 when Basil wrote revealing unhappiness that Atarbius had not made contact with him.[6] In this letter we sense Basil's desire to have his seniority acknowledged and we see an open recognition that his theological goals can only be achieved through concrete alliances. The situation was rendered even more complex because of the multiple lines of communication running between the two cities: Basil was able to address the clergy of the city independently of their bishop and he clearly had his own supporters there. Atarbius himself seems to have avoided Basil, and we find Basil writing again, having heard that Atarbius was teaching 'Sabellian' doctrines. Basil's *Letter* 210, written in 375, was addressed directly to the Neocaesarean elite. The letter attacks 'Sabellian' doctrine but also goes to some lengths to explain the deep connections of family and precedent that tie him to Neocaesarea. Basil plays on personal and family ties to create an audience for his theological voice, which is then inevitably heard within the context of those personal and family ties.[7]

Amphilochius was Gregory Nazianzen's maternal cousin and another well-educated Cappadocian who had turned to the ascetic life. Basil wrote to him in 372, calling him to visit Caesarea and to take up a form of asceticism more communal and ecclesial in nature. In 373 Amphilochius became bishop of Iconium (capital of the new province of Lycaonia) and not only became one of Basil's stronger supporters but also adopted an air of deference to the older man that seems to have greatly pleased Basil. We have already seen some of Basil's letters to Amphilochius from the mid-370s and noted that the *On the Holy Spirit* was dedicated to him. In 376 a council in Iconium issued a synodal letter in support of the Holy Spirit's divinity: the synodal letter, which survives from this council shows clear signs

---

[6] *Ep.* 65.
[7] In *ep.* 210 Basil also appeals to Anthimus of Tyana as a supporter of his theology: by now their rift had been healed.

of Basil's influence. Unfortunately little of Amphilochius' corpus survives, making his theological skill difficult to assess: but he was a clear and articulate supporter of pro-Nicene theology.[8]

We can also pursue the complex intertwining of the personal and the theological in the case of Basil's relationship with Eustathius of Sebaste. Eustathius had become bishop of Sebaste in Armenia sometime before 358 and attended Basil of Ancyra's council in 358. Previous to this he seems to have been a supporter of the emerging Homoians. After the ruin of the Homoiousians in 360 Eustathius was deposed and became one of the Homoiousian ambassadors to Rome who accepted Nicaea. Eventually in 372 or 373 he regained his see. Eustathius was an important influence on the younger Basil's understanding of the ascetic life.[9] We do not know the extent to which Basil shared the radical vision of his early ascetic mentor, but their relationship seems to have been close.[10] Relations between Basil and Eustathius seem to have been still amicable in 371,[11] but in 372 or 373 two of Eustathius' associates who had been living with Basil began a campaign of slander against him, probably alleging that his pneumatology tended towards Sabellianism. This accusation resulted in a call from Meletius (who was in exile in Armenia) and Theodotus of Nicopolis, a prominent bishop from the same region, for Basil to come and answer these charges. During his trip to Armenia in the wake of Valens' charge to reorganize the Church there, Basil was able to convince Meletius and Theodotus of his orthodoxy, although he seems not to have met with both together at the planned meeting. During the same trip Basil also met with Eustathius, who agreed to a pro-Nicene statement of faith.[12] Eustathius' statement did not end the rift: both men have seem to have soon returned to pressing their charges against each other. For Eustathius, Basil was tainted both by his pneumatology and by his earlier friendship with Apollinaris; for Basil, Eustathius was backsliding on his commitment to Nicaea and demonstrating an 'Arian' doctrine of the Spirit. The personal conflict is of importance here for two reasons. First, it resulted in some further disruption to Basil's attempt to create alliances within the Church in Asia Minor. Second, these tensions also created opportunities for those opposed to

---

[8] The synodal letter of the 376 assembly is to be found at PG 39, 93–8. There also survives a creed which seems to originate with Amphilochius: see R. Ambramowski, 'Das Symbol des Amphilochius', *ZNTW* 29 (1930) 129–35. On Amphilochius' theology Holl, *Amphilochius* is still an excellent point of departure.

[9] On Eustathius' asceticism see Elm, '*Virgins of God*', 106–11. Eustathius and some of his practices were condemned at a council at Gangra in Paphlagonia. Unfortunately we cannot date this council with certainty: the dates proposed vary between 340 and 370.

[10] As I noted at the beginning of Ch. 8, Basil may have travelled with Eustathius around Palestinian and Egyptian monastic sites.

[11] *Ep.* 79.   [12] The statement and Eustathius' signature are preserved at *Ep.* 125.

pro-Nicenes to cause disruption in the ongoing work of alliance-building. Thus, when Theodotus of Nicopolis died in 375, Basil's candidate for the post was passed over in favour of one supported by Eustathius and the imperial authorities. Eustathius seems to have died around 377.[13]

Basil's attempts to build a pro-Nicene consensus in Asia Minor—and the setbacks he faced—need also to be seen in the context of a complex set of relationships between Basil, western bishops, Alexandria, and Antioch. Basil's attempts to negotiate between these centres of power clearly indicate that the path towards mutual recognition was long and that issues of mutual recognition were interwoven with long-standing suspicion and personal feuds. At the centre of Basil's regional concerns was Antioch: a major Christian centre riven by internal schism. Basil's concern with Antioch and his wide regional alliances reveal how much his concerns were those of a bishop on the eastern edge of the empire: Raymond Van Dam notices that he seems to accord most importance to figures in a 'tall quadrangle, stretching from the Black Sea south through the Eastern Mediterranean to the Nile River',[14] from his estates in Pontus down through Antioch and the border cities of the Euphrates, past Palestine to Egypt and Alexandria. We last discussed Antioch in the context of Athanasius' attempts to settle disputes between those supporting Meletius and those supporting the 'old-Nicene' party around Paulinus.[15] If anything the situation became worse in the 360s because of Paulinus' consecration to the episcopate by Lucifer of Cagliari. The two supposedly Nicene communities now had rival claimants to the see. Further, Meletius spent a considerable portion of his episcopate in exile: under Valens he was in exile from 365 to 366 (returning during Procopius' revolt) and again from 371 to 378. Thus, for much of Basil's episcopate Meletius was not in possession of his see, although he seems to have exercised control from his exile in Armenia.

One of Basil's other important regional allies was Eusebius, bishop of Samosata, a strategically important city near Edessa and close to the borders of the empire. Eusebius had become bishop in 361 and seems to have been close to Basil of Ancyra and to Gregory Nazianen's father. In Basil of Caesarea's letters to Eusebius we see a respect for the senior bishop's 'kindness' that reveals him treating Eusebius as something of a patron.[16] Indeed, Gregory Nazianzen

---

[13] These comments on Eustathius need to be read in the light of the brief discussion of the emergence of the 'Macedonians' in Ch. 8.
[14] Raymond Van Dam, *Families and Friends in Late Roman Cappadocia* (Philadelphia: University of Pennsylvania Press, 2003), 152.
[15] See Ch. 7.   [16] See *Ep.* 48, 30, 34.

and his father had sought Eusebius' help in the election of Basil himself.[17] Eusebius was driven into exile in Thrace in 374 for his pro-Nicene sympathies and a number of letters survive both from Basil to Eusebius' community and to Eusebius in exile. As in the case of Meletius, Basil continued to solicit Eusebius' support and to treat him as an important player in the region. Basil's concern to ally himself with Eusebius reveals the wide-ranging nature of the ecclesiastical alliances he sought to build. Eusebius was clearly a Greek-speaker and his name suggests a Greek background, but Samosata will have contained many Syriac- and Armenian-speaking Christians and should probably indicate to us that the boundaries between these linguistic groups were considerably more porous than scholars have often assumed.

Basil believed the deep internal divisions among eastern bishops—especially the mistrust older 'Nicenes' maintained towards Basil and Meletius—might be healed if there were clear support from Rome and the west for his party and for Meletius. In 371 Basil attempted to involve Athanasius in a grand plan to get intervention from Damasus of Rome in the affairs of the east. He was, however, concerned to get Damasus to condemn Marcellus, showing the extent to which eastern suspicion over western support for Marcellus persisted.[18] At the same time, Basil was clear that solving the divisions in the Antiochene Church meant supporting Meletius: a position not likely to be acceptable either to Athanasius or to the western bishops.

Attempts to organize a mission to Rome were pre-empted by a messenger from the west whom Basil presents as bringing messages of support for Meletius (which seems unlikely). They were further interrupted by a letter arriving from Damasus conveying the results of a council that had been held sometime in the 368–72 period. Basil attempted to reorganize and get Meletius also to write to the west. Throughout this period it is not entirely clear how Basil understood the function of Athanasius in his plans. While it is likely Basil hoped to build on Athanasius' status in the west to enhance the chances of this embassy, Basil was clearly pursuing a course of his own focused on shoring up the status of Meletius, a course that he must have known was a hard sell in Alexandria.

When the Sabinus who had carried Damasus' letter east returned home, Dorotheus, who was both one of Meletius' deacons and Basil's designated envoy, travelled with him carrying letters to various western bishops.[19] A year later one Evagrius, later the translator into Latin of Athanasius' *Life of Antony*, came east carrying a letter

---

[17] Gregory Nazianzen, *Ep.* 42. [18] *Ep.* 66–9. [19] *Ep.* 90–2.

from Damasus asking Basil to send another embassy and a signed statement agreeing to the statement of faith Damasus had already sent. In this response one sees with clarity the full difficulty of these attempts at rapprochement. Damasus simply did not trust Basil's faith: he perhaps had in mind Liberius' previous willingness to trust Eustathius, and he probably saw eastern demands for a condemnation of Marcellus as something of a ruse hiding a theology insufficiently Nicene. From Basil's letter reporting Damasus' response to Eusebius of Samosata we learn that Damasus had sent back Basil's letter because it was insufficient 'to the more strict of the people there'.[20] At least part of the problem seems to have stemmed from the presence in Rome of Athanasius' successor Peter. When Athanasius died in May 373 Peter was almost immediately driven into exile: travelling to Rome he seems to have reinforced Damasus' suspicions of Basil and Meletius.

This response from the west, coupled with what seems further support from some western bishops for Paulinus in Antioch, seems to have convinced Basil that serious western support was unlikely. Not until 375 did he write to Meletius suggesting that Meletius should send an embassy west.[21] It is noticeable, however, that writing to Eusebius of Samosata (who seems to have suggested this course of events), Basil admits that he has very little idea what can be done to achieve a reconciliation.[22] Philip Rousseau argues that increasingly Basil's concern was to get western bishops to intervene in the east with caution, attending more carefully to the complexity of pro-Nicene networks, rather than offering support to divisive individuals (Paulinus in Antioch) or to small factions.[23] While this shows the care with which Basil had thought through his own political project, it may also have been highly unrealistic.

This latest embassy to the west returned with a letter from Damasus condemning 'Arianism' and Apollinaris, but not really addressing Basil's concerns. Basil's response addressed to the western bishops shows his mastery of the rhetorical arts, and also his growing frustration. Basil argues that 'Arianism' per se is no longer the issue: heretics *within* the Church are far more dangerous. He names Eustathius of Sebaste as constantly shifting in opinion, Apollinaris as a Judaizer, and Paulinus in Antioch as tending towards Marcellan doctrines. Only a common council, he now argues, could solve these problems.[24] Amand de Mendieta argues that the famous *Tomus Damasi* from a Roman council of early 378 formed part of Damasus'

---

[20] *Ep.* 138. [21] *Ep.* 120. [22] *Ep.* 239.
[23] Rousseau, *Basil*, 310 ff. [24] *Ep.* 263.

response.[25] The theology of this text is considered briefly in Chapter 10, but at this point the struggle of Basil to get help from the west ended with his death and in failure. This account of Basil's attempts to build pro-Nicene alliances demonstrates the difficulty of using Basil's later significance to interpret his effect on his contemporaries. More generally, this account of Basil's work should also stand as a general introduction to the questions we must ask when we seek to grasp the interaction of the personal and the theological in the gradual emergence and triumph of pro-Nicene theology.

EPHREM THE SYRIAN

In discussing Basil we had cause to mention Eusebius of Samosata. Samosata was only 75 miles north-west of Edessa as the crow flies, where we find another major pro-Nicene figure writing in the mid-360s and early 370s—Ephrem the Syrian. We lack the evidence that would give us a clear sense of how Ephrem adapted and represented earlier fourth- and third-century Syriac theology: we can, however, clearly trace in his work the lines of an anti-Homoian and possibly anti-Heterousian theology that closely mirrors theological concerns and statements made in his Greek pro-Nicene contemporaries. Judging by his renown in the late fourth century[26] and his status in Syriac tradition he must have played a major role in nurturing and strengthening pro-Nicene theology in his region. The work of locating Ephrem's theology in a pro-Nicene context and of assessing his knowledge of Greek theology in the late fourth century is in its infancy. In this brief discussion I assume, in line with recent scholarship, that the location of Edessa and Nisibis on a strategic highway from Antioch to the Roman frontier with Persia meant that despite linguistic differences Christians in these cities would have been well aware of events further west.[27] Moreover, Ephrem's Trinitarian theology appears to possess features that clearly locate it as a pro-Nicene theology of the 360s and 370s. Examining this theology provides us with another excellent example of how pro-Nicene theology could be expressed in a wide variety of terminologies and contexts.

Despite later tradition Ephrem was not a member of an organized ascetic community on a Greek model: he belonged to a group known

---

[25] E. Amand de Mendieta, 'Basile de Césarée et Damase de Rome', in J. N. Birdsall and R. W. Thompson (eds.), *Biblical and Patristic Studies in memory of Robert Pierce Casey* (New York: Herder, 1963), 140–1.
[26] See Sozomen, *Hist eccl.* 3. 16, Jerome, *Vir. ill.* 115.
[27] For introductions to scholarship on the Hellenization of Syria see Sebastian Brock, 'Syriac Culture, 337–425', *CAH* xiii. 708–19, Ute Possekel, *Evidence of Greek Philosophical Concepts in the Writings of Ephrem the Syrian*, CSCO subsidia, 102 (Louvain: Peeters, 1999), ch. 1.

as the *bnay qyāmâ* or 'sons of the covenant' who lived singly and celibately, had made a special commitment at baptism, and who saw themselves as living lives that attempted to imitate the angelic life of Christians after the general resurrection. Ephrem seems also to have been ordained as a deacon and to have fulfilled a pastoral and educational role for his bishop.[28] He began his work in the important military border town of Nisibis. The first bishop under whom he served, Jacob of Nisibis, had attended the Council of Nicaea. Ephrem worked in Nisibis until the death of Julian in 363. In the consequent humiliating treaty with the Persians the Romans were forced to evacuate and hand over the city of Nisibis. Like many other inhabitants of the city, Ephrem made his way 150 miles west to Edessa, halfway to Antioch. There he experienced at first hand the attempts of Valens to promote Homoian interests when Bishop Barsai of Edessa was exiled in 371. Ephrem died in 373.

The majority of Ephrem's works are poetic in form, possibly intended for use in liturgical settings. The two terms for the works in verse, *memre* and *madrashe*, are conventionally translated as 'homilies' and 'hymns', a terminology which is somewhat misleading. They seem to have been gathered together into themed groups by Ephrem, his disciples, and later redactors of his corpus. This complex history only adds to the complexities of dating. In some cases we can be clear on internal grounds—most of the so-called *Hymns on Nisibis* being an important example[29]—in others we are at a loss. Here, however, I assume the conventional dating of the two collections which focus most directly on the errors of non-Nicene theology: the 87 *Hymns on Faith* (ending with the powerful six hymns *On the Pearl*) were probably written during his years in Edessa, while the 6 *Sermons on the Faith* are possibly to be dated to his last years in Nisibis. On internal evidence we can make the general statement that the earliest likely date for the theology to be found in any of these texts is the late 350s.

It has frequently been assumed that Ephrem's main opponents are Heterousian theologians. It far more likely that the Homoian theology promoted by Valens is his target.[30] He does, however, know the name of Aetius, and it seems reasonable that news of the turmoil in Antioch in the late 350s—including the widespread reaction to

---

[28] On early Syrian asceticism see the excellent essay (which also summarizes previous currents in research) by Sidney H. Griffith, 'Asceticism in the Church of Syria: The Hermeneutics of Early Syrian Monasticism', in Vincent Wimbush and Richard Valantassis (eds.), *Asceticism* (New York: Oxford University Press, 1998), 220–45.

[29] The title is slightly misleading. *HNis* 26–34 concern the tumult in Edessa and Harran over Valens' pro-Homoian activity.

[30] I am grateful to Mark Weedman for sharing with me an unpublished paper from the 1998 NAPS conference arguing that Ephrem's opponents were Homoian.

Eudoxius' promotion of Aetius—would have made its way down the main highway through Edessa towards such an important centre as Nisibis. In the *Hymns on Faith* Ephrem attacks non-Nicenes who are rationalist and who see the Son as a product of the divine will alone. He is also familiar with anti-Nicene use of Proverbs 8: 22 and Mark 13: 32. His attacks on the rationalism of his opponents seem primarily directed towards their taking literally scriptural statements which appear to subordinate the Son: Heterousians do not need to be understood here. Similarly, the anti-Nicene question 'did the Father beget the Son willingly or unwillingly?' was used frequently by Homoians all across the empire, as was Proverbs 8: 22. The discussion of Mark 13: 32 seems to offer a little more specific evidence: Basil attributes anti-Nicene use of this verse to 'Anomoeans', and Gregory Nazianzen treats anti-Nicene use of the verse as one of the ten texts discussed in *Oration* 29. It is important to note, however, that the texts that occur in *Oration* 29 are not uniquely Heterousian or Eunomian: Athanasius provides evidence that Mark 13: 32 was used by Eusebians in the 340s.[31] It seems then most likely that Ephrem's polemical context is one in which he faces Homoian theologies, although these may include some radical Homoian trends influenced by Aetius' teaching in Antioch.

Ephrem's theology—in ways parallel to a number of other pro-Nicene writers in Greek and Latin—depends upon an account of the distinction between God and creation. Father, Son, and Spirit are all located on the far side of this boundary.[32] Ephrem emphasizes that the Son's generation is incomprehensible because of the break or chasm between the created and the uncreated:

Tell me how you have depicted in the inmost part of your mind that birth which is very far away from your inquiry? Do you think that there is just a short space in the middle, between you and searching it? Seal your mouth with silence! Do not let your tongue dare! Know yourself, O created one,

---

[31] Athanasius, *C. Ar.* 3. 26, 42 ff.

[32] On Ephrem's Trinitarian theology, especially with reference to *HdF* see first Edmund Beck, *Die Theologie des hl Ephraem in seinen Hymnen über den Glauben*, Studia Anselmiana, 21 (Rome: Pontificium Institutum S. Anselmi, 1949), and idem, *Ephräms Trinitätslehre: Im bild von Sonne/Feuer, Licht und Wärme*, CSCO subsidia, 62 (Louvain: Peeters, 1981). Paul S. Russell, *St. Ephraem the Syrian and St. Gregory the Theologian Confront the Arians*, Mōrān 'Eth'ō 5 (Kottayam: St Ephrem Ecumenical Research Institute, 1994) offers some useful methodological reflection but is imprecise in his account of 'Arians' and of pro-Nicene terminologies. His work also offers a modern translation of many key passages. Sidney H. Griffith, 'Setting Right the Church of Syria: Saint Ephraem's *Hymns Against Heresies*', in Mark Vessey and Williams E. Klingshirn (eds.), *The Limits of Ancient Christianity: Essays on Late Antique Thought and Culture in Honor of R. A. Markus* (Ann Arbor: University of Michigan Press, 1999), 97–114, although not writing about *HdF*, offers extremely useful reflections on the polemic context of Ephrem's work.

made one, son of a moulded thing. For the chasm is a great, limitless one, between you and the Son as regards investigation.[33]

Ephrem offers a sophisticated account of the distinction between God and creation, emphasizing the mysteriousness of God even though God is in all things:

> In every place is your mystery, Lord, and from every place are you hidden. Even though your mystery be in the heaven, yet [the heaven] does not know what you are. Even though your mystery is in the depths of the sea, from the sea you are concealed ... You are wonderful on all sides: when we search for you, you are near and far.[34]

From other texts we find that God is infinite, not limited by category of space and is simple in the sense that he is beyond division; he is also self-sustaining and perfect.[35] Ephrem's account of the divine attributes is thus basically identical to that found in any Greek or Latin pro-Nicene. However, the state of Ephrem's knowledge of Greek philosophy is not clear. Most importantly, recent scholarship has begun to move beyond earlier portrayals of Syriac thought in this period as *sui generis* and as opposed to Greek conceptual structures. Ute Possekel has, for example, shown that Ephrem's conception of space—and of God as enclosing but not enclosed—reveals a debt to Stoic sources and also to some aspects of middle Platonic tradition.[36] She in turn builds on Edmund Beck's identification of Stoic positions in Ephrem's psychology.

The incomprehensibility of the divine mystery is overcome via a theology of names and an account of the revelatory qualities of the created order.[37] Ephrem conceives of Scripture and the natural world as offering (through providence) points of departure for speaking about God, and he sees the names that we use of God as revealing the mysteriousness of God. In the many interpretations of that nature that flow from God's action in creating and above all in the Incarnation and Scripture, we begin to shape an awareness of the still-hidden God.[38] The symbolic quality of the natural world appears to depend on an understanding both of the Word as the agent of creation and on a sense of God's active ordering of things so that we may speak of the hidden mystery.[39] Ephrem also

---

[33] *HdF* 15. 4–5. I am very grateful to my colleague Roberta Bondi for assistance with translation through this section.

[34] *HdF* 4. 9–11.   [35] *HdF* 45 is particularly clear in this regard.

[36] Ute Possekel, *Evidence of Greek Philosophical Concepts*, ch. 6.

[37] On this theme see Sebastian Brock, *The Luminous Eye: The Spiritual World of Saint Ephrem* (Kalamazoo, Mich.: Cistercian Publications, 1985), chs. 2–5; Thomas Koonammakkal, 'Divine Names and Theological Language in Ephrem', *SP* 25 (1993), 318–23.

[38] *HdF*. 10 and 26.

[39] See *HdF* 4. 9, 6. 3; *HdVirg*. 20. 12, 6. 8. See P. Yousif, 'Symbolisme christologique dans la Bible et dans la nature chez s. Ephrem de Nisibe', *Parole d'Orient*, 8 (1977), 5–66.

distinguishes between 'true' and 'borrowed' names for God, a distinction connected both to his account of revelation in Christ and in Scripture. Borrowed names are names and terms used by God that are most true of human existence. Ephrem seems to have in mind terms used by Scripture to describe God's various appearances in the Old Testament (he is an 'old man', a 'warrior', he is 'angry' and 'repents') and names used of the Incarnate Christ stemming from the assumed body. These we must understand as not describing God truly.[40] The true names of God are titles used of the divine nature or persons that form an interrelated whole, none of which may be rejected. The names of Father, Son, and Spirit, Being and Creator are all in this category.[41] In this complex theology of names we encounter something which mirrors both the accounts of ἐπινοίαι found in Basil and Gregory of Nyssa, and Origen's own theology of divine names. The state of our knowledge of the development of Syriac theology prevents our arguing for any common source here: we can only note that across pro-Nicene contexts theologies of divine names are shaped by accounts of the Incarnation as revealing the still-hidden divine nature and serve to reinforce the paradoxical texture of all speech about Father, Son, and Spirit.

When Ephrem considers Father, Son, and Spirit his work emphasizes the paradox of the irreducible persons and the unitary divine nature, with terminology emphasizing the shared nature in the Son's generation. He makes use of some technical language, but also relies heavily on a few cherished analogical resources. One of the most distinctive is his use of the sun, its light and heat:

Lo, there is a likeness between the sun and the Father, the radiance and the Son, the heat and the Holy Spirit . . . and though it be one, a trinity can be seen in it. That incomprehensible thing, who can explain it? One is many, a one that is a three and a three that is one . . . The sun is distinct from its ray; they are distinct [yet alike] since his ray is itself also the sun. Yet no one speaks of two suns, though his ray is also the sun over things below . . . Distinguish the sun from its ray for me, and both from the heat, if you can . . . Look at the likenesses among the creatures, and do not be divided about the Trinity, lest you perish.[42]

Here we find statements balancing unity and diversity and also an analogy emphasizing unity through a shared being in generation. The sun, light, and heat analogy enables Ephrem to emphasize shared being between the three—and he uses the analogy here to

---

[40] See esp. *HdF* 31.
[41] *HdF* 4. Ephrem also assumes that we appropriate some of these 'true' names, such as when we use the term 'father' of ourselves: our task is never to assume this means such terms are univocal, see *HdF* 63.
[42] Ephrem, *HdF* 73. 1, 11, 20. On this text see Beck, *Trinitätslehre*, 75 ff.

move directly to state the paradox of the three and the one—but it also offers a clear account of the Father as the source of the power and action of Son and Spirit. Ephrem does not clearly state the doctrine of inseparable operation, but he clearly speaks of the power and action of God being present in all three persons.[43] Elsewhere we find him coming close to the doctrine of inseparable operation in the same manner as Athanasius comes close: the Son works in creation not as another divine principle but as the Father's speaking:

> (11) ... His Son sufficed for his voice ... (13) ... it was not the things made that he commanded to make themselves: by the hand of One by One they were created. The Father gave the command with his voice, the Son finished the work.[44]

Ephrem also interweaves the analogy of the sun with others:

> The sun is our light, and no one is able to know it, how much less to know man and still less God. The light of the sun is not subsequent to it, neither was he at any time without it. The light is the second, and the warmth is the third; they depart not from it, nor are they identical with it ... The second is blended with him, though distinguished from him and the third is mingled with him, distinguished, blended and mingled. ... There is a marvel in all these things that makes us silent. Man also is compounded of three, and will rise in the resurrection, when he is perfected entirely.[45]

Ephrem uses analogies both to offer some account of the paradox of the Trinity and to emphasize that any analogy should reveal a paradox beyond our comprehension. The same pattern is apparent when he uses the concept of the divine Word to describe God's mystery in terms of the eternal presence of God's unchanging thought in comparison to human thinking:

> In the beginning he created all things, while his thought was with him without any beginning. He has no thinking as people do, that he could be changed in any new way as with a child of flesh. His movement was not new, nor was his thought fresh.[46]

The analogy with human thinking serves both to draw our imagination forward and to indicate to us where any such analogy fails:

> The truth of John! When he watched you he represented you—you who are Word and God, and are unfathomable, in order that man could trace out a form in his mind ... His nature is hidden and manifest, revealed that it is, but hidden as to what he is.[47]

The use of the language of mingling is also distinctive in Ephrem:

> Mixed with Him [the Father] and divided from Him, He is in His bosom

---

[43] Cf. *HdF* 40. 8 ff.   [44] *HdF* 6. 11, 13.   [45] *HdF* 40. 1–2, 4.
[46] *HdF* 26. 2.   [47] *HdF* 33. 1–3.

The East from Valens to Theodosius

and on his right hand. If he were not mingled with him, His beloved would not be in his bosom. If he were not separated from Him he would not sit at His right hand ... They are one in their one will but two in their two names. They do not have two wills but they do have two titles. Fatherhood is the name of the Father and it is his name which safeguards his glory. Begottenness is the name of the Son and it is his name which safeguards his generation. The distinguishing characteristic of the Father is his name and the explanation of the Son is in his name. In the order of their names is guarded the order of their genealogies.[48]

This passage is of particular interest because it moves from emphasizing the mingling of the distinct persons to more formal statements of Trinitarian theology. First, Ephrem insists on the one will of the persons, a principle that we have already seen in other pro-Nicene theologians. When he seeks to distinguish Father and Son in the following sentences he turns to the names which he takes to indicate order and hierarchy within the one Godhead. It seems from this short text, and from other emphasis on the significance of the divine names, that while we cannot say for certain that Ephrem sees the names and the relationships of the persons as their only distinguishing marks, he does present them as the only points of reference for our attempts to distinguish the persons.

The study of Ephrem's Trinitarian theology is in its infancy. The work of Edmund Beck remains not just seminal but virtually the only extended critical resource. In particular the work of understanding how Ephrem not only borrows from and participates in Greek intellectual cultures, but how he participates in the wider Trinitarian developments of his day has far to go. From the discussion here I can, however, make one point. When we read Ephrem against the background of his pro-Nicene contemporaries we need to move beyond assuming that his love of imagery and paradox is what marks his theology as essentially Syriac and un-Hellenic. It is precisely in the way that he uses the paradox of the divine triuinity without deploying a clear and fixed metaphysical vocabulary that marks him as typically pro-Nicene. Whereas previous study has frequently assumed that the presence or not of discernable equivalents to Greek philosophical terminology is the point of reference for indicating depth of contact with the Greek world, this book's account of pro-Nicene theology should suggest alternative routes for investigation.

[48] *SdF* 2.

II. The Emergence of Pro-Nicene Theology

THE MEANING OF THE TERM 'PRO-NICENE'

Throughout the last two chapters I have used the term 'pro-Nicene' on the basis of a short definition in Chapter 7: it is time now to expand on and defend that definition. I take three central principles to identify a theology as fully pro-Nicene:[49]

1. a clear version of the person and nature distinction, entailing the principle that whatever is predicated of the divine nature is predicated of the three persons equally and understood to be one (this distinction may or may not be articulated via a consistent technical terminology);
2. clear expression that the eternal generation of the Son occurs within the unitary and incomprehensible divine being;
3. clear expression of the doctrine that the persons work inseparably.

The first and second of these points represent two of the fundamental themes whose development enabled the emergence of pro-Nicene theology. The unity of nature was understood to imply that the three persons were of equal ontological standing—all possessed the fullness of what it was to be God. It was also assumed by pro-Nicenes that the particular characteristics of the three persons still enabled us to speak of a certain order of progression within the Godhead. At the same time, new clarity about the simplicity and immateriality of the Godhead enabled a clear insistence that the generation of the Son (and the 'spiration' of the Spirit) did not involve a dividing of the divine being.[50] Michel Barnes helpfully distinguishes between earlier fourth-century usage in which the Father/Son relationship is used to show continuity of nature and fully pro-Nicene usage in which the Father/Son relationship is used only to show that the persons are distinct because now the eternal generation occurs a priori within the unitary and simple Godhead.[51]

My use of the term pro-Nicene is initially defined against those accounts that present the fourth-century Trinitarian controversies as having one solution: the clearer restatement of an original Nicene theology. This theology is understood as defended (if not defined) by Athanasius, taken up and given more precision by the

---

[49] Vaggione, *Eunomius*, 273–5, 364–8, presents the 'Nicene' victory as resulting from a relaxation in ἀκρίβεια on the part of key pro-Nicene polemicists. While my account obviously is in many ways compatible with that of Vaggione, I would also want to emphasize that pro-Nicenes develop a new or different sense of where ἀκρίβεια is important.

[50] These themes are discussed much more fully in Chs. 10–12.

[51] Michel René Barnes, 'Divine Unity and the Divided Self: Gregory of Nyssa's Trinitarian Theology in its Psychological Context', *Modern Theology*, 18 (2002), 53. As I will comment later, pro-Nicene authors often incorporate earlier arguments alongside more fully pro-Nicene arguments.

Cappadocians, and passed to a naturally well-disposed west in translation and with inevitable misunderstanding. The main problem with such accounts is that the evidence for the crucial shifts in and assumptions of this narrative is weak. There is no one original Nicene theology that continues unchanged through the century. Extensive influence of Athanasius' theology on the Cappadocians is difficult to prove. Western accounts are not simply dependent on eastern translations and there was a significant and persistent non-Nicene presence in parts of the west. The theologies that constitute pro-Nicene orthodoxy are not reducible to one point of origin or to one form of expression.

The other significant way of considering the solution to the fourth-century controversies has been to suggest the Trinitarian theologies of the Cappadocians represent a retreat from the Nicene theology of Athanasius. This thesis was advocated by the German Protestant scholars Theodor Zahn and Friedrich Loofs in the late nineteenth century and taken up strongly by Adolf von Harnack (and henceforth I will refer to it as the 'Harnack thesis'). For Harnack 'Cappadocian' theology, which he treats as a unity, is just an adapted Homoiousian theology. Whereas Athanasius argued that *homoousios* meant *unity* of substance, 'Cappadocian' theology focuses on the three beings who *share* a common substance, rather than on the divine unity which is mysteriously threefold. Because the Cappadocians also insist on the Father's person as the source of the Trinity, Harnack sees them as offering a modified version of Origen's Trinitarian theology, not Athanasius' original 'Nicene' theology.[52] Although Harnack does not use the term himself, there has been a persistent tradition of referring to this supposed reinterpretation of Nicene theology as 'neo-Nicene' theology.

In recent continental European scholarship there has been continued debate over the term 'neo-Nicene' and much criticism of the Harnack thesis. Adolf-Martin Ritter, in his 1965 *Das Konzil von Konstantinopel und sein Symbol*, argued strongly against the thesis on the grounds that the Cappadocians understood the unity of the divine essence in a way functionally identical to that of Athanasius. For

---

[52] Adolf von Harnack, *The History of Dogma*, vol. iv, tr. Neil Buchanan (New York: Russell & Russell, 1958), 84–5: 'If up till now orthodox faith had meant the recognition of a mysterious plurality in the substantial unity of the Godhead, it was now made permissible to turn the unity into a mystery, i.e. to reduce it to equality and make the threefoldness the starting-point; but this simply means that Homoiousianism was recognised which resolved to accept the word *homoousios*. And to this theology, which changed the substantial unity of substance expressed in the *homoousios* into a mere likeness or equality of substance, so that there was no longer a threefold unity, but a trinity, the future belonged, in the East, though not to the same extent in the West . . . The unity of the Godhead, as the Cappadocians conceived of it, was not the same as the unity which Athanasius had in his mind.'

Ritter, in the fourth appendix to his text, differences in terminology mask a strong similarity: even the Cappadocian account of the Son and Spirit's origin from the Father actually delivers a similar account of divine unity. Ritter also points out that the one *ousia*, three *hypostases* formula did not stem from Homoiousian theologians, but rather from a development of themes parallel to those advocated in Athanasius.[53] However, it is important to note that Ritter's account preserves one of the central assumptions of the Harnack thesis, that the central line of transmission to be considered is that between Athanasius and the Cappadocians.

More recent work by Christoph Markschies, Manlio Simonetti, Volker Drecoll, and Basil Studer (to give just a few examples) has continued to pursue debate over this thesis.[54] For Studer, the Cappadocian use of the one *ousia*, three *hypostases* formula *is* an advance on Athanasius' defence of *homoousios* because the distinct existence of the persons is better respected while the unity is still preserved. Studer's account here follows the increasingly prominent scholarly position that Athanasius' theology offers a strongly unitarian Trinitarian theology whose account of personal differentiation is underdeveloped. In addition Studer begins to question some of the terms of the existing debate by noting, on the one hand, that the one *ousia*, three *hypostases* formula does not hold the central position it is often accorded. He also notes that the term *homoousios* is not used with precision at Nicaea and that later arguments for *homoousios* always involve *constructing* accounts of its meaning. Thus, it is a mistake to ask whether or not Cappadocian theology represents a departure from an 'original' Nicene theology. 'Neo-Nicene' theology remains, for Studer, an acceptable term, but only in a strongly revised account. Despite the subtleties of Studer's account, the Harnack thesis continues to shape the debate: he still assumes that the character of the transition from Athanasius to the Cappadocians is the fundamental question to be considered.[55]

---

[53] Adolf-Martin Ritter, *Das Konzil von Konstantinopel und sein Symbol*, Forschungen zur Kirchen- und Dogmengeschichte, 15 (Göttingen: Vandenhoeck & Ruprecht, 1965); idem, 'Zum homousios von Nizäa und Konstantinopel: Kritische Nachlese zu einigen neueren Diskussionen', in Adolf-Martin Ritter (ed.), *Kerygma und Logos: Beiträge zu den geistesgeschichtlichen Beziehungen zwischen Antike und Christentum. Festschrift für Carl Andresen zum 70* (Göttingen: Vandenhoeck & Ruprecht, 1979), 404–23.

[54] Manlio Simonetti, 'Dal Nicenismo al Neonicenismo: Rassegna di Alcune Pubblicazioni Recenti', *Augustinianum*, 38 (1998), 5–27; Studer, 'Una Valutazione Critica del Neonicenismo', *Augustinianum*, 38 (1998), 29–48; Drecoll, *Trinitätslehre*; Markschies, 'Was ist lateinischer "Neunizanismus"?', *Zeitschrift für Antikes Christentum*, 1 (1997), 73–95.

[55] Hanson's *The Search*, is another example of a work which never moves beyond this assumption, although without acknowledging the question directly. Hanson's treatment of the 360–80 period is somewhat hampered by its form as an extended summary catalogue of individual figures and movements.

Our point of departure for moving this debate forward must be increased subtlety in our speech about 'original' 'Nicene' theology. As we have seen, Athanasius' theology in the 340s and 350s is not *the* 'original' Nicene theology, but a development from *one of* the original theologies that shaped Nicaea. His theology is part of a wider movement that saw a number of distinct traditions come to view Nicaea as a credal standard and to develop theologies in which it could be interpreted against Homoian and then Heterousian theologies. If we are to speak more accurately about the theologies emerging in the early 360s that came to constitute Theodosian orthodoxy we will need to find a way to identify the common themes of those theologies without presupposing either one point at which a torch was passed to this generation, or even that there was one torch to be passed on.

It is also vital to note that although I use 'pro-Nicene' primarily to indicate theologies recognized as orthodox by the Council of Constantinople and by subsequent imperial decrees, many of the distinctive elements of such theologies appear much earlier than 380. It is not, however, possible to identify one point in time at which pro-Nicene theology emerged across the Mediterranean, and thus the temporal referent of 'pro-Nicene' has to be flexible. Because the emergence of distinctive, pro-Nicene themes was, in most cases, the result of an evolution it is not always possible to identify clearly points at which an individual theology is most appropriately termed pro-Nicene. Hence, I also use pro-Nicene to refer to theologians who seem to be the direct precursors of that later orthodoxy but whose theology still falls short of it in some respects. The most important Greek example is the later Athanasius while in Latin we might point to Hilary, Phoebadius of Agen, or Marius Victorinus.

Some scholars prefer a more differentiated terminology that distinguishes between different stages of pro-Nicene theology. Michel Barnes in particular uses neo-Nicene and pro-Nicene to refer to two stages of development.[56] By neo-Nicene, and using it in a sense virtually opposite to its usage in German scholarship, Barnes refers to the first generation of theologians offering an interpretation of Nicaea: Athanasius being a key example. In his *Power of God* Barnes typifies a neo-Nicene theology by two marks. First, it is one that presents the Word as the one power of God and argues that the Word is coeternal with the Father because God is never without God's power. Pro-Nicene theologies are those that argue God is one power in the sense that God is one nature or substance: the Son is the power of God in possessing, as does the Father, the one power of

---

[56] Barnes, *Power of God*, 169–72.

the divine nature. Barnes also argues that although pro-Nicene theology emerges after neo-Nicene theology, the emergence of the latter does not mean the suppression of the former: both continue, often in the same authors. In more recent work Barnes refines his criteria of distinction, pointing to the two different use of the Father/Son relationship I used a few paragraphs ago.

While Barnes and I agree on the plural character of original Nicene theology, he thinks it possible to distinguish that original plural Nicene theology from an intermediate neo-Nicene stage. My suspicion is that this latter move is problematic: Barnes's terminology for the second stage can potentially designate a theology at any point between 325 and the emergence of the pro-Nicene. Accordingly, I have focused only on distinguishing between original Nicene theologies, as explored in Chapter 4, and the slowly emerging pro-Nicene theologies of the 360s onwards.

THE ACCESSION OF THEODOSIUS

At a number of points in the fourth century extra-ecclesial political events fundamentally shape the controversy: the rise of Constantine; the sole rule of Constantius after 351; the death of Constantius in 361; the turmoil created by Julian's reign. To this list must now be added a fifth: the battle of Adrianople in 378. At this battle against Goths crossing the Danube and seeking to settle in Thrace, a large Roman army was defeated and, by some estimates, as many as two-thirds of the troops were wiped out. The Emperor Valens was among those killed.[57] The empire was presented with two immediate crises: the need to find a replacement for Valens and the need to hold back the Goths.[58] Just as the victories of Constantius in 350–3 created the conditions for the rise of the Homoians, now the rise to power of a new emperor enabled the victory of the pro-Nicene cause.

The Emperor Valentinian had died at the end of 375 in the middle of other campaigns against German tribes (though he died not from

---

[57] For this story see the *CAH* xiii. 94–104. On the conflict with the Goths see Peter Heather, *Goths and Romans 332–489* (Oxford: Clarendon Press, 1991).

[58] Adrianople is sometimes presented as a catastrophic event for the empire, one of the key steps on the way towards the 'fall' of its western half. In reality, this is too simple a view: Theodosius was able to contain the threat from the Goths and negotiate a treaty within a year. The disastrous nature of Adrianople may stem from the loss of troops and the consequent need to incorporate ever greater numbers of German tribal warriors into the army, and from the treaty which handed over large tracts of land to the settlers. But for the purposes of my story the significance of Adrianople stems from the death of Valens and the rise of Theodosius. Normal life and travel and communication continued throughout almost all the eastern empire: and this normality enabled the vast amount of ecclesiastical activity of the 378–81 period. I am grateful to Tom Burns for discussion of this point.

wounds inflicted in battle but choked to death after a fit of anger at barbarian ambassadors). He had been succeeded by his 16-year-old son Gratian (who had been co-emperor since 367). Gratian himself was only two days away from Valens' army when the disaster happened. It was thus on the shoulders of Gratian and his advisers that the task fell of finding a successor to Valens. Gratian chose Theodosius, a military officer whose father had been one of Gratian's father's key military commanders in the west in the late 360s and early 370s.[59] Theodosius himself had been in charge of military operations in Moesia at the age of only 28.[60] Theodosius' father had been disgraced and executed in mysterious circumstances in late 375 or early 376 after the death of Valentinian and since then Theodosius had been in retirement in Spain.[61] Theodosius was brought east, given command of the fight against the Goths in the autumn of 378, and eventually declared Augustus in January 379 at the age of 32 or 33. Theodosius and Gratian managed to contain the threat from the Goths over the next two to three years, but only at the cost of permitting many tribes to settle on Roman land with treaties highly advantageous to the settlers.

The story of ecclesiastical events after Adrianople is initially parallel to that following Constantius' death in 361 some sixteen years before. The end of the previous emperor's policy coupled with a period of military uncertainty and the need of the new regime to garner support stimulated all the parties to try to increase their influence. The authority that had promoted Homoian interests was now gone and the other parties were now able to promote their own platforms with more openness. Realignments that had occurred behind the scenes could now be tested and strengthened openly. After Adrianople Gratian issued a decree permitting the return of exiled bishops and freedom of worship to all except Manichees, Eunomians, and the followers of Photinus.[62] A number of important players in the ongoing controversy were affected by this decree: Meletius was able to return to Antioch, Gregory of Nyssa returned to Nyssa after being in exile for two years, Eusebius of Samosata

---

[59] On the accession of Theodosius, and the complexities involved in a Spanish emperor adapting to the Constantinoplitan scene see John Matthews, *Western Aristocracies and Imperial Court AD 364–425* (Oxford: Clarendon Press, 1975), chs. 4 and 5.

[60] And thus Theodosius also had recent military experience near the very region now under threat.

[61] A still very useful account of Theodosius' role is to be found in R. Q. King, *The Emperor Theodosius and the Establishment of Christianity* (Philadelphia: Westminster Press, 1960).

[62] Socrates, *Hist eccl.* 5. 2, Sozomen, *Hist. eccl.* 7. 1. My understanding of the order of events here is much influenced by T. D. Barnes, 'The Collapse of the Homoeans in the East', *SP* 29 (1997), 3–16. In particular, it is important to note that Theodosius' policies were the continuation of Gratian's actions immediately after Adrianople.

returned from exile; Eunomius himself also returned to Constantinople.[63] Gratian's actions may themselves have followed on a relaxation of Valens' own position in 378 as the threat from the Goths became clear.[64] It was in the context of this upheaval in ecclesiastical life that some of the key texts of pro-Nicene polemic were written. I will begin once again with events in the east; the west is considered in the next chapter.

One of the first and most important stages in this upheaval seems to have been a council called in 379 by Meletius in Antioch.[65] We know little about the details of this meeting: the ancient sources are surprisingly quiet. We do know that Meletius and Eusebius of Samosata were key members and that Gregory of Nyssa was there. It is at least likely that this meeting met with the approval of Theodosius, although he was fully occupied in Thrace and may well have simply been unable to exert much control. We cannot tell the extent to which Theodosius was already known as a pro-Nicene supporter.[66] This council seems to have issued a pro-Nicene statement (perhaps by agreeing to a statement sent east by Damasus),[67] and written to Theodosius. It is highly probable that this council also called on Gregory Nazianzen to go to Constantinople to try and sustain the pro-Nicene community there: his activity in the capital is discussed in the next chapter.

It would, however, be a mistake to assume that divisions among pro-Nicenes were now over. What we see in Antioch is a move on the part of one alliance of pro-Nicenes centred around Meletius and Basil. Tensions between this group and the Egyptians, as well as between this group and the western bishops would persist. These tensions both indicate theological differences, and represent the interplay of traditional regional and inter-diocesan rivalries. The long-standing antipathy of Athanasius and his successors Peter and Timothy to Meletius persisted even though Meletius' supporters by the late 370s included a number of theologians—such as Gregory

---

[63] Kopecek, *Neo-Arianism*, ii. 441. He interprets Gratian's decree as permitting Eunomius' return but refusing Eunomian groups the right to assemble for worship. There is a good possibility that this decree was issued prior to the battle, Gratian following the usual procedure of allowing exiles to return in times of crisis.

[64] Socrates, *Hist. eccl.* 4. 32–5, Sozomen, *Hist. eccl.* 6. 37. On these events see the excellent discussion of Vaggione, *Eunomius*, 305–7; Barnes, 'Collapse', 3–6.

[65] Hanson, *The Search*, 803, and Simonetti, *La Crisi*, 446, review the evidence for the council.

[66] McGuckin, *Gregory of Nazianzus*, 236, argues that the direction of Theodosius' policy was already becoming clear following a joint declaration with Gratian in Milan in 379 (*C. Th.* 16. 5. 5). Williams, *Ambrose*, 157 ff. presents a strong argument that this edict may not have been aimed at non-Nicenes. The nature of the decree will probably remain unclear.

[67] Damasus finally agreed to recognize Meletius after the death of Basil. The evidence for this aspect of the council's work is slim but convincing. See the text printed at Eduard Schwartz, 'Über die Sammlung' des Cod. Veronesis LX; *ZNTW* 35 (1936), 19–23.

Nazianzen and Gregory of Nyssa—whose theology can hardly be thought of as demonstrating an ex-Homoiousian reserve.

This attempt by some pro-Nicenes to seize the initiative was mirrored within other groups. During the late 378 to early 380 period Eunomius took up Basil's attack of the early 360s and composed his *Apologia apologiae* ('Apology for the apology').[68] Early in 380 we find Eunomius and two Heterousian bishops in Constantinople consecrating a bishop for a Palestinian diocese. The four bishops then travelled to Antioch to hold a Heterousian council that seems to have been intended to reorganize Heterousian activity throughout the east.[69] We not only see sudden activity on the part of pro-Nicenes and Heterousians: similar moves can be seen among some looking back to the Homoiousian legacy. We know of councils meeting around 376 that endorsed the Dedication creed or the formula ὅμοιος κατ' οὐσίαν: among these groups Eustathius of Sebaste seems to have been prominent. Sozomen reports that in late 378 or 379 some of those who had been reconciled with Liberius of Rome (presumably he refers here to the embassy of 'Homoiousians' to the west in the early 360s) now tried to repossess the churches from which they had been exiled and convened a council at Antioch in Caria at which they reaffirmed the ὅμοιος κατ' οὐσίαν and rejected *homoousios*.[70] But, as Sozomen tells us, many refused to go along with this reassertion of a Homoiousian identity and actively sought to promote pro-Nicene interests.

---

[68] My account of events here is much indebted to Kopecek, *Neo-Arianism*, vol. ii, ch. 7 for the theology of Eunomius, *Apologia apologiae*, see pp. 441–92; for the events of the years after 378 see pp. 493 ff. and Vaggione, *Eunomius*, 306 ff.

[69] See Vaggione, *Eunomius*, 318; Kopecek, *Neo-Arianism*, ii. 496.

[70] Sozomen, *Hist. eccl.* 7. 2.

10
Victory and the Struggle for Definition

GREGORY NAZIANZEN

As we saw in the last chapter, Gregory Nazianzen was sent to Constantinople by the Antiochene council of 379.[1] The pro-Nicene faction in the capital was small and riven by internal dispute. Nevertheless, we should be wary of underestimating Gregory's support: he lived and preached in a villa complex given to him for the purpose by his cousin Theodosia (the sister of Amphilochius of Iconium).[2] Part of the complex was dedicated as a small church called the Anastasia ('resurrection'). Thus what is frequently presented as a marginalized group was also one with some wealthy and aristocratic support. We can trace a sequence of *Orations* Gregory preached during his first months in the capital, but the highlight came in the summer and autumn of 380 when he delivered the five orations which were later published and known as the *Theological Orations*.[3] The five seem to have been intended for publication from the first and stand as a manifesto of Gregory's position during this mission in Constantinople. Consideration of their theology both reveals something of Gregory's own particular genius and some of the ways some pro-Nicenes had now come to place the paradox of the divine unity and multiplicity at the front and centre of their theological writing. Such a focus enabled the development and performance of an interwoven epistemology and spirituality.

One of the most distinctive characteristics of Nazianzen's Trinitarian theology is the manner of his emphasis on the harmony of unity and diversity in the Godhead. For Gregory, the generative

---

[1] We should not assume that Gregory was sent as the intended bishop of the city or that he assumed he was the rightful bishop. While in his orations he speaks of himself in such terms, he was also careful not to assume the office was his when Theodosius arrived.

[2] Previous accounts of his time in Constantinople are surpassed by McGuckin, *Gregory of Nazianzus*, chs. 5 and 6. McGuckin is particularly helpful on the chronology of these years. Much still remains to be said, however, about Gregory's Trinitarian theology. See Holl, *Amphilochius*, 158–96; John McGuckin, 'Perceiving Light From Light in Light: The Trinitarian Theology of St. Gregory the Theologian', *Greek Orthodox Theological Review*, 39 (1994); John Egan, 'Primal Cause and Trinitarian Perichoresis in Gregory Nazianzen's *Oration* 31', *SP* 27 (1993); idem, 'Towards a Mysticism of Light in Gregory Nazianzen's *Oratio* 32.15', *SP* 18 (1989), 473–82; J. Bernardi, *La Prédication des Pères cappadociens: Le Prédicateur et son auditoire* (Paris: Presses Universitaires de France, 1968).

[3] On the circumstances of the *Orations* see McGuckin, *Gregory of Nazianzus*, 278 ff.; Bernardi, *La Prédication*, 380 ff.

nature of God eternally produces the triunity as the perfection of divine existence. Gregory does not argue to this position, he treats it as a point of departure:

> Monotheism, with its single governing principle, is what we value—not monotheism defined as the sovereignty of a single person (after all, self-discordant unity can become a plurality) but the single rule produced by equality of nature (φύσεως ὁμοτιμία), harmony of will, identity of action (ταυτότης κινήσεως), and the convergence towards their source (πρὸς τὸ ἓν τῶν ἐξ αὐτοῦ σύννευσις) of what springs from unity ... though there is numerical distinction, there is no division in the being. For this reason, a one eternally changes to two and stops at three—meaning the Father, the Son and the Holy Spirit. In a serene and non-temporal, incorporeal way, the Father is parent of the 'off-spring' and originator of the 'emanation' ... [but] we ought never to introduce the notion of involuntary generation.[4]

Similarly, in an oration probably composed in the same months as the *Theological Orations* we find him speaking of

> A perfect Trinity consisting of three perfect (Τριάδα τελείαν ἐκ τελείων τριῶν), we must abandon the concept of a monad for the sake of plenitude (διὰ τὸ πλούσιον), and go beyond a dyad (for the Trinity is beyond the matter and form which constitutes bodies), and we must define a Trinity for the sake of perfection (διὰ τὸ τέλειον).[5]

In articulating this position, Gregory has developed an important strain of earlier pro-Nicene thought. As we have seen, some earlier Nicene accounts present the Son as the intrinsic wisdom and power of the Father. Athanasius in particular presents the eternal generation of the Son as the Father's intrinsic wisdom to be the expression of the Father's perfection. One driving factor behind such arguments was the need to show that the distinction between Father and Son does not involve any diremption of the simple divine being.[6] Once fully pro-Nicene theologies emerged in which all three persons were described as irreducible, then the pressure grew to show not only how this three-in-oneness did not contradict the divine simplicity, but also how this three-in-oneness was an expression of what it meant to be God. One way in which this was accomplished was through arguments about the unity of the divine being and action in the three. Gregory of Nyssa and Basil's presentations of the one divine action as constituted by the three, with the Spirit constantly perfecting that action, in part attempts to display how the

---

[4] *Or.* 29. 2.   [5] *Or.* 23. 8.
[6] For an example of the latter see Athanasius, *Serap.* 1. 28: 'There is, then, a Triad, holy and complete, confessed to be one God in Father, Son and Holy Spirit, having nothing foreign or external mixed with it, not composed of one that creates and one that is originated, but all creative; and it is consistent and in nature indivisible, and its activity is one.'

three together constitute the perfect divine unity.⁷ Gregory Nazianzen's particular argument that the triunity constitutes a perfect overcoming of duality is an extremely rare one in late fourth-century Christian writing, but it is one that follows a trajectory sketched by previous pro-Nicenes.

Gregory's account also points forward to the later concept of *perichoresis*. This concept (in a Trinitarian context) I take to involve not only saying that the three persons are in or with one another beyond any spatial differentiation, but also asserting that the persons are in or with one another through a dynamic movement towards unity and each other.⁸ In the section of *Oration* 29 quoted above we have already seen Gregory speak of a 'convergence towards the source' in the existence of the divine persons. In *Oration* 42, again delivered very closely in time to the *Theological Orations*, we read,

The three have one nature—God. The principle of unity (ἕνωσις) is the Father, from whom the other two are brought forward and to whom they are brought back, not so as to coalesce (συναλείφεσθαι), but so as to cleave together (ἔχεσθαι).⁹

Gregory here understands the persons qua persons as continually returning to their source, remaining distinct and yet inseparable. The divine unity described in material or metaphysical terms as the unity of one light and power is simultaneously the outgoing and return of the divine being and will that results in three who are distinct and yet one.

Oration 29's use of the language of 'convergence' (σύννευσις) deserves further comment. Gregory's source is probably Plotinus. Plotinus once uses the term to describe the movement of multiplicity towards unity in the cosmos and once of the movement internal to Intellect that moves it towards its image The Good.¹⁰ Whereas Gregory of Nyssa and possibly Basil picked up Plotinus' usage when talking about the cosmos, only Gregory Nazianzen uses the term to describe the divine persons. It is in such usage that we see the force of André de Halleux's insistence that one cannot understand Gregory by questioning whether his trinitarianism is 'essentialist' or 'personalist'. The dynamism in Gregory's account does not come from a 'personalist' emphasis over against an

---

⁷ Augustine's account of Trinity as a constant cycle of love is another such example: not so much an attempt to demonstrate philosophically the necessity of God as three, but an attempt to show how we may see the divine threeness as constituting the divine perfection.

⁸ The former understanding is present for example at Athanasius, *Serap*. 3. 4. See also Hilary, *De trin*. 3. 1 ff., Basil, *Spir*. 63. The discussion of Prestige, *God in Patristic Thought* (London: Heineman, 1936), ch. 14, is still useful here.

⁹ *Or*. 42. 15. In exegesis of this passage I am indebted to Egan, 'Primal Cause'.

¹⁰ Plotinus, *Ennead* 2. 2. 1 and 3. 8. 11.

'essentialist' use of essence and nature language.[11] In this case, it is through the adaptation of Plotinus' non-personalist metaphysical language that Gregory sets out a new dynamism in his account of the Trinity.

It is at this point that we need to note Gregory's use of the term σχέσις (relation) in trinitarian contexts. Two famous texts may be quoted:

'Father' is a name neither of substance nor of activity, but of relationship, of the manner of being (σχέσεως δὲ καὶ τοῦ πῶς ἔχει πρὸς τὸν υἱὸν ὁ πατήρ, ἢ ὁ Υἱὸς πρὸς τὸν Πατέρα), which holds good between Father and Son. Just as with us these names indicate kindred and affinity, so here too they designate the sameness of stock, of parent and offspring.[12]

In what particular, then, it may be asked, *does the Spirit fall short of being Son? If there were not something missing, he would be Son.* We say there is no deficiency—God lacks nothing. It is their difference in, so to say, 'manifestation' or mutual relationship, which has caused the difference in names.[13]

In neither of these texts does relationship designate a mode of existence (Gregory's usage thus mirroring Basil's). In the text from *Oration* 29 Gregory responds to a charge that the names must designate either distinct essences or energies. If the first, so the argument goes, then they are distinct in status, if the latter then Son and Spirit are not truly distinct persons. Gregory's response is to continue to *assume* that the persons are one in the Godhead and of equal status, and to show how a pro-Nicene can understand the designation of the personal names as performing a function other than designating essences or energies. In designating relations the names designate only the relationships of the persons with the others; they tell as nothing about the mode of existence of a divine person in the abstract. 'Relation' in Gregory's theology is thus a category that primarily serves to uphold the paradoxical unity in distinction as consonant with Scripture.

Although Gregory's account of the unity of the three persons is both innovative and creative, it is also at times problematic. It has puzzled commentators for centuries that Gregory seems to present both Father *and* the Trinity as a whole as the cause of all:

In a nutshell, the Godhead exists undivided in separate beings. It is as if there were a single intermingling of light, which existed in three mutually connected suns (ἐν ἡλίοις τρισὶν ἐχομένοις ἀλλήλων). When we look at the Godhead, the primal cause, the sole sovereignty, we have a mental picture of the single whole, certainly. But when we look at the three in whom the

---

[11] See André de Halleux, 'Personnalisme ou Essentialisme Trinitaire chez Les Pères Cappadociens', *Revue Théologique de Louvain*, 17 (1986), 129–55, 265–92.
[12] *Or.* 29. 16.   [13] *Or.* 31. 9.

Godhead exists, who derive their timeless and equally glorious being from the primal cause, we have three objects of worship.[14]

In other texts Gregory speaks directly of the Father as the 'cause' of the Son, but here the Godhead in general seems to be the cause of all three.[15] Although it may be that Gregory is being simply incoherent, John Egan suggests that a number of commentators are right to argue that Nazianzen's expression in this passage is loose and that he intends us to see the Father as the primal cause *and* as the source of his own being.[16] We may also argue that as Gregory sees the Father fully sharing 'his' being in generation and spiration, so he would probably accept that the Godhead can loosely be spoken of as both caused by the Father and as itself the primal cause.

Although Gregory presents 'He who is' as the one true name of God,[17] it is light imagery that is particularly prominent. In *Oration* 31 Gregory makes connections that are fundamental in his use of light imagery, linking God as threefold light and God as illuminator:

'He was the true light that enlightens every man coming into the world'— yes, the Son. 'He was the true light that enlightens every man coming into the world'—yes, the Spirit. These are three subjects and three verbs—he was and he was and he was. But a single reality was. There are three predicates—light and light and light. But the light is one, God is one. This is the meaning of David's propehtic vision: 'In thy light we shall see light.' We receive the Son's light from the Father's light in the light of the Spirit.[18]

The same perspective is repeated outside the *Theological Orations*:

God is light . . . he is in the world of thought, what the sun is in the world of sense, presenting himself to our minds in proportion as we are cleansed . . . himself contemplating and comprehending himself, and pouring himself out upon what is external to him. That light, I mean, which is contemplated in the Father and the Son and the Holy Spirit, whose riches is their unity of nature, and the one outleaping (ἔξαλμα) of their brightness.[19]

The sources for Gregory's use of this imagery have not yet been satisfactorily identified.[20] In the first place, Gregory draws on

---

[14] *Or.* 31. 14.   [15] *Or.* 29. 15.

[16] This is the conclusion of Egan in his 'Primal Cause'.

[17] See H. Althaus, *Die Heilslehre des heiligen Gregor von Nazianz* (Münster: Aschendorff, 1972), 159, citing *Or.* 30. 18.

[18] *Or.* 31. 3.

[19] *Or.* 40. 5. cf. *Or.* 28. 31. The statement that God's place in the intelligible world mirrors the sun in the material world is paralleled at *Or.* 28. 30 and is a reference to Plato, *Republic* 508c, especially as this theme was interpreted through Middle Platonic tradition.

[20] The centrality of light imagery to Gregory Nazianzen has not prompted extensive modern consideration: see Egan, 'Towards a Mysticism of Light', C. Moreschini, 'Luce e purificazione nella dottrine di Gregorio Nazianzeno', *Augustinianum*, 13 (1973): The point of departure remains John Egan, 'The Knowledge and Vision of God according to Gregory Nazianzen: A study of the Images of Mirror and Light', diss., Institut Catholique de Paris 1971.

traditional exegesis of the light imagery in John's gospel. We can also draw connections between Gregory and Origen's use of the terminology of illumination.[21] But the use of light imagery is not unique to Christians in the late antique context. Christian discussion was engaged with the light language used both in developing Platonic tradition but also in a number of ancient ritual and religious contexts. John McGuckin, argues that Gregory in his *Hymn of Lament*, recasts the story of his baptism into the language of the mystery cults. A key part of this recasting involves the use of light imagery.[22] We can also point to Plotinus' account of the light that provides an illumination enabling approach to the Good. In this case Plotinus seems to be clear that all other intelligible light is an image of the Good, not part of it.[23] The Good is the source of the 'divine' light in us that draws us towards the Good and yet that second light is not part of the Good itself. John Egan argues that such distinctions may have influenced Gregory, enabling him to use the imagery of light without denying the distinction between Creator and creation.[24] Whether or not Gregory directly draws on Plotinus, Egan is correct to note that for Gregory illumination by divine light *entails* rather than denies the apophatic character of human knowledge of God. Through and in the Spirit's light we are drawn towards a light that exceeds our grasp. The infinite character of the divine light enables a slow removing of the dark veil between human beings and God. But also note how this conception of illumination is intertwined with an account of the dazzling light of the *Triune* God. The light that constitutes God is in part beyond our grasp *because* it is the 'outleaping' of the three who are one.[25]

Gregory's theology did not meet with universal approval even among those in Constantinople who favoured Nicaea. On one side, those who came from a Homoiousian background were unhappy with Gregory's assumption of the Spirit's place in the Trinity. On the other side, there were many Egyptians in the capital who attended his congregation and he reports the disruption that they at times caused. Their opposition probably stemmed from Alexandrian unhappiness at Gregory's links with Meletius. It would not be surprising, however, if reports of Gregory's teaching back to

---

[21] e.g. Origen, *Comm. John* 13. 23.

[22] McGuckin, *Gregory of Nazianzus*, 67–75.

[23] Plotinus, *Enn.* 6. 7. 16. With this text Egan, 'Towards a Mysticism of Light', 475 ff., parallels *Enn.* 1. 2. 2, following Ferwerda.

[24] Egan, 'Towards a Mysticism of Light', 474.

[25] The links between Gregory's Trinitarian theology and his conception of theological method and human purification is discussed in Chs. 11–13.

Alexandria found his terminology for the distinctions between the persons uncongenial. But here we can only surmise.[26]

An important part of Gregory's work in Constantinople was the shaping of Basil's memory. By constructing himself as Basil's heir he was able to increase his authority and to present himself as part of a wide and respected pro-Nicene coalition. As already noted it was around this time that Eunomius finally responded in published form to Basil's own *Contra Eunomium* with his *Apologia apologiae* ('Apology for the apology'). At the very time Gregory was preaching in the Anastasia, Eunomius was only miles away, living on his estate in Chalcedon, teaching and hoping for influence with the new emperor. The memory of Basil was thus an issue of constant and contemporary debate. In 381, probably just before the Council of Constantinople (discussed below), Gregory of Nyssa came to Constantinople and Nazianzen arranged a public reading of sections of Nyssa's own *Contra Eunomium*, which was then in the process of being composed in response to the *Apologia apologiae*.[27]

Finding the two Gregorys in Constantinople engaging in common pro-Nicene polemic and defending the legacy of Basil draws us to consider the unity of the group known as 'the Cappadocians'. We can identify a number of good reasons for speaking of these three as a group. They were closely linked by a web of family and regional ties. They shared significant involvement in the defence of some fundamental theological principles. Their understandings of theological method show significant overlap. Nevertheless, we should not allow these similarities to hide from us their differences. Gregory of Nyssa seems to have had connections to continuing Marcellan groups in Asia Minor, groups towards whom Basil seems to have been strongly opposed. Nyssa also demonstrates an account of the unity of the divine nature and power that is considerably more developed than Basil's. Gregory Nazianzen's theology is shaped by different terminologies and concerns. We do not find in Nazianzen any extended discussion of ἐπίνοια, for example. We also find in Nazianzen a subtly different theology of the Spirit that places less emphasis on the Spirit as completing the divine action, and we do not see extended reflection on the creation's existence as a set of

---

[26] I am convinced by John McGuckin's redating of *Oration* 42 to before Gregory's falling out with Maximus (*Gregory of Nazianzus*, 191). If, however, one does redate this oration, then it is interesting to ask why Gregory goes out of his way (and with such courtesy) to insist on the common orthodoxy of his own followers and the Egyptian visitors. The most likely answer is the long history of Egyptian suspicion of those in communion with Meletius.

[27] As John McGuckin points out (*Gregory of Nazianzus*, 349–50), this reading may have constituted one of the most intellectually high-powered meetings among pro-Nicene theologians, including Jerome, Gregory Nazianzen, Gregory of Nyssa, Evagrius, and possibly Diodore of Tarsus, Amphilochius, and Meletius!

immutable and divinely ordained natures. While one can draw a series of deep connections between Nyssa's theology and Basil's, it is not clear that the particularities of Nazianzen's theology are obviously closer to Basil's than, say, those of Didymus the Blind. The set of familial and geographical connections we find between 'the Cappadocians' warrants the common term if used with caution, but caution is of great importance.

IMPERIAL DEFINITION

The constant background to Gregory's work in Constantinople was Theodosius' own developing religious policy. It was soon clear that Theodosius would pursue a pro-Nicene line. In February 380 Theodosius issued an edict insisting on the profession of 'Nicene' faith, defined as that taught by Damasus, bishop of Rome, and Peter, Athanasius' successor in Alexandria. Three things about this decree are of interest here. First, the decree is addressed not to the prefect of the city, but to the people of Constantinople. It is possible that this reflects a situation in which Theodosius wished to make a clear statement, but one in which he realized the difficulty of actually enforcing any such decree without his own presence. The decree served as a prelude to more precise action in the future. Second, the decree names Peter of Alexandria and Damasus of Rome as the two standards of orthodoxy. This probably reflects both Theodosius' own status as a western pro-Nicene, and the influence of Acholius the bishop of Thessalonica. As I discussed in an earlier chapter, Thessalonica and its surrounding area had a local tradition of supporting an old-Nicene/Athanasian line in theology and its bishops were under the provincial control of the bishop of Rome.[28] Theodosius had his temporary headquarters in the city and when he fell seriously ill in the middle of 380 Acholius baptized him. In his later decrees the citation of Rome and Alexandria ceases and Theodosius adopts a mode of definition more in tune with the traditions of the Meletian/Basilian pro-Nicenes.

Third, Theodosius does not define orthodoxy by reference to Nicaea alone, but by outlining a basic logic of belief in the Trinity:

It is our will that the peoples who are ruled by the administration of our clemency shall practise that religion which the divine Peter the apostle transmitted to the Romans ... [that which] is followed by the Pontiff Damasus and by Peter, bishop of Alexandria ... [that is] we shall believe in the single deity of the Father, the Son and the Holy Spirit, under the concept of equal majesty and of the Holy Trinity.[29]

---

[28] See Chapter 2, p. 51.   [29] *C. Th.* 16. 1. 2.

With this text we need to compare two others. The first is the decree issued by Theodosius in January 381 in Constantinople forbidding 'heretics' the right to assemble for worship. Here Theodosius writes:

> That man shall be accepted as a defender of the Nicene faith ... who confesses that Almighty God and Christ the Son of God are one in name, God of God, light of light, who does not violate by denial the Holy Spirit ... that man who esteems ... the undivided substance of the incorrupt Trinity, that substance which those of the orthodox faith call, employing a Greek word, *ousia*.[30]

The third text is Theodosius' decree *Episcopis tradi* of 382 (the story of events between the second and third of these texts is told below). The beginning of the text runs:

> We command that all churches shall immediately be surrendered to those bishops who confess that the Father, the Son and the Holy Spirit are of one majesty and power, of the same glory, and of one splendour, to those bishops who produce no dissonance by unholy distinction, but who affirm the concept of the Trinity by the assertion of three persons and the unity of the Divinity ... [31]

In all three of these texts Theodosius and his advisers offer a short formula that will serve as a practical marker of orthodoxy. The last two are addressed to specific individuals and possibly are so addressed in response to requests from officials who, after 381, needed to know how to decide claims on disputed churches.[32] We see in these texts how clearly pro-Nicenes had been able to establish the logic of three divine persons within the unitary Godhead as a fundamental identity marker. The second text is particularly interesting in that it incorporates a number of allusions to Nicaea itself ('God from God, Light from Light'; the reference to *ousia* language) but these references are ordered within a basic statement of a pro-Nicene Trinitarian logic: Son and Spirit are to be understood within the 'undivided substance of the incorrupt Trinity.' It is the interpretation of Son and Spirit as 'within' the one divine existence that actually constitutes the key marker of orthodox identity in all three of these texts. It is noteworthy that the texts do not invoke the language of *homoousios* and only the last makes any reference to a technical terminology for distinguishing persons and essence: but even there the emphasis is not on a particular terminology but on

---

[30] *C. Th.* 16. 5. 6. 2.   [31] *C. Th.* 16. 1. 3.

[32] On the nature and function of the Theodosian legislation (and its relationship to earlier Roman legal material) see Caroline Humfress, 'Roman Law, Forensic Argument and the Formation of Christian Orthodoxy (III–VI Centuries)', in Susanna Elm, Eric Rebillard, and Antonella Romano (eds.), *Orthodoxie, christianisme, histoire* (Rome: École Française de Rome, 2000), 125–47.

Victory and the Struggle for Definition

acknowledging the true existence of Father, Son, and Spirit. I return to the character of these definitions in the following chapter.

THE COUNCIL OF CONSTANTINOPLE

In 381 Theodosius summoned a council to meet in Constantinople.[33] It seems unlikely that this meeting was intended as a universal council to rival Seleucia/Ariminum or Nicaea itself. In 378 or 379 there may have been a plan by Gratian to call a council in his own half of the empire, but we have no firm evidence.[34] Theodosius probably consulted with Gratian, but his initial intention seems to have been more limited than a general council of the east, perhaps a council focused on the civil 'diocese' of Oriens. Those present at the council initially came from a fairly restricted area and the majority from areas known to be favourable to Meletius. Its most immediate concerns were to settle affairs in Constantinople and to attempt a rapprochement with the 'Macedonians', but it is also likely that Theodosius intended this to set an example for his half of the empire.[35]

Our knowledge of the council is surprisingly patchy. We have no surviving acts nor any copy of the theological definition that followed the council's creed.[36] Most surprisingly, there is no certain account of the creed itself until the Council of Chalcedon. There are, however, enough hints to attempt a reconstruction of events and to make it fairly certain that this council did issue the creed later associated with it.[37] Meletius was the initial president of the council. When Theodosius had entered Constantinople in November 380 he had given the Homoian Demophilus the chance to remain as bishop if he subscribed to Nicaea. When he did not he was exiled and Theodosius accepted Gregory Nazianzen as de facto bishop. It was, however, the first session of the council that formally recognized

---

[33] On the council see Hanson, *The Search*, 791 ff.; Simonetti, *La Crisi*, 527–41; Ritter, *Das Konzil von Konstantinopel*; Reinhard Staats, *Das Glaubensbekenntnis von Nizäa-Konstantinopel* (Darmstadt: Wissenschaftliche Buchgesellschaft 1996).

[34] See below in discussion of the Council of Aquileia. See especially the discussion in Williams, *Ambrose*, 161 ff.

[35] Socrates, *Hist. eccl.*. 5. 8, Sozomen, *Hist. eccl.* 7. 7, and Theodoret, *Eccl. hist.* 5. 8 all indicate that agreeing on a bishop for Constantinople was a key task for the council. As we shall see, however, Theodosius seems to have been concerned that the council also clearly affirm a pro-Nicene faith for his half of the empire.

[36] One reason for the lack of knowledge of the council was persistent western disinterest in the council, in part because of the claims Constantinople's canons made for the authority of the bishop of Constantinople. Similarly, Rome's continuing recognition of Paulinus in Antioch even after Flavian's election (discussed below) can only have increased their lack of interest.

[37] On this particular question see the still-seminal account of Kelly, *Early Christian Creeds*, ch. 10.

him. One of the first acts of the council seems to have been an attempt to reconcile a group of Homoiousian/Macedonian bishops to the Nicene creed: this failed but may have been the occasion for the drawing up of what became known as the Nicene-Constantinopolitan creed.

Suddenly, Meletius died and Gregory Nazianzen became president of the council. The direction of the meeting soon began to shift with the arrival of Acholius of Thessalonica and a delegation of Egyptian bishops headed by Timothy of Alexandria. According to Gregory these new arrivals came at the behest of Theodosius,[38] but do not seem to have been among those initially invited. It seems probable that, following the failure of negotiation with the Macedonians, Theodosius decided the presence of those he still took to be key arbiters of orthodoxy would secure a pro-Nicere triumph as an example for the whole east. Two questions now dominated proceedings. The first was a replacement for Meletius. Gregory Nazianzen promoted Paulinus, the leader of the old Nicene/Eustathian party in Antioch. By an agreement reached in Antioch in 379 Meletius and Paulinus had recognized each other as bishop; whoever died first would be succeeded by the surviving partner. The Syrian bishops at the council (to whom it fell to elect a successor) did not wish to abide by the agreement: Paulinus seems not to have attracted much support beyond his original community. Exactly what happened remains unclear, but it seems unlikely that the whole council elected a new bishop. Hanson suggests that the bishops of Syria made a compromise choice at the council and the formal consecration then took place after the council in Antioch itself.[39] They elected Flavian, a priest who had been a close associate of Diodore of Tarsus. Flavian was a member of Paulinus' community and over the next few years proved himself able to bring together many from both Paulinus' and Meletius' communities.

The second question concerned Constantinople itself. It seems likely that the Egyptian bishops had attempted to raise the question of Gregory's legitimacy (based on Nicaea's prohibition of bishops moving from see to see) from the moment of their arrival. A few months previously Peter of Alexandria had encouraged Maximus, an Egyptian supporter of Gregory's, to usurp his place.[40] The plot failed, but the attitude of the Egyptians was clear. In the council itself Gregory seems to have quickly made himself unpopular. He

---

[38] Gregory Nazianzen, *De vita sua* 1798.   [39] Hanson, *The Search*, 809 ff.
[40] The whole incident is helpfully related by McGuckin, *Gregory of Nazianzus*, 311 ff. Maximus had been consecrated bishop and he pursued his claim with some vigour before the emperor and in the west. The council seems to have formally rejected his claim in its first session.

supported the wrong candidate for Antioch and had strongly opposed any compromise with the Homoiousians. At some point he seems also to have lost the support of Theodosius. Gregory offered his resignation on a point of principle and it was accepted. In Gregory's place Nectarius, an unbaptized civil official in Constantinople, was chosen. Gregory's successor was both an associate of Diodore and known to Theodosius himself. The details, as far as we can surmise them, of this council indicate the problems with later presentation of the meeting as an 'ecumenical' reaffirmation of Nicaea. Even though it was a fait accompli that Constantinople would endorse 'Nicene' faith in some form, what that meant was still the subject of considerable debate and any decision was inseparable from complex ecclesiastical politics. I want now to consider the theological statements produced by the council.

The creed probably read as follows:

We believe in one God, the Father Almighty, maker of heaven and earth and of all things visible and invisible; and in one Lord Jesus Christ, the Son of God, the Only-begotten, begotten by his Father before all ages, Light from light, true God from true God, begotten not made, consubstantial with the Father, through whom all things came into existence, who for us men and for our salvation came down from the heavens and became incarnate by the Holy Spirit and the virgin Mary and became a man, and was crucified for us under Pontius Pilate and suffered and was buried and rose again on the third day in accordance with the Scriptures and ascended into the heavens and is seated at the right hand of the Father and will come again with glory to judge the living and the dead, and there will be no end to his kingdom; and in the Holy Spirit, the Lord and Life-giver, who proceeds from the Father who is worshipped and glorified together with the Father and the Son, who spoke by the prophets; and in one holy Catholic and apostolic Church; we confess one baptism for the forgiveness of sins; we wait for the resurrection of the dead and the life of the coming age.[41]

In his *Early Christian Creeds*, J. N. D. Kelly somewhat exaggerates when he writes of the differences between this creed and the original Nicaea being so extensive that, in the context of fourth-century creeds, Constantinople is better regarded as a new creed rather than an adaptation of Nicaea's. However, Kelly expands on his comment to offer a seminal account of the creed[42] focused around exploring the difference between commitment to the precise wording of Nicaea, and fidelity to the 'faith' represented by Nicaea. As we know, faithfulness to Nicaea as a text and to some of its key terminology had become increasingly important in the 360–80 period following the promulgation of the Homoian creed. We know,

---

[41] Here I follow Hanson's translation, *The Search*, 816.
[42] Kelly, *Early Christian Creeds*, ch. 10.

however, that the creed of Nicaea was not used directly for catechetical purposes or in worship: the theology for which the creed was a cipher rather came to shape the interpretation and presentation of local baptismal creeds—at times by the insertion into existing creeds of phraseology from Nicaea. In this context faithfulness to Nicaea still did not rule out a certain flexibility of how one formally stated the 'Nicene' faith. Kelly argues that in debate with the 36 Homoiousian bishops, it was necessary to state in a simple form the 'Nicene faith' and that someone did so using a creed that mixed some local credal tradition with phrases from Nicaea and a fuller statement of the Spirit's divinity. Nobody intended this creed as a replacement for Nicaea, merely as a statement of Nicaea's faith. Thus, part of the reason for the *lack* of reference to this creed until the council of Chalcedon in 451 is the *lack* of intention of its framers that the Constantinople creed serve as a precise marker of orthodoxy.

It is within this context that we need to assess the differences between this creed and that of Nicaea 325. Hanson provides a list of twelve differences, eight of which seem to imply no difference in doctrine, but perhaps indicate an attempt on the part of the creed's architects to move the text of Nicaea a little closer to the Old Roman creed.[43] One of the remaining four changes is the addition of the anti-Marcellan 'and his kingdom will have no end': by 381 such an expression was traditional and to be expected. This leaves three changes: (1) the addition of the extended statement about the Spirit; (2) the omission of 'from the *ousia* of the Father'; (3) the omission of Nicaea's anathemas. The last is most easily dealt with: the creed was not designed to exclude a party present at the council who might be taken to hold those views and thus no such anathemas were needed. The omission of 'from the *ousia* of the Father' has, as Hanson puts it, 'caused much heart-searching among scholars'.[44] For some this omission resulted from negotiation with Homoiousians. Many Homoiousians would, however, have been perfectly happy with the phrase, and were far more likely to have been offended by the statement that the Spirit is worshipped *with* (συν) the Father and the Son. Hanson ultimately argues that it was overlooked in a context where the precise wording of the creed as a whole was not a concern.[45] I

---

[43] For the list see Hanson, *The Search*, 816. For the argument that accommodation with the Old Roman creed is important see Luise Ambramowski, 'Was hat das Niceno-Constantinopolitanum (c) mit dem Konzil von Konstantinopel 381 zu tun?', *Theologie und Philosophie* 67 (1992), 481–513 Ambramowski's account is persuasively adapted by Staats, *Das Glaubensbekenntnis*, ch. 5, esp. 165–70.

[44] Hanson, *The Search*, 817.

[45] Its absence is also an indication either that Athanasian emphasis on the phrase was no longer of interest even to the Egyptians, or, more likely, that the creed was drawn up before they arrived.

suggest we can also note that while in some circles (particularly Athanasian circles) the phrase was taken to be of importance, it probably meant far less to those in the circles of Basil and Meletius. The increasing importance of *homoousios* as a watchword in previous decades probably also helped to displace the phrase.

Interpreters of the creed's clauses concerning the Spirit have frequently wondered about the absence of the term *homoousios*. The discussion usually takes its point of departure from Gregory Nazianzen's comments that at the council the pure Nicene faith was adulterated in the name of compromise.[46] Constantinople's account of the Spirit seems to mirror Basil's cautious strategy of insisting that we accord the Spirit equal glory and honour, but refrain from using the terms God or *homoousios*. We need first, however, to reconsider Basil's supposed reserve.[47] As I have already indicated, Basil's reserve on the Spirit tends to increase not decrease through his career, and reflects not a failure to subscribe to basic pro-Nicene logic, but the care with which he tried to combine clarity with advances towards Homoiousians in a still-fluid situation. We need also to note the differing roles of the two Gregorys: while Nazianzen's view of Constantinople is fairly clear, Nyssa's views were probably quite different.

Anthony Meredith points to the three uses of *sun-* as a qualifier in quick succession in the Spirit clauses of Constantinople as very possibly the result of Nyssa's influence. While Basil once himself describes the three as συνδοξάξοντες, one of the very terms used in this creed, the repetition of συν here, combined with the use of συνπροσκυνούμενον ('worshipped with'), seems to reflect Nyssa's personal emphasis in his *On the Holy Spirit: Against Macedonius* (*c.*380). In this text, and here I move beyond Meredith's argument, Nyssa frequently returns to the question of what follows from our according equal worship to the Spirit. He argues that if we worship the Spirit we must also imagine the Spirit involved in the same activities as Father and Son and hence sharing the same nature. Interestingly, Gregory is here able to present at least some of his opponents as sharing the principle of according the Spirit equal worship.[48]

There was thus an ongoing tradition of debate about the character of the worship accorded the Spirit: a debate we may also see a few

---

[46] For his open disapproval see *De vita sua* 1755–8. The revised and later published version of his final oration before the bishops contains a pro-Nicene statement that seems directly opposed to the council's mood: see *Or.* 42. 14–18. For his attempt to preserve Basil's memory from charges that he was unsound on the Spirit's divinity see *Or.* 43. 69.

[47] In this discussion I have been greatly helped by Anthony Meredith's excellent demonstration of the ambiguities here in his 'Pneumatology of the Cappadocian Fathers'.

[48] Gregory of Nyssa, *Spir.* (GNO 3/1 95).

years earlier in Basil's *On the Holy Spirit*. For Gregory, invoking emphasis on the *common* worship and glorification of the Spirit inexorably leads to the conclusion that the Spirit is of equal ontological status with the Father and the Son. For some who may not have made those leaps so clearly, this phraseology seemed more acceptable than anything Nazianzen might have suggested. Thus, the very ambiguity of Constantinople's pneumatological clauses enabled it to serve not only as a negotiating tool to draw in as many Homoiousians and ex-Homoiousians as possible, but also as a cipher for the robustly pro-Nicene theology of a Gregory of Nyssa. We may see here, then, the subtle pragmatism of Basil's younger brother. If this account is correct then we must term the creed a 'compromise' only with great caution. A desire to accommodate need not also mean a willingness to compromise.

Although the detailed statement of faith which accompanied Constantinople's creed does not survive, Theodoret's *Ecclesiastical History* preserves a letter from a council in Constantinople in 382, which included some of the same bishops and responded to western unhappiness at the decisions of the 381 council concerning the sees of Constantinople and Antioch. This letter offers a definition of Trinitarian orthodoxy intended to be compatible with western statements. The letter says,

> [Nicaea] is the faith of our baptism; it is the faith that teaches us to believe in the name of the Father, of the Son and of the Holy Spirit. According to this faith there is one Godhead (θεότης), Power (δυνάμις), and Substance (*ousia*) of the Father and of the Son and of the Holy Spirit; the dignity being equal, and the majesty being equal in three perfect hypostases, i.e. three perfect persons (πρόσωπα). Thus there is no room for the heresy of Sabellius by the confusion of the hypostases, i.e. the destruction of the personal properties (ἰδιοτήτες); thus the blasphemy of the Eunomians, of the Arians, and of the Pneumatomachi is nullified, which divides the substance (*ousia*), the nature (φύσις), and the godhead (θεότης), and superimposes onto the uncreated consubstantial and coeternal Trinity a separate nature, created, and of a different substance.[49]

This text does not follow Theodosius' legislation in focusing on the logic of the relationship between persons and essence without reference to technical terminology: it achieves the same result by *supplementation* of terminology. Θεότης, *ousia*, and φύσις are used for the divine nature, while *hypostasis*, πρόσωπον, and ἰδιοτήτες are used to indicate the divine persons; variety in terminology is not of concern as long as the logic embodied in such terminologies is preserved. To

---

[49] Theodoret, *Eccl. hist.* 5. 9. This text, in the last sentence quoted here, offers an excellent example of the ways in which articulating the logic of the persons and essence for pro-Nicenes was dependent on also articulating the divine simplicity . . .

give one small example, the letter allows πρόσωπον as a synonym for *hypostasis*: while we find the Cappadocians sometimes using πρόσωπον, its appearance here indicates the recognition that those who preferred πρόσωπα to *hypostases* were not necessarily unorthodox.[50] Both this text and Theodosius' legislation seem to reflect a situation in which distinct and developing theological traditions were able to recognize each other while still engaged in a continual persuasion towards terminological convergence.

The Council of Constantinople does not mark the end of Trinitarian debate in the eastern empire. Indeed, Constantinople was not even the end of Theodosius' attempts to entice non-Nicene groups into the pro-Nicene fold. Attempts to seduce those unhappy with pro-Nicene pneumatology continued for some years. In 383 Theodosius even summoned a council of all 'sects' for a general discussion of the faith. Socrates and Sozomen report that on the suggestion of Nectarius Theodosius asked the representatives of each sect to say whether they revered the earliest Christians who lived before the current divided state of the Church and then whether they were prepared to defer to the witness of those Christians.[51] Socrates reports that this suggestion caused consternation among all present: everyone had now become sensitive to the ways in which pre-Nicene texts could not easily be used by any of the late fourth-century theological parties! Each party was asked to provide a statement of faith: only those provided by the pro-Nicenes and the Novatianists[52] were found acceptable. Surviving legislation from later in 383 and 384 appears to show Theodosius coming down hard on dissenting groups: 'Eunomians', 'Arians', and 'Macedonians' are three names that consistently appear in lists of groups beyond the bounds of orthodoxy.[53] At the same time, however, Socrates reports Theodosius following the pragmatic policy of his predecessors in tolerating dissenting groups as long as they built their churches outside the walls of cities. Socrates lists only one exception: the Eunomians, who had met in private houses

---

[50] My argument here suggests something of a corrective to de Halleux's magisterial ' "Hypestase" et "Personne" ', in that de Halleux suggests too strongly that there was a consensus in terminology apparent by 381. Accordingly, he misses the consciousness with which the logic inherent in parallel terminologies could be expressed.

[51] Socrates, *Hist. eccl.* 5. 10, Sozomen, *Hist. eccl.* 7. 12.

[52] Novatianists were a sect whose origins lay in Novatian's own stand against the terms under which those who had lapsed during the Decian persecution (249–50) were received back into the Church. He was elected bishop of Rome in opposition to Cornelius and eventually a sect appeared that seems to have had a presence in Italy and in Asia Minor. The Novatianists had a Trinitarian doctrine that probably owed much to their founder and were accepted as basically orthodox if schismatic throughout the 4th cent.

[53] *C. Th.* 16. 5. 11, 12, 13.

inside the walls of Constantinople and attempted to win over new supporters.[54]

We cannot clearly trace the fortunes and ultimate decline of the various groups in the east that opposed pro-Nicenes after the 380s. This decline was not swift: anti-'Arian' writings were produced into the 420s and many of the non-Nicene groups flourished beyond this date. Indeed, it was in the years immediately after Constantinople 381 that some of the key pro-Nicene texts were produced, much of Gregory of Nyssa's anti-'Arian' writing being an excellent example. This 'end' to our narrative is thus only the *beginning* of the end of non-Nicene theology in the east.

THE WEST AD: 365–400

The last events in the west we discussed were the pro-Nicene campaigns of the early 360s. One feature of those campaigns was the caution with which they had to be conducted. Even though Valentinian I (366–75) has gone down in history as a Nicene emperor, his public policy was one of pragmatic non-interference—even if privately he had a harsh and unforgiving temper: it was this imperial policy that formed the background to pro-Nicene activity until 375. Thus, while small synods could profess Nicaea's creed, we have no evidence that pro-Nicenes had the means to depose (rather than just censure or excommunicate) Homoian bishops. In fact pro-Nicenes only rarely attempted the direct removal of their opponents. In one well-known incident Hilary travelled to Milan in 364 to campaign against Auxentius, the Homoian bishop. This attack ended in Hilary being ordered to leave Milan as a threat to public order. Pro-Nicenes could expand their influence primarily by pushing for the appointment of like-minded bishops on the deaths of Homoian incumbents. The patchy evidence that we possess indicates that the conciliar condemnation of Homoians by pro-Nicene synods continued through the 370s, but that Homoian theology continued to be a potent force, especially in Illyria and in northern Italy.

Two western figures from the 370s and 380s demand mention here, Damasus, bishop of Rome 366–84, and Ambrose, bishop of Milan 374–97. Damasus had been a deacon in Rome under Liberius, had briefly supported Felix, who supplanted Liberius during the latter's exile in 356–8, and was elected in a disputed and divisive contest after Liberius' return and death in 366. Throughout most of his episcopate Damasus was opposed by Ursinus, the minority

---

[54] Socrates, *Hist. eccl.* 5. 20. On the fate of Eunomius and his followers during Theodosius' reign see Vaggione, *Eunomius*, ch. 8.

candidate. While he became increasingly unpopular with Valentinian, the emperor Gratian encouraged him and gave the Roman see increasing judicial powers over the western Church. From his election Damasus was resolutely pro-Nicene, kept up relations with Athanasius (and his successor Peter), and wrote on more than one occasion to Basil of Caesarea. As we saw in the last chapter, however, Damasus' relations with Basil were hampered by his strong support for Paulinus in Antioch (see above) and suspicion of Basil's own theology, but his letters offer some important summary statements of his Trinitarian theology. His *ep.* 2 which survives in fragmentary form, and *ep.* 4 (also known as the *Tome of Damasus*), which stems from a Roman council of 377 or 378, are the most important. Damasus' theology follows Tertullian in its terminology, but has a pro-Nicene clarity in expressing the unity of the divine being and action. Damasus was not a particularly original theologian, but he shows how western pro-Nicene theologians could rely on their own traditional figures, such as Tertullian and Novatian, but under influence from eastern theology via such figures as Hilary and Eusebius of Vercelli.[55]

Ambrose of Milan was a provincial governor and an unbaptized catechumen when he was chosen as successor to the Homoian bishop of Milan Auxentius in 374.[56] The circumstances of his election are somewhat murky: the prefect Petronius Probus had probably been responsible for his appointment as governor and seems to have done much to secure his election as bishop. Probus seems to have done so in the hope of dislodging Homoian power in Milan: Ambrose's predecessor, Auxentius, had resisted all pro-Nicene attempts to remove him since 355 and had managed retain the support of Valentinian. Valentinian eventually agreed to Ambrose's appointment, but for the first few years of his episcopate, Ambrose seems to have tried to promote himself as a non-partisan figure and he took little action against Homoians. Towards the end of 375 Valentinian died in Illyricum after a choking fit brought on by rage at an embassy from the Quadi. Valentinian's 16-year-old son Gratian had already been appointed as another Augustus eight years before to ensure the succession. Unfortunately, the troops who had seen Valentinian die were many miles from Gratian in Trier and in order to prevent ambitious generals taking their chance Valentinian's 4-year-old son Valentinian II was also proclaimed Augustus, an action that would lead to much confusion.

---

[55] Damasus, *Ep.* 4 is considered briefly in Ch. 11.
[56] Here see Williams, *Ambrose*, chs. 4 ff.; Neil McLynn, *Ambrose of Milan: Church and Court in a Christian Capital* (Berkeley: University of California Press, 1984); Christoph Markschies, *Ambrosius von Mailand und die Trinitätstheologie* (Tübingen: J. C. B. Mohr, 1995).

By 378 there was considerable pressure on Ambrose from Homoians in Milan, aided by an influx of refugees from Illyricum following the battle of Adrianople and the Gothic incursions. In this fiercer polemical climate Ambrose was forced to defend himself and wrote a two-volume *On the Faith* at the request of Gratian. In this text Ambrose insists above all on the one divine power evident in Father and Son. He offers no technical vocabulary to distinguish Father and Son, betraying not so much a modalist reading of the relationship as a rather clumsy portrayal.[57] Ambrose does not seem to have tried to counter the specific theology of his Homoian opponents, relying instead on the tactic of condemning Arius in general terms. However, within two or three years Ambrose had written three more books to add to his *De fide* and a work *On the Spirit*. This new activity seems to have been prompted in part by attacks on his first two books by Homoians and by requests from Gratian for further elaboration.[58] The last three books show a much more detailed engagement with Homoian theology, while the *On the Holy Spirit* is deeply indebted to the work of Didymus the Blind, to Basil's *On the Holy Spirit*, and possibly to Athanasius' *Letters to Serapion*. Ambrose devotes a great deal of space in these books to refuting Homoian exegesis, arguing both that Father and Son share the same works and hence the same nature and power, and that the incarnate Son's human activity does not reveal him to lack the fullness of divinity.

We find an excellent example of the first theme in book 4:

> (5. 63) If then the Son can, by virtue of a common hidden power of the same nature which he has with the Father, both see and act in an invisible manner ... what remains for us but to believe that the Son, by reason of indivisible unity of power, does nothing, save what he has seen the Father doing (6. 69) ... and it is impossible that the work of the Son should not be in agreement with the Father's will, when what the Son works, the Father works also, and what the Father works, the Son works also ... For the Father appointed naught save by the exercise of his Power and Wisdom, for as much as he made all things wisely, as it is written, 'in wisdom you have made them all', and likewise God the Word made naught without the Father's participation. ... (71–2) [commenting on Jesus' thanking of the Father at John 11: 40 for 'hearing' him following the raising of Lazarus] It is for our sakes, therefore, that he renders thanks, lest we should suppose the Father and the Son are the same person, when we hear of one and the same work being wrought by the Father and the Son.

This passage focuses on Homoian exegesis of texts (such as John 5: 19) that appear to indicate Father and Son undertaking different

---

[57] Ambrose, *De fide* 1. 2.   [58] Williams, *Ambrose*, 148 ff.

tasks and hence being of unequal power and nature. Note that in this passage Ambrose uses two different arguments based on notions of power. In the first case, he insists that the Son possesses the one power which stems from the common divine nature.[59] This is clear above in sections 63 and 71–2. In the second case, Ambrose argues that Father and Son are one because the Father works always through the Son who is the Power of God (section 69). In this combination of arguments we see once again how fully pro-Nicene theologies were able to incorporate earlier arguments. Ambrose's most basic picture of the divine nature is of a unitary nature exhibiting a unitary power, but within this picture he can incorporate earlier arguments that present the Son as the Father's power and therefore as eternally present with the Father. We can glimpse how strong a unity Ambrose sees following from the unity of power in the last section of the passage quoted above: Jesus offers thanks to the Father in order that we do not suppose—and the implication is that naturally we should—the Father and Son to be one person because of their common power![60]

Ambrose offers some accounts of the distinction between unity of nature and distinction of persons that are typically pro-Nicene:

The substance of the Trinity is, so to say, a common essence in that which is distinct, an incomprehensible, ineffable substance (*est quaedam indistincta distinctae incomprehensibilis et inenarrabilis substantia trinitatis*). We hold the distinction, not the confusion of Father, Son and Holy Spirit; a distinction without separation, a distinction without plurality . . . We know the fact of distinction, we know nothing of the hidden mysteries, we pry not into the causes, but guard the mysterious signs (*sacramenta*) vouchsafed unto us.[61]

While Ambrose seems to draw extensively on Hilary's earlier pro-Nicene writing, he also exemplifies a pro-Nicene Latin theology influenced by later generations of Greek theology—and one more fully pro-Nicene. Unlike Hilary, Ambrose does not use the traditional Latin idea of the Son's unique generation as a fundamental point of departure for explaining the relationship between Father

---

[59] Cf. *De fide*, 4. 3. 35: 'No separation, then, is to be made of the Word from God the Father, no separation in power, no separation in wisdom, by reason of the unity of the divine substance . . . Nor again is the power of the one increased by the power of the other, for there are not two powers, but one power; nor does Godhead take on Godhead, for there are not two Godheads, but one Godhead (*nec enim virtus virtute angetur, quia non duae virtutes, sed una virtus, nec divinitatis divinitatem accipit, quia non duae divinitates, sed una divinitas*). We, contrariwise, shall be one in Christ through power received and dwelling in us.'

[60] Both are also interestingly incorporated in *De fide* 4. 8. 88: 'For the Son is always with the Father, and in the Father—with the Father through the distinction without division of the eternal Trinity (*per distinctionem indissociabilem trinitas aeternae*), in the Father through the unity of the divine nature (*per divinae unitatem naturae*).'

[61] *De fide* 4. 8. 91.

and Son. One might say that whereas Hilary saw the Son's *nativitas* as the central mystery, Ambrose sees the common operation of the three who are one in the divine substance as the central mystery.[62] In these later books of the *De fide* Ambrose uses the pairing *persona* and *natura* a number of times,[63] but his terminology remains flexible: for the individual persons he also uses *substantia, proprietas,* and occasionally *nomen,* seeming to avoid *persona*.

Ambrose also now offers a sophisticated account of the Son's eternal generation, insisting on its unique and incomprehensible nature. One of the most extended accounts occurs at *De fide* 4. 9, answering the standard anti-Nicene question 'Did the Father beget willingly or unwillingly?'

> (103) But in the eternal generation there is no foregoing condition, neither of will nor of unwillingness ... for to beget depends not upon possibility as determined by will, but rather appears to stand in a certain right and property of the hidden being of the Father (*sed in iure quodam et proprietate paterni*). For just as the Father is not God because he wills to be so, or is compelled to be so, but is above these conditions ... even so, the putting forth of his generative power is neither of will nor of necessity ... [108 offers an argument based on the intrinsic existence of light and radiance] (115) [with ref. to Isa. 53: 8] I read about the distinguishing characteristic of the divine generation, not its nature (*proprietatem legi divinae generationis non qualitatem*).[64]

Ambrose also argues in the same section of text that if we thought of the Father as having lacked the presence of the Son at some stage then we would be saying that there was 'a time when God lacked the fullness of divine perfection'.[65] Ambrose is here able to express the idea of the divine perfection consisting in the generation of Son with a clarity that may well stem from his knowledge of Greek theology.

In 381 Ambrose completed his series of Trinitarian works for Gratian by composing his *On the Spirit*. Ambrose draws much here from Didymus and Basil, a borrowing that Jerome was later to cast as plagiarism and which prompted Jerome to translate Didymus' own treatise into Latin to show up the crime. Whether or not Ambrose hoped to hide his sources, the work was probably written in haste ready for Gratian's visit to Milan at Easter 381. Despite his borrowings the treatise has little that will surprise the reader of even the early books of the *De fide*. Ambrose bases his argument on

---

[62] And this theme is central from the beginning of the *De fide*, e.g. 1. 3. 23–5.
[63] e.g. *De fide* 3. 15, 5. 3.
[64] *De fide* 4. 8. 104–16. At *De fide* 1. 2. 16 Ambrose even uses generation as a way of distinguishing Father and Son in a manner that looks very much like Hilary: '... not that the Father is one person with the Son; between Father and Son is the plain distinction that comes of generation'.
[65] *De fide* 4. 9. 111.

common operations: the Spirit's activities are also those attributed to Father and Son and, just as Father and Son share one nature, so must Father, Son, and Spirit. Where the Spirit alone is spoken of as acting we know that all are present just as when any divine person is described as acting alone. Ambrose offers an account of the Spirit as the gift that enables our sanctification, but does so by emphasizing that the Spirit is the source and principle of goodness in the same way as Father and Son are.[66] As such the Spirit's grace is the same as the Father's: the Spirit is poured forth from the mouth of God without any division or loss occurring in the Godhead with which the Spirit is one.[67] As with other pro-Nicene writers Ambrose's pneumatology applies arguments to the Spirit developed in polemic over the Son. The result of so doing is to offer an account of Christian existence as directly shaped and inspired by the triune presence. Indeed, Ambrose's discussion of the Spirit as God's presence and as the love of God poured into our hearts (Rom. 5: 5) may have been one of the inspirations for Augustine's own later theology of the Spirit. Like other fourth-century pro-Nicenes, Ambrose has little to say about the place of the Spirit in the Godhead in distinction from the Son: we should note the particularly clear argument at *De fide* 2. 76 that it is because of the unity of nature that Scripture speaks of both Father and Son sending the Spirit. Ambrose adds that because of the same unity we should even speak of the Spirit sending the Son.

Ambrose the ecclesiastical politician was probably more influential on the Church in the 370s and 380s than Ambrose the theologian. Although the young emperor initially followed the policies of toleration pursued by his father Valentinian, he fell increasingly under the sway of Ambrose. Influenced also by Theodosius' policies in the east, he began to pursue a much more directly pro-Nicene line. The high point of this new policy was the small council held at Aquileia (just inland from the northern coast of the Adriatic) in 381. Gratian appears initially to have envisaged a fairly large council, probably to encourage a wide-scale pro-Nicene settlement. But at the beginning of 381 he seems to have been persuaded by Ambrose to restrict the number of those present, including a restriction on the numbers of known Homoians invited. This may have occurred because of Gratian's own embarrassment at being pre-empted by Theodosius' actions in calling a council to Constantinople: Ambrose provided a way to save face when invitations to eastern bishops would have been ignored.[68] Thus when the council met in September only around 25 bishops were present, mostly from northern

---

[66] *Spir.* 1. 69.   [67] *Spir.* 1. 97.   [68] Such is the argument of McLynn, *Ambrose*, 124 ff.

Italy. To their surprise the two main Homoian prelates present, Palladius of Ratiaria and Secundianus of Singidunum, found themselves on trial. Under Ambrose's management they were duly condemned and deposed, the council asking Gratian to assist in removing them from their sees. We are extremely fortunate in possessing not only a terse set of acts from the council, but also an account from the Homoian side, which gives us a clear picture of how Ambrose and his associates engineered the condemnation of these prominent Homoians.[69]

The council appears to have been well informed about the recent meeting in Constantinople. While modern students of the period have tended to see similar doctrinal purpose behind the two meetings, the bishops at Aquileia were unhappy with many of Constantinople's decisions. While the formulae of faith that council produced may have been acceptable, its accompanying ecclesio-political choices were not. A letter survives among Ambrose's corpus from 'Ambrose and the other bishops of Italy', that seems to have been issued by the council. The letter protests against the election of Paulinus to Antioch, against both Gregory and Nectarius to Constantinople, and against the failure of the bishops in Constantinople to consult with Rome. In the following year a small council met in Rome that again recognized Paulinus, declared the two bishops who had elected Nectarius to be deposed, and made considerable claims for the see of Rome. At this meeting were present three envoys sent west from the council that had met earlier in 382 in Constantinople, largely to respond to Aquileia (and whose statement of faith we considered earlier in the chapter). Although we are coming to the end of the narrative section of this book, we end not with mutual agreement, but with a combination of gradual doctrinal convergence amid continuing ecclesiastical rancour.[70]

The Council of Aquileia does not mark the end of Homoians in the west, but it is an important juncture. After 381 Homoians do not seem to have held any of the major sees in the west and they seem to have begun the process of becoming a clearly distinct group. Their theology continued to develop, however, and Latin Homoians produced a great deal of written material over the following decades. Ambrose himself was to face a serious conflict in 385–6 when, after Gratian's death, Valentinian II proclaimed freedom of worship for those who held to the Council of Ariminum, and tried to get control

---

[69] Edited and translated by Roger Gryson, *Scolies Ariennes sur le concile d'Aquilée*, SC 267 (Paris: Cerf, 1980).

[70] The letter from Aquileia is to be found at CSEL 82/3 (1982), 201–4. For the Roman council of 382 see Sozomen, *Hist. eccl.* 7. 11. On these events in general see Simonetti, *La Crisi*, 548–52; Hanson, *The Search*, 820–3.

of a major church in Milan for their worship. Ambrose won this battle, in part because the Milanese court felt the threat of another claimant to the throne who was a strong Nicene, but the incident shows Homoian Christians continued to be an important presence in some areas of the west. In fact, non-Nicene Christianity in the west grew in importance through the fifth century with the breakdown of centralized Roman order. Many of the Germanic peoples who came to control the territory of the Roman west were Homoian in theology.[71]

The last event in the west that I want to mention here is the anti-Homoian activity of Augustine of Hippo, who had been in Milan during the tense time of 385–6. Augustine's Trinitarian theology was formed in this anti-Homoian milieu, as his early texts demonstrate. In the early 400s his *On the Trinity* engages in some detail with patterns of Homoian exegesis, although we do not know if this was for him a primarily literary engagement or whether he was actually meeting resistance from Homoian communities. In 418 we know that Augustine engaged in a fierce polemical battle with one Maximinus, and the anti-Homoian texts which date from this period show a continuing engagement with the Latin anti-Homoian tradition. Augustine may thus be read as one of the greatest Latin pro-Nicenes of these years. I offer a reading of his theology from this perspective in Chapter 15.

ON NOT ENDING THE STORY

My narrative in the first nine chapters of this book intentionally does not begin or end at clear points. The more one realizes that these controversies arose out of tensions among existing theological trajectories, the more it becomes a mistake to identify one temporal point of departure. Similarly, older narratives in which a clear end is identified fly in the face of evidence that controversy continued into the fifth century. I want to end this chapter, and the narrative section of the book, by indicating three more contexts in which pro-Nicene theologies continued to develop. Pointing to these three contexts will also involve indicating one or two figures whose careers fit within the period that I have covered, but who did not receive any, or any extensive, discussion. This last section thus serves to highlight some of the ragged edges of my canvas as a whole.

When we think about Antioch and the decades after 381 it is the Christological controversies that come most immediately to mind.

---

[71] On the later development of the Homoian community see Maurice Wiles, *Archetypal Heresy: Arianism through the Centuries* (Oxford: Clarendon Press, 1996), ch. 2.

Nevertheless, that should not lead us to forget that in the 370–400 period a number of the very figures central to the early stages of those controversies began their theological careers fighting non-Nicene theology. Diodore of Tarsus (d. *c*.390) we have already encountered as a supporter of Meletius and as a leading figure at Constantinople. Unfortunately, because of his later condemnation in connection with the Christological controversies, only fragments of his work on the Trinity and on the Spirit survive. Diodore was the teacher of two other figures associated with Antioch, John Chrysostom (*c*.347–407) and Theodore of Mopsuestia (*c*.350–428), and from these more extensive contributions to pro-Nicene literature survive. From Chrysostom, who eventually became the bishop of Constantinople, we possess series of homilies on John and on 1 Corinthians, both of which focus much attention on anti-Heterousian argument, and both of which were written around 390. We also possess a striking series of homilies *On the Incomprehensibility of God* directed against Heterousians. The series consists of two sets, the first delivered in Antioch in 386–7, the second ten years later in Constantinople.[72] Baptismal lectures discovered in the 1950s also add to our knowledge of Chrysostom's pro-Nicene teaching on the Trinity.

Although much of Theodore's corpus is also lost because of later condemnation, we do possess a set of catechetical lectures that survive only in Syriac, the first half of which takes the form of a commentary on a creed close to that of Nicaea. We are not certain of the date of their delivery, some scholars have argued for 388–92, when Theodore was a priest in Antioch, others for the time of his episcopate in Mopsuestia (392–428). These texts from John and Theodore not only provide evidence for the continuing importance of anti-Heterousian polemic, but also evidence for the complex development of pro-Nicene theology after 381. Chrysostom's homilies, for example, demonstrate a close engagement with some themes from 'Cappadocian' theology, raising questions about how Trinitarian theology in Antioch developed after Meletius' death. The narrative of such development and cross-fertilization lies outside the scope of this book: indeed, it is a task that has not yet been undertaken in any depth.

When we turn south to Alexandria we see most immediately two authors who are not discussed in any detail in this book, Didymus the Blind (310/13–398) and Cyril of Alexandria (d. *c*.444). The anti-'Arian' writings of these two theologians raise for us the question of how Athanasius' theology and legacy was preserved and or altered in

---

[72] Some themes from this series of homilies are discussed in Ch. 12.

Alexandria. Didymus' *On The Holy Spirit* was used by Ambrose in his own work of that name and after translation by Jerome *c*.385–90 it influenced other Latin theologians. Cyril of Alexandria's anti-'Arian' works and his commentary on John written in the first decades of the fifth century demand mention here because, while Cyril continues to draw on Athanasius' work, he also accepted some standard features and terminologies of pro-Nicene theology not found in his illustrious predecessor. Noting the continuing development of pro-Nicene theology in Alexandria opens up the question of how that development involved interchange between distinct pro-Nicene traditions and how certain terminologies gradually came to be increasingly widespread.

I have already indicated the continuity of the development of pro-Nicene theology in Latin-speaking authors. When we consider the work of figures such as Ambrose and Augustine we not only see the continuing development of pro-Nicene thought after 381. We also begin to see how the interaction between Nicene and non-Nicene Christianities entered a new phase in the west with the gradual falling apart of Roman rule over the western half of the empire. Augustine's encounters with actual Homoians during the latter half of his career were encounters with Homoians moving south from Italy in the wake of instability there and with Homoians who had connections outside the empire, in the Gothic federations that would soon play a central role in the life of western Christianity. In the west the beginning of the fifth century does not mark the end of the Trinitarian controversies as much as the beginning of a new phase. In this new phase pro-Nicene and Homoian communities were more clearly delineated as distinct, but the polemic between them continued.

III
Understanding Pro-Nicene Theology

11
On the Contours of Mystery

Chapters 11–13 identify three theological strategies shared by pro-Nicene theologians. By a theological strategy I mean a pattern of argumentation, a way of relating together particular themes, and a tendency to highlight particular themes or topics for discussion: a strategy is thus a matter of both form and content. These three strategies lie at the heart of what I term the pro-Nicene 'life of the mind'. My exploration of these three strategies is not intended as a summary of all that pro-Nicenes say or share, nor is it the only way one might proceed to explore the character of pro-Nicene theologies. My argument, however, is that these three strategies are the shared core of pro-Nicene Trinitarianism, and pro-Nicenes gradually come to view the whole of the Christian theological matrix through the lens they offer. It needs also to be borne in mind that there is no 'final' stage in which we can view a 'complete' pro-Nicene theology: pro-Nicene theology continued to develop. Pro-Nicene theologians also continued to grow in their abilities to see the consequences of core pro-Nicene themes, during this period we see a number of disputes that demonstrate the still-evolving nature of pro-Nicene theology.[1]

Many of the themes I explore in these chapters have already been discussed in connection with Basil's mature work in Chapter 8, and in discussion of other figures in Chapters 7, 9, and 10. The juxtaposition of 'eastern' and 'western' figures throughout this part of the book also intentionally pushes further arguments already made to the effect that 'east' and 'west' cannot serve as fundamental categories of division for pro-Nicene Trinitarian theologies. There are indeed a number of divisions between Greek and Latin theologies (although different differences will be between different sets of Greeks and Latins), but we can better explore these differences by re-learning the fundamental shared core of

---

[1] For instance one might cite the persistence in some pro-Nicene contexts of conceptions of the divine glory as a bodily form. See Alexander Golitzin, ' "The Demons suggest an illusion of God's glory in a form": Controversy over the Divine Body and Vision of Glory in some Late Fourth, Early Fifth Century Monastic Literature', *Studia Monastica*, 44 (2002), 13–43 and my own 'Shine Jesus Shine: On Relocating Apollinarianism', *SP*, forthcoming. One could also cite the letter from Consentius to Augustine (preserved as *ep.* 119 in Augustine's corpus) in which Consentius can summarize many pro-Nicene principles clearly, but confesses he is unable to understand the divine simplicity and immateriality.

pro-Nicene Trinitarian beliefs. These three chapters seek to establish a basic framework for considering those differences and similarities in more detail. Chapters 14 and 15 then consider the Trinitarian theologies of Augustine and Gregory of Nyssa against this background, further reinforcing the shared heritage of pro-Nicene thought.

CULTURE, *HABITUS*, AND THE LIFE OF THE MIND

Before proceeding further it may be helpful to offer a discussion of the theoretical basis for my use of the phrase 'the life of the mind', in relation to the terms culture and *habitus*. Such a discussion will make clearer the intended scope and intended limits of the next three chapters. My use of the term 'culture' stems from discussions in cultural anthropology, and a summary definition might be: a system of learned patterns of behaviour (including thought, speech, and human action), ideas, and products that together shape conceptions of the order of existence and interactions with other cultures.[2] 'Cultures' do not necessarily have clearly defined boundaries and we participate in more than one.[3] A culture may be appropriated by people in a variety of circumstances and social locations:[4] such appropriation will involve ongoing acts of interpretation and decisions about priority to fit a new culture alongside the other cultures in which a person participates.

To identify a culture here may be to speak of a particular collection or *bricolage* of practices and ideas that may themselves be found in other cultures, and to identify a style of interaction with other cultures. In a recent study Kathryn Tanner attempts to describe Christian 'culture' as a relational cultural activity, not defining itself solely by possessing particular cultural materials or rituals not shared with other cultures, but by particular modes of using borrowed materials and interacting with material in other cultures. Christian identity is thus formed 'not so much by a boundary as at

---

[2] For a good discussion of parallel terminology see Kathryn Tanner, *Theories of Culture: A New Agenda for Theology* (Philadelphia: Fortress Press, 1997), chs. 2 and 3.

[3] Sometimes the notion of a culture in older anthropological theory implies a closed system, often allied with a geographical or racial unity. My own use draws on the way more recent theorists have emphasized the difficulty of identifying a culture with a specific group or social location. See the discussion of this problem and the further literature cited at Tanner, *Theories*, 53 ff.

[4] I have used the language of 'appropriation' here, but one could present essentially the same argument with different nuances via the use of Homi Bhaba's language of mimicry. Such a usage might serve as an excellent tool for examining the gradual spread of certain formulae and terminologies between and within pro-Nicene theological traditions. Similarly discussion of 'hybridity' in the development of cultures might also serve as an excellent tool for exploring other dimensions of the emergence of a pluralistic pro-Nicene culture.

one'; it is formed by the distinctive cultural processes of adaptation and modification that constitute Christian activity.[5] One might point also to Michel de Certeau's hints at an understanding of Christian tradition as being defined not so much by reference to a particular content, but by equal reference to a mode or a particular practice of handing on.[6] In both cases these practices of adaptation and of 'handing on' are themselves motivated by particular patterns of attention and thought, particular combinations of ideas and narratives intrinsic to a culture, by what Pierre Bourdieu terms a *habitus*. Thus any simple distinction between cultural materials and modes of cultural activity is heuristically useful but ultimately problematic. Styles of cultural activity are themselves shaped by cultural materials: *habitus* provides us with a lens for looking beyond any simple dualism here.

In his sociological/anthropological theory Bourdieu defines a *habitus* as 'a system of durable, transposable dispositions, structured structures predisposed to function as structuring structures, that is, as principles which generate and organize practices and representations'. Earlier in his career Bourdieu was also willing to define *habitus* as 'a matrix of perceptions, appreciations, and actions'.[7] In evolving the concept of *habitus* Bourdieu's concern was to remain sensitive to the complexities of describing action and choice without imposing the theoretical assumption either that action is merely the determined outcome of societally imposed norms or that it is the result of unconscious innate characteristics. Against these Bourdieu has tried to evolve a way of speaking about a structure of perceptions and dispositions that are learned and which then come to function as the roots of practice. The dispositions and inclinations of a *habitus* provoke adaptation to new situations in specific ways, particular judgements of taste and styles of cultural practice. In investigating pro-Nicene theology we are watching literate Christians articulate the ideas and practices that they think together shape and constitute an appropriate Christian *habitus*. Considering pro-Nicene theology from this perspective helps us to see how its evolution involved not simply the evolution of disconnected ideas, but the development of interrelated conceptions of the Christian *habitus*—of the Christian imaginative universe—and of a collection of intellectual practices seen as consonant with that *habitus*. A number of critics, notably Michel de Certeau, have correctly seen Bourdieu's

---

[5] Tanner, *Theories*, 110–19. Here I paraphrase Tanner.
[6] Michel de Certeau, *Faiblesse de Croire* (Paris: Éditions du Seuil, 1987), 112.
[7] Pierre Bourdieu, *Outline of a Theory of Practice*, tr. R. Nice (Cambridge: Cambridge University Press, 1977), 72.

habitus as still too static a conception.[8] For these critics, despite Bourdieu's intentions, his notion of *habitus* assumes the inability of people to resist the determination of force of a cultural system. Certeau identifies a complementary notion of 'tactical' behaviour by which members of a seemingly monolithic culture subvert and adapt aspects of a whole that they can never grasp as a totality. Certeau's work gives a somewhat more complex texture to investigations of the effect of culture and unity and plurality within a cultural group.[9] Thus, in order to emphasize that I understand a *habitus* as something that both evolves and that takes similar but subtly different forms in different contexts, I will speak less technically of the pro-Nicene life of the mind.

My focus on *intellectual* habits here should not be taken as antipathy towards examinations of the structure of pro-Nicene orthodoxy that focus on the evolution of particular material social practices, or as antipathy towards most versions of the principle that dispositions and habits are formed and exist within the context of actual performance. There are indeed very specific social material practices linked with pro-Nicene episcopal and well-educated lay Christians, particular styles of rhetorical display and argumentation, and particular material structures, such as processes of book production, styles of epistolary interchange, and practices of communal ritual exchange. It is also clearly the case that studying the structure of the social practices that shaped pro-Nicene writers and the communities of Christians with which they interacted adds much to our understanding of what it was to be counted orthodox in this context. Nevertheless, that late fourth-century Christian writers inhabited a context marked by these material practices does not forbid an investigation which focuses on that aspect of their imaginative world concerned with fundamental doctrines and intellectual practices. Indeed, there are also some good reasons for asserting that developments in ideas were at the core of the evolution of pro-Nicene theologies. Unless one wishes to take an exclusively materialist view of intellectual history, it was the slow coming together and internal evolution of theological ideas and strategies of thought that enabled the mutual recognition that gave rise to pro-Nicene theology or theologies. My intention, however, is that such a statement should be read as entirely consonant with insisting that particular

[8] That we are studying an *emergent habitus*—and that the emergence and maintenance of a *habitus* involves a constant negotiation over time—points to the place at which Certeau's critique of Bourdieu is most important.

[9] See Michel de Certeau, *The Practice of Everyday Life*, tr. S. Rendall (Berkeley: University of California Press, 1984), 29–60. De Certeau's work here may be usefully paralleled with Roland Barthes's early accounts of the formation of 'myths' and the complexities of appropriation, see his *Mythologies*, tr. A. Lavers (New York: Hill & Wang, 1972).

personal and social networks were the context through which this collection of themes developed.[10] In other words, while my focus in this book does, of course, reveal certain theoretical assumptions about the nature of intellectual development, it is intended to be easily supplemented and enhanced by other modes of studying pro-Nicene culture.

At this point someone might well ask why I have not spent time trying to draw out the links between the life of the mind and the culture of my pro-Nicene elite theologians and that of the mass of less well educated Christians. I have no objection to attempts to widen my suggestion that we need to consider pro-Nicene theology as a 'culture', but there are two key theoretical issues which considerably complicate such a project. On the one hand, the sheer lack of pertinent literary remains renders such a project complex.[11] Although one may gain some perspectives from archaeological evidence of cultic practice and artistic style, attempting a reconstruction of the *habitus* formed by Christian belief in non-literate Christians will always remain a matter for conjecture. On the other hand, however, I suggest that we need to be particularly careful about how we impose on the late fourth century modern distinctions between elite and non-elite Christians or between 'theologians' and 'ordinary' Christians. Such a theoretical division can only be deployed once the character of the division in a particular social setting has been discussed. The character of late fourth-century theology seems to provide evidence of a different and much denser set of connections between literate and non-literate Christians than can be observed in modern Christianity. For examples, we can note two features that link those involved in the production of theological texts in the late fourth century and other contemporary Christians:

1. The language of Scripture is taken as the primary and most trustworthy language for Christians developing their account of the world and the importation of philosophical themes and technical language is conceived not as a necessary *transposition* of ideas, but as an *elucidation* of the text of Scripture. Thus, it seems fair to suppose a fairly close connection between the narrative and symbolic

---

[10] I think of approaches typified by the work of Elizabeth Clark on Origenism. See especially her programmatic essay, 'Elite Networks and Heresy Accusations: Towards a Social Description of the Origenist Controversy', *Semeia*, 56 (1992), 79–117. To give an idea of the range of approaches to which I point here I would argue that, in a less theoretically focused manner, some of John Matthews's implicit method has a number of areas of overlap with Clark's work. See esp. his *Western Aristocracies*.

[11] I am indebted to Elizabeth Clark for sharing with me the manuscript of her forthcoming *History-Theory-Text* (Cambridge, Mass.: Harvard University Press, 2004). The book is particularly important for examining ways in which the field of early Christian studies is necessarily skewed towards intellectual history by the very nature of the available sources.

languages of Christians with very different levels of education. Even where we frequently see preachers arguing that their congregations understand terms too literally and do not understand how the text speaks in human terms of an immaterial God, it is still clear that preacher and audience are linked by shared commitments to the significance of the plain sense of Scripture.[12] Thus the exegetical arguments that are so central to fourth-century controversy are based on assumptions about the nature of the scriptural text that seem to link preacher and audience.

2. Late fourth-century theologians frequently write—especially in homiletic contexts—with the express goal of linking their own modes of reflection and imagination to those of non-literate and non-elite Christians by invoking a common spiritual progress as the setting for all Christian social practice. Although one should never assume that such an invocation matches or creates a social reality, it is probably fair to assume (in conjunction with my other suggestions concerning the scriptural nature of fourth-century theology) that this concern reveals a dense web of interconnection between the imaginary habits of different types of Christians even while differences were certainly present (and probably differences over the immateriality or materiality of spiritual realities were stark).

This, I hope, gives a sufficient account of the theoretical context within which I deploy some key terms. I do not think that the following chapters describe 'Christian culture', or even the 'culture' of late fourth-century orthodoxy in all its senses. I do think I have described the central imaginative, doctrinal matrix of pro-Nicene theologies as that which was intentionally aimed at shaping the Christian *habitus*.

STRATEGY I: SPEAKING OF UNITY AND DIVERSITY IN THE TRINITY

Towards simplicity

The first and the most fundamental shared strategy is a style of reflecting on the paradox of the irreducible unity of the three irreducible divine persons. Pro-Nicenes reflect on this mystery, I shall argue, always bearing in mind the absolute distinction between God as the only truly simple reality and creation. Bearing this principle in mind pro-Nicene discussion of the divine persons remains highly austere, and discussion of the individual persons is strongly shaped by the consequences of the divine distinction and simplicity. Thus

---

[12] For 'plain sense' see Ch. 1.

this strategy concerns the basic contours of pro-Nicene understandings of appropriate patterns of speech about the triune God. The strategies sketched in the following two chapters reveal, on the one hand, how the evolution of this first strategy affected pro-Nicene theologies of salvation, anthropologies, and epistemologies and, on the other hand, ways in which those wider developments in turn nurtured the practice considered as my first strategy. Those developments nurtured this first strategy by shaping a complex imagination of what it meant to be created, Christian, en-souled, and seeking purification. It was this complex imagination—a set of images, intellectual strategies, habits of thought—that formed the context for the practice of speaking directly of the Triune God. Thus, it is important to note that my trajectory through these three chapters is not one of isolating all that pro-Nicenes share in their accounts of the Trinity but, first, their fundamental shared principles, and then, second, the imaginary complex that was understood to be the context for all articulation of those principles. My argument in this chapter has two steps: first I identify some of the basic principles of pro-Nicene discussion of divine unity, leading to the use made of divine simplicity; second, I show how pro-Nicenes mine a variety of 'analogical sites' in their accounts of the Trinity, but always bear in mind God's transcendence of our categories of division. The doctrines of appropriation and inseparable operation lie at the heart of the enterprise.

The unity of God

It is fundamental to all pro-Nicene theologies that God is one power, glory, majesty, rule, Godhead essence, and nature. In summaries of pro-Nicene Trinitarian theology found across the Mediterranean, and in countless asides in the course of exposition and polemical argument, the assertion that God is a unity in these respects is universal.[13] Summary accounts of pro-Nicene theology tend to focus on identifiably philosophical terms such as *ousia*, φύσις, natura, and *essentia*. It is, however, important to note that pro-Nicenes use many other terms for the divine unity, drawn from a variety of (often scriptural) sources, whose metaphysical senses modern readers tend to miss. Thus, for example, terms such as 'light', 'power', and 'glory' should not be read as 'merely metaphorical' simply because modern thought does not accord them any dense or technical description. Each one of these terms has its own history, and each deserves its own scholarly treatment—although in many cases that treatment

---

[13] e.g. Damasus, *Ep.* 2 (*Ea gratia*: PL 13. 350–1); Gregory of Nyssa, *Ablab.* GNO 3/1. 44, 50; Augustine, *Doc.* 1. 5. 6; Epiphanius, *Panarion* 76. 45; Ambrose, *De fide* 1. 1. 9; 1. 2. 16; 4. 3. 36; Gregory Nazianzen, *Arc.* 3. 40–82; Basil, *Spir.* 18. 44; Didymus, *Spir.* 76, 81.

remains to be delivered. To these terms we should also add the terms carrying both philosophical and legal histories of usage: Damasus of Rome and Gregory Nazianzen, for example, both use terminology expressing the one rule and authority in the Godhead.[14] On the one hand, we can read such language as related to philosophical language describing the one divine creative action and power (and perhaps parallel to Nyssa's insistence that *theotes* is named from the divine activity of beholding and supervising[15]). On the other hand, we should also see such language as related to a long semi-legal tradition discussing the nature of a ruler's authority.

Within this context pro-Nicenes make use of a wide variety of terminology for the persons: πρόσωπον, *hypostasis*, τρόπος ὑπάρξεως, *persona*, for example. I have also observed that for some theologians the use of standard generic terms for the persons is rare and might even be said to have been avoided: Athanasius and Didymus the Blind are excellent examples here. Pro-Nicenes were of course keen to give a coherent account of the terminology they deployed, particularly to show that the logic of differentiation implied in their divisions between essence and persons did not involve them in denying the unity of God. All pro-Nicenes show, however, remarkably little interest in developing a detailed account of what it means to be a divine *hypostasis* in any generic sense. To be a little more precise, one does not find in pro-Nicenes extended attempts to develop an ontology of divine personhood. (I return to this question later in the chapter.)[16]

Inseparable operation and simplicity

One of the most important principles shared by pro-Nicenes is that whenever one of the divine persons acts, all are present, acting inseparably. In Chapter 15 I provide summary statements of this doctrine from Hilary, Ambrose, and Augustine:[17] to them can be added this passage from Gregory of Nyssa:

If ... we understand that the operation of the Father, the Son, and the Holy Spirit is one, differing or varying in nothing, the oneness of their nature must needs be inferred from the identity of their operation. The Father, the Son, and the Holy Spirit alike give sanctification, and life, and light, and comfort, and all similar graces. And let no one attribute the power of sanctification in an especial sense to the Spirit, when he hears the saviour in the Gospel saying to the Father concerning his disciples, 'Father,

---

[14] *Tom. Dam.* (*Ep.* 4), 20; *Or.* 29. 2, 42.   [15] See below, p. 355.
[16] I return directly to this topic below, pp. 295–6. Discussions elsewhere in the book of Basil (pp. 198ff.), Gregory of Nyssa (pp. 357–9), Gregory Nazianzen (pp. 246–7), and Augustine (pp. 375ff.) provide a number of detailed examples to substantiate this point.
[17] Ch. 14, p. 369.

sanctify them in thy name.' . . . As we say that the operation of the Father, and of the Son, and the Holy Spirit is one, so we say that the Godhead is one . . .[18]

Understanding what is intended by this principle is, however, as complicated as understanding the consequences of any of the individual terminologies mentioned in the previous paragraph. Inseparable operation does not mean that the three persons are understood as merely co-operating in a given project. To begin to grasp the importance of the concept we need to turn to the doctrine of divine simplicity with which it is closely connected.

For pro-Nicenes God is non-composite: God has no parts, is incapable of division, and is not composed of a number of elements. In other words, God is simple. Most pro-Nicenes also add that God is infinite and is present everywhere, immediately and yet not as creatures are present to each other.[19] As Christopher Stead has shown, however, 'simplicity' in early Christian hands is a concept deployed rather loosely. By the late fourth century speaking of the divine nature as simple is usually taken also to include a number of non-necessary corollaries, in particular that as simple God must be unique and incomprehensible.[20] It will be important for the argument of this chapter, however, to show that although simplicity is not defined with great precision, it is used consistently. Earlier in the book I argued that during the fourth century the very 'grammar' of divinity was at issue. Within pro-Nicene theology we find a very clear if often implicit set of rules for such language. Pro-Nicenes assume the impossibility of there being degrees of divine existence, and they assume God to be the only truly simple reality. The generation of the Son and the breathing of the Spirit thus occur *within* the bounds of the divine simplicity. Because God is indivisible the persons cannot be understood to work as three divided human persons work. Linking divine simplicity and inseparability of operation draws us inexorably towards

---

[18] Gregory of Nyssa, *Trin.*; See also e.g. Ephrem, *HdF* 6. 5; Basil, *Spir.* 22. 53; Didymus, *Spir.* 105, 145.

[19] On the complexities of ascribing infinity to God in pro-Nicene thought see Leo Sweeney, 'Augustine and Gregory of Nyssa: Is the Triune God Infinite in Being?', in Joseph T. Lienhard *et al.* (eds.), *Augustine: Presbyter Factus Sum*, Collectanea Augustiniana 3 (New York: Peter Lang, 1993).

[20] Stead, *Philosophy in Christian Antiquity*, ch. 11. Discussions of this theme in Gregory of Nyssa still sometimes strongly differentiate Gregory's account of the divine infinity from Augustine's, on the basis that Nyssa defines infinity in temporal terms, Augustine in spatial. I am not convinced one can make much of this difference. In many places Nyssa does not treat temporal infinitude as the controlling theme of his conception: e.g. *Cant.* 5: 'The blessed eternal nature surpassing all understanding contains all things in itself and is limited by nothing. For no name or concept can impose limits to it: not time, place, colour, form, image, bulk, quantity, dimension, or anything else.'

the persistent pro-Nicene assertion that the nature of God is unknowable.

Knowing and not knowing

Pro-Nicenes universally assert that God's nature or essence is incomprehensible. Explanations as to why vary but are broadly compatible. We can summarize them as arguing that God's existence does not fit in the categories that characterize the created order. Alongside these statements of divine incomprehensibility, pro-Nicenes also speak of right and wrong belief about God and about growth in knowledge of God. How, then, do they understand the sort of knowledge that is possible, and how do they speak of ignorance and growth simultaneously? Pro-Nicenes in fact approach this problem via a number of strategies, one of the most common of which is to distinguish between different modes of knowing. We have already seen Basil distinguishing between essence, power, and energies, and between an incomprehensible nature and comprehensible ἰδιώματα.[21] I also made brief reference to his *Letter* 235 in which he distinguishes a variety of possible objects of knowledge:

a thing is knowable with respect to number, and size and power, and manner of subsistence, and time of generation ... Our position is that we confess that we know what is knowable about God, and yet to know anything ... that escapes our comprehension (κατάληψις) is impossible.

In Chapter 12 I show how Gregory of Nyssa continues and develops Basil's work through exploration of very similar philosophical dynamics. An insistence on the distinction between unknowable essence and knowable operations is also found in many Latin pro-Nicenes, even outside the anti-Heterousian polemical context that shaped the Cappadocian writers.[22] In both Basil and Gregory of Nyssa we find the argument that knowledge of the divine nature is impossible just as knowledge of *any* nature in itself is impossible.

Basil's use of the term κατάληψις in the quotation above brings us to another way in which pro-Nicenes speak of different modes of knowing: allusion to Stoic epistemological terminology.[23] The term κατάληψις was originally used by Zeno to describe the last of three stages in cognition. At this final stage true cognition is reached in an observer (or thinker) who not only perceives what is and assents to it, but does so with a clarity that prevents them from being persuaded that their perception is false. The term is not used with such precision by pro-Nicenes: they seem unaware of Zeno's insistence

---

[21] See pp. 195ff.   [22] For examples see Barnes, *Power of God*, 149–72.
[23] For an introduction to Stoic epistemology see Keimpe Algra *et al.* (eds.), *The Cambridge History of Hellenistic Philosophy* (Cambridge: Cambridge University Press, 1999), ch. 9.

on it being impossible to persuade one from a true cognition. Rather the term indicates only cognition that results from assent to clear and true perception of what something is. The term κατάληψις is frequently rendered into Latin as *comprehensio*, and Augustine's famous insistence that 'if you comprehend something, it is not God'[24] provides us with an example of a Latin author using the same Stoic terminology as Basil or Gregory of Nyssa.

But in Latin and Greek authors we should not assume that this Stoic terminology gives a precise account of what knowledge is and is not possible of God. In his *Letter* 235 Basil follows his seemingly precise account of the modes of possible knowledge with a much less precise account of the many dimensions of knowledge that are possible:

[knowledge of God] is the apprehension (σύνεσις) of him who has created us, and the understanding (κατανόησις) of his wonder, and the keeping (τήρησις) of his commandments and intimacy (οἰκείωσις) with him.

All that is here ruled out is θεωρία or contemplation of God's *ousia*. In parallel fashion Gregory of Nyssa's *Commentary on the Song of Songs* frequently links God's infinite nature and the possibility of infinite progress in knowledge:

the person looking at the divine, invisible beauty will always discover it anew since he will see it as something newer and more wondrous in comparison to what he has already comprehended. He continues to wonder at God's continuous revelation; he never exhausts his desire to see more because what he awaits is always more magnificent and more divine than anything he has seen.[25]

In these texts precise distinctions between knowledge of God's essence and knowledge of other aspects of God has given way to a more poetic statement focusing on the possibility of growth in insight. When he discusses knowledge of God—especially in Trinitarian contexts—Augustine also turns to more poetic languages of 'touching' and 'cleaving to' God even while he denies the possibility of achieving real understanding of God.[26]

The philosophical imprecision of these accounts appears to be of

---

[24] *Serm.* 117. [25] *Cant.* 11.

[26] Augustine is an interesting case. In some circumstances, especially anti-sceptic contexts, he insists strongly on the possibility of knowing that God exists and that God is truly Good. In *Ep.* 147 he has to admit, in the face of scriptural evidence, the possibility of human minds having a vision of God in this life. In Trinitarian discussions, however, Augustine insists much more strongly on the impossibility of sight of God or of understanding of the Trinity. On these questions see Roland Teske, 'St. Augustine and the Vision of God', in Frederick Van Fleteren *et al.* (eds.), *Augustine: Mystic and Mystagogue* (New York: Peter Lang, 1994), 287–308; Michel René Barnes, 'The Visible Christ and the Invisible Trinity: Mt. 5: 8 in Augustine's Trinitarian Theology of 400', *Modern Theology*, 19 (2003) 329–55.

little concern to most pro-Nicenes.[27] I suggest this is because, for deeply held *theological* reasons, pro-Nicenes consider it impossible to deliver precision about human growth towards God. Through these accounts, however, one common principle is clear. Pro-Nicenes argue that we can have no knowledge of God in which we can rest as if we finally understood: all knowledge of God is useful within what we might term an anagogic context. This stricture deeply conditions how pro-Nicenes understand the possibility of analogy in Trinitarian contexts.

The process of analogy

Pro-Nicenes assume that one can draw no analogies between God and creation that will either deliver knowledge of God's essence or that can involve us in grasping clearly where and why any analogy fails. That this is a virtually universal pro-Nicene position is in some ways easy to miss because of the variety of ways in which it is expressed: some pro-Nicenes argue against the applicability of strict analogy, others deploy the terminology of analogy while simultaneously insisting on its inadequacy. For example, Augustine directly denies the possibility of *analogia* in the technical sense of a proportion (*proportio*) between two things because no one can ever grasp the proportion between the analogates. As an alternative he then deploys a flexible vocabulary of terms broadly synonymous with *similitudo* (likeness) to indicate a form of general 'likeness'.[28]

We find a similar procedure in Gregory Nazianzen. At *Oration* 31. 10 Gregory offers an extended performance of appropriate use of analogy in theology.[29] Gregory first insists it is futile to search for analogies for the immutable in the changing world, but agrees to find a ὁμοίωσις ('likeness'). He then, against Pneumatomachians, uses Adam, Eve, and Seth to illustrate the possibility of two things coming from the same source without both being offspring. This ὁμοίωσις is taken to demonstrate only 'the possibility of our position'. At 31. 31 Gregory tells us he has long sought for some sort of εἰκών (image) to illustrate the relationships between the persons, but he has failed: 'if a faint resemblance comes my way, the more significant aspect escapes me ...'. In the next few paragraphs, right at the end of the *Theological Orations*, Gregory simply eschews the possi-

---

[27] Some pro-Nicenes offer sophisticated reflection on epistemology in general but turn to a less precise often poetic language when knowledge of God is discussed. This is, I suggest, no accident.

[28] See my ' "Remember that you are Catholic" (*serm.* 52, 2): Augustine on the Unity of the Triune God', *JECS*, 8 (2000), 39–82.

[29] Norris, *Faith Gives Fullness to Reasoning*, 194–6, offers a useful discussion of this passage, terming it a 'locus classicus' of both Gregory's Trinitarian theology and theological method.

bility of finding a satisfactory analogy for the Trinity and holds up the centrality of confessing the bare logic of union and distinction in worship.[30]

In his *Catechetical Oration* Gregory of Nyssa clearly insists that analogies can be drawn: but the language in which he describes the process is significant. We apply our own attributes to the 'transcendent nature' ἀναγωγικῶς. This does not serve to 'express the ineffable depth of the mystery in words' although it can 'according to an ineffable measure, give some sense (τινὰ κατανόησιν) of our teaching on the knowledge of God'.[31] Thus analogy enables our defence of pro-Nicene and scriptural principles but only as long as we understand that the knowledge we have gained functions within the anagogic process.[32] In *this* context we need to become skilled at understanding how appropriate analogical resources are ordained not simply to illustrate, but to inculcate constant attention to the ongoing task of progression towards the infinite mystery.[33] The same emphasis is seen ever more clearly in both the *Life of Moses* and the *Commentary on the Song of Songs*.[34] While we could extract distinct theories of analogical predication from all three of the theologians considered here, in the course of their texts such predication is displayed primarily as a process of making judgements, and judgements in which one displays clearly the ultimate failure of any given analogy; the face of the divine transcendence and simplicity. Indeed, none of these authors spends extended time setting out a theory in the abstract: through displays of appropriate predication pro-Nicenes attempt to display how and where analogy can help the imagination while never focusing our attention away from the distinction between God and world.[35]

---

[30] *Or.* 31. 33: 'I resolved to keep close to the more truly religious view and rest content with few words ... safeguarding to the end the genuine illumination I had received from [the Spirit], as I strike out a path through this world. To the best of my powers I will persuade all men to worship Father, Son and Holy Spirit as the single Godhead and power, because to him belong all glory, honor and might for ever and ever. Amen.'

[31] *Cat. or.* 2–3.

[32] To the discussion of Word and Spirit at the beginning of the text one can compare the discussion of the incarnation at *Cat. or.* 10–11. There Gregory speaks of the appropriateness of examining the soul/body relationship to understand the incarnation. The incomprehensibility of this relationship should encourage us towards ever more focused awareness of the incomprehensibility of the union of natures in Christ and towards a better understanding of what should and should not be investigated. Good analogical reasoning here helps to shape a particular style of attention and faith.

[33] To this discussion one should compare the account of the ways in which Scripture deploys analogies for the Word's generation in forms that display their own failure in Gregory's *Ref.* 9 (GNO 2/2. 348 ff.).

[34] Cf. the discussion of Basil in Ch. 8.

[35] My attention to 'judgement' here follows David Burrell's use of Gilson's account. See David B. Burrell, 'From Analogy of "Being" to the Analogy of Being', in Thomas Hibbs and John O'Callaghan (eds.), *Recovering Nature: Essays in Natural Philosophy, Ethics and*

III. Understanding Pro-Nicene Theology

The function of simplicity

For pro-Nicene authors the assertions that God is simple, truly distinct from the creation, and thus beyond our comprehension provide the central point of reference for all analogical practice in Trinitarian terminology. We can begin by noting some examples of how divine simplicity functions in a range of Greek and Latin authors. In all cases the examples I offer are unremarkable: that is, they are to be found en passant in sections of longer arguments and appear to be offered on the assumption that readers will share similar assumptions.

Interwoven through the initial sections of Nyssa's *Refutation of Eunomius' Confession* are assertions that God is eternally immutable, indivisible, simple, and existing without participation in anything, the 'absolutely existent'. Nyssa uses these descriptions to develop an account of speech about God. On the one hand, he asserts that the divine nature is 'above every name' and hence not to be spoken of as we speak of created things. On the other hand, he insists that the incarnate Word gives authority to use scriptural terms for addressing God, and tries to educate his readers not to claim the ability to describe the divine essence. The conjunction of terms describing God as unique, simple, and incomprehensible thus shapes a fundamental distinction between the divine existence and the created order.[36] This distinction between created and uncreated is a continual presence in pro-Nicene texts. For example, Didymus argues in a predictably pro-Nicene way that we should not import into our speech about the unity of the persons divisions seen in material objects and assumptions about movement and distinction seen in beings who are 'in' space, unlike God. He repeats his point with regard to the 'coming forth' of the Son and asserts that we only understand the words of the Son about his generation and the scriptural discussion of the Spirit's procession by faith and by a faithful assumption that the very mode of these processions is ineffable. Considering divine simplicity thus shapes how we think of our speech about God.[37]

For a Latin example, we can note first the culmination of book 7 of Hilary's *On the Trinity*.[38] Hilary offers an account of divine simplicity at the end of a section trying to show that any faithful account of the Son's generation has to admit that the Son has all that the Father has. Hilary argues that all analogies—and here he speaks

Metaphysics in Honor of Ralph McInerny (Notre Dame, Ind.: University of Notre Dame Press, 1999), 259. I return to Burrell later in this chapter and to this specific point at the end of Ch. 12.

[36] Gregory of Nyssa, *Ref.* 1–3.   [37] Didymus, *Spir.* 25. 112–26. 114.
[38] Hilary, *De trin.* 7. 27–30.

primarily of physical analogies—enable us to know 'in part' (*parte cogniscimus*) and to refute 'heretics'. But our discussion of analogies against the background of acknowledging divine simplicity should also make us realize that it would be best just to repeat the scriptural terms God himself has licensed for our use.[39] Similarly, at *On the Faith* 4. 9. 104, Ambrose considers his response to the standard anti-Nicene question 'did the Father generate the Son by will or unwillingly?' He argues that an opposition between compulsion and temporal, arbitrary choice does not apply in the divine nature. As perfect the divine nature stands outside the context of lack or external affect that form central conditions of created existence. Hence, he argues, the Father's will to beget and the act of begetting are an intrinsic part of the Father's ineffable nature. The combination of a belief in divine perfection and distinction from the creation fundamentally shape Ambrose's discussion of the divine unity.[40]

Thus, in pro-Nicene texts the primary function of discussing God's simplicity is to set the conditions for all talk of God as Trinity and of the relations between the divine 'persons', to shape the judgements that we make in speaking analogically, not to offer a description of divine being taken to be fully comprehensible.[41] Pro-Nicenes are loose and inconsistent in their definitions of simplicity, but this inconsistency does not necessarily prevent them *using* the doctrine in very similar ways. The language of simplicity is inseparable from the language of divine incomprehensibility and gives rise to 'formal features' of divine being that should govern all our speech about God. In using the language of 'formal features' I am adapting David Burrell's account of Aquinas.

Burrell argues that when Aquinas describes God as simple he is not indicating a property of the divine nature:

---

[39] Hilary, *De trin.* 7. 30: 'These things, I have stated, are only brought in for the sake of a comparison, in order to impart to us a knowledge of the faith, and not as things suitable to the dignity of God ... not, indeed, that any comparison does adequate justice to the nature of God, since it is fitting and just to believe God when he testifies regarding himself.'

[40] In many ways Ch. 15's discussion of Augustine is an extended example of this use of divine simplicity.

[41] Christopher Stead argues that early Christian writers tend to draw on a number of different senses of simplicity to talk about God without ever being clear which they prefer. Moreover, he argues that there are a number of problems with a coherent concept of divine simplicity. On the one hand, Stead argues that no coherent account of the personal distinctions can be given against this background. On the other hand, he argues that only the Plotinian view in which the truly simple is free from knowing and discursive thought is coherent: but this would mean that God could not exercise providential care over the creation. Christians, obviously enough, could not accept such a position and should thus renounce belief in the divine simplicity. Stead is, I think, correct in his charge that the authors with whom we are concerned here draw on a variety of unacknowledged sources for their accounts, and that they do not always explain coherently what they mean by simplicity. However, I would also argue that Stead has simply missed the function of this terminology in pro-Nicene authors.

we do not include 'simpleness' in that list of terms we wish to attribute to God—classically, 'living', 'wise', 'willing'. It is rather that simpleness defines the manner in which such properties might be attributed to God . . . 'formal features' are not so much said of a subject, as they are reflected in a subject's very mode of existing, and govern the way in which anything whatsoever might be said of that subject.[42]

Burrell then argues that such formal features shape the way that we speak of God:

the demand for attention to analogous uses of language will be established as one establishes 'the distinction' through these formal features of divinity. For it is they that remind us how God transcends our capacity to know objects, and not just quantitatively—there being a lot about God that we don't know; but they remind us in such a way that we will constantly need to ask ourselves how our concepts might be used of divinity—not simply whether or not they apply.[43]

It is, I suggest, in pro-Nicene theology that we first see simplicity functioning in the manner Burrell describes so well in the theologies of the thirteenth century. Of course, thirteenth-century theologians exhibit attitudes towards and styles of use of philosophy very different from those exhibited by the subjects of this book, but some of their fundamental concerns are directly mirrored in pro-Nicene thought.[44] We have, then, arrived at the heart of this first strategy and at a fundamental aspect of the pro-Nicene life of the mind: reflection on the distinction between Creator and creation is the context within which all speech about God (including the God-given language of Scripture) must be considered and examined. From this point we can turn again to the analogical practice of pro-Nicenes and see how this practice is shot through with attention to the distinction we have observed.

SPEAKING OF GOD

We must, however, be cautious about speaking of pro-Nicenes using analogies to illustrate 'the divine unity' or 'the three persons'. I have already indicated the importance of not reading discussions of divine unity as necessarily separate from discussions of the three

---

[42] Burrell, *Knowing the Unknowable God: Ibn-Sina, Maimonides, Aquinas* (Notre Dame, Ind.: University of Notre Dame Press, 1986), 38–50, here 46–7. I have also found extremely helpful his 'Distinguishing God from the World', in Brian Davies (ed.), *Language, Meaning and God: Essays in honour of Herbert McCabe* (London: Chapman, 1987), 75–91.

[43] Burrell, *Knowing the Unknowable God*, 47.

[44] It is against this background that I can now discuss pro-Nicene use of analogy. Burrell himself has recently made nicely clear that the use of analogy to speak of a simple God requires a certain notion of created existence as participation: see his 'From Analogy of "Being" to the Analogy of Being'. I turn to this theme of Burrell's work in Ch. 12.

persons: we need now to complement that observation with two further qualifications.

1. When pro-Nicenes deploy analogies their purpose is often to illustrate *aspects* of Trinitarian theology: the generation of the Son, inseparable operation, the difference between Son and Spirit. Pro-Nicenes may well use an analogy differently when illustrating different aspects of the Triune mystery. We should, then, for the most part avoid talking of pro-Nicenes using different and discrete analogies 'for the Trinity' and speak instead of certain aspects of the creation functioning as 'analogical sites' that may be explored and mined in different and complementary ways, just as an archaeological site may be explored in the search for understanding different aspects of an ancient context. This we have seen through the examples of emerging pro-Nicene theologies in Chapters 7–10 and we see it again in discussion of Gregory of Nyssa and Augustine in Chapters 14 and 15.

2. What we might term analogical supplementation and deconstruction is also a central feature of pro-Nicene practice. Different analogies are used together or are displayed side by side; analogies are also displayed only in order to demonstrate the inadequacies of other analogies or to enable the reader to see where they themselves fail.[45] Again, we have seen some of this already in previous chapters, and in this chapter my discussion of the remarkable series of analogies offered and then universally rejected in the final sections of Gregory Nazienzen's *Oration* 31 could easily be repeated and extended as an example. A recent essay by Sarah Coakley explores the sheer variety of imagery used by Gregory of Nyssa in Trinitarian contexts, providing another extended example. In what follows I have explored the use of just one particularly ubiquitous analogical site to show the complexity of its use.[46]

GOD AND THE UNITY OF MIND

At the beginning of his *Catechetical Oration* Gregory of Nyssa prominently deploys language about the Father and Son that relies on picturing the Father and his Word as parallel to a person and his

---

[45] For examples of this process see Gregory Nazianzen, *Or.* 31. 31 ff. Gregory of Nyssa, *Cant.* Ref. 9, Augustine, *Trin.* 11, *Serm.* 117.

[46] Sarah Coakley, 'Re-thinking Gregory of Nyssa: Introduction—Gender, Trinitarian Analogies, and the Pedagogy of *The Song*', *Modern Theology*, 18 (2002), 431–43. It will already be clear that I have no time for the idea that there is a basic Greek/Latin Trinitarian divide according to a supposed preference for 'psychological' or 'social' analogies. Part of my purpose in the following section is not only to illustrate the ubiquity of analogies based on 'psychological' material, but also to show that it may be used in a wide variety of ways.

or her 'word'.[47] In deploying this language he follows a near-universal practice of using the analogy, but one of many paths through its resources. One of the strongest uses of this analogy occurs in Athanasius, although his usage really only approaches a fully pro-Nicene usage. At *Oration* 1.28, to take one example, Athanasius argues that the Son is the Father's wisdom, while at 1.20 he argues that the Father's essence has its fullness and plenitude in the existence of the Son as Wisdom and Word. The Father's existence as Father and true God seems to be constituted by the presence of his own proper Wisdom and Word. When the analogy is used by authors more fully pro-Nicene, such as Nyssa, it must be used in a manner that illustrates both the unity between the divine 'speaker' and the word and the real distinction of the word and speaker, so that modalist connotations are held off.

It is sometimes asserted that while Greeks use external speech or an external word as an analogy for the Son, Latins, following Augustine, use the concept of an internal word. The picture is much more complex than this. In both languages theologians are agreed on the possibility of using the mind's act of 'generation' as a model for understanding the Word: it is the act of generating without material division that such analogies offer. Even in Greek writers 'internal' examples sometimes appear: Athanasius' discussion of a person and her or his wisdom is one such; below I provide others from Basil and Nazianzen. The real differences, at least in part, stem from different responses to non-Nicene use of the same set of analogies. Whereas a writer such as Nyssa speaking of a person and an external word immediately insists that in God such a word is not temporary or of inferior status, Augustine, responding to Ambrose's caution about any such analogy, speaks of an internal word to emphasize (like Athanasius) the lack of inferiority between word and generator.

The use of the analogical resources provided by a thinker and his or her word is, of course, unsurprising given the first verses of John's Gospel. But we may also turn observations made in discussing Basil into a more general observation. Pro-Nicenes naturally and universally see the mind or soul as a key site on which to reflect when thinking about the existence of the Word and the character of divine existence. We have already seen Basil discussing the origin of both Son and Spirit with 'mental' or 'psychological' language.[48] In his *Oration* 12, we see Gregory Nazianzen speak of the unity between the persons as that between three aspects of the mind.[49] The question is not, however, whether all pro-Nicenes use this imagery from time to time, but how they use it.

---

[47] *Cat. or.* 1. [48] See 270ff. [49] PG 37. 385–6.

In a recent paper Michel Barnes[50] argues that Nyssa does not use psychological language in Trinitarian theology in ways parallel to those of modern theologians: he is not primarily interested in using clear and unitary psychological language as a way of defining what it means to be a divine person or God. The basic context for Nyssa's use (and implicitly for the use of virtually all fourth-century writers) is the attempt to consider how the apparent or real divisions of the human soul can serve as a language for describing the unity of the Godhead. Whether one has a unitary, di- or trichotomous psychology one experiences the soul as divided, as unable to achieve true unity. Hence, while the immaterial soul provides a key resource for thinking about God, the unity we speak of in God is inconceivable: our actual disunity always highlights the distinction between the divine existence and our own. Psychological unity thus offers a particularly important point of departure for reflecting on a God who demonstrates a unity beyond any psychological experience we have.

Augustine is of course famous for exploring the distinction and unity of memory, intelligence, and will as an analogical site. It is important to note that Augustine builds on common pro-Nicene themes. First, he relies on the common assumption that the human being is in the image of God in possessing a creative, rational mind.[51] Second, he builds on the long tradition of using the 'psychological' analogy of a person and her or his word. Third, he also stands in a long tradition of relating discussion about the unity of God to discussion about the unity of the soul. Elsewhere I have argued that Augustine's use of this analogical site in the *De trinitate* follows a similar logic to that Barnes identifies in Gregory of Nyssa. Augustine uses this analogy in ways that draw on our imagination of mental processes to provide a key analogical base for imagining three things that are distinct and yet form an inseparable unity. Simultaneously, however, Augustine wants his readers to see their own inability to grasp the unitary process they describe as essential to being in the image of God, and he wants his readers to see that the divine unity exceeds our imagination.[52] Thus Gregory of Nyssa and Augustine both offer particularly developed reflections on the soul as image of God, and both identify the soul as an analogical site which demonstrates its own insufficiency to the anagogical imagination.

---

[50] Michel Barnes, 'Divine Unity and the Divided Self'.
[51] The common nature of this belief is discussed in Ch. 13.
[52] Lewis Ayres, 'Memory, Intelligence and Will', in Lewis Ayres and Vincent Twomey (eds.), *The Mystery of the Trinity in the Fathers of the Church* (Dublin: Four Courts Press, 2005, forthcoming).

What kind of unity?

I make no attempt here to summarize the wide range of analogical resources used by pro-Nicenes: nevertheless we can say that we never find descriptions of the divine unity that take as their point of departure the psychological inter-communion of three distinct people. The phraseology of this sentence is intended precisely: I mean that we do not find pro-Nicene authors offering as an analogical base for discussing the unity of God the sort of unity observed between three people engaged in a mutual project or sharing a common goal. The essential divisions observed in such cases would render this analogy fundamentally insufficient. Where we do see the analogy of three rational beings used it is noticeable both that the terminology used of the individual persons is not defined by reference to a distinct psychological content and that the persons are always described as having an essential and metaphysical unity through the indivisibility of φύσις: in such texts it is most frequently the logic of difference and unity between individuals as distinct members of a general class that is at issue. How then should we characterize the unity that pro-Nicenes see between the three divine persons?

A long-running scholarly debate has asked whether the terminologies used by the Cappadocians and especially Basil entail a 'generic' or 'numerical' unity. The Basilian account (or that of the Cappadocians as a whole) has sometimes been taken to demonstrate a merely generic as opposed to a 'truly' Nicene 'numerical' account of unity. This debate serves as a useful point of departure for considering pro-Nicene usage in general. While this scholarship has offered some excellent analysis of the complex sources for the terminologies used it has largely failed to consider the contexts within which these terminologies are set. We cannot assume that we have understood how a theologian understands the divine unity and distinction if we only explore the sources of a particular terminology and the vision of unity and diversity implied in that terminology itself.

Thus, taking further the discussion of Chapter 8, we do not get an accurate picture of the unity of which Basil speaks by focusing only on the terminology he deploys. We need also to consider how that terminology is qualified by his general statements about the nature of divine existence. Most obviously, Basil insists that the divine *ousia* and the generation of the Son are incomprehensible: the way in which the one divine *ousia* encompasses the three persons is unknown to us. The comparison of Basil's and Athanasias' accounts of divine unity would, then, need to consider how they serve to support and are shaped by the architectonic themes in a given theology. For example, Basil sees good accounts of divine unity as drawing the Christian's mind to the incomprehensibility of the divine existence and to recognizing the unsuitability of positing any ontological hierarchy of divine being. Indeed, we might even argue that Basil's account is better than Athanasius' for shaping attention to the paradoxical diversity and unity as the necessary context for the belief in traditional Christian language about the divine persons. We could then go on to ask in more detail how well the differing accounts of the 'Cappadocians' serve the functions they each and commonly make central. Christopher Stead has observed that the concepts of 'numerical' and 'generic' unity are themselves too vague to serve as useful dividing markers. My addition to his extremely important observation is to note that even the particular unity implied by a given terminology (if it can be determined) needs to be placed in the context of an author's theology more widely if we are to understand how they envisage the Trinitarian unity.

It is also vital to note that pro-Nicenes are still stumbling towards a clear sense of how to defend their terminologies for persons and essence, and few consistently use one terminology. At the same time it is rarely observed just how infrequently such terminologies receive lengthy discussion. Such extended discussions are not found as extensive parts of catechetical treatises or sermons, nor in the major polemical works against Eunomius. Taking 'the Cappadocians' as an example, we find only some short discussions in Basil's letters, two short texts by Gregory of Nyssa, and virtually nothing in Nazianzen. Scholars have tended to treat those few texts devoted to this issue as non-polemically driven summary texts which take us to the heart of Cappadocian theological concerns. In the case of Basil and Gregory of Nyssa the existence of such a terminology and the distinction it preserves is of importance: but even where the terminology is discussed at length it is usually given relatively brief explanation in the context of insistence on the incomprehensibility of the divine essence and the need for attention to the incapacities of human knowledge of God.

The *Ad Petrum*, probably an early text from the pen of Gregory of Nyssa, offers an excellent brief example. Although the first few sections of the text focus on the relationship between individual and particular (and have received some excellent scholarly analysis), the major part of this short text does not.[53] After his initial consideration the author argues that the best way to take forward or fill out (ἀνιχνεῦσαι) the account is to dwell on inseparable operation. An exposition of this doctrine follows that emphasizes the impossibility of apprehending any separation between the persons even while they are known by their distinguishing marks (ἰδιώματα). This is in

---

[53] On this text see Hübner, 'Gregor von Nyssa als Verfasser'; Zachhuber, *Human Nature*.

turn followed by an extended analogy for the persons' unity based on the indistinguishable boundaries between the colours in a rainbow. The purpose of the illustration, says the author, is to demonstrate the possibility of continuing to think through what initially seem the irrational dogmas of faith. Although we cannot comprehend the divine nature, we can proceed by careful use of analogy and example to show that faith contains a certain rationality. Thus the movement of the text as a whole carefully qualifies the short technical discussion offered in its initial sections. That technical account is 'filled out' not only by a description of inseparable operation: statement of the latter doctrine serves (as it so often does) as a point of departure for emphasizing the virtue and yet limit of all analogical thinking. Without considering this movement of argument we may seriously misunderstand the extent to which pro-Nicenes see their technical language delivering comprehension of the divine existence.[54]

We can, of course, consider the sources and coherence of the various terminologies used by pro-Nicenes and we may well conclude that those terminologies are either incoherently deployed or point to an account of unity and differentiation that is highly problematic alongside other pro-Nicene claims. Thus, although as a general principle it is true that discussions of terminology need to be interpreted in the light of the other principles articulated in this chapter, it should not be assumed that there are no differences in the ways that pro-Nicenes imagine unity and distinction in the Godhead. My suggestion is simply that investigating these differences will need to take into account not only particular terminologies, but also how those terminologies and analogies are deployed and conditioned.

One further tentative suggestion is possible: pro-Nicenes consistently emphasize that our understanding of the distinction between persons and essence must be governed by awareness of the distinction between God and world. In part because of the need to refuse any hint of the materialist or otherwise problematic connotations that had seemed to accrue to 'Nicene' accounts since 325, pro-Nicenes made the incomprehensibility of the divine relationships a cornerstone of their position in ways that should make us wary of attempts to read off notions of unity simply from the connotations

---

[54] The text of the *Ad Petrum* has traditionally been read from beginning to end in a fairly direct manner. Unfortunately the argument of the text may not actually be constructed in this way. One can read the text as offering its initial defence of terminology and then its explanation of inseparable operation as the initial stages in a polemic against those who have argued that Heb. 1: 3, because of its insistence that Christ is the image of the Father's *hypostasis*, prevents us speaking of three *hypostases*. In the future I intend to offer a more extended version of this argument.

of particular terminology used. Of course, at different points in the history of Trinitarian theology the terminologies used for distinguishing divine persons and divine unity may be governed more or less by insistence on our lack of comprehension: my suggestion here is that pro-Nicenes are actually notable for the clarity with which they allow statements of incomprehensibility to so govern their technical vocabulary. It is thus the principle of divine simplicity and incomprehensibility articulated so clearly in the late fourth century that makes the question 'what type of unity?' impossible to answer in the categories recent scholarship has offered us, and difficult to answer in any short fashion.

What is a divine person?

In the light of the foregoing discussion we can now try to summarize how pro-Nicenes conceive of a divine person in the abstract. First, divine persons are irreducible within the irreducible essence. We cannot make their mode of existence more understandable by presenting them in 'Sabellian' fashion as aspects of God or roles of God, but nor can we assume that they possess different natures, wills, or activities within the one Godhead. The distinctions between them are real: but we do not know what it is to exist distinctly in this state. Hence statements of the general form Father is not Son, Son is not Father, and Spirit is neither Father nor Son are some of the clearest we can make precisely in that they deliver only a logic of relationship.[55]

Second, while pro-Nicenes do not talk about the divine persons by offering detailed accounts of the ontology of personhood, they do use the analogical site of human mind and reason to illuminate both our speech about the unity of God and about what it is to be a person within that unity. We have already seen some of the ways in which human rationality is used as a site for exploring the character of the Trinitarian unity. In discussing Basil we also saw some of the ways in which he used the human mind as a site to explore the individual divine persons. What we saw there can be raised to the level of a general comment about pro-Nicene theology. There is a natural fittingness to using the rational human in the image of God as a parallel to a divine person: but this never means that the three persons are treated as three distinct human individuals.

Thus, in the course of attempts to articulate what it means for the persons to be equal in status we do frequently see insistence on each person possessing the attributes intrinsic to divine nature. In his

---

[55] Cf. e.g. Epiphanius, *Anc.* 10; Gregory Nazianzen, *Or.* 31. 9; Athanasius, *C. Ar.* 3. 4; Augustine, *Serm.* 52. 2; Gregory of Nyssa, *Ref.* 5–6 (GNO 2/2. 314–15); *Simpl.* (GNO 3/1. 66 ff.).

Catechetical Oration, for example, Gregory of Nyssa first insists that the Son must possess life. He then insists that because the Word is simple the Word does not participate in life, but is its own life and hence must possess will and be both wise and omnipotent. Because the very term 'Word' signifies relation to the Father Word and Father must be distinct.[56] But while such passages appear to give further density to the idea of a divine person it is important to note that, for example, when rationality or a capacity for willing is attributed to the Son, it is the unitary divine will that is spoken of: within the simple Godhead, the distinct Word possesses the fullness of the indivisible Godhead. Similarly, in book 15 of the *De trinitate* Augustine insists that each divine person possesses memory, understanding, and will. But again, the assertion is necessary lest anyone think of the persons as performing a partial function within the Godhead. Augustine's insistence draws us to the full consequences of the logic or grammar of divine simplicity, and provides us with some key principles for developing our understanding of the Trinitarian unity and diversity. He does not, however, use the attributions of memory, understanding, and will to the divine persons to encourage us to think we can understand what it is like to be a divine person by analogy with our own experience of personhood. Because we accord these qualities to divine persons in their perfect form and within the context of the divine simplicity, we do not know what it is for divine persons to possess such qualities: as David Burrell says the analogy here is analogical. Thus for both Augustine and Gregory of Nyssa we will grow in understanding of the individual persons the more we understand their co-inherence and con-joint operation. The more we can imagine the irreducibility of persons within the simplicity of the Godhead, the more we can speak appropriately about them.

INSEPARABLE OPERATION AND APPROPRIATION

It is at this point that we must return to the principle of inseparable operation. Inseparable operation sets bounds to how we envisage the persons but it does not do so *only* by indicating that we are to think of them as more a unity in our sense than a plurality. It is true that pro-Nicenes do intend to place restrictions on the way that we imagine the unity of God. Most clearly, if we were to imagine God as three potentially separable agents or three 'centres of consciousness' the contents of whose 'minds' were distinct, pro-Nicenes would see us as drawing inappropriate analogies between God and

---

[56] e.g. at *Cat. or.* 1.

created realities and in serious heresy. Pro-Nicenes insist that we cannot imagine the diversity of divine persons in the simple Godhead in ways that would import distinctions that we observe between material objects in the world.

But, at the same time, the doctrine of inseparable operation also sets bounds to or shapes how we envisage the diversity of the persons by shaping habits of speech that keep us attentive to the mystery of God's unity and diversity. Learning to speak of Father, Son, and Spirit as inseparably operating while still affirming that any one of the divine persons is not the other two, and that each possesses the fullness of the Godhead, does not so much lead us to an easy imagining of their diversity and unity as it defers our comprehension and draws our minds to the constantly failing (even as constantly growing), character of our interpretation of what is held in faith. The development of such attention to the mysteries of divine triunity is, ideally, the shaping of an ongoing process of analogical judgement, a process in which we learn to display a balance between admitting human inability to comprehend the divine and appropriately exploring the providentially ordered resources of the language of faith.

Closely linked to the doctrines of divine simplicity and inseparable operation is the practice of appropriation. Appropriation is the practice of attributing to one divine person an attribute or action that is common to the Godhead and thus to all divine persons: because the persons work inseparably in the context of the divine simplicity we frequently speak about something as characteristic of a divine person although it is in fact equally true of all divine persons. Appropriation is, for pro-Nicenes, an important habit of Christian speech because it is central to Scripture's own speech about the divine persons. Appropriation is sometimes presented as an 'Augustinian' doctrine: in fact, Augustine's clarity about the doctrine—which may be seen in Chapter 15—is simply the clearest statement of a common pro-Nicene principle.

A few examples from one Greek author will suffice. In the first book of his *Contra Eunomium* Gregory of Nyssa focuses much of his argument around the consequences of believing the divine simplicity to encompass Father, Son, and Spirit.[57] The argument is aimed at Eunomius' supposition that the Father alone is simple. For Gregory this means that Eunomius actually teaches three distinct beings possessing different natures in an ontological hierarchy. Against such an account Gregory asserts that divine simplicity admits of no degrees and that in God there are no distinct qualities

---

[57] *Eunom.* 1. 19.

adhering in a prior subject. Thus we cannot speak of any degrees of perfection or goodness:

> Nothing which possesses wisdom or power or any other good, not as an external gift, but rooted in its nature, can suffer diminution in it: so that if anyone says that he detects beings greater and smaller in the divine nature, he is unconsciously establishing a composite and heterogeneous nature.[58]

The significance of the passage lies in the reference to the terms wisdom and power, accorded to the Son at 1 Cor. 1: 24. While Nyssa continues to speak of the Son as the Wisdom of God he has also established a principle, based on the notion of divine simplicity, that the Son cannot be said to possess more or less wisdom than the Father or Spirit because the divine wisdom is a unity.[59] Even though Gregory does not possess a technical terminology for appropriation, he understands Scripture and Christians to be engaging in just this practice.

The same argument is found in his short *To Eustathius on the Holy Trinity* but with clearer reference to the doctrine of inseparable operation. There we find that there is one life-giving power in which Father, Son, and Spirit are included and that consequently all attributes are fully possessed by all three divine persons without degree. Repeating and expanding on the same argument Gregory asserts that where Scripture attributes a work to one person all are involved, and that the inseparability of operation reveals an identity of nature in which no divine attribute is more or less true of any one person.[60] Throughout this text Gregory attempts to inculcate a practice speaking with Scripture, being attentive to where and how Scripture speaks and trying to mirror that speech in our own. Nyssa, like all pro-Nicenes, understands one of the central dimensions of Scripture's speech to be its condescension to the level of created reality in revealing God and yet its anagogic function in leading the human imagination to see the necessary path beyond those human categories. We speak with Scripture when we deploy scriptural titles and analogies in the light of Scripture's own dynamic of revealing and drawing.

The doctrine of appropriation thus epitomizes the pro-Nicene dynamics I have been exploring through this chapter. As we come to understand that, and how Scripture and Christian speech constantly appropriate common divine attributes to particular persons (just as divine actions are appropriated to individual divine persons), we are

---

[58] *Eunom.* 1. 19.
[59] Cf. *Eunom.* 1. 34. Here the further point is made that Father and Son are one not as two people are one in the sense that they do not share accidental virtues in particular proportions as do two people who have become wise over time. Any virtue they possess as one is both part of their nature and a unity.
[60] Gregory of Nyssa, *Trin.* (GNO 3/1. 11 ff.). Cf. *Simpl.* (GNO 3/1. 66 ff.).

drawn into an understanding of the complexity and mystery of human speech about God. We grow in such understanding, however, the more we are attentive to the divine simplicity (and that each unitary attribute must be possessed equally by the persons). Nevertheless, this attentiveness is not simply an act of intellectual surrender, admitting the complete failure of our speech but continuing to speak in a manner that we know to be invalid. Appropriation is, rather, part of the anagogic life of the mind central to pro-Nicene Trinitarianism. Gregory here (or Augustine a generation later) is shaping structures of the Christian imagination and habits of Christian speech in which we speak both of the individual persons as embodying divine attributes, but do so while cultivating habits of attention to the divine simplicity. In exploring this tension in our speech we perform a central aspect of the way that the text of Scripture is understood to shape a movement of the intellect and imagination beyond (or into) its language and towards the divine mystery.

It is also important to realize both that assuming the centrality of this practice in Scripture's and our speech about God does not mean either that there is no basis in the nature of the divine existence for appropriation, or that a unitary divine substance is assumed to be more real than the persons. In the latter case, for both Gregory and Augustine the unitary divine attributes are not predicated of a divine nature somehow prior to the persons, rather the divine attributes are predicated of a nature constituted by the three persons existing in a mode of union beyond our comprehension. In the former case, the manner in which Scripture models appropriation enables a real movement towards understanding of the divine action and the movement of the divine life: sticking with my examples, both Gregory and Augustine see Scripture's presentation of the Spirit's role in sanctification as vital in shaping our understanding of how God acts towards us and the character of the divine life itself. At the same time, however, both assume that understanding that the gifts of wisdom and holiness brought by the Spirit are or reflect the one wisdom and holiness that marks the divine life deepens our understanding of the Spirit's work.[61] The same is also true of the Son's status as the power and wisdom of God.

---

[61] As we see, for example, at Gregory of Nyssa, *Simpl.* (GNO 3/1. 66): 'all the supreme and divine names which are applied by the Scriptures to the Father and the Son are also to be contemplated in the Holy Spirit—immortality, blessedness, goodness, wisdom, power, justice, holiness—every excellent name is predicated of the Holy Spirit as it is predicated of the Father and of the Son, with the exception of those by which the Persons are clearly and distinctly divided from each other ... By this then we apprehend that the Spirit is above creation.' Understanding that attributing any one of these qualities to the Spirit is an act of appropriation enables the Christian to grasp the true nature of the Spirit and thus to understand better the character of salvation. Augustine, *Trin.* 15. 17. 29 ff.

It is within the context of the doctrines of divine simplicity and inseparable operation that we also find Greek and Latin pro-Nicenes articulating the principle that we know the persons only by their relationships of origin.[62] The austerity of this principle, however, is held alongside the discipline of appropriation. We can thus perhaps describe pro-Nicene approaches to describing the persons and nature of the Trinity as moving between two poles: towards an assertion that the bare logic of differentiation is all that may be said, and simultaneously towards analogical descriptions that shape one's awareness of the sheer difficulty of thought's struggle to encompass what remains beyond our epistemic grasp.

CONCLUSION

The central argument of this chapter has been that to understand how pro-Nicenes conceive of the irreducible divine unity and irreducible divine persons, we must first understand how pre-Nicenes attempt to locate such discussions within a discourse that displays its own insufficiency. The pro-Nicene life of the mind finds its core in attention, on the one hand, to the distinction between Creator and creation and, on the other hand, to the dynamics not simply of 'revelation', but of the divine economy that condescends to our categories but does so only to draw us slowly towards a contemplation of the divine realities of which they speak.[63]

In a previous paper I questioned the usefulness of asking where theologies 'begin'.[64] In the standard narrations of classical Trinitarian theology found during the past hundred years it is a commonplace to speak of the west 'beginning' with the unity of God while the east 'begins' with the three persons. Much of the latter half of this book is aimed at showing the unsustainable nature of this division. At the same time it is important to note the intensely problematic assumption that theologies 'begin' somewhere in the abstract.

---

[62] Cf. Gregory Nazianzen, *Or.* 31. 9; Gregory of Nyssa, *Ablab.* (GNO 3/1. 47 ff.) *Simpl.* (GNO 3/1. 66–7); Augustine, *Trin.* 6. 2. 3.

[63] My focus in this and the next two chapters is on some fundamentals of pro-Nicene theological practice, the basic structures of pro-Nicene theological culture. One important alternate next step that might have been taken from the end of this chapter, however, would have been to investigate common themes among pro-Nicene presentations of the individual persons of Father, Son, and Spirit. That is a large task for which I intend only to lay the groundwork for future work here. It should be clear, however, that pursuing such an investigation would involve being attentive not only to how individual theologians and traditions present the three persons, but also to how they relate their presentations to their (perhaps implicit) understandings of appropriation and common operation. Thus, for example, comparing the attributes and roles accorded the Spirit should involve also seeing how those attributes are also understood as common, and how according those attributes or roles shapes an account of Spirit in relation to Son and Father.

[64] Ayres, 'Remember that you are Catholic'.

At the simplest level different texts by different pro-Nicenes 'begin' at different points: with statements of faith, with outlines of a polemical context, with particular verses that are contested. Few, if any, pro-Nicene texts have a 'systematic' format in which 'the One God' and 'the Triune God' are dealt with in a clear order.

Questions about where pro-Nicenes 'begin' their Trinitarian theology must, then, be read as questions about what is of deepest concern to those theologians, or about those themes to which they constantly return. But if so, then I suggest that the deepest concern in pro-Nicene Trinitarian theology is shaping our attention to the union of the irreducible persons in the simple and unitary Godhead. Pro-Nicenes 'begin' as much with the process, with the practice of reflection they seek to perform and inculcate, as with the formal principles they espouse: the former is the necessary context for the latter. This is not to say that there are no divisions between pro-Nicene traditions or that (if carefully defined) 'east' and 'west' cannot function usefully as markers of division at some level. It does, however, mean that there is a fundamental continuity of deepest concern at the heart of pro-Nicene Trinitarian theology: they 'begin', insofar as any theology can be said to 'begin', at the same point.

12
'The First and Brightest Light'[1]

In the previous chapter I focused on the practice of attention to the mystery of God's triunity at the heart of pro-Nicene thought. For pro-Nicenes appropriate attention to the divine unity or divine persons was shaped by the cultivation of awareness of the distinction between God and creation and by a complex analogical process that conditions all that we might say in propositional terms about how pro-Nicenes understand the divine. Such a conception of Trinitarian theology per se affected how pro-Nicenes conceived of the character of existence and the character of the world in which they existed: conceptions of cosmology and soteriology were irrevocably marked by the rise of pro-Nicene dynamics. In turn, the reshaping of these other theological areas provided a wider context that nurtured and shaped pro-Nicene Trinitarian theology itself. Accordingly, if we are to understand the character of pro-Nicene trinitarianism we will need to explore some of these shared cosmological and soteriological dynamics. In this chapter I consider pro-Nicene accounts of Christology and cosmology, setting the wide stage for the next chapter's consideration of anthropological issues. For the sake of space I have, through Chapters 12 and 13, provided fewer examples, focusing on demonstrating continuity between Greek- and Latin-speaking pro-Nicenes.

STRATEGY II: CHRISTOLOGY AND COSMOLOGY

Introduction: the virtues of De Régnon

At this intersection I will draw attention to two related themes: the Christological determination of the notion of spiritual purification; the interweaving of Christology and ontological speculation in pro-Nicene thought. It is particularly important to see how pro-Nicene theologies use their accounts of the Son's eternal generation to shape accounts of creation and redemption. English-language scholarship on the fourth century has often presented the development of pro-Nicene theology as bringing an end to earlier 'Logos theology'.[2]

---

[1] Gregory Nazianzen, *Or.* 40. 37.
[2] e.g. Hanson, *The Search*, 872: 'we must observe that the doctrine of the Trinity ... as finally accepted by the Church actually put an abrupt stop to one train of development ...

By 'Logos theology' such scholars refer to the tradition going back to the Apologists of treating the Logos as mediator between Creator and creation. In such theologies the Logos is the means by which the transcendent divine Father creates and interacts with the creation. Our first task is to see that pro-Nicene theology did not simply bring an end to 'Logos theology'.

The late nineteenth-century French historian of Trinitarian theology Theodore De Régnon has been increasingly cited over recent years, in part because of an article by Michel Barnes showing the influence of De Régnon's division of the history of Trinitarian theology into 'patristic' and 'scholastic' paradigms, the latter beginning with Augustine and pointing forward to the achievements of medieval Latin scholasticism. In a very simplified and usually directly reversed form, De Régnon's account became the basis for many twentieth-century accounts of the wonders of Greek Trinitarian theology and the errors of Latin theology. De Régnon's account is the basis not only for much western Christian theological writing but even for Vladimir Lossky's understanding of Trinitarian history.[3]

While it is vital for my own account of late fourth-century trinitarianism that we move beyond De Régnon's periodizations—and beyond their distorted echo in recent historical narratives—De Régnon's work contains much more than this famous paradigm. On the question of 'Logos theology' his position particularly deserves discussion. Michel Barnes notes that French-language scholarship has sustained a far more vibrant debate about the fate of 'Logos theology', in part because De Régnon himself argued for considerable continuity between pre- and post-Nicene theologies.[4] Barnes gives a useful survey of this French debate: I want to turn back to De Régnon's own account. De Régnon argues that Greek

---

The centuries-old, much-used, one can almost say Catholic, concept of the pre-existent Christ as the link between an impassible Father and a transitory world, that which made of him a convenient philosophical device, the *Logos*-doctrine dear to the heart of many orthodox theologians in the past, was abandoned.' The immediately following sentence is a beautiful vignette of Hanson's sometimes simplistic views of the developments of the 4th cent.: 'This was rather a return to Scripture than a development of dogma.' The same all-or-nothing attitude that Hanson takes to the presence of Logos theology is also taken with regard to a whole host of other traditions in his 'The Transformation of Images in the Fourth Century', *SP* 17/1 (1982), 97–113.

[3] See Michel René Barnes, 'De Régnon Reconsidered', *Augustinian Studies*, 26 (1995), 57–8. It is particularly important to note that De Régnon's use of epochal divisions (following the earlier work of Jacques Marie Ginoulhiac) is not a distinction between Greeks and Latins; pre-Augustinian Latin theology is as much a part of the 'patristic paradigm as the theology of any of the Cappadocians.

[4] Barnes, 'De Régnon Reconsidered', 55, 58–71.

theologies of the fourth century face a basic problem:[5] Once Father and Son are coequal members of the Godhead, in what sense can the Son be said to be the Father's image? The Son cannot truly be said to be the image of the Father's essence, as the one divine essence simply *is* the Son's own essence as well. Nor can the Son be truly the image of the Father's personal qualities because if they were shared by the Son they would not be the Father's own. De Régnon poses this question only to argue that it misunderstands the subtleties of Trinitarian theology.[6] Once one realizes that the persons constitute the essence, then new approaches to the question are possible.

De Régnon's answer depends on his assertion that an 'image' not only imitates, but also reveals that of which it is an image. In this light, De Régnon proposes that we consider the essential goodness of the Father's being. He argues that for late fourth-century writers the Father's goodness naturally (but not from necessity) gives rise to an image (the Son) which reveals the Father's essential nature *as* Goodness. This revealing image is part of the perfection of the Father's existence. The ontological unity of the two secures the revelatory image as an eternal expression of the perfect divine existence. Thus pro-Nicenes do not abandon earlier presentations of the Word as 'image', but bring out more deeply some central themes of earlier theologies while radically modifying other key aspects.

De Régnon then argues that the theme of the interior word as image for the Son's production in scholastic tradition (beginning with Augustine) incorporates and enhances the central point of the Greek tradition. The transformation of Logos theology into a discussion of the Word's eternal procession on the model of the production of the 'inner word' focuses attention ever more clearly on the manner in which the Son's existence is the perfection of the Father's mode of being and yet still mediatorial. De Régnon offers an excellent point of departure for exploring the ways in which pro-Nicenes transform but do not abandon earlier Logos theology. In what follows I have not attempted a full-scale defence of his thesis, but have assumed its plausibility as a heuristic tool for exploring the common thrust of Greek and Latin discussion of the divine Word.

PURIFICATION IN CHRIST'S BODY

By speaking of the 'Christological determination' of purification and ascent I mean that pro-Nicenes take the soul's formation to be shaped by the action of Christ as incarnate (and crucified, resur-

---

[5] Theodore De Régnon, *Études de théologie positive sur la sainté Trinité* (Paris: Retaux, 1898), nos. XVII *passim* and XIX, 361–78.

[6] He takes the question from Dionysius Petavius (1583–1652).

rected, and ascended) Word. In particular, pro-Nicenes envisage the process of salvation as occurring through participation in Christ, through, in some sense, a union of the Christian with Christ's person. Despite holding to a variety of notions of human capability and agency in the process of sanctification, and to a wide range of pre-Chalcedonian Christologies, pro-Nicenes treat the Word present in Christ as the ultimate agent in the process of redemption.[7]

Nyssa on transformation in Christ

As an initial example I will consider Nyssa's sermon on 1 Cor. 15: 28 ('When all things are subjected to him, then the Son himself will also be subjected to him who put all things under him, that God may be all in all.'). Pro-Nicenes inherited an anti-Marcellan exegesis in which this text demonstrated the permanence of the Son's kingdom. In his sermon Nyssa explains how Christ's kingdom is both permanent and universal through an exposition of[8] Christian formation reaching its end in a two-stage union. First, all Christians are unified with Christ through the control of passions and an ordering of soul and body that is a true imitation of Christ. At this point, 'all are subjected to the one who rules over all ... One body has been formed with the good as predominant; our body's entire nature is united to the divine, pure nature.'[9] In the second stage, the union of all with Christ brings all to share what Christ has from the Father, and thus the kingdom is led into subjection to the Father:

> Unity then means to be one body with him. When the good pervades everything, then the entirety of Christ's body will be subjected to God's vivifying power ... Christ unites all mankind to himself, and to the Father through him ... he who is in the Father effects our union with this very same Father.[10]

The links between soteriology and Christology seen here are typically pro-Nicene. The closeness of the Word to the Father means that our union with Christ is a real union with the one life of God. Because Father and Son share eternally in the one power of God, Christ's body (and hence our bodies) are directly affected by the life of God.

The full extent to which pro-Nicene concerns have shaped Nyssa's picture can be seen when we consider his account of the transformation of the human being in Christ. Attention to God's

---

[7] One might object that 'ultimate' here is somewhat vague: this is intentionally so. While all pro-Nicenes appear to agree on the role of the Word they differ in where and the ways in which they see the Word actually effecting change.

[8] This short text is extensively commented on by Reinhard Hübner, *Die Einheit des Leibes Christi bei Gregor von Nyssa* (Leiden: Brill, 1974), 27–66.

[9] *In 1 Cor. 15. 28*, PG 44. 1316.   [10] *In 1 Cor. 15. 28*, PG 44. 1317, 1320.

immediate but non-competitive[11] presence in the world reshapes existing traditions of reflection on the transformation of the individual soul. Reflection on this transformation must now speak both of the mystery of God's presence to the soul and the mysterious character of unity in the person of Christ. These themes can be seen in Nyssa's account of 'deification' or *theosis*. Nyssa is cautious in his terminology and reluctant to speak of Christians 'becoming divine'.[12] Reluctant or not, however, Nyssa actually offers one of the most considered accounts of this theme in the later fourth century.[13] At a number of points Nyssa describes the soul's imitation of the divine through imagining a shaping of the soul's life or activity such that it eventually displays nothing but the activity (ἐνέργεια) of love. This activity both transforms the soul into a perfect image (achieving its natural end) *and* draws the soul into union with the life of God.[14]

We need also to note the extent to which he insists on the impossibility of speaking about God's presence in terms of spatial location or intensity of degree. In true pro-Nicene fashion Gregory insists that God is immediately present everywhere and that God transcends all things equally. Appropriate attention to the all-pervading, all-powerful nature of the Triune God can only be sustained when we move beyond language that considers God's activity in those terms we use of competing created agents. This can be seen particular clearly in the *Catechetical Oration*:

If then all things exist in him and he exists in all things, why are [some people] shocked at a scheme of revelation (οἰκονομία) which teaches that God became man, when we believe that even now he is not external to man? It must be granted that even if the mode (τρόπος) of the presence of God in

---

[11] By 'non-competitive' presence I mean that God's presence in the world does not compete with objects in the world for space or time. God may be closer to me than all else without displacing any object in the world.

[12] The seminal literature on this theme is to be found in Jules Gross, *La Divinisation du chrétien d'après les pères grecs: Contribution historique à la doctrine de la grâce* (Paris: J. Gabalda, 1938); Myrrha Lot-Borondine, *La Déification de l'homme selon la doctrine des Pères grecs* (Paris: Cerf, 1970); David O. Balás, Metousia Theou: *Man's Participation in God's Perfections According to Saint Gregory of Nyssa*, Studia Anselmiana, 55 (Rome: IBC Libreria Herder, 1966); H. Merki, *Homoiosis Theou* (Fribourg, Switzerland, 1952). Verna E. F. Harrison, *Grace and Human Freedom According to St. Gregory of Nyssa* (Lewiston, NY: Edwin Mellon Press, 1992), esp. ch. 3. My suggestions in the following paragraphs are intended to be consonant with and build on some of the best of this work. In particular I would point to Merki's insistence on the dynamism of the imago Dei in Nyssa and to both Merki and Balás's insistence that it is through the honing of the soul's natural sharing in the perfections of God that we share or participate in God (for a brief statement of this principle by Nyssa himself see *Hom. op.* 16).

[13] Ayres, '*Theosis* and the Dynamics of Nicene Theology', *St Vladimir's Theological Quarterly*, forthcoming.

[14] e.g. *Anim.*, PG 46. 94–7; *Hom. op.* 12. 9–11.

us is not the same as in that instance, nevertheless, the presence in us now and then is equal (κατὰ τὸ ἴσον). In the one case he is united to us insofar as he sustains existing things. In the other case he united himself with our nature, in order that by its union with the Divine it might become divine.[15]

To understand the distinction between different 'modes' of presence even while there is equality of degree, we need first to note that Gregory insists on the mysteriousness of God's action. Not only do we no more understand how God acts on us than we understand how the soul acts on the body, but even the true life that is God's own nature is incomprehensible. Thus the life that is the perfection of the soul's existence is an incomprehensible life.[16] Indeed, the soul's own mysteriousness is reflected in the creation as a whole: insofar as they image the divine nature all natures are hidden from us.[17] How then can we shape a discourse attentive to the mystery of the soul's reshaping? From one point of view Gregory severely restricts our speech, ruling out a variety of tempting strategies for describing God's presence. At the same time, however, he encourages us to deploy specifically scriptural terminology and narrative, understood in the context of general pro-Nicene principles. Thus, in the passage quoted above the two 'modes' of divine presence are described through narration: philosophical terminologies are used to articulate such narration but their explanatory power is strictly limited. When Gregory describes the purified soul's existence as a mirror of the divine life, he knows his language skirts a site where the languages of unity and distinction are intensely problematic: the purified soul existing in the immediate presence of the divine life with an intimacy beyond our telling.

Even from this brief exploration we can identify four themes that have reached their current form under pressure from pro-Nicene emphases:

1. Sanctification and redemption are understood as participation in the body of Christ, as union with the person of Christ. This theme receives a particular pro-Nicene emphasis through Gregory's understanding of the Word's intimate union with the Father, a union manifested in the Word's sharing in the one divine power.

2. The theme of being one with Christ is shaped by growing pro-Nicene clarity about the distinction between God and creation. Pro-Nicene accounts of the unity of the divine persons and their

---

[15] *Cat. or.* 25.
[16] *Mos.* 2. 234–5: '... absolute being is true life. If, therefore, the life producing nature surpasses knowledge, that which is apprehended is in no way life.'
[17] e.g. *Eunom.* 2. 106.

existence 'within' a simple divine Godhead conditions Gregory's vision of the Word as mediator.

3. Nyssa's account of what it means to be taken up into the divine life revolves around an account of the purified soul reflecting the Word in whose image it is made and exhibiting its own mysterious 'union' with the divine life present in it. Once again, this emphasis is shaped by Gregory's insistence on the distinction between Creator and creation. This account of the soul has consequences for how Nyssa understands Christian identity: at the same time as Nyssa focuses on individual transformation, he also insists that there is a true unity in the body of Christ. True human identity is now to be found within a greater unity and life and outside the realm of our experience as 'individuals'. The mysteriousness of human and Christian identity serves as a constant reminder of the divine mystery.

4. Insistence on the mysterious, incomprehensible nature of God shapes a particular set of intellectual and contemplative practices. We see this here, for example, in the way that Gregory calls us to avoid the language of degree, but allows us the language of different 'modes' of divine presence. In the next chapter we will see further ways in which the discourse of mystery is shaped.

Augustine on transformation in Christ

To show the widespread nature of these four themes among pro-Nicenes I want now to turn to Augustine. From late in the 390s Augustine speaks of the Word's union with humanity in the person of Christ as the means of our salvation. Around 396 or 397 we find him writing:

> Just as he ascended, you see, and still didn't depart from us, so we too are now there with him . . . if he has attached us to himself as his members in such a way that even with us joined on he is his very same self (*ut etiam nobis coniunctis idem ipse sit*, . . . we too are going to ascend, not by our own virtue, but by our and his oneness (*sed nostra et illius unitate*).[18]

Augustine comes more and more clearly to focus on the way in

---

[18] *Serm.* 263. 2–3. This text is quoted and the Christological determination of Augustine's account of Christian existence discussed in my 'The Christological Context of *De Trinitate* XIII: Towards Relocating Books VIII–XV', *Augustinian Studies*, 29 (1998), 111–39. For a later presentation see *Ep. Io. tr.* 1. 2: 'But how could he who made the sun be seen in the sun except that "he has pitched his tent in the sun and he, as a bridegroom coming out of his bridal chamber, has rejoiced as a giant to run the course" . . . the true Creator . . . in order that he might be seen by carnal eyes that see the sun . . . showed his flesh in the manifestation of this natural daytime light. And the bridal chamber of that bridegroom was the womb of a virgin, for two have been conjoined in that virginal womb . . . he has made himself the bridegroom and the bride, because not two, but one flesh—for "the Word was made flesh and dwelt among us". To that flesh the Church is joined, and there comes to be the whole Christ, head and body.'

which the mysterious unity of the two natures in Christ's person functions as the means of our redemption.

Augustine's account of the unity of the body of Christ has what we might term a dramatic dimension. The head has gone before, the life of the 'limbs' is hidden in Christ. Augustine frequently dwells on the tensions of this situation, balancing strong statements of Christ's presence with equally strong assertions of our current failure to see the true nature of Christian existence:

> Now, what does he, ascending from us, yet all the while not withdrawing from us, leave with us except himself? For he is our peace, who has made both one. Therefore he himself is peace for us both when we believe that he is and when we shall see him as he is. For, as long as we are in the corruptible body, which weighs down the soul, when we walk by faith, not by sight, he does not abandon those journeying apart from him, how much more, when we have come to the sight itself, will he fill us with himself?[19]

Using a very different terminology from Nyssa, Augustine sees the ultimate vision of God at the end of this journey as a 'seeing' of God with the eyes 'of the heart' as well as (possibly) with the physical eyes, a 'seeing' of God in all, filling all and as the end of all desire.[20]

Augustine's mature texts demonstrate close attention to the complex nature of identity in the body of Christ.[21] I want to draw attention to two passages from the seventh of his homilies on 1 John. In the first Augustine explains the basis for his startling assumption that the epistle's 'God is love' entails 'love is God':

> How then . . . 'love is of God,' and now 'love is God'? The Son is God of God; the Holy Spirit is God of God. And these three are one God not three Gods. For God is Father and Son and Holy Spirit . . . If the Son is God and the Holy Spirit is God and he in whom the Holy Spirit dwells loves, therefore love is God, but God because [it is] of God. For you have both in the epistle, both 'love is of God' and 'love is God'.[22]

In other words, because love is said to be 'of God', in the same way that Son and Spirit are 'of God', and because love comes from the Spirit's presence (one of Augustine's favourite texts, Rom. 5: 5 clearly speaks of true love coming into the soul from outside), love itself is God.

Augustine then turns to the phenomenology of Christian life:

> 'God is love.' What sort of face does love have? What sort of form does it have? No one can say. Nonetheless it does have feet, for they lead to the

---

[19] *Io. ev. tr.* 77. 3.   [20] *Civ.* 22. 29–30.
[21] For what follows see my 'Augustine, Christology and God as Love: An Introduction to the Homilies on 1 John', in Kevin Vanhoozer (ed.), *Nothing Greater, Nothing Better: Theological Essays on the Love of God* (Grand Rapids, Mich.: Eerdmans, 2001), 67–93.
[22] *Ep. Io. tr.* 7. 6.

Church. It does have hands, for they are stretched out to the poor man . . . It does have ears, about which the Lord says, 'he who has ears to hear, let him hear.' They are not members separated by places, but by means of the understanding he who has love sees the whole at one time. Dwell and you will be a dwelling, abide and you will be an abode.[23]

In the loving action of Christians God can be 'seen' if our faith truly guides our thinking.[24] This renewal in Christ is a renewal of the image of God within us. In his early *On the Greatness of the Soul* he insists the renovation of the soul 'cannot take place at all, unless we are remade in the image of Him who gave us that image to keep as a most precious treasure'.[25] Fifteen to twenty years later Augustine comments on the importance of following Christ in his *On the Trinity*: 'through the example of him who is the image let us not depart from God, since we too are the image of God'.[26]

Returning to the passage from the seventh homily on 1 John quoted above, on pro-Nicene grounds Augustine establishes that salvation comes through the uniting of Christians to Christ's person, and that the love that is God is truly present in the Christian community revealing the Triune God. He then draws his audience to recognize a paradox. We do not see that which constitutes our identity as Christian. Faith teaches that God is revealed to the body of Christ, and that in that one body the head infuses the members with the presence of God; as yet we fail to see that we are one person in Christ. Augustine articulates this paradox to indicate the necessity of a form of life that will enable us to reinterpret what seems to appear before our eyes:

For even that man to whom it was said 'Because you have seen, you have believed,' did not believe the thing that he saw, rather, he saw one thing, but believed another; for he saw the man, he believed the God . . . But even though things that are seen are said to be believed, as each one says that he has believed his own eyes, nevertheless this is not the faith that is built up in us. But from those things that are seen we are brought to a point that those things that are not seen are believed.[27]

Our identity is transformed through life in the body of Christ: it is there that we learn our mysteriousness to ourselves and the true complexities of learning to see the *imago Dei* necessarily present but hidden within us.[28] In his homilies on 1 John, Augustine points to the transformed (or being-transformed) soul as the 'abode' of the divine presence. We see here another strong parallel with Nyssa, but

---

[23] *Ep. Io. tr.* 7. 10.

[24] Most notably in *Trin.* 8. 7. 11, a passage discussed in the next chapter.

[25] *Quant.* 28. 55   [26] *Trin.* 7. 3. 5.   [27] *Io. ev. tr.* 79. 1.

[28] Cf. *Trin.* 10. 8. 11–9. 12 and discussion of this passage in my 'Memory, Intelligence and Will'.

it is one that needs careful consideration. There has been occasional discussion in scholarly literature about the possible place of 'deification' in Augustine's work.²⁹ I do not wish to enter the scholarly discussion over the terminology of 'deification' here, merely to insist that in overlapping and yet distinct language we find in Augustine and Gregory of Nyssa important formal similarities driven by common pro-Nicene concerns: Augustine exhibits all four of the themes I identified in Gregory:

1. As in Gregory the drama of redemption is the story of incorporation into Christ's person.

2. As in Gregory, the pro-Nicene account of the distinction between God and world is fundamental. It is the Word's status as coeternal 'within' the simple Godhead that enables the Word to act as the focus of salvation, and it is the coequal divinity of the three persons that shapes Augustine's account of the paradoxical structure of the body of Christ infused with the love of God.

3. For Augustine, what it means to be taken up into the divine life revolves around his account of the purified soul, which must both reflect the one in whose image it is made and exhibit its own mysterious 'union' with the divine life present in it. A complex discussion of Christian identity begins to emerge from this discussion at both the level of the soul's own mysteriousness to itself and at the level of the individual's place within the body of Christ. The mysteriousness of our identity, shaped in the light of pro-Nicene principles in turn helps to nurture our attention to the mysteriousness of the Triune God.

4. Augustine also shapes modes of thinking and speech that will focus Christian awareness of how the mysterious presence of the coeternal Word shapes Christian practice and identity. Once again, this Christian discourse of mystery will be taken up in the next chapter.

---

[29] V. Capánaga, 'La Deificatión en la soteriología augustiniana', in *Augustinus Magister: Congrès International Augustinien, Paris 21–24 septembre 1954* (Paris: Études Augustiniennes, 1954), ii. 745–54; P. Wilson-Kastner, 'Grace and Participation in the Divine Life in the Theology of Augustine of Hippo', *Augustinian Studies*, 7 (1976), 135–57; G. Bonner, 'Augustine's Conception of Deification', *JThS* NS 37 (1986), 369–86; J. Oroz Reta, 'De l'illumination à la déification de l'âme selon Saint Augustin', *SP* 27 (1993), 364–82. The main problem with this literature is that while it emphasizes a theme that is certainly present in Augustine, it has not yet sufficiently explored the variety of ways in which Augustine talks of Christ's presence. At times, especially perhaps in the *Ennarationes in Psalmos*, Augustine can speak as if adopting a theory of the imputation of grace. Even here, however, he still understands Christ to be the effective agent in salvation and still uses an account of our existence in Christ's person to destabilize the seeming certainties of identity. See T. J. Van Bavel, *Recherches sur la christologie de Saint Augustin*, Paradosis 19 (Fribourg: Éditions Universitaires, 1954), 74 ff.; M. Fiedrowicz, *Psalmus vox totius Christi: Studien zu Augustins Ennarationes in Psalmos* (Freiburg: Herder, 1997).

Gregory and Augustine, in their concern to attend carefully to the distinction between Creator and creation, throw into relief constant pressures on pro-Nicene soteriology. These pressures are present even in those pro-Nicenes who make make more overt use of the terminologies of *theosis* and participation in God, as are many of the strategies that we find so fully developed in the two authors considered here.

Pro-Nicene reflection on salvation in Christ is of importance for the practice of Trinitarian theology in two ways. First, and most generally, it is here that we see the basic structuring principles of the process of purification that pro-Nicenes think constitutes Christian life. The action of the immediately present consubstantial Word drawing Christians towards God in union with him provides their point of departure. In particular, and second, I have noted here how this strategy begins to point towards the importance of rethinking one's identity within the body of Christ. A destabilization of the certainties of identity calls forth new attention to how the language of faith may enable exploration of this now contested site.[30] Having begun to examine pro-Nicene understandings of Christian existence I want now to turn to the Christological character of pro-Nicene ontological reflection. This investigation will help to flesh out hints given in the past few pages about pro-Nicene imagining of a world created and redeemed 'in' Christ.

EXISTENCE IN THE WORD

In this section of the chapter I will argue that we should avoid thinking of pro-Nicenes as constructing 'Christian ontologies'—ontological systems grounded in a particular philosophy or philosophical proposal. Rather, we should focus on exploring the ways in which pro-Nicenes adapt and negotiate a number of theological and philosophical traditions in their reflection on the created order. In such adaptation pro-Nicenes pursue common strategies, even while their conceptions of creation may differ in some significant respects. An account of the Word as the consubstantial expression of the divine perfection is at the heart of these shared strategies

A number of modern writers have suggested that with the emergence of pro-Nicene theology, or in one or other individual pro-Nicene figures, we see the emergence of a new 'Christian' ontology.

---

[30] It is not, of course, that earlier generations of Christians had not also sought to problematize the seeming certainties of identity through a notion of participation in Christ: one has only to look at texts such as Ignatius' letters or Cyprian's *On the Lord's Prayer* to see that this is so. The difference lies in the thoroughgoingness with which pro-Nicenes relate that destabilizing of identity to the immediate action of the consubstantial word.

There are two prominent proposals. The first points to Gregory of Nyssa's account of infinity and the distinction between God and world, and is found clearly in Ekkehard Mühlenberg.[31] The second, associated particularly with John Zizioulas, argues that in Basil's theology for the first time all things originate from a 'person',[32] and 'person' is now the fullest expression of existence. Zizioulas's proposal quickly falls apart in the face of the evidence. While it is true to say that Basil sees the person of the Father as the source of all, insistence on the incomprehensibility of what it means for the Father to be a 'person' means that this statement entails only that the universe is the product of a willed agency. Jews and Christians prior to the fourth century would have happily agreed. Similarly, the fact that the world is the product of a 'person' does not entail that 'being' is necessarily 'personal'. Basil and Gregory of Nyssa develop accounts of creation in which the basic units are indivisible natures constituted by intrinsic powers, without any sense that these are 'personal realities'. We do not find, then, the Cappadocians attempting to construct a Christian ontology based on the primary reality of the person over against non-Christian ontologies.

Mühlenberg's thesis offers much more substantial content. Indeed, some of his key arguments parallel those of Chapter 11. Nevertheless, Mühlenberg both fails to explore ways in which previous traditions had created the conditions for Gregory's presentation and he fails to note the ways in which Gregory's argument is part of a much wider pro-Nicene emphasis on the distinction between God and world.[33] We must, I suggest, move away from looking at individual pro-Nicenes as potential sources for hermetically sealed ontological systems, and look instead at their fundamental orientations towards ontological questions and at the strategies used to negotiate complex inherited traditions. I would like to suggest that there are two particularly important strategies that pro-Nicenes pursue. The

---

[31] Ekkehard Mühlenberg, *Die Unendlichkeit Gottes bei Gregor von Nyssa* (Göttingen: Vandenhoeck & Ruprecht, 1966). A similar account is found in von Balthasar's account of *diastema*: Hans Urs von Balthasar, *Presence and Thought: An Essay on the Religious Philosophy of Gregory of Nyssa*, tr. Mark Sebanc (San Francisco: Ignatius Press, 1995).

[32] A key example of his argument is to be found at Zizioulas, *Being as Communion* (Crestwood, NY: SVS Press, 1985), 87–8: 'Now, however, [with the Cappadocians] the term *hypostasis* was disassociated from that of *ousia* and became identified with that of *prosopon*. But this latter term is *relational*, and was so when adopted in trinitarian theology. This meant that from now on a relational term entered into ontology and, conversely, that an ontological category such as *hypostasis* entered the relational categories of existence. To be and to be in relation.' As problematic as Zizioulas's ontological reasoning is his use of 'person' in Trinitarian contexts: see Turcescu, ' "Person" versus "Individual" '.

[33] Mühlenberg uses his account of the difference between Creator and creation to deny the possibility of any doctrine of *theosis* in Gregory. In my account it is precisely this distinction that renders possible that doctrine. See above and my '*Theosis* and the Dynamics of Nicene Theology'.

first interweaves understandings of the created order's structure with questions of Trinitarian and soteriological doctrine. The second is an increasing attention to the semiotics of the created order, attention to the ways in which the created order leads human minds to contemplation of the Creator. As examples I will consider aspects of two commentaries on the Genesis narrative of creation, one by Basil, the other by Augustine.

Basil on the created order

Basil's nine Hexameron homilies[34]—delivered probably in 378— engage a variety of classical traditions that speak of the structure of the universe and the means of its creation. Throughout Basil expands and explores the narrative of Genesis with a variety of ancient theoretical reflections and science, and yet is always attentive to points at which that material needs itself to be adapted to 'the way the words [of Scripture] run'.[35] In this complex negotiation we see Basil not so much constructing a 'Christian ontology' as shaping strategies that will give a pro-Nicene cast to his ontological reflection.[36]

The most obvious of these strategies is to present the created order as the product of a Trinitarian God whose power is infinite. Basil emphasizes the power of God by utilizing a pro-Nicene account of the Word's unity with God. Because we conceive of the eternally present Word as 'the divine will and the first impetus of divine intelligence', he argues, we see that God's creative act involves no thinking or speaking, no need to express the desire to create. Thus, when we read in Genesis of God 'speaking' at the creation we should take the words as a sign of the triune God's activity, of the joint working of Father and Son.[37] Understanding that this reality is only hinted at by a text in human words draws us to recognize the distinction between God's activity and ours: 'everywhere the dogmas of theology have been mystically (μυστικῶς) sown into the narrative ἱστορία)'.[38] Μυστικῶς here indicates that Basil sees the text of Genesis as intended to stimulate and guide reflection on the character of the divine action and power.

---

[34] For an interesting read of these homilies from a different angle see Rousseau, *Basil of Caesarea*, 318–49. There is also a very useful introduction by Stanislas Giet in SC 26 bis. Here I have quoted only from homilies 1–9, although I agree with van Esbroeck in SC 160 that 10 and 11 are probably also genuine.

[35] For this term see the discussion of 4th-cent. exegesis in Ch. 1.

[36] Of course, one could take the path of simply reconstruing what a 'Christian ontology' is and then Basil might well be an excellent example of the phenomenon. My concern is that he is not an example of the sort of thing modern writers such as Zizioulas and Mühlenberg have in mind.

[37] *Hex.* 3. 2.   [38] *Hex.* 6. 2.

'The First and Brightest Light'   315

These pro-Nicene emphases heighten a presentation of the power of God in creating that long pre-dates the emergence of pro-Nicene theology. In the first homily Basil argues that the phrase 'God created heaven and earth' deploys a construction in which an agent engages in a specific activity to emphasize that the power of God exceeds this one activity:

> In the same way that the potter, after having made with equal pains a great number of vessels, has not exhausted either his art or his talent, so the maker of the universe, whose creative power, far from being bounded by one world, could extend to the infinite, needed only the impulse of his will to bring the immensities of the visible world into being . . . 'In the beginning God created'—it is he, beneficent nature, goodness without measure, a worthy object of love for all beings endowed with reason . . . it is he who 'in the beginning created heaven and earth'.[39]

In true pro-Nicene fashion it is the infinite and transcendent quality of the divine power that is the focus of Basil's interest in the activity of creating. When Basil offers his account of the created order itself we find that its most basic structure consists of a series of unchangeable natures decreed in the act of creation, each possessing its own intrinsic power that gives rise to the distinctive activities we experience.[40] Although we cannot trace the same argument clearly in Basil, it is noticeable that Gregory of Nyssa sees the unitary and unchangeable natures of creation as intentionally reflecting God's own unitary nature.[41]

Throughout his exposition Basil is concerned to shape a mode of attention to the created order: we may come to see the diverse activities of created natures reflecting the initial and ongoing harmonious action of the Word in all things and thus grow in appreciation of the providential and immediate action of the Triune God,[42] while, from the human point of view, we may speak of shaping patterns of attention: but as will be clear by now these patterns correspond in cosmological terms to an account of creation's semiotic structure. The same theme is seen in Basil's discussion of the potential figural function of created realities. Basil offers a number of statements about the teleological and signifying nature of creation. For example, 'the world is a work of art displayed for the beholding of all people, to

---

[39] *Hex.* 1. 2.   [40] *Hex.* 6. 3; 9. 2.   [41] See Ch. 13, pp. 350–1.

[42] *Hex.* 9. 2 The same theme may be seen in Basil's account at *Hex.* 1.8, where he argues that we never encounter a nature free from qualities: if we remove all qualities we find literally nothing. Basil uses this observation as the point of departure for outlining the virtues of placing 'limits' on investigation that will enable appropriate cultivation of and attention to faith in the infinite power of the Creator. The context for Basil's opinion, and a detailed account of Gregory of Nyssa's clear divergence from it is to be found in Richard Sorabji, *Matter, Space and Motion. Theories in Antiquity and their Sequel* (London: Duckworth, 1988), ch. 4.

make them know him who created it'.[43] In the fifth homily Basil argues that we should read each aspect of creation as a figure of God's intentions for humanity and his redemptive activity. Thus 'the sight of a vine, when observed by an intelligent eye, serves to remind you of your nature'. Basil next argues that we should not only remember John 15's image of the Son as the vine on whom Christians are the fruit: we should also call to mind Isaiah 5: 1 and Matthew 21: 33's account of the Lord's chosen as themselves vines in a vineyard.[44] Just prior to this discussion Basil similarly meditates on the relationship between the growth of seeds in a field and the sower parable of Matthew 4.[45]

In the ninth homily Basil focuses on the ordered manner in which natural kinds reproduce themselves. The order we observe is as a sign of the care of God and of the Word's structuring role in reproduction. We see that, once set in motion, creation constantly obeys the Creator. We see how individual animals display an innate sense of self-care and preservation demonstrating the care with which God created all. One aspect of such innate self-preservation is attention to future needs, something we see clearly in the way ants focus on communal construction for their common future good.[46] In all these things the Creator infuses impulses that make up for animals' deficiency in reason: we, on the other hand, possess by nature the reason and the virtues that should enable us to live in conformity with nature—a phrase synonymous with being in conformity with the will and care of the Creator.[47] It might seem as if Basil is here just offering a Christianized Stoic natural theology in which the phenomenon of οἰκείωσις (natural affiliation and appreciation[48]) should point us to the need for our own purification and self-preservation. But at the end of his account Basil states that the beasts offer a proof (ἀπόδειξις) of the faith (πίστις). Basil here seems to mean quite precisely that the self-preservative instincts of beasts without reason should demonstrate to one with faith that God gives to creatures the power to attain their appointed goals. When we view the creation with the eyes of faith we see the 'unapproachable wisdom' of God calling us to the particular destiny that we now so easily ignore or deny. Basil's final move is to argue that contemplation of ourselves is the necessary culmination of contemplation of creation and the surest aid to contemplation of the divine.[49]

Basil brings to bear a variety of philosophical and scientific theories from his day to tease out the text of Genesis. At all times,

---

[43] *Hex.* 1. 7. [44] *Hex.* 5. 6. [45] *Hex.* 5. 5.
[46] *Hex.* 9. 2–3. [47] *Hex.* 9. 4.
[48] For an introduction to the complex phenomenon of οἰκείωσις see *CHHP* 677 ff.
[49] *Hex.* 9. 6.

however, he does so with fundamental pro-Nicene principles in mind. I suggest we can identify two broad arguments that mark the text as pro-Nicene:

1. First, there is a strong emphasis on presenting the creation as revelatory of the Triune God's infinite power. Meditation on the Son's existence as the coeternal Word of the Father, as the eternal expression of the Father, serves as a key pointer to the character of God's infinite power and to the immediate character of God's action in creating.

2. This first emphasis intrinsically involves attention to the semiotics of the created order. The figural nature of creation points us always to a God beyond comprehension who is to be approached by a process of purification and reflection on the mysterious nature of the human soul. Basil's theological epistemology is further conditioned by his undercutting of the knowledge that we think we have of things themselves. Things in the world are both mysterious in their natures and only truly approached when seen as reflecting the God who ordered them and is mysteriously present in them. Basil's account of the created order serves to destabilize seeming epistemological certainties in order to reshape attention to what is in the light of the mysterious triune power. These themes will receive further expansion at the third 'intersection'.

Augustine on the created order

The Hexameron tradition is one found in Greek and Latin Christianity. Basil's homilies were translated into Latin within a very few years and used by Ambrose in his own longer work on the same subject in 386. Further examples of the genre are available in a variety of early Christian languages.[50] Augustine's own corpus offers four different discussions of the early books of Genesis, the most extensive being his *On the Literal Interpretation of Genesis*, begun in 401. This text draws on Ambrose and, it has been convincingly argued, on a translation of Basil's own text. Augustine's *Literal Interpretation* is, however, a much longer text than Basil's and engages in a wider range of speculation.

I will focus here on demonstrating Augustine's pursuit of the same fundamental themes we saw in Basil, beginning with Augustine's use of a pro-Nicene Trinitarianism to shape an account of the relationship between world and God. That Genesis presents God 'speaking' or 'commanding' is not to be understood as the Father ordering the Son, nor does it indicate a temporal sequence in God's

---

[50] See M. Alexandre, *Le Commencement du livre Genèse I–V: La Version grecque de la Septante et sa réception* (Paris: Beauchesne, 1988).

conceiving of and creating the world.[51] Rather, in the first case, the Word's giving of life in the act of creating makes sense only when we understand that the Son possesses life from the Father and in union with the Father.[52] In the second case, the Father's 'speaking' of his coeternal Word demonstrates the existence of the 'eternal reason' of each thing in the Word. God's Word, as the expression of God's nature, is already the expression of all the possible creatures and their kinds. The act of creation is a transforming of this potential into actual being by the Word. The Word 'rules and holds' all in existence and in a special sense is the 'Life and Light' of human beings. Within the unified action of God here the Spirit is also spoken of as enabling all things to continue in existence.[53]

Thus, Augustine's understanding of the Word as existing coeternally with God, as the Father's Word, provides the basis for an account of the immediacy of God's role in creation. The collapsing of any hierarchy beyond the created order serves to demonstrate the intimacy of the creation's relation to God. Augustine makes this latter point particularly clear in book 5:

Although the divine being is beyond words and cannot be spoken of in any way with human language without recourse to expressions of time and space, nevertheless He who made us is nearer to us than many things which have been made. For in Him we live and move and have our being.[54]

Augustine does not focus here on the infinite nature of the divine power as Basil did, but his sense of the Creator as omnipotent source of all is directly congruent with Basil's. While some modern readers have presented Augustine's account of creation as 'Neoplatonic', comparison with Basil shows how misleading such a simple attribution can be. Both authors make use of material from a variety of philosophical traditions and accept many Platonic and Stoic dynamics. But, at the same time, a complex process of adaptation is taking place to serve common pro-Nicene ends.

Staying with book 5 of the *Literal Interpretation*, we may note a second parallel with Basil. In both cases we can trace a similar attention to the semiotics of the created order. Although Augustine does spend some time discussing how the actions of non-humans serve as calls to us to live out human virtues—and here he may be directly dependent on Basil[55]—he spends much more space exploring how the unfolding of created types and the overall harmony of the created order, if properly contemplated, demonstrates the care and providence of God. This is not surprising given the importance Augustine places on the existence of 'seminal reasons' in all things

---

[51] *Gn. litt.* 2. 6.   [52] *Gn. litt.* 2. 6. 12.   [53] *Gn. litt.* 2. 6. 14.
[54] *Gn. litt.* 5. 16. 34.   [55] *Gn. litt.* 5. 15. 24–16. 25.

and on the structuring function of number. In book 5, Augustine takes the example of seeds growing into plants to emphasize that creation is an ongoing process in which God constantly enables things to unfold along paths whose origins are an intrinsic part of their natures.[56] At a number of points in this text Augustine argues that when we seek the true end of human life we actually seek our appropriate place in God's order *and* that creation itself is a conversion towards God given by and in the Word.[57]

One of Augustine's concerns through the first books of the work is to shape a circular process of reflection in which our interpretation of the nature and creation of the cosmos is guided by the principles of pro-Nicene Trinitarianism and in which, in turn, we learn to see the cosmos reflecting the glory of that Triune Godhead. For example, in book 2 Augustine argues that the character of God's creating in the Word depends on our understanding the principle of inseparable operation:

> But we may further ask whether we must suppose, from the words of Scripture 'And God said, "Let there be a firmament" ', that the Father has, as it were, given an order to the Son . . . By what words would the Father order the Son to perform a work, since the Son is the original Word of the Father by which all things have been made? Perhaps we should say that by the words of Scripture . . . is indicated the utterance which is the Word of the Father, the only-begotten Son, in whom all created things have their being even before their creation. Whatever is in Him is life. For whatever had been made by Him is life in Him. This is the life, to be sure that creates, whereas the creature is dependent upon Him.[58]

Recognizing that the Son is not ordered to create leads Augustine to offer an account of the dependence of all things on the Word as coeternal with the Father, as possessing life itself and as the foundation for an ordered creation reflecting the eternal 'speech' of God. Augustine thus seeks to develop what in Basil we would term a θεωρία, in which we realize ever more deeply how the creation is immediately 'in' God even though God escapes our comprehension. We see one of the most striking feature of this θεωρία—one to which we shall return in the next chapter—when Augustine argues that the working of God should be more easily seen than the natures of things themselves. A pro-Nicene account of existence in the Word

---

[56] e.g. *Gn. litt.* 5. 23. 44–6.
[57] e.g. *Gn. litt.* 1. 4. 9–5. 10. On this important theme see Marie-Anne Vannier, *'Creatio', 'conversio', 'formatio', chez S. Augustin* (Fribourg: Éditions Universitaires, 1991). Rowan D. Williams, ' "Good for Nothing"? Augustine on Creation', *Augustinian Studies*, 25 (1994), 9–24.
[58] *Gn. litt.* 2. 6. 12.

leads to the need for us to rethink our most basic interpretations of sense data.[59]

Moving briefly beyond his *Literal Interpretation* Augustine also frequently treats the ordering of creation as enabling us to describe the creation as itself a poem or beautifully ordered speech, revealing to us that all things are ordered providentially.[60] Similarly, in an exegesis that seems to be a particular development of his own, Augustine sees all things as ordered according to measure, number, and weight following Wisdom 11: 21. Augustine uses this exegesis to argue that things possess stability of being only because of their ordering 'in' the Word.[61] Augustine, like Basil, appropriates a variety of Christian and non-Christian accounts of creation as part of the process of working both from and towards pro-Nicene principles, but through these two different accounts we find some important common pro-Nicene strategies. I have suggested two:

1. A common use of pro-Nicene Trinitarian principles to articulate an account of God's immediate presence to, care for, and yet distinction from the created order. The foundation of this emphasis lies in pro-Nicene development of the theology of the Word, now understood as a coequal person 'in' the simple Godhead.

2. A common conviction that the creation is intended to draw the human soul towards God, and that, hence, it has an intentional semiotic structure. In both authors, the immediacy of God's presence to and governance of the creation serves to shape the character of the creation's semiotic structure so that it constantly points not simply 'above' or 'beyond' itself but to a mysterious presence 'within' and sustaining all that is. Both Basil and Augustine attempt to undercut our seeming epistemological certainty in the world in order to shape a new attention to things as they exist in God. As we shall see in the next chapter we see here one of the ways in which pro-Nicene theology shapes a theological epistemology and understanding of Christian existence around and orientated towards contemplation of the pro-Nicene Godhead.

In this discussion of pro-Nicene 'ontologies' I have suggested two common pro-Nicene themes on the basis of a comparison of only two texts. Not only will this suggestion need filling out from a considerable range of authors if it is to stand, it will also need filling out

---

[59] *Gn. litt..* 5. 16. 34.

[60] For some texts see Carol Harrison, *Beauty and Revelation in the Thought of Saint Augustine* (Oxford: Clarendon Press, 1992), 116–22.

[61] e.g. *Gn. litt.* 4. 3. 7. See also my 'measure, number and weight', in A. Fitzgerald (ed.), *Augustine: An Encyclopedia* (Grand Rapids, Mich.: Eerdmans, 1999), 550–2 with further bibliography.

'The First and Brightest Light' 321

via a complex study of how ontological presuppositions such as these appear in a variety of genres and styles of writing.[62] Nevertheless, this comparison between Basil and Augustine begins to reveal some of the ways in which the emergence of pro-Nicene Trinitarian theologies also involved the emergence of particular accounts of the cosmos itself. In these accounts the very textuality of the cosmos is reconceived in the light of pro-Nicene accounts both of the Creator/creation distinction and of the consubstantial Word. Comprehension of the cosmos as text is deferred and the task of reading is interwoven with appreciation of the dynamics of pro-Nicene faith. It is the Word's status as both image and expression within the consubstantial Trinity that grounds and forms these developments: a 'Logos theology' transformed but not abandoned. What we have seen here also adds further density to the dynamics discussed in the first half of the chapter: this account of the world existing in the Word and the consequent consideration of the semiotic function of the created order shape a wider and wider context for the destabilization of seeming epistemological certainties and the necessity of re-conceiving existence in the light of the language of faith—a movement that is the context for the next chapter's consideration of pro-Nicene strategies regarding the soul's purification and the reading of Scripture.

INTERLUDE 1: 'PARTICIPATION' IN PRO-NICENE THEOLOGY

During the preceding section of the chapter a number of readers will have expected statements about the 'participation' of the creation in the Creator (or in the Creator's perfections).[63] There has been a great revival of interest in this theme in recent years, especially among those who see 'classical' Christian thought as possessing an ontology of participation over against various modern ontologies. I have already indicated two of the most important points that can be made with respect to pro-Nicene understanding of 'participation'. First, for pro-Nicenes, it is the mysteriousness and incomprehensibility of such participation that is of paramount importance. Commitment to such mysteriousness follows from an account of the Trinity's immediate presence in creation and shapes a

---

[62] It is beyond the scope of this book to offer an extensive discussion of the ways in which pro-Nicene Christological developments—and the rather underdetermined nature of pro-Nicene Christology—create the dynamics of the Christological controversies in the decades that follow.

[63] I say 'participation' because the term must stand as a cipher for a wide range of terminology in Greek and Latin. In recent theology I think especially of the work of John Milbank. His recent work is concerned particularly with the human making as participation in God. I return briefly to Milbank's work in Ch. 16.

complex vision of theological discourse attentive to its anagogic function and the necessity of destabilizing our epistemic, 'certainties'. Second, much scholarly work needs to be undertaken on the ways in which pro-Nicenes adapt existing themes in the construction of their cosmologies and ontologies. The scholarship does not yet exist that would provide materials for a summary history of how theologians from distinct trajectories used, appropriated, and deployed different notions of participation.

In addition to making these two points I want to suggest categories for further work in this area. In very general terms we can say that pro-Nicene theologies developed two broad 'grammars of participation'. In each case pro-Nicenes agree that the mode of participation under discussion is beyond full human comprehension. In both cases pro-Nicenes also shape discourses that combine high degrees of austerity about these modes of participation with an account of the ways in which attention to scriptural/Christian language and narratives is fundamental for our going on speaking about them. The first grammar governs discussion of the relationship between the divine persons. Here we must immediately be very cautious about the terminology of 'participation'. While many at the beginning of the fourth century would have spoken of the Son participating in the Father, in pro-Nicene theology such accounts are drastically curtailed. Son and Spirit can no longer be said to possess their attributes by sharing in the Father's attributes: generation and 'spiration' result in divine persons who have the fullness of the Godhead in themselves. Any terminology of participation that indicates possession of an attribute by dependence on that attribute's true source is ruled out.

The second grammar concerns the relationship between God and the creation. Here participation language continues to be used, but receives a particular pro-Nicene cast. Pro-Nicenes show a heightened sensitivity to the ways in which the created order mirrors the divine incomprehensibility and the extent to which it may serve as a training ground for our apprehension of the divine. The creation shares in and imitates divine qualities and modes of existence in a variety of ways consequent on its ordered division. The governing, rational soul of humanity occupies a special place in imitating the divine nature: but it is essential to note how, for pro-Nicenes, the mysteriousness of the soul is itself *part of* its imitation of the divine nature. At all levels the creation contains in itself a relation to the Creator that constitutes the core of its mysteriousness. Insofar as the creation functions as a semiotic structure pointing to the Creator it should inculcate a sense of our failure to comprehend the Creator's nature. The creation's existence 'in' the Word is governed by an awareness of the Word's place as a coequal member of the Triune and yet simple God, distinct from the world but intimately present to and in it. The character of the Logos's presence cannot be conceived on the basis of any created analogy, nor can the character of the Logos's 'possession' in perfect form of any of those goods we know in the world. In the light of all else in this chapter and the last we can push further. Pro-Nicene accounts of the participation of the creation in the Triune Creator need to be investigated not purely by consideration of particular terminology used, but also by seeing how that terminology is governed by patterns of argument that shape our understanding of its texture: where and how must we, for pro-Nicenes, display reserve, where and how may we go on speaking? We thus need to focus attention on the habits of discourse that pro-Nicenes see as sustaining appropriate attention to the paradoxes of participation. Although my concern is not with participation per se, Chapters 11–13 reveal some of the most basic common habits important here.

I want to end this interlude by suggesting that one other aspect of David Burrell's discussion of analogy can help in more detailed exploration of this theme. In an essay published in a *Festschrift* for Ralph McInerny, Burrell reiterates a frequently overlooked aspect of his earlier work: for Aquinas the language of 'participating' in God (or God's perfections) is a corollary of a theology of creation in which God is truly distinct. Burrell's argument may be glimpsed in two quotations: first:

> The role of participation, then, is to remind us that there could be no such set of [analogical] terms were the universe itself not derived from a source from which all that is, and notably what is perfect about what-is, flows. So the ontological ground of the set of terms lies in the fact that all-that-is participates in the One from whom everything derives, and their proper use demands that we bring this grounding fact to awareness. Yet we can only assert it, knowing as little as we do how to express this all-important 'distinction' and the consequent relations obtaining between creator and creatures.

> Christian analogical language does not override the distinction between God and world, because it is set in the context of a notion of creation which asserts that all 'flows' from God *and* that God is distinct from the creation. Speech about the creation must thus govern our analogical discourse if it is to remain aware of its true nature.[64]

---

[64] Burrell, 'From Analogy of "Being" to the Analogy of Being', 258. Later on the same page we find: 'if we fail to advert to creation, understood precisely as participation, then [we will assume] that there can be no properly analogical predication unless there be a common feature ... predicable of both God and Socrates. But the presence of such a common feature would effectively deny "the distinction" of creator from creature.' I am grateful to Sarah Coakley for drawing my attention to this essay.

The second quotation is from the next page:

> a properly analogous use of analogous terms demands an awareness that we are functioning as creatures ourselves in a created *order* whose principles remain unknown to us, yet whose lineaments can be glimpsed from time to time. Creatures can be just in their fashion, and hence properly be said to be so: the term 'just' can be predicated of them inherently, without there being a proportional similarity between God's justice and theirs. For as the cause of being, the creator is not an extrinsic cause of creatures, since their very to-be is to-be-in relation to the creator.[65]

The first sentence repeats one of the key themes of the first quotation: the context for appropriate analogical predication is awareness of a created order whose principles lie in God. But then Burrell introduces a further theme. Because God is understood as not extrinsic to things—the distinction between God and world not placing God as a peculiarly distant 'thing'—we use analogical predication here analogically. The order of the world calls us to speak of justice in people as found perfectly in God, but we cannot speak of a proportional similarity between human justice and its perfection. Burrell's argument not only amplifies his other accounts of how divine simplicity functions to govern speech about God, it also shows how such a conception of speech about God is interwoven with a particular account of creation as participation. Not only can this argument further help us to see how pro-Nicene accounts of creation are essential to their Trinitarian theologies but it also provides a model for the further investigation of pro-Nicene cosmology.

[65] Burrell, 'From Analogy of "Being" to the Analogy of Being', 259.

13
'Walk Towards Him Shining'[1]

STRATEGY III: ANTHROPOLOGY, EPISTEMOLOGY, AND THE READING OF SCRIPTURE

The material considered in the last chapter sets the stage of existence as a Christian for pro-Nicenes. Pro-Nicenes wish Christians to see themselves embedded within a cosmos that is also a semiotic system that reveals the omnipresent creating consubstantial Word. In our state of ignorance one of the tasks of the Christian life is the relearning of the language of creation in the Word: this relearning is itself part of the reimagining of ourselves in Christ. These themes thus both reinforce and shape the discourse of Trinitarian theology outlined in Chapter 11. In this chapter I focus on two further aspects of pro-Nicene theological culture: shared accounts of the soul's purification and the reading of Scripture. The two themes discussed here are interwoven with those explored in the last chapter and provide further density to my account of the reshaping of thought and imagination that is at the heart of pro-Nicene Trinitarianism. Taken together, Chapters 11, 12, and 13 sketch the fundamental aspects of that theological culture pro-Nicenes take to be the necessary context for all appropriate speculation about the work of God in the world and about the Trinity itself.[2]

DUAL-FOCUS PURIFICATION

Although pro-Nicenes do not share a detailed common anthropology, one can indicate some common themes.[3] There is a common insistence on the division between body and soul and a common sense that the soul governs the body and enables the human being to

---

[1] Gregory Nazianzen, *Or.* 40. 37.
[2] It may seem that my account is overly intellectualist in not considering in any detail the sort of ascetic and liturgical practices that pro-Nicenes may also have considered necessary. My discussion of dual-focus purification should, however, make it clear that the 'aesthetics of faith' I describe must be located within bodily and ritual practices that are appropriate to shaping the soul's attention. Discussion of what we might identify as common practices will have to await another occasion.
[3] By this statement I mean that pro-Nicenes hold to a variety of positions within ancient anthropological debates: we find, for example, different assumptions about the relationships between the soul and the passions, and different assumptions about the character of divisions within the soul.

fulfil its vocation in the created order.⁴ There is also consensus on *some* key aspects of what it means for human beings to be in the *imago Dei*. Prominent pro-Nicenes speak of the soul as the location of the image: Athanasius, Augustine, Gregory of Nyssa, and Gregory Nazianzen all hold this opinion.⁵ Though even here there is diversity: Epiphanius gives one of the most intriguing accounts in which the image is present in the whole person. In the course of listing a range of opinions and denying that the soul is simply the image, that the body is the image and that virtue is the image he argues that the *imago* is mysteriously present in no one part and yet rests in the whole person. Nevertheless, Epiphanius, like all pro-Nicenes is clear that the soul is at the core of the image.⁶ Pro-Nicenes also agree that the soul's ability to exercise rationality and govern the body and lesser creatures stems from its status as *image*. Pro-Nicenes do, however, disagree on the extent to which the image is retained, obscured, or lost in the human soul after the fall.

Against the background of these broad agreements, I want to focus on one particular consensus. All pro-Nicene authors believe that at the heart of the purification necessary for Christians lies a reordering of human knowing and desiring.⁷ Across psychologies that draw on different ancient traditions, we can speak of Christians sharing a common account of spiritual progress in the context of a 'dual-focus' anthropology.⁸ An anthropology is 'dual-focus' where problems with unsanctified human thinking and action—and the cure for those problems—are described by exploring how human beings should possess a trained soul that animates the body and attends to their joint τέλος in the divine presence through contemplation of God. Once again I will offer both Greek and Latin examples to show

---

⁴ e.g. Augustine, *Quant.* 33. 70–34. 78; Gregory of Nyssa, *Anim.* (PG 46. 29).

⁵ Augustine, *Conf.* 13. 32. 7; Gregory of Nyssa, *Hom. op.* 5; Gregory Nazianzen, *Or.* 38. 11; Ephrem, *HdF* 11. See also Athanasius, *Incarn.* 3 and 11, but note that Athanasius presents the rational soul as a sharing in the being of the Logos. The human being is an image of God insofar as he or she shares in the Logos, the true image. Behind this broad agreement there is also a remaining debate about the extent to which the soul is the image in conjunction with the body or by itself. On the notion of *imago Dei* in this period see the survey of A.-G. Hamman, *L'Homme, image de Dieu* (Paris: Desclée, 1987); R. Bernard, *L'Image de Dieu d'après saint Athanase* (Paris: Aubier, 1952); John Edward Sullivan, *The Image of God: The Doctrine of St. Augustine and its Influence* (Dubuque, Ia.: Priory Press, 1963), ch. 5.

⁶ Epiphanius, *Panarion* 70. 2. 3–5. 4. It is noticeable that even Epiphanius' argument against the image being the soul by itself rests on good pro-Nicene principles: (1) we cannot observe the image because that of which it is the image infinitely exceeds our grasp; (2) the soul has divisions and hence cannot by itself image the indivisible God; (3) the soul exists in a state of ignorance, unlike God.

⁷ And this itself may exist in the context of a number of different theories of the way in which the soul is affected by the passions.

⁸ I owe the phrase 'dual-focus' to conversation with Michel Barnes, one of many acts of what he likes to call continuing lend-lease.

how dual-focus accounts of purification were shaped by and contribute to pro-Nicene Trinitarian theology.

Ambrose and Augustine on the dynamics of faith

We can begin with Ambrose's *On the Mysteries*, written in the late 380s. This short text offers an introduction to the theology of baptism and the eucharist. Towards the middle of the text Ambrose discusses the washing away of sins at baptism and the consequent task given to Christians.[9] That task is to allow the image of God to 'shine' forth in a twofold manner: the purified desire of the soul must shine with the gift of true faith in the presence of Christ and Spirit in the sacrament; those who exhibit (or struggle to exhibit) this faith also exhibit virtuous practices and 'good works'.[10] Here we see two of three themes I want to identify in Ambrose's text. First, a dual-focus anthropology lies at the heart of the picture. Second, this dual-focus anthropology raises questions concerning the inter-relationship between the body's action and the soul's growth in contemplation. Ambrose makes no explicit attempt here to offer a rationale for the interconnection of these two, in part, I think, because he repeats something of a commonplace. We will, however, see such a rationale shortly.

At the end of the treatise, Ambrose attempts to answer someone who still sees the bread and wine as they appear, not as body and blood.[11] Ambrose argues that faith in the incarnation—the logic of the mysterious presence of the consubstantial Word in Jesus—provides a focus for the pure soul that enables a 'seeing' of the bread as body in the light of faith. Just as the Word created all things and was able to effect the incarnation because of his power, so Christ effects the change of elements.[12] Ambrose does not provide an explanation but an exhortation to faith dependent on pro-Nicene theology. Appropriate faith in the power of the consubstantial Word should lead to an interior strengthening of the soul and a trust in the transformations of eucharist and individual that faith narrates.[13] Ambrose does not resolve the tension between what we

---

[9] *Myst.* 7. 34.
[10] *Myst.* 7. 38: 'The Church is likened to a flock of these [goats], having in itself the many virtues of those souls which through the washing lay aside the superfluity of sins, and offer to Christ the mystical faith and the grace of good living . . .'; 7. 41: 'Place me as a seal upon your heart, that your faith may shine forth in the fullness of the mystery. Let your works also shine and set forth the image of God in whose image you were made.'
[11] *Myst.* 9. 50.   [12] *Myst.* 9. 52–4.
[13] *Myst.* 9. 54–5: 'He himself speaks of his blood. Before the consecration it has another name, after it is called blood. And you say, Amen, that is, it is true. Let the heart within confess what the mouth utters, let the soul feel what the voice speaks. Christ then feeds his church with these sacraments, by means of which the soul is strengthened.'

should believe about the eucharistic elements and what appears to our untransformed senses; instead he shapes what Peter Cramer calls an 'aesthetics' of 'seeing-in-faith'.[14] Cramer identifies this as an aesthetics because Ambrose focuses on our sensual experience of eucharistic presence, not simply saying 'don't believe your eyes', but calling the congregation to feel and sense the paradox of this present state of moving towards a new seeing in faith. At this point we see the third theme I want to highlight in Ambrose's text: discussing the reformation of the soul in a dual-focus context shapes an ongoing reflection on the paradoxes and aesthetics of faith in the light of pro-Nicene accounts of Christ's action and the failings of unreformed perception.

Elsewhere we find Ambrose describing more directly how lack of virtuous practice affects the mind. In his *On the Holy Spirit* Ambrose refers to the Spirit as the fount of the water of grace shaping the Church. We may partake within ourselves (Prov. 5: 15–16) so long as we do not 'lay up treasures on the earth, where rust and moth destroy' (Matt. 6: 19). Ambrose reads these two texts together as a command to avoid 'the filth of vices', which in turn 'dim the keen vision of the mind'.[15] Stating a key principle of dual-focus anthropologies, Ambrose sees vice as distorting the focus of the soul on God. From here he argues that if someone loses their grasp of the truly divine power welling forth into the Christian, they will develop doctrines that do not recognize the unity of the Spirit with the Father. Arius and Photinus are both named as examples.[16] Amid the polemic in this text we see a distinctively pro-Nicene linking of appropriate spiritual progress and growth in correct doctrinal belief.[17] Whether one conceives of the training of soul and body as controlling or eliminating the passions, only by this training can the soul appropriately 'govern' the body while attending to the Good 'in' which it exists. Achieving clarity in the soul's vision is directly associated with learning to speak of (or 'see') the presence of the unmediated and consubstantial Word and Spirit in the soul. Pro-Nicene insistence on shaping patterns of speech about God governed by the formal conditions of the divine simplicity and infinity is here incorporated into a conception of Christian life as spiritual discipline.

---

[14] Peter Cramer, *Baptism and Social Change* (Cambridge: Cambridge University Press, 1993), 65. One could also approach the question of the aesthetics of faith by considering the extent to which one might read pro-Nicenes within a tradition of 'spiritual senses'.

[15] *Spir.* 1. 16. 181 ff.   [16] *Spir.* 1. 16. 183.

[17] On these themes and Ambrose's own asceticism see Peter Brown, *The Body and Society: Men, Women and Sexual Renunciation in Early Christianity* (New York: Columbia University Press, 1988), 341–65.

The same approach is seen in Ambrose's most famous catechumen. Augustine's basic adherence to a dual-focus anthropology is well known: it is one of the central features of book 12 of *On the Trinity*, to take just one famous text.[18] Of particular interest here, however, is Augustine's reflection on the relationship between bodily action and the soul's contemplation. In book 8 of *On the Trinity* Augustine sets out the incarnation's purpose as the culmination of an extended discussion of fallen humanity's inability to see God, and to understand the unity and distinction of the divine persons.[19] The incarnate Christ chooses a form of life intended to teach humility, one consequence of which is a greater attention to *inner* realities. Imitation of Christ's action will teach us that in the act of love we 'rest in' the God who 'is love' (Wisd. 3: 9; 1 John 4: 8). By imitation of Christ's humility we are drawn to see the importance of our learning to love, and to see that love is itself the presence of God. Imitation of Christ's humility should thus lead to a reconceiving of the character of the soul's life in the light of scriptural teaching. The task is not just to 'look within' to see God—we have lost the ability to so look and to understand what we see. Rather, the task is conjointly to undertake patterns of action and to learn a new language with which to 'see' the soul as existing in the illuminating presence of God.

Thus Augustine does not believe that we come to see the soul in the presence of God simply through deeper self-examination.[20] Rather, the language of faith, the principles of Trinitarian theology, may themselves provide us with terms for speaking of the soul's nature and the nature of love. If, Augustine argues here, we know in faith that the soul or love is both triune and a unity because it is in the image of God, then the language of that faith can guide our investigation into the image itself. We can use the principles of Trinitarian theology to describe our love as threefold, even in the face of the seemingly unitary phenomenon that appears to us. The process is, however, circular: such a reading of love, and eventually of the soul itself enables a gradual reformation of our seeing. This example draws on texts I explored in Chapter 11's discussion of the use of the self as an analogical site: but here we see how the pro-Nicene understanding of analogical practice is intertwined with pro-Nicene accounts of dual-focus purification.

In Ambrose and Augustine, then, we see three common themes:

1. Dual-focus anthropologies are at the heart of accounts of the soul's ailments and purification.
2. In the context of dual-focus anthropologies, the reformation of

---

[18] *Trin.* 12. 1. 1–3. 3.   [19] *Trin.* 8. 7. 11.   [20] Ayres, 'Memory, Intelligence and Will'.

the soul is understood to enable Christian bodily action, and that action is, in turn, understood to aid the development of appropriate contemplation of the mysterious and immediate presence of Christ and the Spirit in the Christian soul.

3. Whereas the last chapter revealed pro-Nicenes using Christological and cosmological reflection to shape a particular form of attention to the creation as existing in the immediate presence of God, here we find pro-Nicenes focusing in particular on the Christian life as the site within which a complementary aesthetics of faith is shaped: the two dimensions together are the vital context for the practice of Trinitarian theology outlined in Chapter 11. Once one begins to see both of these dimensions it becomes ever clearer that the deferment of epistemological rest discussed in the last chapter is not quietist, but characteristic of an ongoing process of epistemological and anthropological reformation and purification.

Nyssen and Nazianzen on the aesthetics of faith

Gregory Nazianzen also understands the basic task involved in moving towards the vision of God as involving both not thinking of God in material terms and refocusing the gaze of the mind away from its obsession with the material world. In *Oration* 40 (*On Holy Baptism*) Gregory speaks of baptism initiating a process of purification: 'And since we are double-made, I mean of body and soul, and the one part is visible, the other invisible, so the cleansing also is twofold . . .'.[21] Later in the same oration Nazianzen speaks of the 'light of our ruling power directing our steps according to the will of God'.[22] Gregory here also insists that true contemplation is interwoven with, if not dependent upon, appropriate action:

> . . . let us kindle ourselves for the light of knowledge. This will be done by sowing unto righteousness, and reaping the fruit of life, for action is the patron of contemplation (πρᾶξις γὰρ θεωρίας πρόξενος), that among other things we may learn also what is the true light, and what the false . . . Let us lay hold of the Godhead; let us lay hold of the First and Brightest light. Let us walk towards him shining . . .[23]

Nazianzen's use of light imagery in this passage points us to the complex and typically pro-Nicene manner in which this picture is Christological. The 'first and brightest light' is the *one* light of the Godhead, that which presents itself to our minds in proportion to our love for God. At the same time that one light is Christ, whose immediate presence restores and illumines our souls.[24]

---

[21] *Or.* 40. 8. [22] *Or.* 40. 8. [23] *Or.* 40. 37.
[24] *Or.* 40. 10. At this point we can also note that Nazianzen's sense of Christ as agent of salvation is fundamentally the same as that expressed in the texts from Nyssa considered in the

'Walk Towards Him Shining' 331

While *Oration* 40 is concerned with baptism, much of Nazianzen's *Oration* 28, the second of the *Theological Orations*, is devoted to speaking of the transcendent Triune Godhead, and here we begin to see Nazianzen's own 'aesthetics of faith'. Nazianzen offers a typology of religions indexed against different ways in which people are overcome by the passions. In what seem to be allusions to traditional Roman and Hellenic gods, Gregory speaks of those who 'make gods of their emotions'.[25] Those whose reason leads are able to make some progress, although the senses continually intrude. Those like Solomon and Paul, given true wisdom by God, attempt not the direct sight of God, but only to understand the distance that separates them from God.[26] Nazianzen proceeds to offer a vision of θεολογία that takes as its informing theme the wise person's ability to wonder at the distinction between Creator and creation. Only now does Gregory offer us an extended meditation on the creation, leading us through Scripture's praise of its order and beauty as a display of the divine intelligence. This anagogy leads us to realize the human mind's inability to grasp 'the all-transcending nature'.[27]

Thus in *Oration* 28 we see Nazianzen sketching an aesthetics of 'seeing-in-faith' parallel to that found in Ambrose and Augustine. More strongly developed in the *Theological Orations*, however, is what we might term a complementary aesthetics of 'speaking-in-faith'. Nazianzen uses his succession of religious types in *Oration* 28 not only to point towards awareness of God's incomprehensibility as the highest form of human religiosity, but also as a context for the polemic of *Orations* 29 and 30. It is in the light of this ordering of types that Nazianzen turns to the importance of proclaiming a faith that 'they dishonour, but we worship'. In what follows Nazianzen pursues two tactics in his characterization of appropriate theological argument. We can see the first in *Oration* 29 when Gregory tries to

---

previous chapter. E.g. *Or.* 30. 6: 'But as the "form of a slave" he comes down to the same level as his fellow-slaves ... he bears the whole of me, along with all that is mine, in himself, so that he may consume within himself the meaner element.' Note also, at the end of the same section the exegesis of 1 Cor. 15. 28: 'The Son will not revert to disappear completely in the Father ... God will be "all and in all" when we are no longer what we are now ... with little or nothing of God in us, but are fully like God, with room for God and God alone ... Paul is a special witness here. What he predicates of "God" without further specification in this passage, he elsewhere assigns clearly to Christ ... "Christ is all and is in all" (Col. 3. 11).'

[25] *Or.* 28. 13 ff.: 'although every thinking being longs for God, the First Cause, it is powerless, for the reasons I have given, to grasp him. Tired with the yearning it chafes at the bit and careless of the cost, it tries a second tack. Either it looks at things visible and makes of these a God ... or else it discovers God through the beauty and order of things seen ... (14) Others again have taken as patronal deities whatever objects of special beauty happened to strike their sight. There are yet others, more emotional, more sensual, who have paid divine reverence to statues ... (15) Men of worse passions even made gods of their emotions ...'.
[26] *Or.* 28. 21.   [27] *Or.* 28. 31.

show how logical and syllogistic argument may be adapted in the context of an appropriate realization of the divine difference from human existence. He not only attempts to refute his opponents' arguments, but also to perform appropriate reasoning with the principles of pro-Nicene theology.[28] This is apparent, for example, in Gregory's response to the non-Nicene question 'since when has the Spirit been proceeding?'[29] He attacks by demonstrating that the question itself makes temporal assumptions that do not apply.[30] He similarly attacks the question 'how, then, can the process of begetting not involve subjection to change?' Appropriate attention to God as unlike anything in the created order delivers one from assuming that the (scriptural) terminology of begetting must imply change.[31] Thus the context for these arguments is the θεωρία described in *Oration* 28.

The second tactic can be seen when Nazianzen turns to the scriptural description of Christ later in *Orations* 29 and 30. His clear articulation of the principle that scriptural material may be attributed either to the pre-incarnate Word or to the incarnate Word is frequently noted.[32] It is less frequently noted that Nazianzen presents the speech that follows from employing these principles as a form of attention or contemplation. At the end of *Oration* 29 Nazianzen makes the famous statement that 'faith is the fulfilment of our reasoning'. (ἡ γὰρ πίστις τοῦ καθ' ἡμᾶς λόγου πλήρωσις)[33] 'Faith' here seems to be a reference both to the principles of pro-Nicene belief Gregory has used to organize scriptural material and to the sets of statements that we confess to be true of the Word and the incarnate Word. But in the sentences before this famous statement Gregory echoes the language of *Oration* 28: the task for us is, first, to use logic to demonstrate the incompleteness of anti-Nicene exegesis. But, second, we should seek to show the importance of confession

---

[28] There is much useful literature exploring Gregory's debt to various logical and rhetorical schools. Much of the best of this is summed up in F. W. Norris, 'Of Thorns and Roses', *Church History*, 53 (1984), 455–64; and idem, *Faith Gives Fullness to Reasoning*, 25–39, 132–58. While Norris correctly notes that Nazianzen adapts his philosophical borrowings for theological purposes, my suggestion here is that we need also to attend to the way the structure of the *Theological Orations* is intended to create a context for the deployment of such argumentation.

[29] For example, at *Or.* 29. 16 ff. There Gregory famously explores how to avoid the trap of the Heterousian question 'does "Father" designate substance or activity?' by pursuing two strategies. First, he emphasizes the usefulness of the term relationship (*schesis*) in Trinitarian contexts. Second, at 29. 17 ff. he then places this point in a wider context by launching into a long discussion of pro-Nicene patterns of predication and outlining an overall approach to those passages which might seem to offer amunition to his opponents.

[30] *Or.* 29. 3: 'Since as long as the Son has *not* been proceeding but being begotten in a non-temporal way that transcends explanation. We cannot, though, explain the meaning of "supra-temporal" *and* deliberately keep clear of any suggestion of time.'

[31] *Or.* 29. 4. [32] *Or.* 29. 18. [33] *Or.* 29. 21.

(or worship) through offering paradoxical exegesis of the Son as both human and divine, a paradox necessary 'in the face of the vastness of the realities (τοῦ μεγέθους τῶν πραγμάτων)'. To undertake such exegesis is to perform appropriate speech in the face of mystery, to perform the tensions of speaking in faith.

The same strategy can be seen in Oration 30's exegesis of the scriptural titles for the Son. The practice of predication Gregory encourages is intended to form part of the θεολογία outlined in Oration 28:

There you have the Son's titles. Walk in a God-like way (θεϊκῶς) through all [the titles] that are sublime, and with fellow-feeling through all that are bodily, so that you may ascend from below to become God, but even better, treat all in a God-like way, because he came down from above for us.[34]

The adverb 'God-like' (θεϊκῶς) is a rare one in Gregory's corpus, but we can see what he means by reference to its use in Oration 38 (On the Theophany). Here the term describes the manner in which we should celebrate the feast: we should do so not with riotous feasting, but by a cleansing of the mind and senses so that the discourse of Gregory's homily may provide 'delights' that are permanent. Gregory then offers a summary of the simplicity of the divine nature and of the condescension of God in drawing us through creation, illumination, and redemption to share in the divine life. To go through the Son's titles θεϊκῶς is to read, speak, and think through them aware of the ways in which the creation points to the incomprehensible Creator and the distinction between God and world.[35]

For one further example of the pro-Nicene aesthetics of faith, we can turn to Gregory of Nyssa's short address *Concerning Those Who Have Died*. The text considers the appropriate attitude towards those who have died and takes as its point of departure the natural desire of the soul for the Good. After death the soul migrates towards the source of Goodness, and in this life we should conceive of the soul's appropriate attitude as one focused towards the rest that will come when the soul finally reaches the Good.[36] The natural

---

[34] *Or.* 30. 21.
[35] Lim, *Public Disputation, Power and Social Order in Late Antiquity*, 158–71, uses Gregory's *Theological Orations* as an example of the mystification of theological discourse in the late 4th cent., which he sees as fundamentally a power-play by bishops seeking to bolster their authority in an increasingly public and ever-contentious Christian community. Gregory is, indeed, clearly trying to restrict the bounds of discussion in his community but he is also trying to shape a particular community of discourse: argument is restricted through being relocated within a wider θεωρία. Thus, my concern is not to deny the reality of the ways in which pro-Nicenes used their theologies to shape and construct communities, but to highlight other dynamics at work in the same contexts.
[36] *Mort.* GNO 9. 39.

power of choice that should be the source of our ability to reflect the divine power has become distorted such that our desires and cravings now serve only to distract the soul.[37] The high point of the text comes in an address by the soul to humanity:

> What is seen is transitory whereas what is invisible is eternal. But once we have turned our minds to the invisible nature within us, we must truly believe in it, even though it escapes our perception.[38]

The soul's address thus begins with a paradox: human beings are now only capable of knowing the material conditions of this life, being ignorant of the true life of the soul 'within'. And yet, *both* lives remain hidden from us: the operations of our bodies remain a mystery despite our focus on them, showing the full reality of the ignorance in which we pass our time. In faith we can only love what we do not know (the Lord of Deut. 6: 5) with our heart and soul and strength.[39]

The soul then exhorts humanity to make a series of leaps of reason and imagination toward realizing the true life of the soul. We must gradually recognize in faith the need for a death to this life so that the soul may become accustomed to 'hearing unutterable words'. The 'soul's eye' 'tastes' that the Lord is Good (Ps. 33: 9), 'smells' the odour of Christ (2 Cor. 2: 14), and 'touches' the Word (1 John 1: 1).[40] This exhortation to a life beyond our accustomed experience ends in a call to observe the natural progress of nature in a growing seed, echoing Basil's use of the same analogy in his *Hexameron*. The progress towards maturity we see in the growing seed and the Pauline call to a life of reformation to which the soul exhorts us follow the same pattern: by both we are led to choose a new mode of life in which the corrupting impulses of the passions are rejected.[41]

The final twist comes in a peroration concerning the resurrected body. Much of the first two-thirds of the text could be read as advocating the soul's flight from the body. At the end of the text, however, Gregory directly controverts such a reading. He tells us that we must avoid inappropriately derisory speech about the body and learn to love it in accord with Paul's 'law' of Eph. 5: 29. But we can only love the body truly as we sense its future transformation, as we reflect on the process of procreation that marks bodily life and see it as a pointer towards the need for a new life to take form in us.[42] In all of these authors—Ambrose, Augustine, Gregory Nazianzen, and Gregory of Nyssa—we see, then, three common themes:

---

[37] *Mort.* GNO 9. 32–6.   [38] *Mort.* GNO 9. 40.   [39] *Mort.* GNO 9. 45.
[40] *Mort.* GNO 9. 47.   [41] *Mort.* GNO 9. 52–3.   [42] *Mort.* GNO 9. 61–3.

1. Dual-focus anthropologies are at the heart of accounts of the soul's ailments and purification.

2. In the context of dual-focus anthropologies, the reformation of the soul is understood to enable Christian bodily action, and that action is understood to aid the development of appropriate contemplation of the mysterious and transforming presence of the consubstantial Word. The dynamics of Christ's immediate and yet hidden presence shape how the process of purification is understood.

3. Dual-focus accounts of purification are accompanied by attention to the paradoxes of faith and by the development of an aesthetics of faith that further reshapes our epistemological certainties within the Christological and cosmological context explored in the last chapter. Within such a life the practice of pro-Nicene Trinitarian theology acts as both goal and architectonic principle for our contemplation as a whole.

REREADING SCRIPTURE

I want now to turn to the pro-Nicene reading of Scripture. In most important ways pro-Nicene reading practices are simply those shared by virtually all Christian readers in the fourth century. The distinctive character of pro-Nicene exegesis is to be found in subtle twists given to common reading practices, and in links drawn between these reading practices and the principles of pro-Nicene Trinitarianism.[43] Thus, the basic pro-Nicene assumptions about Scripture can be stated in summary fashion, and the reader pointed back to the first chapter. Like almost all early Christian writers, pro-Nicenes read Scripture as a providentially ordained resource for the Christian imagination. It is an intrinsic part of Scripture's purpose to enable description of the God who acts *and* of the structure of the cosmos within which God acts: the reshaping of the cosmological imagination is a central aspect of the Incarnate Word's mission.

---

[43] Although I have spoken here about pro-Nicenes in general, some readers will find it strange that I have not shaped this discussion around discrete 'Alexandrian' and 'Antiochene' traditions. These two categories can be highly misleading when they are taken to describe a fundamental division between late 4th-cent. exegetes. In the first case, many of the 'grammatical techniques' that formed the most basic principles of exegetical practice (and which, in particular, are so central to the shaping of the doctrinal exegesis of which I spoke in Ch. 1) are simply common currency among theologians supposedly belonging to either 'school'. In the second case, even when we consider the particular figural practices that are frequently taken as the markers of an 'Alexandrian' approach, we find that these techniques are widely shared among people who have little meaningful connection with that city. To call Nyssa, Ambrose, and Augustine 'Alexandrian' in their reading of the Psalms, for instance, reveals only the problematic nature of the category. Third, that particular figures from Alexandria played a role in opposing particular figures associated with Antioch in a particular controversy at the end of the 4th cent. is certainly the case: it is far less certain that this should enable the

III. Understanding Pro-Nicene Theology

Scripture shapes the description of the journey in the Church and in Christ toward full sight of the divine glory. Within this context pro-Nicenes continue to make use of the range of grammatical and figural techniques discussed in Chapter 1. We can, however, identify two ways in which pro-Nicenes subtly adapt previous tradition.

The pro-Nicene σκοπός

Interpretation of Scripture is governed by a pro-Nicene rule of faith. Creeds, pre-existing rules of faith, and passages of Scripture traditionally used as hermeneutical keys, are all given a pro-Nicene cast. This reshaping enables a subtle shifting of how the σκοπός of Scripture is understood and, in turn, how one understands the σκοπός of Scripture will influence how one understands the function and the very texture of the text—its manner of signifying, its perspicacity, the character of the faith we should place in it. We may see this particularly clearly in catechetical contexts. Although, well past the end of the fourth century, the Nicene-Constantinopolitan creed was not used directly in catechetical or liturgical contexts, pro-Nicene faith was conveyed to catechumens through commentary on existing local baptismal creeds.

Daniel Williams has explored how Ambrose's treatment of the Milanese creed follows such a strategy:[44] Rufinus' *Commentary on the Apostle's Creed* (c.400) offers another excellent example. This is an important text not only because of its widespread use in later Latin Christianity, but also because Rufinus constructed the text with open acknowledgement of a debt to previous Greek examples of such literature. He alludes to Gregory of Nyssa's *Catechetical Oration* and appears to be in some debt to Cyril of Jerusalem's own *Catechetical Lectures*. We see Rufinus' basic strategy in his comments on the initial clauses of the Aquileian creed. Rufinus explicates 'I believe in God the Father Almighty' by explaining that, first, God is infinite, incorporeal, simple, and incomprehensible and then, second, that 'Father' is a title to be understood as a necessary correlative of the eternal 'Son' and image:

> Thus, the very title by which God is called 'Father' proves that a Son coexists side by side (*pariter subsistere*) with the Father. I would rather, however, you did not discuss how God the Father generated the Son, and did not plunge too inquisitively into the depths of the mystery. There is a danger that, in prying too persistently into the brightness of inaccessible

---

construction of a general typology of 4th-cent. exegesis. Fourth, while supposedly 'Alexandrian' principles are widely shared, writers who can be clearly labelled 'Antiochenes' are far shorter in supply and it is not at all certain that they can be simply lumped together as a clearly distinct school.

[44] Williams, 'Constantine and the "Fall" of the Church'.

light, you may find yourself deprived of the tiny glimpse (exiguum ipsum) which is all the good God vouchsafes to mortals. Alternatively, if you judge this a subject which justifies every sort of scrutiny, first employ your mind on things which concern ourselves . . . First of all explain, if you can, how the mind within you generates its word, and what the spirit of memory in your mind is. Explain how these, for all their diversity in reality and operation, form a unity in substance or nature . . . [*other examples follow*]. Even if you can explain each of these mysteries, you must realize that the mystery of divine generation is different from and loftier than they in proportion as the Creator is more powerful than His creatures . . . We must believe, then, without argument, that God is Father of his only-begotten Son, our Lord . . . [*scriptural texts follow*]. Is anyone entitled to thrust himself argumentatively between these statements of the Father and the Son, dividing the Godhead . . . denying the truth of what the Truth affirms?[45]

Rufinus wishes his catechumens to hear scriptural discussion of Father and Son as inviting the deployment of a notion of mystery shaped by pro-Nicene principles. Rufinus attempts to shape his catechumens' imaginations to hear the words of Scripture both in the light of pro-Nicene principles and as a text comprehensible only in the light of a particular spiritual transformation. Thus it is not precise enough to say that Rufinus wishes the text to be heard as pro-Nicene in theology: he wishes the text to be heard and read as a particular type of text, a text whose meaning is intertwined with a spiritual ascent that it itself teaches.

This reading is reinforced when Rufinus discusses the descent into Hell. He begins by referring to the omnipresence and omnipotence of God and by insisting that when the creed speaks of the 'upper' and 'underworld', it is accommodating itself to our spatial imaginations.[46] That which the Incarnate Christ undergoes for us is the result of the divine power's action, culminating in the placing of the human body of Christ at the Father's right hand.[47] At this point the mysteriousness of the text of Scripture is relocated by basic pro-Nicene principles: Christ's being seated at the right hand of the Father is mysterious precisely *because* this story cannot refer to any change in the Word's status as coeternal with the Father in the indivisible Godhead. The clause must, therefore, concern the elevation of Christ's humanity. Again, the σκοπός of Scripture revolves around the action of the incomprehensible and omnipresent God becoming incarnate in the world: because Scripture focuses on this story, it can only be read faithfully by one who understands the structure of the soul's ascent to a true vision of the Creator.

By way of comparison with Rufinus' text I want to turn away

---

[45] *Symb.* 4.   [46] *Symb.* 29.   [47] *Symb.* 31–2.

from the directly catechetical genre to Augustine's *Sermon* 117, an anti-'Arian' sermon on John 1: 1–3. Most notably we read:

> We are not now discussing, brothers and sisters, possible ways of understanding the text, In the beginning was the Word . . . it wasn't read in order to be understood, but in order to make us mere human beings grieve because we don't understand it, and make us try to discover what prevents our understanding, and so move it out of the way, and hunger to grasp the eternal Word, ourselves thereby being changed from worse to better.[48]

Augustine ties good interpretation of the text to a sense of Scripture as teaching the actions of the Triune, simple, and incomprehensible God.[49] Through the sermon Augustine sketches how the Word must be understood as an unformed form, the form of all things beyond any created or material form we can imagine. Through the latter parts of the sermon Augustine links the incomprehensibility of these verses to Christ's offer of refreshment in Matthew 11: the careful reader will sense how Scripture leads us in a pro-Nicene spiritual progress, an internal and external, or dual-focus reorientation.[50]

In what we have seen thus far, in Rufinus and Augustine, the σκοπός of Scripture intrinsically includes the journey of the soul in Christ towards union with and understanding of the Triune Godhead. For a brief Greek example, we can turn to Chrysostom's *Homilies on the Incomprehensibility of God*.[51] Throughout the second homily Chrysostom presents Paul as the archetypal theologian: heterousian claims to be able to discuss the mode of the Son's generation are the product of their failing to identify with Paul's claim that 'we are fools for Christ's sake' (1 Cor. 4: 10). This foolishness consists in holding fast to what is revealed in faith and in appropriate dread of the incorporeal, omnipresent, and omnipotent God.[52] Chrysostom then offers an account of the power of God in creating

---

[48] *Serm.* 117. 3.

[49] When Augustine comments on John 1 his standard practice is to assert the incomprehensibility of the first three verses, while asserting that the remaining eleven speak of the Son's descent into flesh enabling us to begin comprehending.

[50] *Serm.* 117. 17: 'What does he say himself, after all, to the weak and infirm, so that they may recover that kind of sight and to some extent at least attain to or brush against the Word through which all things were made, "Come to me, all you who toil and are overburdened, and I will refresh you" . . . He is calling the human race . . . You were thinking, no doubt, that the Wisdom of God was going to say, "learn how I made the heavens and the stars . . ." Is that the sort of thing you were thinking she would say? No; but first this: that I am meek and humble of heart . . . Confess your infirmity, lie there patiently in the presence of the doctor. When you have caught hold of his humility, you start rising up with him.'

[51] These homilies are the first five of a series against Heterousians, delivered in Antioch (*c*.386) and then in Constantinople. The introduction by Jean Daniélou in SC 28. 9–63 is still a good point of departure.

[52] *Incomp.* 2. 7–8.

'Walk Towards Him Shining'

that is typically pro-Nicene. At its end Paul is again invoked: John argues that while Paul does not directly say 'how great a distance there is between God and man', he presents us with an example of exactly this at Rom. 9: 20 ff. in likening God to the potter who has an absolute claim over the clay.[53] When we read in Philippians of Paul's insistence on the imperfect quality of his own knowledge, Chrysostom argues, we should recognize that 'Paul's cry is louder than a trumpet blast as he instructs the entire world to be content and satisfied with the measure of knowledge which has been granted to it.' It is at this very point that Chrysostom then presents Paul (on the basis of 2 Cor. 13: 3) as speaking with the voice of Christ.[54] Paul's call to faith is not simply a tirade against human reasoning, but a call to participation in a journey of spiritual purification and preparation:

'I do not think of myself as having understood' are the words of a man who is making it clear that he has arrived at a certain point of his journey, that he is going on and will advance further, but that he has not completely reached the end.[55]

Once again, in pro-Nicene fashion the σκοπός of Scripture is understood as focused around the creating and salvific activity of the distinct and yet intimately present Triune God. Because Scripture is understood to speak of and aid in the transformation of the soul in the light of this God's character and action, the nature of Scripture as a text has itself been subtly reconfigured.

The complexity of scriptural semiotics

At this point we have arrived at a second theme shared between pro-Nicene exegetes. In the theological postscript to his *Arius*, Rowan Williams speaks of the victors of the fourth-century controversies as realizing with new clarity the complexity of speech about God and the need to bring out the 'strangeness' of Scripture, the need to render it 'more difficult' in order that its 'simplicities' be better understood.[56] This can be seen clearly in the extent to which pro-Nicenes offer accounts of Scripture's revelatory ability in which understanding is incremental and deferment of comprehension endless. The scholarship on conceptions of sign as used in exegetical contexts during this period is vast. My aim here is only to indicate briefly ways of approaching that body of scholarship with particular questions in mind about how late fourth-century developments reveal concerns flowing from the development of pro-Nicene Trinitarianism.

[53] *Incomp.* 2. 34–5.   [54] *Incomp.* 2. 40–1.   [55] *Incomp.* 2. 47.
[56] Williams, *Arius*, 236.

A parallel between two contexts will demonstrate the point. We have already encountered the use of ἐπίνοια and ἔννοια in the Cappadocians. The development of this terminology represents a subtle adaptation and transformation of Origenist tradition: in particular a recasting of the progress in knowledge that ἐπίνοια may be said to promote. Although the complexity of Origen's texts defeats attempts at simple synthesis, it is noticeable that Origen not only offers some remarkably positive assessments about the possibility for speech about God based on God's having spoken to Israel and the Church, but he does so while also offering a high estimation of the mind's ability to comprehend spiritual realities and the divine.[57] This position is indeed combined with statements about the unspeakability of God, but it is worth noting, for example, that Origen is able to present the silence preserved by Paul about the third heaven as appropriate to the *knowledge* he possessed.[58] In this context the process of ἐπίνοια delivers something very different from its use in Basil or the two Gregorys. In the latter context the process of ἐπίνοια is only understood when one sees the tension between the (divinely given) ability to use scriptural language to speak about God and the incomprehensibility of the divine nature towards which one's desire and θεωρία reach.

Augustine's own practices demonstrate similar concerns. I want here to point to only two threads that run through Augustine's extremely complex account of signification and Scripture. First, Augustine's distinction between 'things' and 'signs' in the first book of *On Christian Teaching* evolved under the clear pressure of pro-Nicene dynamics.[59] Augustine's insistence that there is truly only one true 'thing' that is not also a sign means that speech about Father, Son, and Spirit is only now a gesturing towards the *one* thing that remains beyond all signs as source. There is no possibility of Son and Spirit sharing a distinct ontological status that might allow them to stand as signs towards and thus more comprehensible than the Father. Augustine's account of the soul's ability to conceive of itself as a point within a chain of signifying realities between material things and the world is similarly conditioned by the radical distinction between creation and the Triune God. God provides both a significatory universe and the scriptural text as a combined guide for the soul's ascent, but our acts of signifying continually fail in the face of the Triune God's simplicity.

This tension is partly negotiated in Augustine through development in his understanding of the Incarnation. Michael Cameron has

---

[57] e.g. Origen, *Orat.* 8.2, 21.1, 24.2.
[58] I am here indebted to the helpful account of Mortley, *From Word to Silence*, ii. 63–84.
[59] *Doc.* 1. 4. 4–5. 5.

recently offered a new typology of the interaction between Augustine's understanding of the significatory function of Scripture and developments in Augustine's understanding of the unity of natures in the Incarnation.[60] Cameron argues that Augustine moves from an initially 'disjunctive' perspective, in which signs arbitrarily represent the intelligible world, into a 'conjunctive' perspective, in which realities may intrinsically possess a signifying quality and lead us to appropriate speech about spiritual realities. Augustine develops this conjunctive perspective as he develops an account of the sacramental character of the union of natures in Christ. The Word's mysterious union with a human being in the person of Christ provides the model for the mysterious character of language's signification. The literature on Augustine's semiotics is vast, but has only infrequently drawn connections with his Trinitarian theology and with pro-Nicene developments more widely. My point here is that the basic lines of his account clearly fit within the broader pro-Nicene Trinitarian context, and deserve to be studied from this perspective.

CONCLUSION

Considered together, my three strategies demonstrate how pro-Nicene Trinitarianism stood at the core of a theological vision, or more precisely, how pro-Nicene Trinitarianism began to effect changes and adaptations throughout whole theologies. The development of pro-Nicene understandings of the paradox of unity and diversity in the Godhead not only occurred in the context of a developing sense of the distinction between God and world. It also developed alongside the evolution of subtly transformed accounts of the spiritual progress that constitutes Christian life. Pro-Nicenes were only following long-established tradition in understanding Christian life as a purification for contemplation of the divine life: nevertheless, emphasis on the coequal status of the Word and on the simplicity of the divine existence resulted in a deferring of our cognitive rest and in the construction of a new attention to the paradoxes and tensions of speaking, seeing, tasting, and touching in Christian existence. The aesthetics of faith inherent in pro-Nicene

[60] Michael Cameron, 'The Christological Substructure of Augustine's Figurative Exegesis', in Pamela Bright (ed.), *Augustine and the Bible* (Notre Dame, Ind.: University of Notre Dame Press, 1999), 74–103; See also Rowan Williams, 'Language, Reality and Desire in Augustine's *De doctrina*', *Literature and Theology*, 3 (1989), 138–50 for some helpful further reflections. Robert Markus, *Signs and Meanings: World and Text in Ancient Christianity* (Liverpool: Liverpool University Press, 1996), ch. 1. There is also much to be gleaned from G. Strauss, *Schriftgebrauch, Schriftauslegung und Schriftbeweis bei Augustin* (Tübingen: J. C. B. Mohr, 1959).

theologies is the natural counterpart of their theological conditioning of our seeming epistemological certainties and results in a reshaping of the texture of faith and of one's imagination of the world itself. The development of this new account of the Christian life for purification was not so much a consequence of developments in Trinitarian theology: it was an essential part of those developments, offering a context within which appropriate thought about the Triune God could grow.

We see in these strategies apparent in pro-Nicene writing the lineaments of the pro-Nicene life of the mind. I say 'lineaments' in the sense of distinguishing features, in the sense of some aspects or features of a reality that lies still partially hidden. We cannot know what it was like to think and write as a late fourth-century pro-Nicene: our evidence is only in patterns of text-composition, styles of recording and performing certain patterns of paradox. Nevertheless, what we can see coalesces towards an account of the life of the mind constantly concerned to develop awareness of and attention to the mysteriousness of the divine existence, to the graciousness of God's self-revelation and drawing of humanity into the divine life. The theological strategies that I have explored thus offer an initial sketch of that life of the mind, of the *habitus* at the heart of the culture of pro-Nicene Trinitarianism.

INTERLUDE II: ASCETIC PORTABILITY

A number of scholars concerned with the changes effected by the 'triumph' of Christianity and the appearance of the early Byzantine state have linked the end of late antiquity and the rise to prominence of ascetic discourse. Peter Brown, Averil Cameron, and Robert Markus have all argued that there is a connection between the development of a hierarchical 'Christian' empire in the east—lacking some of the supposed cultural openness of an earlier age—and the rise of ascetic discourse.[61] Asceticism offered images of the monastic community, and accounts of the control of soul and body originally developed in ascetic communities as models for Christians as a whole. At the same time, members of ascetic communities, and those living out the values of such communities but not members of them, came increasingly to control episcopal and other dominant positions within the Church.

Averil Cameron has recently tried to highlight the complexity of this process. She argues that the 'transference of the undoubtedly

---

[61] See Brown, *Power and Persuasion in Late Antiquity*, Robert Markus, *The End of Ancient Christianity* (Cambridge: Cambridge University Press, 1990); Averil Cameron, *Christianity and the Rhetoric of Empire*.

hierarchical and coherence-seeking side of Christian discourse to the political sphere' was accompanied by more 'paradoxical' and 'humane' aspects of Christianity.[62] Much scholarly work remains necessary on these accounts of large-scale social change: there is a noticeable ease with which scholars considering these shifts slip into a profoundly modern discourse about the end or closure of the openness and vibrancy that marks the classical worlds—despite the fact that many of these scholars have argued eloquently for the study of late antiquity against an older perception that the second century saw the close of the truly creative and classical. Nevertheless, something of fundamental importance *is* identified in their accounts of the increasing significance of ascetic models of Christian life.[63] I want to suggest here that much of the theological groundwork for these shifts occurred through the emergence of pro-Nicene theology.

Among the major pro-Nicene theologians it is fairly easy to trace the influence of ascetic models of Christian life infusing accounts of the purification necessary for Christians. At the same time, however, we can trace what we might call an argument for the 'portability' of ascetic practice and literature. When non-Nicene theology is seen to result both from a failure to maintain appropriate attention to the mysteriousness of God and from an inappropriately trained soul, it is not surprising that in the homilies of many pro-Nicene authors there is a conscious attempt not simply to encourage people to join ascetic communities, but to encourage those who continue to live within non-sexual-renunciant families to adopt practices that stem from ascetic contexts. Describing and encouraging the portability of ascetic practice may thus be seen as intrinsic to pro-Nicene theology and catechesis. A great deal of scholarly work is necessary to trace the patterns of development here and to sketch useful typologies: but such investigation would help to illuminate our understanding of the broad shifts in Christian development that occur from the fourth to the seventh centuries and beyond.

---

[62] Averil Cameron, 'Ascetic Closure and the End of Antiquity', in Vincent L. Wimbush and Richard Valantassis (eds.), *Asceticism* (New York: Oxford University Press, 1998), 147–61. The problem with Cameron's phraseology is, perhaps obviously enough, that it does not really question the categories: it simply argues that a little human 'openness' managed to sneak into early Byzantium before the monks and emperors shut the door!

[63] By asceticism I mean a discipline based on Stoic and Platonic conceptions of the good life and on late antique psychological and medical notions. It is a discipline aimed at achieving self-control, at controlling and counteracting a range of the 'passions', from appetitive passions for food and sex to states such as anger, jealousy, and avarice. Asceticism is not primarily a dualistic phenomenon and it is not an end in itself. The ascetic practitioner aims to transform him or herself into a vehicle of the divine will and to realize the intended nature of human existence as in the image of God. In offering this definition I am adapting the definition that Susanna Elm offers (in turn adapting Weber's). See '*Virgins of God*', 13–14.

14
On Not Three Gods: Gregory of Nyssa's Trinitarian Theology

[T]he sacred company of the prophets and Patriarchs . . . from the names which express the manifold variety of his power, lead men, as by the hand, to the understanding of the divine nature, making known to them the bare grandeur of the thought of God; while the question of His essence, as one which it is impossible to grasp . . . they dismiss without any attempt at its solution.[1]

INTRODUCTION

In this chapter I offer an account of the fundamental structures of Gregory of Nyssa's Trinitarianism as an alternative to the commonly assumed narrative of him as a 'pluralistic' and typically 'eastern' theologian. I will argue that Gregory uses an account of God's unitary power, activity, and causality as the basis for approaching the paradox of the divine diversity and unity. At the same time, also through his deployment of power terminology, Gregory also offers an ontological and epistemological foundation for human knowledge of God that sets the stage for any analogical description of the Godhead. Only when we see how this account of divine creative power and ontological difference grounds a vision of human speech about God will we begin to see what it means for Gregory to confess the incomprehensible unity of the incomprehensible and yet irreducible distinct divine persons. This chapter considers Gregory as a detailed example of the ways in which pro-Nicene theologies are only comprehensible when their account of the Triune unity and distinction are considered in the broader epistemological and anthropological context I have sketched in the last three chapters. The next chapter turns to another example: Augustine of Hippo. Taken together, these two chapters add further weight to my argument that distinc-

---

[1] Gregory of Nyssa, *Eunom.* 2. Throughout this chapter, contrary to practice in the rest of the book but to enable easy following of the argument, I have given references to *Ablab.* in both the GNO and NPNF.

tions between 'east' and 'west' 'Greek' and 'Latin' are inadequate and misleading when used to categorize pro-Nicene theologies.

It may seem strange that I have chosen to focus on Gregory's *To Ablabius: On Not Three Gods* (to which I will refer in the text as *Ad Ablabium*), given that this text is often taken as a paradigm of Gregory's supposed commitment to beginning with divine plurality rather than unity, or even as a paradigm of his supposed commitment to 'social' Trinitarian analogies. I will argue, however, that Gregory's purpose in the *Ad Ablabium* is actually to point the reader away from speculating about the possibility of a 'social' analogy and towards the very themes I outlined in the previous paragraph as the necessary context for exploring the divine unity and diversity. Thus, the *Ad Ablabium* is paradigmatic because it offers a summary of the positions advocated in such texts as the *Contra Eunomium* and the *Catechetical Oration*—and I would argue that when a short summary of Gregory's account of the divine nature is needed the *Catechetical Oration* is probably the most useful.

THE POLEMICAL CONTEXT OF *AD ABLABIUM*

It is important first to get a sense of the polemical charge that Gregory faces in the *Ad Ablabium*. This charge is that Gregory's theology (and Cappadocian theology more widely[2]) implied the existence of 'three Gods' because it was susceptible to the logic of distinctions pertaining between three distinct people. Gregory talks initially of Ablabius bringing forward charges made by 'opponents of the truth', and elsewhere in the text he refers to those whose charges Ablabius brings forward as 'adversaries'. It is these 'opponents of the truth' who have deployed the analogy of three people to show what they take to be a logical implication of Cappadocian theology. Ablabius seems to have been unable to answer the charge and has requested help. Note that his opponents are not asking whether or not Gregory thinks the divine persons are like three human persons in communion, they are interested only in the degree of individuation the analogy reveals in Cappadocian Trinitarianism.

The charge that Gregory faces probably originates with the problematically named 'Macedonians'.[3] The text of the *Ad Ablabium* itself does not provide us with many clues as to the origin of the

[2] Although in general it is important to distinguish the theologies of Basil and the two Gregorys, here Gregory is encountering a charge first faced by Basil, and now being faced by the two Gregorys. The charge, as I hope to show, goes to the heart of a concern shared by all three thinkers.

[3] For a brief outline of the nature of 'Macedonian' theology and the problems of using the term see Ch. 8. There is also some evidence that the same charge was pressed by Heterousians.

charge. In Gregory's *Refutation of Eunomius' Confession*, however, Gregory speaks of 'those who keep repeating against us the phrase "three Gods" '.[4] Gregory's comment occurs in the middle of a long exposition of Eunomius' text, in which he frequently speaks of Eunomius by name. At this point he offers an extended account of the Spirit's divinity, arguing that the attribution of sanctification to the Spirit alone is mistaken: such activity is that of the whole Trinity together. Then begins the short discussion of the anonymous group who charge that Gregory teaches 'three Gods'. Such people—and suddenly Gregory speaks of his adversaries in the plural—would only have a point if it were first true that pro-Nicenes taught that God was a duality to which we then discussed whether another should be added. However, God is always one, even though we confess the names of Father, Son, and Spirit. Gregory then says that it is time to resume his refutation of Eunomius' text. Gregory seems to indicate that the charge originates with those who, despite a willingness to accept the divinity of the Son, doubt the divinity of the Spirit and, thus, seem not yet to have grasped the essential unity of the Godhead as pro-Nicene theology has come to present it.

The character of the debate is further revealed by references elsewhere in the Cappadocians. Most directly, at *Oration* 31. 13–15 Gregory of Nazianzus attempts to argue against those who say that if the term 'God' may be used three times of Father, Son, and Spirit then are there not a plurality of powers and hence a plurality of Gods? Nazianzen carefully identifies this charge as originating primarily with those who are 'fairly sound' on the Son but who doubt the Spirit's divinity. He even tells us that such people press their charge by alleging that the unity of the pro-Nicene Trinity fails because it is *only* equivalent to the unity of three people. Nazianzen argues that those who worship the Father and the Son but not the Spirit might be accused of ditheism. If they were, he argues, they could only respond by articulating an understanding of Father and Son as *together* constituting the one God. In effect their response would be to argue that unity is not disrupted by the distinctions between the *hypostases*. Thus, Nazianzen concludes, the response of such people against those who might accuse them of ditheism is structurally identical to the response that these people should expect from those who worship Father, Son, *and* Spirit: acknowledging commonality of substance does not necessarily involve admitting that the substance itself is divided. Thus there are not three Gods, and the analogy of three people does not apply. Even from this brief summary of Nazianzen's argument it is clear that the point at issue

---

[4] Gregory of Nyssa, *Ref.* 14.

concerns the very grammar of divinity itself.[5] While Macedonian polemic was concerned with the question of the Spirit's divinity, at a deep structural level the Macedonians were also resisting, or not yet grasping, the basic pro-Nicene grammar of divinity. Thus, noting that the charge probably comes from Macedonian circles helps us to see the task that Gregory faces in the *Ad Ablabium*. The problem that he faces is not fundamentally one of explaining how the Spirit is also divine, where both sides in the dispute share a common account of divinity and of the nature of the union between Father and Son. Rather, it is the very character of divine unity that is at issue.

THE STRUCTURE OF THE *AD ABLABIUM*

In the following sections I will offer a sequential reading of the text as a whole. In each section my procedure will be to place the arguments of the text in the wider context of other relevant discussions in Gregory's corpus. Looking at the text in this way will help to show how Gregory not only fights on a number of polemical fronts simultaneously, but also how his general strategy is to shift the battle on to ground he has already made his own and away from just skirmishing around the division of universal and particular terminologies.

The text is short but surprisingly complex and a summary of the argument may be helpful.

At the beginning Gregory introduces the problem and almost immediately tells Ablabius that those who have raised this charge have failed to distinguish between strict linguistic use (in which natures are indivisible and human nature is not divided between three human beings) and common usage (in which we use the phrase 'three men' as if human nature could be divided). Because, strictly speaking, natures are indivisible, speaking about three *hypostases* does not imply the existence of 'three Gods' because the nature of divinity cannot actually be divided. Having given this answer Gregory admits that this is unlikely to be sufficient, given the persistence of the common usage.

Progress, he tells us, can only be made by exploring the name 'Godhead'. Gregory then goes on to argue that names for the divine nature do not describe God directly, but each one describes the action of God: the divine nature remains unknown. 'Godhead'

---

[5] This account of the polemical context of *Ablab.* may be further reinforced by Basil's insistence at *Spir.* 18. 45 that 'we do not say "one, two, three", or "first, second, and third"' and by his strong insistence that ranking the Spirit with Father and Son does not mean that the divine nature and power is now threefold.

itself (θεότης) stems from our observation of God's act of watching over, seeing or beholding (θέα), and in our observation of this action we see all three persons engaged in the same action. If their action is one then the power which gives rise to that action is one, and the divine nature itself, although unknown, must be one.

At this point, around halfway through the text, Gregory admits that the argument is not yet sufficient because, in created natures, we often see things involved in common operations that are appropriately spoken of as three: three orators or farmers, for instance. Gregory then argues at some length that the action of the three divine persons is shown to be one action not three distinct but similar actions and that, hence, the power that originates them must also be one. The one divine power is constituted by Father, Son, and Spirit fulfilling their roles in every unitary divine action. Towards the end of the text Gregory tells us that, even if the main argument he has pursued is not accepted, his first argument was by itself sufficient. Gregory concludes by telling us that all divine attributes should be spoken of in the singular and that the persons may be differentiated by us only according to their causal relationships.

This text thus offers two main arguments: the first argues that natures are strictly indivisible; the second attempts to show that his opponent's charge has no force when placed in the context of an appropriate theology of the divine action and power. It is the second argument that most directly gets us to the heart of Gregory's Trinitarian theology. On this basis we can divide up the structure of the text by identifying how Gregory interweaves these two discussions. In the following diagram, the letters A and B indicate the two basic lines of argument I take Gregory to be pursuing, while the Arabic numerals indicate the different stages of those individual arguments through the course of the text:

A.1 We do not speak of three Gods because natures are not divisible: even 'three men' is a loose and misleading usage.

B.1 Natures and their intrinsic powers are known by the operations of those powers, and the divine operation is always observed to be one. Therefore the divine power and nature is indivisibly one.

Question: But surely this doesn't really solve the problem? Three people performing the same operation are still distinct: for example, three people speaking in court are correctly called three orators.

B.2 True, but operations reveal also the ways in which natures and powers are individuated, and the divine nature is seen to be always one, with a threefold order, and not to be individuated in the same way as individual people relate to their common substance.

A.2 Anyway, natures are not divisible.

Conclusion: The combination of B.1 and B.2 best supports our speech about both appropriate unity and appropriate distinction.

My argument will be that, while A.1 and A.2 take up most directly the charge that has been referred to Gregory, it is B.1 and B.2 (arguments originally developed through his controversy with Eunomius) that constitute the argument Gregory thinks conclusive and which we should treat as fundamental in his Trinitarian theology. In the following two sections I examine them in turn.

ARGUMENT A: CREATION AND THE INDIVISIBILITY OF NATURES

The first and last sections of the argument pursue the strategy that has received most attention in the meagre scholarship on this letter.[6] At the beginning of the text Gregory argues that the everyday usage of 'three men' to designate three instances of the generic 'man' is technically mistaken (A.1). This is so because each 'nature' ($\phi\acute{u}\sigma\iota\varsigma$) is uncompound and we should not allow common usage in serious philosophical argument. Indeed, says Gregory, we would run a great danger if we were to transfer such patterns of speech to God: for we know without doubt that God is one. This is so, continues Gregory, 'even though the name of Godhead extends through the Holy Trinity'. Gregory then uses this comment as a point of departure for turning to the first main section of the text, which considers the meaning of 'Godhead' and the nature of theological language (B.1).[7]

---

[6] On this letter see, most recently, G. Christopher Stead, 'Why not Three Gods? The Logic of Gregory of Nyssa's Trinitarian Doctrine', in Hubertus R. Drobner and Christoph Klock (eds.), *Studien zu Gregor von Nyssa und Die Christlichen Spätantike* (Leiden: Brill, 1990), 149–63. Stead's article considers only the logic of differentiation (almost entirely what I have designated argument A). Stead notes that the argument is applicable to the differentiation of both material things and angels, but then insists—on the weak grounds that Gregory argues his logical point from the example of three humans and usually about three biblical saints that (p. 160)—'underlying Gregory's confusion is the thought that ideal humanity, the human race at its best, would provide an analogy for the Holy Trinity'. Unlike many modern commentators Stead thinks Gregory is deeply confused, and he refrains from endorsing his understanding of the project as a whole. Nevertheless, following much modern scholarship, he presents us with the evidence for concluding that Gregory does not intend to draw any detailed or dense analogy between three people and the Triune God, but still insists that this is precisely Gregory's intention.

[7] *Ablab*. GNO 3/1. 42; NPNF V. 332: ' "Hear, O Israel, the Lord thy God is one Lord," even though the name of Godhead extends through the Holy Trinity. This I say according to the account we have given in the case of human nature, in which we have learnt that it is improper to extend the name of the nature by the mark of plurality. We must, however, more carefully examine the name of "Godhead" . . .'.

Towards the end of *Ad Ablabium* Gregory returns again to his opening argument (A.2). Once again Gregory tells us that 'natures' are in themselves free from accidents and indivisible. Those whose charge has made its way to Gregory through Ablabius have failed to see that talk of the divine persons being distinct 'Gods' as three human beings are three 'men' is simply illogical given the character of the universal term 'man' and the indivisibility of natures.

It is important to note that Gregory's argument in these sections of the text (A.1 & 2), whether or not it reveals a flawed confusion of logic and ontology to modern eyes, is not concerned with deriving an analogy from the interrelatedness of human community. The argument he offers rests not on an account specifically of human nature (let alone of human 'community'), but on an ontological or cosmological conception of natures in general. This much is apparent when a similar statement about the indivisibility of natures occurs en passant at *Contra Eunomium* 3. There Gregory considers the parallel between, on the one hand, the generation of the Son by the Father and, on the other hand, the relationship between the moisture in the grape on the vine and the moisture in wine. This is an appropriate parallel, Gregory argues, because there is true community of nature between the grape and the wine: the moisture found in the unpicked grape is essentially the same as that found in the wine.[8] Gregory here offers logically the same argument, and he does so without any need to offer the particular example of three people sharing a common nature.

The same account of indivisible natures can be found at the heart of his consideration of the first days of creation, the *Apologia in Hexaemeron*. Gregory insists that things may be changed from one nature into another, but that natures in themselves are fixed in the act of creation and are indivisible. He writes,

in the generation of countless animals we see differences according to types and bring them into general harmony by remarking that that each one of them is 'exceedingly' good ... each one by itself has a perfect nature. A horse is certainly not a cow; the nature and properties of each is conserved, not by a corruption of nature but by the power of their being (ἀλλ' εἰς τὴν τοῦ εἶναι δύναμιν ἔχουσα).[9]

Here Gregory deploys an understanding of the 'power' (δύναμις) inherent in each nature to explain their indivisibility: the creation is an act of God's power and follows an ordered sequence in which

---

[8] *Eunom.* 3. 4.

[9] *Hex.* PG 44. 92. On this understudied text see Eugeino Corsini, 'Nouvelles perspectives sur le problème des sources de l'Hexaëméron de Grégoire de Nysse', *SP* 2 (1957), 94–103; John F. Callahan, 'Greek Philosophy and the Cappadocian Cosmology', *Dumbarton Oaks Papers*, 12 (1958), 29–58.

God, after creating dark unformed matter, endows the dark matter with the light and fire of his own power. Then, through the delegated action of this power, individual natures come into being. The Word infuses a power into the creation which, in line with God's will, and mirroring the divine power, diversifies into a variety of distinct and unitary natures each with its own 'natural, divinely endowed power'.

Thus, Gregory's insistence that natures are indivisible is a cosmological doctrine (although, as we shall see, one in turn shaped by his pro-Nicene concerns). For Gregory this account is necessary both for human knowledge of God to be possible, and for understanding the creation's dependence on and autonomy from the Creator. Because natures are the basic principles in which God contemplated the creation, they are indivisible. If they were divisible, then our contemplation could not provide knowledge of God's created activity and hence of God. In the first section of *Ad Ablabium* Gregory deploys only one aspect of his account, that natures are by definition inseparable. In later sections of the argument, however, Gregory uses the same account to build a more subtle refutation of the charge which he faces. To those later sections we should now turn. As we leave this section of the *Ad Ablabium*, it is important to note that I have not considered in detail how Gregory understands this indivisibility to apply in the particular case of human beings. While this question has received a good deal of treatment in the scholarship, Gregory himself quickly moves on from this particular argument to what I am arguing is the main theme of his text. I shall do likewise.

ARGUMENT B: NATURES, POWERS, ACTIVITIES, AND KNOWLEDGE

... whosoever searches the whole of revelation will find therein no doctrine of the Divine nature, nor indeed of anything else that has a substantial existence, so that we pass our lives in ignorance of much, being ignorant first of all of ourselves as men, and then of all things besides. For who is there who has arrived at a comprehension of his own soul?[10]

The main section of the text (B.1–2) begins when Gregory insists that we cannot allow loose and misleading patterns of human speech to be transferred to the Godhead and that we can best clear up the charge he faces by considering the nature of 'Godhead' itself. This main section of the text is divided into two related discussions separated by a short interlude.

The first discussion (B.1) introduces the idea that terms used to

[10] *Eunom.* 2. 106.

describe God do not describe God's nature, they describe things 'around' (περί) the divine nature, things through which the divine nature may be known.[11] Gregory adds that all the terms we use for God work by creating a particular sense (ἰδίαν διάνοιαν). This sense takes as its point of departure some feature of our world that reflects the activity of God, and then negates or intensifies that core significance in the attempt to speak worthily of God. Such terms do indicate something that may appropriately be thought or spoken of the divine, but they do not 'reach' the divine nature. For example, calling God 'Giver of Life' draws our attention to what is given, not directly to the nature of the giver. With these moves Gregory begins to outline an ontological and epistemological foundation for theological language that follows the course set out by Basil in his anti-Eunomian polemic. For both Gregory and Basil this point identifies a key divergence from Eunomius: no term, not even any scriptural term, can be understood to signify the divine nature directly.[12] Also like Basil, Gregory frequently deploys the terminology of ἐπίνοια (and in the passage of *Ad Ablabium* just discussed ἰδίαν διάνοιαν functions as a synonym for ἐπίνοια).[13] From the act of mental dissection that is ἐπίνοια we may acquire a sense of an object that remains hidden from direct perception. We call God 'Giver of Life' and by abstraction we term God 'Life': by reflecting on God's act of creating all things we learn to speak of God as uncreated.

For Gregory it is vital that we build up our set of appellations for God in a way that preserves appropriate reverence and reserve: participating in the established practice of those who already undertake this discipline and sharing their assumptions about what may be reverently said of God is a prerequisite for the good use of ἐπίνοια. The process of ἐπίνοια is also circular (but at its best virtuously so): each act of abstraction needing to enhance, change, and yet stay in conformity with the whole of one's set of appellations for God. Thus Gregory understands the good practice of ἐπίνοια to be part of a spiritual process, an ἄσκησις of heart and mind. God's activities and the text of Scripture enable a process of ἐπίνοια by which we can speak of the divine being, but, Gregory writes, 'in applying such appellations to the divine essence, "which passes all understanding", we do not seek to glory in it by the names we employ, but to guide our own selves by the aid of such terms towards the comprehension of the things which are hidden' (πρός τὴν τῶν κρυπτῶν κατανόησιν).[14]

---

[11] *Ablab.* GNO 3/1. 43; NPNF V. 332.
[12] e.g. Basil, *Eunom.* 1. 14–15; 2. 32; Gregory of Nyssa, *Eunom.* 7. 4–5.
[13] A paradigmatic text in Gregory discussing this theme is *Eunom.* 2. For fuller discussion of the term's history and use in Basil see Ch. 8, pp. 191ff.
[14] Gregory of Nyssa, *Eunom.* 2 (GNO 1/1. 270; NPNF V. 265). See also *in Cant.* 1.

To understand the main argument of the *Ad Ablabium* to which Gregory is beginning to turn here we need also to note two aspects of the philosophical traditions from which Gregory draws his nature and power terminology. First, the link between natures and intrinsic powers in Gregory's cosmology is of importance both for his Trinitarian theology and in his account of human knowledge of God. In two recent articles and a book Michel Barnes provides us with the key elements we need to understand Gregory's arguments. In the first article Barnes sets out the differing traditions of 'transcendental causality' that are operative in Gregory and Eunomius' account of the relations between the three divine persons. In Gregory, the divine nature is inherently productive, expressed through the doctrine that the unitary and simple divine power is intrinsic to the indivisible divine nature. Gregory of course insists that such natural productivity and expression is willed not necessary, but his account makes a great deal of use of natural metaphors, such as the example of a fire and its heat, to emphasize the reality of the ontological union between a nature and its power. It is in such a context that the Son may be presented as both the power of God—in which case inseparable from the Father—and called *the* power only by appropriation, there being only one divine power intrinsic to the divine nature. In offering this model of 'transcendent causality' Gregory demonstrates his debts to a long philosophical and medical tradition which intimately associates the nature or reality of an existent and its power. Gregory's most immediate 'intellectual precedent and authority' (to use Barnes's words) for the deployment of this tradition of power terminology in a transcendent context is Plotinus, especially as evident in *Ennead* 5. 4.[15]

In Gregory's account of how theological language reaches only what is 'around' the Godhead, and in his account of God's ordering of creation in terms of natures and powers, we see him making use of another facet of this philosophical tradition. Indeed, Gregory again seems to be following Plotinus' lead: both writers not only talk of a power as being intrinsic to a nature, but also metaphorically present a power as being 'around' a nature. In *Ennead* 5. 1, a text which makes a frequent appearance in Cappadocian theology, Plotinus describes the power that each thing exhibits as 'a surrounding reality directed to what is outside'.[16] In *Ennead* 5. 4 Plotinus uses this very same language about both *nous* and *psyche* to indicate how their generative nature expresses itself in creation. Here, the talk of powers being 'around' natures serves as a way of indicating that

---

[15] See Barnes, 'Eunomius of Cyzicus and Gregory of Nyssa, 81.
[16] Plotinus, *Ennead*, 5. 1. 6.

although powers are the cause of the activity of νοῦς and ψυχή outside themselves, the natures themselves remain somehow unknown and distinct.[17] Gregory too speaks of theological language as reaching that which is 'around' the divine nature, that is, the divine nature's power which gives rise to divine activity in the world. This metaphorically spatial language nicely indicates the distinction between knowing the power of a nature and knowing a nature directly and is often reinforced, as at *Ennead* 5. 1 by means of the analogy of the sun and its rays.

However, and second, Gregory talks not only of nature and power, but also of activity (ἐνέργεια), and here we come to the second article by Michel Barnes. In distinguishing these three terms Gregory employs a technical sequence of causal language in which[18] activities *ad extra* are set in motion by a nature's power and it is by observing activities that we may recognize the power that is operative. For example, Gregory speaks in the *Ad Ablabium* of 'the various activities of the transcendent power' through which the power is known directly after he has indicated that natures remain unknowable except through activities.[19] At this point nature is interchangeable with power.[20] Gregory's theology thus incorporates ontological and cosmological doctrines into a complex system of thought which provides the constant foundation for his articulation of pro-Nicene

---

[17] Plotinus, *Ennead*, 5. 4. 2.

[18] See Barnes, 'The Background and Use of Eunomius' Causal Language', in Michel Barnes and Daniel H. Williams (eds.), *Arianism after Arius: Essays on the Development of the Fourth Century Trinitarian Conflicts* (Edinburgh: T. & T. Clark, 1993), 217–36. Barnes's paper is concerned primarily with the presence of the sequence essence, activity, product in Eunomius and its precedents. However, en passant he remarks on the significance that stems from Gregory's retention of 'power' in the sequence between essence and activity. This different sequence helps to shape a very different account of divine causality. In Eunomius' sequence and tradition the link between essence and activity is not a necessary one and thus, deploying such a sequence to describe the Son as 'product' of the Father's activity serves to indicate the necessary subordination (and lack of coeternity) that the Son must possess. Gregory, on the other hand, retains 'power' in the sequence and, because a power is intrinsic to a nature and necessarily contains the causal capacity of that nature, speaking of the Son as the Father's power helps to shape a very different account of the divine generation.

[19] *Ablab.* GNO 3/1. 44; NPNF V. 333. Cf. Origen, *Princ.* I. 2. 12. 411–16 (cited by Barnes, 'Background and Use', 231) for a direct precedent. Cf. *Eunom.* 1. 30–2, where the same threefold sequence and the same virtual equivalence of power and nature is to be found.

[20] Note here Barnes, *Power of God*, 297–305. Barnes argues that in *Ablab.* Gregory focuses his argument on ἐνέργεια language because of the polemic context. Ἐνέργεια language had become linked to debate over the Spirit, with some ex-Homoiousians presenting the Spirit as an ἐνέργεια. Gregory's concern is to relocate ἐνέργεια language into his own metaphysical sequence so that talk of the Spirit's ἐνέργεια points to the power that such an activity reveals. Barnes's argument—with which I agree—is not intended to supplant his account of the importance of δύναμις terminology: the focus on ἐνέργεια here is a focus intended to draw us to recognition of the centrality of power in his causal sequence. Because I am concerned to present *Ablab.* as paradigmatic I have not discussed Nyssa's particular use of ἐνέργεια language here in any detail.

Trinitarian theology. The flexibility of this language is also a key point in its favour when it is used not only to describe the character of created reality, but also to shape an account of the Creator, who is conceived as both creating a world in His own image and yet as being truly distinct from it. When it suits his purpose Gregory deploys different aspects of nature, power, and activity terminology in the attempt to characterize human knowledge of God. We must watch carefully to spot the allusions that Gregory makes to this terminology, but we should beware of mistaking his complex and ad hoc allusion for simple incoherence. It is time now to return to the course of the first main section of the argument (B.1).

Having insisted that we know only the power of a thing not its nature, Gregory goes on to argue that 'Godhead' (θεότης) is itself a term which originates in observation of the divine activity of seeing or contemplating. However, Father, Son, and Spirit all seem to be engaged in the *same* activity of seeing and contemplating. Thus, says Gregory, if the activities of the three are the same, then the power which gave rise to them is the same and the ineffable divine nature in which that power is inherent must also be one.[21] The divine nature remains unknown but its power is revealed to be one.[22] Gregory has thus offered a refutation of the charge that his teaching implies three Gods, but one considerably more sophisticated than his first attempt (in section A.1) concentrating solely on the logic of differentiation. However, the force of this second refutation will only be felt by someone who first accepts the significance of knowledge following observation of activity and then accepts Gregory's account of how divine activity is described in Scripture.

Gregory seems to be arguing that the 'three Gods' charge is best faced by opening a discussion about two fundamental questions: what do we mean by 'divine nature'? how it is possible for us to speak of divine nature? As Gregory knows well, these two questions are inseparable: he sets up a foundation for our speaking of God, but only by also beginning to offer an account of the divine nature and

---

[21] *Ablab.* GNO 3/1. 43–4; NPNF V. 332–3: 'Hence it is clear that by any of the terms we use the Divine Nature is not itself signified, but some one of its surroundings (τι τῶν περί) is made known ... Since, then, as we perceive the varied operations of the power above us, we fashion our appellations from the several operations that are known to us ... He surveys all things and overlooks them all, discerning our thoughts, and even entering by His power of contemplation those things that are not visible, [hence] we suppose that Godhead (θεότης) is so called from beholding (θέα) ... Now ... let him consider this operation, and judge whether it belongs to one of the persons whom we believe in the Holy Trinity, or whether the power extends throughout the Three Persons ... For Scripture attributes the act of seeing equally to Father, Son and Spirit.'

[22] The principle that operations reveal natures is often treated as a fundamental of Cappadocian theology. At least in the case of Gregory it is not so: operations reveal powers while natures remain unknown.

its activity. The epistemological question must receive an ontological and a cosmological answer, but the cosmology is already shaped by a consideration of how God creates and of how the creation imitates that divine nature. Of course, Gregory's answers to these questions already also contain an answer to the question of whether the divine nature can be divided. Nevertheless, his purpose should not be understood solely as one of fixing the cards so that the 'Macedonian' will lose. Rather, we should understand him as indicating that questions about the divine nature can only be faced once one has in place appropriate conceptions of the relations between Creator and creation and of the character of human knowledge of God. In other words, articulating the pro-Nicene grammar of divinity necessarily involves articulating an account of the relationship between Creator and creation.

Having introduced the text's central argument Gregory now admits, in a rhetorically sophisticated interlude, that his main argument seems so far to have offered no reason why we should not speak of three Gods.[23] In fact, he argues, the attempt to argue only from the unity of operations might seem to make pro-Nicene theology even more susceptible to the charge that has been raised. There seem to be plenty of cases where we admit common operation but are also clear that distinct individuals are involved. Thus, for example, we speak of many orators or farmers without reference to any shared nature. On the other hand, says Gregory in a quick aside, if we did suppose that we could actually know the divine nature, then the observation of the unified divine action in creation would seem to emphasize the importance of subsuming the persons under a unitary Godhead. But, he continues, since that course is forbidden to us because we want to argue only from operations, it seems that the argument is weak. The interlude ends by Gregory saying that he has tried to highlight the possible response of his adversaries so that the direction of his argument may become clearer. This short passage serves a number of purposes. On the one hand, it cleverly serves to put off the charge that the question posed is simply not being faced; on the other hand, it serves to highlight what has so far been missing from Gregory's account. While he has indicated the unity of the persons in their activity, Gregory has not yet offered a fully convincing account of the link between the common actions of the divine persons and the indivisibility of the divine nature. The answer comes in the second half of the work's main section (B.2) where Gregory offers a more extensive account of the link between inner divine causality and operation *ad extra*.

[23] *Ablab.* GNO 3/1. 46; NPNF V. 333.

His first step in B.2 is to indicate the distinction between the inseparable union of the divine persons in their activity and the accidental or coincidental activity of human persons undertaking a common project. Different human persons may undertake the same task but they do not directly participate in the action of others and each one possesses his or her own special sphere of activity.[24] In other words, in terms hinted at here but developed in more detail in the *Ad Graecos*, the actions of human beings demonstrate an interrelated causal matrix which reveals human beings to have a substance that may be individuated in a way characteristic of the created order. Not only do individual persons possess their own activity, they also reveal themselves to be impermanent and to be caused by previous generations of human beings.[25] Operations thus reveal the character of the powers and natures with which they are connected. However, in the case of the Father we find no individual activity in which the Son does not also work. Similarly, the Son has no 'special activity' without the Spirit. Whatever sort of individuality and difference exists between the three divine persons it is not the sort of individuality we observe in an existent that has its own self-caused and distinct activity. The divine persons, thus, do not simply act together, they function inseparably to constitute any and every divine activity towards the creation. Gregory goes on to articulate his position further by developing his account of inner divine causality. He talks of the power or action of God 'issuing from the Father as from a spring, [being] brought into operation by the Son, and perfecting its grace by the power of the Spirit' (ἐκ μὲν τοῦ πατρὸς οἷον ἐκ πηγῆς τινος ἀφορμώμενος, ὑπὸ δὲ τοῦ υἱοῦ ἐνεργούμενος, ἐν δὲ τῇ δυνάμει τοῦ πνεύματος τελειῶν τὴν χάριν . . .).[26]

This phrase, and others like it, have sometimes been taken to indicate the 'personal' character of Gregory's Trinitarian theology, as if Gregory were telling us that the divine persons co-operated, at the Father's initiative, to bring to fruition every divine action. Unfortunately, although such a reading correctly highlights the position of the Father in this sequence, it misses key elements of Gregory's argument. Gregory, of course, does not want to deny that the divine persons possess their own distinct and irreducible hypostatic existence. However, he uses a model of causality to present the

---

[24] *Ablab.* GNO 3/1. 47; NPNF V. 334: 'Thus, since among men the action of each in the same pursuits is discriminated, they are properly called many, since each of them is circumscribed from the others within his own environment, according to the special character of his operation' (ἑκάστου αὐτῶν εἰς ἰδίαν περιγραφὴν κατὰ τὸ ἰδιότροπον τῆς ἐνεργείας ἀποτεμνομένου τῶν ἄλλων).

[25] For the discussion in *Ad Graecos* see esp. GNO 3/1. 23–4.

[26] *Ablab.* GNO 3/1. 50; NPNF V. 334.

three not as possessing distinct actions, but as together constituting *just one distinct action* (because they are one power). Gregory here makes no attempt to apply psychological categories to explain what it means for the persons to be distinct within the unitary divine power and deploys no language that obviously relies on metaphors of co-operation.[27]

Gregory can now present his second answer to the critique of pro-Nicene theology in a more sophisticated and powerful form. The activity of divine persons shows God's power (and hence the divine nature) not to be individuated as is human nature. Here it may help to call to mind an aspect of Gregory's theology that is alluded to in the *Ad Ablabium*, but which I discussed earlier in this chapter: God has created a world whose order and structure is (at infinite remove) a reflection of God's own power. This cosmological foundation helps Gregory assert that through observing God's activity we see that the divine action or will is the will of the Father that proceeds through the Son to the Spirit, and yet without that will being only the action of the Father, or being the action of three together.[28] It is, thus simply inappropriate to speak of three Gods, because we do not observe three distinct actions in the divine activity. However, this observation does not serve only the purpose of indicating that the three have a unitary 'motion and disposition of the good will' (μία ... τοῦ ἀγαθοῦ θελήματος κίνησίς τε καὶ διάδοσις),[29] it also serves to emphasize the incomprehensible nature of the divine power. Gregory does not allow us to argue that what we observe in the divine activity is just one acting power comparable to any one power in the created order: the divine power is one and yet Scripture and the confession of the Church insist that the persons are three. Gregory's ontology is intrinsic to his argument, but he uses this ontological reflection as a further way of vindicating the uniqueness and ineffability of the divine nature.

In the final few pages of the text (my section A.2), Gregory both turns back to the initial answer he had given to Ablabius' question based on his understanding of the indivisibility of natures, and

---

[27] Unless we take the mere ascription of a distinct role and a distinct name within the divine action to indicate 'psychological' content. If we do so, our language has become so general that we might just as well attribute 'psychological' content to the discrete parts of the computer on which this paper is being written. However, just to repeat, my point is not that Gregory does not conceive of the persons as truly distinct, but that ascribing true distinctness to the Trinitarian persons is not necessarily equivalent to ascribing dense psychological content to them.

[28] e.g. *Ablab.* GNO 3/1. 48; NPNF V. 334: 'From Him, I say, who is the chief source of gifts, all things which have shared in this grace have obtained their life. When we inquire, then, whence this good gift came to us, we find, *by the guidance of the Scriptures* that it was from the Father, the Son and the Spirit ...' (italics added).

[29] *Ablab.* GNO 3/1. 48; NPNF V. 334.

offers a few more hints about the importance of grasping a unitary divine causality. That Gregory is willing to revert to his initial argument at this stage—and that he even hints at a third argument which would argue that 'Godhead' cannot be the name of a nature because God is above every name—may be taken simply to be evidence of Gregory's willingness to provide Ablabius with a variety of polemical resources. However, one might also argue that in pursuing this multi-pronged tactic Gregory demonstrates a keen awareness of how his theology is attempting to argue for a theological epistemology that many of his contemporaries may have found too austere.[30]

Gregory also turns here to those who might think his insistence on the unity of the divine nature serves to confuse the distinctions of the persons. It is, he insists, only in the causal relationships between the persons that we can make any distinctions. The sequence of the one divine action *ad extra* reflects the nature and order of God's *internal* generation, and in both the same sequence of causality is operative. Nevertheless, this internal order does not reveal the nature of the persons as such, but only their mode of having or exercising that which remains ineffable. Thus because persons and essence are identical, that in which the persons consist also remains unknown:

when we learn that he [the Father] is unbegotten, we are taught how he exists (ὅπως ... εἶναι), and how it is fit that we should conceive Him as existing, but what He is we do not hear in that phrase.[31]

Thus, we may speak of the way in which a person contributes to the divine activity—and thereby we understand something more of the divine power—but the nature itself that the divine persons share remains ineffable. In Chapter 8 I noted that in Basil the phrase τρόπος ὑπάρξεως served to identify not a metaphysically dense notion of personhood but merely the mode of origination of the persons. In Gregory of Nyssa the phrase is more frequently used, but with equal austerity of meaning (and directly still only of Son and Spirit).[32] What we know of the persons is their modes of origination and the characteristics attributed to them by Scripture—as long as all attributes are understood to be those of the one simple Godhead. The language of individuation itself serves here to emphasize that the nature of a divine person remains ineffable.

CONCLUSION: THE ESSENTIAL NYSSA

for we, who are initiated into the mystery of godliness by the divinely inspired words of the Scripture do not see between the Father and the Son

---

[30] *Ablab.* GNO 3/1. 55; NPNF V. 336. [31] *Ablab.* GNO 3/1. 57; NPNF V. 336.
[32] Sherwood, *Earlier Ambigua*, 159 ff.

a partnership of Godhead, but a unity ... (οὐχὶ κοινωνίαν θεότητος ... ἀλλ' ἑνότητα).³³

The *Ad Ablabium* does not centrally argue for three human persons as a useful analogy for the Trinity. At the beginning and end of the text Gregory is indeed directly concerned with whether his account of the Godhead falls prey to the same logic of differentiation that operates between three people. However, the bulk of *Ad Ablabium* is taken up with drawing out a related but distinct argument that does not begin with a particular understanding of differentiation or individuation in the Godhead (although it does result in such an account). Rather, this main argument of the text begins by establishing an account of the character of human knowledge of God and an account of the ontological principles on which our speech of the Trinity should be founded. This account provides, for Gregory, the necessary background against which we should offer any account of the logic of differentiation of the divine *hypostases*, and against which we should offer any analogy for the character of their communion. In this light perhaps we should begin to teach and read Gregory assuming different texts to be paradigmatic. Rather than turning first to the *Ad Ablabium* I suggest we make far more use of three texts: *Catechetical Oration, Refutation of Eunomius' Confession,* and *Contra Eunomium 2*.³⁴

At the end of this investigation I will set out three observations about the wider character of Gregory's Trinitarian theology that follow from my discussion of the *Ad Ablabium*.

1. Gregory's various deployments of the sequence nature–power–activity, and his insistence that, while operations reveal their originating powers, natures remain unknown and ineffable, is the cosmological and ontological foundation on which his account of Trinitarian theology is built. However, these reflections deliver not simply Gregory's account of God's ineffability, but his account of what I have termed the texture of God's ineffability. In the first of his homilies on *The Song of Songs* Gregory writes in general terms,

the unlimited [divine] nature cannot be accurately contained by a name; rather, every capacity for concepts, and every form of words and names, even if they seem to contain something great and befitting God's glory, are unable to grasp his reality. But starting from certain traces and sparks, as it were, our words aim at the unknown, and from what we can grasp we make conjectures by a kind of analogy about the ungraspable ... the wonders visible in the universe give material for the theological terms by which we

---

³³ Gregory of Nyssa, *Ref.* 40. (GNO 1/2. 328).
³⁴ Non-Patristic specialists should note that the *Eunom.* 2 which appears as NPNF V. 101 ff. is actually *Refutation of Eunomius' Confession*; the true *Eunom.* 2 appears as NPNF V. 250 ff.

call God wise, powerful, good, holy, blessed, eternal, judge, saviour, and so forth ... the human mind is unable to find any description, example, or adequate expression of that beauty ...[35]

In this passage, Gregory's well-known insistence on the divine infinity founds a complex account of theological analogy. On the one hand, the creation seems to provide points of departure for our talk of God (and here Gregory should not be thought of as conceiving of creation as a separate source from Scripture: scriptural narrative and terminology is taken to direct our attention appropriately to the ways in which creation mirrors the divine existence through the presence of delegated power). On the other hand, Gregory insists that God remains at infinite remove from our understanding; the divine power creates a context in which human beings may move in trust and in truth towards God, but God is not comprehended.

Elsewhere in Gregory's theology—such as in the *Ad Ablabium*—we seem to find the logic of natures, powers, and activities enabling a more concrete account of the relationship between the activities we observe and the realities initiating them. But, as we have seen in this chapter, even here Gregory uses his account of Creator and creation to force upon us a deliberate and focused *askesis* of the imagination, insisting that the logic of ineffable natures known through the activity of their intrinsic powers is fundamental to the structure of the creation itself. The particular discipline of epistemological reserve and cultivated attention to Scripture (and to the creation in Scripture's light) that Gregory shapes is thus founded on a developed theology of the divine infinity and power and a developed account of the created order and ontological difference.

2. In the last sentence of his summary of Gregory's Trinitarian theology Richard Hanson reports, but makes little of, Karl Holl's 1904 description of Gregory's God as a life-imparting power (ζωοποιός δύναμις) in three forms.[36] In fact, Holl's brief account provides a good basis for discussing the general conception of Gregory's Trinitarian theology that shines through the complex argument of the *Ad Ablabium*. Holl both saw Gregory's account of the simple and ineffable divine power prefigured in Basil, and, in its particular and extensive development, as the theme which distinguished Gregory's account from that of the other 'Cappadocian' theologies. For Holl, Gregory makes his own a theme that the other Cappadocians treat as one among many themes. Holl also sees Gregory's vision of what is revealed in—and active in—the scriptural account of salvation history as revolving around the revelation

---

[35] *Cant.* 1.   [36] Hanson, *The Search*, 730.

of a threefold divine power. In this way Gregory provides himself with the basis for a soteriology which draws together an understanding of God's salvific divine power restoring the creation and a theology of creation in which God has shown himself in creation as the one whose inexhaustible power sustains and exists always in an economy of infinite plenitude. In this theology of redemption Christ's being one with the divine power, being *the* divine power is the basis for the incorporation of all into the life and power of Christ.[37]

Importantly, Holl also treats Gregory's account of the divine power which *is* the threefold being of Father, Son, and Spirit as the point of departure for his brief treatment of the ways in which the persons are differentiated.[38] As I hinted towards the end of the last section of the chapter Gregory's talk of the individuation of the persons is itself not intended to result in one account of the difference between them, but rather to emphasize the conditions under which we must speak of difference and the conditions under which we speak of unity. The mode of the persons' individuation remains hidden from us, although Gregory insists that only confession of the reality and eternity of the hypostatic distinctions can do justice to the account of God's activity with which Scripture presents us.

It is noteworthy that Holl assumes in Gregory the presence of a subtle subordination of Son and Spirit and suggests that he has failed to follow through on the logic of his own theology. Holl's argument here is a reflection of the late nineteenth-century argument that 'Cappadocian' Trinitarianism was always marked by Basil's failure to leave behind his Homoiousian past. Holl's own failure, it seems to me, is to note how Gregory's understanding of the unity of the divine power and nature is intended to govern statements about the causal order within the Trinity just as much as it governs his account of the differentiation of divine persons. Gregory insists that the order we perceive in scriptural discussion of the Trinity does not involve spatial or temporal separation or sequences because of the unity and simplicity of the divine essence. Similarly each person possess the fullness of the Godhead, there are no degrees in being God. Thus his understanding of divine unity

---

[37] These themes may be particularly clearly seen in Gregory's homily on 1 Cor. 15: 28. There is a detailed discussion of the text in Hübner, *Die Einheit des Leibes Christi*, 27–66; see also Ch. 12. Part of the significance of this text lies in the way that it shows particularly clearly how the polemical conflict around the Son's status and what I have termed the grammar of divinity had, for Gregory, clearly soteriological consequences. See also *Eunom.* 5. 5, where Gregory discusses the transformation of the Christian through the indwelling of God's power: this passage opens a number of avenues for exploring Gregory's technical vocabularies for the theme of *theosis*.

[38] Holl, *Amphilochius von Ikonium*, 209 ff.

and simplicity is intended to render the divine distinctions ultimately incomprehensible: they cannot be equated with any distinctions in the created order. Of course, even if I am right, this does not mean that there is no hierarchy in Gregory's account. It means we cannot assume the order and hierarchy in the Trinity to bring along an ontological subordinationism. The priority of the Father as cause—even if it is the priority of one who eternally gives rise to a mutuality of loving exchange—is in some sense still a priority.

3. Like most other pro-Nicenes Gregory uses a variety of terminologies for describing the relationship between the divine unity and persons; *ousia*, φύσις, *hypostasis*, and πρόσωπον are all brought into service when it is deemed necessary.[39] As we have seen, however, the deployment of these terminologies does not result in Gregory offering us a dense account of divine personhood as such. Gregory does tell us, of course, that we can distinguish the persons with causal language. Now, given the structure of modern readings of Gregory, it is only to be expected that mention of this argument will result in the question being posed 'what degree of distinction does this causal language involve?' I suspect that the nearest we can come to the answer that Gregory might give to this question is to repeat that given with reference to pro-Nicenes more generally in Chapter 11: 'we do not know'. Scripture demands that we confess a logic of eternal distinction which insists that insofar as we can talk of God as an eternal and distinct reality, so too we can speak of Father and Son and Spirit as eternally distinct realities. At the same time Scripture demands that we speak of a unitary divine power and nature, *and*, for Gregory, it demands of us analogical talk that attempts to explore the resonances and implications of the character of God's action as narrated in Scripture. For those modern commentators who accept the account of east and west as differentiated by a preference for social or mental analogies, failure to deploy some sort of social analogy of necessity implies a failure to distinguish the three persons appropriately. However, such an equation is not a necessary one and its deployment reveals a lack of understanding of the peculiarly modern preoccupations that make it seem plausible.

[39] For summary discussion see Lienhard, 'Ousia and Hypostasis'.

15
The Grammar of Augustine's Trinitarian Theology

INTRODUCTION: THE MODERN ATTACK ON AUGUSTINE

In much modern appropriation Augustine is treated as the source and exemplar of a distinctively western style of Trinitarian theology.[1] Ironically, while this division of Trinitarian theologies into 'eastern' and 'western' began, in its modern form, as a way of indicating the superiority of 'western' and scholastic theology, in recent writing the same division has been used to highlight the supposed deficiencies of the west.[2] Denigration of Augustine's Trinitarianism, however, continues to occur even as Augustinian scholars have begun to revise radically the accounts of his Trinitarian theology that have been standard since the early years of this century.[3] Unfortunately, the critique of Augustine's Trinitarianism to be found in much modern theological writing does not occur actively against this recent trend in Augustinian scholarship—engaging directly and in detail with original texts and attempting to refute these new scholarly arguments—but largely in ignorance of it.

There are a number of different charges made against Augustine. Some have charged Augustine's Trinitarian theology with being insufficiently Trinitarian, with being focused overly much on the unity of God and with being reliant on an alien Platonic metaphysics which serves to prevent a fully Trinitarian theology.[4] For instance, Cornelius Plantinga sees two forces at work in Augustine's Trinitarianism: his attention to biblical material draws him towards a

---

[1] For extended treatment of aspects of this chapter see my ' "Remember that you are Catholic" '. Michel René Barnes, 'Re-reading Augustine's Theology of the Trinity', in S. T. Davis, D. Kendall, and G. O'Collins (eds.), *The Trinity: An Interdisciplinary Symposium on the Doctrine of the Trinity* (Oxford and New York: Oxford University Press, 1999), 145–76, presents a complementary perspective to that essay.

[2] Barnes, 'De Régnon Reconsidered'; idem, 'Augustine in Contemporary Trinitarian Theology', *Theological Studies*, 56 (1995), 237–50.

[3] For a list of relevant scholarship here see the initial notes to my ' "Remember that you are Catholic" '.

[4] For example, Catherine Mowry LaCugna writes (*God For Us: The Trinity and Christian Life* (San Francisco: HarperCollins, 1991), 214): 'Augustine's point of departure in *De Trinitate* was the unity of the divine essence shared by the three divine persons'. On p. 10 she nicely shows how this account of Augustine may be taken to be the first step in a story of western failure at Trinitarian theology.

pluaralistic social Trinitarianism while his commitment to a Platonic doctrine of God's unity and simplicity draws him to corrupt the biblical account and towards the focus on God's unity that has been so consistently a mark of western theology.[5] One related charge that has come especially from Orthodox theologians is that Augustine's theology is insufficiently personal. This critique alleges that, because Augustine focuses so strongly on the unity of God, he fails to be attentive to the Father's status as personal foundation of the divine communion. In the strongest of these critiques Augustine's doctrine of *filioque* stands as proof that he saw the Trinity founded in the unitary divine essence.[6]

My aim in this chapter is to offer an account of the fundamental grammar of persons and essence in Augustine's Trinitarian theology, showing that this grammar provides us with one of the clearest examples of a fundamentally pro-Nicene Trinitarianism. This grammar, this set of rules or principles, provided the basis both for Augustine's reading of Scripture and for his articulation of more detailed presentations of the doctrine (in part through the use of likenesses or analogies).[7] The first section of the chapter discusses some of the key principles apparent in Augustine's early Trinitarian theology and his debt to Platonism. The second shows how Augustine articulated his mature Trinitarian theology through a particularly sophisticated deployment of the notion of divine simplicity.

---

[5] Cornelius Plantinga, 'Social Trinity and Tritheism', in R. J. Feenstra and C. Plantinga Jr. (eds.), *Trinity, Incarnation and Atonement: Philosophical and Theological Essays* (Notre Dame, Ind.: University of Indiana Press, 1989), 21–47. The assumption that biblical material necessarily and obviously results in a 'social' Trinitarianism is itself a questionable if not somewhat naive assumption given the length and sophistication of the exegetical debates in this history of Trinitarian theology and the peculiarly modern character of 'social Trinitarianism' as Plantinga defines it.

[6] Vladimir Lossky, *The Mystical Theology of the Eastern Church* (Cambridge: James Clarke, 1957), 57 writes of filioquist theologies: 'The relationships of origin which do not bring the Son and the Spirit back directly to the unique source, to the Father—the one as begotten, the other as proceeding—become a system of relationships with the one essence: something logically posterior to the one essence.' Of course this *may* occur, but whether it *necessarily* occurs is a very different question: my suggestion is that there is no indication that Augustine's pneumatology does not entirely satisfy Lossky's own description, given on pp. 56–7, that '[t]he nature is inconceivable apart from the persons or as anterior to the three persons, even in the logical order'. As we saw in Ch. 12, this critique finds one of its loudest advocates in John Zizioulas, who places much emphasis on a supposed reorientation of ontology towards a basis in the person by the Cappadocians, e.g. at *Being as Communion*, 88: 'By usurping the ontological character of *ousia*, the word *person*//*hypostasis* became capable of signifying God's being *in an ultimate sense*. The subsequent developments of trinitarian theology, especially in the West with Augustine and the scholastics, have led us to see the term *ousia*, not *hypostasis*, as the expression of the ultimate character and the causal principle ($\dot{\alpha}\rho\chi\acute{\eta}$) in God's being.' I will argue here that, for Augustine, neither person nor *ousia* can express the 'ultimate character' of God's being (I suspect Lossky would have argued against Zizioulas's extravagant claim here) or the causal principle in God. The 'causal principle' is ultimately the Father.

[7] See my ' "Remember that you are Catholic".'

Ultimately, however, we will best understand this mature account when we see that it is also an articulation of the very epistemological and anthropological dynamics that we have seen shared between pro-Nicene theologians and present so clearly in Gregory of Nyssa.

THE EARLY AUGUSTINE: PRO-NICENE OR PLATONIST?

When the origin of Augustine's Trinitarian theology is discussed two interrelated strategies are frequently found. On the one hand, Augustine's earliest writings are often considered primarily against the background of Neoplatonic writing, and on the other hand, Augustine is usually considered without reference to his immediate theological forebears, the Latin theological tradition of the fourth century. In this attitude we see echoes of the nineteenth-century thesis that Augustine converted first to Neoplatonism and only secondly to Christianity. This two-stage thesis has been long discredited, in part because it misses the complex intertwining of some Platonic themes with virtually all Christianity of the fourth century. Nevertheless, some Platonic themes were central to the development of Augustine's Trinitarian theology. Hence we need to begin by thinking both about the character of this Platonism, and then about the sources for his earliest assumptions in Trinitarian theology.

In book 7 of the *Confessions*[8] Augustine sets out for us what was perhaps the most important shift in his understanding of God, a shift to a position that basically remained with him until his death. He tells us that he had originally conceived of God as an extended, and perhaps infinitely diffused, material substance. Augustine tells us that the most fundamental problem he saw with this account was that God's materiality must imply God's divisibility.[9] However, through reading some 'books of the Platonists' at the same time as he was returning to his Christianity, Augustine came to a new account of God. This account involved five interrelated elements described at *Confessions* 7. 10. 16 ff. First, Augustine realized that God was the immaterial 'light' of 'Truth itself': eternal and everywhere present. Second, Augustine realized that God was distinct from all, and yet calling to and drawing all things towards Truth through a benevolent providence. Third, Augustine realized that God was Being itself. 'Truth itself' was identical with the real source of all existence, and thus the incorporeality and infinity of Truth itself did not mean that God was literally nothing (*nihil*). Fourth,

---

[8] The argument of the next few paragraphs is related to that of Lewis Ayres and Michel René Barnes, 'God', in A. Fitzgerald (ed.), *Augustine: An Encyclopedia* (Grand Rapids, Mich.: Eerdmans, 1999), 384–90.

[9] *Conf.* 7. 1; cf. 7. 5.

Augustine realized that all things that are not Being itself exist only by participation in God and through the gift of Being from God. Thus he can say of himself, 'unless my being remains in Him, it cannot remain in me'.[10] Fifth, Augustine discovered a paradoxical relationship between the soul and God. On the one hand, the soul was immaterial and 'above' the material reality of the body, and when discovered to be such served as a pointer to the nature of God. On the other hand, the soul was still mutable and served only to reveal the incomparable and infinitely surpassing reality and 'light' of the divine.[11]

If we were to add one more point to this list, but a point that does not clearly appear at *Confessions* 7. 10. 16, it would be that God was simple. At *Confessions* 4. 16. 28 Augustine describes God as 'marvellously simple and unchangeable' (*mirabiliter simplicem atque incommutabilem*). This is taken to imply the foolishness of trying to think of God as subject to accidental predication: imagining God as having greatness or beauty as qualities of a divine nature or substance. Instead, God *is* inseparably and eternally greatness or beauty itself. There is no division possible between being and attributes in the God who simply is those qualities that we want to predicate of God. Divine simplicity is treated as an essential corollary of Augustine's conception of God as immaterial, unchangeable, and as Truth itself (although it is by no means simply a 'Neoplatonic' idea).[12]

It is important to note that at *Confessions* 7. 10. 16 Augustine does not offer a comprehensive account of what the Platonic texts said about God. This summary is, rather, an account of elements in those texts that provided a great leap forward in his understanding of God: it is a partial account of how some themes provided answers to questions raised by his engagements with such movements as Manichaeism and Scepticism. Indeed, the picture is further complicated when we see that Augustine's encounter with these texts occurred *during* his slow return to Christianity and *after* his initial encounter with Ambrose of Milan and with Ambrose's spiritual exegesis of the Old Testament. Augustine's eclectic borrowings from Platonism thus took place in the context of an existing knowledge of and some degree of commitment to Christian doctrine.[13] These texts provided a fundamental intellectual orientation enabling him to articulate

---

[10] *Conf.* 7. 11. 17.
[11] For Augustine's understanding of the soul's power and place see *Quant.* 1. 2–2. 3, 34. 77.
[12] It is only a little later in his career (e.g. *Io. ev. tr.* 1. 1. 8) that Augustine ascribes infinity to God's being. See the excellent discussion of Leo Sweeney, 'Divine Attributes in *De doctrina christiana*: Why does Augustine not List "Infinity"?', in Duane Arnold and Pamela Bright (eds.), *De doctrina christiana: A Classic of Western Culture* (Notre Dame, Ind.: University of Notre Dame Press, 1994), i. 195–204.
[13] *Conf.* 7. 5. 7.

more coherently the doctrine that he had begun to treat as authoritative.[14] As his theological knowledge grew, he encountered figures whose own theology was already marked by strong commitment to many of the very principles that he had learned from his Platonic reading (writers such as Hilary and Ambrose).[15] Indeed, there is little in his first borrowings from Platonism that he could not have found through close reading of Ambrose or (if it were possible) Gregory of Nyssa.

As an important example of the eclectic character of these borrowings we can note that at *Confessions* 7. 9. 13–14 Augustine describes his excitement at first reading these texts and seeing in them parallels to Father and Son and their interrelationship. This passage is revealing because it shows that Augustine came to those texts with an existing knowledge of Trinitarian theology, and in particular of a pro-Nicene theology which insists on the Son's coeternal divinity. When Augustine goes on to describe what he took from those texts it is notable that he does not describe himself as taking away any specific details of the ways in which the three Neoplatonic *hypostases* related together. Although some scholars have attempted the task, it is extremely difficult to make any certain equations between Neoplatonic characterizations of the three *hypostases* and Augustine's earliest allusions to the Trinitarian persons. Recent work by Nello Cipriani in particular has shown that such allusions as may be there in Augustine's earliest texts probably demonstrate engagement with Ambrose and especially Victorinus, and it is *their* engagement with Neoplatonic texts that may partially be reflected in Augustine.[16] Hence, we must look elsewhere for

---

[14] The complex character of his debt to 'Platonism' is highlighted at the end of book 3 of his *Contra Academicos* (AD 387). At 13. 17. 37 ff. Augustine describes himself as becoming a member of the 'Platonic' school to combat 'Academic' scepticism. But, following Cicero, the 'Platonic' school is presented as the underlying movement of all Classical philosophy except Epicureans and some Sceptics. Thus, Augustine can confess membership of this 'school' while holding in the same work to a theory of cognition and of the unity of the soul that owes most to ancient Stoicism. *Contra Academicos* itself may indeed quote or refer to some Plotinian texts directly, but little is confessed as central that could not have been found at the time of Cicero (who died c.230 years before the birth of Plotinus). Belonging to this school involves acceptance of the immateriality and reality of Truth and the soul, of the participation of beings in Being, and of the possibility of reliable knowledge (3. 17. 37). Note also that Augustine sees himself as belonging to this school even as he sees Christ as the ultimate authority.

[15] That Augustine's sources for his account of God as immaterial, simple, and as Being itself were, at least initially, texts that modern scholars term 'Neoplatonic' is open to little doubt. Whether the ideas he took from them were uniquely Neoplatonic is another question entirely. I have explored how little his belief in these characterizations of God distinguishes him from predecessors such as Hilary or Basil—both of whom could articulate very similar principles without ('probably without' in the case of Basil) knowledge of strictly *Ne*oplatonic texts—in my ' "Remember that you are Catholic" '.

[16] Nello Cipriani, 'Le Fonti Cristiane della Dottrina Trinitaria nei Primi Dialoghi di S. Agostino', *Augustinianum*, 34 (1994), 253–312.

Augustine's Trinitarian Theology

evidence of the most fundamental principles of Augustine's early Trinitarianism.

We might begin this task by noting the significance of a text that has been greatly neglected in the study of Augustine's Trinitarian theology, his *Letter* 11. The letter was written in 389, only three years after his conversion, and contains one of his earliest discussions of Trinitarian theology.[17] Augustine presents a key principle thus:

> For, according to the Catholic faith, the Trinity is proposed to our belief and believed—and even understood by a few saints and holy persons—as so inseparable that whatever action is performed by it must be thought to be performed at the same time by the Father and by the Son and by the Holy Spirit . . . the Son does not do anything which the Father and the Holy Spirit do not also do . . .[18]

Augustine does not argue for the doctrine of inseparable operations, but states it as an inherited part of tradition, and thus provides us with a key indicator that we must locate his earliest Trinitarian theology within the Latin pro-Nicene tradition. Although the doctrine has already been discussed it may be helpful to provide some more examples here from Latin pro-Nicenes.

In his *On the Holy Spirit* of c.387–90 Ambrose writes:

> If then the peace of the Father, the Son and the Holy Spirit is one, the grace one, the love one and the communion one, the working is certainly one, and where the working is one, certainly the power cannot be divided nor the substance separated . . . And not only is the operation of the Father, Son and Spirit everywhere one but also there is one and the same will, calling and giving of commands.[19]

Similarly, we find Hilary writing some years before,

> And since He [Christ] wished, therfore, to confess the power of his nature He stated: 'This Son can do nothing of Himself, but only what He sees the Father doing' . . . Because He was aware of His Father's power and strength that was with Him, the Son asserted that He could do nothing by Himself except what He saw the Father doing . . . all the things that the Father does the Son does in a like manner. This is the understanding of the true birth and the most complete mystery of our faith . . .[20]

For both Hilary and Ambrose the common working of the divine persons stems from the fact that they are of the same substance and the same power. Thus, *Letter* 11 enables us to observe that

---

[17] Other key discussions before AD 389 are to be found at *Ord.* 2. 5. 16; *Beata v.* 4. 34–5; *Sol.* 1. 1. 2–4; *Mor.* 1. 16. 26–9.
[18] *Ep.* 11. 2.   [19] Ambrose, *Spir.* 1. 12. 131; 2. 10. 101.
[20] Hilary, *De trin.* 7. 17–18.

Augustine's earliest understanding of the Trinitarian persons sits within the traditions of late fourth-century (Latin) pro-Nicene theology.

Letter 11 offers some account of the relations between the persons, but a more extended account of Augustine's early understanding of the three persons can be seen in the short *On the Faith and the Creed* (*De fide et symbolo*) of AD 393, a short commentary on the creed read to African bishops assembled in Hippo. Here we read that the Word was made by him who is 'from himself (*de seipso*)'. The existence and consubstantiality of the Word demonstrates that, unlike any human speaker, the Father has the power to reveal himself perfectly.[21] The Father is also the personal source of the Son's coequal nature: 'The Son as Son has received existence from the Father . . . the Son owes the Father his existence, but owes him also his equality with the Father.'[22] At the same time, we cannot claim comprehension of the ineffable God: no corporeal analogy can reveal to us the workings of the divine nature of 'he who is'. Augustine's concerns here again reflect those of the Latin anti-Homoian tradition. One of his central concerns in the Christological sections of this text is to show the equality of Father and Son who are of 'one substance'. He makes use of a key anti-Homoian verse in claiming that the Father does all things through the Word who is 'the Power and Wisdom of God' (1 Cor. 1: 24), and he shows himself well aware of other key texts in dispute, such as Prov. 8: 22 and those texts which seem to point to the Son's subordination. We should also notice the emphasis he places on the Son being from the Father's substance: this principle enables us to talk of a true revelation of the Father through the Son.

Augustine then comes to the Spirit and the question of origin becomes more complex. He asserts two basic principles: the Spirit is not begotten like the Son; the Father is the ultimate source of the Spirit (and thus the Spirit is not begotten by the Son at one remove from the Father). As for all pro-Nicenes, further progress in describing the nature of the Spirit's procession (beyond simply saying that it is different from that of the Son) is difficult. Augustine turns to an argument he describes as that of others: 'some have even dared to believe that the Holy Spirit is the communion (*communio*) or deity so to speak of the Father and Son'.[23] Augustine goes on to suggest that

---

[21] *F. et symb.* 3. 4–4. 5. [22] *F. et symb.* 9. 18.

[23] *F. et symb.* 9. 19. This use of *deitas* is odd, but nevertheless note that in context the phrasing in no way indicates that this *deitas* is any sort of divinity prior to the persons and their relations of origin. This *deitas* clearly originates with the Father (BA 9. 56): *ut, quoniam Pater Deus et Filius Deus, ipsa deitas, qua sibi copulantur et ille gignendo Filium et ille Patri cohaerendo, ei a quo est genitus aequatur.* In other words: that which joins Father and Son is counted as equal with the one who generates the Son.

the Spirit is the love between Father and Son and is also called the love of God with reference to humanity because it is by the Spirit that we are enabled to follow Christ. Although Augustine has previously described the Spirit as the gift of God, as the finger of God, and as the love of God, this is the first attempt he makes to describe the Spirit as the communion of Father and Son. The attempt does not occupy much text and is rather clumsy. Nevertheless, the passage shows evidence of engagement with his predecessors: allusion to Victorinus is probably to be found in the idea of Spirit as the communion of Father and Son, while allusion to Ambrose and to Jerome's translation of Didymus the Blind's *De Spiritu Sancto* is possibly behind the odd (and not repeated) equation of communion and 'deity'.[24]

Augustine admits that others think such a theology does not accord the Spirit truly substantial existence, because the join between two bodies is not itself a body. To defend the idea of Spirit as communion we see Augustine making subtle if highly condensed and suggestive use of his Platonic resources. In a few short sentences Augustine argues that the Spirit is only thought to be insubstantial by those who conceive of the joining (*copulatio*) between Father and Son as the joining of two material bodies, and thus think that when the two joined bodies are separated the join does not remain. However, Augustine argues, once we realize that God is immaterial and simple then we will see that the analogy between the joining of two material bodies and the joining of Father and Son is mistaken. In God there are no relationships that are not eternal and essential to God, there is nothing in God that is not eternally part of what it is to be God. Hence it is not the case that the love between Father and Son is only a temporary aspect of Father and Son. That love is inseparable from the reality, being, or substance of both and thus the Spirit may be conceived as love *and* as a divine and substantial person. The significance of this argument is that Augustine again attempts to advance on his sources through applying the explanatory resources of his Platonic account of God's nature to deal with a problem he has read about in and inherited from earlier Latin

---

[24] The links to these figures are not clear but, given Augustine's insistence throughout this text that his opinions are built on those of predecessors, we can point to some possible parallels. Marius Victorinus, *Hymn* 1, line 3 describes the Spirit as *copula* of Father and Son. Ambrose, *Spir.* 3. 10. 59 uses the term *theotes* and links it with John 3: 6: a loose reading of this text in conjunction with an assumption that the Spirit was the *copula* or *communio* of Father and Son could well have contributed to Augustine's account. *Spir.* also appeals to Rom. 5: 5 at a number of significant points in ways that closely accord with Augustine's usage (which itself becomes significantly more frequent after 393). Didymus' contribution is less obvious (and more problematic: Jerome's translation was probably finished only in 390; if we could establish a clear link it would demonstrate the degree to which Augustine was keeping up with the very latest literature).

pro-Nicene tradition. In the case of Father and Son he has insisted—in a way that would have made Ambrose or Hilary proud—that the generation of the Word by the Father does not imply subordination because the generation and its product are subject to the rules of God's immaterial and ineffable nature: now we see him applying the same methodology to pneumatology.

After discussing the Spirit, Augustine admits there is an important distinction between believing rightly about the Trinity and growing in understanding of it. The distinction is one we find throughout Augustine's career: appropriate belief should form a basis for the continuing struggle to articulate a reasoned account of that belief. Augustine insists that we should begin by *believing* that

> the Father is God and the Son is God and the Holy Spirit is God; that there are not three Gods, but that the Trinity is One God; that the persons are not diverse in nature but are of the same substance (*neque diversos naturae, sed eiusdem substantiae*); that the Father is always the Father and the Son always the Son and the Holy Spirit always the Holy Spirit.[25]

To this expression we might add the following complementary statement from a little earlier in the text:

> [we must believe] that Trinity is one God. Not that Father, Son and Spirit are identical (*non ut idem sit Pater qui et Filius et Spiritus sanctus*). But Father is Father, the Son is Son and the Holy Spirit is Holy Spirit, and this Trinity is one God, as it is written 'Hear O Israel, the Lord thy God is one God.'[26]

These two quotations set out Augustine's fundamental grammar of the relations between persons and essence: the persons are irreducible, and yet God is one. In the attempt to show how we may deploy these principles, we have already seen Augustine turning to what we might term his complementary grammar of divine simplicity. In the next section of the chapter we will see that in his mature work Augustine maintains the same pro-Nicene principles and comes to articulate them in increasingly sophisticated ways using the same grammar of divine simplicity. In so doing Augustine develops an account of divine simplicity found in earlier Latin pro-Nicenes but offers a theology that stands as one of the high points of pro-Nicene Trinitarianism.

THE MATURE AUGUSTINE: PRO-NICENE SIMPLICITY

We can now turn to his *Sermon* 52 (*c.* AD 410). This sermon, which concerns the story of Christ's baptism in the Jordan at Matt. 3:

---

[25] *F. et symb.* 9. 20.   [26] *F. et symb.* 9. 16.

13 ff., anticipates some key aspects of the latter half of the *De Trinitate*. The sermon begins with a problem: in the descent of the dove onto Jesus and the sounding of the voice from heaven acclaiming Christ (Matt. 3: 16–17) we are presented, says Augustine, with 'a sort of separated Trinity' (*quasi separabilem Trinitatem*): each of the three persons seems to be accorded a different action. Augustine immediately imagines himself open to a charge from an imaginary interlocutor:

But one may say to me: 'Show the Trinity to be inseparable: remember that you are Catholic and that it is to Catholics that you are speaking.'[27]

Once again the doctrine of inseparable operation is taken as a well-known and fundamental doctrinal rule. The doctrine is then given a gloss which shows how clearly this is a doctrine about the unity of three irreducible persons:

... the Father, Son and Holy Spirit are a Trinity inseparable; one God not three Gods. But yet so one God, as that the Son is not the Father, and the Father is not the Son, and the Holy Spirit is neither the Father nor the Son, but the Spirit of the Father and of the Son. This ineffable Divinity, abiding ever in itself, making all things new, creating, creating anew, sending, recalling, judging, delivering, this Trinity, I say, we know to be at once ineffable and inseparable.[28]

How is it that such a faith may be seen as consonant with the separation between the persons seemingly apparent at Matt. 3: 13 ff.? To solve this apparent conflict between Scripture and traditional confession, Augustine says that he will first consider the relationship of Father and Son. To do so he brings forward John 1 and Wisdom 8: 1, which taken together indicate that the creating and the ordering of the world are jointly the work of the Father and the Son.[29] Having made his way via Scripture back towards the doctrine of inseparable operation, which had seemed initially against Scripture, Augustine restates the paradox caused by inseparable operation. He does so by drawing attention to a basic problem: should we say that the Father was also born of the Virgin? 'God forbid,' he says, 'we do not say this, because we do not believe it.'[30] Indeed, he continues, the creed seems to make it clear that the Father was not born of a virgin, did not suffer and did not rise again: these are, the creed teaches us, the work of the Son. Thus, Augustine's tactic in

---

[27] *Serm.* 52. 2
[28] *Serm.* 52. 2. Only slightly mischievously, I would suggest that Lossky's stress on the 'apophatic' character of a very similar formula, while also stressing its basic rule-providing character (*The Mystical Theology of the Eastern Church*, 54) nicely mirrors Augustine's own intention.
[29] *Serm.* 52. 5.   [30] *Serm.* 52. 6.

this restatement of the problem is to draw attention to the problems of a 'Patripassian' reading: a reading that over, or wrongly, emphasizes the inseparability to the extent of contradicting the creed. However, this argument has so far only brought us back to our starting point: if the creed is right then we seem to have a clear example of the Son doing something that the Father does not. Augustine moves us forward by first stating the answer he thinks necessary in his own words and then demanding that it must be proved by the Scriptures. The answer in sum is that,

The Son indeed and not the Father was born of the Virgin Mary; but this very birth of the Son, not of the Father, was the work both of the Father and the Son. The Father indeed suffered not, but the Son, yet the suffering of the Son was the work of the Father and the Son.[31]

The sections which follow list scriptural testimonies that demonstrate the congruence of this extended formula with Scripture's accounts of the Son's birth, death, and resurrection. At the end of this demonstration Augustine leaves us with a general principle 'You have then the distinction of persons, and the inseparableness of operation.'[32] This extended discussion repeats all the basic elements of the rules for Trinitarian discourse that we saw in *Letter* 11 and *De fide et symbolo*. Augustine sets out his principles in formulae that advance on the early formulations, but which are in clear continuity with them. For instance, the virtue of the formula in the last paragraph is that it enables us to insist clearly that the Son alone becomes incarnate and that the union of the Incarnation involves the second person of the Trinity in a way that it does not involve the other divine persons. Nevertheless these formulae insist that we must still speak of the Incarnation being the work of the undivided Godhead. At the same time this formula is compatible with the insistence that through that union Christ's human nature is united with the Trinity as a whole.[33]

The formulae we have seen in *Sermon* 52 are austere: they are an attempt to set out appropriate rules for an orthodox reading of Scripture and for orthodox talk of God. To use a terminology I outlined earlier, they are an attempt to set out what we must believe rather than a detailed articulation of Trinitarian belief. However, it is important to note that in these statements of belief, we have not as yet seen any evidence to sustain the charge that Augustine 'begins' with the unity of God in a way that promotes the divine essence as prior to the persons. I want now to turn to those mature texts in

---

[31] *Serm.* 52. 8.   [32] *Serm.* 52. 14.

[33] For a brief account of the importance of this theme in Augustine and further bibliography see my 'The Christological Context of *De trinitate* XIII'.

which he does attempt to offer a more detailed articulation of what it means to say that there are three persons and one God.

To approach these texts we must begin by reiterating an epistemological fundamental. Augustine consistently argues that fallen humanity is drawn to imagining God according to the characteristics of material objects: to apply to God the grammar of material objects.[34] Within this general critique Augustine diagnoses as a particular problem our tendency to separate persons from essence, to treat the essence as something 'behind' the persons. In his *Letter* 120 (*c.* AD 410) Augustine argues that we must not conceive of the relationships between the persons according to material analogies. The three should not be imagined as three large objects spatially bounded, nor as touching, nor as arranged in any shape, such as a triangle (*in modum trigoni*). Augustine goes to argue, on the one hand, against any attempt to conceive of the persons as somehow limited and the divinity as infinite, and, on the other hand, against any assertion that the substance of the Trinity is different from the Father, the Son, and the Spirit. Augustine says,

... the Father, the Son and the Holy Spirit are the Trinity, but they are only one God; not that the divinity, which they have in common, is a sort of fourth person, but that the Godhead is ineffably and inseparably a Trinity ...
You know that in the Catholic faith it is the true and firm belief that the Father and the Son and the Holy Spirit are one God, while remaining a Trinity ... the Trinity is of one substance and *[the] essence is nothing else than the Trinity itself* (*ut ipsa essentia non aliud sit quam ipsa trinitas*).[35]

Augustine then says that the very word 'substance' here is confusing because it makes us think of a unitary 'thing' separate from the three persons. Augustine suggests that 'divinity' (*divinitas*) or 'essence' (*essentia*) are better terms, the latter in particular being closer to the Greek *ousia* and better reminding us of God's status as Being itself.[36] Thus we again find a hint that, for Augustine, the best way we can articulate what we mean by the unity of God and the irreducibility of the persons is by attention to the grammar of divine simplicity rather than the grammar of materiality. To see such an articulation in action more extensively we can turn to book 7 of *De Trinitate*, although we must first and briefly place that book in the context of books 5 and 6.

At the beginning of *De Trinitate* 5 Augustine describes what it

---

[34] e.g. *Io. ev. tr.* 1; *Serm.* 53 and 117. [35] *Ep.* 120, 3. 13, 3. 17.
[36] His concern here perhaps also reflects uncertainty in immediately preceding Latin tradition about the best term to use, see pp. 183–4. His use of *essentia* may stem from Gregory of Elvira's usage at *De fide* 11 and 56.

means for God to be one essence or *ousia* by reference to God as Being itself, the only being that is unchangeable and hence not capable of possessing accidents.[37] His summary of God's attributes here reiterates the very themes we saw at *Confessions* 7. 10. 16 and enables Augustine to insist that we must continually guard our speech so that God is not described as if God were a thing like other things. Augustine then begins to consider whether words used of God always describe God's essence or whether they sometimes describe things accidental to God. He does so in response to Homoian claims that all terms used of God describe God's substance and thus 'unbegotten' describes the substance of the Father while 'begotten' describes the substance of the Son. Augustine first argues that the Homoians are right to say that nothing accidental may be predicated of God. Following an argument with which we are now familiar, Augustine says that God is simple, that is, in God all qualities are identical with God's essence—to be is the same as to be wise, to use a key Augustinian example. Nevertheless, Augustine continues, not all things said of God are directly predicated of God's substance. Such an assumption would mean a series of basic contradictions or incoherencies in Scripture. We can see one immediately in the Homoian suggestion that both 'begotten' and 'unbegotten' are spoken according to substance. If these two terms are understood to be directly about God's substance then they indicate a distinction between Father and Son such that the two cannot be 'of one substance'. But, argues Augustine, by the same rules John 10: 30's 'I and the Father are one' would then also have to be applied to God's substance and would indicate that there was no such distinction! The Homoian suggestion seems initially attractive but results in a basic incoherence.[38]

Augustine's famous solution to this problem is that the only category we may discern in our talk of God other than talk according to essence or substance is talk according to relation.[39] We may summarize his twofold solution in these terms: we can, on the one hand, say that God 'is' something. By so doing we mean that this quality or term is essential to God, it is essential to what Father, Son, and Spirit are. In any such case we are not to think that there is more essence in two or three than in one divine person or that the essence is something from which the three persons stem. On the other hand,

---

[37] *Trin.* 5. 2. 3–3. 4.   [38] *Trin.* 5. 3. 4.
[39] *Trin.* 5. 5. 6–6. 7. One of the classic studies of this theme in *Trin.*, I. Chevalier's *Saint Augustin et la pensée grecque: Les Relations trinitaires* (Fribourg: Collectanea Friburgensia, 1940) argued that Augustine's account of relation owed much to Gregory Nazianzen's use of σχέσις. Although this thesis is sometimes repeated in modern appropriation, recent scholarship has recognized that it is unsustainable.

we can talk of Father, Son, and Spirit insofar as they are related to each other. In this case, to give an example, we may say that Father is eternally Father and Son is eternally Son without meaning that they are distinct substances or that the Son is only accidental, separable from what it is to be God. In such a case we are saying that Father and Son are terms which indicate relationships, but that those relationships are essential to being God.

In this way we have found a coherent language for talking about the unity of God's being (according to substance) and we have found a way to talk about the distinctions between the persons without simply contradicting what we say about God's unity (according to relation). This twofold language also enables us to talk of God's unity and of the distinct persons without implying that the distinctions are somehow secondary to the shared substance—terms which are used 'according to relation' designate relations that are eternally so. Thus far the argument is relatively well known: but we must follow him further if we are to grasp how well the grammar of simplicity helps Augustine to articulate his Nicene Trinitarian theology. Augustine's insistence that God is not material and that the essence is not prior to the persons should already have enabled us to see that Augustine's God is not one thing or substance with secondary internal divisions. Nevertheless, there is more to be said.

In the first half of book 7 Augustine asks whether each of the persons may be called God singly or whether the term is only appropriate when used of the three together. He begins to answer by offering a *reductio ad absurdum* to demonstrate the consequences of saying that the Father is wise 'in the same way that he speaks'.[40] The Father speaks *through* the Word: is he then wise '*through* his Wisdom'? Much of book 6 has been concerned with refuting non-Nicene (and earlier Nicene) exegesis of 1 Cor. 1: 24. That argument is now being repeated as a preliminary to book 7. If we were to say, as some previous Nicene exegesis had done,[41] that the Father was wise *through* the eternal presence of the Father's Wisdom then the same argument would pertain about Power (because the two terms are joined in 1 Cor. 1: 24): the Father would be or have Power only through the presence of his Power to him. The logical consequences of this picture would be that the Father was only God because of the Son's presence: at its most absurd the Son would be the deity of the Father! For Augustine this last leap may be made because the Father's 'power' must be essential to and expressive of the Father's divinity. Obviously enough it makes no sense to think of the Father as being wise—let alone being God—by participation in something

---

[40] *Trin.* 7. 1. 1.   [41] See *Trin.* 6. 1. 1.

else: to assert this of God would ultimately mean that the Father simply wasn't God 'in himself'.[42] To understand Augustine's alternative account of how the Son may be the Wisdom of God while the Father is still wise 'in himself' it may be helpful to divide his argument into three steps.

1. Augustine first insists that 'every essence which is spoken of relatively is something apart from that relative predication'.[43] Note that, at this stage in the argument, Augustine is not talking of divine essence with reference to the Trinity as a whole, he is talking only about the person of the Father. He is insisting that the persons are not just relations. The Father is something in himself and only *because* the Father is such an essence can the Father be spoken of in relation. In fact this point follows both from Augustine's insistence that to be in relation implies the existence of something which may be in relation, and it follows from the argument that because the Father is God and God is simple, therefore the Father must be wise in Himself, in his essence. To call the Father God implies that the Father is in Himself wisdom itself, Being itself. The individual reality of the Father is thus affirmed.

2. The Father generates the Son. More precisely we may say that the Father generates the Son's essence: what the Son *is* has been generated by the Father. Just as the Son is light from light, Augustine says, so too the Son is wisdom generated from wisdom and even *essentia de essentia*.[44] However, this does not mean that the Son is only a part of the Father or not truly a person in himself. To explain why, Augustine turns again to the grammar of divine simplicity. If the Son is Wisdom (as 1 Cor. 1: 24 tells us) and if the Son is God (as the creed and John 1: 3 tells us) then the Son must be wise in himself, he must be Wisdom itself. To use the term God of the Son must mean that as wisdom itself the Son is not wise, or powerful, or good, or God by participation in anything else: calling the Son God means that *all* the arguments Augustine has applied to the Father must now be applied to the Son. The grammar of simplicity means that we must say that if God the Father is to generate another, a Son, both the generator and the generated must be wisdom and God in themselves: the grammar of simplicity allows us to say truly that 'the Father has

---

[42] In what follows I have used the terms 'him' and 'himself' when talking specifically of Father and Son. By this use I am not intending to claim anything about the 'gender' of God, simply to distinguish discussion of the Father as a particular person from discussion of God in 'Godself'. In neither case am I intending to imply that God has one or three 'selves' in modern terms.
[43] *Trin.* 7. 1. 2: *omnis essentia quae relative dicitur est enim etiam aliquid excepto relativo.*
[44] *Trin.* 7. 2. 3.

given the Son to have life in himself' (John 5: 26). Thus Augustine is using simplicity as a tool for exploring the unity and multiplicity that the principles of Nicene Trinitarian belief commend: and in so doing we see that a simple being may generate another who is also coequal and simple.

3. However, the language of divine simplicity enables and demands a further step. If the Son is wisdom itself, and the Father is wisdom itself, then we can go a step further and say that the Son's essence must be identical with the Father's essence. There cannot, obviously enough, be two instances of wisdom itself. However, note that this unity does not result from the fact that our grammar forces us to speak of an underlying or shared substance to the three persons, as many material analogies would. A material grammar could only allow us to imagine the unity of the three by drawing an analogy with a material substance shared within three objects, a material substance that would be the ground of or basis for their unity. The grammar of simplicity, however, provides very different linguistic resources for us to speak of the unity of the three. When we apply this grammar to the principles of Trinitarian theology we find that we, first, have found a language in which to talk of the generation of Son from Father as the begetting of one who is truly consubstantial, one who is truly also wisdom and life in himself. But, if we consistently apply this grammar, then we must say that the three persons are both distinct and also one in the unity of existence and wisdom itself. Although the unity and multiplicity of the triune communion stills remains beyond our final comprehension, this language draws speech and imagination beyond the possibilities that a purely material grammar provides. This language draws us to the individual reality of the persons and then immediately to their unity without the need to imagine a substance or thing which provides that linkage.

Thus, summing up these three steps: The Father generates the Son who is light from light, wisdom from wisdom, and essence from essence. The Son is an essence in Himself, not just a relationship: to talk of the person of the Son is to talk of the Son's essence. And yet, because the Father's and the Son's essences are truly simple, they are of one essence. Because the principles of his Trinitarian faith tell him that the Spirit is also God and is a distinct person, the same arguments apply to all three persons. Thus, in using the grammar of simplicity to articulate a concept of Father, Son, and Spirit as each God, and as the one God, we find that the more we grasp the full reality of each person, the full depth of the being that they have from the Father, the more we are also forced to recognize the unity of their being.[45] We do not find the unity by focusing on something different from the persons: it is focusing on the persons' possession of wisdom and existence 'in themselves' that draws us to recognize their unity. The triune communion *is* a consubstantial and eternal unity—but there *is* nothing but the persons. Of course, Augustine's attempt to work towards a concept of the unity of God's essence is not intended as a proof: Augustine takes the unity of God's essence to be a truth of faith. It is perhaps better to say that Augustine is making use of the grammar of simplicity to articulate a reasoned presentation of the fundamental principles of Trinitarian faith, as we have seen them set out consistently in *De fide et symbolo* and *Sermon* 52.[46] It is also important to reiterate my earlier point that Augustine does not think we can thus comprehend the divine essence: all we have done is to show how our talk of God may be given some coherent structure without slipping from the bedrock of right belief.

Much of this sophisticated argument is reiterated at *De civitate Dei* 11. 10. Here Augustine defines simplicity in his standard manner: to call something simple is to say that its being is identical with its attributes: 'it "is" what it is said to "have" '. Augustine offers two arguments why God must be simple. First, things which are not simple are corruptible and changeable because they may lose qualities: God is not so. Second, things which are not simple possess their qualities through participation: but God possesses, or better is, nothing through participation, and thus God can most fittingly be described as simple. Hence Augustine argues, we must speak about the generation *and* relation of the divine persons in the context of God's simplicity. That which the simple God 'begets' will be equally simple. The begetter and the begotten here we call Father and Son: the simple Father begets a Son who is equally simple. Once again, the Father is the source of the divine essence and simplicity.

---

[45] One might take this question further by consideration of *Trin*. 15. 17. 27 ff. There Augustine repeatedly insists that the Spirit proceeds from the Father principally (*principaliter*) in the sense that the Spirit proceeds also from the Son because the Father gives it to the Son that the Spirit so proceeds as joint communion. Of course there are many further issues about this theology to discuss: however, it should be clear that Augustine clearly sees the Father as the personal source of both Son and Spirit. He also insists (*Trin*. 15. 17. 29) that we should not imagine a temporal sequence of procession, Son first and *then* the Spirit from both. Our temporal language of procession points to an eternal procession of the persons. As with a number of other pro-Nicenes Augustine accords the Son a necessary role in the procession of the Spirit because of the unity and simplicity of the divine essence.

[46] We can also say that the analogies proposed in the course of *Trin*. 8–14 arise because of the impossibility of grasping the unity and multiplicity of God directly through the grammar of simplicity. Augustine offers the account we have seen here in books 5–7 and then slowly moves towards the same argument from a different analogical base in books 8–14, focusing much more directly on why we find it so hard to grasp the argument and on how we must be reformed to grow in knowledge and love of God.

Each of these divine persons, 'in Himself', has a being in which being and qualities are identical, and each may be said not only to be living (to have life), but to be *life itself* (John 5: 26). And thus the being of these two is also the same: they are of one being or substance.

Book 7 of *De Trinitate* also hints at an important argument we find in full form in book 15. There Augustine offers a short summary of the argumentation which led to the discussion of the conjoint action of *memoria*, *intellegentia*, and *voluntas* when focused on God as a 'likeness' for the Trinitarian communion.[47] Augustine ends this summary with two criticisms of the analogy. First, this triad is found in the human being but is not identical with the human being: the Trinity itself is identical with God, not something *in* God (*Trin.* 15. 7. 11). Second, the three terms of Augustine's final analogy should not be taken as each equivalent to a person of the Trinity: the Father is not somehow equivalent to memory, the Son to intelligence, and the Spirit to will. Importantly, Augustine argues that this cannot be so by directly drawing a parallel with the argument in book 7 that the Father is not wise because the Son is continually present, but because Father and Son share the one wisdom that is identical with God's simple essence.[48] If God is a simple essence and yet irreducibly Trinitarian, then each of the three persons must possess as their own the one memory, intelligence, and will. Later in book 15 he writes: 'all together possess and each one possess all three of these in their own nature'.[49] None of the persons is dependent on the others for anything that is essential to God although the essence of the three persons is one. Thus, not only does the doctrine of divine simplicity provide a grammar for asserting the generation of the persons from the Father, but it also provides a grammar for ensuring the irreducibility of the persons in Trinitarian language.

CONCLUSION: THEOLOGY IN THE WORD

Augustine consistently and specifically rules out the idea that the divine essence is prior to the divine persons. He also clearly maintains the Father as the personal source of the divine simplicity and essence. Using the grammar of simplicity Augustine argues that we should beware of speaking even about a substance in which the three persons are 'contained': there is nothing but the three coeternal and consubstantial persons. As we saw in Chapter 11, David Burrell's remarkable book *Knowing the Unknowable God* offers us tools to

---

[47] *Trin.* 15. 6. 10. On this theme see my 'Memory, Intelligence and Will'.
[48] *Trin.* 15. 7. 11.
[49] *Trin.* 15. 17. 28: *ut omnia tria et omnes et singuli habeant in sua quisque natura*.

understand how pro-Nicenes made use of the absolute distinction between God and world that they identified.[50] When we have grasped this distinction—or, better, understood that this distinction prevents us grasping—we must search to see if there is any language that will help us articulate the structure of Christian belief beyond just restating its most fundamental principles. For Augustine the grammar of simplicity is turned to just that task. It is ironic that the role 'Platonism' plays in Augustine's doctrine of God is virtually the opposite of that it is taken to play by those who commonly criticize the 'Platonism' in his theology. The grammar of God's simplicity, partially stemming from those Platonist engagements serves not to make God a unitary essence or to replace biblical exegesis with discussion of the three Neoplatonic *hypostases*. Rather, that grammar serves to enhance the explanatory power of a fully Nicene Trinitarianism in which the order of Trinitarian generation is preserved, and in which Father, Son, and Spirit are all equally bound by the terms of divinity without ceasing to be 'other' to each other. Augustine's Platonism serves the cause of good exegesis.

This chapter has considered only some aspects of Augustine's Trinitarian theology. If my approach here is correct, though, the groundwork is laid for a more extensive rereading. At every point we would first, however, need to pursue Augustine's version of the pro-Nicene reflection on the character of human speech about God. We would have to note, first, the importance Augustine places on the incomprehensibility of the divine nature to human (and especially fallen) intelligences, and, second, on the need for Christians to struggle to grow in the ability to imagine the divine through the cultivation of appropriate faith and practice. The development and purification of the Christian intellect occurs within an *askesis* of the Christian as unified body and soul, as an embodied rational being located within the Christian sacramental community. From the period before the writing of the *Confessions* until his death, Augustine presented this process of purification within a Christological perspective.[51] Within this Christology, one of the functions of the Incarnate and resurrected Christ is to lead our intelligences beyond their obsession with the material to imagine the immaterial reality of the divine as the source of our material world. In pursuing these themes we would be considering how Augustine's thought manifests those very themes with which we were concerned in Chapters 11–13.

Thus, all Christian talk of God finds itself located *within* this reformation and reorientation of the Christian: indeed, we may see

---

[50] D. Burrell, *Knowing the Unknowable God*, esp. chs. 2 and 3.
[51] See my 'The Christological Context of *De trinitate* XIII'.

that Augustine locates the enterprise of theological reflection within the economy of redemption in three key ways. First, we can only understand the task the theologian faces by grasping something of the nature and purpose of the redemptive drama as a whole. Only when we see how that drama represents God's speaking in the world so that we may no longer be subject to it and to its powers can we grasp the full task of attempting to talk of God. Second, Augustine's conception of theological reflection is, more particularly, part of the Christian's participation in the mystery of dying, rising, and ascending with Christ: only *within* this movement may the inner and the outer person be restored and the mind come to imagine God, as far as it may, without delusion or self-deceit. Third, the exegesis of Scripture provides the point of departure for the enterprise of Trinitarian theology and for the conjoint exercise of the rational powers that is central to that enterprise: but we can only come to see what is involved in reading this Scripture through seeing how that text fits within God's overall redemptive economy. Only then may we see how the materialism of scriptural texts about the divine challenges us to move beyond the material and to begin to develop a grammar of divine distinction from the world—in Augustine's case to begin to develop a grammar of divine simplicity—in order to secure God's fully Trinitarian nature. Thus, struggling to apply the grammar of simplicity to the Triune God plays, for Augustine, a small part in the movement of the human being, in Christ, towards God as the creator and source of all wisdom and power and truth. In presenting these dynamics as the prism through which one views the principles of pro-Nicene Trinitarianism Augustine reveals himself to share a wide set of fundamental assumptions with Gregory of Nyssa. Each thinker represents a particular articulation of those shared assumptions, and their particularity is the product of being located in different local traditions, of having different philosophical and polemical engagements, and of being in different generations. But against the background I have sketched in Chapters 11-13, our reading of these two theologians must begin from the assumption that they offer two compatible articulations of the legacy bequeathed to later generations by pro-Nicene Christians across the late antique Mediterranean and Near East.

16
In Spite of Hegel, Fire, and Sword[1]

The theoretical status of each discipline holds less to the definition that it ascribes to itself than to its relation with others, that is, its inscription in a network of reciprocal determinations. A renewal is therefore not possible if one is pigeonholed inside of a (or each) discipline: one thus necessarily confirms the system that is implied by its specific place in the constellation of an epistemological classification ... Structural innovation takes place only in interdisciplinarity, wherever boundaries and significant divisions of a system can be challenged.[2]

I: NARRATION FROM MODERNITY

The previous few chapters have sketched an account of some basic shared structures of pro-Nicene theology in part in conscious opposition to those commonplace narratives that allege late fourth- and early fifth-century Trinitarian theology to be fundamentally divided into eastern and western varieties and to be a product of the overcoming of Christian thought by 'Greek' philosophical categories. I have suggested a model for understanding the unity and differences among pro-Nicene theologians in the hope of shifting the questions that we ask about the emergence and structure of late fourth-century orthodoxy. In so doing I have been questioning narratives widespread not only in mostly older early Christian scholarship, but also in current systematic theology.[3] I do not intend to

---

[1] With apologies to the hymnody of Frederick Faber. I am particularly grateful to Michel Barnes, Andy Gallwitz, and Medi Volpe for discussion of and editorial help with this chapter. Barnes's excellent 'Augustine in Contemporary Trinitarian Theology' offers an account that overlaps much with my own critique here (especially in its focus on the importance of understanding the meta-narrative that accompanies particular uses of Augustine).

[2] Michel de Certeau, 'The Social Architecture of Knowledge', tr. Tom Conley, *Culture in the Plural* (Northfield, Minn.: University of Minnesota Press, 1997), 98.

[3] The presence of these narratives may not seem to need demonstration, but it is important to note the wide range of theologians in whom they are present. See e.g. Robert W. Jenson, *Systematic Theology*, i (New York: Oxford University Press, 1997), 115 ff., Colin Gunton, *The Promise of Trinitarian Theology* (Edinburgh: T. & T. Clark, 1991), ch. 3; Jürgen Moltmann, *History and the Triune God*, tr. John Bowden (London: SCM Press, 1990), 80 ff., Wolfhart Pannenberg, *Systematic Theology*, i, tr. G. W. Bromiley (Grand Rapids, Mich.: Eerdmans, 1991), 322–4; LaCugna, *God For Us*, chs. 2 and 3, James McClendon, *Systematic Theology*, ii (Nashville: Abingdon, 1994), 296–8, David Brown, *The Divine Trinity* (London: Duckworth, 1985), 276–85; William Placher, *A History of Christian Theology: An Introduction* (Philadelphia: Westminster Press, 1983), 79. The basic narrative of an east/west division in Trinitarian

spend further space attacking those narratives head-on: my case has, I hope, been made clearly enough. My concern in this final chapter is with a number of questions about what it means and should mean to treat pro-Nicene theology as an authority within modern Christian thought. My argument is thus likely to be of interest to only some of the possible audiences I outlined in the Introduction. I should also add that my argument here is consciously aimed at theologians in communions that hold Nicaea to be a normative statement: those who do not may find the argument at least intriguing, insofar as they have been convinced by my argument that pro-Nicenes offer a plausible reading of Scripture.

Previous summary treatments of the fourth century have frequently ended with discussion of modern ramifications of the disputes and modern systematic theologians frequently use narratives of the fourth century to delineate options available to the modern Trinitarian theologian: in some sense then it is clear that pro-Nicene theology continues to be authoritative for modern Trinitarians. On the one hand, however, I want to argue that engagement with pro-Nicene theology is usually fairly shallow and, on the other hand, that this stems from the very culture of modern systematic theology. That culture inculcates views of how one understands and deploys anything pre-modern counted as authoritative that prevent a more serious engagement. Thus, while I have been concerned to refute what I take to be unsustainable narratives of the period, I do not think that simply trying to replace those narratives with more historically accurate accounts will by itself stimulate a deeper engagement with pro-Nicene theology and better Trinitarian theology in the present.

The particular narratives I have been opposing fit into a category of narratives about pre-modern theology that are not extrinsic to modern systematic theology and thus easily replaced. Rather, such narratives have become intrinsic to Trinitarian theology within modern systematics in two ways. First, they frequently serve as quasi-confessional statements, indicating existing options, setting out a narrative that results in a range of possibilities for current use, or they narrate a story of error such that certain modern assumptions seem necessary.[4] Thus a narrative that sketches a distinction

theology traceable to or exemplified in Augustine and the Cappadocians is present in these texts in a number of versions and used in a number of ways. In some very recent texts we see writers aware of recent refutations of this narrative, but unwilling to engage in any critical appreciation of such scholarship, merely noting it and continuing business as usual. e.g. David Coffey, *Deus Trinitas: The Doctrine of the Triune God* (Oxford: Oxford University Press, 1999), 25.

[4] One of the clearest examples is Pannenberg's building of arguments around brief but large-scale historical surveys. The frequent result is that those arguments are dependent on older secondary sources whose concerns and contexts are never examined. See Pannenberg, *Systematic Theology*, vol. i, pp. xi, 60.

between eastern and western alternatives frequently serves to sketch a menu of options that the modern theologian can choose to develop. Similarly, the story of the supposed errors of western Trinitarianism serves to persuade the reader that a turn to 'eastern' emphases is necessary. Second, narratives of the pre-modern are intrinsic to modern systematics because they are frequently interwoven with meta-narrative assumptions about the course of intellectual history that subtly serve to render necessary the assumptions of modern systematic discourse. I will argue that the narratives of the fourth century deployed by modern systematic theologians are frequently interwoven with assumptions about how theology should be practised and about how theology has developed that hold at arm's length the real challenge that pro-Nicene theologies offer. Thus, for example and in broad terms, modern Trinitarian theology invokes some of the formulae produced within the fourth century but simultaneously argues that the theological methods that produced those formulae are untenable in modernity.[5]

Thus it seems to me that an attempt to argue about how pro-Nicene theology may best serve as resource and authority for modern Trinitarian theology must take the form of a wider critique of the culture of systematic theology as such, an uncovering of the conditions that make it possible, and a sketch of the sort of theological culture that would enable a deeper and more attentive engagement with those texts and figures that should remain the source of all later Christian thinking.[6] Throughout this investigation I understand pro-Nicene theology to be functioning as an authority when its basic principles are treated as a foundation for subsequent theological reflection and its theologians as a constant point of departure in the articulation of Trinitarian belief in subsequent periods and cultural contexts.

Of course, when I speak of *the* culture of modern systematic theology I might seem to reify the extremely diverse set of fields that currently come under the rubric of systematics. Thus, to be more accurate, I want to identify some assumptions and strategies of thought that appear within a variety of modern theological styles,

[5] I make no claim to be the first to raise this rather obvious point. E.g. Andrew Louth, *Discerning the Mystery: An Essay on the Nature of Theology* (Oxford: Clarendon Press, 1983), 100: '... the Fathers, and creeds, and councils claim to be interpreting Scripture. How can one accept their results if one does not accept their methods?'

[6] It is important to note that my concern here is with the consideration of basic Christian doctrines. There are, of course, other aspects of theological thinking (such as Christian ethical reasoning) whose modalities may well take different forms. I assume, however, that re-emphasizing contemplation of the Scriptures as the core of attention to major doctrines, and re-emphasizing contemplation of the Trinity as the goal of Christian life will have significant consequences for theological practice as a whole. I offer little speculation as to how that might look.

but which all have their origin in the development of Protestant systematic theology in the eighteenth and nineteenth centuries and in the differentiation of that discipline from historical theology and biblical studies. These assumptions and strategies shape a culture apparent through a wide range of sub-fields, Protestant and Catholic. I will begin by sketching some of the meta-narrative assumptions mentioned above and which help to sustain the modern discipline of systematics. I will then turn to the evolution of systematic theology both as a theoretical proposition and as a material profession. Sketching something of both aspects is essential in showing the peculiar relationships between the reading of Scripture and the appropriation of modern historical consciousness that so shapes the sub-structures of argument and authority in systematic theology. These sketches will enable me then to locate some of the most basic dynamics of recent Trinitarian theology within this wider culture as a prelude to suggesting how a deeper engagement with pro-Nicene theology depends upon a reconfiguring of theological practice.

Meta-narrative strategies

We can identify a number of meta-narrative strategies that are interwoven with the particular narratives of the pre-modern used by systematicians and which serve to justify the practices of the modern discipline. I will briefly identify three that are of particular importance in connection with Trinitarian theology. The three are closely interwoven:

1. First, there is the strategy of assuming that modern theological method must differ from the methods of pre-modernity because of supposedly necessary features of post-Enlightenment rationality. This strategy frequently reads pre-modernity as a gradual anticipation of modernity, which is in turn understood as the fulfilment of pre-modernity's 'best' modes of thinking and inquiring. Sometimes this thesis is stated boldly, in other cases it appears as a cast given to a variety of narratives. For instance, the assumption can be seen clearly in the ways that pre-modern biblical exegesis has frequently been treated by both liberals and many conservative theologians as primarily a story of attempts which find their full flowering with the emergence of modern 'critical' exegesis.

One of the most significant forms of this strategy is the Enlightenment narrative concerning heteronomous authority in the 'pre-critical' period.[7] It is a commonplace in modern systematic

---

[7] Edward Farley's *Ecclesial Reflection: An Anatomy of Theological Method* (Philadelphia: Fortress Press, 1982), ch. 5 offers a particularly egregious example of this contrast. In other forms it is fairly common. See, for example, Pannenberg, *Systematic Theology*, i, 214–55;

theology that pre-modern theology demonstrates modes of submission to authority necessarily unsustainable after the Enlightenment. The assumption is based not on the principle that the wide variety of Englightenment and post-Enlightenment philosophies offer very particular challenges for theological reflection (which is obviously true), but that the challenge presented by modernity's philosophical children can *only* be faced by a significant reconsideration of the principles of authority.

This is one clear context in which we find narratives of pre-modern theology functioning as basic confessions of faith. Modern narration of pre-modern Trinitarianism tends to extract from them abstract principles that are taken to be still sustainable in modernity while simultaneously relativizing the principles and methods of the theologies under investigation. It is in this way, I suspect, that the narratives about eastern/western, Latin/Greek theologies have become so fundamental for recent Trinitarian theology even while the challenge presented by the theological culture sustaining those theologies is ignored. A set of Trinitarian models (or sometimes supposedly characteristic analogies) is extracted and then used to mark out the boundaries of modern Trinitarian theology even as it is assumed that the methods of exegesis by which those models were shaped and the analogies used are assumed to be unsustainable. A peculiarly modern narrative about the character of pre-modern authority guides the way the pre-modern is understood and appropriated. Gradually an Enlightenment argument about the character of pre-modern understandings of authority (one I obviously take to be unsustainable in itself) has itself become an authoritative assumption that underlies a wide variety of narratives.

2. Second, there is the strategy of presenting classical Christian theology as unsustainable because of its debt to 'Greek metaphysics', or because of its 'Platonizing' of Christianity. This debt is taken either to result in a speculative theology unrelated to Christian social practice, or it is taken to result in the overcoming of some fundamental 'biblical' themes, frequently present as 'dynamic' in distinction from 'static' ontological categories.[8] This rhetoric continues to be deployed despite clear rejection of the opposition by many New

---

Walter Kasper, *Theology and Church*, tr. Margaret Kohl (New York: Crossroad, 1989), 1–16; Roger Haight, *Dynamics of Theology* (New York: Paulist, 1990), 89–90; Stanley Grenz and Roger Olson, *Twentieth Century Theology: God and the World in a Transitional Age* (Downers Grove, Ill.: InterVarsity Press, 1992), 15–26; McClendon, *Systematic Theology*, ii. 298.

[8] e.g. Cornelius Plantinga, 'The Social Analogy of the Trinity', *Thomist*, 50 (1986), 325–52.

Testament scholars[9] and despite the increasingly strong rejection of the idea that theology's subservience to Greek metaphysics involved it in any sort of 'onto-theology'.[10]

Claims about the metaphysical bondage of Christian thought are not simply part of modernity's dislike of metaphysics per se: they are also closely related to post-Enlightenment thought's suspicion of the idea that contemplation of the divine might be the goal and root of theology, wanting instead to focus Christian attention on the 'practical' and on the narrative of Christ's ministry as transformative of human possibility.[11] On the one hand, suspicion of the contemplative—and a concomitant suspicion of a conception of the text of Scripture as intended to draw Christians towards contemplation—feeds suspicion of any attempt to systematize accounts of God in Godself. On the other hand, there is a sense that ontological categories placed at the heart of a basic summary of faith can only take

[9] See particularly Troels Engberg-Pedersen, (ed.), *Paul Beyond the Judaism/Hellenism Divide* (Louisville, Ky.: Westminster John Knox, 2001), esp. the essay by Dale Martin, 'Paul and the Judaism/Hellenism Dichotomy: Toward a Social History of the Question' (29–61). For examples of the opposition used in different ways see Pannenberg, *Systematic Theology*, i, 332–4; Joseph O'Leary, *Questioning Back* (Minneapolis: Winston Press, 1985), 176, 178 ff. (O'Leary's book is one of the most succinct and open use of the fairly widespread Heideggerean thesis about 'onto-theology'); Jürgen Moltmann, *The Trinity and the Kingdom of God*, tr. Margaret Kohl (London: SCM, 1981), 10, 129. Moltmann's use of the theme is particularly complex: God as absolute substance is a Greek philosophical idea, while the doctrine of the Trinity is not. Accepting the standard east/west narrative, Moltmann presents the 'western' Trinity as corrupting Trinitarian doctrine by adopting the 'Greek' philosophy of absolute substance. As in the case of the distinction between Augustine and the Cappadocians or east and west, we also find here figures aware of scholarship identifying the fundamental problem with this account but avoiding serious re-evaluation. E.g. David Cunningham, *These Three are One: The Practice of Trinitarian Theology* (Oxford: Blackwell, 1998), 25–6. One recent very useful account of modern attacks on the category of 'substance' and their failings is provided by William Alston, 'Substance and the Trinity', in Gerald O'Collins et al. (eds.), *The Trinity* (Oxford: Oxford University Press, 1999), 179–201. This basic distinction is also at work in such passages as this from LaCugna, *God For Us*, 54: 'The Cappadocians (and also Augustine) went considerably beyond the scriptural understanding of economy by locating God's relationship to the Son (and the Spirit) at the "intradivine" level ... Our Patristic predecessors in both East and West approached the Christian doctrine of God as a metaphysics of God's trihypostatic *ousia*.' Here particular modern assumptions about appropriate biblical exegesis—Patristic exegesis isn't really acceptable exegesis—enable the characterization of Patristic trinitarianism as metaphysics in opposition to 'what the scripture says'.

[10] One of the more notable recent admissions that Aquinas does not succumb to 'onto-theology' is that of Jean Luc Marion, 'Saint Thomas d'Aquin et l'onto-théo-logie', *Revue Thomiste*, 95 (1995), 31–66. Protestant theologians have been slow to follow Eberhard Jüngel's own admission that traditional Catholic theology does not hold to an onto-theological *analogia entis*, see *God as the Mystery of the World*, tr. Darrell L. Guder (Edinburgh: T. & T. Clark, 1983), 282 ff.

[11] This general tendency has been well documented and is apparent, like the others I have identified, in liberal and conservative theologies across a range of denominations, from liberal Protestants to Catholics and figures such as Stanley Hauerwas. Pro-Nicene thought is not, of course, unconcerned with the ethical, but the ethical is located within the context of dual-focus anthropologies where contemplation of God is the source of appropriate action. See Matthew Levering, *Scripture and Metaphysics: Aquinas and the Renewal of Trinitarian Theology* (Oxford: Blackwell, 2004), esp. ch. 1.

away from an appropriate focus on Jesus' supposed lack of metaphysical speculation. This last trope reveals a fascinating set of modern concerns: theological practice begins not from the plain sense of Scripture[12] but from reconstructions of Jesus as a human being like us; all that Scripture says to offer a cosmology and an account of God's action within that must be a secondary accretion to the particular life of the man Jesus.

In fact, the opposition Greek and Hebrew, or Greek philosophy and Christian theology, is one of the most important examples of a wider narrative trope that relies on oppositions between idealized thought forms. Some versions of this trope are of course one of the more lamentable aspects of early Christian heresiology, but it is also important to note that a particular version of engagement via typification has been important within modern theological thought. Relating the history of a doctrinal theme as the story of two competing and abstract ideas has enabled systematicians to invoke the history of Christian thought without the need for deep textual and contextual engagement. Such a style of narration in part continues ancient heresiological usage, but it does so in a mode reflecting post-Enlightenment concerns. The reduction of the past to a variety of continuous options enables the grasping of that past in order that its contents may present options for modern thought, usually via some sort of 'translation' of those ideas into a form shaped by a particular modern philosophy. This brings us to the third strategy I want to identify.

3. The third and perhaps most subtle strategy involves both assumptions about the nature and function of philosophy and about the appropriate use of the text of Scripture. This strategy presents philosophies as self-enclosed systems of thought that frequently overcome those theologians who attempt to appropriate them and that are only naively used piecemeal to expand on and explore the plain sense of Scripture. The former case is seen particularly clearly in narratives that make use of the second narrative strategy I identify and argue that Christian thought is, at a particular stage in history, shaped by one particular philosophy—Neoplatonism or Aristotelianism for example. In such cases an originally Protestant polemical strategy has taken a post-Enlightenment cast to prevent serious engagement with the history of Christian doctrine. That original polemical form aimed at the 'Aristotelianism' of late medieval scholasticism—or at the 'Platonism' of some Patristic and

---

[12] Where, as I hope previous chapters show, metaphysical statements and questions are constantly intimated. When I use the phrase 'plain sense' in this chapter I do so in line with the definition in Ch. 1.

medieval authors—itself builds on an ancient heresiological trope but is here allied to a notion of returning to the original gospel and to notions of *sola Scriptura*. Once an Enlightenment sense of the importance of re-conceiving previous thought in a systematic manner and on necessary foundations (following developments in the notion of what a philosophy must be) has become widespread, it is only a short step for theologians to assume as a working model that the history of Christian thought presents them with a history of accommodations to particular philosophies, or negotiations between self-enclosed philosophies and the Gospel. This perception has become widespread in much modern theology, and is consequently understood as a universal trope that may be projected onto pre-modern thought.

In the latter case, the attempt to explore and explain the plain sense of Scripture (either individual terminologies or longer passages) by the use of philosophical resources—such as using an account of the way common activities reveal common essence to interpret John 5: 19, or an understanding of the relation of powers to natures to interpret 1 Cor. 1: 24—is seen as a naïve distorting of the text. Such assumptions are tied both to modern assumptions about the paramount importance of historical-critical methods, and to modern (and specifically idealist) understandings of the function of philosophy. When philosophies are seen as self-establishing accounts that must offer a synthetic account of history and spirit then piecemeal adaptation seems to restrict the character of the theologian's engagement with the scope of the particular philosophy.[13]

Looking ahead to the argument of the latter half of this chapter, in a theological culture where the reading of a scriptural text takes the sort of pluralistic form I outlined in the first chapter, very different patterns of engagement are followed. Engagement here is a complex and piecemeal affair between Christian, inherited Jewish, and Greek and Roman philosophical traditions. By 'piecemeal' I mean that particular philosophical doctrines, separated from others taken to be intrinsically related to them in their original context are

---

[13] Such a perspective may be nicely seen in Paul Tillich's understanding of the relations between philosophy (understood in an idealist tradition) and theology. The philosopher attempts to conceive 'reality as such', 'the *logos* of reality as a whole'. The theologian essentially aims at the same question but begins always from reality experienced as the 'new being' in Christ. The theologian is, hence, engaged in a constant dialogue with and move towards the philosophical, towards the universal *logos* and (as Romantic hero) constantly runs the risk of overstepping the bounds of ecclesial authority and tradition. In such an account the piecemeal engagement studied in this book can only seem a sub-set of the truly important engagement between conceptions of the universal *logos*. See his *Systematic Theology*, vol. i (Chicago: University of Chicago Press, 1951), 18, 22 ff., 53–9. While Tillich's account is very much his own, his dynamics are apparent in many who inherit idealist notions of philosophy. Such traditions of course differ considerably from those influenced by Kantian and neo-Kantian attempts to focus discussion on ethics rather than ontology.

used to elucidate particular themes or terminologies or passages from Scripture. For example, both Gregory of Nyssa and Augustine adapt themes from Plotinus: neither, however, makes any extensive use of the complex discussions concerning the interrelationships between the three primary *hypostases* that so fascinated the latter. Rather, discussions that Plotinus would have assumed to be pertinent to only the One or Nous are drawn on and melded together to discuss the Christian Trinity. Both similarly draw on aspects of Stoic epistemological terminology (in many cases using elements of that terminology in dismembered and re-membered forms that would seem perverse to non-Christian Neoplatonists): both feel free to condemn other aspects of Stoic tradition that are antithetical to their purposes. Athanasius, as we saw, makes use of earlier theological discussion of what it means to speak of something being 'proper' to a substance, but he adapts and manipulates a tradition he may well have encountered only in theological adaptation in figures such as Eusebius of Caesarea and Origen. This piecemeal engagement is deeply shaped by a complex notion of the scriptural text as the primary resource for the Christian imagination, as a text that may be explicated through the use of whatever lies to hand and that may be persuasively adapted. What counts as 'persuasive adaptation' is, of course, something constantly under negotiation and argument.

All three of these strategies are present in the particular narratives I have sought to oppose in this book. All three also obstruct dense engagement with pro-Nicene theology by hiding the need for a dialogue between significantly distinct theological cultures and the possibility of considering pro-Nicene arguments in detail as sentences that may still be spoken today. One might say that the use of narrative in modern systematics serves both to prevent good historical work (insofar as it continues to insist on the anticipatory character of the pre-modern) and reconfigures the character of appeals to authoritative formulae and texts (insofar as it assumes the unsustainability of the practices that shaped those texts and qualifies any assent to the formulae of a pre-modern era). History and authority in theology are reconfigured in the direction of modernity's necessary reworking of the pre-modern. To understand this dynamic in more detail we will need to consider some of the fundamental dynamics of systematic theology as such.

II: THE FORMS OF SYSTEMATICS

The origins of systematic theology lie in German Protestant theological shifts in the eighteenth and nineteenth centuries, building on the development of dogmatics since Melanchthon's *Loci communes* in the mid-sixteenth century.[14] The evolution of systematics as a distinct discipline involved a conscious self-distinction between itself and historical or biblical study. Edward Farley helpfully distinguishes between earlier divisions of theology into constituent sub-fields, in which the sub-fields name merely different literatures or different aspects of one field of knowledge, and nineteenth-century accounts in which theology is divided into a series of disciplines each with its own methodology and rationale. In such accounts anyone attempting to conceive the field as a whole is faced with the dual task of finding some guiding principle under which to relate the disciplines and giving an account of the various rationales of the individual disciplines.[15] This division of the field at a theoretical level was accompanied by a slow growth of distinct professions. With the rise of these distinct professions theology also perfectly illustrates Pierre Bourdieu's observation that the development of a profession (in this case a number of professions) involves the evolution of theoretical justifications for the existence of each discipline as a distinct discipline.[16]

This development of the common modern fourfold division of theology into the four sub-fields of systematics, Church history or historical theology, biblical studies, and practical or pastoral theology occurred for many reasons. The influence of post-Renaissance interest in historical development and historical context is, however, fundamental.[17] The development of a biblical studies that assumed

---

[14] For the Protestant developments particularly important here see Edward Farley, *Theologia: The Fragmentation and Unity of Theological Education* (Philadelphia: Fortress, 1983). Richard Muller's *Post-Reformation Reformed Dogmatics*, 4 vols., 2nd edn. (Grand Rapids, Mich.: Baker, 2003) covers the period up to the late 18th cent. with extraordinary thoroughness. There is also some useful material in Wolfhart Pannenberg, *Theology and the Philosophy of Science*, tr. Francis McDonagh (Philadelphia: Westminster Press, 1976) and en passant in Claude Welch's *In This Name: The Doctrine of the Trinity in Contemporary Theology* (New York: Charles Scribner's, 1952). See also Gerhard Sauter, 'Dogmatik', *TRE* ix. 41–77. By identifying Melanchthon as a point of departure I do not mean to ignore the wealth of scholarship that locates the early reformers against the background of late medieval theology. I do, however, mean to identify the discussion that takes form in the 16th cent. around the need for a literature summarizing the basic doctrinal loci of Scripture, as an important point of departure in the development of modern Protestant systematics.

[15] Farley, *Theologia*, 49–66, 105.

[16] Pierre Bourdieu, 'The Market of Symbolic Goods', in *The Field of Cultural Production* (New York: Columbia University Press, 1993), 114: 'The process of differentiation among fields of practice produces conditions favourable to the construction of "pure" theories (of economics, politics, law, art etc.), which reproduce the prior differentiation of the social structures in the initial abstraction by which they are constituted.'

[17] When I speak of modern historical consciousness in the pages that follow I am fundamentally pointing to a concern that better understanding of documents, people, and events follows on a closer and closer attention to their immediate historical circumstances. This very general definition needs refining as, in different periods, 'historical consciousness' is inseparable from other qualifiers. Thus in the 18th and 19th cents. this sense is interwoven with a

the importance of reading Scripture only within the context of the cultures of its production combined with the development of a historical theology dependent on the methods gradually shaping secular historical studies to create new, and transform existing, divisions in theology. This adaptation of modern historical consciousness was further conditioned by Enlightenment questions about the value of authority and the manner in which dogmatics might continue to establish itself as a science. Even many of those theological traditions that refused Enlightenment critiques of pre-modern uses of authority in Christianity nevertheless sought ways of articulating the possibility of dogmatic theology in direct opposition to Enlightenment agendas.[18]

Wolfhart Pannenberg provides one useful way of articulating the distinction that occurred: whereas pre-modern discussion of the truth of Christian doctrines involved argument from a truth assumed on the basis of divine revelation and the Church's authority, Pannenberg argues that 'modern' theology argues towards the truth of Christian belief by demonstrating the coherence of those doctrines with that which is more widely taken to be true (whether understood as history or philosophy).[19] Of course this characterization can serve only as a heuristic device, but it has particular usefulness because it can serve to identify a range of Protestant conceptions of dogmatics over the past two hundred years, from theologies that assume the importance of translating basic Christian beliefs via a post-Enlightenment philosophy to many of those that hope to defend against this need. Pannenberg's phrasing also inadvertently captures the widespread assumption that the apologetic and systematic task after the Enlightenment must involve accommodation to a new philosophical reality and clarity about truth over against pre-modern conceptions of authority.[20] Pannenberg's concern here is not with the piecemeal engagement

critique of tradition as a legitimate vehicle of interpretation, with a sense of progress in understanding and frequently with a materialist sense that events and ideas are entirely the product of particular confluences of social, economic, and political force. See Peter Reill, *The German Enlightenment and the Rise of Historicism* (Berkeley: University of California Press, 1975), Joseph M. Levine, *Humanism and History: Origins of Modern English Historiography* (Ithaca: Cornell University Press, 1987); Hayden White, *Metahistory: The Historical Imagination in Nineteenth-Century Europe* (Baltimore: Johns Hopkins University Press, 1972). I return later in the chapter to ways in which recent historiographical theory offers new resources for the historical theologian.

[18] My brief discussion of the dynamics of modern Catholic theology offers one of the clearest examples of this phenomenon.

[19] Pannenberg, *Systematic Theology*, i. 21 ff.

[20] At this point I have considerable sympathy for John Milbank's account of the ways in which many moderns construe the relations of philosophy and theology in 'The Theological Critique of Philosophy in Hamann and Jacobi', in John Milbank et al. (eds.), *Radical Orthodoxy* (London and New York: Routledge, 1999), 21–37.

between the plain sense and other sentences found to be persuasive, but with the need for theology to justify its statements in the face of a new and governing construal of what constitutes truth. Thus in those who accept an Enlightenment agenda—which is very different from accepting a particular set of Enlightenment conclusions—narration of the past must always be propaedeutic to the establishment of Christian thought on some other grounds than the authority of the past.[21]

In the wake of these developments the relationship between modern theological formulation and pre-modern thought could never merely be that of the relationship between present and past in the abstract (if such a thing is ever possible): the past would always be viewed through (or against) Enlightenment notions of progress and understandings of authority in pre-modern thought. Thus narratives of the theological past—whether it is assumed to be surpassed or to present an inestimable content needing new translation—gradually became intrinsic to the self-understanding of systematic theology as such. But as this process happens the practices by which pre-modern theologians shape an argument to be authoritative are lost to view because they are now read *in toto* as failing basic tests of what counts as authoritative. Because these shifts are both theoretical and institutional the gradual adoption of professional distinctions that emerged under the influence of those in favour of some basic Enlightenment assumptions has had the effect of reinforcing a view of interdisciplinary relations—and thus of the very character of systematic theology—even among those who refuse some basic Enlightenment assumptions about pre-modern theology. These Enlightenment and idealist dynamics created the fundamental agenda for virtually all appropriation of modern historical theory by Christian theologians: the question for us must be whether the modes of historical understanding developed in this light were the only ones possible.

If we turn away from systematic theology as such for a moment, the rise of Church history or historical theology is also a story that must be understood both as the rise of a theoretical discipline under the influence of post-Renaissance and Enlightenment notions of historicity and as the rise of an academic discipline or profession gradually distinct from 'systematic' theology.[22] This distinction took

[21] Even Catholic apologetic theology in the 19th cent. found itself needing to effect a triangulation between dogmatic formulae, biblical texts, and new conceptions of reason: seen, for example, in the way that many American Catholic writers accepted the originally Protestant tradition of rationalistic 'evidences' in arguing for Christian faith. See E. Brooks Holifield, *Theology in America* (New Haven: Yale University Press, 2003), ch. 20.

[22] For strong account of the dynamics of professionalization within modern academic professions see Jan Goldstein, 'Foucault among the Sociologists: The "Disciplines" and the History of the Professions', *History and Theory*, 23 (1984), 171–92.

III. Understanding Pro-Nicene Theology

form either through understanding historical theology as a propaedeutic or as simply a historical discipline with no intrinsic relationship to the practice of systematics. During the early and mid-nineteenth century the great Catholic and Protestant thinkers of Tübingen demonstrate the tensions apparent in those who struggled to see studying the historical course of Christian thought as an intrinsic part of good dogmatics. Ferdinand Christian Baur offers a wonderfully integrated vision of the mutual interaction between historical theology and dogmatics. Through grasping the whole of the course of theological development and comprehending its fundamental dynamics and moments, the dogmatician can grasp what is unchanging and attempt to offer a system for the present. Of course Bauer understands that this present offering will eventually become further material for the historian, but the theoretical configuration of the various disciplines is clear: the investigation of the path is the mining of a source (and, note, one that can be grasped) to face the challenges of the present: the past has authority insofar as it is grasped for the present and from the present.[23]

In the context of Catholic Tübingen the work of Johann Sebastian Drey offers a fascinating parallel. Here we find a perspective much more attentive to the significance of the Church's dogmatic formulations. But, at the same time, historical investigation is still understood as the task of grasping the dynamic of the past so that, in idealist fashion, the coherence of the intelligible vision it offers may be grasped and articulated. The possibility of such grasping depends on the correspondence between the human mind and the divine mind.[24] Both Drey and Bauer represent an attempt to interrelate dogmatics and historical theology and they do so by means of Hegelian or at least idealist assumptions. As a result the unity between historical theology and dogmatics they both suggest is ultimately achieved by grasping the truth and *necessity* of the dogmatic whole revealed in history. The two are related via the possibility of a panoptic perception of their necessary unity. The speculative moment in which the truth of doctrine is grasped is understood as the culmination of the historical task rather than as a feature of historical investigation. The possibilities of post-Renaissance historical consciousness are thus once again adapted via a perspective that necessarily removes authority from credal and dogmatic

---

[23] See Peter Hodgson, *The Formation of Historical Theology: A Study of Ferdinand Christian Bauer* (New York: Harper & Row, 1966), esp. ch. 5.

[24] See Wayne L. Fehr, *The Birth of the Catholic Tübingen School: The Dogmatics of Johann Sebastian Drey* (Chico, Calif.: Scholars Press, 1981), esp. ch. 5. Alistair McGrath, *The Genesis of Doctrine* (Oxford: Blackwell, 1990), 138 ff. offers some extremely useful comments on the development of historical theology in 19th-cent. Germany.

formulae as such. While these two figures illustrate one of the most interesting attempts to re-relate historical theology and dogmatics (or systematics) such attempts have largely been out of vogue since the mid-nineteenth century. In the past hundred years while the historical study of the history of Christianity has become ever more pluriform, systematicians have generally adopted styles of using history as propaedeutic that lack theoretical justification.

If one of the most fundamental ways in which this evolution of disciplines imported a fundamentally Enlightenment set of assumptions into theological practice was the division between historical theology and systematics and the use of summary narratives by systematicians, then one of the most fundamental breaks with pre-modern practice that this division endorsed and promoted was the refiguring of the relationship between doctrinal exposition and close reading of Scripture.[25] Just as the rise of systematic theology must be traced to the Renaissance and Reformation, so too the rise of modern biblical studies is a long story, and one that need not be even sketched here. We need here to note only two things. First, the development of modern biblical studies and its concomitant guild structure within the overall shifts I have sketched further affected the ways pre-modern interpreters of Scripture might be viewed as authoritative in their own right. Second, the increasing division between systematic theology and biblical study is one important factor reducing the ability of modern Trinitarian theologians to engage the foundational documents of pro-Nicene theology and the creeds and conciliar material that they may well acknowledge as 'authoritative'. For theologians working within such divisions it becomes difficult to see the interactions between those credal formulae and the wider sets of principles and intellectual/spiritual practices understood to ground those creeds. As I have tried to show, those practices take form as a method of engaging the text of Scripture and as an aesthetics of faith: close attention to their performance will be fundamental to good interpretation of those formulae and principles, and good continuing articulation of pro-Nicene orthodoxy is likely to involve us in being able to perform practices that are in a high degree of continuity with those that sustained its original expression.

In the last decades of the twentieth century the field of systematics

---

[25] Hans Frei, *The Eclipse of Biblical Narrative: A study in Eighteenth and Nineteenth Century Hermeneutics* (New Haven: Yale University Press, 1974), offers much here, but does not focus directly on the ways in which the developments he traces were interwoven with the professionalization of theology and its diremption into distinct fields. Appendix A of Frei's *Types of Christian Theology* (New Haven: Yale University Press, 1992), 'Theology in the University' (95–132), although unfinished at the time of his death, sketches for us how he would perhaps have used the earlier material to speak about the shifts I am identifying here.

III. Understanding Pro-Nicene Theology

in the English-speaking world became increasingly diverse, at least on the surface. While many systematic theologians do remain attentive to the great German figures of the twentieth century, 'process' theologians, 'liberation' theologians, and many 'feminist' theologians (to name just a few sub-fields that cross denominations) respond to a diverse range of concerns and adopt distinct philosophical and ideological agendas.[26] Nevertheless, this seemingly distinct set of fields usually assumes some common principles from the history of systematics as a discipline and can be fairly seen as participating in a common systematic theological culture. For example, thinkers in all of the sub-fields I mentioned in the previous sentence tend to assume that the evolution of modern disciplines was necessary and hence 'critical' thought will have to abide by the disciplinary divisions between systematic and biblical studies (even if abiding by this division means lamenting it and trying to seek ways to bring the 'two' together). Similarly, thinkers across this range of disciplines tend to use common narrative tropes about the pre-modern, and assume similar relationships between historical and systematic theology. As we shall see, not only have the majority of significant modern Trinitarian theologies originated with thinkers participating in this common culture, Trinitarian theology has been particularly influenced by a number of other common post-Enlightenment and idealist concerns.

The story that I have told is one centred in the Protestant world and this is so because while Catholic theology and education has a long and venerable history throughout modernity, in recent decades the disciplinary divisions and theoretical understandings that mark the Protestant fourfold division have significantly shaped understandings of professional education and specialization among Catholic thinkers. While some important pockets of Catholic theology have resisted many of the implications of this division—especially where the various modern Thomisms still hold sway—it is noticeable that in the English-speaking world Catholic Trinitarian theology in the last forty years has largely been the province of those who either accept the fourfold division or accept many of its basic premises. For my purposes here, then, the story that I need to sketch is that of how those dynamics came to influence Catholic thought.

Even before this relatively recent adoption of a Protestant schema, some of the most basic themes of Catholic theology's development

---

[26] The foundations of the systematics must be studied in a broader European context and many of the major figures of the field have been German. Nevertheless, the structures of the discipline in current theology are also closely related to particular cultures and educational contexts: my concern here is with systematics in the English-speaking world.

parallel Protestant theology's reaction to the Enlightement.[27] During the late seventeenth and early eighteenth century commentaries on Thomas and on the *Sentences* marked by different school allegiances were already being replaced by manuals based on exposition of basic dogmatic truths of faith. This shift was then given a particular texture by the desire to articulate more formal systems in the later seventeenth century in reaction to Wolf's philosophy. Here the need to show deductively the relationship between theological material and a particular underlying idea mirrors comparable moves found in Protestant literature. In a manner also parallel to Protestant developments we see the emergence of theological encyclopaedias which take account of emerging divisions within the field of theology by subsuming them under one or other unifying concept, the work of F. A. Staudenmeier being a particularly important example.

The paths of Protestant and Catholic theologies were kept apart in the nineteenth century in part because of the place of positive dogmatic formulation within Catholic ecclesiology and in part because of the revival of Scholasticism which took place especially in the second half of the century and which culminated in the officially sanctioned development of various Thomisms following the encyclical *Aeterni Patris* in 1879. While it may seem as if these developments show Catholic theology pursuing a very different path from that of Protestant theology, it is vital to note the extent to which the revival of Scholasticism was motivated by a concern for a philosophy that could oppose Kantian critique of positive religion.[28] Interestingly, in many of these systems, summary narratives serve to introduce particular Thomisms as the modern culmination of a unified past in ways that are directly parallel to the styles of narration found in Protestant theologies.[29] Even though the development

---

[27] A still useful survey of the development of Catholic conceptions of theology since the 17th cent. is to be found in Yves Congar, *A History of Theology*, tr. Hunter Guthrie (New York: Doubleday, 1968), 177–202.

[28] For this story see Gerald A. McCool, *Nineteenth Century Scholasticism: The Search for a Unitary Method* (New York: Fordham University Press, 1977). I have found John Inglis, *Spheres of Philosophical Inquiry and the Historiography of Medieval Philosophy* (Leiden: Brill, 1998) particularly helpful in articulating how, across a broad field of approaches, 19th-cent. adaptations of Thomas and of scholasticism more broadly tended to have in view the construction of a philosophy that would oppose Kant and/or Descartes. He summarizes (p. 276): 'While significant medieval thinkers transformed philosophy into theology, philosophers in the modern period would transform medieval theology back into philosophy. Working within this tradition Kleutgen and Stöckl ... used specific medieval texts [*specifically Aquinas*] to construct a theory of knowledge, metaphysics, and ethics that allowed them to oppose what they took to be the subjectivism of Descartes, Kant, and the German idealists, as well as the materialism of ancient Greece and the modern world.'

[29] Reginald Garrigou-LaGrange, *The Trinity and God the Creator. A Commentary on St. Thomas's Theological Summa, 1a, q. 27–119*, tr. F. C. Eckhoff (St Louis: Herder, 1952), introd., offers an excellent example of such a narrative.

of Catholic biblical studies moved more slowly in the directions Protestant scholars had already pursued, developments in nineteenth-century Catholic understandings of the need for a Catholic philosophy that could both ground theology and oppose post-Enlightenment traditions helped to reshape views of what counts as an authoritative argument among theologians. Is it too speculative to see these developments as helping to prepare the ground for the headlong rush of Catholic biblical scholars into professional guilds and methodologies so championed by their Protestant colleagues?

Although the story of nineteenth-century Catholic theology is important insofar as we see Catholics following parallel tracks to Protestants in their reaction to the Enlightenment and its aftermath, it is only when we turn to the institutional shifts after the Second Vatican Council that we see Catholic theology finally adopting some of the deep structures of Protestant response to the Enlightenment. Commentators on the teaching of Catholic theology in both seminaries and undergraduate contexts in the decades before Vatican II report much turmoil over the manner in which theology should be taught and the usefulness of the manuals then in use. The problems were perceived to lie in the failure of the older apologetic approach in these manuals and in a failure to take account of the modern philosophical trends. After Vatican II these problems were addressed by an adoption both of more recent trends in Catholic thought but also by a very quick adoption of the Protestant fourfold schema discussed above. Thus, Joseph White, in his study of seminary education, notes the high degree of continuity in the textbooks used to teach dogmatics through the twentieth century up until the post-Vatican II period. At that point not only do manuals change but the very name of the subject changes in many places to systematic theology.[30] My point here is not about the value of the books being replaced but that this shift takes the form of adopting an originally Protestant schema. Of course much of the material taught would have been very distinctively Catholic: but form here is essential as it reflects a gradual separation of disciplines and thus a revising of the practices by which authoritative arguments are made and deployed.

The character of the shift can be seen in the two treatments of theology produced by Michael Schmaus. His 1960 *Katholische Dogmatik* was superseded by a post-Vatican II *Der Glaube der*

---

[30] Joseph M. White, *The Diocesan Seminary in the United States: A History from the 1780s to the Present* (Notre Dame, Ind.: University of Notre Dame Press, 1989), chs. 16 and 17. Much can be learned about parallel developments in the teaching of theology to undergraduates from Patrick W. Carey and Earl C. Muller (eds.), *Theological Education in the Catholic Tradition: Contemporary Challenges* (New York: Crossroad, 1997).

Kirche, itself translated and adapted for the United States market as *Dogma*. This last is particularly clear about the changes that characterize the new approach: 'whereas formerly [dogmatic theology] considered itself the center of the theological enterprise ... more recently, as a result of general developments in theology and of the statements of the Second Vatican Council, it has come to see more clearly that it occupies one position within a totality'.[31] Schmaus goes on to articulate the relationship between 'Biblical theology' and dogmatics as one in which the former interprets what the Scripture says and dogmatics, consisting of historical theology and systematic theology, initially traces the interpretation of Scripture in different contexts (first comes that of 'Greek philosophy') and demonstrates continuity of development down to modern expressions of Catholic dogma. As systematic theology it attempts the production of a system (but always fails before the eschaton) and attempts to pass judgement on the 'intellectual, cultural and religious movements of its time'.[32] On the one hand, the task of understanding 'what Scripture says' has been handed over to another discipline and the interpretations of Scripture found in Christian tradition can most certainly express dogma correctly, but they are no longer of primary significance for understanding the text itself. On the other hand, and once again, the organization of disciplines places the overall systematic/speculative moment as the culmination of tracing a historical course; while a scholar such as Schmaus himself may have been able to undertake serious historical scholarship as well as systematic work, lesser scholars and students are now presented with a rhetoric of historical theology (and historical theology understood as grand summary narrative) as propaedeutic to construction in the contemporary philosophical context. Catholic theology's path beyond the older apologetic synthetic manuals is to adopt the form (and hence even aspects of content) of post-Enlightenment Protestant thought.[33]

These developments in the Protestant and Catholic world are, however, not a monolithic story of 'betrayal'. The development of intellectual traditions is complex and without awareness of that complexity lines of possible engagement with modern 'systematics'

---

[31] Michael Schmaus, *Dogma*, vol. i: *God in Revelation* (New York: Sheed & Ward, 1968), 288.

[32] Schmaus, *Dogma*, 294.

[33] Once again we see the importance of the professionalization of theology into a fourfold system. While it is true that among those pressing for new styles of theology after Vatican II were many members of the 'nouvelle théologie' that I have held up as providing resources beyond the current state of affairs, figures such as DeLubac and Congar, the force of professionalization seems to have easily overcome their own strong antipathy to some modern theological divisions—especially that between dogmatics and the reading of Scripture.

would remain hidden. At the beginning of *After Virtue*, MacIntyre offers a bleak account of modern writers deploying terms whose meaning is no longer known to them: 'emotivism' hides itself under the guise of a language from an older era.[34] MacIntyre's analysis (which one can easily apply to modern Trinitarian theology) may be adapted to explain my point here. Authors who repeat fragments of a language they do not understand are also engaged in a mimicry that sustains the presence of that earlier speech. This presence may create fissures in a language that tries to hold up for celebration its own re-articulation of earlier theology; a presence enabling some to make occasional complex moves beyond the general intellectual trajectories of modern theology. Thus many theologians have inevitably found their theological discourse shaped by the language and confessions of earlier periods in ways that created fissures in their discourse and made them bearers of traditions they sought to re-articulate or suppress.[35] I think here, for example, of the way in which Barth's conscious and active engagement with sixteenth- and seventeenth-century dogmatics—often via later compilations such as that by Heinrich Heppe—as an alternative to the concerns of nineteenth-century theologies serves to modify the post-Kantian epistemological concerns that are also embedded in his theology.[36] In the same way Schleiermacher's *Glaubenslehre* far less consciously draws into its world dynamics of faith and reason that introduce a constant element of instability.[37]

In the Catholic context such fissures in theological texts are in some ways more likely and far more common. An ecclesiology in which the authoritative language of credal confession and its interpretation within tradition remains the basis for catechism and official documentation is both more likely to encourage the Catholic

---

[34] Alasdair MacIntyre, *After Virtue: A Study in Moral Theory* (London: Duckworth, 1985), chs. 1 and 3.

[35] We should also note that many Church communities sustain practices that push against the direction of the use of the Bible within academic theology. Increasing interest in such communities has helped to create a climate within which the exploration of alternatives to modernity's construals of theological practice is of wide interest. For some extremely diverse examples see Mary McClintock Fulkerson, *Changing the Subject. Women's Discourses and Feminist Theology* (Minneapolis: Fortress Press, 1994), 239–98; Michael Cartwright, 'Ideology and the Interpretation of the Bible', *Modern Theology*, 9 (1993), 141–58; McGrath, *The Genesis of Doctrine*, 159 ff.; Vincent Wimbush, 'The Bible and African Americans: An Outline of an Interpretive History', in Cain Hope Felder (ed.), *Stony the Road we Trod* (Minneapolis: Fortress, 1991), 81–97.

[36] It is noticeable that much modern reading of Barth ignores his own interest in these figures and his own sense that engaging their theologies was a key factor in his reshaping of dogmatic practice. See Bruce L. McCormack, *Karl Barth's Critically Realistic Dialectical Theology* (Oxford: Clarendon Press, 1995), 334–6.

[37] Eugene Rogers, 'Schleiermacher as an Anselmian Theologian: Apologetics, Dogmatics, Aesthetics, and Proof,' *Scottish Journal of Theology*, 51 (1998), 342–79.

theologian to engage the course of that tradition and is more likely to disrupt any simple account of the need to 'translate' credal language into a new philosophical idiom. The past couple of decades have also witnessed the beginnings of a fracturing of the theological disciplines through conscious critique of modernity's intellectual preoccupations. These moves have opened a number of avenues that may be more sympathetic to the direction I pursue here. To give some current examples from the English-speaking context one might point to the 'Radical Orthodoxy' movement,[38] to the work of such post-liberal writers as Hans Frei, George Lindbeck, Stephen E. Fowl, Gene Rogers, and Bruce Marshall, to British theologians such as Sarah Coakley, John Webster, and Rowan Williams. One could also point to a number of Catholic writers who have become suspicious of much recent theology's modes of engagement with pre-modern traditions, figures such as Michael Buckley, Frederick Bauerschmidt, William Cavanaugh, Nicholas Lash, and Matthew Levering.[39]

The sketch I have offered here is necessarily cursory, but the main thrust of the argument is, I hope, clear. The use of narrative within modern systematic culture is one feature of a culture of authority in theology dependent on reaction to some of the most fundamental Enlightenment and post-Enlightenment dynamics of thought. My argument is not that theologians do not treat the fourth century as authoritative, but that the fourth century is only allowed to be authoritative within modern systematics in ways already shaped by particular modern and supposedly necessary constructions of authoritative argument and thus only in ways that hide the true challenge of those models of authoritative argument present in fourth-century texts themselves. This culture has shaped theological practice not only at a theoretical level but also and importantly at the material level of modern professional guild distinctions

---

[38] The relationship between the positions I advocate in this chapter and the programme of 'Radical Orthodoxy' will probably be of interest to a number of readers. While there are some significant similarities of concern, I would, nevertheless, want to question the extent to which 'Radical Orthodoxy' remains still too much another modern systematic theological option. This is so particularly when one considers the modes of theological practice deployed by such interesting figures as John Milbank and Catherine Pickstock. In these writers we find no overt theology of Scripture and little account of the process of transformation in Christ. From this perspective one can think of their assumptions about the practice of theology as closer to those of modern systematics than to pre-modern theologians. I am grateful to John O'Keefe and others for the opportunity to explore this perception in the Annual Theology and Philosophy Lecture at Creighton University in 2000.

[39] This list is by no means exhaustive and it consciously crosses a number of 'school' allegiances. My suggestions to all concern the manner in which the character of argument about and exposition of basic Christian doctrines should be understood once some of the characteristic preoccupations of 'modern' theology have been questioned.

within theology: the evolution of these disciplinary boundaries has served to reinforce the methodological principles with which I have been concerned. A deeper engagement with the legacy of pro-Nicene theology will involve both a deeper awareness of the deep structures of modern theological practice (which remain central even as the discipline(s) seems to become ever more diverse) and a rethinking of how appropriate argument within theology is to be envisioned.

III: LOCATING THE 'REVIVAL'

Against this background, I want now to describe two of the determining dynamics of modern Trinitarian theology. My intention is both to draw out the extent to which a great deal of modern Trinitarian theology is dependent on particular modern philosophical concerns, and to do so in a way that draws out the extent to which those concerns involve both a narration of the pre-modern and a rejection of some of the basic tenets of classical Trinitarian theology.[40] While those making use of these philosophical traditions may continue to subscribe to those tenets it will require a great deal of care if that subscription is not to become more formal than material. At the same time the fact that the project(s) of modern Trinitarian theology are imbued with the culture of systematic theology means that understandings of authoritative arguments prevail that further serve to disrupt detailed and dense engagement with the sources of classical Trinitarian theology.

The influence of Hegel

Our point of departure here must be the influence of Hegel: the German systematic theological tradition that has so shaped recent Trinitarian theology is incomprehensible without grasping the significance of his influence.[41] While few accepted the entirety of

---

[40] At a number of points through this chapter I have moved without acknowledgement between speaking of 'pro-Nicene' and 'classical' Trinitarianism. While the two are by no means identical, I take it that the former is the foundation and core of the latter. Readers may well ask if I am arguing that a Trinitarian theologian must be an expert in pro-Nicene theology. No: I am arguing that for the development of good Trinitarian theology that takes classical credal formulae as normative a theologian should aim to participate in a theological culture in continuity with pro-Nicene culture (such as the one I sketch here) and develop close attention either to pro-Nicenes or to those whose Trinitarianism embodies the fundamentals of pro-Nicene Trinitarianism within a compatible theological culture: a medieval theologian (or perhaps a more modern figure such as Dionysius Petavius or Scheeben).

[41] Samuel M. Powell's recent *The Trinity in German Thought* (Cambridge: Cambridge University Press, 2001) has much to offer anyone seeking to understand the course of Trinitarian theology within German Protestantism. Powell unfortunately assumes an account of the 'fall' of Trinitarian theology a little too easily and sees a continuity between Augustine, Thomas, and Idealism by which I am not persuaded.

Hegel's reconstruction of Christianity, many of Hegel's dynamics found their way even into the thought of those who opposed his system as a whole. It is thus important that we bear in mind some of the most important of those dynamics in the paragraphs that follow.

Hegel makes his elegant end-run around the Kantian epistemological restriction of theology by relocating the particular moments of thought and feeling within an ontology of the self-differentiation and realization of *Geist*. The particular epistemological restrictions Kant describes are taken to reflect Kant's own failure to see that the structures of mind and thought he identifies are only one stage in a process that leads far beyond them. Thus the problems in discussing realities beyond the mind's categories highlighted by Kantian epistemology are relocated by offering an ontology within which these categories are no longer determinative of theological discussion. The same move also constitutes an attack on Schleiermacher and on Pietist attacks on Hegel. For Hegel these trends were similar restrictions of the scope and possibility of theology that overlooked the actual and enduring significance of traditional Christian dogmatic teaching. Within Hegel's system, however, these teachings are 'preserved' by his attempt to bring to full clarity their 'philosophical' content.[42]

It is in the structure of this 'philosophical recovery' that we see some of his most characteristic reinterpretations of Christian Trinitarian belief. First, Hegel—as John Milbank observed some years ago—presents the Spirit in his Trinitarian scheme as a *necessary* hermeneutic moment.[43] The Spirit—or the moment of Spirit—enables the realization of *Geist* in and as community. The significance of the move lies not only in the skill with which Hegel accords the Spirit a role which makes the divine triunity seem less contingent (a move which might, of course, be a profound mistake however well executed), but also in the fact that his finding the Spirit a role fulfils an essentially Protestant dynamic *separating* the Son and the Spirit (a theme to which I will return). Hegel is as complex as ever here: he at least reflects the principle that the *operationes ad extra* are indivisible insofar as he clearly presents each stage of the unfolding of *Geist* as the unfolding of the concept that implicitly is already threefold (God in and for Godself). Nevertheless, when he comes to play out the philosophical content of Son and Spirit he can

---

[42] G. W. F. Hegel, *Lectures on the Philosophy of Religion, One-Volume Edition: The Lectures of 1827*, tr. Peter Hodgson (Berkeley: University of California Press, 1988), 389 ff. In the interpretation of Hegel I have found particularly useful Dale M. Schlitt, *Hegel's Trinitarian Claim* (Leiden: Brill, 1984); Cyril O'Regan, *The Heterodox Hegel* (Albany, NY: SUNY Press, 1994).
[43] John Milbank, *The Word Made Strange* (Oxford: Blackwell Publishers, 1997), ch. 7.

do so only by also separating out the two stages through invoking a temporal dynamic. Because Spirit operates both as the name for a Trinitarian person and as a controlling concept for his system as a whole, Hegel can clearly present the realization of the Spirit as a distinct moment beyond the Son's. Even if we must, in Hegel's case, bear in mind the sophistication with which he deploys the concept of God in Godself, his separation of the roles of Son and Spirit and his lack of interest in the notion of the Body of Christ in favour of the Spirit-filled community take up themes from previous Protestant tradition and reinforce the direction of its arguments.

In speaking of Hegel's pneumatology we come to his conception of *Geist* coming to full realization *through* interaction with the world. For Hegel, to maintain an account of the immutable God distinct from the world is to remain in the sphere of representation and to be alienated from the reality of Spirit. Hegel here sets the stage for a variety of post-Hegelian reinterpreted Christianities in which God either becomes with the world or is affected by the events of created history in a manner parallel to our own experience of suffering. Hegel insists that not only difference but also anguish and suffering are grounded in the differentiation of God.[44] It is noticeable that this attempt to give new vitality to the notion of God offers little argument against earlier Enlightenment rejection of pre-modern negotiations of divine immutability and presence. Hegel just adds to the seeming weight of the consensus that pre-Enlightenment accounts need significant correction. What for them was, at some stage, argument, has become for him assumption.

Some of the most basic of Hegel's reinterpretative moves found their way into much subsequent Trinitarian theology, initially in the Protestant world, eventually in other communions as well. As I noted at the beginning of this section few are 'Hegelians' *tout court*, and it is because his influence on Trinitarian theology has been so widespread and diverse that many of his own arguments and assumptions have become accepted as the necessary common currency of discussion. Hegelian (and subsequent idealist) influence is clearest on the central German tradition of recent Trinitarian theology, in such figures as Pannenberg, Moltmann, and Jüngel (I briefly discuss the influence of this tradition on Karl Rahner below). Their influence on English-speaking theology continues to be immense, as can be seen, for instance, in the recent and extremely interesting *Systematic Theology* of Robert Jenson. It is important to note that this engagement with the Hegelian legacy has occurred in the theological culture discussed above; occurring in a context when

---

[44] Hegel, *Philosophy of Religion*, 432 ff., 470 ff.

pre-modern methods of attention to Scripture are under suspicion if not simply forgotten and in a context where the supposedly authoritative statements of credal and conciliar tradition are engaged in an attenuated and ahistorical manner (because the methods that sustained them are rejected), it becomes all the easier for the sheer novelty of these Hegelian dynamics and the challenge to them represented by classical Trinitarian theology to be ignored.[45]

The Trinitarian revival

It has become commonplace in the last thirty or forty years to speak of a revival in Trinitarian theology, and to assume that in the previous century or two the doctrine was seriously neglected. My focus here will be on the theologies linked with this recent revival, but it is important to notice that claims for a revival in Trinitarian theology have been made in a number of circles since the early nineteenth century in both Protestant and Catholic contexts.[46] If there is, however, something distinctive about this particular revival it is that whereas the revivals of the nineteenth century saw themselves as recovering a doctrine lost during the Enlightenment and its aftermath, recent revivalists have frequently seen themselves as both overcoming the Enlightenment and rectifying the problems inherent in western theological tradition. A few writers interweave this story with post-Harnackian claims that the Hellenization of Christianity

---

[45] Cyril O'Regan offers one of the most interesting re-readings of the Hegelian tradition as a recapitulation of a Gnostic tradition within modern Christianity. See *The Heterodox Hegel*. See also his new multi-volume project sketched in its opening volume, *Gnostic Return in Modernity* (Albany, NY: SUNY Press, 2001). Even if one is suspicious of the possibility of describing an intrinsically 'Gnostic' dynamic, he makes clear the extent to which one who does not accept the necessity of a re-articulation of Christian faith after the Enlightenment challenge is certain to find the fundamental dynamics of Hegelian thought pushing against the central and formative tradition of Christian Trinitarianism.

[46] Thus, for example, Isaac Dorner frequently identified a mid-19th-cent. Trinitarian 'revival' after a period in which only Hegelians had kept the doctrine alive. Claude Welch argues that among Catholic theologians there is a Trinitarian revival under way in the 1940s: *In This Name*, 101. Rather than offering a simple 'fall' and 'revival' of Trinitarian doctrine it might make more sense to speak of the rise of anti-Trinitarian thought concomitant with shifts in models of theological practice during the 17th and 18th cent. This anti-Trinitarianism at times achieves prominence, especially in academic contexts, but is always accompanied (at both academic and popular levels) by other streams of thought that offer a more robust Trinitarian perspective. The question I am asking is whether many of the forms of this consciously Trinitarian theology are frequently (and especially in recent decades) overcome by strains of thought that undermine their continuity with the tradition they seek to uphold or recover. In Protestant contexts aspects of the early story of the rise of anti-Trinitarian thought—and its links with shifts in theological method—have recently been excellently explored by Richard Muller, *Post-Reformation Reformed Dogmatics, vol. iv: The Divine Triunity*, and Philip Dixon, *Nice and Hot Disputes: The Doctrine of the Trinity in the Seventeenth Century* (London: T. & T. Clark, 2003). The story of Catholic Trinitarianism since the 17th cent. remains largely unexplored.

itself overcame a truly Trinitarian theology.[47] Little scholarship is offered to back up the historical narration, one senses that much of the argument rests on the reader's willingness to accept the persuasiveness of the three narrative tropes I explored above.[48]

Despite these varying perspectives on the origins of the lack that must be overcome, the main themes of this most recent 'revival' can be summarized under two headings. First, many pursue fundamentally Hegelian strategies to articulate God's Trinitarian involvement in history.[49] Sometimes the expressed sources for these positions are not openly Hegelian—we see both appeal to other philosophical sources and appeal to scriptural material supposedly rid of later Greek influence—but one does not have to be a particularly skilled intellectual archaeologist to recognize that Hegel's thought set the context within which such modern moves become possible.[50] Second, many revivalists attempt to counter what is taken to have become a functionally unitarian account of God by finding strategies to emphasize plurality within the Trinity. One of the most important strategies pursued is to describe the divine persons via attributing to them a psychological density parallel to that found in human persons and via an account of their mutual interaction that relies heavily on aspects of the interrelationship of human persons.

This project owes more to early twentieth-century personalist philosophies than to Hegelian themes, but Hegel's account of the person as defined through self-transcendent love and sacrifice is not irrelevant here (especially when the project is pursued by projecting human experience of alienation and anguish into the separations between the persons evident in the crucifixion). It is here also that we begin to see a Kantian sub-theme in modern Trinitarianism: the persons are more and more present as autonomous self-establishing

[47] Thus, for example, LaCugna, *God For Us*.

[48] One of the most ironic discussions of the functional unitarianism of previous western tradition is actually that of Karl Rahner at *The Trinity*, tr. Joseph Donceel (London: Burns & Oates, 1970), 9 ff. While asserting that Christians have become 'mere monotheists' he cites (nn. 3–4) 16 articles and books written between 1927 and 1958 that attempt to shape a Trinitarian spirituality or make the Trinity central to Christian theology. Even without citing any of the relevant literature in English this does not seem to indicate quite such a desert as he alleges. Later in the text (p. 25 n. 22) he also testifies to the extensive debate in Catholic theology during the 1940s and 1950s concerning the nature of the Spirit's indwelling.

[49] In such complex figures as Barth and Balthasar the Hegelian influence is more subtle but still important. See for example Rowan Williams, 'Barth on the Triune God', in Stephen Sykes (ed.), *Karl Barth: Studies of his Theological Method* (Oxford: Clarendon Press, 1979), 147–93.

[50] It is probably worth noting that the shape of process thought (now very much declining in significance) is also fundamentally Hegelian: both in the Hegelian tradition's subtle influence on Whitehead and, importantly, in the way that recent process accounts of God have tended to buy in wholesale to the basic structure of Hegel's account of previous theology and have accepted many Hegelian trends apparent through recent theological thinking. David Burrell, 'Does Process Theology Rest on a Mistake?', *Theological Studies*, 43 (1982), 125–35.

individuals whose depth of love is seen in their mutual co-operation. It is important, however, to note that fully 'social' Trinitarian theologies, theologies that openly advocate viewing the persons in the manner described above are less common than either those which do not offer a detailed account of divine personhood but which assume a mode of discourse that speaks *as if* the persons functioned in this way, or than those which qualify the analogy between human and divine persons, but functionally speak as if there is such a direct parallel, neglecting the consequences of the divine simplicity and unity of operations. This move enables many to abandon the principle that the persons' operations *ad extra* are indivisible (at least by assuming that a valid form of the doctrine is that each person contributes something to a common project) and to focus on ways in which each Trinitarian person is distinctly involved in creation and redemption. In other contexts the same strategy enables the drawing of parallels between the nature of God as Triune and the relational nature of the Church and human community.[51]

As I will explore later in this chapter, such moves involve theologians not only in reconceiving the sort of unity one imagines within God, but also in being less attentive to pre-modern accounts of how the body of Christ functions in the drama of redemption. The shaping of Trinitarian theology one sees here has noticeably moved away from the epistemological reserve intrinsic to pro-Nicene thought. These moves need also to be understood as dependent on the wider move away from pre-modern modes of reading Scripture, and thus on shifts in what counts as authoritative argument. The meta-narrative strategies I identified at the beginning of this chapter are present in these revivalist strategies as assumptions about the character of authority and theology in

---

[51] Thus fully 'social' Trinitarianism is perhaps clearest in the work of Plantinga, 'The Social Analogy', and Richard Swinburne, *The Christian God* (Oxford: Clarendon Press, 1994). Miroslav Volf, *After Our Likeness: The Church as the Image of the Trinity* (Grand Rapids, Mich.: Eerdmans, 1998) offers a slightly different social notion of the Trinity, but again one dependent on misunderstanding the function of the divine unity and simplicity, and on the persuasiveness of modern notions of personhood: see 202–3 (where the notion of a unitary substance or nature is dispensed with in favour of a 'perichoretic' notion of relation) and 215 ff., where the unity of the persons as 'separate centers of action' is understood as a community of absolute equality in which, I suppose, the unity can only be understood as the product of the eternal and free wills of the persons themselves. Elizabeth Johnson, *She Who Is* (New York: Crossroad, 1997) on the basis of the standard critique of pre-modern 'metaphysics', turns to the idea of communion that occurs through freedom in loving as the basis of unity (e.g. 216 ff., 227 ff.). Catherine LaCugna, *God For Us*, criticizes both the evils of classical conceptions of the unity of substance and the projection of the model of egalitarian loving communion onto God in Feminist and Liberation theologies (243–88), but then (300 ff.) constructs her own account around a narration of the roles of the divine persons in salvation based on the principle that God is 'immutably personal' (301). In effect this enables her then to talk as if there were most fundamentally three free agents who come together (even if they do so eternally) (e.g. 292–300).

pre-modernity. As a result the credal formulae of the fourth century are no longer subject to any dense consideration and largely function as authorities insofar as they can be used as points of departure for dynamics taken from modern philosophical or psychological concerns. The patterns and techniques of exegesis that ground them are similarly ignored.

When we turn to Catholic Trinitarian theology we find that talk of a revival is equally loud and that the main lines of that revival follow those in the Protestant world. There are one or two notable differences: the Hegelian conceptions of God's becoming via an involvement with the creation that are so important within Protestant trinitarianism are still less frequently overtly present within Catholic thought. Within a context where authoritative theological pronouncements by the Church are still deeply imbued with an insistence on the divine immutability it has been much more difficult for theologians consciously Catholic to adopt Hegelian dynamics. At the same time the vitality of a continuing strand of thinkers willing to advocate the significance of Thomas for modern theology (at least in part as a continuation of *ressourcement* attempts at the recovery of a more historically sustainable account of Thomas) has offered a clear counterpoint to the increasing influence of 'revivalist' dynamics.

Nevertheless, Catholic Trinitarian revivalists are very close to their Protestant counterparts both in their interest in introducing an increased plurality into God, their willingness to adopt a Hegelian or idealist paradigm in order to speak of God's involvement in history, and their participation in modern Protestant theology's use of narrative. Karl Rahner's 1967 essay on the Trinity that was soon translated and published as his short *The Trinity* was fundamental in shaping this agenda within Catholic theology: Rahner provides us with an excellent example of the way that Hegelian and idealist dynamics can become fundamental in a thinker otherwise 'committed' to credal principles that push in very different directions. Although Rahner did not directly deny the Thomistic principle that God's relationship with the world is not 'real' in God (that is, that this relationship does not affect God's being), he pushes the boundaries of the doctrine of divine immutability as far as he can by his usual method of asserting the traditional formulations to be true while introducing as points that have been somewhat neglected positions opposed to those traditional formulations.[52] The idealist

---

[52] e.g. Karl Rahner, 'On the Theology of the Incarnation', *Theological Investigations*, iv, tr. Kevin Smyth (Baltimore: Helicon Press, 1966), 113–14 n. 3: 'If we do call [the Incarnation] a change, then, since God is unchangeable, we must say that God who is unchangeable in himself can change in another (can in fact become man). But this "changing *in* another" must

direction of Rahner's thought is further seen in the way he articulates his substitution of 'manner of subsisting' (*distinkte Susbsistenzweisen*). The concept serves better than the modern understanding of person because that concept would indicate that God consists of three distinct centres of consciousness and action whereas God is only one. But God is one such centre with just two 'basic activities of Spirit' (*Grundvollzüge des Geistes*) of knowledge and love: this we know from the 'metaphysics of spirit'.

Moreover this conception of God is better than the 'classical psychological' analogy because the latter cannot demonstrate the necessity of the Word's existing as utterance: only the metaphysics of Spirit delivers this. Rahner ends his essay by suggesting that his model is also superior in that it can be seen as beginning not from any analysis of the isolated individual but from the experience which results from God's action in history, from a knowledge of the movement of the human spirit in history, its transcendence and openness towards the future.[53] In these arguments we see the extent to which Rahner has moved far beyond the patterns of analogical judgement I have argued are central to pro-Nicenes such that it is only an idealist account that can sufficiently demonstrate the necessity of doctrine formulations in the modern context. At the same time it is important to note the ways in which Rahner's account makes use of the standard styles of narration found in modern systematic theologies: brief summaries of positions are offered only so that the new challenges of modernity may take centre stage as demanding a rethinking of the basic dynamics of pre-modernity's confusions (confusions frequently due to polemical context).

It is also fascinating to note that while Rahner's account has this strongly idealist focus, there is a certain incoherence in the ways that he also helped to prepare the way for Catholic theologians to leave behind the doctrine appropriation and push towards very strongly pluralistic accounts of the persons' action! Bruce Marshall notes Rahner's strong concern to argue that each of the persons has 'non-appropriated relations' with human beings in the process of salvation. Rahner's brief account of these relations seems remarkably close to Thomas's understanding of appropriation (rather than to

---

neither be taken as denying the immutability of God in himself nor simply be reduced to a changement [*sic*] of the other ... We must maintain methodologically the immutability of God, and yet it would be basically a denial of the incarnation if we used it alone to determine what this mystery could be ... This we can and must affirm, without being Hegelians. And it would be a pity if Hegel had to teach Christians such things.' One might have hoped that a Catholic theologian would maintain such a doctrine a little more than 'methodologically'.

[53] Karl Rahner, *The Trinity*, 109–20, originally as Johannes Feiner and Magnus Löhrer (eds.), *Mysterium Salutis: Grundriß heilsgeschichtlicher Dogmatik*, ii (Zurich and Cologne: Benziger, 1967), 389–97.

what Rahner condemns as the Thomist doctrine of 'mere' appropriations), but he locates his category of 'non-appropriated' relations within a wider critique of the doctrine in Catholic theology in the 1960s that attempted to focus Christians' attention on the 'economic' Trinity and led to the sort of highly pluralistic accounts found in such figures as Catherine LaCugna.[54]

The general structure of the moves found in Rahner are followed in much subsequent Catholic Trinitarian theology. Walter Kasper's theology represents another trend in Catholic thought, and another historically Protestant shift. Kasper's *The God of Jesus Christ* expends much effort on attempting to be 'biblical' in his account of the Father's priority. As John Milbank points out, one of Kasper's basic moves is a 'Catholic transcendentalism' that uses the Kantian legacy to characterize the freedom of the persons and qualify the sense that the persons are only in relation. In his attempt to recover the Father's *monarchia* as a way round a fairly standard narrative of the western tradition's failings, Kasper emphasizes the gratuity of the Father's gift to Son and Spirit rather that focusing on a model of the Father as essentially Father, being God in the eternal and defining act of sharing. Modern notions of personhood here do not simply introduce too much division into the Trinity, they run the risk of corrupting the basic pro-Nicene sense of the mysterious and incomprehensible union of the Godhead.[55]

At a number of points I have indicated where my brief characterizations overly simplify a complex situation: the path of recent Catholic Trinitarianism is also much more complex than my picture might suggest. In part this is so because, despite the large-scale rejection of Thomist theologies, some remain who actively use these resources. I have also presented this story as one in which Catholics adapt themes from a historically Protestant movement. While I would argue that this is an accurate diagnosis, one irony deserves note. At some key points the narratives of pre-modern theology deployed within this cross-denominational revival in Trinitarian theology have their origin in Catholic and Thomistic contexts.

---

[54] See Bruce Marshall, *Trinity and Truth* (Cambridge: Cambridge University Press, 2000), 254 ff., esp. 255 n. 23. Rahner, e.g. at *The Trinity*, 73 cites Heribert Mühlen's 'Person und Appropriation', *Münchener Theologische Zeitschrift*, 16 (1965), 37–57. Mühlen's account is then later acknowledged by Lacugna, *God For Us*, 108 (although Mühlen's own Trinitarianism was much closer to Rahner's model). It is also worth noting that Rahner's discussion of the interrelationship between the immanent and economic Trinities also pushes in the direction of focusing attention on the distinctness of the persons as revealed through God's actions: in Rahner an idealist conception of Spirit reigns in what in later thinkers tends towards social Trinitarianism. On the problems with the very distinction of economic and immanent Trinities see Bruce Marshall, 'The Trinity', in Gareth Jones (ed.), *The Blackwell Companion to Modern Theology* (Oxford: Blackwell, 2004), 183–203.

[55] Milbank, *Word Made Strange*, 174 ff.

Thus, most fundamentally, the narrative about the separation between eastern and western theologies finds its origin in Theodore De Régnon's history of Trinitarian theology in the late nineteenth century.[56] Focus on the importance of the 'psychological' analogy in understanding Latin theology is another example. While this conception is frequently projected onto Augustine as its source, in many neo-Thomist writers following De Régnon and yet pushing his argument further, Augustine's 'failure' is described precisely as a failure to align each person of the Trinity clearly with a mental function![57] The overcoming of this lack is taken to be apparent in Thomas. Once we note that Thomas's position is not quite so simple as that attributed to him in this regard we begin to see the central role in the development of a standard narrative about the supposedly classical psychological analogy played by neo-Thomism itself. Thus, even the rejection of neo-Thomism may involve a continuing adherence to one of its key contributions to the history of Trinitarian theology.

The story of Orthodox theology's reaction to modernity is far less well known and well researched. In some respects, and given the story I am telling in this chapter, it is worth noting that the need to tell that story is itself hidden by those strands of Orthodox scholarship that have supported the neo-Patristic and neo-Palamite synthesis so prominent in Vladimir Lossky and George Florovsky. Once one is convinced that a synthetic restatement of the Fathers is both possible and will enable us to step back beyond any periods of 'corruption' of the tradition, then the story of that 'corruption' hardly needs to be told. The extent to which this presentation was itself part of a polemic against alternative construals of Orthodoxy is not usually noted by those enthusiastic about the portrayal of the Fathers one finds there.[58] While this turn towards a neo-Patristic synthesis has enabled some Orthodox theologians to maintain serious engagement with the legacy of Nicaea, it is noticeable that in a number of prominent Orthodox theologians the same 'revivalist' dynamics are seen that we have encountered elsewhere. The work of John Zizioulas is particularly noteworthy—and the ease within which he is considered and engaged within Catholic and Protestant theology is an interesting indication of a shared inheritance! At the

---

[56] On which see Barnes, 'De Régnon Reconsidered'. It is particularly important to note Barnes's exposition of the many ways in which De Régnon's account is transformed in its adaptation. Most fundamentally, De Régnon is not concerned primarily with differences between Greek and Latin but with a historical periodization: pre-Nicene Latins for him demonstrate the dynamics of a pattern that finds its high point in the Cappadocians.

[57] E.g. Garrigou-LaGrange, *The Trinity and God the Creator*, 68.

[58] Though see now Paul Valliere, *Modern Russian Theology. Bukharev, Soloviev, Bulgakov. Orthodox Theology in a New Key* (Grand Rapids, Mich.: Eerdmans, 2000).

same time, however, the prominent Hegelian trends of the recent 'revival' are far rarer than in other contexts.

The theological strategies pursued in the literature of this Trinitarian 'revival' almost universally assume all or some of the meta-narrative strategies I identified at the beginning of this chapter. Moreover, they occur as part of the culture of modern systematics that reconfigures the manner in which the pre-modern can be understood as authoritative and its arguments engaged. Thus it is not surprising that the narratives of the pre-modern used by theologians within this tradition frequently serve to hide the possibility of meaningful dialogue with pro-Nicene theology. The distinction between the practice of theology and the reading of the scriptural text, combined with a thoroughly modern sense of what does and does not count as 'biblical', helps to make the modern solutions that recent Trinitarian theology deploys seem plausible. Within this system there is little possibility for a meaningful engagement with pro-Nicene Trinitarianism and the full tragedy of systematic theologians in Churches committed to the Nicene creed becomes apparent.

IV: AFTER THE PASSING: A THEOLOGY OF THEOLOGY

By now it should be clear that the challenge to modern Trinitarian theologies from pro-Nicene theologies stems from a difference in theological culture: the principles of classical Trinitarian theology were sustained by a culture taken to be essential to the appropriate use of and belief in them, but a theological culture very different from that shaped by the broad field of modern systematic theology. In some manner scholarship on the fourth century has recognized for a hundred and fifty years that a theological culture grounds the formulations of pro-Nicene theology. Newman himself presented the pre-Nicene age as possessing a depth of spiritual insight into the nature of the Gospel that did not need the external structures of a developed Trinitarian doctrine. He then argued that at the heart of fourth-century 'Nicene' theology is a mode of reverence and awe, an attention to the mysteriousness of doctrine largely identical with the attention to the mystery of faith to be found in the pre-Nicene era.[59] Newman makes little attempt to analyse the theological practices shaping these modes of attention: but they are often used to distinguish his fourth-century heroes from the nineteenth-century targets of his polemic. More recent writing has also tended to point to modes of theological practice as the heart of

---

[59] John Henry Newman, *The Arians of the Fourth Century* (Notre Dame, Ind.: Notre Dame University Press, 2001 (reprint of 1871 edn. with introd. and notes by Rowan Williams)), 134–50.

the pro-Nicene genius, but rarely is any attempt made to question how far contemporary Christianity can or should sustain those modes even as it holds to the central insights or formula sustained by them.

In the light of the first three sections of this chapter I want to suggest some basic dynamics of a theological culture sustainable in the twenty-first century and yet which would enable pro-Nicene theology to serve as usefully and continually authoritative for modern Trinitarian theology. In large part I suggest in what follows ways in which modern theologians can shape a theological culture that seeks as far as it can to appropriate the culture of pro-Nicene theologians themselves. Proceeding in this manner will help to make even clearer the character of the challenge that pro-Nicene thought offers to modern systematics and to Trinitarian theology in particular.

Two basic dimensions of any such attempt will be to outline the interrelationships between doctrinal formulae and the text of Scripture, and to outline the ways in which modern historical dynamics are appropriated into this culture. But these dimensions must, I suggest, first be approached by noting one shared fundamental of pro-Nicene theologies. At the heart of attempting to appropriate and engage pro-Nicene theological culture lies the task of asking how Christians considering their most fundamental doctrines may see the task before them as one of contemplating the Scriptures even while they are persuaded by many modern historicist assumptions. But, for pro-Nicenes, interpretation of the scriptural text is a site for focusing the interrelationships between epistemology, anthropology, and the nature of human speech about God. It is thus the case that pro-Nicene understandings of the status of Scripture and of appropriate reading practices offer not so much a theology of Scripture as one theological activity, but a 'theology of theology' in all its aspects.[60] As I argued in Chapters 11–13, at the heart of shared pro-Nicene understanding is an account of the life of the mind resulting from an analysis of the need for human purification, an analysis of the nature of rational human existence in the Logos, and an account of how God's economy of salvation involves the incarnate Word restoring the creation. The methodological challenge of pro-Nicene

---

[60] In expressing these opinions in print over the past few years I have often received the reply that it is incoherent to argue for the application of modern historiography to the development of doctrine but to argue against it in the case of the biblical text. 'On the Practice and Teaching of Christian Doctrine'; and with Stephen E. Fowl, '(Mis)reading the Face of God: The Interpretation of the Bible in the Church', *Theological Studies*, 60 (1999), 513–28. This attack seems to rest on a misunderstanding. I have not argued that modern historical critical modes of investigation should not be used, but that they are not *necessary* for Christians reading their scripture as Scripture. The texts of non-scriptural writers in the Christian tradition do not hold scriptural status even if they are authoritative.

theology is also thus a firmly doctrinal challenge about the 'theology of theology' that we adopt.

When I argue that the core of theological practice, the exploration and articulation of Trinitarian and Christological doctrine, should be seen as a contemplation of Scripture I may be easily misunderstood. It might seem as if I am endorsing a modern Protestant project either of a Barthian character or one related to older traditions of Protestant orthodoxy. It might seem as if I am identifying the plain sense of Scripture as the source of revealed propositional knowledge, above and distinct from the Church's creeds, or identifying Scripture as an objective 'word' addressed to humanity from without.[61] Such an account might seek to overcome the culture and institutional structure of modern systematics by arguing that all theology must be grounded in the plain sense of the text (or more likely in the 'literal' sense understood as the one 'meaning' of the text). While I will obviously hold significant common ground with someone arguing such a position, there are also very significant differences. In fact, the best way to sketch an account of what I mean by speaking of this aspect of theology as a contemplation of Scripture is not via a formal dogmatic account of the interrelationship between Scripture and Tradition, but by describing how the plain sense of Scripture read grammatically and figurally can function as the core of the theologian's attention when thinking about basic Christian doctrines, offering a phenomenology of the theologian's patterns of attention. This account will obviously imply some more formal principles, but the question of how our doctrinal attentions and imaginations should take form is for the moment the more urgent task.

Theology and the contemplation of scripture

Most importantly, by saying that theology is fundamentally a contemplation of Scripture I mean that it should form the penultimate focus of the theologian's attention: ultimate attention must be reserved for the mystery of God revealed in Christ. In more Thomistic language we might say that the text of Scripture provides our point of access to the principles of a science identical with God's own self-knowledge.[62] As object of penultimate attention Scripture should serve as the fundamental resource for articulating and

---

[61] One of the clearest recent statements of a project combining strands of both is John Webster, *Holy Scripture: A Dogmatic Sketch* (Cambridge: Cambridge University Press, 2003). Richard A. Muller, *Post-Reformed Dogmatics*, vol. ii: *Holy Scripture*, offers an excellent summary of the evolution of accounts of Scripture in Protestant orthodoxy before the 19th cent.

[62] *Summa Theologiae*, Ia, q. 1, a. 6. I argue more extensively in these terms in my 'On the Practice and Teaching of Christian Doctrine', 38 ff. I have also been much influenced here by Eugene Rogers, *Thomas Aquinas and Karl Barth: Sacred Doctrine and Natural Knowledge of God* (Notre Dame and London: Notre Dame University Press, 1995).

exploring the Church's credal faith and provides the ultimate point of reference in the human task of shaping the imagination and intellect towards the vision of and life within the Triune God that constitutes the end of Christian life. Gregory Nazianzen's account of analogical practice in the *Theological Orations*, discussed in Chapter 12, can serve as an excellent example of what I envisage. The scriptural text both enables human knowledge of God through being understood to demand of us an analogical practice that constantly seeks to articulate and explore its resources, and it continually forces us to acknowledge the limits of that knowledge: the end result of that exploration is a recognition of the divine mystery. In Chapters 12 and 13 I alluded to Augustine's sense of the movement of the imagination and the affections as they are transformed in faith. In a forthcoming paper I argue that Augustine's use of *regula fidei* and some virtually synonymous phrases has two dimensions. On the one hand, it is used to indicate the basic narrative of Christian faith or the basic propositions of Christian faith. On the other hand, Augustine identifies the movement of the soul's attention intrinsic to Christian faith as itself the rule.[63] Learning to inhabit this movement and learning to use it as an index against which to read the plain sense remains, I suggest, intrinsic to the good reading of Scripture. Of course, making these remarks reminds us again that the reconstruction of theological practice I suggest involves reconstructing a theology of theology: it is as much doctrinal as 'methodological'.[64]

---

[63] 'Augustine on the Rule of Faith: Rhetoric, Christology, and the Foundation of Christian Thinking', *Augustinian Studies*, forthcoming.

[64] There is an interesting parallel between arguing for this account of a theology of theology and against one of the tendencies of modern social Trinitarianism. A number of modern theologians use a notion of the relationships between the three divine persons as a model for ideal societal and ecclesial structure. It will be clear from previous discussion that I see such arguments as finding little foundation in pro-Nicene thought and as frequently insufficiently attentive to the nature of theological analogy. At the same time, however, it is important to note that while pro-Nicenes do from time to time make direct comparisons between the character of the unity between the persons and the ideal character of relationships within the Church, such discussions are closely related to their accounts of the body of Christ as the locus of Christian formation. First, such discussions are almost always extrapolations from observations about particular scriptural discussions of the ways in which the Church is called to exhibit and participate in the relationship between Father and Son or in the love of the Spirit and are thus less likely to be reliant on abstract accounts of relationship projected onto the divine life. Second, the same attention to scriptural discussion of these topics locates any discussion of the relationship between our community and divine 'community' within ecclesiology. The manner in which we may imitate the divine love is learnt by slow progress within the body of Christ: by our beginning to share in that divine life as members of Christ's body. Thus the unity of the Church is not to be primarily found in direct comparisons between unity and diversity in God and between human beings, but by reflection on the unity and diversity appropriate in the body of Christ during the process of purification and sanctification, a unity and diversity at this point in the drama of salvation. We find here one way in which revising our account of appropriate theological method may effect changes in our approaches to discussing Trinitarian theology and its applications.

III. Understanding Pro-Nicene Theology

As object of attention in this context the text also demands of us the formation of a theological epistemology. My discussion in Chapters 8 and 13 of Basil and Gregory of Nyssa's adaptation of Origen's understanding of ἐπίνοια may be a model here: the plain sense of the text serves as the only true point of departure for us to speak of God's actions, and yet we do so best in awareness that the integration of our speculations and articulations remains beyond us.[65] Note also that throughout Chapters 11–13 I argued that an understanding of the character of human speech about God was sustained in pro-Nicenes through accounts of the place of Scripture in the ascent of Christian minds. It is, then, a central question whether pro-Nicene Trinitarianism can be sustained in theological cultures that do not sustain pro-Nicene accounts of dual-focus purification and the pro-Nicene aesthetics of faith sketched in Chapters 11–13.

I suggest that we might consequently understand appropriate attention to the text of Scripture as constituted by attention to two sets of relationships.[66] First, the Christian considering basic Christian doctrines should understand the plain sense of the text as appropriately organized and summarized by the Church's basic credal formulations such that in articulating and exploring the resources of basic Christian doctrines the plain sense can always be used as a linguistic resource for presenting those doctrines and exploration of the plain sense by grammatical and figural techniques can always lead to those doctrines.[67] The discussion of Augustine's

---

[65] As another example of how taking this principle seriously might affect a contemporary Trinitarian theology, I can point to the possibility of engaging with a new seriousness the great austerity with which pro-Nicenes describe the notion of a divine person. We need not understand this austerity as inevitably leading to and demanding a more complex account of Trinitarian persons. As we have seen, Pro-Nicene theologies focused on the need to shape a discourse about the divine that would both take Scripture as its point of departure and that would also locate interpretation within an account of human purification. This need was met in accounts which took scriptural accounts of God's action as guides for a process of thought which ended (in this life) in a growing and complex 'sight' of the paradox of the one and three. Understanding the austerity of our notion of divine person thus we may begin to see again the centrality of the doctrines of inseparable operations and appropriation. Christian understanding of the mysteriousness of God's action in the world may be shaped by growth in attention to the patterns of appropriation revealed in Scripture. We learn to worship and speak of this incomprehensible reality through learning how appropriating attributes to particular divine persons helps us grasp the mysteriousness of the triune communion: how, for instance, speaking of the Son as Wisdom and the Spirit as love draws us to recognize the exchange of love that is the being of the Triune God.

[66] Thus when I speak of 'attention to the plain sense' I mean a form of attention that intrinsically involves other forms of attention which function to structure appropriate reading of Scripture.

[67] These statements are in no way intended to deny the usefulness of historical critical investigations of the scriptural text or of the historical course that led to those fundamental dogmatic formulae. It is, however, to suggest the importance of understanding that the text of Scripture can be read in multiple ways. In the current context arguing for a conscious adoption of some pro-Nicene exegetical practices will also involve arguing for the possibility of

use of simplicity in Chapter 15 may stand as an excellent example of the practice to which I refer. Pro-Nicene accounts of the distinction between Creator and creation, of the nature of human speech about the divine, form both the context for interpreting credal formulae and are understood as the guide to exploration of the plain sense of the Scripture. It is here that we see the circular or spiral nature of this theological structure: the plain sense both functions as ultimate point of reference in the articulation of Trinitarian doctrine and that doctrine not only guides the doctrinal content found in Scripture, it also shapes an account of how Scripture leads the imagination into mystery and silence. I take up the question of the need for a concomitant historical examination of credal and other authoritative formulae as part of this spiral process below.

Second, the plain sense of Scripture should be understood to govern the appropriation of philosophical resources, but the appropriation of philosophical resources for exploring the plain sense should be understood as a vital task in articulating Trinitarian theology. The governing of philosophical appropriation by the plain sense can perhaps be understood best by reference to Bruce Marshall's insistence (following Donald Davidson) on a principle of charity in the attempt to 'take every thought captive'. Marshall's concern is to describe the process by which sentences from non-Christian discourses are seen to be consonant with or useful in explicating the plain sense of Scripture understood as normed by the Church's dogmatic commitments:

> Charity about truth shapes the interpretation of whatever discourse the Christian community encounters; the goal of interpretation is to find a way of understanding that discourse which allows it to be held true, that is, to find a place for it within the world . . . opened up by the Scriptural text. At the same time there is an important dissimilarity between the theological 'principle of charity' and that invoked by Davidson in the philosophy of language . . . the best interpretation of initially alien discourse will not necessarily be the one which maximizes the truth of that discourse by the community's own standards . . . The Christian interpretation of initially externalized discourse . . . may involve giving such discourse and worldviews in important respects a different sense than they originally had . . . Sometimes even the best available interpretation, applying the principle of

plurality in reading. I suspect that the possibility of good Christian theology partially rests on accepting that the plain text of Scripture may be read as consonant with Christian belief. This commitment need not prevent engagement with the work of the historical critical exegete: but it will demand of the theologian a constant engagement with the assumptions of that exegesis about the nature of texts and the function of Scripture. For some account of how such a discussion might proceed see Stephen E. Fowl, *Engaging Scripture*.

charity, may still require that a certain discourse or even whole worldview be rejected . . .'[68]

Negotiation between the plain sense and other material shapes a method by which the theologian seeks to integrate knowledge with Christian belief by an ongoing process of dogmatically normed experimentation: as I hope is becoming clear, however, such a process should also, I suggest, be governed by the character of the knowledge that one takes to be possible of God at this stage in the drama of redemption and by constant attention to the historical life and development of theology. My discussions of the adaptation of Stoic, Aristotelian, and Platonic resources by the Cappadocians in the search for terminologies to distinguish nature from personal property or the use of a variety of traditions by Gregory of Nyssa in explicating 'power' terminology all provide examples that illustrate the style of argument I recommend.

A credal theology

If we are to understand attention to the scriptural text in the manner I suggest then theologians will need to develop a new attention to the Church's creeds and articles of faith as guides for the reading of the plain sense. Over the course of the period we have studied, less formalized notions of inherited faith have begun to give way to the idea of creeds as precise markers of the limits of faith. Frequently, however, it is a pre-Nicene understanding of the *regula fidei* that has captured the interest of many seeking to appropriate early Christian exegesis. This concern, however, frequently seems to circumvent the growing awareness in the fourth and fifth centuries that shifts in the public life of the Church and the Trinitarian controversies themselves rendered necessary more precise doctrinal formulations: modern Christians wishing to remain classical Trinitarians avoid such formulae only by way of romanticism. Insofar as attention to such formulae presupposes ecclesiological principles—most importantly that the body of Christ in the Spirit is able to make such determinations[69]—developing attention to these formulae is going to

---

[68] Marshall, 'Absorbing the World', 75–7. This quotation should be read alongside the other given at the end of Ch. 1.

[69] By designating this as a necessary form of attention I am, of course, implying a formal account of the interrelationship between Scripture and tradition. Without discussing this *in extensor* I can at least own up to preferring an account of their interrelationship in the broad orbit of those developed by *ressourcement* theologians such as Congar and DeLubac. These accounts seem of importance (especially to anyone seeking to renew engagement with pro-Nicene theology) because, first, they articulate a view of Church and tradition as the context for reading of Scripture at the same time as articulating an account of the reading of Scripture as the ultimate (or penultimate) concern of the doctrinal theologian. Second, the same accounts offer an important revision of earlier post-Enlightenment accounts of the character

involve the intention to develop awareness of the range and interrelationship of such formulae over time (thus, for example, a theologian seeking to be faithful to Chalcedon on the basis of its place in the Church's teaching must also, by the same token, develop some familiarity with the further and central Christological determinations of Constantinople 553).[70] This is not to demand omnicompetence before statements are made, but it is to call for a certain structure to the patterns of attention developed by those who consider basic Christian doctrines. It also indicates one point at which my sketch of a modern theological culture that can sustain serious engagement with pro-Nicene thought must also move beyond the pro-Nicene.

At this point we can also see the general outlines of how the retrieval of the relationship between doctrine and the plain sense of Scripture may combine with a different adaptation of some modern historiographical emphases to suggest alternatives to the culture of modern systematics. Theologians should share a sense that good understanding of the foundational statements of Christian faith—credal and conciliar formulae, fundamental articulations of those documents—is consequent upon careful historical investigation of the circumstances of production and the history and adaptation of the language used within them. The application of this fundamental principle of modern historical consciousness will, I suggest, find particularly persuasive the emphasis of much recent historiography that much caution is necessary in the deployment of

---

of 'revelation' by identifying the person of Christ as the revelation from which Scripture and tradition stem. Yves M.-J. Congar, *Tradition and Traditions*, tr. Michael Naisby and Thomas Rainborough (San Diego: Basilica Press, 2002).

[70] Is the theological enterprise inherently Catholic? This is a difficult question to answer, dependent in part on how one defines 'Catholic'. Nevertheless, some observations may be offered. First, classical Protestant Trinitarian theology is necessarily parasitic for its concepts and possibilities on the concrete existence of the continuous Catholic tradition. The pretence of a simple engagement between now and 'the Fathers' almost always involves an implicit attempt to hide from the manner in which later Christological and Trinitarian development and definition guide what 'the Fathers' are taken to say (perhaps especially when those 'fathers' are taken to simply repeat what Scripture teaches rather than being understood as authoritative interpreters of a pluralistic text). At the same time, of course, Catholic theologies that neglect the development of doctrine beyond 451 face the same problems (and it is here ironical that some reformed theologians have much to teach those who think of themselves as 'Catholic'!). Faithful appropriation of Patristic trinitarianism thus involves openness to engagement with the whole of the continuous tradition, and can rarely be successful while characterizing one period or another as 'fallen'. Theologies which are unable to sustain the broad pre-modern Catholic tradition of reading Scripture will also find it difficult to sustain dense engagement with the doctrinal heritage they may uphold. The foundation for a Protestant theology would thus seem to lie precisely in a self-justification as a necessary and constant *protesting* theology within the common Catholic thought-world. This is, perhaps, one of the most useful of Stanley Hauerwas's points about the structure of theology: see, for instance, his 'Reformation is Sin', *Sanctify them in the Truth* (Edinburgh: T. & T. Clark, 1998), 241–4.

III. Understanding Pro-Nicene Theology

epochal characterizations and summary narratives. Similarly, against some of the fundamental assumptions of nineteenth-century historiography, those holding to these theoretical perspectives have become increasingly conscious that the isolation of 'context' is a complex task. One cannot simply isolate one context that will reveal the unitary meaning of a text and the very attribution of causality always involves the placing of an event or text into a problematic relationship with something subsequent to it.[71] These perspectives provide further resources for resisting the modes of narration common in modern systematics, and for developing new skills of attention to particular credal texts and authoritative theologians as a foundation for reading the plain sense of the Scripture.

Recovering a sense of the plain sense of Scripture as read in the history of the Church and through the lens of the Church's authoritative statements will also radically condition the tendency to view the history of the Church as the history of an inevitable progress demanding further translation into the present. On the one hand, this is so because if the plain sense of Scripture is the focus of our attention then readings of it are to be ranked and considered as part of a Christian conversation over time not simply as stages in a historical narrative of progression. On the other hand, if the historical investigation of texts and figures is understood as the ever deeper entering of a conversation about the plain sense then one will be pushed away from considering theological texts as the product of a particular philosophy towards questioning the ways in which particular philosophical resources promote persuasive or unpersuasive readings of particular scriptural texts. The same approach will reinforce the movement away from seeing modernity as providing a necessary reorientation of Christian doctrine. Thus, and perhaps

---

[71] These trends are excellently summarized in Elizabeth Clark's *History-Theory-Text* (Cambridge, Mass.: Harvard University Press, 2004). The complexity of the act of narration is excellently explored in Michel de Certeau, 'The Historiographical Operation', in *The Writing of History*, tr. Tom Conley (New York: Columbia University Press, 1988), 56–113. The problem of the attribution of causality is perhaps captured with particular verve by Walter Benjamin at the end of his 'Theses on the Philosophy of History', see *Illuminations: Essays and Reflections*, tr. Harry Zohn (New York: Schocken Books, 1968), 263: 'Historicism contents itself with establishing a causal connection between various moments in history. But in fact a cause is for that very reason historical. It became historical posthumously, as it were, through events that may be separated from it by thousands of years. A historian who takes this as his point of departure stops telling the sequence of events like the beads of a rosary. Instead, he grasps the constellation which his own era has formed with a definite earlier one. Thus he establishes a conception of the present as the "time of the now" which is shot through with chips of Messianic time.' On the one hand, Benjamin's own understanding of the peculiar character of modernity and the manner in which quotation of the past may offer a disruptive window onto the pre-modern offers much for those trying to envisage the possibility of a move beyond some of modernity's theological methods. On the other hand, Benjamin, in perhaps overly dramatic fashion, nicely illustrates the reconstruction from the future that accompanies any exercise in the attribution of causality.

paradoxically to many readers, there is possible a fruitful alliance between the adaptation of recent historiography by theologians and a recovery of theology as a contemplation of the plain sense of Scripture.[72]

None of this is to suggest that theologians must lose the speculative, integrative moment of considering doctrine, or that the historical investigation of individual texts and loci is not also part of the gradual imagining of the course of Christian thought. It does mean, however, first, that this moment occurs as *part of* the historical investigation of the fundamentals of Christian faith and that even suggestion about the contemporary formulation and articulation of doctrine is inseparable from that historical investigation. The idea that the conceptual moment occurs after understanding the course of history so far and as an exercise of (at least limited) conceptual freedom from it—an idea embedded within our professional theological structures—may be left behind in favour of better understanding of the past and better contemporary engagement.[73] We do not need the modern culture of 'systematic' theology in order to articulate the interrelationship between doctrines and to face the challenges of late modernity. Second, it means that the unity of theology may be understood as lying in the unity of God's mysterious action: the investigation of doctrinal loci does not need to find a unity in a particular modern philosophical schema: it needs to hazard connections between the articles of faith understood as nodes of the divine mysterious action. In this manner Scheeben's attempt to

---

[72] Historical and philosophical exploration of the meaning of the plain sense in an ecclesially normed context thus involves a wide range of styles of investigation, and I intentionally attempt no suggestions about possible genres of theological writing. It may, however, be helpful to add that—just as in pro-Nicene literature—the modes of investigation I have outlined may be understood as forms of attention to Scripture even when they are not materially constructed as running commentaries on the plain sense. I suggest, however, that one way in which connection with the text of Scripture in a Trinitarian discussion may be flexibly maintained is through constant attention to the movement of faith into the mystery of God (in part through the theological epistemology assumed and deployed). The cultivation of awareness of and participation in this movement—the movement that is taken to be at the heart of Scripture's transformative function in the economy of salvation—will intrinsically involve a sense of the ways in which the plain sense serves to shape our attention to the mysteriousness of God and thus the move 'away' from the plain sense in the sense of writing in genres that are not running commentary may be understood as a part of a spiral in which one is constantly drawn back to that sense and the sense of the mystery of God's action.

[73] It is helpful here to notice the links between the Catholic Tübingen school, Schleiermacher, and contemporary notions of 'creative authorship' drawn by John Thiel in his *Imagination and Authority: Theological Authorship in the Modern Tradition* (Minneapolis: Fortress Press, 1991). Thiel's account nicely shows how modern notions of creativity in theological authorship have their origins in Idealist and Romantic conceptions of relationship with tradition. He rightly indicates that there are aspects of authorial self-conception that are real theoretical gains in this tradition: but his account of the balance that he hopes may be achieved in modern Catholic thought still assume that the problem must be conceived in terms of a Romantic stepping out beyond the bounds of tradition.

argue for such a perspective within the nineteenth-century context still has much to teach.[74]

The sketch I have offered here suggests a context for doing Trinitarian theology that both undermines some of the central ways in which modern systematics makes use of narratives of the pre-modern and assumes as necessary modern philosophical reconstruction. As well as undermining these aspects of modern Trinitarianism this sketch suggests how authoritative argument might be developed and deployed in a manner that would enable Trinitarian theology to be both more historically attentive to the foundations of Trinitarian faith and still attentive to philosophical and cultural questions that face new generations of Christians. It is important to note that I am not simply arguing that the Hegelian/Idealist and 'social' thrusts of much modern Trinitarianism are simply wrong because they do not accord with the structures of pro-Nicene thought. While Chapters 11–13 do indeed suggest that some of these dynamics are extremely hard to reconcile with the legacy of Nicaea, my more fundamental challenge is that modern Trinitarians do not offer arguments for these dynamics that are or should be convincing. By and large they lack a theological culture in sufficient continuity with Nicene thought to show how these modern trends might be read alongside careful attention to foundational credal formulae and alongside the text of Scripture. The evolution of new modes of theological practice may well enable theologians to argue for some of the main thrusts of modern Trinitarian thought or it may push Trinitarian theology in directions that take us beyond modernity's preoccupations. The jury must as yet remain out until they have a clearer sense of how to argue!

In offering this sketch I do not think that I am offering a vision of theological practice as clearly defined as that of many 'systematic' methodologies. We can, I think, set out some of the key themes essential to good doctrinal practice and we can identify some strategies that one might follow, but this is far from offering a clearly spelled out vision. While the 'treasures of darkness' (Isaiah 45: 3) are still bestowed upon us in the form of the length and breadth and height and depth of the mystery of Christ revealing the Father in the Spirit, we are more in the dark about how we should speak and share those mysteries than many of our pro-Nicene forebears. I

---

[74] Matthias Scheeben, *The Mysteries of Christianity*, tr. Cyril Vollert (St Louis and London: Herder 1946), 733–61. His account follows development of the idea that (737–8): 'The supernatural truths ... are grouped directly not around the created nature, but around the divine nature.' There is little scholarship on Scheeben's work. E. Paul, *Denkweg und Denkform der Theologie von Matthias Joseph Scheeben* (Munich: E. Hueber, 1970) provides references to the earlier literature and a good introduction to his thought.

assume, however, that attempting to embody the forms of attention I have suggested would at least take us a little way forward.

V: ON THE DEVELOPMENT OF DOCTRINE

Throughout this chapter questions of authority have been central. But, as I indicated at the outset, a number of questions of authority are involved. I have focused on the question of how theologians should invoke credal formulae and authoritative texts from the Christian tradition in the construction of persuasive arguments. As the argument progressed it will have probably become clearer that I operate with a strong sense of the fundamental and enduring value not only of creed but also of those theologians taken to offer paradigmatic articulations of those creeds and who reveal the theological cultures understood to be central to understanding those creeds. Such a position raises questions about the relationship between accepting such texts as authoritative and asserting the centrality of careful historical consideration of sources and development.[75] At a number of moments during the rise of the modern study of early Christian theology this relationship has been the source of much tension: especially when accounts of the developments of Christian belief have seemed either to relativize credal statement or to reveal the process of development as one in which political force or worldly bishop seems to have had too strong a hand. Even though my own argument is strongly revisionist in its advocacy of the gradual development of pro-Nicene theology and even though I have not attempted to present this development as one that occurred apart from political and ecclesio-political forces, there is possible a fruitful understanding of the relationship between credal authority and historical scholarship.

The relationship between Nicene doctrine and that of the pre-Nicene Church has long been an important site for the exploration of these questions. Where Arius has increasingly been seen as a representative of a wider tradition that seems to have been part of the mainstream of Christian thought—and probably within the bounds of what might be considered the boundaries of pre-Nicene orthodoxy—the situation is even more complex. Here the question is not one only of the relationship between a pre-Nicene implicit belief and a post-Nicene explicit version, but also one of the emergence of pro-Nicene theology from a more pluralistic and diverse context.

[75] In articulating my position here I have learnt much from Rowan Williams, 'Doctrinal Criticism: Some Questions', in Sarah Coakley and David Pailin (eds.), *The Making and Remaking of Christian Doctrine* (Oxford: Clarendon Press, 1993), 239–64.

III. Understanding Pro-Nicene Theology

Over the last two hundred years these questions have been faced through a variety of theories of doctrinal development. The emergence of these theories is in many ways another part of the story of modern theology's appropriation of Hegelianism and Romanticism. This can be seen most clearly in the ways that such theories have tended to use 'vitalist' metaphors likening the development of doctrine to the growth of an organism. It is frequently noticed, of course, that the theories of development seen in the nineteenth-century Tübingen school and in such figures as John Henry Newman are attempts to hold together the reality of growing attention to historical development with the need to show the continuity of Christian teaching in a Catholic context. Those theories that were not broadly vitalist in this way (especially Thomist models from the first half of the twentieth century) have tended to work on a rationalist model in which the earliest deposit of Christian faith was seen as the foundation for the developed faith of later centuries, broader propositional content being slowly deduced from logical principles. In liberal Protestant contexts development could of course much more easily be seen as a basic story of departure from an original kernel or the carrying of that kernel through history with various accretions.

Nicholas Lash, in his survey of theories of doctrinal development, importantly notes that during the second half of the twentieth century grand theories of continuous evolution or development tended to give way as theorists became increasingly attentive to the cultural shifts marking different periods of Christian history. In such contexts theories of continuity seemed to assume an unsustainable cultural homogeneity down the centuries. In this light historians of theology have focused on tracing small-scale shifts rather than attempting to offer theories of overall development and magisterial narratives.[76] The constant dangers here are that the assumption of cultural incompatibility forestalls clear investigation of continuity and that without ongoing thought of the question of doctrinal development Christians, necessarily bound to asserting fundamental continuity in their faith, rely on older models in an unexamined manner. We must, then, continue to consider how we conceptualize doctrinal development.

Henri de Lubac's long 1948 article 'The Problem of the Development of Dogma' offers what remains one of the most insightful commentaries on the debate over theories of doctrinal

---

[76] Nicholas Lash, *Change in Focus: A Study in Doctrinal Change and Continuity* (London: Sheed & Ward, 1973).

development.⁷⁷ De Lubac here is arguing against Catholic accounts of development that focused on ensuring continuity in propositional content. For de Lubac such accounts miss a basic theological truth: 'revelation' is the action of God in Christ: all subsequent reflection on that action is already abstraction from what is necessarily in essence mystery. Such abstraction may well be necessary, and the Spirit-led development of that abstraction also essential, but we can only consider the idea of development in the light of awareness of the mystery at its core. When we speak, as we must, of the explicit being present in the implicit here we cannot describe the relationship solely in terms of seed and developed organism or in terms of the unexplored consequences of propositions: much will always remain mysterious about how the explicit is present.

De Lubac does not see himself offering a theory of development, only some suggestions about what must be taken as fundamental in these discussions. I would like to add to those suggestions. One of the rarely noticed features of virtually all modern theories of doctrinal development is that they assume success in such a theory involves providing a way in which the paths of continuity in doctrine can be traced and understood by the human observer. Only by such a revealing of continuity in change does such a theory provide a way of opening theology to historical development while preserving Christians' certainty in their beliefs. This assumption is, however, not only theoretically problematic for anyone who has read a little about the structure and problems of narrative, it is also theologically problematic. For Christians working with a theology of the Triune God's maintenance and guidance of the Church surely we should no more expect to be able to trace the paths of that continuity with certainty than we expect to be able to locate the history of grace in the Church with certainty. I do not mean that we cannot conceive of the Church being able to judge the appropriate structure of a faith resulting from development, but that there are good theological reasons (let alone historical ones) for supposing that we will not always find it possible to follow the steps by means of which the Spirit guided the expression of the Apostles' faith until it emerged into pro-Nicene theology.

Christian theologians, I suggest, find themselves negotiating a narrow path. On the one hand, they must attempt to narrate the continuity of their core beliefs with those of the apostles. They should do so because of scriptural texts that speak of Christ's guarantee that the Church will be maintained in truth through the

---

⁷⁷ Henri de Lubac, 'The Problem of the Development of Dogma', *Theology in History*, tr. Anne Englund Nash (San Francisco: Ignatius, 1996), 248–80.

presence of the Spirit and because the Church is the body of Christ, being led in the Spirit to share in the relationship of God, Word, and Spirit. Christians are thus called as part of their membership of the body of Christ to narrate a story of the Spirit's presence in the body and a story of the head of the body leading the limbs towards the Father. But, on the other hand, the path by which the Spirit leads occurs under the ultimate agency of the Spirit (bearing in mind, of course, the principle of inseparable operation!): the narratives that we attempt will always ultimately fail this side of the *eschaton*. Thus the Christian historian may go astray both by thinking that no such continuity is possible and by thinking that she or he has it within their power to prove that continuity: there is a complex negotiation here that cannot easily be summarized. It is, I suggest, this paradox that makes the Christian historian possible and gives texture to her enterprise: attention to the complexity of history especially in light of modern historicism is not incompatible with belief in the Spirit's shaping of that history. Of course, the Christian historian is likely to be suspicious of blanket claims to a lack of continuity in Christian teaching, but she also need not think that it is within her power to demonstrate that continuity to her opponents—her work need not be a desperate attempt to demonstrate a continuity that must ultimately be beyond the human grasp.

At the end of his elegant *Archetypal Heresy: Arianism through the Centuries*, Maurice Wiles questions whether the monographs of Rowan Williams and Richard Hanson give sufficient reason for their claim that the victory of the pro-Nicenes was the victory of truth: 'the satisfactory nature of the outcome of the debate is affirmed rather than argued . . .'.[78] Wiles's question is one that he has asked throughout his scholarly career with his characteristic clarity and openness. How would I sketch the elements of an answer? In the first place I suspect that one would have to argue that pro-Nicene theology offers a more coherent reading of the plain sense of Scripture. But, of course, this answer, at whatever length it was developed, would be unlikely to persuade Professor Wiles unless it also converted him to the understanding of Scripture's function implied in the answer. The realization that this is so is instructive insofar as it reveals that questions about the persuasiveness of pro-Nicene theology are also questions about the nature of theology itself.

But, at the same time, any answer to Wiles's question would have to be one about the status of the Church and its teaching authority. I do not mean that it would be a useful answer to say that pro-Nicenes

---

[78] Wiles, *Archetypal Heresy*, 180.

are right because the Church says they are! Rather, the Church's maintenance of this faith down the centuries, in spite of Hegel, fire, and sword, may itself be something of an answer to those who already believe that the work of God in Christ culminates in drawing people into the body of Christ and guiding that body in the Spirit towards the vision of God. Thus, the ability to answer Professor Wiles's question depends on wider faith commitments, not on offering evidence fitting some objective historiographical criteria.

My point in this conclusion is that belief in an authoritative credal faith does not need to have the effect of silencing the historian, rendering impossible the adaptation of some aspects of modern historical consciousness: it may perform precisely the opposite function.[79] Christian historians go astray when they feel that the possibility of Christian faith depends on their own ability to demonstrate the continuity of doctrine. In the knowledge that we are unlikely to demonstrate the continuity of doctrine's development, but in the faith that we must try, the Church's authority and the historian's craft may coexist for the good of the Church. Thus, for many of his contemporaries even Newman's heavily qualified emphasis on the development of doctrine and on the emergence of classical Christian doctrine of God seemed dangerous. His focus seemed to lead all too easily to a justification of claims for the Church's magisterium: if doctrine develops thus, perhaps only the Church's possession of an inspired teaching office can guide the truly historically attentive Christian. To modern ears this seems a strange paradox to be sure: but perhaps his contemporaries had seen the heart of the matter.

---

[79] At the end of this chapter, as at the beginning, it is important to bear in mind that my concern is only with the fundamentals of Trinitarian and Christological doctrine. How the Church's teaching office might proceed in a manner which respects the hierarchy of truths and which respects the character of Christian charity are questions beyond my scope here; for an example of the questions involved see Nicholas Lash's elegant 'On not Inventing Doctrine', *Tablet* (2 Dec. 1995), 1544.

Epilogue:
On Teaching the Fourth Century

In this epilogue I offer brief answers to two questions that arise in the context of teaching the fourth century. First, what are the most fundamental narrative pointers one can use to introduce the course of these controversies—how might one summarize the narrative I have offered? Second, what texts should one treat as exemplary and fundamental for understanding the century?

A SUMMARY

My hope is that the following summary can serve as the model for the construction of others along similar lines, and that drawing attention to the decisions one must make in constructing such a summary will itself help teachers and scholars think through how they present these controversies:

1. Probably in the year 318 a controversy erupted in Alexandria between a priest, Arius, and his bishop Alexander. This controversy concerned the relationship between God the Father and the Son or Word. Alexander taught that the Son, although 'between created and uncreated', was always with the Father, and eternally generated from the Father. Arius objected, emphasizing that there was only one God, the Father, and the Son existed by the will of the Father from 'before the ages' but not eternally and without sharing the Father's being. Thus this initial controversy concerned questions both of the status of the Word or Son of God and about the very nature of God.

2. After some initial meetings in Alexandria and elsewhere, in AD 325 a council of bishops (mostly from the eastern half of the Roman empire) met at the behest of the emperor Constantine at the city of Nicaea to deal with a number of controversial issues including this dispute. The council issued a creed which said that the Son was generated 'from the essence of the Father' and was hence 'homoousios' (the same thing or being or essence) with the Father. The creed also condemned anyone who said that the Son was from an *ousia* or *hypostasis* other than that of the Father. Arius was condemned and exiled.

Epilogue: On Teaching the Fourth Century

3. This dispute reflected and, in turn, stimulated tension between different theological trajectories present at the time it erupted. Many of the eastern trajectories owed much to the development of different trends found in Origen's thought. Some of these trends emphasized the closeness between Father and Son and the Son's sharing of the Father's being by the deployment of unitarian language and with often strongly material analogies (e.g. the Son as light from light). Other trajectories focused on the distinctions between Father and Son and emphasized the special status of the Father as alone 'true God'. All of these trajectories shared a basic understanding of the way theology focused around attention to the text of Scripture. The decision at Nicaea did not solve the tension between these traditions and its terminology seems to have been chosen, at least in part, as an ad hoc tool to censure Arius. This can in part be seen from the fact that Arius was eventually readmitted to communion on the basis of a statement that did not include the technical terms of Nicaea. However, to many the creed seemed strongly to favour the unitarian tendency among these existing trajectories.

4. Arius himself is of little significance in the years that follow. Indeed, during the years 326–50 the term *homoousios* is rarely if ever mentioned. While the council appears to have been well known because of its size and association with Constantine, its creed was not seen as the authoritative statement of faith by anyone whose writing survives (no precisely worded creed occupied such a position). A great deal of controversy was caused in the years after the council by some supporters of Nicaea whose theology had strongly unitarian tendencies. Chief among these was Marcellus of Ancyra, who had been an important figure at the council and may have significantly influenced its wording. Marcellus and his followers were condemned by a number of meetings during these years and the absence of Nicaea and its terminology from debate is probably due to the modalist trajectory into which it seemed so easily to fit.

5. During his exile Marcellus went to Rome and there met Athanasius (AD 339–40), who had been exiled from Alexandria for maladministration. Partly in conjunction with Marcellus, Athanasius developed an account of his opponents as being part of a conspiracy on the part of supporters of the now dead Arius. One key technique in his polemic was to offer an account of Arius' theology and then present later credal decisions and the writings of his enemies as those of 'Arians'. This rhetorical construction of 'Arianism' seems to have begun before Athanasius' exile, but it is only in his *First Oration* that we see a fully developed version. This terminology was accepted by many western theologians, and increasingly by some

easterners in later decades. The years between 325 and 350 are thus highly complex because although we do see a clash of theological traditions throughout this period, many of the participants see themselves involved in a dispute as much about ecclesiastical discipline as anything else. Many westerners, for instance, seem to have read strong eastern antipathy to Athanasius as being primarily theological, when in fact it may have been equally due to dislike of his personality and ecclesio-political actions in Egypt.

6. Once we begin to grasp the problems with Athanasius' rhetorical unmasking of 'Arians' then we need to look beyond the Athanasian terminology of an 'Arian' conspiracy to get a more accurate sense of how to understand non-Marcellan and non-Athanasian eastern theologies during this period. It is perhaps possible to speak of a broad insistence on the part of many eastern theologians during these years that there is a basic distinction between Father and Son that must be protected in theological formulation. However, at the same time, we consistently see an insistence that there is an ineffable closeness between Father and Son such that the Son's being can be said to be from the Father in some indescribable sense, and that the Son is (to use one prominent phrase cf. Wisd. 7: 25; Heb. 1: 3) 'the exact image of the Father's substance'. Many of those who, for instance, were able to sign up to the 'Dedication' creed of 341 at Antioch were happy with such language but probably found both Arius' language and the Athanasian/Marcellan theology unacceptable. Nicaea appears to have seemed dangerously modalist to many of them.

7. The controversy shifted considerably during the 350s, in part because of the stance of the emperor Constantius. Constantius (a son of Constantine who came to control the whole empire over the 350–3 period) broadly supported the position of those who moved towards a theology which was strongly anti-Marcellan and very suspicious of any theologies which did not distinguish clearly and hierarchically between Father and Son. By the last few years of the decade (especially after the Sirmium 'manifesto' of 357 and the councils of 359–60) the leaders of this group advocated a theology we can term as 'Homoian'. Homoians argued that the Son is 'like' (*homoios*) the Father although distinct and ontologically inferior. They increasingly claimed to reject any explanation of the Father/Son relationship that used any form of 'essence' terminology. This attempt to ban essence terminology was not an irenic move, but one which tried to rule out some readings of some traditional terminologies (such as describing the Son as 'light from light') in favour of a more strongly subordinationist picture.

8. The most subordinationist wing of this theological movement

is represented by Aetius and his disciple Eunomius. They both insisted that Father and Son were unlike if one wanted to talk about 'essence': although there are other ways in which it is appropriate to speak of likeness between them. Their teaching was unacceptable to many within the broad eastern tradition mentioned under 6 above. Their teaching seems also to have affected perception of the Homoian movement generally and produced a strong reaction. During the 370s and 380s Eunomians increasingly became a distinct ecclesial group with their own bishops and churches.

9. One group who strongly opposed the Homoian radicals and the whole Homoian project of trying to prevent the use of 'essence' language, focused around Basil of Ancyra. His theological approach claimed the Dedication creed as its own ancestor and described the Son as 'like the Father according to essence'. These people rapidly became known as Homoiousians. Although the number of bishops we can clearly identify with this group is small, there are occasions on which many seemed to have been sympathetic to their approach, perhaps because they seemed attentive to some of the themes of what I have referred to as the broad eastern tradition. Indeed, we have to be careful throughout this period of speaking about 'ecclesiastical parties' without always bearing in mind that these groups were very fluid, unstructured, and may have got ad hoc support from those whose thought cannot easily be tied clearly to one or other trajectory.

10. In 359–60 Constantius called two councils, which met and sent delegations to him. Under pressure from Constantius these meetings promulgated a creed which was Homoian. Constantius intended this creed to function as a universal point of reference and a universal confession of faith. Many opponents of the creed (including prominent Homoiousians such as Basil of Ancyra himself) were exiled at this point.

11. In the wake of this seeming Homoian triumph, the 360s were actually a period in which a variety of different groups began to coalesce around the Nicene creed as the only alternative that would unite those opposed to the Homoian creed. Athanasius and his supporters were able to recognize as orthodox the theologies of some who had previously supported a broadly Homoiousian position and others from the broad eastern traditions that had previous opposed him. One key tactic followed in this rapprochement and promoted by Athanasius was to ask for confession of Nicaea as a sign of orthodoxy but to refrain from inquiring further (Basil of Caesarea is one who eventually followed Athanasius' policy here directly). At the same time many western theologians also followed Athanasius' lead. Athanasius and the others who were prepared to coalesce around

Nicaea also had to be clear about the principles within which it could be understood, admitting that none of them wished to divide God's immaterial being or treat the persons as other than truly distinct from each other. During these two decades we also see the beginnings of an evolution of terminologies that will distinguish what in God is one from what is three: a statement that God is one in nature, power, glory, or essence is combined with a statement that there are three persons, hypostases, or 'things'. This balance of statements is understood as the context for interpreting Nicaea's terminology, and marks the full emergence of 'pro-Nicene' theology. This last development also occurs through polemic against some groups who doubted the full divinity of the Spirit.

12. In 381 this process of rapprochement resulted, through the help of the pro-Nicene emperor Theodosius, in the Council of Constantinople. This council (although our knowledge of it is amazingly patchy) promulgated a revised version of Nicaea's creed, which removed the phrase 'from the Father's essence'; added, in anti-Marcellan vein, 'and his kingdom shall have no end'; and added clauses on the Spirit to insist (though without directly asserting that the Spirit was God) that 'with the Father and the Son He is worshipped and glorified'. Theodosius also promulgated a decree in the eastern half of the empire, *Episcopis tradi*, that defined Christian orthodoxy by reference to the basic logic of Trinitarian belief (neither dividing the essence nor confusing the persons) and by pointing to a list of those with whom one should be in communion.

13. The theologies which came during the 360–80 period to recognize each other as orthodox and to interpret Nicaea within the context of confessing God to be mysteriously one and three we can refer to as 'pro-Nicene'. These theologies were not identical, but shared a common commitment to the beliefs that God was one power, nature, and activity; that there could be no degrees in divinity; that the divine persons were irreducible although all sharers in the divine being without any ontological hierarchy; that human beings would always fail to comprehend God and that one could only make progress towards knowledge and love of God through entering a discipline and practice that would reshape the imagination. The theologies of Basil of Caesarea, Gregory of Nyssa, and Gregory Nazianzen are three key examples of pro-Nicene theologies, as are the western theologies of figures such as Eusebius of Vercelli, Ambrose, and Augustine of Hippo, and the theologies of the later Athanasius, Didymus the Blind, and Cyril of Alexandria. Theologies such as those of Athanasius and Hilary of Poitiers show many of the features of these later theologies but not all.

14. These theologies, distinct but with shared themes and

Epilogue: On Teaching the Fourth Century

principles, take forward and produce some convergence among a number of the different theological trajectories that run through the century. On the one hand, they incorporate developed versions of the broad eastern tradition that we find represented in some aspects of the Dedication creed and which so strongly opposed Marcellus. On the other hand, these theologies also incorporate trajectories such as Athanasius' own strongly unitarian account and much of the pro-Nicene western thought. By focusing on the shared logic of belief running between these trajectories, the emergence of pro-Nicene orthodoxy also functioned as a continual persuasion to each trajectory to seek convergence with the others. Various groups of non-Nicene Christians continued to be a real force within the Christian world through the next century, but increasingly they became distinct ecclesial groups with their own episcopal hierarchies and organizational structures.

IDENTIFYING PARADIGMATIC TEXTS

The other important choice we make as teachers of these controversies is in selecting original texts for students to consider. I suggest it is particularly important here that we do make such a selection: the best prophylactic against older narratives and against simplistic reductions in many brief textbook surveys is close reading of small sections of text. I offer this as a list of paradigmatic texts to be used in illustrating the structure and varieties of pro-Nicene theology:

1. Gregory of Nyssa, *Catechetical Orations*
2. Gregory of Nyssa, *Refutation of Eunomius' Confession*
3. Gregory Nazianzen, *Theological Orations*
4. Augustine, *Sermons 52, 117*
5. Augustine, *On the Trinity*, books 4 and 15.
6. Rufinus, *Commentary on the Apostles' Creed*.

Bibliography

ANCIENT AUTHORS

For each author I have provided reference to the original text used, and to available translations into English, where possible.

Alexander of Alexandria

Ep. Alex.   *Letter to Alexander of Byzantium* (*he philarchos*). Opitz, *Werke*, III/1 (U. 14); tr. Rusch, *Trinitarian Controversy*.

Ep. om.   *Letter to all Bishops* (*henos somatos*). Opitz, *Werke*, III/1 (U. 4b); tr. Rusch, *Trinitarian Controversy*.

Ambrose

De fide   *On the Faith*. CSEL 78; NPNF II. 10.
Myst.   *On the Mysteries*. CSEL 73; NPNF II. 10.
Spir.   *On the Holy Spirit*. CSEL 79; NPNF II. 10.

Arian Scholia

Gryson, *Scolies Ariennes sur le Concile d'Aquilée*, SC 267.

Athanasius

Ad Afros   *Letter to the African Bishops*. PG 26; NPNF II. 4.
Apol.   *Apology for his Flight*. Opitz, *Werke*, II/2–3; NPNF II. 4.
Apol. sec.   *Apology against the Arians* (*Apologia Secunda*). Opitz, *Werke*, II/1; NPNF II. 4.
C. Ar.   *Orations against the Arians*. Metzler/Savvidis, *Werke* I/1; NPNF II. 4.
C. Gen.   *Against the Nations*. Ed. and tr. Robert W. Thompson, Contra Gentes *and* De Incarnatione (Oxford: Clarendon Press, 1971).
Const.   *Apology to Constantius*. PG 25; NPNF II. 4.
Decr.   *On the Decrees of Nicaea*. Opitz, *Werke* II/1; NPNF II. 4.
Ep. cath.   *Catholic Letter*. Martin Tetz, 'Ein enzyklisches Schreiben der Synode von Alexandrien (362)', *ZNTW* 79 (1988), 262–81.
Incarn.   *On the Incarnation*. Ed. and tr. Robert W. Thompson Contra Gentes *and* De Incarnatione (Oxford: Clarendon Press, 1971).
Sent.   *On the Opinion of Dionysius*. Opitz, *Werke* II/1; NPNF II. 4.
Serap.   *Letters to Serapion Concerning the Holy Spirit*. PG 26.

Ancient Authors 437

	529–676; C. R. B. Shapland, *The Letters of Saint Athanasius Regarding the Holy Spirit* (London: Epworth Press, 1951).
Synod.	*On the Councils of Ariminum and Seleucia.* Opitz, *Werke* II/1; NPNF II. 4.
Tom.	*Letter to the People of Antioch.* PG 26. 795–810; NPNF II. 4.

(Letters from Arius, Constantine, Eusebius of Nicomedia, Eusebius of Caesarea, and Paulinus of Tyre are quoted from Opitz, *Werke*, III/2.)

Augustine of Hippo

Acad.	*Against the Academics.* CCSL 29; ACW 12.
Beata v.	*On the Blessed Life.* CCSL 29; FoC 1.
Civ.	*City of God.* CCSL 47–8. Tr. and ed. R. W. Dyson, *The City of God against the Pagans*, Cambridge Texts in the History of Political Thought (Cambridge: Cambridge University Press, 1998).
Conf.	*Confessions.* CCSL 27; tr. Henry Chadwick, *Saint Augustine: Confessions* (Oxford: Oxford University Press, 1991).
Doc.	*On Christian Teaching.* CSEL 80; *Augustine: On Christian Teaching*, tr. R. P. H. Green (Oxford: Clarendon Press, 1995).
Ep.	*Letters.* I have referred only to *ep.* 11, 14, 119, 120. For these see CSEL 34/1–2. FoC 12, 18. For details of other letters see the table by Robert Eno in Fitzgerald, *Augustine Encyclopedia*, 299–305.
Ep. Io. tr.	*Tractates on the First Letter of John.* SC 75. FoC 92.
F. et symb.	*On the Faith and the Creed.* CSEL 41; FoC 27.
Gn. litt.	*On the Literal Interpretation of Genesis.* CSEL 28; ACW 41, 4
Io. ev. tr.	*Tractates on the Gospel of John.* CCSL 36; FoC 78, 79, 88, 90, 92
Mor.	*On the Catholic and Manichaean Ways of Life.* CSEL 90; FoC 56
Ord.	*On Order.* CCSL 29; FoC 1.
Quant.	*On the Greatness of the Soul.* CSEL 89. ACW 9.
Serm.	*Sermons.* I have referred only to *serm.* 52, 117 (and *RB* 74 (1964), 15–35 for *serm.* 52). For these see PL 38; WSA. For details of other sermons see the table by Eric Rebillard, Fitzgerald, *Augustine Encyclopedia*, 774–89.
Sol.	*Soliloquies.* CSEL 89; FoC 2.
Trin.	*On the Trinity.* CCSL 50/50A; FoC 45.

Basil of Caesarea

Ep.	*Letters.* Ed. Yves Courtonne, *Saint Basile, Lettres*, 3 vols., Collection Guillaume Budé (Paris: Les Belles Lettres, 1957, 1961, 1966); tr. Roy J. Defferrari, *Saint Basil. The Letters*, 4 vols., Loeb Classical Library (Cambridge, Mass.: Harvard University Press, 1950–3).

Eunom.	Against Eunomius. SC 299 & 305.
Hex.	On the Hexameron. SC 26; FoC 46.
Spir.	On the Holy Spirit. SC 17; tr. Blonfield Jackson, rev. David Anderson. St. Basil the Great On the Holy Spirit (Crestwood, NY: St Vladimir's Seminary Press, 1980).

Cyril of Jerusalem

Cat. lect.	Catechetical Lectures. PG 33; LCC 4.

Damasus of Rome

Ep.	Letters. PL 13.

Didymus the Blind

Spir.	On the Holy Spirit. SC 386.

Ephrem the Syrian

HdF	Hymns de Fide. CSCO 154/155 (with German trans.).
HdVirg	Hymns on Virginity. CSCO 223/224 (with German trans.); Kathleen McVey; Ephrem the Syrian Hymns (Mahwah, NJ: Paulist Press, 1989).
HNis	Nisibene Hymns. CSCO 92/93, 102/103 (with German trans.); NPNF 000.
SdF	Sermones de Fide. CSCO 212/213 (with German trans.).

Epiphanius of Salamis

Anc.	Ancoratus. GCS 25.
Panarion	Panarion (Medicine Chest). GCS 25, 31, 37; tr. Frank Williams, The Panarion of Epiphanius of Salamis, 2 vols. (Leiden: Brill, 1987).

Eunomius of Cyzicus

Apol.	Apology. Ed. and tr. Richard P. Vaggione, Eunomius: The Extant Works (Oxford: Oxford University Press, 1987).

Eusebius of Caesarea

Dem. evang.	Demonstration of the Gospel. GCS 6; tr. W. J. Ferrar, The Proof of the Gospel. Being the Demonstratio Evangelica of Eusebius of Caesarea, 2 vols. (London: SPCK, 1920).
Eccl. theol.	Ecclesiastical Theology. GCS 14.
Marcell.	Against Marcellus. GCS 4.
Prep.	Preparation for the Gospel. PG 21; tr. E. H. Gifford, Eusebii Pamphili Evangelicae Praeparationes, libri XV, 4 vols. (Oxford, 1903).
Vit. Const.	Life of Constantine. GCS 1/1; Averil Cameron and Stuart G. Hall (tr. and introd.), Eusebius: Life of Constantine (Oxford: Clarendon Press, 1999).

Eustathius of Antioch

De engastrimytho CCSG 51.

Gregory Nazianzen

Arc.	*Poemata Arcana.* C. Moreschini and D. A. Sykes, St. Gregory of Nazianzus, *Poemata Arcana* (Oxford: Clarendon Press, 1997).
Or.	*Orations.* SC 247, 309, 406, 270, 284, 250 (*The Theological Orations*), 318, 358, 384. Some of the Orations are translated in NPNF II. 7. See also Frederick W. Norris (introd. and comm.), Lionel Wickham and Frederick Williams (tr.), *Faith Gives Fullness to Reasoning: The Five Theological Orations of Gregory Nazianzen* (Leiden: Brill, 1991).

Gregory of Nyssa

Ablab.	*On Not Three Gods To Ablabius.* GNO 3/1; NPNF II. 5.
Anim.	*On the Soul and Resurrection.* PG 46; NPNF II. 5.
Cant.	*Commentary on the Song of Songs.* GNO 6; Gregory of Nyssa, *Commentary on the Song of Songs*, Casimir McCambley OCSO (Brookline, Mass.: Hellenic College Press, 1987).
Cat. or.	*Catechetical Oration.* SC 453; tr. Cyril Richardson in Edward R. Hardy (ed.), *Christology of the Later Fathers*, Library of Christian Classics (Philadelphia: Westminster Press, 1954), 268–325.
Eunom.	*Against Eunomius.* GNO 1 & 2; NPNF II. 5.
Graec.	*To the Greeks: From Common Notions.* GNO 3/1; tr. Daniel F. Stramara, *Greek Orthodox Theological Review*, 41 (1996), 381–91.
Hom. op.	*On the Making of Man.* PG 44; NPNF II. 5.
In 1 Cor. 15	PG 44; Casimir McCambley, 'A Treatise on First Corinthians 15.28', *Greek Orthodox Theological Review*, 28 (1983).
Mort.	*Concerning Those Who Have Died.* GNO 9.
Mos.	*Life of Moses.* GNO 7/1; tr. Abraham J. Malherbe and Everett Ferguson, Gregory of Nyssa, *The Life of Moses* (Mahwah, NJ: Paulist Press, 1978).
Petr.	*To His Brother Peter.* Preserved as Basil's *Letter* 38: see above.
Ref.	*Refutation of Eunomius' Confession.* GNO 1/2; NPNF II. S, 101–34.
Simpl.	*On the Faith to Simplicius.* GNO 3/1; NPNF II. 5.
Spir.	*On the Holy Spirit Against Macedonius.* GNO 3/1; NPNF II. 5.
Trin.	*On the Holy Trinity.* GNO 3/1; NPNF II. S.

Gregory Thaumaturgus

Phil.	*To Philagrius [On Consubstantiality].* PG 46; FoC 98.

Hilary of Poitiers

C. ant. Par.	Collectio antiariana Parisiana. CSEL 65; tr. Lionel Wickham, *Hilary of Poitiers: Conflicts of Conscience and Law in the Fourth-Century Church*, Translated Texts for Historians, 25 (Liverpool: Liverpool University Press, 1997).
C. Const.	Against Constantius. SC 334.
De trin.	On the Trinity. SC 443 & 448; FoC 25.
Synod.	On the Synods. PL 10; NPNF II. 9.

Irenaeus

Adv. haer.	Against Heresies. SC 263–4, 293–4, 210–11, 100, 152–3; ANF 1.

John Chrysostom

Incomp.	Homilies on the Incomprehensibility of God. SC 28 (bis); FoC 72.

Lactantius

Inst. div.	Divine Institutes. CSEL 19; ANF 7.

Marcellus of Ancyra

Frag.	Fragments. Vinzent, *Markell von Ankyra*; tr. in Dowling, *Marcellus of Ancyra*.

Marius Victorinus

Adv. Ar.	Against the Arians. SC 68; FoC 69.

Novatian

Trin.	On the Trinity. CCSL 4; FoC 67.

Origen

C. Celsum	Against Celsus. SC 132, 136, 147, 150, 227; Henry Chadwick (Cambridge: Cambridge University Press, 1965).
Comm. John	Commentary on John. SC 120, 157, 222, 290, 385; FoC 80, 89.
Orat.	On Prayer. GCS 3; ACW 19.
Princ.	On First Principles. SC 252, 253, 268, 269, 312; tr. Henry Butterworth, *Origen: On First Principles* (Gloucester, Mass.: Peter Smith, 1973).

Philostorgius

Hist. eccl.	Ecclesiastical History. GCS 21 (collection of surviving fragments).

Phoebadius

C. Ar.	Against the Arians. CCSL 64.

Plotinus
Enn.   Enneads. Ed. and tr. A. H. Armstrong, *Plotinus The Enneads*, 7 vols., Loeb Classical Library (Cambridge, Mass.: Harvard University Press, 1966–88).

Rufinus
Symb.   *Commentary on the Apostles' Creed*. CCSL 20; ACW 20.

Socrates
Hist. eccl.   *Ecclesiastical History*. PG 67; NPNF II. 2.

Sozomen
Hist. eccl.   *Ecclesiastical History*. GCS 50; NPNF II. 2.

Sulpicius Severus
Chron.   *Chronicles*. CSEL 1; NPNF II. 3.

Tertullian
Adv. Prax.   *Against Praxeas*. Ernest Evans, *Tertullian's Treatise Against Praxeas* (London: SPCK, 1948).

Theodoret
Eccl. hist.   *Ecclesiastical History*. GCS 44; NPNF II. 3.

Theodosian Code
CTh.   *Theodosian Code*. T. Mommsen (ed.), *Theodosiani libri XVI cum constitutionibus Sirmondianis* (Zurich: Weidmann, 1971); C. Pharr, *The Theodosian Code and the Sirmondian Constitutions* (Princeton: Princeton University Press, 1952).

SECONDARY SOURCES

ALEXANDRE, M., *Le Commencement du livre Genèse I–V: La Version grecque de la Septante et sa reception* (Paris: Beauchesne, 1988).

ALGRA, KEIMPE, et al. (eds.), *The Cambridge History of Hellenistic Philosophy* (Cambridge: Cambridge University Press, 1999).

ALSTON, WILLIAM, 'Substance and the Trinity', in Gerald O'Collins et al. (eds.), *The Trinity* (Oxford: Oxford University Press, 1999), 179–201.

ALTHAUS, H., *Die Heilslehre des heiligen Gregor von Nazianz* (Münster: Aschendorff, 1972).

AMAND DE MENDIETA, E., 'Basile de Césarée et Damase de Rome', in J. N. Birdsall and R. W. Thompson (eds.), *Biblical and Patristic Studies in memory of Robert Pierce Casey* (New York: Herder, 1963).

——'The Pair Κήρυγμα and Δόγμα in the Thought of Basil of Caesarea', *JThS* NS 16 (1965), 129–42.

——*The 'unwritten' and the 'Secret' Apostolic Traditions in the Theological Thought of Basil of Caesarea*, Occasional Paper 13 (Edinburgh: Scottish Journal of Theology, 1965).

AMBRAMOWSKI, LUISE, 'Was hat das Niceno-Constantinopolitanum (C) mit dem Konzil von Kønstantinopel 381 zu tun?', *Theologie und Philosophie*, 67 (1992), 481–513.

AMIDON, PHILIP R. (tr. & ed.), *The Panarion of St Epiphanius, Bishop of Salamis: Selected Passages* (New York: Oxford University Press, 1990).

ANASTOS, MILTON V., 'Basil's *Kata Eunomiou*, A Critical Analysis', in Paul J. Fedwick, *Basil of Caesarea: Christian, Humanist, Ascetic* (Toronto: Pontifical Institute of Medieval Studies, 1981), 67–136.

ANATOLIOS, KHALED, *Athanasius: The Coherence of his Thought* (London and New York: Routledge, 1998).

ARMSTRONG, A. H. (ed.), *The Cambridge History of Later Greek and Early Medieval Philosophy* (Cambridge: Cambridge University Press, 1967).

ARNOLD, JOHANNES, 'Begriff und heilsökonomische Bedeutung der göttlichen Sendungen in Augustinus *De Trinitate*', *Recherches Augustiniennes*, 25 (1991), 3–69.

AYRES, LEWIS, Augustine on the Rule of Faith: Rhetoric, Christology, and the Foundation of Christian Thinking', *Augustinian Studies*, forthcoming.

——'Memory, Intelligence and Will', in L. Ayres and V. Twomey (eds.), *The Mystery of the Trinity in the Fathers of the Church* (Dublin: Four Courts Press, forthcoming).

——'Shine Jesus Shine: On Relocating Apollinarianism', *SP*, forthcoming.

——'Deification and the Dynamics of Pro-Nicene Theology: The Contribution of Gregory of Nyssa', *St Vladimir's Theological Quarterly*, 49 (2005), 375–95.

——'The Discipline of Self-Knowledge in Augustine's *De Trinitate* Book X', in Lewis Ayres (ed.), *The Passionate Intellect: Essays on the Transformation of Classical Traditions Presented to Professor Ian Kidd*, RUSCH VII (Brunswick, NJ: Transaction, 1995), 261–96.

——'The Christological Context of *De trinitate* XIII: Towards Relocating Books VIII–XV', *Augustinian Studies*, 29 (1998), 111–39.

——'measure, number and weight', in A. Fitzgerald (ed.), *Augustine: An Encyclopedia* (Grand Rapids, Mich.: Eerdmans, 1999), 550–2.

——'On the Practice and Teaching of Christian Doctrine', *Gregorianum*, 80/1 (1999), 33–94.

——' "Remember that you are Catholic" (*serm.* 52, 2): Augustine on the Unity of the Triune God', *JECS*, 8 (2000), 39–82.

——'Augustine, Christology and God as Love: An Introduction to the Homilies on 1 John', in Kevin Vanhoozer (ed.), *Nothing Greater, Nothing Better: Theological Essays on the Love of God* (Grand Rapids, Mich.: Eerdmans, 2001), 67–93.

——'Athanasius' Initial Defense of the Term ὁμοούσιος: Re-reading the *De decretis*', *JECS* 12 (2004) 337–59.

——and BARNES, MICHEL RENÉ, 'God', in A. Fitzgerald (ed.), *Augustine: An Encyclopedia* (Grand Rapids, Mich.: Eerdmans, 1999), 384–90.

——and FOWL, STEPHEN E., '(Mis)reading the Face of God: The Interpretation of the Bible in the Church', *Theological Studies*, 60 (1999), 513–28.

—— and JONES, GARETH, *Christian Origins: Theology, Rhetoric and Community* (London and New York: Routledge, 1998).
BALÉS, DAVID O., Metousia Theou: *Man's Participation in God's Perfections According to Saint Gregory of Nyssa*, Studia Anselmiana, 55 (Rome: IBC Libreria Herder, 1966).
BARDY, GUSTAVE, *Recherches sur Saint Lucien d'Antioche et son école* (Paris: Beauchesne, 1936).
BARNARD, LESLIE W., 'The Antecedents of Arius', *VigChr*, 24 (1970), 172–88.
—— *The Council of Serdica 343 AD* (Sofia: Synodal Publishing House, 1983).
BARNES, MICHEL RENÉ, 'The Arians of Book V, and the Genre of *De Trinitate*', *JThS* NS 44 (1993), 185–95.
—— 'Augustine in Contemporary Trinitarian Theology', *Theological Studies*, 56 (1995), 237–50.
—— 'The Background and Use of Eunomius' Causal Language', in Michel Barnes and Daniel H. Williams (eds.), *Arianism after Arius: Essays on the Development of the Fourth Century Trinitarian Conflicts* (Edinburgh: T. & T. Clark, 1993), 217–36.
—— 'De Régnon Reconsidered', *Augustinian Studies*, 26 (1995), 51–79.
—— 'Divine Unity and the Divided Self: Gregory of Nyssa's Trinitarian Theology in its Psychological Context', *Modern Theology*, 18 (2002).
—— 'Eunomius of Cyzicus and Gregory of Nyssa: Two Traditions of Transcendental Causality', *VigChr* 52 (1998), 59–87.
—— 'The Fourth Century as Trinitarian Canon', in Lewis Ayres and Gareth Jones (eds.), *Christian Origins: Theology, Rhetoric and Community* (London and New York: Routledge, 1998), 47–67.
—— '"One Nature, One Power": Consensus Doctrine in Pro-Nicene Polemic', *SP*, 29 (1997), 205–23.
—— *The Power of God: Dunamis in Gregory of Nyssa's Trinitarian Theology* (Washington, DC: Catholic University of America Press, 2000).
—— 'Re-reading Augustine's Theology of the Trinity', in S. T. Davis, D. Kendall, and G. O'Collins (eds.), *The Trinity: An Interdisciplinary Symposium on the Doctrine of the Trinity* (Oxford and New York: Oxford University Press, 1999), 145–76.
—— 'The Visible Christ and the Invisible Trinity: Mt. 5. 8 in Augustine's Trinitarian Theology of 400', *Modern Theology*, 19 (2003), 329–55
BARNES, TIMOTHY D., *Athanasius and Constantius* (Cambridge, Mass.: Harvard University Press, 1993).
—— 'The Collapse of the Homoeans in the East', *SP* 29 (1997), 3–16.
BARTHES, ROLAND, *Mythologies*, tr. A. Lavers (New York: Hill & Wang, 1972).
BAUER, WALTER, *Orthodoxy and Heresy in Earliest Christianity*, tr. and ed. Robert A. Kraft *et al.* (Philadelphia: Fortress Press, 1971).
BECK, EDMUND, *Ephräms Trinitätslehre: Im bild von Sonne/Feuer, Licht und Wärme*, CSCO subsidia, 62 (Louvain: Peeters, 1981).
—— *Die Theologie des hl Ephraem in seinen Hymnen über den Glauben*,

Studia Anselmiana, 21 (Rome: Pontificium Institutum S. Anselmi, 1949).
BEHR, JOHN, *The Way to Nicaea*, The Formation of Christian Theology, 1 (Crestwood, NY: St Vladimir's Seminary Press, 2001).
BENJAMIN, WALTER, *Illuminations: Essays and Reflections*, tr. Harry Zohn (New York: Schocken Books, 1968).
BERNARD, R., *L'Image de Dieu d'après saint Athanase* (Paris: Aubier, 1952).
BERNARDI, J., *La Prédication des Pères cappadociens: Le Prédicateur et son auditoire* (Paris: Presses Universitaires de France, 1968).
BETTENSON, HENRY S., *The Later Christian Fathers* (Oxford: Oxford University Press, 1970).
BIANCHI, EUGENE C., and RUETHER, ROSEMARY RADFORD (eds.), *A Democratic Catholic Church: The Reconstruction of Roman Catholicism* (New York: Crossroad, 1992).
BLONDEL, MAURICE, *The Letter on Apologetics and History and Dogma*, tr. Alexander Dru and Illtyd Trethowan (Edinburgh: T. & T. Clark, 1994).
BLOWERS, PAUL M., 'The *regula fidei* and the Narrative Character of Early Christian Faith', *Pro Ecclesia*, 6 (1997), 199–228.
BOFF, LEONARDO, *The Trinity and Society*, tr. P. Burns (New York: Orbis, 1988).
BONNER, G., 'Augustine's Conception of Deification', *JThS* NS 37 (1986), 369–86.
BOURASSA, F., 'L'Intelligence de la foi', *Gregorianum*, 59 (1978), 375–432.
——'Théologie trinitaire chez s. Augustin', *Gregorianum*, 58 (1977), 675–725.
BOURDIEU, PIERRE, *The Field of Cultural Production* (New York: Columbia University Press, 1993).
——*Outline of a Theory of Practice*, tr. R. Nice (Cambridge: Cambridge University Press, 1977).
BOWERSOCK, G., *Julian the Apostate* (Cambridge, Mass.: Harvard University Press, 1978).
BOYS-STONES, G. R., *Post-Hellenistic Philosophy* (Oxford: Clarendon Press, 2002).
BRAKKE, DAVID, *Athanasius and the Politics of Asceticism* (Oxford: Clarendon Press, 1995).
BRENNECKE, HANNS CHRISTOF, *Hilarius von Poitiers und die Bischofsopposition gegen Konstantius, ii: Untersuchungen zur dritten Phase des arianischen Streites (337–361)* (Berlin: De Gruyter, 1984).
——'Lukian von Antiochien in der Geschichte arianischen Streites', *Logos: Festschrift für Luise Abramowski* (Berlin: De Gruyter, 1993), 170–92.
——*Studien zur Geschichte der Homöer: Der Osten bis zum Ende der homöischen Reichskirche* (Tübingen: J. C. B. Mohr, 1988).
BROCK, SENASTIAN, *The Luminous Eye: The Spiritual World of Saint Ephrem* (Kalamazoo, Mich.: Cistercian Publications, 1985).
——'Syriac Culture, 337–425', *CAH* xiii. 708–19.
BROWN, DAVID, *The Divine Trinity* (London: Duckworth, 1985).
BROWN, PETER, *The Body and Society: Men, Women and Sexual Renunci-*

ation in Early Christianity (New York: Columbia University Press, 1988).
——*Power and Persuasion in Late Antiquity: Towards a Christian Empire* (Madison: University of Wisconsin Press, 1992).
BUNGE, GABRIEL J. 'Hénade ou Monade? Au subjet de deux notions centrales de la terminologie evagrienne', *Le Muséon*, 102 (1989), 69–91.
——'The "Spiritual Prayer": On the Trinitarian Mysticism of Evagrius of Pontus', *Monastic Studies*, 17 (1986), 191–208.
BURNS, PAUL, 'Hilary of Poitiers, Confrontation with Arianism', in Robert C. Gregg (ed.), *Arianism: Historical and Theological Reassessments*, Patristic Monograph Series, 11 (Philadelphia: Philadelphia Patristic Foundation, 1985), 287–302.
BURRELL, DAVID B., 'Distinguishing God from the World', in Brian Davies (ed.), *Language, Meaning and God: Essays in Honour of Herbert McCabe* (London: Chapman, 1987), 75–91.
——'Does Process Theology Rest on a Mistake?', *Theological Studies*, 43 (1982), 125–35.
——'From Analogy of "Being" to the Analogy of Being', in Thomas Hibbs and John O'Callaghan (eds.), *Recovering Nature: Essays in Natural Philosophy, Ethics and Metaphysics in Honor of Ralph McInerny* (Notre Dame, Ind.: University of Notre Dame Press, 1999), 253–66.
——*Knowing the Unknowable God: Ibn-Sina, Maimonides, Aquinas* (Notre Dame, Ind.: University of Notre Dame Press, 1986).
BURRUS, VIRGINIA, *'Begotten, not Made': Conceiving Manhood in Late Antiquity* (Stanford, Calif.: Stanford University Press, 2002).
CALLAHAN, JOHN F., 'Greek Philosophy and the Cappadocian Cosmology', *Dumbarton Oaks Papers*, 12 (1958), 29–58.
CAMERON, AVERIL, 'Ascetic Closure and the End of Antiquity', in Vincent L. Wimbush and Richard Valantassis (eds.), *Asceticism* (New York: Oxford University Press, 1998), 147–61.
——*Christianity and the Rhetoric of Empire: The Development of Christian Discourse* (Berkeley: University of California Press, 1991).
——and GARNSEY, PETER (eds.), *Cambridge Ancient History*, xiii: *The Late Empire AD 337–425* (Cambridge: Cambridge University Press, 1998).
CAMERON, MICHAEL, 'The Christological Substructure of Augustine's Figurative Exegesis', in Pamela Bright (ed.), *Augustine and the Bible* (Notre Dame, Ind.: University of Notre Dame Press, 1999), 74–103.
CAPÁNAGA, V., 'La Deificatión en la soteriología augustiniana', in *Augustinus Magister: Congrès International Augustinien, Paris 21–24 septembre 1954* (Paris: Études Augustiniennes, 1954), ii. 745–54.
CAREY, PATRICK W., and MULLER, EARL C. (eds.), *Theological Education in the Catholic Tradition: Contemporary Challenges* (New York: Crossroad, 1997).
CARTWRIGHT, MICHAEL, 'Ideology and the Interpretation of the Bible', *Modern Theology*, 9 (1993), 141–58.
CAVALCANTI, ELENA, *Studi Eunomiani* (Rome: Pontificium Institutum Orientalium Studiorum, 1976).

CERTEAU, MICHEL DE, *Culture in the Plural*, tr. Tom Conley (Northfield, Minn.: University of Minnesota Press, 1997).
—— *Faiblesse de Croire* (Paris: Éditions du Seuil, 1987).
—— *The Practice of Everyday Life*, tr. S. Rendall (Berkeley: University of California Press, 1984).
CERTEAU, MICHEL DE, *The Writing of History*, tr. Tom Conley (New York: Columbia University Press, 1988), 56–113.
CHADWICK, HENRY, *The Church in Ancient Society: From Galilee to Gregory the Great* (Oxford: Clarendon Press, 2001).
—— 'The Origin of the Title Oecumenical Council', *JThS* NS 23 (1972), 132–5.
—— 'Ossius of Cordova and the Council of Antioch', *JThS* NS 9 (1958), 292–304.
CHEVALIER, I., *Saint Augustin et la pensée grecque. Les Relations trinitaires* (Fribourg: Collectanea Friburgensia, 1940).
CHILDS, BREVARD, 'The *sensus literalis* of Scripture: An Ancient and Modern Problem', in H. Donner et al. (eds.), *Beiträge zur Alttestamentlichen Theologie, Festschrift für Walter Zimmerli zum 70* (Göttingen: Vandenhoeck & Ruprecht, 1977), 80–93.
CIPRIANI, NELLO, 'Le Fonti Cristiane della Dottrina Trinitaria nei Primi Dialoghi di S. Agostino', *Augustinianum*, 34 (1994), 253–312.
CLARK, ELIZABETH A., 'Elite Networks and Heresy Accusations: Towards a Social Description of the Origenist Controversy', *Semeia*, 56 (1992), 79–117.
—— *History-Theory-Text* (Cambridge, Mass.: Harvard University Press, 2004).
—— *The Origenist Controversy: The Cultural Construction of an Early Christian Debate* (Princeton: Princeton University Press, 1992).
—— *Reading Renunciation: Asceticism and Scripture in Early Christianity* (Princeton: Princeton University Press, 1999).
COAKLEY, SARAH, 'Re-thinking Gregory of Nyssa: Introduction—Gender, Trinitarian Analogies, and the Pedagogy of *The Song*', *Modern Theology*, 18 (2002), 431–43.
COFFEY, DAVID, *Deus Trinitas: The Doctrine of the Triune God* (New York: Oxford University Press, 1999).
CONGAR, YVES, *A History of Theology*, tr. Hunter Guthrie (New York: Doubleday, 1968).
—— *Tradition and Traditions*, tr. Michael Naisby and Thomas Rainborough (San Diego: Basilica Press, 2002).
CORSINI, EUGENIO, 'Nouvelles perspectives sur le problème des sources de l'Hexaëméron de Grégoire de Nysse', *SP*, 2/1 (1957), 94–103.
COX MILLER, PATRICIA, 'Origen and the Witch of Endor', in *The Poetry of Thought in Late Antiquity: Essays in Imagination and Religion* (Aldershot and Burlington, Vt.: Ashgate, 2001).
CRAMER, PETER, *Baptism and Social Change* (Cambridge: Cambridge University Press, 1993).
CROUZEL, HENRI, *Bibliographie critique d'Origène* (The Hague: Nijhoff, 1971 (with suppl. 1982)).

—— *Origen*, tr. A. S. Worrall (Edinburgh: T. & T. Clark, 1989).
CUNNINGHAM, DAVID, *These Three are One: The Practice of Trinitarian Theology* (Oxford: Blackwell, 1998).
DALEY, BRIAN E., 'Divine Transcendence and Human Transformation: Gregory of Nyssa's Anti-Apollinarian Christology', *SP* 32 (1997), 87–95.
—— 'The Giant's Twin Substances: Ambrose and the Christology of Augustine's "Contra Sermonem Arrianorum" ', in Joseph T. Lienhard et al. (eds.), *Augustine: Presbyter factus sum*, Collectanea Augustiniana, 2 (New York: Peter Lang, 1993), 477–95.
—— 'Nature and the "Mode of Union": Late Patristic Models for the Personal Unity of Christ', in Stephen T. Davis, Daniel Kendall, and Gerald O'Collins (eds.), *The Incarnation: An Interdisciplinary Symposium on the Incarnation of the Son of God* (Oxford: Clarendon Press, 2001), 164–96.
—— 'Origen's De Principiis: A Guide to the Principles of Christian Scriptural Interpretation', in John Petruccione (ed.), *Nova et Vetera: Patristic Studies in Honor of Thomas Patrick Halton* (Washington, DC: Catholic University of America Press, 1998), 3–21.
DANIÉLOU, JEAN, 'Eunome l'Arien et l'exégèse néo-platonicienne du Cratyle', *Revue des Études Grecques*, 49 (1956), 412–32.
DAVIS, S. T., KENDALL, D., and O'COLLINS, G. (eds.), *The Trinity: An Interdisciplinary Symposium on the Doctrine of the Trinity* (Oxford and New York: Oxford University Press, 2000).
DAWSON, DAVID, *Allegorical Readers and Cultural Revision in Ancient Alexandria* (Berkley: University of California Press, 1992).
—— 'Figural Reading and the Fashioning of Christian Identity in Boyarin, Auerbach and Frei', *Modern Theology*, 14 (1998), 181–96.
—— *Figural Reading, the Fashioning of Identity and the Suppression of Origen* (Berkeley: University of California Press, 2002).
DE HALLEUX, ANDRÉ, 'Personnalisme ou Essentialisme Trinitaire chez Les Pères Cappadociens', *Revue Théologique de Louvain*, 17 (1986), 129–55, 265–92 (repr. in *Patrologie et Œcuménisme: Recueil d'études*, Bibliotheca Ephemeridum Theologicarum Lovaniensum, XCIII (Leuven: Leuven University Press, 1990), 215–68).
—— 'La Reception du Symbole Œcumenique, de Nicée à Chalcédoine', *Ephemerides Theologicae Lovaniensis*, 61 (1985), 5–47 (repr. in *Patrologie et Œcuménisme: Recueil d'études*, Bibliotheca Ephemeridum Theologicarum Lovaniensum, XCIII (Leuven: Leuven University Press, 1990), 25–67).
DE LUBAC, HENRI, *Histoire et Esprit: L'Intelligence de l'Écriture d'après Origène* (Paris: Aubier, 1950).
—— *Medieval Exegesis*, vols. 1 and 2 (Grand Rapids, Mich.: Eerdmans, 1998, 2000).
—— 'The Problem of the Development of Dogma', *Theology in History*, tr. Anne Englund Nash (San Francisco: Ignatius Press, 1996), 248–80.
—— ' "Typologie" et "allegorisme" ', *Recherches de science religieuse*, 34 (1947), 180–226.

DE MARGERIE, BERTRAND, *The Christian Trinity in History*, tr. Edmund J. Fortman (Still River, Mass.: St Bede's Publications, 1982).

——'La Doctrine de saint Augustin sur l'Esprit-Saint comme communion et source de communion', *Augustinianum*, 12 (1972), 107–19.

DE RÉGNON, THEODORE, *Études de théologie positive sur la sainté Trinité* (Paris: Retaux, 1898).

DE RIEDMATTEN, HENRI, 'La Correspondance entre Basile de Césarée et Apollinaire de Laodicée', *JThS* NS 7 (1956), 199–210, 8 (1957); 53–70.

DIGESER, ELIZABETH DEPALMA, *The Making of a Christian Empire: Lactantius and Rome* (Ithaca, NY: Cornell University Press, 2000).

DILLON, JOHN, 'Logos and Trinity: Patterns of Platonist Influence on Early Christianity', in Godfrey Vesey (ed.), *The Philosophy in Christianity* (Cambridge: Cambridge University Press, 1989), 1–13.

—— *The Middle Platonists 80 BC to AD 220* (London: Duckworth, 1977).

DIXON, PHILIP, *Nice and Hot Disputes: The Doctrine of the Trinity in the Seventeenth Century* (London: T. & T. Clark, 2003).

DOIGNON, JEAN, *Hilaire de Poitiers avant l'exil* (Paris: Études Augustiniennes, 1971).

DÖRRIE, H., '*Hypostasis*, Wort- und Bedeutungsgeschichte', *Nachr. Akad. Göttingen*, 3 (1955), 35–92.

DOVAL, ALEXIS, *Cyril of Jerusalem, Mystagogue* (Washington, DC: Catholic University of America Press, 2001).

DOWLING, MAURICE JAMES, *Marcellus of Ancyra: Problems of Christology and the Doctrine of the Trinity*, diss. (Queen's University, Belfast, 1987).

DRECOLL, VOLKER HENNING, *Die Entwicklung der Trinitätslehre des Basilius von Cäsarea: Sein Weg vom Homöusianer zum Neonizäner* (Göttingen: Vandenhoeck & Ruprecht, 1996).

DRISCOLL, JEREMY, *The 'Ad Monachos' of Evagrius Ponticus: Its Structure and a Select Commentary*, Studia Anselmiana, 104 (Rome: Pontificio Ateneo S. Anselmo, 1991).

DROBNER, HUBERTUS R., 'Grammatical Exegesis and Christology in St. Augustine', *SP* 18 (1990), 49–63.

——*Person-Exegese und Christologie bei Augustinus* (Leiden: Brill, 1986).

DUVAL, Y. M., 'La "Manœuvre fraudulense" de Rimini à la recherche du Liber adversus Ursacium et Valentem', in *Hilaire et son temps: Actes du colloque de Poitiers, 29 septembre–3 octobre* (Paris, 1969), 51–103.

——'Traduction latine inédite du symbole de Nicée et une condemnation d'Arius à Rimini: Nouveau fragment historique d'Hilaire ou pièces des actes du concile?', *Revue Bénédictine*, 82 (1972), 7–25.

EDWARDS, MARK, 'The Arian Heresy and the Oration to the Saints', *VigChr* 49 (1995), 379–87.

——'Did Origen Apply the Word *Homoousios* to the Son?', *JThS* NS 49 (1998), 658–70.

——*Origen Against Plato*, Ashgate Studies in Philosophy & Theology in Late Antiquity (Burlington, Vt.: Ashgate, 2002).

EGAN, JOHN, 'The Knowledge and Vision of God according to Gregory Nazianzen: A Study of the Images of Mirror and Light', diss. Institut Catholique de Paris, 1971.

―― 'Primal Cause and Trinitarian Perichoresis in Gregory Nazianzen's *Oration* 31', *SP* 27 (1993).
―― 'Towards a Mysticism of Light in Gregory Nazianzen's *Oratio* 32.15', *SP* 18/3 (1989), 473–82.
ELM, SUSANNA, 'The Diagnostic Gaze: Gregory of Nazianzus' Theory of Orthodox Priesthood in his *Orations* 6 *De pace* and 2 *Apologia de fuga sua*', in Elm et al. (eds.), *Orthodoxie, christianisme, histoire* (Rome: École Française de Rome, 2000), 83–100.
―― '*Virgins of God*': *The Making of Asceticism in Late Antiquity* (Oxford: Clarendon Press, 1994).
ENGBERG-PEDERSEN, TROELS (ed.), *Paul Beyond the Judaism/Hellenism Divide* (Louisville Ky.: Westminster John Knox, 2001).
FARLEY, EDWARD, *Ecclesial Reflection: An Anatomy of Theological Method* (Philadelphia: Fortress Press, 1982).
―― *Theologia: The Fragmentation and Unity of Theological Education* (Philadelphia: Fortress Press, 1983).
FEHR, WAYNE L., *The Birth of the Catholic Tübingen School: The Dogmatics of Johann Sebastian Drey* (Chico, Calif.: Scholars Press, 1981).
FERGUSON, EVERETT (ed.), *Encyclopedia of Early Christianity* (London: Garland, 1998).
FIEDROWICZ, M., *Psalmus vox totius Christi: Studien zu Augustins Ennarationes in Psalmos* (Freiburg: Herder, 1997).
FLORENSKY, PAVEL, *The Pillar and Ground of the Truth: An Essay in Orthodox Theodicy in Twelve Letters*, tr. Boris Jakim (Princeton: Princeton University Press, 1997).
FLOROVSKY, GEORGES, 'St. Athanasius' Concept of Creation', *SP* 6 (1962), 36–57 (repr. in *Aspects of Church History*, Collected Works, iv (Belmont, Mass.: Nordland, 1975), 39–62).
FORTE, BRUNO, *Trinity in History: Saga of the Christian God*, tr. P. Rotondi (New York: Alba, 1989).
FORTMAN, EDMUND J., *The Triune God: A Historical Study of the Doctrine of the Trinity* (Philadelphia: Westminster Press, 1972).
FOWL, STEPHEN E., *Engaging Scripture* (Malden, Mass.: Blackwells, 1999).
FREDE, MICHAEL, 'Epilogue', in Keimpe Algra et al. (eds.), *The Cambridge History of Hellenistic Literature* (Cambridge: Cambridge University Press, 1999), 771–97.
FREI, HANS, *The Eclipse of Biblical Narrative: A Study in Eighteenth and Nineteenth Century Hermeneutics* (New Haven: Yale University Press, 1974).
―― 'The Literal Sense: Does it Stretch or Will it Break?', *Theology and Narrative: Selected Essays* (Oxford and New York: Oxford University Press, 1993), 117–52.
―― *Types of Christian Theology* (New Haven: Yale University Press, 1992).
GADAMER, HANS GEORG, *Truth and Method* (London: Sheed & Ward, 1975).
GARRIGOU LAGRANGE, REGINALD, *The Trinity and God the Creator. A*

Commentary on St. Thomas's Theological Summa, 1a, q. 27–119, tr. F. C. Eckhoff (St Louis: Herder, 1952).

GARVIE, ALFRED E., *The Christian Doctrine of the Godhead* (London: Hodder & Stoughton, 1925).

GATTI, MARIA LUISA, 'Plotnius: The Platonic Tradition and the Foundation of Neoplatonism', in Lloyd P. Gerson (ed.), *The Cambridge Companion to Plotinus* (Cambridge: Cambridge University Press, 1996), 10–37.

GELZER, H., et al. (eds.), *Patrum Nicaenorum Nomina* (Stuttgart and Leipzig: Teubner, 1995).

GIRARDET, KLAUS MARTIN, 'Constance II, Athanase et l'édit d'Arles (353): A propos de la politique religieuse de l'empereur Constance II', in Charles Kannengiesser (ed.), *Politique et Théologie chez Athanase d'Alexandrie* (Paris: Beauchesne, 1974), 63–91.

GOLDSTEIN, JAN, 'Foucault among the Sociologists: The "Disciplines" and the History of the Professions', *History and Theory*, 23 (1984), 171–92.

GOLITZIN, ALEXANDER, ' "The Demons suggest an illusion of God's glory in a form": Controversy over the Divine Body and Vision of Glory in some Late Fourth, Early Fifth Century Monastic Literature', *Studia Monastica*, 44 (2002), 13–43.

GONZALEZ, JUSTO L., *A History of Christian Thought*, vol. i, rev. edn. (Nashville: Abingdon, 1987).

GRANT, ROBERT M., 'The Book of Wisdom at Alexandria: Reflections on the History of the Canon and Theology', *SP* 7 (1966), 462–72.

GREEN, F. W., 'The Later Development of the Doctrine of the Trinity', in A. E. J. Rawlinson (ed.), *Essays on the Trinity and the Incarnation* (London: Longman, 1932).

GREGG, ROBERT C., 'Cyril of Jerusalem and the Arians', in Robert C. Gregg (ed.), *Arianism: Historical and Theological Reassessments*, Patristic Monograph Series, 11 (Philadelphia: Philadelphia Patristic Foundation, 1985), 85–109.

——and GROH, DENIS E., *Early Arianism: A View of Salvation* (Philadelphia: Fortress Press, 1981).

GRENZ, STANLEY and OLSON, ROGER, *Twentieth Century Theology: God and the World in a Transitional Age* (Downers Grove, Ill.: InterVarsity Press, 1992).

GRIBOMONT, JEAN, 'Eustathe le philosophe et les voyages du jeune Basile de Césarée', *Revue d'Histoire Ecclésiastique*, 54 (1959), 115–24.

GRIFFITH, SIDNEY H., 'Asceticism in the Church of Syria: The Hermeneutics of Early Syrian Monasticism', in Vincent Wimbush and Richard Valantassis (eds.), *Asceticism* (New York: Oxford University Press, 1998), 220–45.

——'Setting Right the Church of Syria: Saint Ephraem's *Hymns Against Heresies*', in Mark Vessey and Williams E. Klingshirn (eds.), *The Limits of Ancient Christianity: Essays on Late Antique Thought and Culture in Honor of R. A. Markus* (Ann Arbor: University of Michigan Press, 1999), 97–114.

GRILLMEIER, ALOYS, *Christ in Christian Tradition*, I, 2nd edn. (London: Mowbrays, 1975).

GROSS, JULES, *La Divinisation du chrétien d'après les pères grecs: Contribution historique à la doctrine de la grâce* (Paris: J. Gabalda, 1938).
GRYSON, ROGER, *Scolies Ariennes sur le concile d'Aquilée*, SC 267 (Paris: Éditions du Cerf, 1980).
GUNTON, COLIN, *The Promise of Trinitarian Theology* (Edinburgh: T. & T. Clark, 1991).
GWATKIN, H. M., *Studies of Arianism* (Cambridge, 1882).
HAHN, AUGUST, *Bibliothek der Symbole und Glaubensregeln der Alten Kirche* (Breslau: Morgenstern, 1877).
HAIGHT, ROGER, *Dynamics of Theology* (New York: Paulist, 1990).
HALL, STUART, 'The Creed of Sardica', *SP* 19 (1989), 173–84.
HALVINI, DAVID WEISS, *Plain and Applied Meaning in Rabbinic Exegesis* (New York: Oxford University Press, 1991).
HAMMAN, A.-G., *L'Homme, image de Dieu* (Paris: Desclée, 1987).
HAMMERSTAEDT, J., 'Hypostasis', *RAC* 16 (1985), 986–1035.
HANSON, RICHARD P. C., 'The Influence of Origen on the Arian Controversy', in L. Lies (ed.), *Origeniana Quarta*, Innsbrucker theologische Studien, 19 (Innsbruck: Tyrolia, 1987), 410–23.
—— *The Search for the Christian Doctrine of God: The Arian Controversy 318–381 AD* (Edinburgh: T. & T. Clark, 1988).
—— 'The Transformation of Images in the Fourth Century', *SP* 17/1 (1982), 97–113.
HARNACK, ADOLF VON, *The History of Dogma*, vol. iv, tr. Neil Buchanan (New York: Russell & Russell, 1958).
—— 'Die Hypotyposen des Theognost', *TU* 9 (1903), 73–92.
HARRIES, JILL, *Law and Empire in Late Antiquity* (Cambridge: Cambridge University Press, 1999).
HARRISON, CAROL, *Beauty and Revelation in the Thought of Saint Augustine* (Oxford: Clarendon Press, 1992).
HARRISON, VERNA E. F., *Grace and Human Freedom According to St. Gregory of Nyssa* (Lewiston, NY: Edwin Mellon Press, 1992).
HAUERWAS, STANLEY, *Sanctify Them in the Truth* (Edinburgh: T. & T. Clark, 1998).
HAUSCHILD, W.-D., *Die Pneumatomachen. Eine Untersuchung zur Dogmengeschichte des vierten Jahrhunderts*, diss. (University of Hamburg, 1967).
HAYKIN, MICHAEL A. G., *The Spirit of God: The Exegesis of 1 and 2 Corinthians in the Pneumatomachian Controversy of the Fourth Century* (Leiden: Brill, 1994).
HEATHER, PETER, *Goths and Romans 332–489* (Oxford: Clarendon Press, 1991).
HEFELE, JOSPEH, *Histoire de Conciles* i/2 (Paris: Letouzey et Ané, 1907).
HEGEL, GEORG WILHELM FREDERICK, *Lectures on the Philosophy of Religion*, iii: *The Consummate Religion*, ed. and tr. Peter C. Hodgson et al. (Berkeley: University of California Press, 1985).
—— *Lectures on the Philosophy of Religion, One-Volume Edition. The Lectures of 1827*, tr. Peter Hodgson (Berkeley: University of California Press, 1988).

HEIL, UTA, *Athanasius von Alexandria: de Sententia Dionysii*, PTS 52 (Berlin: De Gruyter, 1999).
HEINE, RONALD E., *Gregory of Nyssa's Treatise on the Inscription of the Psalms: Introduction, Translation and Notes* (Oxford: Clarendon Press, 1995).
—— *Perfection in the Virtuous Life*, Patristic Monograph Series, 2 (Philadelphia: Philadelphia Patristic Foundation, 1975).
HERON, ALISDAIR, 'Some Sources used in the *De Trinitate* ascribed to Didymus the Blind', in Rowan Williams (ed.), *The Making of Orthodoxy* (Cambridge: Cambridge University Press, 1989), 173–81.
HESS, HAMILTON, *The Early Development of Canon Law and the Council of Sardica* (Oxford: Clarendon Press, 2002).
HINSON, E. GLENN, *The Early Church: Origins to the Dawn of the Middle Ages* (Nashville: Abingdon, 1996).
HODGSON, PETER C., *The Formation of Historical Theology: A Study of Ferdinand Christian Bauer* (New York: Harper & Row, 1966).
HOLIFIELD, E. Brooks, *Theology in America* (New Haven: Yale University Press, 2003).
HOLL, KARL, *Amphilochius von Ikonium in seinem Verhältnis zu den grossen Kappadoziern* (Tübingen: J. C. B. Mohr, 1904).
HOLMES, AUGUSTINE, *A Life Pleasing to God: The Spirituality of the Rules of St. Basil* (London: DLT, 2000).
HÜBNER, REINHARD M., *Die Einheit des Leibes Christi bei Gregor von Nyssa* (Leiden: Brill, 1974).
—— 'Gregor von Nyssa als Verfasser de Sog. *Ep.* 38 des Basilius', in Jacques Fontaine and Charles Kannengiesser (eds.), *Epektasis: Mélanges patristiques offerts au Cardinal Daniélou* (Paris: Beauchesne, 1972), 463–90.
—— *Der paradox Eine: Antignosticher Monarchianismus im zweiten Jahrhundert*, ed. Markus Vinzent (Leiden: Brill, 1999).
HUMFRESS, CAROLINE, 'Roman Law, Forensic Argument and the Formation of Christian Orthodoxy (III–VI Centuries)', in Susanna Elm, Eric Rebillard, and Antonella Romano (eds.), *Orthodoxie, christianisme, histoire* (Rome: École Française de Rome, 2000), 125–47.
HUNT, E. D., 'Did Constantius II Have "Court Bishops"?', *SP* 21 (1989), 86–90.
INGLIS, JOHN, *Spheres of Philosophical Inquiry and the Historiography of Medieval Philosophy* (Leiden: Brill, 1998).
IRVINE, MARTIN, *The Making of Textual Culture: Grammatica and Literary Theory 350–1100* (Cambridge: Cambridge University Press, 1994).
JAUSS, HANS ROBERT, 'Literary History as Challenge to Literary Theory', *Towards an Aesthetic of Reception* (University of Minnesota Press, 1981).
JENSON, ROBERT W., *Systematic Theology*, i (New York: Oxford University Press, 1997).
—— *The Triune Identity* (Philadelphia: Fortress Press, 1982).
JOHNSON, ELIZABETH, *She Who Is* (New York: Crossroad, 1997).
JONES, A. H. M., *The Cities of the Eastern Roman Empire* (Oxford: Clarendon Press, 1971).

JÜNGEL, EBERHARD, *God as the Mystery of the World*, tr. Darrell L. Guder (Edinburgh: T. & T. Clark, 1983).
KANNENGIESSER, CHARLES, *Athanase d'Alexandrie évêque et écrivain: Une lecture des traités contre les Ariens*, Théologie historique, 70 (Paris: Beauchesne, 1983).
—— 'Divine Trinity and the Structure of *Peri Archon*', in Charles Kannengiesser and William L. Petersen (eds.), *Origen of Alexandria: His World and His Legacy* (Notre Dame, Ind.: University of Notre Dame Press, 1988), 231–49.
KASPER, WALTER, *The God of Jesus Christ*, tr. Matthew J. O'Connell (London: SCM, 1983).
—— *Theology and Church*, tr. Margaret Kohl (New York: Crossroad, 1989).
KASTER, ROBERT A., *Guardians of Language: The Grammarian and Society in Late Antiquity* (Berkeley: University of California Press, 1988).
—— 'Notes on Primary and Secondary Schools in Late Antiquity', *Transactions of the American Philological Association*, 113 (1983), 323–46.
KELLY, J. N. D., *Early Christian Creeds*, 3rd edn. (London: Longman, 1972).
—— *Early Christian Doctrines*, 5th edn. (London: Longman, 1977).
KING, R. Q., *The Emperor Theodosius and the Establishment of Christianity* (Philadelphia: Westminster Press, 1960).
KINZIG, WOLFRAM, *In Search of Asterius: Studies on the Authorship of the Psalms* (Göttingen: Vandenhoeck & Ruprecht, 1990).
—— MARKSCHIES, CHRISTOPH, and VINZENT, MARKUS, *Tauffen und Bekenntnis: Studien zur sogenannten* Traditio apostolica, *zu den* Interrogationes de fide *und zum Römischen Glaubensbekenntnis* (Berlin: De Gruyter, 1998).
KLEIN, RICHARD, *Constantius II und die christliche Kirche* (Darmstadt: Wissenschaftliche Buchgesellschaft, 1977).
KOONAMMAKKAL, THOMAS, 'Divine Names and Theological Language in Ephrem', *SP* 25 (1993), 318–23.
KOPECEK, THOMAS A., *A History of Neo-Arianism*, 2 vols. (Philadelphia: Philadelphia Patristic Foundation, 1979).
KÖSTERS, OLIVER, *Die Trinitätslehre des Epiphanius von Salamis. Ein Kommentar zum 'Ancoratus'* (Göttingen: Vandenhoeck & Ruprecht, 2003).
LACUGNA, CATHERINE MOWRY, *God For Us: The Trinity and Christian Life* (San Francisco: HarperCollins, 1991).
LAMPE, GEOFFREY W. H., *A Patristic Greek Lexicon* (Oxford: Oxford University Press, 1961).
LANG, UWE, 'The Christological Controversy at the Synod of Antioch in 268/9', *JThS* NS 51 (2000), 54–80.
LASH, NICHOLAS, *Change in Focus: A Study in Doctrinal Change and Continuity* (London: Sheed & Ward, 1973).
LATOURETTE, KENNETH, *A History of Christianity* (New York: Harpers, 1953).
LEBON, J., 'La Position de Saint Cyrille de Jerusalem dans les luttes provoquées par l'arianisme', *Revue d'Histoire Ecclésiastique*, 20 (1924), 181–210, 357–86.

LE BOULLUEC, A., *La Notion d'hérésie dans la littérature Grecque IIe–IIIe siècles*, 2 vols. (Paris: Études Augustiniennes, 1985).
LEROUX, J. M., 'Acace évêque de Césarée de Palestine (341–365)', *SP* 8 (1966), 82–5.
LEVERING, MATTHEW, *Scripture and Metaphysics: Aquinas and the Renewal of Trinitarian Theology* (Oxford: Blackwell, 2004).
LEVINE, JOSEPH M., *Humanism and History: Origins of Modern English Historiography* (Ithaca, NY: Cornell University Press, 1987).
LIENHARD, JOSEPH T., 'Acacius of Caesarea: Contra Marcellum. Historical and Theological Considerations', *Cristianesimo nella Storia*, 10 (1989), 1–22.
—— 'The Arian Controversy: Some Categories Reconsidered', *Theological Studies*, 48 (1987), 415–36.
—— *Contra Marcellum: Marcellus of Ancyra and Fourth Century Theology* (Washington, DC: Catholic University of America Press, 1999).
—— 'Did Athanasius Reject Marcellus?', in Michel Barnes and Daniel H. Williams (eds.), *Arianism after Arius: Essays on the Development of the Fourth Century Trinitarian Conflicts* (Edinburgh: T. & T. Clark, 1993), 65–80.
—— 'Ousia and Hypostasis: The Cappadocian Settlement and the Theology of "One Hypostasis"', in S. T. Davis, D. Kendall, and G. O'Collins (eds.), *The Trinity: An Interdisciplinary Symposium on the Doctrine of the Trinity* (Oxford and New York: Oxford University Press, 2000), 99–121.
LIM, RICHARD, *Public Disputation, Power and Social Order in Late Antiquity* (Berkeley: University of California Press, 1995).
LINDBECK, GEORGE A., *The Nature of Doctrine: Religion and Theology in a Postliberal Age* (Philadelphia: Westminster Press, 1984).
LIPATOV, N. A., 'The Statement of Faith Attributed to St Basil the Great', *SP* 37 (2001), 147–59.
LOGAN, ALISTAIR H. B., 'Marcellus of Ancyra and the Councils of 325: Antioch, Ancyra, and Nicaea', *JThS* NS 43 (1992), 428–46.
—— 'Marcellus of Ancyra, Defender of the Faith against Heretics—and Pagans', *SP* 37 (2001), 550–64.
—— 'Origen and Alexandrian Wisdom Christology', in Richard P. C. Hanson and Henri Crouzel (eds.), *Origeniana Tertia* (Rome: Edizioni dell'Ateneo, 1985), 123–9.
—— 'Origen and the Development of Trinitarian Theology', in L. Lies (ed.), *Origeniana Quarta*, Innsbrucker Theologische Studien, 19 (Innsbruck: Tyrolia, 1987), 424–9.
LÖHR, WINRICH, *Die Entstehung der homöischen und homöusianischen Kirchenparteien: Studien zur Synodalgeschichte des 4. Jahrhunderts* (Bonn: Wehle, 1986).
—— 'A Sense of Tradition: The Homoiousian Church Party', in Michel Barnes and Daniel H. Williams (eds.), *Arianism after Arius* (Edinburgh: T. & T. Clark, 1993), 81–100.
LÖHRER, M., 'Glaube und Heilsgeschichte in *De Trinitate* Augustins', *Freiburger Zeitschrift für Philosophie und Theologie*, 4 (1957), 385–419.

LORENZ, RUDOLF, 'Die Eustathius von Antiochien zugeschreibene Schrift gegen Photin', *ZNTW* 71 (1980), 109–28.
LOSSKY, VLADIMIR A., *The Mystical Theology of the Eastern Church* (Cambridge: James Clarke, 1957).
LOT-BORONDINE, MYRRHA, *La Déification de l'homme selon la doctrine des Pères grecs* (Paris: Cerf, 1970).
LOUTH, ANDREW, *Discerning the Mystery: An Essay on the Nature of Theology* (Oxford: Clarendon Press, 1983).
—— 'The Use of the Term ἴδιος in Alexandrian Theology from Alexander to Cyril', *SP* 19 (1987), 198–202.
LUIBHÉID, COLM, *Eusebius of Caesarea and the Arian Crisis* (Dublin: Irish Academic Press, 1981).
LYMAN, J. REBECCA, 'Ascetics and Bishops: Epiphanius on Orthodoxy', in Susanna Elm, Eric Rebillard, and Antonella Romano (eds.), *Orthodoxie, christianisme, histoire* (Rome: École Française de Rome, 2000), 149–61.
—— *Christology and Cosmology: Models of Divine Activity in Origen, Eusebius, and Athanasius* (Oxford: Oxford University Press, 1993).
—— 'A Topography of Heresy: Mapping the Rhetorical Creation of Arianism', in Michel Barnes and Daniel H. Williams (eds.), *Arianism after Arius* (Edinburgh: T. & T. Clark, 1993), 45–62.
MCCLENDON, JAMES, *Systematic Theology*, ii (Nashville: Abingdon, 1994).
MCCLINTOCK FULKERSON, MARY, *Changing the Subject: Women's Discourses and Feminist Theology* (Minneapolis: Fortress Press, 1994).
MCCOOL, GERALD A., *Nineteenth Century Scholasticism: The Search for a Unitary Method* (New York: Fordham University Press, 1977).
MCCORMACK, BRUCE L., *Karl Barth's Critically Realistic Dialectical Theology* (Oxford: Clarendon Press, 1995).
MCGRATH, ALISTAIR, *The Genesis of Doctrine* (Oxford: Blackwell, 1990).
MCGUCKIN, JOHN, 'Perceiving Light From Light in Light: The Trinitarian Theology of St. Gregory the Theologian', *Greek Orthodox Theological Review*, 39 (1994).
—— *Saint Gregory of Nazianzus: An Intellectual Biography* (Crestwood, NY: St Vladimir's Seminary Press, 2001).
MACINTYRE, ALASDAIR, *After Virtue: A Study in Moral Theory* (London: Duckworth, 1985).
MCLYNN, NEIL, *Ambrose of Milan: Church and Court in a Christian Capital* (Berkeley: University of California Press, 1984).
MARION, JEAN LUC, 'Saint Thomas d'Aquin et l'onto-théo-logie', *Revue Thomiste*, 95 (1995), 31–66.
MARKSCHIES, CHRISTOPH, *Ambrosius von Mailand und die Trinitätstheologie* (Tübingen: J. C. B. Mohr, 1995).
—— 'Was ist lateinischer "Neunizanismus"?', *Zeitschrift für Antikes Christentum*, 1 (1997), 73–95.
MARKUS, ROBERT, *The End of Ancient Christianity* (Cambridge: Cambridge University Press, 1990).
—— 'The Problem of Self-Definition: From Sect to Church', in E. P. Sanders (ed.), *Jewish and Christian Self-Definition*, i: *The Shaping of Christianity in the Second and Third Centuries* (London: SCM, 1980), 1–15.

MARKUS, ROBERT, *Signs and Meanings: World and Text in Ancient Christianity* (Liverpool: Liverpool University Press, 1996).
MARROU, H. I., *Education in Antiquity*, tr. George Lamb (Madison: University of Wisconsin Press, 1956).
MARSHALL, BRUCE D., 'Absorbing the World: Christianity and the Universe of Truths', in Bruce Marshall (ed.), *Theology and Dialogue: Essays in Conversation with George Lindbeck* (Notre Dame, Ind.: Notre Dame University Press, 1990), 69–102.
—— *Trinity and Truth* (Cambridge: Cambridge University Press, 2000).
—— 'The Trinity', in Gareth Jones (ed.), *The Blackwell Companion to Theology* (Oxford: Blackwell, 2004), 183–203.
MARTIN, ANNIK, *Athanase d'Alexandrie et l'Église d'Égypte au ive siècle* (Rome: École Française de Rome, 1996).
—— 'Le Fil d'Arius: 325–335', *Revue d'Histoire Ecclésiastique*, 84 (1989), 297–333.
MARTIN, DALE, 'Paul and the Judaism/Hellenism Dichotomy: Toward a Social History of the Question', in Troels Engberg-Pedersen (ed.), *Paul Beyond the Judaism/Hellenism Divide* (Louisville, Ky.: Westminster John Knox, 2001), 29–61.
MATTHEWS, JOHN, *Western Aristocracies and Imperial Court AD 364–425* (Oxford: Clarendon Press, 1975).
MAYER, CORNELIUS P. (ed.), *Augustinus Lexicon* (Stuttgart and Basle: Schwabe & Co., 1986).
MEIJERING, E. P., 'Athanasius on the Father as the Origin of the Son', *God, Being, History: Studies in Patristic Philosophy* (Amsterdam: North Holland, 1975), 89–102.
MEREDITH, ANTHONY, 'The Pneumatology of the Cappadocian Fathers and the Creed of Constantinople', *Irish Theological Quarterly*, 48 (1981), 196–212.
MERKI, H., *Homoiosis Theo. Von der platonischen Angleichung an Gott zur Gottahnlichkeit bei Gregor von Nyssa* (Fribourg, 1952).
MESLIN, MICHEL, *Les Ariens d'Occident* (Paris: Éditions du Seuil, 1967).
MILBANK, JOHN A., 'Divine Triads: Augustine and the Indo-European Soul', *Modern Theology*, 14 (1997), 451–74.
—— 'The Theological Critique of Philosophy in Hamann and Jacobi', in John Milbank *et al.* (eds.), *Radical Orthodoxy* (London and New York: Routledge, 1999), 21–37.
—— *The Word Made Strange* (Oxford: Blackwell, 1997).
MINGANA, A., *Woodbrooke Studies*, v: *Commentary of Theodore of Mopsuestia on the Nicene Creed* (Cambridge: Heffer, 1932).
MOINGT, JOSEPH, 'La Théologie trinitaire de S. Hilaire', *Hilaire et son Temps* (Paris, 1969), 159–73.
—— *Théologie Trinitaire de Tertullian*, 4 vols. (Paris: Aubier, 1966–9).
MOLTMANN, JÜRGEN, *History and the Triune God*, tr. John Bowden (London: SCM, 1990).
—— *The Trinity and the Kingdom of God*, tr. Margaret Kohl (London: SCM, 1981).

Moreschini, C., 'Luce e purificazione nella dottrine di Gregorio Nazianzeno', *Augustinianum*, 13 (1973).
Morgan, Teresa, *Literate Education in the Hellenistic and Roman Worlds* (Cambridge: Cambridge University Press, 1998).
Mortley, Raoul, *From Word to Silence*, ii: *The Way of Negation, Christian and Greek* (Bonn: Hanstein, 1986).
Mühlen, Heribert. 'Person und Appropriation', *Münchener Theologische Zeitschrift*, 16 (1965), 37–57.
Mühlenberg, Ekkehard, *Die Unendlichkeit Gottes bei Gregor von Nyssa* (Göttingen: Vandenhoeck & Ruprecht, 1966).
Muller, Richard A., *Post-Reformation Reformed Dogmatics*, 4 vols., 2nd edn. (Grand Rapids, Mich.: Baker, 2003).
——*Post-Reformed Dogmatics*, vol. ii: *Holy Scripture*, 2nd edn. (Grand Rapids, Mich.: Baker, 2003).
Neuschafer, Bernhardt, *Origenes als Philologe*, 2 vols. (Basle: Friedrich Reinhardt, 1987).
Newman, John Henry, *The Arians of the Fourth Century*, ed. Rowan Williams (Notre Dame, Ind.: Notre Dame University Press, 2001).
Norris, Frederick W., *Faith Gives Fullness to Reasoning: The Five Theological Orations of Gregory Nazianzen*, tr. Lionel Wickham and Frederick Williams (Leiden: Brill, 1991).
——'Of Thorns and Roses', *Church History*, 53 (1984), 455–64.
O'Keefe, John, 'A Letter that Killeth: Toward a Reassessment of Antiochene Exegesis', *JECS* 8 (2000), 83–104.
O'Leary, Joseph S., *Questioning Back* (Minneapolis: Winston Press, 1985).
Orbe, Antione, *La Epinoia: Algunos preliminaires históricos de la distinción kat' epinoian* (Rome, 1955).
O'Regan, Cyril, *Gnostic Return in Modernity* (Albany, NY: SUNY Press, 2001).
——*The Heterodox Hegel* (Albany, NY: SUNY Press, 1994).
Oroz Reta, J., 'De l'illumination à la déification de l'âme selon saint Augustin', *SP* 27 (1993), 364–82.
Osborn, Eric, *Tertullian, First Theologian of the West* (Cambridge: Cambridge University Press, 1997).
Owen, I., '$Ἐπινοέω, ἐπίνοια$ and Allied Words', *JThS* 35 (1934), 368–76.
Palanque, Jean-Rémy, et al., *The Church in the Christian Roman Empire*, tr. Ernest C. Messenger (London: Oates & Washbourne, 1949).
Pannenberg, Wolfhart, *Systematic Theology*, vol i, tr. G. W. Bromiley (Grand Rapids., Mich.: Eerdmans, 1991).
——*Theology and the Philosophy of Science*, tr. Francis McDonagh (Philadelphia: Westminster Press, 1976).
Patterson, Lloyd G., *Methodius of Olympus: Divine Sovereignty, Human Freedom, and Life in Christ* (Washington, DC: Catholic University of America Press, 1997).
——'Methodius, Origen and the Arian Dispute', *SP* 17/2 (1982), 912–23.
Paul, E., *Denkweg und Denkform der Theologie von Matthias Joseph Scheeben* (Munich: E. Hueber, 1970).

PLACHER, WILLIAM C., *A History of Christian Theology: An Introduction* (Philadelphia: Westminster Press, 1983).
PLANTINGA, CORNELIUS, 'Gregory of Nyssa and the Social Analogy of the Trinity', *Thomist*, 50 (1986), 325–52.
—— 'Social Trinity and Tritheism', in. R. J. Feenstra and C. Plantinga Jr. (eds.), *Trinity, Incarnation and Atonement: Philosophical and Theological Essays* (Notre Dame, Ind.: University of Notre Dame Press, 1989), 21–47.
POSSEKEL, UTE, *Evidence of Greek Philosophical Concepts in the Writings of Ephrem the Syrian*, CSCO subsidia, 102 (Louvain: Peeters, 1999).
POWELL, SAMUEL M., *The Trinity in German Thought* (Cambridge: Cambridge University Press, 2001).
PRESTIGE, GEORGE L., *God in Patristic Thought* (London: Heinemann, 1936).
—— *St. Basil the Great and Apollinaris* (London: SPCK, 1956).
QUASTEN, JOHANNES, *Patrology*, iii: *The Golden Age of Greek Patristic Literature* (Westminster, Md.: Christian Classics, 1992).
RAHNER, KARL, *Theological Investigations*, iv, tr. Kevin Smyth (Baltimore: Helicon Press, 1966).
—— *The Trinity*, tr. Joseph Donceel (London: Burns & Oates, 1970).
REBILLARD, ERIC, 'A New Style of Argument in Christian Polemic: Augustine and the Use of Patristic Citations', *JECS* 8 (2000), 559–70.
REILL, PETER, *The German Enlightenment and the Rise of Historicism* (Berkeley: University of California Press, 1975).
RIST, JOHN, 'Basil's "Neoplatonism": Its Background and Nature', in Paul J. Fedwick, *Basil of Caesarea: Christian, Humanist, Ascetic* (Toronto: Pontifical Institute of Medieval Studies, 1981), i. 137–220.
RITTER, ADOLF-MARTIN, *Das Konzil von Konstantinopel und sein Symbol*, Forschungen zur Kirchen- und Dogmengeschichte, 15 (Göttingen: Vandenhoeck & Ruprecht, 1965).
—— 'Zum homousios von Nizäa und Konstantinopel: Kritische Nachlese zu einigen neueren Diskussionen', in Adolf-Martin Ritter (ed.), *Kerygma und Logos: Beiträge zu den geistesgeschichtlichen Beziehungen zwischen Antike und Christentum. Festschrift für Carl Andresen zum 70* (Göttingen: Vandenhoeck & Ruprecht, 1979), 404–23.
ROBERTSON, DAVID G., 'Stoic and Aristotelian Notions of Substance in Basil of Caesarea', *VigChr* 52 (1998), 393–417.
ROGERS, EUGENE, 'How the Virtues of an Interpreter Presuppose and Perfect Hermeneutics: The Case of Thomas Aquinas', *Journal of Religion*, 76 (1996), 64–81.
—— 'Schleiermacher as an Anselmian Theologian: Apologetics, Dogmatics, Aesthetics, and Proof', *Scottish Journal of Theology*, 51 (1998), 342–79.
—— *Thomas Aquinas and Karl Barth: Sacred Doctrine and Natural Knowledge of God* (Notre Dame and London: Notre Dame University Press, 1995).

ROLDANUS, J., *Le Christ et le homme dans la théologie d'Athanase d'Alexandrie* (Leiden: Brill, 1968).
ROUSSEAU, PHILIP, *Basil of Caesarea* (Berkeley: University of California Press, 1994).
ROWE, WILLIAM V., 'Adolf von Harnack and the Concept of Hellenization', in Wendy Hellman (ed.), *Hellenization Revisited* (Lanham, Md.: University Press of America, 1994), 69–98.
RUSCH, WILLIAM G., *The Trinitarian Controversy*, Sources of Early Christian Thought (Phildelphia: Fortress Press, 1980).
RUSSELL, PAUL S., *St. Ephraem the Syrian and St. Gregory the Theologian Confront the Arians*, Mōrān 'Eth'ō 5 (Kottayam: St Ephrem Ecumenical Research Institute, 1994).
SANTER, MARK, and WILES, MAURICE (eds.), *Documents in Early Christian Thought* (New York: Cambridge University Press, 1975).
SCHEEBEN, MATTHIAS, *The Mysteries of Christianity*, tr. Cyril Vollert (St Louis and London: Herder, 1946).
SCHLABACH, GERALD, ' "Love is the Hand of the Soul": The Grammar of Continence in Augustine's Doctrine of Christian Love', *JECS* 6 (1998), 59–92.
SCHLITT, DALE M., *Hegel's Trinitarian Claim* (Leiden: Brill, 1984).
SCHMAUS, MICHAEL, *Dogma*, vol. i: *God in Revelation* (New York: Sheed & Ward, 1968).
SCHWARTZ, EDUARD, 'Über die Sammlung des Cod. Veronensis LX', *ZNTW* 35 (1936), 1–23.
SEIBT, KLAUS, 'Ein argumentum ad Constantium in der Logos- und Gotteslehre Markells von Ankyra', *SP* 26 (1993), 415–20.
—— *Die Theologie des Markell von Ankyra*, AKG 59 (Berlin: De Gruyter, 1994).
SELLERS, R. V., *Eustathius of Antioch* (Cambridge: Cambridge University Press, 1928).
SESBOÜÉ, BERNARD, *Saint Basile et La Trinité: Un acte théologique au IVe siècle* (Paris: Desclée, 1998).
SHERWOOD, POLYCARP, *The Earlier Ambigua of Maximus the Confessor*, Studia Anselmiana, 36 (Rome: Pontificum Institutum S. Anselmi, 1955).
SIEBEN, H.-J., *Die Konzilsidee der Alten Kirche* (Paderborn: Schöningh, 1979).
SIMONETTI, MANLIO, *La Crisi Ariana nel IV secolo*, Studia Ephemeridis Augustinianum, 11 (Rome: Augustinianum, 1975).
—— 'Dal Nicenismo al Neonicenismo: Rassegna di Alcune Pubblicazioni Recenti', *Augustinianum*, 38 (1998), 5–27.
SLUSSER, MICHAEL, 'The "To Philagrius On Consubstantiality" of Gregory Thaumaturgus', *SP* 19 (1989), 230–5.
—— 'Traditional Views of Late Arianism', in Michel Barnes and Daniel H. Williams (eds.), *Arianism after Arius* (Edinburgh: T. & T. Clark, 1993), 3–30.
SMULDERS, P., *La Doctrine trinitaire de S. Hilaire de Poitiers* (Rome, 1944).
SORABJI, RICHARD, *Matter, Space and Motion: Theories in Antiquity and their Sequel* (London: Duckworth, 1988).

SPANNEUT, MICHEL, 'La Position théologique d'Eustathe d'Antioche', *JThS* NS 5 (1954), 220–4.
——*Recherches sur les écrits d'Eustathe d'Antioche* (Lille, 1948).
SPOERL, KELLY MCCARTHY, 'The Schism at Antioch since Cavallera', in Michel Barnes and Daniel H. Williams (eds.), *Arianism after Arius: Essays on the Development of the Fourth Century Trinitarian Conflicts* (Edinburgh: T. & T. Clark, 1993), 101–26.
——*A Study of the* Kata Meros Pistis *by Apollonarius of Laodicea*, Ph.D. diss. (University of Toronto, 1991).
STAATS, REINHARD, *Das Glaubensbekenntnis von Nizäa-Konstantinopel. Historische unde theologische Grundlagen* (Darmstadt: Wissenschaftliche Buchgesellschaft, 1996).
STEAD, G. CHRISTOPHER, *Divine Substance* (Oxford: Clarendon Press, 1977).
——' "Eusebius" and the Council of Nicaea', *JThS* NS 24 (1973), 85–100.
——*Philosophy in Christian Antiquity* (Cambridge: Cambridge University Press, 1994).
——'The Platonism of Arius', *JThS* NS 15 (1964), 16–31.
——'Was Arius a Neoplatonist?', *SP* 33 (1997), 39–52.
——'Why not Three Gods? The Logic of Gregory of Nyssa's Trinitarian Doctrine', in Hubertus R. Drobner and Christoph Klock (eds.), *Studien zu Gregor von Nyssa und Die Christlichen Spätantike* (Leiden: Brill, 1990), 149–63.
STEENSON, JEFFERY N., 'Basil of Ancyra and the Course of Nicene Orthodoxy', D.Phil. diss. (Oxford, 1983).
——'Basil of Ancyra on the Meaning of *Homoousios*', in Robert C. Gregg (ed.), *Arianism: Historical and Theological Reassessments*, Patristic Monograph Series, 11 (Philadelphia: Philadelphia Patristic Foundation, 1985), 267–79.
STEPHENSON, A. A., 'St. Cyril of Jerusalem's Trinitarian Theology', *SP* 11 (1972), 234–41.
STEVENSON, J. (ed.), *A New Eusebius: Documents Illustrating the History of the Church to AD 337*, rev. W. H. C. Frend (London: SPCK, 1987).
STRANGE, STEPHEN, 'Plotinus, Porphyry, and the Neoplatonic Interpretation of the *Categories*', *ANRW* 2. 36. 2 (1987), 955–74
STRAUSS, G., *Schriftgebrauch, Schriftauslegung und Schriftbeweis bei Augustin* (Tübingen: J. C. B. Mohr, 1959).
STRUTWOLF, HOLGER, *Die Trinitätstheologie und Christologie des Euseb von Caesarea: Eine Dogmengeschichte Untersuchung seiner Platonismusrezeption und Wirkungsgeschichte* (Göttingen: Vandenhoeck & Ruprecht, 1999).
STUDER, BASIL, *The Grace of Christ and the Grace of God in Augustine of Hippo: Christcentrism or Theocentrism*, tr. M. J. O'Connell (Collegeville, Minn.: Liturgical Press, 1997).
——'History and Faith in Augustine's *De Trinitate*', *Augustinian Studies*, 28 (1997), 7–50.
——'La teologia trinitaria in Agostino d'Ippona: Continuità della tradizione occidentale?', in *Cristianesimo e specificità regionali nel mediter-*

raneo Latino (sec. IV–VI), Studia Ephemerides Augustinianum, 46 (Rome: Augustinianum, 1994), 161–77.
—— *Trinity and Incarnation: The Faith of the Early Church* (Edinburgh: T. & T. Clark, 1993).
—— 'Una Valutazione Critica del Neonicenismo', *Augustinianum*, 38 (1998), 29–48.
SULLIVAN, JOHN EDWARD, *The Image of God: The Doctrine of St. Augustine and its Influence* (Dubuque, Ia.: Priory Press, 1963).
SWEENEY, LEO, 'Augustine and Gregory of Nyssa: Is the Triune God Infinite in Being?', in Joseph T. Lienhard *et al.* (eds.), *Augustine: Presbyter Factus Sum* (New York: Peter Lang, 1993), 497–516.
—— 'Divine Attributes in *De doctrina Christiana*: Why does Augustine not List "Infinity"?' in Duane Arnold and Pamela Bright (eds.), *De Doctrina Christiana. A Classic of Western Culture* (Notre Dame, Ind.: University of Notre Dame Press, 1994), 195–204.
—— *Divine Infinity in Greek and Medieval Thought* (New York: Peter Lang, 1992)
SWINBURNE, RICHARD, *The Christian God* (Oxford: Clarendon Press, 1994).
TANNER, KATHRYN, 'Theology and the Plain Sense', in Garret Green (ed.), *Scriptural Authority and Narrative Interpretation* (Philadelphia: Fortress Press, 1987), 59–87.
—— *Theories of Culture: A New Agenda for Theology* (Philadelphia: Fortress Press, 1997).
TESKE, ROLAND, 'St. Augustine and the Vision of God', in Frederick Van Fleteren *et al.* (eds.), *Augustine: Mystic and Mystagogue* (New York: Peter Lang, 1994), 287–308.
TETZ, MARTIN, 'Ante omnia de sancta fide et de integritate veritatis: Glaubensfragen auf der Synode von Serdica (342)', *ZNTW* 76 (1985), 243–69.
—— 'Ein enzyklisches Schreiben der Synode von Alexandrien (362)', *ZNTW* 79 (1988), 262–81.
—— 'Markellianer und Athanasios von Alexandrien: Die markellianische Expositio fidei ad Athanasium des Diakons Eugenios von Ankyra', *ZNTW* 64 (1973), 75–121.
THIEL, JOHN, *Imagination and Authority: Theological Authorship in the Modern Tradition* (Minneapolis: Fortress Press, 1991).
THOMPSON, MARIANNE MEYE, *The God of the Gospel of John* (Grand Rapids Mich.: Eerdmans, 2001).
TILLICH, PAUL, *Systematic Theology*, vol. i (Chicago: University of Chicago Press, 1951).
TORJESEN, KAREN J., *Hermeneutical Procedure and Theological Method in Origen's Exegesis* (Berlin: De Gruyter, 1986).
TORRANCE, THOMAS F., *The Trinitarian Faith* (Edinburgh: T. & T. Clark, 1988).
TROIANO, MARINA, 'Il Contra Eunomium III di Basilio di Cesarea e le Epistolae ad Serapionem I–IV di Atanasio di Alexandria—nota comparativa', *Augustinianum*, 41 (2001), 59–91

TURCESCU, LUCIAN, 'The Concept of Divine Persons in Gregory of Nyssa's *To his Brother Peter, On the Difference between Ousia and Hypostasis*', *Greek Orthodox Theological Review*, 42 (1997), 63–82.
—— ' "Person" versus "Individual", and other Modern Misreadings of Gregory of Nyssa', *Modern Theology*, 18 (2002), 527–39.
—— '*Prosōpon* and *Hypostasis* in Basil of Caesarea's *Against Eunomius* and the Epistles', *VigChr* 51 (1997), 374–95.
ULRICH, JÖRG, *Die Anfänge der Abendländischen Rezeption des Nizänums* (Berlin: De Gruyter, 1994).
VAGGIONE, RICHARD P. C., *Eunomius of Cyzicus and the Nicene Revolution* (Oxford: Oxford University Press, 2000).
VAGGIONE, RICHARD P. C., 'Οὐχ ὡς ἕν τῶν γεννηματῶν: Some Aspects of Dogmatic Formulae in the Arian Controversy', *SP* 17 (1982), 181–7.
VALLIERE, PAUL, *Modern Russian Theology: Bukharev, Soloviev, Bulgakov. Orthodox Theology in a New Key* (Grand Rapids, Mich.: Eerdmans, 2000).
VAN BAVEL, TARCISIUS J., 'God In Between Affirmation and Negation According to Augustine', in J. Lienhard, E. Muller, R. Teske (eds.), *Collectanea Augustiniana: Augustine, Presbyter Factus Sum* (New York: Peter Lang, 1993), 73–97.
—— *Recherches sur la christologie de saint Augustin*, Paradosis 19 (Fribourg: Éditions Universitaires, 1954).
VAN DAM, RAYMOND, 'Emperor, Bishops, and Friends in Late Antique Cappadocia', *JThS* NS 37 (1986), 53–76.
—— *Families and Friends in Late Roman Cappadocia* (Philadelphia: University of Pennsylvania Press, 2003).
VANNIER, MARIE-ANNE, *'Creatio', 'conversio', 'formatio', chez S. Augustin* (Fribourg: Éditions Universitaires, 1991).
VESSEY, MARK, *Ideas of Christian Writing in Late Roman Gaul*, D.Phil. diss. (Oxford University, 1988).
VINZENT, MARKUS, *Asterius von Kappadokien: Die Theologische Fragmente. Einleitung, Kritischer Text, Übersetzung und Kommentar* (Leiden: Brill, 1993).
—— *Markell von Ankyra: Die Fragmente und Der Brief an Julius von Rom* (Leiden: Brill, 1997).
VOLF, MIROSLAV, *After Our Likeness: The Church as the Image of the Trinity* (Grand Rapids, Mich.: Eerdmans, 1998).
VON BALTHASAR, HANS URS, *Presence and Thought: An Essay on the Religious Philosophy of Gregory of Nyssa*, tr. Mark Sebanc (San Francisco: Ignatius Press, 1995).
WEBSTER, JOHN, *Holy Scripture: A Dogmatic Sketch* (Cambridge: Cambridge University Press, 2003).
WELCH, CLAUDE, *In This Name: The Doctrine of the Trinity in Contemporary Theology* (New York: Charles Scribner's, 1952).
WHITE, HAYDEN, *Metahistory: The Historical Imagination in Nineteenth-Century Europe* (Baltimore: Johns Hopkins University Press, 1972).
WHITE, JOSEPH M., *The Diocesan Seminary in the United States. A History*

from the 1780s to the Present (Notre Dame, Ind.: University of Notre Dame Press, 1989).
WICKHAM, LIONEL, 'The Syntagmation of Aetius the Anomean', *JThS* NS 19 (1968), 532–69.
WIDDICOMBE, PETER, *The Fatherhood of God from Origen to Athanasius* (Oxford: Clarendon Press, 1994).
WILES, MAURICE, *Archetypal Heresy: Arianism through the Centuries* (Oxford: Clarendon Press, 1996).
—— 'Eunomius: Hair-Splitting Dialectitian or Defender of the Accessibility of Salvation?', in Rowan Williams (ed.), *The Making of Orthodoxy: Essays in Honour of Henry Chadwick* (Cambridge: Cambridge University Press, 1989), 157–72.
WILKEN, ROBERT L., 'In Defense of Allegory', *Modern Theology*, 14 (1998), 197–212.
WILLIAMS, DANIEL H., *Ambrose of Milan and the End of the Arian–Nicene Conflicts* (Oxford: Clarendon Press, 1995).
—— 'Constantine and the "Fall" of the Church', in Lewis Ayres and Gareth Jones (eds.), *Christian Origins: Theology, Rhetoric and Community* (London: Routledge, 1998), 117–36.
—— 'Defining Orthodoxy in Hilary of Poitiers' Commentarium in Matthaeum', *JECS* 9 (2001), 151–71.
—— 'A Reassessment of the Early Career and Exile of Hilary of Poitiers', *Journal of Ecclesiastical History*, 42 (1991), 202–17.
—— *Retrieving the Tradition and Renewing Evangelicalism: A Primer for Suspicious Protestants* (Grand Rapids, Mich.: Eerdmans, 1999).
WILLIAMS, ROWAN D., 'Angels Unawares: Heavenly Liturgy and Earthly Theology in Alexandria', *SP* 30 (1997), 350–63.
—— *Arius: Heresy and Tradition* (London: DLT, 1987).
—— 'Arius and the Melitian Schism', *JThS* NS 37 (1986), 35–52.
—— 'Barth on the Triune God', in Stephen Sykes (ed.), *Karl Barth: Studies of his Theological Method* (Oxford: Clarendon Press, 1979), 147–93.
—— 'Doctrinal Criticism: Some Questions', in Sarah Coakley and David Pailin (eds.), *The Making and Remaking of Christian Doctrine* (Oxford: Clarendon Press, 1993), 239–64.
—— ' "Good for Nothing"? Augustine on Creation', *Augustinian Studies*, 25 (1994), 9–24.
—— 'Language, Reality and Desire in Augustine's *De doctrina*', *Literature and Theology*, 3 (1989), 138–50.
—— 'The Logic of Arianism', *JThS* NS 34 (1983), 56–81.
—— 'Origen: Between Orthodoxy and Heresy', in W. A. Bienert and U. Kuhneweg (eds.), *Origeniana Septima: Origenes in den Auseinandersetzungen des 4. Jahrhunderts*, BETL CXXXVII (Leuven: Leuven University Press, 1999), 3–14.
—— 'Origen on the Soul of Jesus', in Richard P. C. Hanson and Henri Crouzel, (eds.), *Origeniana Tertia* (Rome: Edizioni dell'Ateneo, 1985), 131–7.
—— '*Sapientia* and the Trinity: Reflections on the *De trinitate*', in B. Bruning *et al.* (eds.), *Collectanea Augustiniana: Mélanges T. J. Van Bavel*

(Leuven: Leuven University Press, 1990) (=*Augustiniana*, 40–1 (1990–1)), i, 317–32.
—— 'The Son's Knowledge of the Father in Origen', in L. Lies (ed.), *Origeniana Quarta*, Innsbrucker theologische Studien, 19 (Innsbruck: Tyrolia, 1987), 146–53.
WILLIAMS, S., and Friell, G., *Theodosius: The Empire at Bay* (New Haven: Yale University Press, 1995).
WILSON-KASTNER, P., 'Grace and Participation in the Divine Life in the Theology of Augustine of Hippo', *Augustinian Studies*, 7 (1976) 135–5.
WIMBUSH, VINCENT, 'The Bible and African Americans: An Outline of an Interpretive History', in Cain Hope Felder (ed.), *Stony the Road we Trod* (Minneapolis: Fortress Press, 1991), 81–97.
WINSLOW, DONALD F., *The Dynamics of Salvation: A Study in Gregory of Nazianzus*, Patristic Monograph Series, 7 (Philadelphia: Philadelphia Patristic Foundation, 1979).
YOUNG, FRANCES, *Biblical Exegesis and the Formation of Christian Culture* (Cambridge: Cambridge University Press, 1997).
—— 'The Rhetorical schools and their Influence on Patristic Exegesis', in Rowan D. Williams (ed.), *The Making of Orthodoxy: Essays in Honour of Henry Chadwick* (Cambridge: Cambridge University Press, 1989), 182–99.
YOUSIF, P., 'Symbolisme christologique dans la Bible et dans la nature chez s. Ephrem de Nisibe', *Parole d'Orient*, 8 (1977), 5–66.
ZACHHUBER, JOHANNES, *Human Nature in Gregory of Nyssa: Philosophical Background and Theological Significance* (Leiden: Brill, 2000).
ZEILLER, J., *Les Origines Chrétiennes dans les provinces danubiennes de l'empire romain* (Paris: De Boccard, 1918).
ZIZIOULAS, JOHN D., *Being as Communion* (Crestwood, NY: SVS Press, 1985).

Index

Acacius of Caesarea 117, 138, 140, 141, 150, 154, 161, 162–4, 169, 170, 171, 172, 198
Acholius of Thessalonica 51, 251, 254
Activity, *see* ἐνέργεια
Adoptionism 72, 74–5, 161
Aetius 138, 145–6, 149, 150, 153, 188, 230–1, 433
Aetius of Thessalonica 51
ἀγέννητος / ἀγένητος 112–13, 143–4, 146, 147–8, 149
ἀκρίβεια 236
Albinus 149
Alexander of Alexandria 15–20, 88, 89, 95, 98, 100, 106, 107, 113, 135, 147, 154, 190, 430
  theology of 43–5
Alexander of Byzantium 43
Alexander of Thessalonica 51–2
Alston, W. 389
Althaus, H. 248
Amand de Mendieta, E. 218, 228–9
Ambramowski, L. 225, 256
Ambrose of Milan 89, 183, 198, 260, 261–7, 269, 279, 287, 290, 334, 335, 367, 368, 369, 371, 434
  De fide 262–4
  Myst. 327–8
  Spir. 264–5, 328
Amphilochius of Iconium 195–6, 199, 210, 215, 219, 224–5, 244, 250
Anastos, M. 191
Anatalios, K. 47
ἀνόμοιος 116, 145, 162, 194
Anthimus of Tyana 223, 224
Antioch, divisions in 69, 174–6, 226–8, 266
Antiochus of Ascalon 199
ἀπαράλλακτος 44–6, 118, 189
  in Asterius 54
Apollinaris of Laodicea 202, 205–6, 207, 225, 228
  and Basil 189–90

'Arian' as polemical category, *see* polemic
'Arian' conspiracy after Nicaea? 105–6
Aristotle 93–5, 200–1, 202
  Arius-Didymus 192
Arius of Alexandria 76, 94, 97, 103, 107, 108–9, 111, 120, 124, 125, 135, 141, 145, 147, 149, 182, 190, 193, 328, 425, 430, 431, 432
  after Nicaea 100–1
  and events AD 318–25 15–20
  theology 54–7
Asceticism 219–20, 225
  definition 343
  influence on Pro-Nicene orthodoxy 342–3
  intrinsic to faith 352–3
Asclepas of Gaza 105
Asterius the Sophist 102, 107, 111, 119, 120, 141, 193
  in Athanasius, *C. Ar.* 116–7
  theology of 53–4
Atarbius of Neocaesarea 224
Athanasius of Alexandria 43, 77, 78, 90, 99, 100, 102–3, 104, 105, 118, 120, 122, 123, 124, 126, 127, 129, 134, 136, 137, 147, 152, 154, 158, 163, 165, 167, 168, 171–7, 184, 186, 187, 193, 196–8, 211, 217–18, 222, 231, 234, 236–9, 242, 245, 246, 256, 260, 268–9, 280, 290, 293, 295, 326, 392, 431, 432, 433, 434, 435
  and 'Arian' as polemical term 106–9
  Apol sec. 108–9
  and Basil 227–8
  C. Ar 110–17
  Cath, ep. 173
  Decr. 140–4
  early allegiance to Nicaea 115
  early theology 45–8
  with Marcellus in Rome 106–7
  Serap. 211–14
  Synod. 171–3
  Tom. 174–6

Athanasius of Alexandria (*cont.*)
  various exiles 140
Augustine of Hippo 32, 214, 246, 265,
    267, 269, 274, 279, 280, 283, 289,
    290, 291, 295, 296, 297, 299, 300,
    308–12, 326, 334, 335, 338, 340–1,
    344, 364–83, 389, 392, 413, 417,
    418, 434, 435
  on aesthetics of faith 329–30
  Conf. 366–7
  on divine simplicity 375–81
  Ep. 11: 369–70
  Ep. 120: 375
  F. et symb. 370–2
  Gn. litt. 317–20
  grammar of trinitarian belief 372–81
  modern critique of 364–5
  and platonism 365–8
  on purification for theology 382–3
  Serm. 52: 372–4
  Trin. 375–81
Auxentius of Milan 260, 261
Ayres, L. 20, 96, 143, 273, 284, 291,
    300, 306, 307, 309, 313, 320, 329,
    364, 365, 366, 368, 374, 381, 382

Balás, D. 306
Bardy, G. 13, 57
Barnard, L. 49, 123
Barnes, T. D. 102, 103, 108, 133, 135,
    140, 144, 152, 173, 241, 242
Barnes, M. R. 11, 22, 23, 41, 54, 58, 59,
    108, 125, 147, 182, 214, 215, 236,
    239–40, 282, 283, 291, 303, 326,
    353–5, 364, 366, 413
Barsai of Edessa 230
Barth, K. 402, 408
Barthes, R. 275
Basil of Ancyra 134, 139, 143, 150, 162,
    186, 188, 190, 193, 194, 197, 198,
    214, 226, 433
  and Athanasius 172–3
  theology of 150–2
Basil of Caesarea 159, 169, 168, 176,
    186, 187–229, 233, 242, 245, 246,
    247, 250, 257, 258, 261, 264, 273,
    279, 282, 290, 292–3, 313, 334, 344,
    345, 352, 359, 362, 368, 418, 433,
    434
  and Aristotle 200–1
  Eunom. 191–209
  Hex. 314–17
  and Homoiousians 188–9

  on knowledge and faith 196–7
  political activity 222–9
  Spir. 215–20
  and Stoicism 199–200
Bauer, F. C. 396
Bauer, W. 78*ff*
Bauerschmidt, F. 403
Beck, E. 231, 233, 235
Behr, J. 22, 76, 94
Benjamin, W. 422
Bernardi, J. 244
Blowers, P. 79
Bonner, G. 311
Bourdieu, P. 275–6, 393
Bowersock, G. 168
Boys-Stones, G. R. 199
Brakke, D. 17, 43
Brennecke, H. C. 12, 57, 109, 137, 138,
    160, 162, 164, 169, 170,
Brock, S. 228, 232
Brown, D. 384
Brown, P. 81, 328, 342
Buckley, M. 403
Burns, P. 179
Burns, T. 240
Burrell, D. 285, 287–8, 296, 323–4,
    381–2, 408
Burrus, V. 81

Cameron, A. 82, 342
Cameron, M. 340–1
Capánaga, V. 311
Cappadocians 145, 187, 205, 236–8,
    268, 345, 362–3, 389, 413
  as a unified group 250–1,
    292–3
Carey, P. 400
Cartwright, M. 402
Cassian 219
Cavalcanti, E. 145
Cavallera, F. 151
Cavanaugh, W. 403
Certeau, M. de 275, 276, 384, 422
Chadwick, H. 18, 108
Chevalier, I. 376
Childs, B. 32
Christ
  role in salvation *c.* 300 76–8
  soul of 29–30, 76–80
  texts referring to incarnate Christ,
    not Word in Alexander 44; in
    Athanasius 113–14
  see also Son, Word

Cicero 368
Cipriani, N. 368
Clark, E. 20, 32, 277, 422
Clement of Alexandria 193
Coakley, S. 289, 403
Coffey, D. 385
Congar, Y. 399, 401, 420, 421
Consentius 273
Constans, Emperor 103, 110, 121–3, 126–7, 129–30, 133
Constantine II, Emperor 103, 104, 110, 133
Constantine, Emperor 99, 100–1, 103, 136
  and Council of Nicaea 17–20, 87–9, 90–1
Constantius, Emperor 103, 117, 122, 123, 127, 129–30, 136, 138, 139, 140, 149, 150, 152, 153, 157, 158, 161, 163, 167, 171, 177, 178, 240, 432, 433
  religious policy 133–4
Corsini, E. 350
Councils:
  Alexandria (339) 109
  Alexandria (362) 173–4, 211
  Ancyra (358) 149–50
  Antioch (268) 79–80, 86
  Antioch (325) 18, 50–1, 86
  Antioch (341) 117–22, 163
  Antioch (349) 144
  Antioch (379) 242
  Aquileia (381) 265–6
  Ariminum (359) 160–1, 173
  Arles (353) 135, 136
  Caesarea (334) 102
  Chalcedon (451) 253
  Constantinople (381) 239, 253–60, 265, 266
  Constantinople (382) 258–9
  Constantinople (553) 421
  Constantinople (360) 164
  Jerusalem (335) 103
  Lampsacus (364) 170
  Milan (355) 135, 136–7
  Milan (345) 129
  Nicaea (325) 18–20, 85–100, 230, 430; course of 88–92; difference between 'judgments' and 'terms' 87, 135–6
  Paris (360) 177–8
  Rome (340) 109
  Rome (377) 261

Seleucia (359) 154, 158, 160, 161–4, 173
Serdica (343) 110, 122–6; Text of 'western' definition of faith 99
Sirmium (351) 134–5
Sirmium (357) 179; text of 'blasphemy' 137–8, 150, 179, 432
Sirmium (358) 152
Tyana (366) 170
Tyre (335) 102–3, 108
Vatican II (1962–65) 400–1
Councils
  before Nicaea 86–7
  function of in general 79ff
Cramer, P. 328
Creeds
  Antioch (325) 99; text 50–1
  Antioch (341) 'Dedication' 144, 153, 154, 179, 243, 432, 435; text 118–9
  Antioch (341) (4th creed) 134, 153 165; text 121–2
  appropriate attention to in modern theology 420–1
  Baptismal creeds 85–6
  Constantinople (360) 158, 189; text 164–5
  Constantinople (381) 254, 336; relationship to Nicaea 255–8; text 255
  fluidity of in mid-4th century 162–3
  'Macrostich' (345) 127, 135, 144, 147
  Nicaea (325) 108, 138, 139–40, 160–1, 163, 167, 169–71, 211, 255–7, 260, 430, 433–4; as minimum condition for communion among pro-Nicenes 171–5, 178, 89, 215, 252; as standard of faith 85–6; at Antioch (341) 119–20; attacked at Sirmium (351) 134–5; Old "Nicene" theology? 98–100, 239; status in West before 360: 126, 135–6, 137; text 19
  Sirmium (359) 'Dated' 158, 160, 161, 164, 165
Crouzel, H. 22
Culture
  defined 12, 274–8
  of systematic theology 385, 386–7, 398
Cunningham, D. 389
Cyprian of Carthage 70, 312
Cyril of Alexandria 213, 268–9, 434

Cyril of Jerusalem 153–7, 164, 336
  Cat. lect. 154–7

Daley, B. 210
Damasus of Rome 184, 227, 228–9,
  242, 251, 260–1, 279, 280
Daniélou, J. 149, 338
Davidson, D. 419
Dawson, D. 22, 32, 37–8
De Halleux, A. 11, 246–7, 259
De Lubac, H. 31, 402, 420, 426–7
De Régnon, T. 302–4, 412
De Riedmatten, H. 189
Declerck, J. 68
Demophilus of Constantinople 253
Dianius of Caesarea 188
Didymus the Blind 264, 268–9, 279,
  280, 286, 371, 434
Dillon, J. 199
Diodore of Tarsus 250, 254, 268
Diogenes Laertius 192
Dionysius of Alexandria 48, 93–4,
  147
Dionysius of Milan 137
Dionysius of Rome 93–4
Dixon, P. 407
Doignon, J. 75, 179
Dorner, I. 407
Dörrie, H. 92
Doval, A. 154
Drecoll, V. H. 187–8, 189, 192, 200,
  211, 221, 238
Drey, J. S. 396
Drobner, H. 35
δύναμις (power) 23, 41, 44, 205,
  216, 239–40, 252, 262–3, 279,
  298, 314–5, 348, 357–8, 361–2
  377
  many in Asterius 53–4
  many in Eusebius 58–9
  and nature in Gregory of Nyssa
    350–4
  and nature in Hilary 182
Duval, Y. M. 161

East / West divisions, see Greek / Latin
  divisions
Edwards, M. 22, 23, 30, 91
Egan, J. 244, 246, 248–9
ἐκ τῆς οὐσίας 97, 114–15, 120, 140–2,
  171–2, 256
Eleusis of Cyzicus 162–3
Elm, S. 81, 151, 188, 225, 343

ἐνέργεια (activity) 56, 63–5, 147–8,
  151–2, 172, 195–8, 214, 215–6
  and δύναμις 354–5
Engberg-Pedersen, T. 389
ἔννοια see ἐπίνοια
Ephrem the Syrian 198, 229–35, 326
Epicurus 192
ἐπίνοια/ἔννοια 25, 151, 159, 191–6, 233,
  250, 340, 352, 418
Epiphanius of Salamis 103, 150, 151,
  152, 158, 159–60, 172, 173, 206,
  279, 295, 326
Eternal generation, see Son of God
Eudoxius of Antioch/Constantinople
  138, 139, 146, 150, 152, 153, 161,
  164, 169, 170, 231
Eufrata 75
Eunomius of Cyzicus 138, 145, 149,
  150, 153, 164, 193, 194, 195, 204,
  215, 241, 243, 250, 293, 297, 346,
  354, 433
  theology of 146–8
Eusebius of Caesarea 17, 18, 52, 76, 87,
  89, 96–7, 101, 111, 119, 120, 138,
  147, 149, 154, 172, 188, 197, 201,
  212–13, 392
  Ep. Caes. 140–4
  at Nicaea 90–1
  theology of 58–60
Eusebius of Nicomedia 19, 88, 94, 97,
  100, 101, 102, 105–6, 107, 109, 117,
  154
  theology of 52–3
'Eusebian' as category, defined 52
Eusebius of Samosata 211, 226–7, 228,
  229, 241, 242
Eusebius of Vercelli 136, 137, 178, 183,
  261, 434
Eustathius of Antioch 68–9, 76, 89, 95,
  99, 101, 102, 105, 175–6, 205
  as anti-Arian writer 107–8
Eustathius of Sebaste 188, 191, 205,
  215, 225, 226, 228, 243
Evagrius (translator) 227
Evagrius Ponticus 219, 250
Evans, E. 70, 74
Exegesis (see also Pro-Nicenes)
  categories for understanding 31–40
  categories of Antiochene and
    Alexandrian 31, 40, 336–9
  and contemplation 389–90, 416–20
  and definition of orthodoxy
    c. 300–400 79–81

in modernity 387–8, 397, 401,
418–19
and philosophy 39–40, 388–92
and a possible new theological culture
415–20

Farley, E. 387, 393
Father
Father as 'personal' source in John
Zizioulas 313
Father as source 16, 27, 237, 357,
378–80; in Basil and Pro-Nicenes
206–7; in Ephrem 233–4; in
Gregory of Nazianzus 248
Father / Son terminology
correlativity of terms 44, 72, 73; in
Alexander 44; in Athanasius 46,
111–12, Son as ἴδιος to Father 114;
in Basil of Ancyra 152; criticized
42; in Cyril of Jeruslem 155–7; in
George of Laodicea 159, 201; as
not implying two co-eternal
principles 44, 72; in Origen 22–3,
97; not used in Aetius 146
Father perfect with Son; in Ambrose
264; in Athanasius 46, 245, 264; in
Basil 206–7; in Gregory of
Nazianzus 245
used to indicate distinction of
persons in Pro-Nicenes 236
Fehr, W. L. 396
Felix of Rome 260
Fiedrowicz, M. 311
Flavian of Antioch 253, 254
Florensky, P. 11
Florovsky, G. 413
Fowl, Stephen E. 32, 403, 415, 419
Frei, H. 397, 403
Fulkerson, M. 402
φύσις 44, 45, 59, 127, 174, 175, 209,
245, 258, 279, 363

Garrigou 413
Garrigou-Lagrange, R. 399, 413
Gatti, M. 199
Gelasius 100
Generation (of Son)
in Ambrose 264, 287
in Athanasius 111–12, 175
in Augustine 378–9
in Basil of Ancyra 151–2, 197
in Basil of Caesarea 197–8, 206–7
in Cyril of Alexandria 155–7

distinction from creation 125
and divine simplicity in pro-Nicenes
286–7
eternal 71, 236, 264–5; in Alexander
45; at Nicaea 91; in Origen 22
from will of God 53, 58, 129, 264,
287; in Aetius 146; in Arius 55; in
Eunomius 147, 198; in Origen 27
in Hilary 181, 184, 286–7
two fundamental trends 41–3
George of Laodicaea 14, 171, 201, 203,
206
theology of 158–60
Giet, S. 314
Girardet, K. M. 135
Goldstein, J. 395
Golitzin, A. 273
grammar, see Trinity
Grant, R. 22
Gratian, Emperor 241, 242, 253, 260,
264, 265, 266
Greek / Latin (and East / West) as
marker of division 6, 109–10,
273–4, 290, 300–1, 302–4, 344–5,
363–5, 388, 413
Gregg, R. 55–6, 77, 154
Gregory of Elvira 178, 375
Gregory of Nazianzus the Elder 188,
226
Gregory of Nazianzus 170, 188, 193,
197, 198, 215–16, 217, 222, 223,
224, 226, 227, 242, 266, 279, 280,
284–5, 289, 290, 295, 300, 304, 325,
326, 334, 376, 417, 434, 435
and Council of Constantinople (381)
253–5
Or. 244–51, 330–3, 346–7
Gregory of Nyssa 196, 203, 210, 214,
215, 216, 217, 223, 233, 241, 243,
245, 246, 250, 257, 258, 260, 274,
279, 280, 281, 282, 283, 285, 286,
289–91, 295–6, 300, 326, 330, 336,
383, 392, 418, 420, 434, 435
Ablab. 344–63
on appropriation 297–9
Cat. or. 306–7
In 1 Cor. 15 305–6
Mort. 333–5
Petr. 293–4
on Trinitarian theology 344–63
Gregory Thaumaturgus 49–50,
218
Grenz, S. 388

Gribomont, J. 188
Griffith, S. H. 230, 231
Grillmeier, A. 49, 77
Groh, D. 55–6, 77
Gross, J. 306
Gryson, R. 138, 266
Gunton, C. 384

Haight, R. 388
Hall, S. 125, 126
Halvini, D. W. 35
Hamman, A. G. 326
Hammerstaedt, J. 92
Hanson, R. P. C. 12, 17, 18, 19, 21, 31, 48, 53, 57, 58, 59, 68, 70, 76, 88, 92, 93, 100, 102, 105, 109, 118, 119, 120–1, 123, 124, 126, 127, 133, 134, 135, 137, 138, 140, 145, 151, 152, 154, 158, 160, 173, 175, 176, 179, 183, 187, 211, 214, 218, 223, 238, 242, 253, 254, 255, 266, 302, 303, 428
Harnack, A. von 31, 49, 237, 238
Harrison, C. 320
Harrison, V. 306
Hauerwas, S. 421
Hauschild, W.-D. 211
Haykin, M. 211
Heather, P. 240
Hefele, J. 170
Hegel, G. W. F. 220, 404–7, 408, 429
Heil, U. 48
Hellenization 31–2
Heppe, H. 402
Heresy, notion of 78*ff*
Hess, H. 86–7, 123
Heterousians (inc. 'Eunomians,' 'Anomoians,' 'Neo-Arians') 139, 144–9, 158, 169, 231, 243, 259–60, 268, 332, 376
 See also Eunomius, Aetius, ἀνόμοιος
Hilary of Poitiers 70, 75, 120, 123, 124, 127, 136, 138, 139, 162, 163, 168, 177–86, 214, 239, 246, 260, 261, 263, 286–7, 367, 368, 369, 434
 De trin. 180–5
 exiled 137
 Synod. 179–80
 theology of 179–85
Historicism, modern 393–4, 395–7
 and development of doctrine 426–9
 and plain sense of Scripture 421–3

Hodgson P. 396
Holifield, E. B. 395
Holl, K. 210, 225, 361–3
Holmes, A. 188
Homoians 42, 144–5, 149–50, 158, 162, 162–4, 165, 169, 176–7, 197, 222, 230–1, 260, 261–2, 265–7, 269, 376, 433
 defined 138–9
 prefigured in Macrostich 128
 ὅμοιος κατ' οὐσίαν 146, 151, 154, 172, 189, 204, 243
Homoiousians 163, 164, 165, 167, 170–1, 177, 179, 184, 194, 196–7, 214–15, 216, 237, 243, 249, 253–8, 433
 appealed to by Athanasius 171–3
 theology of 149–53
Homoiousios 138, 150, 162, 167
Homoousios 23, 25–7, 101, 115, 138, 146, 160, 162, 171–2, 189–90, 195, 237, 243, 252, 430, 431
 in Arius 55
 Athanasius's initial defense of 140–4
 background to 4th century usage 93–4
 in Basil of Caesarea 205–6
 at Nicaea 89–91, 95–7
Hübner, R. 68, 200, 293, 305, 362
Humfress, C. 252
Hunt, E. D. 153
Hyposatsis 45, 54, 55, 57, 59, 63, 69, 118, 125, 128–9, 155–6, 159, 160, 189, 202–3, 238, 258, 259, 280, 294, 363
 in Athanasius 47–8, 174–5
 in Basil 209–10
 at Nicaea 98
 in Origen 25–6

Iamblichus 201
ἰδιώματα / ἰδιότητες 159, 191–204, 258
ἴδιος 114–5
Ignatius of Antioch 312
Image terminology 22, 51, 58–9, 120, 122, 128, 141, 194–5, 304
Incomprehensibility
 of divine nature 142, 155, 282–4, 331–2, 351–2, 355–6, 359, 360–1, 307–8, 379
 of divine persons 292–4

of nature 191, 192, 234, 354
  of soul 307, 334
Ingenerate, *see* ἀγέννητος / ἀγένητος
Inglis, J. 399
Inseparable operations, *see* operations, of divine persons
Irenaeus 212, 213
Irvine, M. 35

Jacob of Nisibis 230
Jenson, R. W. 384, 406
Jerome 151, 154, 229, 250, 264, 269, 371
John Chrysostom 268
  Incomp. 338–9
John Damascene 113
Johnson, E. 409
Jones, A. H. M. 223
Jovian, Emperor 169
Julian, Emperor 167, 168–9, 170, 177, 178, 201, 230, 240
Julius of Rome 109, 110, 117, 126, 136, 140
Jüngel, E. 389, 406

Kannengiesser, C. 110
Kant, I. 405, 408–9, 412
Kasper, W. 388, 412
Kaster, R. 35
Kelly, J. N. D. 86, 88, 253, 255–6
King, R. Q. 241
Kinzig, W. 53
Klein, R. 133
Koonamakkal, T. 232
Kopecek, T. A. 53, 113, 125, 128, 144, 145, 146, 149, 152, 191, 192, 242, 243

Lactantius 70–1,
  theology of 72–3
LaCugna, C. M. 364, 384, 389, 408, 409, 412
Lang, U. 76
Lash, N. 403, 426, 429
Le Boulluec, A. 79
Lebon, J. 154
Leontius of Antioch 127
Leroux, J. M. 138
Levering, M. 389, 403
Levine, J. 393
Liberius of Rome 136, 137, 170, 177, 178, 228, 243, 260
Lienhard, J. T. 11, 41, 52, 53, 58, 62, 64, 102, 106, 119, 138, 203, 363

Light, terminology of 23, 41–2, 48–9, 50–1, 58, 74, 111, 115–16, 120, 141, 190, 212, 233–4, 247–9, 279, 330–1
Lim, R. 81, 333
Lindbeck, G. 403
Lipatov, N. A. 191
Liturgy 56, 218–20
Logan, A. H. B. 18, 19, 22, 23, 25, 62
Logos, see Word
Löhr, W. 150, 158
Loofs, F. 237
Lorenz, R. 68
Lossky, V. 303, 365, 413
Lot-Borodine, M. 306
Louth, A. 34, 115, 386
Lucian of Antioch 17, 52, 57, 119, 120, 145
Lucifer of Cagliari 136, 137, 176, 226
Luibeheid, C. 58
Lyman, R. 21, 58, 79, 106

Macarius of Jerusalem 154
Macedonius of Constantinople, Macedonians 164, 214–18, 345–7
MacIntyre, A. 402
Magnentius, imperial pretender 133
Manicheasim 47, 93, 107
Marcellus of Ancyra 18, 50, 76–7, 89, 95, 96, 97, 99 101, 102, 103, 104, 105, 107, 108, 109, 117, 124, 126, 136, 150, 157, 160, 197, 227, 431, 435
  on eschatology 66–7
  later followers 250
  on power and energy 64–5
  precedents for 67–8
  theology of 62–8
  see also polemic
Marion, J.-L. 389
Markschies, C. 238, 261
Markus, R. 88, 341, 342
Marrou, H. I. 35
Marshall, B. 39–40, 403, 411–12, 419–20
Martin, D. 389
Matthews, J. 241, 277
Maximus (opponent of Gregory of Nazianzus) 254
Maximus of Jerusalem 154
McClendon, J. 384, 388
McCool, G. 399
McCormack, B. L. 402
McGrath, A. 396, 402

McGuckin, J. A. 223, 242, 244, 249, 250, 254
Mclynn, N. 261, 265
Meijering, E. P. 110
Melancthon, Philip 393
Meletius of Antioch 175–6, 197, 203, 205, 225, 226, 227, 228, 241, 242, 249, 250, 253, 254, 257, 268
Melitius, Melitians 16–17, 102, 105
Meredith, A. 216, 257
Meslin, M. 70, 125
Methodius of Olympus 29–30, 149
Milbank, J. 321, 394, 403, 405, 412
Miller, P. C. 34
Moltmann, J. 384, 389, 406
Monarchianism 68, 74–5, 127, 183
Moreschini, C. 248
Morgan, T. 35
Mortley, R. 145, 149, 340
Mühlenberg, E. 313, 314
Muller, E. C. 400
Muller, R. 407, 416
Musonius of Neocaesarea 224

Narratives
  of the 4th century in modern theology 384–5
  function of in systematic theology 385–6, 395
  meta-narrative assumptions 387–91
  narrative continuity as act of faith 421–2
Nectarius of Constantinople 255, 266
Neo-Thomism 399
Neuschäfer, B. 22
Newman, J. H. 187, 414, 426, 429
Norris, F. W. 284, 332
Novatian 70–2, 259

O'Keefe, J. 31, 403
O'Leary, J. 389
O'Regan, C. 405, 407
οἰκείωσις 283, 316
οἰκονομία 220–1, 306
Olson, R. 388
Operations of divine persons,
  Inseparable operation; in Ambrose 262–5, 369; in Athanasius 113–14, 212–13, 216; in Augustine 319, 373–4; in Basil of Caesarea 216; in Ephrem 234; in Gregory of Nyssa 348–9, 355–8; in Hilary 182–3, 369; in modernity 405–6, 409; in Pro-Nicenes generally 280–4, 296–7
  Common operation; in Basil of Ancyra 152, 216; in Origen 28
Orbe, A. 192
Origen of Alexandria 20–30, 97, 120, 125, 149, 193, 212, 213, 214, 233, 237, 249, 340, 354, 392, 418, 431
  and Arius 28–9
  criticized 29–30, 77
  on exegesis 21–2, 82–4
  on *ousia* and *hypostasis* 24–6
  theology of 20–8
Oroz Reta, J. 311
Ossius of Cordoba 18–19, 70, 88, 89, 92–8, 99, 100, 126, 136, 137
Ousia 125, 145, 151, 157, 165, 171–4, 183, 209, 238, 252, 256, 258, 363,
  in Acacius of Caesarea 162
  in Aetius 144–6
  in Athanasius 114–15, 140–4
  attacked 127, 134–5, 137–8, 163
  in Augustine 375–6
  avoided 122, 128
  in Basil of Ancyra 151
  in Basil of Caesarea 190, 192, 194, 197–8, 200
  in Origen 23
  at Nicaea 92–8
Owen, I. 192

Palladius of Ratiaria 266
Pannenberg, W. 384, 385, 387, 393, 394–5, 406
Patterson, L. G. 29
Paul, apostle 151
Paul, E. 424
Paul of Constantinople 105
Paul of Samosata 76, 94
Paulinus of Antioch 176, 205, 226, 228, 253, 254, 261, 266
Persona in Latin pro-Nicenes 183
Petavius, D. 304, 404
Peter of Alexandria 228, 242, 254, 251, 261
Petronius Probus 261
Philostorgius 126, 145, 188
Phoebadius of Agen 139, 178, 180, 183, 239

Photinus of Sirmium 68, 127–8, 134–5, 136, 150, 182, 241, 328
Pickstock, C. 403
Placher, W. 384
Plantinga, C. 365, 388, 409
Plotinus 95, 193, 201, 202, 217, 246, 247, 248, 249, 353, 368, 392
Pneumatomachoi, see Macedonians
Polemic,
  anti-Arian 2, 13–14, 106–9, 180, 182, 228, 259, 431–2; genealogy of in Athanasius 116–17
  anti-Macedonian 259
  anti-Marcellan 122, 127, 150, 178, 197–8, 228, 256, 432, 434
  anti-Sabellian 109, 119, 157, 175, 179, 180–1, 182
Porphyry 95, 200, 201
Posidonius 192, 199
Possekel, U. 228, 232
Potamius of Lisbon 137
Powell, S. M. 404
Power, see δύναμις
πρᾶγμα 25, 45, 128
Prestige, G. L. 74, 189, 209
Procopius 169, 226
Pro-Nicenes
  activities in West after 365: 260–1
  on analogy 111–12, 207–9, 284–9, 323–4, 361, 375, 381, 417
  as not only culture of elite 277–8
  on aesthetics of faith 327–35
  Basil's attempts to build Pro-Nicene alliances 222–9
  on body of Christ 305–12, 409
  on creation as existing in the Word 314–21
  on creation as semiotic 315–17, 318–20
  defined 6, 167–8, 236–40; emergence 434; and Neo-nicene 237–8, 239–40
  on divine unity 279–301
  on ontology 312–21
  on participation 321–4
  on Sanctification 304–12
  on Scripture 277–8, 335–41, 361–2
  on soul 325–6, 327–35
  see also Trinity, 'simplicity, divine'
πρόσωπον 128, 159, 210, 258, 259, 280, 363
Protegenes of Serdica 126, 136

Quasten, J. 203

Rahner, K. 408,
  Hegelian influence on 410–12
Rebillard, E. 81
Reill, P. 393
relation, see σχέσις
Rist, J. 202, 217
Ritter, A.-M. 237–8, 253
Robertson, D. G. 200
Rogers, E. 32, 403, 416
Roldanus, J. 114
Rousseau, P. 187, 191, 208, 222, 223, 228, 314
Rowe, W. 31
Rufinianus 173
Rufinus of Aquileia 338, 435
  Symb. 336–8
Rule of faith 79ff
Russell, P. S. 231

Sabellius, see Polemic
Sauter, G. 393
Scheeben, M. 404, 423–4
σχέσις (relation) 201–2, 247
  in Augustine 376–7
Schleiermacher, F. 402, 405
Schlitt, D. M. 405
Schmaus, M. 400–1
Schwartz, E. 242
Scripture, see Exegesis
Secundianus of Singidunum 266
Seibt, K. 62
Sellers, R. V. 68
Serapion of Thumis 211–14
Sesboüé, B. 187, 200, 209
Sherwood, P. 210, 359
Sieben, H.-J. 87
Simonetti, M. 12, 19, 20, 88, 100, 105, 109, 123, 134, 137, 152, 160, 173, 179, 188, 211, 238, 242, 253, 266
Simplicity, divine 26, 49, 112, 142, 232, 236, 245, 278–9, 281, 367
  in Augustine 375–80
  in pro-Nicenes 286–8
Slusser, M. 49
Smulders, P. 183
Socrates 16, 100, 111, 120, 126, 127, 134, 154, 158, 162, 163, 164, 170, 241, 242, 253, 259, 260
Son
  as created 27, 49, 60, 148
  from Father's *ousia*, before Nicaea 97

Son (cont.)
  knowledge of Father; in Arius 55; in Origen 26
  as ontologically mediating in Alexander 44
  as revealer of Father for Eusebians 120
  as 'spring' from the Father's 'fountain' 42, 50, 73, 74
  as will of God in Athanasius 114
  see also Father / Son terminology, generation, image, Word, Trinity, Power, Light
Sorabji, R. 314
Soul
  and dual-focus purification 325–35
  as image of God 310, 326
  as mirror of divinity 307–8
Sozomen 16, 100, 101, 120, 126, 150, 153, 154, 157, 158, 160, 170, 229, 241, 242, 243, 253, 259, 266
Spanneut, M. 68
Spirit, Holy 148, 208, 245, 265
  in Augustine 370–1, 380
  at Council of Constantinople (381) 256–8
  development of Pro-Nicene doctrine of 211–18, 345–7
  in Hilary 184–5
  in Origen 25–6
Spoerl, K. Mc. 176, 202
Staats, R. 253, 256
Staudenmeier, F. A. 399
Stead, G. C. 56, 92, 93, 97, 98, 147, 281, 287, 349
Steenson, J. 150, 160, 191, 204, 215,
Stephen of Antioch 127
Stephenson, A. A. 154
Stoicism 282–3, 368, 392
Strange, S. 201
Strauss, G. 341
Strutwolf, H. 18, 58
Studer, B. 20, 238
Sullivan, J. E. 326
Sulpicius Severus 135
Sweeney, L. 281, 367
Swinburne, R. 409

Tanner, K. 32, 274
Tertullian 183, 184, 261
  theology of 73–5
Teske, R. 283
Tetz, M. 110, 123, 173

Themistius 201
Theodore of Mopsuestia 268
Theodoret 16, 89, 107, 124, 127, 253, 258
Theodosius, Emperor 51, 187, 169, 259–60, 265, 434
  accession of 240–2
  and Council of Constantinople (381) 253–5
  as definer of orthodoxy 80–1, 251–2
Theodotus of Nicopolis 225, 226
Theognostus 49
θεολογία 331–2
  and οἰκονομία 220–1
theology, modern
  authority in 387–8, 394–7, 403–4
  development of systematic 392–5
  divisions in 393–404
  as inherently catholic 421
  modern Catholic 396, 398–401, 402–3, 410–13
  possible new account of 415–25
  theories of development in 425–9
θεωρία 219–21, 283, 330, 340
Thessalonica, theological tradition of 51
Thiel, J. 423
Thomas Aquinas 287–8, 410, 411–12, 413, 416
Tillich, P. 391
Timothy of Alexandria 242, 254
Torjesen, K. J. 22
Tradition
  in Basil of Caesarea 218–20
  possible theology of 420–3, 425–9
Trinity
  'grammar' of Trinitarian theology 3, 14–15, 175, 258–9, 434
  mind as analogical site 49–50, 289–91, 411, 413; in Basil 207–9
  'mixing' terminology in Syriac theology 234–5
  in modern Catholic thought 410–13
  modern 'revival' of 407–14
  perichoresis 246
  pressures on Pro-Nicene doctrine of Trinity 245–6
  Pro-Nicenes on appropriation 297–300
  Pro-Nicenes on Father as source 207
  Pro-Nicenes on persons as correlative 190, 194–5, 201–4, 245

Pro-Nicenes on unity of Trinity 289–95; almost prefigured in Homoiousians 159–60
Pro-Nicene understanding of Divine persons 292–4, 295–6, 359, 362, 375, 376–80, 418
social analogy for 208, 292–3, 344, 357–8, 360, 365, 409, 417, 424
Subordinationism 21, 362–3
three persons as expressing perfection of God 180, 245–8
Trinity beyond number 346–7
unity of will 235, 245, 358
see also Pro-Nicenes, 'simplicity, divine'
Troiano, M. 221
τρόπος ὑπάρξεως 210–11, 280, 359
Turcescu, L. 201, 209, 313

Ulrich, J. 87
Unoriginate, see ἀγέννητος / ἀγένητος
Ursacius 124–5, 127, 136, 137, 158, 160, 161
Ursinus of Rome 260

Vaggione R. 12, 80, 96, 143, 145, 149, 192–3, 236, 242, 243, 260
on 'interpretive frameworks' 139–40
Valens of Mursa 124–5, 127, 136, 137, 158, 160, 161, 170, 226, 230, 240, 241
Valens, Emperor 138, 154, 169–70, 222–4
Valentinian, Emperor 169, 170, 240, 260–1, 265
Valentinian II, Emperor 261, 266
Valliere, P. 413
Van Bavel, T. J. 311
Van Dam, R. 187, 223, 226
Vannier, M.-A. 319
Vetranio, imperial pretender 133
Victorinus, Marius 139, 171, 204, 239, 368, 371
Vinzent, M. 53, 62

Volf, M. 409
Von Balthasar, H. U. 313, 408

Webster, J. 403, 416
Weedman, M. 230
Welch, C. 393, 407
White, H. 393
White, J. M. 400
Wickham, L. 146, 177
Widdicombe, P. 22, 110
Wiles, M. 149, 266, 428–9
Wilken, R. 31
Williams, D. H. 75, 136, 137, 138, 160, 161, 169, 177, 178, 242, 253, 261, 336
Williams, R. D. 22, 23, 24, 25, 48, 55, 56, 57, 12, 13, 17, 19, 22, 26, 30, 77, 89, 94, 100, 105, 140, 147, 319, 339, 341, 403, 408, 425, 428
on orthodoxy 82–4
Wilson-Kastner, P. 311
Wimbush, V. 402
Wisdom, terminology of 23–4, 41, 112, 116, 141, 152, 298, 377–9
Word, terminology of 27, 41, 42, 71, 73, 76–8, 94, 96, 114, 116, 141, 152, 234, 289–91, 304, 314–16, 322–3, 337–8, 370, 377
Logos theology transformed by Pro-Nicenes 302–4, 314–21
see also Son, Image, Trinity

'X from X' arguments 23, 59, 73, 120, 165, 182

Young, F. 34
Yousif, P. 232

Zacchuber, J. 95, 190, 200, 201, 205
Zahn, T. 64, 237
Zeiller, J. 123
Zeno of Elea 282–3
Zizioulas, J. 313, 314, 365, 413

Milton Keynes UK
Ingram Content Group UK Ltd.
UKHW021307130824
1249UKWH00057B/885